WATER AND SANITATION IN THE WORLD'S CITIES

WATER AND SANITATION IN THE WORLD'S CITIES
LOCAL ACTION FOR GLOBAL GOALS

United Nations Human Settlements Programme
(UN-HABITAT)

Earthscan Publications Ltd
London • Sterling, VA

First published in the UK and USA in 2003 by Earthscan Publications Ltd
for and on behalf of the United Nations Human Settlements Programme (UN-HABITAT)

Copyright © United Nations Human Settlements Programme (UN-HABITAT), 2003

United Nations Human Settlements Programme (UN-HABITAT)
PO Box 30030, Nairobi, Kenya
Tel: +254 2 621 234
Fax: +254 2 624 266
Web: **www.unhabitat.org**

DISCLAIMER
The designations employed and the presentation of the material in this publication do not imply the expression of any opinion whatso-
ever on the part of the Secretariat of the United Nations concerning the legal status of any country, territory, city or area, or of its
authorities, or concerning delimitation of its frontiers or boundaries, or regarding its economic system or degree of development. The
analysis, conclusions and recommendations of the report do not necessarily reflect the views of the United Nations Human
Settlements Programme (UN-HABITAT), the Governing Council of UN-HABITAT or its Member States

HS/682/03E

ISBN: 1-84407-004-2 paperback
        1-84407-003-4 hardback

Typesetting by MapSet Ltd, Gateshead
Page design by S&W Design Ltd
Cover design by Danny Gillespie
Cover photographs © UN-HABITAT Water for African Cities Programme (top) and GHK/Kevin Taylor (bottom)
Printed and bound in the UK by William Clowes, Suffolk

For a full list of publications please contact:
Earthscan Publications Ltd
120 Pentonville Road, London, N1 9JN, UK
Tel: +44 (0)20 7278 0433
Fax: +44 (0)20 7278 1142
Email: earthinfo@earthscan.co.uk
Web: **www.earthscan.co.uk**

22883 Quicksilver Drive, Sterling, VA 20166-2012, USA

Earthscan is an editorially independent subsidiary of Kogan Page Ltd and publishes in association with WWF-UK and the
International Institute for Environment and Development

A catalogue record for this book is available from the British Library

Library of Congress Cataloging-in-Publication Data

Water and sanitation in the world's cities : local action for global goals / United Nations Human Settlements Programme
(UN-HABITAT).
        p. cm.
    Includes bibliographical references and index.
    ISBN 1-84407-004-2 (pbk.) — ISBN 1-84407-003-4 (hardback)
    1. Municipal water supply—Developing countries. 2. Sanitation—Developing countries. I. United Nations Human Settlements
Programme.

    TD327.W353 2003
    363.6'1'091724—dc21

                                                                                                                    2003002259

Printed on elemental-chlorine-free paper sourced from sustainably managed forests

Foreword

The 20th century will be remembered for unprecedented technological advances, the acceleration of globalization and the urbanization across this planet. The closing years of the last century witnessed a slow but steady decline in the proportion of people living in extreme poverty, and several countries are now back on track to achieve universal primary education. Yet, despite these advances, at the start of the new millennium, over a billion of the world's people remain without access to safe drinking water and over twice that number are denied access to adequate sanitation.

World leaders meeting at the Millennium Summit and the following World Summit on Sustainable Development resolved to halve, by 2015, the proportion of people without sustainable access to safe drinking water and basic sanitation. Achieving this goal will not be easy, given the mounting population pressures, rapid urbanization and ubiquitous resource constraints.

Unquestionably, the commitment of policy-makers to translate these global goals into country- and city-level goals and targets will be a necessary first step. The goals may be global in character but they must be implemented locally, where people live and where shelter and services are required.

Strong political leadership and support from national governments will be needed to turn things around. A stable policy environment will be essential to attract fresh investment in water and sanitation. And the urban poor, mostly living in slums and squatter settlements, should, unquestionably, receive the high priority regarding future investment that they deserve.

It will be equally important to put in place effective monitoring mechanisms that will allow the tracking of progress towards safe drinking water and basic sanitation. The global monitoring mechanisms currently available have proved to be incapable of capturing the real aspirations and needs at the local level. We need monitoring mechanisms that will allow local voices to be heard and their perceptions to be relied upon.

The timing of the UN-HABITAT report *Water and Sanitation in the World's Cities* could not be more opportune. The United Nations Millennium Project has just embarked on the identification of the best strategies for meeting the Millennium Development Goals and related targets. By the target year of 2015, nearly 60 per cent of the world's population will make cities their home. Meeting the rapidly growing urban demand for safe water and adequate sanitation facilities will be a daunting challenge. The analytical work in this report and its central finding – that local solutions are key to achieving global goals – should provide a valuable input to the work of the Millennium Task Force.

Anna Kajumulo Tibaijuka
Under-Secretary-General, United Nations
Executive Director, UN-HABITAT

Acknowledgements

Water and Sanitation in the World's Cities was made possible by the generous support of the Swedish International Development Cooperation Agency (Sida) and the Japan Water Resources Association (JAWA).

Water and Sanitation in the World's Cities was prepared under the supervision of Kalyan Ray, Chief of Water, Sanitation and Infrastructure Branch. Key substantive support was provided by Graham Alabaster, Andre Dzikus, Brian Williams and Neeru Singh of the same branch.

An initial outline of the report was prepared by David Satterthwaite of the International Institute for Environment and Development (IIED) in close consultation with UN-HABITAT.

An annotated outline of the report was discussed in a Stakeholders' Consultation organized by UN-HABITAT during the first World Urban Forum held in Nairobi, Kenya, on 10 May 2002. The meeting was chaired by Sir Richard Jolly, Chairman of the Water Supply and Sanitation Collaborative Council, and was widely attended by expert delegates to the World Urban Forum, NGOs and representatives of external support agencies.

The preparation of the report was entrusted to IIED with David Satterthwaite and Gordon McGranahan acting as the main consultants and principal resource persons with support from Hannah Reid. They brought into this work strong personal commitment, extraordinary energy and a rare degree of professionalism to complete this report within an almost impossible deadline.

UN-HABITAT organized an Expert Group Meeting in Nairobi on 12–13 September 2002, to discuss the first draft of the report (Chapters 1–6) prepared by IIED. Experts attending the Meeting included: Jan G Janssens (the World Bank), Bernhard Griesinger (Organization of the American States), Sekou Toure, Henry Ndede and Gazoulit Kawtar (UNEP), Mario Vásconez (CIUDAD), Malick Gaye (ENDA-TM), Piers Cross and Japheth Mbuvi (Water and Sanitation Programme, East Africa), Pushpa Pathak (Water and Sanitation Programme, South Asia), Diana Lee-Smith (SIUPA-CIP), Professor R A Obudho (Nairobi University), Sunita Kapila and John D Skoda (Consultants), David Satterthwaite and Gordon McGranahan (IIED); from UN-HABITAT: Anna Tibaijuka, Daniel Biau, Nefise Bazoglu, Farouk Tebbal, Alioune Badiane, Iouri Moisseev, Andre Dzikus, Graham Alabaster, Brian Williams, Anne-Maj Lahdenpera, James Ohayo, Pireh Otieno, Junko Nakai and Kalyan Ray. Extensive comments and inputs were received from the experts which led to rewriting of several chapters and some reorganization of the report. Arthur McIntosh and K E Seetharam of the Asian Development Bank, Jamie Bartram of WHO, Sandy Cairncross of the London School of Hygiene and Tropical Medicine, Perween Rahman (Orangi Pilot Project-Research and Training Institute) and David Nilsson of Sida could not personally attend the EGM but offered their valuable comments and inputs to the report.

A number of authors were commissioned to write background papers for the report. They included: Sheridan Bartlett, WaterAid (Dar es Salaam), Pedro Jacobi, Jessica Budds, Micheline Duruz, Khatim Kherraz and a team in IIED-America Latina in Buenos Aires (Kimberly Vilar, Jorgelina Hardoy, Florencia Almansi). We are also grateful to the Indian NGO SPARC for making available the preliminary findings from their interviews with 'slum' dwellers in Pune and Mumbai and to David Johnstone for his help and comments on draft texts. Additionally, regional reviews of the report were entrusted to: Perween Rahman for Asia, Albert Wright for Africa and Mario Vásconez for Latin America and the Caribbean. Sandy Caincross and Virginia Roaf (WaterAid) also reviewed the whole draft text and gave valuable comments and suggestions.

The draft report was also widely circulated among professional staff of UN-HABITAT and benefited from their comments. Notable among them are: Daniel Biau, Graham Alabaster, Andre Dzikus, Brian Williams and Junko Nakai. Valuable contributions were also made by Graham Alabaster, Andre Dzikus, James Ohayo and Pireh Otieno.

The report also benefited from the comments received from the World Water Assessment Programme Secretariat, in particular, Gordon Young and Andy Bullock, and from the World Health Organization, in particular Jamie Bartram and Robert Bos.

Henk Verbeek, Eric Verschuur, Salome Gathu, Veronica Njuguna and Emily Njeru of UN-HABITAT and Josie Villamin of the United Nations Office in Nairobi provided valuable administrative support.

Special thanks are due to the people at Earthscan Publications Ltd, in particular Jonathan Sinclair Wilson, Akan Leander and Frances MacDermott.

Kalyan Ray
Chief, Water, Sanitation and Infrastructure Branch
UN-HABITAT

Contents

List of Figures, Tables and Boxes

Figures

Tables

Boxes

List of Acronyms and Abbreviations

BOT	build-own-transfer
CBO	community-based organization
CEMIS	community-based environmental management information system
CEPAL	Comisión Económica para América Latina y el Caribe (UN)
CSO	civil society organization
DALY	disability adjusted life year
DHS	demographic and health survey
DSM	demand-side management
ENDA	Environment and Development Association
GDP	gross domestic product
IIED	International Institute for Environment and Development
IWRM	integrated water resource management
Ksh	Kenyan shillings
N$	Nigerian naira
Na$	Namibian dollars
NGO	non-governmental organization
OPP	Orangi Pilot Project (Pakistan)
PAHO	Pan American Health Organization
PLC	public limited company
PPP	public–private partnership
PRODEL	Programa de Desarrollo Local (Local Development Programme)
Rs	rupee
SEMAPA	Servicio Municipal de Agua Potable y Alcantarillado (Bolivia)
SEWA	Self-Employed Women's Association (Ahmedabad)
Sida	Swedish International Development Cooperation Agency
SPARC	Society for the Promotion of Area Resource Centres
UN	United Nations
UNCHS (Habitat)	United Nations Centre for Human Settlements (Habitat) (*now* UN-HABITAT)
UN-HABITAT	United Nations Human Settlements Programme (*formerly* UNCHS (Habitat))
UNICEF	United Nations Children's Fund
USAID	United States Agency for International Development
WHO	World Health Organization

Introduction

Water and Sanitation in the World's Cities is the first attempt by the United Nations Human Settlements Programme (UN-HABITAT) as the 'city agency' of the United Nations to monitor, analyse and report on a major area of the *Habitat Agenda*, namely 'Environmentally sustainable, healthy and liveable human settlements'.[1] It also responds to the need for international action to achieve Millennium Development Goal 7, specifically addressing two targets: to reduce by half the proportion of people without sustainable access to safe drinking water by 2015; and to achieve significant improvement in the lives of at least 100 million slum dwellers by 2020 (with a specific indicator on sanitation for slum dwellers).[2]

The report has four central themes:

1 The under-estimation by governments and international agencies of the number of urban dwellers who have inadequate provision for water and sanitation, and the very serious health consequences that inadequate provision brings for hundreds of millions of people.

2 The inadequacies in the attention given by governments and international agencies to this, although there are many examples of innovation and ingenuity from around the world which suggest that the barriers to improved provision are not so much technical or financial but institutional and political.

3 The need for improved provision for water, sanitation and drainage to be rooted in the specifics of each locality, including the needs and priorities of its citizens and the local and regional ecology.

4 The need for improved provision for water and sanitation to be within a 'good governance' framework; it is difficult to see how improvements can be made and good quality provision extended to low-income households without more competent city and municipal governments that work with and are accountable to their citizens.

On the first of these themes, hundreds of millions of urban dwellers have inadequate provision for water, sanitation and drainage, which contributes to very large disease burdens and hundreds of thousands of premature deaths each year. Less than half the population in most urban centres in Africa, Asia and Latin America have water piped to their homes, and less than one-third have good quality sanitation. Those living in large cities are generally better served than those in smaller urban centres. However, more than half the population in most large cities in sub-Saharan Africa, and many in Asia, still lack water piped to their homes and good quality toilets. Perhaps as many as 100 million urban dwellers world-wide have to defecate in open spaces or into waste paper or plastic bags ('wrap and throw') because there are no toilets in their homes and public toilets are not available, too distant or too expensive. Low-income urban dwellers are often paying high prices for very inadequate water provision – for instance, purchasing water from vendors at 2–50 times the price per litre paid by higher-income groups, who receive heavily subsidized water piped into their homes.

This raises the issue of why is this so, after 50 years of aid programmes, dozens of official aid agencies and development banks and hundreds of international NGOs with programmes for water and sanitation? And why haven't the promises made by governments been met? In 1977, representatives from most of the world's governments committed themselves to ensuring that everyone would have adequate water and sanitation by 1990.

The problem is not necessarily one of governments lacking funds. In many cities and smaller urban centres, it is possible to improve provision for water and sanitation in low-income settlements while charging their inhabitants less than they currently pay for inadequate provision. This book describes the innovations and ingenuity of certain international agencies, national governments, local governments, non-governmental organizations and community-based organizations in different cities in terms of improving water and sanitation provision. These show that deficiencies in water and sanitation provision can be enormously reduced without a reallocation of national investments and international aid that is politically unfeasible. They show that the targets related to water and sanitation within the latest set of internationally agreed goals – the Millennium Development Goals – are feasible. The need to meet these targets is all the more pressing, given that so many international goals have not been met and another failure will discredit the making of such goals. But to achieve these goals requires a change in attitudes and approaches, especially in regard to urban areas. Many governments and international agencies have inadequate urban policies, based on inaccurate stereotypes about urban areas and those who live in them. They fail to recognize the scale of need in urban areas. They still think that virtually all poverty is located in rural areas. They also fail to support the kinds of local processes that can bring the needed improvements.

Governments and international agencies need to recognize that urban areas have particular needs for water and sanitation that are distinct from rural areas, and they also have particular advantages over rural settlements. It is still common for the same definition of what constitutes 'adequate' or 'improved'

access to water to be applied to all urban and rural areas. For instance, some governments classify everyone who has a water source within 200 metres of their home as having adequate provision for water, but having a public tap within 200 metres of your home in a rural settlement with 200 persons per tap is not the same as having a public tap within 200 metres of your home in an urban squatter settlement with 5000 persons per tap. Urban settlements with large numbers of people concentrated in small areas present particular problems for avoiding faecal contamination if there are no sewers or other means to remove household and human waste. Many urban households have so little space per person that there is no room to fit toilets into each person's home. But urban settlements also provide more opportunities for good quality provision for water and sanitation, because unit costs are generally lower and urban dwellers often have more capacity to pay.

It is difficult to reconcile definitions of 'adequate' water and sanitation provision from a health perspective with definitions that allow data on provision to be easily collected. It would be easy to meet international targets for improving water and sanitation provision if the definition of 'improved provision' were to be set too low. And in one sense, 100 per cent of urban (and rural) dwellers already have access to water and sanitation. No one can live without water. No city develops where there is no water. Virtually all livelihoods (and the economic activities that underpin them) also depend on water, directly or indirectly. Everyone has sanitation in the sense that they have to defecate; again, no one can live without doing so. The issue is not whether they have provision for water and sanitation, but whether they have adequate provision:

- Do they have water that can be safely drunk and used in food preparation (especially for infants and young children, who are particularly at risk from diarrhoeal diseases caught from contaminated food or water)?
- Do they have enough water for washing, food preparation, laundry and personal hygiene?

- Is getting sufficient water very expensive? If it is, this generally means less money for food in low-income households.
- Is getting water very laborious and time consuming? Water is very heavy to carry over any distance, and trips to and from water standpipes or kiosks often take up two or more hours a day.
- Is there a toilet in the home and a tap for hand-washing? If not, is there a well maintained toilet in easy reach? If this is a public toilet and there is a charge for using it, is it kept clean, can low-income households afford to use it and is it safe for women and children, especially after dark?
- Is there provision to remove human wastes and household wastewater?
- Are low-income areas protected against floods?

Any assessment of provision for water and sanitation has to be based on some implicit understanding or explicit definition of 'adequate'. In urban areas in high-income countries, 'adequacy' for water is considered as water that can be safely drunk piped into each home, distributed by internal plumbing to toilets, bathrooms and kitchens, and available 24 hours a day. 'Adequacy' for sanitation is at least one water-flushed toilet in each house or apartment, with a 24-hour guaranteed supply, a wash basin in the toilet or close by where hands can be washed, and facilities for personal hygiene – hot water and a bath or shower. And, of course, there must be an income level that allows all this to be paid for, or provisions to ensure supplies for those unable to meet their bills. If these are used as the criteria for 'adequate provision', as Chapter 1 describes, most of Africa's and Asia's urban population and much of Latin America's urban population have inadequate provision. Indeed, most have levels of provision far below this standard. In many urban centres in these regions, no one has this level of provision, because even piped water supplies to the richest households are intermittent and of poor quality. Most urban centres in Africa and Asia have no sewers, and in most of those that do, only a small proportion of the population is connected.

It can be argued that every urban dweller has a right to a standard of water and sanitation provision that matches the standards in high-income nations. Certainly, this level of provision produces the greatest health benefits. It virtually eliminates diarrhoeal diseases and many other water-related diseases as significant causes of death. As Chapter 2 describes, it brings many other benefits too – including improved nutrition and often higher real incomes and more employment opportunities for many of the poorest urban households. But it is unrealistic to set this standard in most low-income nations, since, with limited resources and limited institutional capacities, getting better provision for everyone is more important than getting very good provision for the minority. If the focus is on getting very good provision, the beneficiaries are likely to belong to the richer and more politically powerful groups.

If we take 'adequate' water to mean a regular piped supply available within the home or in the yard, at least half of the urban population of sub-Saharan Africa and Southeast Asia has inadequate provision (and perhaps substantially more than this). If we took 'adequate' sanitation to mean an easily maintained toilet in each person's home with provision for hand-washing and the safe removal and disposal of toilet wastes, a very large proportion of the urban population of sub-Saharan Africa (50–60 per cent?) and more than half of the urban population in most low-income nations in Asia and Latin America is likely to have inadequate provision. As examples in different chapters will show, public toilets can be 'adequate' in terms of cleanliness, accessibility and cost, but this is rare.

At present, there are no global figures for the proportion of the world's population or of each region's population that have adequate water and sanitation provision. The World Health Organization and UNICEF Joint Monitoring Programme for Water Supply and Sanitation (on whose work this book draws) can only give figures for the proportion with 'improved' provision, because of the lack of data on who has 'adequate' or 'safe' provision. As Chapter 1 describes in more detail, 'improved' provision can include water from public standpipes, boreholes and protected dug wells (with no guarantee that this water is safe to drink), provided that at least 20 litres per person per day is available from a source within 1 kilometre of the person's home. 'Improved' provision for sanitation can include shared pit latrines, with no guarantee that these are easily accessed or clean.

Table I.1 contrasts two different sets of estimates for the number of urban dwellers lacking water and sanitation provision in 2000. The first is based on the definition of 'improved' provision used by the above-mentioned Joint Monitoring Programme (because of the lack of data for measuring 'adequate' or 'safe' provision for most nations). The second set is based on the evidence presented in this book, drawing on all available city studies that have more detailed descriptions of the quality and extent of water and sanitation provision.

Most of the world's governments and international agencies have committed themselves to the Millennium Development Goals which arose from the United Nations Millennium Declaration adopted in September 2000. The most relevant of these for water and sanitation is Millennium Development Goal 7, addressing the following targets:

- Target 10: to halve, by 2015, the proportion of people without sustainable access to safe drinking water.

- Target 11: to achieve, by 2020, a significant improvement in the lives of at least 100 million slum dwellers.

The World Summit on Sustainable Development in 2002 added another relevant target:

- to halve, by 2015, the proportion of people who do not have access to basic sanitation.

If we apply these goals to urban populations, the scale of the funding needed to halve the proportion of urban dwellers who do not have safe drinking water and basic sanitation may be considerably under-estimated for two reasons. First, estimates for the funding needed may be based on large under-estimations as to the number of people lacking adequate provision. For instance, looking at Table I, if there are only 98 million urban dwellers in Asia in need of better water supply (as all but these have 'improved provision') the problem seems soluble financially. If there are 500 million urban dwellers in Asia in need of better water supply, because the 402 million urban dwellers who have 'improved provision' still have very inadequate provision, the picture changes dramatically. The second reason that the funding requirements for urban areas may be considerably under-estimated is the need for investment in infrastructure, facilities and institutions upstream of the pipes and

Region	Number and proportion of urban dwellers without 'improved' provision for:[a]		Indicative estimates for the number (and proportion) of urban dwellers without 'adequate' provision for:[b]	
	Water	Sanitation	Water	Sanitation
Africa	44 million (15 per cent)	46 million (16 per cent)	100–150 million (circa 35–50 per cent)	150–180 million (circa 50–60 per cent)
Asia	98 million (7 per cent)	297 million (22 per cent)	500–700 million (circa 35–50 per cent)	600–800 million (circa 45–60 per cent)
Latin America and the Caribbean	29 million (7 per cent)	51 million (13 per cent)	80–120 million (circa 20–30 per cent)	100–150 million (circa 25–40 per cent)

Table I Estimates as to the number of urban dwellers lacking provision for water and sanitation in 2000 based on who has 'improved' provision and who has 'adequate' provision

Sources: a WHO and UNICEF (2000), *Global Water Supply and Sanitation Assessment 2000 Report*, World Health Organization, UNICEF and Water Supply and Sanitation Collaborative Council, Geneva, 80 pages; *b* based on the evidence presented in Chapter 1.

downstream of the drains to allow better provision.

But estimates for the scale of external funding that is needed can also be over-stated because too little consideration is given to local resources, including the current or potential roles of investments made by households, communities and local governments. The extent to which unit costs can be reduced by community–non-governmental organization (NGO)–local authority (and/or local utility) partnerships can also be under-estimated, which in turn reduces the gap between good quality provision and what low-income households can afford. Many case studies in this book show the possibilities of much better provision financed by local resources.

This highlights another constraint – that the official development assistance agencies were not set up to support households, communities and local governments. Official bilateral aid programmes and multilateral development banks were set up to work with and through national governments. Most seek to support local governments, and some seek to support community initiatives or steer their funding through other institutions that can do this – but this represents a small part of their funding for water and sanitation, except in nations where national governments have supported this stance. And all official development assistance agencies have difficulties supporting a large and diverse range of 'cheap' initiatives by local authorities and NGOs because of the high administrative cost of doing so.

If the Millennium Development Goals of halving the proportion of people lacking adequate water and sanitation provision by 2015 are to be met, along with the goal to have achieved a significant improvement in the lives of at least 100 million slum dwellers by 2020, international agencies will need to develop a greater capacity to support good local governance and the investments and initiatives undertaken by households, communities and local governments. This inevitably means channelling more support to local governments that are committed to improving provision and less to local governments (or national governments) that are not. This can be awkward politically; it may mean some

redirection of funds away from some of the poorest nations because of their government's lack of interest in improving water and sanitation provision and the local governance structures that this needs. It is also inconsistent with poverty reduction goals to penalize poor groups in nations that have unrepresentative and anti-poor governments. Here, international agencies need to consider how to support local initiatives directly, including those undertaken by community organizations, residents' groups and local NGOs. This will usually require new funding channels and local institutions through which such funding is channelled. This is not incompatible with better local governance in that, as many examples given in Chapters 5 and 7 show, supporting representative organizations of the urban poor to develop better water and sanitation provision helps build good local governance from the bottom up.

There is also the need for improved provision for water, sanitation and drainage to be rooted in the specifics of each locality, including the needs and priorities of its citizens. Some of the most compelling evidence for the need for changed approaches in this book comes from interviews with low-income households. These reveal just how poor water and sanitation provision is, even when their settlement is officially classified as having 'improved provision' or even when the local authority reports that everyone has house connections. They raise issues that are rarely seen in technical discussions of water and sanitation – for instance, as shown by interviews with women in Pune and Mumbai that are reported in Chapters 1 and 2:

- The difficulties in getting water from public taps and of the conflicts that often occur at the tap, including the pressure from those in the queue behind you not to take 'too long' or take 'too much water'.
- How heavy it is to fetch and carry enough water for domestic use to and from a standpipe, even if this is less than 100 metres away from one's home.
- The indignity of having to defecate in the open and the sexual harassment that

women and girls suffer when having to do so.

- The opposition that people so often face collecting water from a standpipe in a neighbouring settlement (why are you using 'our tap'?).
- How disgusting it is to have to use public toilets that are not cleaned and well maintained, 'the insects that climb up our legs,' the need to use public toilets only once a day because low-income households cannot afford to use them more often, children's reluctance to use public toilets (for all the above reasons and because they have difficulty waiting in queues), and how dangerous public toilets can be for women and girls to use, especially after dark.

These are also a reminder of how progress towards more adequate water and sanitation provision in any city for those with low incomes is always a political struggle – as it was when provision improved so much in what are today the world's high-income countries. Most of the examples of better provision in this book arose because of government institutions responding to democratic pressures or through partnerships between water and sanitation utilities and communities, or through autonomous actions by community organizations which governments permitted (or at least did not prevent).

The need for improvements to be rooted in local realities is also important from an ecological perspective. This is particularly so in a world where fresh water is increasingly in short supply in more and more places, and where finite fresh water resources are often being over-used, depleted and polluted. City-based demands for fresh water by businesses and affluent residents should not over-ride the needs of other users (as they often do). But here, as in the other main themes of this book, this discussion is complicated by the great diversity of circumstances among the tens of thousands of urban centres around the world. Accurate generalizations are not easily found. Inaccurate generalizations abound. As Chapters 3 and 4 discuss, the inadequacies in water and sanitation provision in many cities

and smaller urban centres have nothing to do with a shortage of water resources in their regions. Most deficiencies in urban water and sanitation provision are caused by other factors. The amount of water required to achieve adequate water and sanitation provision is small compared with the demands associated with other uses of water. Urban centres in water-scarce regions can, and often do, make a special effort to improve residents' access to these scarce resources. What is perhaps more remarkable than water-scarce cities is the number of cities that have increased their population more than fiftyfold in the last century (and their draw on fresh water resources much more than fiftyfold) and still have not run out of water. Even some of the world's largest cities still meet their water needs from local sources.

One issue that falls under the discussion of the need for provision for water, sanitation and drainage to be rooted in the specifics of each locality is the need for less certainty by international 'experts' and agencies and more willingness to listen to those with inadequate provision and to support local innovation. As the issue of water scarcity has become more central to discussions both of environment and of development, so new generalizations are made and new policies are proposed by national governments and international agencies. There are lots of strong opinions about what should be done among politicians, senior staff from international agencies and national governments and 'experts', especially the experts who advise international agencies. Amongst most international agencies, priorities are set, policies are designed or changed, programmes are developed and projects set in motion with little or no consultation with those who suffer the worst water and sanitation provision.

In recent years, for example, increasing private sector involvement in water and sanitation utilities has been put forward as a widely applicable means of improving water and sanitation provision. As shown in Chapter 5, however, many of the most critical obstacles to improved provision persist when private sector participation increases, and in some circumstances privatization heightens (rather than reduces) the political conflicts surrounding water and sanitation provision. Rapid and radical shifts in private sector involvement often provide little scope for measures promoting the interests of those without adequate water and sanitation. Also, the urban centres and neighbourhoods most in need of improvements in water and sanitation provision tend to be those that are least attractive to private investors and operators. Moreover, where the public sector lacks the will or capacity to provide urban water and sanitation, it often also lacks the will or capacity to regulate private provision effectively. In some circumstances, increasing private sector involvement may be an appropriate response to local water and sanitation problems. Much depends on local conditions, on the forms that private sector involvement actually takes, and on what else is being done to improve water and sanitation provision. It is not a 'solution' that should be promoted internationally in the name of those who currently lack adequate water and sanitation. As Chapter 7 emphasizes, the stress should be on getting the best out of public, private and community organizations.

Similarly, there is a great deal of discussion internationally of the need to take a more integrated approach to water resources management. Within this integrated approach, there is a tendency to view demand-side water management principally as a means of preventing water from being wasted. In many of the more deprived urban settlements, however, the major challenge is not to find new ways of saving water, but to find new ways of making more water available, and ensuring it is put to good use. As described in Chapter 6, demand-side management can also play a role here, but only if it is taken to include issues of sanitation, hygiene behaviour and giving deprived groups more influence over their own water and sanitation systems. So for demand-side water management, it is critical to adapt new approaches to local conditions, and to ensure that local voices – including especially the voices of those without adequate provision – are heard and have an influence.

Meeting the Millennium Development Goals for water and sanitation means that the

voices, opinions and priorities of slum and pavement dwellers in Indian cities, and the inhabitants of Humura in Nairobi and of some informal settlements in Cali that are reported in this book, get to influence the policies and practices of the international development agencies (as well as influencing their own local governments). There is a huge physical and institutional distance between decision-making structures in most international agencies and 'the poor', who are meant to be their clients but who have no formal channels to influence priorities and hold these agencies to account. But as Chapter 7 describes, there are some hopeful signs on this – international agencies who recognize the need for solutions to be developed within each local context in ways that ensure the solutions are influenced by those lacking adequate provision.

There is also the long established tradition among commentators on development issues and environment issues of judging urban areas as 'parasitic' or seeing them as 'places of privilege' to which fewer resources should be steered, including those needed to improve water and sanitation provision. This helps explain why water and sanitation provision in urban areas has received inadequate attention. It is common for judgements to be made about cities 'unfairly' drawing water from rural areas and damaging the rural ecology in doing so. There are certainly instances where such judgements are justified, but many specialists assume that this is the norm. It is not. And even where it does happen, it is rarely the city poor who benefit. There is an urgent need for more priority to be given to improving water and sanitation provision in urban areas, but this should not be at the expense of rural investments. Indeed, this book's claim that the inadequacies in water and sanitation provision in urban areas are under-estimated is likely to be valid for most rural areas too. And as Chapter 2 describes, there is no clear line between what is rural and what is urban. A sizeable proportion of the people with the world's worst water and sanitation provision live in settlements with between 1000 and 20,000 inhabitants. In some nations these are considered rural, in others urban. This suggests the need to consider water and sanitation provision in rural and urban areas together. However, as noted above, for water, sanitation and drainage, most urban contexts are different from rural contexts because of the size and spatial concentration of the population and the number of non-agricultural enterprises – all of which need water and all of which produce wastewater. In a nation which defines urban areas as settlements with 2500 or more inhabitants, the best means of improving water and sanitation provision in 'rural' villages of 1000–2499 inhabitants may have much in common with improving provision in many market towns and agricultural service centres that have between 2500 and 10,000 inhabitants. But the means used for these villages and small urban centres will not have much in common with the means needed for a city of 1 million plus, or a metropolitan region of 10 million plus inhabitants.

The fourth central theme of this book is that deficiencies in water and sanitation provision in cities are often as much the result of inadequacies in the institutions with responsibilities for providing water and sanitation, and the governance structures within which they operate, as a lack of funds. This makes the task of improving provision more difficult. This helps explain why progress has been so limited. Unlike most subjects related to environment and development, there is very little disagreement about the need for better water and sanitation provision in Africa, Asia and Latin America. There may be disagreements about where the priorities should be (with many being anti-urban), about who the best providers are (public, private, community) and about the best technologies to use. But the need for better provision is very rarely questioned. In 2002, Nelson Mandela made the need for improved provision for water one of the central points in his speech to the World Summit on Sustainable Development. During the summit, *The Economist* emphasized that the need to help the world's poorest secure safe drinking water and adequate sanitation was the least controversial of all the priorities discussed at the summit, and even used the image of someone drinking from a cup as its cover photo.[3] But many of the same points

were made 26 years earlier at the UN Conference on Human Settlements in 1976 and at a subsequent UN Water Conference in 1977. Here too, there was a very firm and broad consensus among government representatives and staff from international agencies about the importance of better water and sanitation provision. In some key aspects, better water and sanitation provision in urban areas is also ideally suited to funding from international agencies, because well designed and managed systems need capital upfront (which is what most agencies provide) and then deliver their benefits over many years or even decades.

Good water and sanitation provision in cities needs competent city and municipal authorities that are accountable to their citizens and able to manage improved provision – whether as providers themselves or as the institution that provides the legal and regulatory framework for other providers (whether large-scale private, small-scale private, non-profit, NGO or community based). Most aid agencies and development banks backed away from large capital projects in urban areas during the 1980s because local governance structures proved unable to manage and maintain them. As a result, most such agencies now have 'good governance' programmes – although many still underestimate the importance of applying these to local governments. But supporting improvements in city and municipal governance is never easy for international agencies. These agencies were not set up to do so, and it can be difficult to promote such ends when their official counterparts, national governments, are reluctant to let local governments have the power, resources and fund-raising capacities they need to be effective. But in the end, it is difficult to see how most international goals and targets, including those directly or indirectly related to water and sanitation, can be met without more competent, effective, accountable local governments. The quality of local governments and their capacity to represent, support and work with their citizens has great relevance for the achievement of sustainable development, within which good quality water and sanitation provision is so important.

Notes and references

1   UNCHS (Habitat) (1997), *The Habitat Agenda*, HS/441/97E, UNCHS (Habitat), Nairobi, Chapter IV, Section C. Available at: www.unhabitat.org/unchs/english/hagenda/ch-4c-5.htm.

2   The Millennium Development Goals arose from the United Nations Millennium Declaration adopted by the United Nations General Assembly (the Millennium Assembly) in September 2000.

3   *The Economist*, 31 August 2002, page 66.

Provision for Water and Sanitation in Cities

 Introduction

This chapter reviews the quality and extent of provision for water and sanitation in urban areas. It highlights how the inadequacies in provision in much of Latin America and Asia and most of Africa are much worse than most international statistics suggest. As such, they are key contributors to poverty and premature death. It also highlights how too little attention is given to sanitation. Many people still assume that clean water is the main issue, as can be seen in international conventions and declarations that forget to mention sanitation. It must be remembered that human excreta is extremely dangerous unless disposed of safely. Where provisions for water and sanitation are inadequate, the diseases that arise from faecally contaminated food, water and hands are among the world's leading causes of premature death and serious illness; such diseases also contribute much to under-nutrition, as diarrhoeal diseases and intestinal parasites rob people's bodies of nutrition. Good provision for sanitation should virtually eliminate these health burdens.

This chapter is also about definitions. Less than half of the urban population of Africa, Asia and Latin America has adequate provision for water and sanitation. Yet 85 per cent of the urban population in these same regions has 'improved' water and 84 per cent has 'improved' sanitation. Both of these statistics are correct; the statistical evidence for both is robust. Here, we explain how this is possible and the important differences between what is defined as 'improved' provision and what is considered 'adequate' or 'safe' provision. 'Improved' provision for water is often no more than a public tap shared by several hundred people with an intermittent supply of water. 'Improved' sanitation is often no more than a latrine, to which access is difficult, shared among many households.

This chapter also makes clear why it is so difficult to reach low-income groups in urban areas with good quality provision for water and sanitation. Most of the world's urban population lives in low- and middle-income nations in Africa, Asia and Latin America and the Caribbean. A significant proportion of these people have incomes that are so low that they can afford no more than US$0.01–US$0.05 a day on water and sanitation. If piped water is not available at this price, they will use any other available water source that is cheaper or free (for instance, drawing from polluted and faecally contaminated lakes, rivers or shallow wells). Tens of millions of urban dwellers defecate in the open or into plastic bags or waste paper (what is often termed 'wrap and throw') because they have no toilet they can use. Many such people live in such cramped conditions (5–6 persons in a small room) that there is no room in their homes for toilets. Many are tenants and their landlords make no provision for sanitation in the rooms they rent. This is the challenge facing governments and international agencies intent on improving provision.

Judging who has adequate provision

Official statistics on provision for water and sanitation suggest that it is only a minority of urban dwellers who are unserved, even in low-income nations in Africa, Asia and Latin America. For instance, even in Africa, by the year 2000, 85 per cent of the urban population had 'improved' provision for water and 84 per cent had 'improved' provision for sanitation. The total number of urban dwellers worldwide lacking improved provision by the year 2000 (173 million for water, 403 million for sanitation) is obviously a serious problem, but greatly reducing this should be relatively easy, given that urban centres concentrate people in ways that usually reduce unit costs for improving provision. Much of the urban population is willing and able to pay for improved provision. Problems seem much more serious in rural areas, where most of those lacking improved provision live. Indeed, if international commitments to halve the proportion of people lacking water and sanitation by 2015 are to be met, this would imply giving priority to rural areas.

But what if the hundreds of millions of urban dwellers who are said by government statistics or household surveys to have improved provision for water and sanitation still have very inadequate provision, which also means very large health burdens from water-related diseases? This chapter seeks to demonstrate that this is the case and to present the evidence for this. It is not claiming that the official statistics are wrong, but it is suggesting that most governments and international agencies misinterpret these statistics and, in so doing, give a false impression of the extent of provision for water and sanitation in urban areas. It also suggests that new benchmarks need to be set to monitor global trends on provision for water and sanitation in urban areas.

Everyone has access to water in some form since no one can live without water. The issue is not whether they have access to water but whether the water supplies are safe, sufficient for their needs, regular (for instance available 24 hours a day and throughout the year), convenient (for instance piped to their home or close by) and available at a price they can afford. Similarly, for sanitation, everyone has to make some provision for defecation, even if this is defecating on open land or into an open drain (as is the case for tens of millions of urban dwellers). The issue is not whether they have provision for sanitation but whether they have a quality of provision that is convenient for all household members (including women and children), affordable and eliminates their (and others') contact with human excreta and other wastewater (which may also be contaminated with excreta) within the home and the wider neighbourhood. If households do not have toilets in the home, do they have access to toilets close by that are well maintained, affordable and accessible without queues? Are there toilets that children are happy to use? As Chapter 2 will describe, children are frightened to use many toilets. If the toilets are not connected to sewers, there is also the issue of what happens to the excreta (for instance, is it polluting groundwater or going into open drains?) and also the provision for the disposal of households' wastewater. If they are connected to sewer systems, there is the issue of whether the outputs from these systems are polluting other people's waters.

Thus, any assessment of provision for water and sanitation (in cities, smaller urban centres or rural areas) has to begin with a definition of 'adequate provision' against which to compare actual provision. In high-income nations, the need for all urban households to have water piped to their home that is safe (ie drinkable) and regular (available 24 hours a day), internal plumbing (so piped water is available in bathrooms, kitchens and toilets) and their own sanitary toilet within the house or apartment (usually connected to sewers) is unquestioned. These expectations can be used as the standards. Virtually all urban dwellers in high-income nations live in houses, apartments or boarding houses that meet these standards. These standards may also be set and achievable in well-governed cities in middle-income nations, as demonstrated by cities such as Porto Alegre[1] and Seoul.[2] These are good standards too from a public health viewpoint, as will be elaborated later in this chapter and in Chapter 2. They are also the standards preferred by households so long as they are not too expensive, because they eliminate a lot of hard work and drudgery fetching and carrying water and getting rid of human wastes and wastewater. But by these standards, most of the urban population in Africa and Asia and much of the urban population in Latin America and the Caribbean have inadequate provision both for water and for sanitation. Indeed, large sections of the urban population in these regions have levels of provision that are nowhere near this standard. Hundreds of millions of people only have unsafe and inconvenient water sources, compete with hundreds of others to get water from distant standpipes, have to share dirty, poorly maintained toilets with dozens of other people, or have no toilets at all within the home. This fact will surprise no one who works in cities and smaller urban centres in these regions but it does seem to contradict the official international statistics on provision for water and sanitation, which suggest that it is only a minority of urban dwellers that lack provision.

But there is a danger in setting the standards for adequate provision too high. In any city or smaller urban centre where large sections of the population have very inadequate provision (and low incomes), and where there are limited resources available for improving provision, setting too high a standard could work to the disadvantage of those with the worst provision. It could mean that all available resources go to providing a small proportion of the population with high standards – and of course, it will generally be the higher-income groups and those with greater political muscle who benefit from this. In such circumstances, it can be argued that the priority should be to ensure that everyone has improved provision, with higher standards provided to areas of the city where the inhabitants are willing and able to pay the full cost of this. From a public health perspective or a poverty reduction perspective, it is better to provide a whole city's population with safe water supplies by means of taps within 50 metres of their home than to provide only the

richest 20 per cent of households with water piped to their homes.

But care needs to be taken in setting lower standards. Set the standards too low and the problem appears to disappear. A survey that asks households whether they have access to piped water can find that most say yes, whereas a more detailed set of questions about whether they have safe, sufficient, convenient, affordable water supplies produces very different results. Obviously, there is little point in ascertaining the proportion of people whose homes are connected to a piped water system if there is no water in the pipes (which is the case for many urban households). The value of piped water supplies is also diminished if water is only available irregularly and the quality of the water in the pipe is very poor. One-third of the urban water supplies in Africa and in Latin America and the Caribbean and more than half of those in Asia operate intermittently, and many do not disinfect their water.[3] The problems of intermittent supplies are particularly serious in many cities in North Africa and the Middle East.[4]

Assessments of provision for water and sanitation are complicated when water piped to the home and internal plumbing and sanitary toilets in each housing unit are not the norm. If a lower standard than 'water piped to the home' is set, then 'adequate provision' has to consider not only whether a household has a water source close by but the regularity of the water supply and issues of water quality and price. For urban settings, consideration must be given to ease of access as well as distance, since being within 100 metres of a single public tap may be adequate in a small settlement but very inadequate in a high-density settlement, as hundreds of people compete for access to it. Interviews with low-income dwellers often reveal difficulties that external agencies do not anticipate: the need to queue for two hours or more to get enough water; the difficulty in getting enough water from a standpipe for household needs, because of pressure from others in the queue not to take too much; the unreliability of supplies to the standpipes (water is often available for only a few hours a day) and low water pressure, both of which act to increase waiting times; and the physical effort needed to fetch and carry water from distant standpipes or other sources.

In addition, households that lack convenient access to good quality and reasonably priced water supplies often rely on multiple sources – for instance, getting (expensive) water from vendors for drinking and cooking, and using (cheaper) river or well water for laundry and washing. It is difficult to develop common standards for such varied sources. Other issues such as seasonal variations in quality or reliability also have to be considered.

Similarly, for sanitation, if ensuring provision for all households of a sanitary, easily cleaned and maintained toilet inside their house, apartment or shack is unrealistic, consideration needs to be given to how to ensure access to shared, community or public facilities that are close, easily accessed, cheap and clean. Assessments of 'adequacy' should pay attention to whether there is adequate provision for disposing of excreta, wastewater and storm and surface run-off. Similarly, assessments should include some consideration of health behaviour, since reducing the incidence of diseases caused by human excreta (the so-called 'faecal–oral' diseases, of which diarrhoeal diseases are the most common) depends not only on the availability of water and sanitation but on hand-washing and personal hygiene.

It is clear from many case studies that public, communal or shared toilets are important for large sections of the urban poor in many nations. Yet there is surprisingly little discussion of these in the general literature on water and sanitation. Particular care is needed in assessing whether public, communal or shared provision of toilets is adequate. Urban populations with communal or public toilets close by may be assumed to be adequately served when large sections of the urban population do not use them – for instance, because parents do not have time to accompany their children and young girls to these toilets (and of course young children have great difficulty in waiting and queuing), or because women and children are afraid to visit them, especially after dark. Few official studies of

provision for water and sanitation acknowledge the high proportion of people who defecate in the open in many urban centres in Africa and Asia, and the particular problems that women and girls face in terms of harassment and sexual abuse as a result of doing so.

 Setting standards

Perhaps the most relevant basis for setting standards for water and sanitation provision is the extent to which provision reduces the very large health burden that arises from inadequate provision. Chapter 2 documents just how large this health burden is and how it is difficult for those who do not experience it to recognize its significance and its contribution to poverty. Non-health criteria for provision are also important – for instance, price and convenience – but these are partially covered by a focus on reducing health burdens, in that high prices and inconvenient supplies lead to lower levels of water use that are then reflected in higher health burdens. Of the many diseases associated with inadequate water and sanitation, the faecal–oral diseases are among the most significant in terms of health impact (although there are many other important diseases related to inadequate provision: see Chapter 2 for more details). Figure 1.1 illustrates how the risks of human contamination from faecal–oral diseases vary with different levels of provision for water, sanitation and hygiene. This illustrates the difficulty of setting appropriate benchmarks for assessing the provision for water and sanitation, since – even if we ignore the variation at each level – it is unclear where within Figure 1.1 to draw the line between 'adequate' and 'inadequate' provision.

The dividing line between those who have adequate provision and those who do not could be set close to the top of this figure, so that those who have access to shared standpipes and pit latrines are classified as adequately served – but as the figure suggests, the risk of human contamination from faecal–oral pathogens with this level of provision remains very high. This dividing line does not measure who has safe water, or who has sufficient provision for water, or who has safe sanitation. The dividing line can be set right at the bottom

Figure 1.1 How the risk of transmission of faecal–oral pathogens varies according to the quality of provision for water, sanitation and hygiene

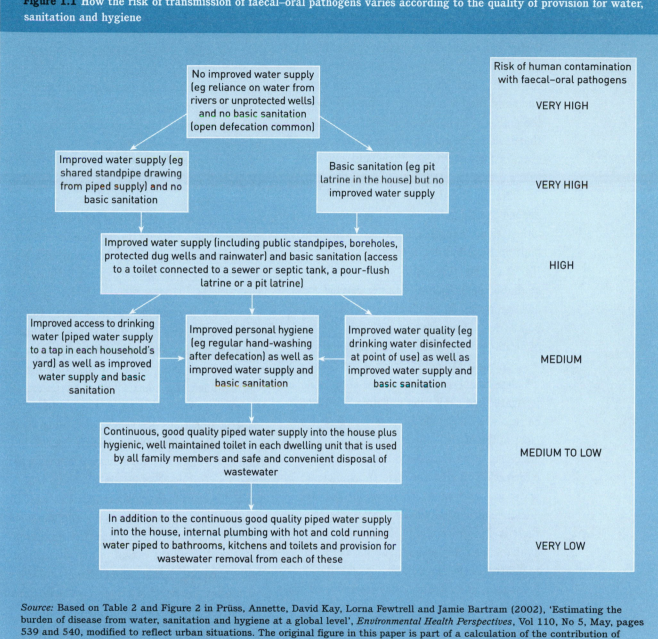

Source: Based on Table 2 and Figure 2 in Prüss, Annette, David Kay, Lorna Fewtrell and Jamie Bartram (2002), 'Estimating the burden of disease from water, sanitation and hygiene at a global level', *Environmental Health Perspectives*, Vol 110, No 5, May, pages 539 and 540, modified to reflect urban situations. The original figure in this paper is part of a calculation of the contribution of deficiencies in provision for water, sanitation and hygiene to global disease burdens: see Chapter 2 for more details.

of the figure where the risk of human contamination from faecal–oral pathogens is very low, but this implies a quality of provision with unit costs that are unrealistic in most urban centres in low-income nations and many middle-income nations.

This suggests the need for assessments that use more than one benchmark – for instance, assessing who has improved, adequate and good provision. This would allow a focus on ensuring improved provision for everyone and supporting better than improved provision wherever possible. At present, global assessments of provision for water and sanita-

tion only assess who has improved provision. For water supply, improved provision means 'reasonable access' to a water supply from a household connection, a public standpipe, a borehole, a protected dug well, or a protected spring and rain water connection. At least 20 litres per person per day must be available from a source within 1 kilometre of the user's dwelling. For sanitation, 'improved' provision means access to a private or shared toilet connected to a public sewer or a septic tank, or access to a private or shared pour-flush latrine, simple pit latrine or ventilated improved pit latrine.[5]

The lack of data

Detailed assessments of who has improved and better than improved provision depend on good data. The most urgent need for better data on the quality and extent of provision for water and sanitation is obviously at the level where the deficiencies in provision are to be tackled – that is, data for each household in each urban area, or for districts or municipalities within urban areas.

National and global assessments are also needed to help guide national governments and international agencies, but these should be built up from detailed local assessments. Unfortunately, there is little detailed data available on the quality of provision for water and sanitation for much of the world's urban population. There are two problems: the level of detail and the extent of the coverage.

In regard to detail, most of the data on which national or global surveys of provision for water and sanitation rely are drawn from censuses or household surveys that do not ask most of the critical questions regarding the adequacy of provision – so they cannot provide information on who has 'safe and sufficient' water and adequate sanitation. For instance, questions are usually asked about whether there is a piped supply to the house or water available on the premises, but not about the regularity of the supply, the respondent's perception of its quality, the cost and whether the household uses other water sources.[6] The case studies given in later sections of this chapter show how many cities and smaller urban centres have piped water systems in which water is in the pipes for only a few hours a day (or less), and the piped water itself is unfit for drinking. Similarly, assessments of provision for sanitation are often based on the type of toilet that people use, but the health risks from using toilets in many urban settings may be more linked to the number of people sharing each toilet than to the kind of toilet used.[7] It is rare for data to be collected on the extent of toilet sharing. For instance, in demographic and health surveys (which are the main sources of data on provision for water and sanitation in many low-income nations), no information is gathered about the time that households spend accessing shared, communal or public facilities or the frequency with which these facilities are cleaned.[8]

In addition, the criteria used in most censuses or household surveys for drawing the line between who has and does not have adequate provision for water and sanitation do not recognize important differences between rural and urban contexts. For instance, many censuses or household surveys consider that the availability of water within 100 metres of the home indicates adequate access to water, yet water taps every 100 metres in a village of 100 persons is not the same as water taps every 100 metres in a high-density squatter settlement with 100,000 inhabitants.

Thus, we end up with a paradox: the worse the quality of provision for water and sanitation, the more sophisticated the data need to be to ascertain what should be done. For instance, if a household has a regular supply piped to the home that is not too expensive, no questions are needed regarding all the other water sources the members use, their quality or their ease of access. If a household has a water-flushed toilet in the home that only the household members use, and which is connected to sewers, this eliminates the need for many questions about how the excreta is disposed of and the extent of provision for toilet cleaning. Ascertaining the quality of sanitation provision is also particularly complicated when there are no facilities within a home, and people rely on shared, communal or public facilities. Box 1.1 highlights the complications of ascertaining whether water and sanitation provision is adequate. To ascertain whether households have adequate water and sanitation provision would require far more questions than those currently included in censuses or household surveys.

There is also the issue of coverage. There are no data on water and sanitation provision for most (urban and rural) households in many low-income nations. The only recent data on water and sanitation provision come from household surveys that are based on representative samples of the population. These may be able to provide accurate statistics on the proportion of the population that has (for

Box 1.1 The many complications in determining whether provision for water and sanitation is adequate

Complications in determining the adequacy of water supplies

People often use more than one water source, and it is difficult to ascertain the quality, accessibility, regularity and cost of each, and whether its use is a problem (ie, it is not so much of a problem if people are using a cheaper, more accessible water supply that is not of drinking water quality if this is used only for laundry or washing).

There may be large variations in the water sources that households use over time – for instance, the availability of some sources varies seasonally, and people might switch to more contaminated sources during water shortages when vendors put up their prices.

There may be large variations in the water sources that households use in different areas of a settlement, reflecting differences in available water resources (eg, between those who live close to communal facilities and those who do not).

There may be large variations in the adequacy of provision within a settlement depending on household income (ie, high-quality provision for households able to spend more than a certain amount on water).

What seems like an adequate supply (eg, a water tap inside the home) often is not (eg, there is no water in the pipes, water is available only very irregularly or is of poor quality).

The 'problem' may be perceived very differently by different household members, especially by those who have most responsibility for obtaining the water or for the tasks that require water.

What seems like a 'reasonable' charge for water sold by water kiosks or vendors when viewed as the cost charged per pot can still be very expensive for poor households, especially if this is the only water source that people have access to.

The legal basis for households to qualify for official provision is often unclear, and is often complex or ambiguous if people live in informal or illegal settlements and/or are renters.

Complications in ascertaining the adequacy of provision for sanitation

Good sanitation needs good quality provision in the home (eg, the toilet), the immediate surrounds (eg, connection to a sewer or to a pit or septic tank that does not contaminate the groundwater or other people's water) and the neighbourhood (provision to ensure no human contact with excreta and to make sure that wastewater is removed safely).

To be effective, everyone must use it (so issues of easy access and children's use of it are important: do tenants get access to toilet facilities?)

The 'adequacy' of provision may be perceived very differently by different household members, especially by those who have most responsibility for cleaning and maintaining the toilets.

Good sanitation needs good provision for anal cleaning, hand-washing and maintenance.

Additional issues for the hundreds of millions of people who have only shared, communal or public toilets

Ease of access for each member of a household (close enough for children to use; accessible at night and with public lighting in the roads/passages to it and inside it; not dangerous for women/girls to get to it and use it at night).

Quality of provision to keep it clean and quality of maintenance (especially difficult if toilet facilities are shared among several households, or if they are communal or public toilets that do not generate revenues to ensure good management and cleaning).

Cost of use (what seems like a cheap price per use may be very expensive for low-income households, even if each family member uses it just once a day).

Additional issues in many cities

What happens to water and sanitation provision during periods of high rainfall (ie, flooding of pit latrines and septic tanks, contamination of some water sources)?

Are there problems with blockages in drains (very common where there is inadequate or no provision for regular house-to-house solid waste collection)?

---

instance) water on the premises and access to a latrine (but not for most of the issues raised in Box 1.1), but they do not show where the people lacking such provision live. These surveys usually have a sample size large enough to allow the statistics on provision to be disaggregated to 'rural' and 'urban' populations and sometimes to a few specific cities (or just the largest city in the nation). But it does not help a city utility or a local authority

much to know that 38 per cent of the households within their boundaries lack water on their premises but not to know which households, which neighbourhoods and which districts these people live in.

The records of the utilities or agencies responsible for providing water and sanitation should be a good information source about the quality of provision for each household – but obviously, these generally only have details for those households to which these agencies provide services. As the case studies in this chapter will show, it is common for half or more of the households in a city to lack connection to the water supply system, and for three-quarters or more to lack connections to sewers or drains. In most small urban centres in low- and middle-income nations (and many larger urban centres) there are no sewers at all, so local utilities have no information on provision for sanitation. However, the quality and extent of water and sanitation provision may be under-estimated if only the records of water and sanitation companies are drawn on. These rarely record the households that have invested in provision for sanitation. They may not record the piped water and sanitation systems installed by communities. For instance, in Karachi, in a high proportion of the *katchi abadis* [informal settlements] in which around half the population live, there are piped water systems and sewers that were installed by self-help, not by government agencies.[9]

Censuses are generally the only information sources that provide details of provision for each household; the quality and level of detail of their data on water and sanitation may be limited for the reasons outlined above, but at least this is information on each household. But in many nations, there has been no census for many years and international agencies are reluctant to fund them. In many nations where censuses have been held, the data on water and sanitation provision by household or by neighbourhood are not available to city authorities or to water and sanitation utilities. As Chapter 7 will describe, there are cities where detailed, house-by-house and shack-by-shack assessments of water and sanitation provision have been built from the bottom up by city authorities, local NGOs and even federations of the urban poor, but these are the exception, not the rule.

This explains why global and regional assessments of water and sanitation provision for the world's urban (and rural) populations (which have to draw primarily on existing censuses and household surveys) are not able to measure the proportion of people with access to safe and sufficient water and good quality sanitation, and have a very limited ability to identify where those with inadequate provision are. They can only provide estimates of the proportion within each nation (or large city) with improved provision. Global assessments can only be as detailed as the censuses and household surveys on which they draw.[10] Ironically, the nations where the need for better provision is greatest are generally the nations with the most inadequate information bases.

Provision for water and sanitation in each of the world's regions

Table 1.1 shows the proportion of the urban population in each of the world's regions that had access to improved water supply and sanitation in 2000. The WHO/UNICEF *Global Water Supply and Sanitation Assessment 2000 Report* (Assessment 2000) from which these figures come describes the difficulties mentioned above in assessing whether provision for water is adequate, and explains that its figures do not measure the proportion of people with adequate provision.[11] Adequate provision would mean the supply of 'safe' water (ie, water that can be safely drunk and used for cooking) of a sufficient volume to allow for all domestic needs including food preparation and cooking, washing, laundry and other aspects of personal hygiene. The assessment does not estimate the proportion of people with safe or adequate supplies, but those with access to improved water supply – which is taken to include household connections, public standpipes, boreholes, protected dug wells, protected springs and rain water collection. It was not possible for the assessment to get data on whether the water was safe, and many case studies have shown that, in urban settings, it is common for water from all these different sources to be contaminated.

Table 1.1 suggests that in 2000, there were 173 million urban dwellers unserved with improved provision for water – 98 million in Asia, 44 million in Africa, 29 million in Latin America and the Caribbean and 3 million in Europe. This appears as a serious problem but could be judged as not requiring a high priority. After all, if 93 per cent of the urban population of Asia and Latin America and 85 per cent of the urban population of Africa have improved provision, then this simply requires a programme focusing on particular urban areas, in particular countries where provision is particularly poor, and minor improvements in provision elsewhere. But individual city studies and the data collected by the Assessment 2000 for large cities[12] suggest that, if it were possible to widen the assessment to measure the proportion with access to safe, sufficient supplies, the number of urban dwellers inadequately served would be much higher – perhaps as much as four times higher. So it is no longer a problem of reaching a small proportion of the urban population, but implies that existing systems of provision are not adequately serving 30–60 per cent of the urban population in most nations.

Table 1.1 suggests that provision for sanitation in urban areas is more of a problem than for water – but again, that it is a minority who suffer. In Latin America and the Caribbean, only 13 per cent of the urban population do not have improved provision; in Africa, only 16 per cent; in Asia, 22 per cent. The assessment recognizes the difficulties in assessing whether provision for sanitation is adequate and it does not estimate the proportion of people with adequate sanitation, but those with improved sanitation (which includes any toilet connection to a sewer or septic tank, a pour-flush latrine or a pit latrine). Shared latrines are included in 'improved' while public latrines and service or bucket latrines are not. No assessment was possible regarding the availability of water for hand-washing or personal hygiene. This means that the benchmark for assessing improved provision for sanitation is up at the top of Figure 1.1.

If a choice was made to use water-flushed toilets connected to sewers as the standard because they perform best in terms of reducing faecal–oral diseases, then the number of urban dwellers with inadequate provision for sanitation would probably be three times as many as indicated in Table 1.1 – not 400 million but 1200 million. Of the population of a sample of 43 large African cities, the assessment showed that 82 per cent lacked toilets connected to sewers. For the large cities in Asia, it was 55

Table 1.1 The proportion of urban populations with access to 'improved' water supply and sanitation, 2000

Region	Urban population (millions)	Proportion with 'improved' provision (%)	Number of people unserved (millions)
Global			
Urban water supply	2845	94	173
Urban sanitation		86	403
Africa			
Urban water supply	297	85	44
Urban sanitation		84	46
Asia			
Urban water supply	1352	93	98
Urban sanitation		78	297
Latin America and the Caribbean			
Urban water supply	391	93	29
Urban sanitation		87	51
Oceania			
Urban water supply	21	98	0
Urban sanitation		99	0
Europe			
Urban water supply	545	100	3
Urban sanitation		99	8
Northern America			
Urban water supply	239	100	0
Urban sanitation		100	0

Source: WHO and UNICEF (2000), *Global Water Supply and Sanitation Assessment 2000 Report*, World Health Organization, UNICEF and Water Supply and Sanitation Collaborative Council, Geneva, 80 pages.

Table 1.2 The proportion of households in major cities connected to piped water and sewers

Region	House or yard connection for water (%)	Connected to sewer (%)
Africa	43	18
Asia	77	45
Latin America and the Caribbean	77	35
Oceania	73	15
Europe	96	92
North America	100	96

Source: WHO and UNICEF (2000), *Global Water Supply and Sanitation Assessment 2000 Report*, World Health Organization, UNICEF and Water Supply and Sanitation Collaborative Council, Geneva, 80 pages. These figures are based on information provided for 116 cities. In no region was there a representative sample of large cities, although the figures for each region are likely to be indicative of average levels of provision for major cities in that region.

per cent; for those in Latin America and the Caribbean, it was 65 per cent (see Table 1.2). In general, large cities have higher proportions of people connected to sewers, so if data were available for the proportion of all urban dwellers with toilets in their homes connected to sewers, coverage would be less than that shown in Table 1.2.

A decision to use 'water-flushed toilets available in each dwelling unit connected to sewers' as the benchmark for adequate sanitation is increasingly criticized by environmentalists because of the ecological disadvantages that sewer systems can bring. But if decisions about provision for sanitation were made only on public health grounds, then in most city contexts – with high densities, very small lot sizes and many multiple-storey buildings – water-flushed toilets connected to sewers would be the sanitation system of choice. Sewer-based systems have the great advantage of removing wastewaters too, and often provide additional drainage capacity during storms. They should also protect groundwater from contamination by human excreta. Sewers are the only technology regarded as adequate in cities in high-income nations, and the extension of sewers to entire city populations during the second half of the 19th century and the early part of the 20th century brought very large health gains in Europe and North America. It is worth recalling that infant mortality rates of 100–200 per 1000 live births were common in cities in Europe and North America only 100 years ago.[13] Water-based sewerage can have ecological disadvantages, especially where there are shortages of fresh water and in large cities where the very large volume of sewage overwhelms any capacity for treatment. However, these disadvantages are not inherent to sewer systems but to the way they are used and the ways in which water use and re-use are managed (see Chapter 6 for more details).

It would also be inappropriate to set a standard for sanitation that had a cost far beyond the means of low-income households. Sewers are generally more expensive per household served than on-site systems such as pit latrines. However, as described in Chapter 7, the Orangi Pilot Project in Pakistan has demonstrated that the unit costs of sewers can be reduced to the point where even low-income households in Karachi can afford them.[14]

But to assume that only urban households with water-flushed toilets connected to sewers in the home have adequate provision for sanitation would over-state the case, since many urban residents are adequately served with on-site sanitation such as toilets connected to septic tanks or pour-flush latrines, or good quality, easily cleaned pit latrines.[15] In many urban settings, neither the funding nor the institutional structure exists to allow the construction of sewers to serve most of the population. Water-flushed toilets are also not much use if water supplies are too irregular, expensive or difficult to obtain to allow regular flushing. However, it does highlight how the scale of the 'sanitation gap' is very dependent on what is said to be 'adequate'. On-site sanitation also means that human excreta is still in the settlement; in over-crowded city settings where space is at a premium, it is difficult to ensure good maintenance and regular and safe sludge removal from latrines or septic tanks. In cities or city districts where flooding is common, pit latrines and septic tanks regularly over-flow, spreading human excreta everywhere with very serious public health implications.

One of the central themes of this book is that the deficiencies in water and sanitation provision in urban areas are much worse than the figures in Table 1.1 suggest. Later sections in this chapter will present more evidence for this. For instance, they will show the very large deficiencies in water and sanitation provision in urban areas in many African and Asian nations where officially more than 90 per cent of the urban population have improved water and sanitation. This includes nations which claim that 99 per cent of their urban population have improved water supplies when detailed studies of their major cities show that 30–50 per cent of their population have very inadequate provision. Similarly, this includes nations which claim that more than 95 per cent of their urban population have improved sanitation when detailed city studies show that 30–50 per cent of the population have very poor quality latrines (which are often difficult to access) or defecate in the open or into bags or waste paper.

The assessment on which the figures in Table 1.1 draw is not at fault. It is very clear that its figures do not show the proportion of people with safe water supplies and adequate provision for sanitation. It recognizes that 'the definition of safe or improved water supply and sanitation facilities sometimes differed not only from one country to another, but also for a given country over time'.[16] It notes that some of the data from individual countries 'often showed rapid and implausible changes in level of coverage from one assessment to the next'.[17] In addition, the quality and level of detail in the Assessment 2000 is a considerable advance on earlier assessments. The advance in this assessment was achieved by drawing primarily on household surveys (ie, data from consumers) and national reports and censuses rather than, as previously was the case, exclusively on information from service providers. But details of coverage were inevitably limited by the (limited) range of questions asked about water and sanitation within these surveys. As noted earlier, neither censuses nor household surveys give sufficient attention to assessing the quality of water and sanitation provision. In addition, the assessment questionnaires that were completed for all nations did not include any methodology for discounting coverage figures to allow for intermittence or poor quality of the water supplies.[18]

What is a greater problem is the way that national governments and international agencies use these official figures – and the confusions inherent in the targets set by many international agencies. For instance, for many years, official statistics on water and sanitation provision presented by international agencies gave figures for the proportions of rural and urban populations in each nation that have 'access to safe water' when the criteria used in most nations for collecting the statistics were clearly not measuring adequacy or adequate access for 'safety'. Recent reports have tended to present figures for the proportion of rural and urban dwellers with improved provision for water, drawing on the Assessment 2000. For instance, in the *Human Development Report 2001*,[19] UNDP draws on the assessment figures for provision for water and presents figures for the proportion of people not using improved sources, but it does not include a definition of 'improved'. This report lists figures for the 'population using adequate sanitation facilities' which are incorrect; it gives the proportion with improved provision, not adequate provision. The World Bank in its *World Development Report 2000/2001* gives figures for 'access to sanitation' and 'access to improved water sources' in urban areas with no qualifications given in the table[20] and little recognition in the technical notes that give definitions of what these mean in regard to their inadequacy. For instance, the text of the technical notes states that 'Access to sanitation is the percentage of the population with disposal facilities that can effectively prevent human, animal and insect contact with excreta'[21] but it is clear from the examples given later in this chapter that this is not so. One of the characteristics of many 'state of the world' reports on environment and development over the last 15 years is the inclusion of tables with a great array of statistics that purport to summarize conditions in each of the world's nations. Some of these, including those for water and sanitation provision, are also broken down into rural and urban areas. The sections that follow this one demonstrate the false impressions that the use of these statistics on water and sanitation in urban areas can give. One hopes that the statistics for aspects of environment and development other than water and sanitation provision are more accurate.

The rest of this chapter is devoted to examining the quality of water and sanitation provision in urban areas of Africa, Asia and Latin America and the Caribbean and to highlighting the very large number of urban dwellers with inadequate provision, and how this is much larger than the number lacking improved provision. This is not to say there is no need for improved provision elsewhere. For instance, more than 10 per cent of the urban population in many urban centres in Eastern Europe do not have water piped into their home, and a significant proportion of urban households suffer from deficiencies in provision for sanitation.[22] There are also issues regarding the quality of disinfection for urban water supplies and the quality of pollution control (including sewage treatment), not only in Eastern Europe but also in Western Europe and North America. But this book has chosen to focus on where the quality and extent of water and sanitation provision is worst and, generally, where the possibilities for improvement are weakest, because of weak institutions and lack of funding.

 ## The regions where provision needs the greatest improvements

Provision for water and sanitation in urban areas of Asia

Table 1.3 shows the proportion of the urban population in Asian nations with access to improved water supply and sanitation in 2000, while Table 1.4 shows the provision for water in selected cities drawing from an Asian Development Bank survey in the mid-1990s. Table 1.4 gives more detail than Table 1.3 in that it shows the proportion of households with house taps, access to public taps, and how those who lack piped water supplies obtain water. Box 1.2 gives short summaries of the extent of water and sanitation provision in selected Asian cities; most of these summaries show that large sections of these cities' populations lack adequate provision.

It is clear from these tables and Box 1.2 that there are very large variations in the quality and extent of water and sanitation provision. For instance, all or virtually all of the populations of cities such as Singapore, Hong Kong, Seoul and Kuala Lumpur have water piped into their homes for 24 hours a day. But there are also many examples of cities in which less than one-third of the population have water piped into their homes, and in many cities water supplies are unreliable and intermittent.

This information on Asian urban areas makes evident the difficulties discussed earlier in this chapter regarding the best benchmark to use in assessing the quality of provision. In the cities mentioned above that have high-quality provision for virtually all their inhabitants, the governmental standard of adequate provision for water is very different from that used to measure the proportion of the urban population with access to improved water supplies in Bangladesh, India, Indonesia, Pakistan, the Philippines, Sri Lanka and Vietnam – the standard used to produce the figures shown in Table 1.3. Or, to put it

Table 1.3 Proportion of the urban population in Asian nations with access to improved water supply and sanitation

Country	Percentage of urban population with improved coverage for	
	Water supply	Sanitation
Afghanistan	19	25
Bangladesh	99	82
Bhutan	86	65
Cambodia	53	58
Cyprus	100	100
Democratic People's Republic of Korea (North Korea)	100	100
India	92	73
Indonesia	91	87
Islamic Republic of Iran	99	86
Jordan	100	100
Kazakhstan	98	100
Krygyzstan	98	100
People's Democratic Republic of Laos	59	84
Lebanon	100	100
Maldives	100	100
Mongolia	77	46
Myanmar	88	65
Nepal	85	75
Oman	41	98
Pakistan	96	94
Philippines	92	92
Republic of Korea (South Korea)	97	76
Saudi Arabia	100	100
Singapore	100	100
Sri Lanka	91	91
Syrian Arab Republic	94	98
Thailand	89	97
Turkey	82	98
Uzbekistan	96	100
Vietnam	81	86
Yemen	85	87

Source: WHO and UNICEF (2000), *Global Water Supply and Sanitation Assessment 2000 Report*, World Health Organization, UNICEF and Water Supply and Sanitation Collaborative Council, Geneva, 80 pages.

Table 1.4 Provision for water supplies in Asian cities, mid-1990s

City	Percentage of population with house taps	Percentage of population served by public taps	Persons per public tap	Other
Almaty (Kazakhstan)	39.8	27.8	150	No data; utility estimates 99% coverage
Bandung (Indonesia)	31.4	10.4	100	58% without piped water; relying mostly on tubewells and dug wells
Bangkok (Thailand)	62.8	0.0		Utility claims 82% coverage; those not served draw on wells, ponds and rain water
Beijing (China)	99.9	0.1	115	99.9% coverage with house taps but most such taps serve several families
Bishkek (Kyrgyzstan)	64.5	12.2	42	Utility estimates 98% coverage
Calcutta (India)	24.1	20.3	75	34% without piped water; use mostly tubewells and dug wells
Cebu (Philippines)	20.9	1.6	128	77% without piped water; 47% getting water from wells and rest from vendors
Chennai (India)	68.0	26.4	150	97% coverage claimed by utility but other figures dispute this – see Box 1.2
Chiangmai (Thailand)	64.8	0.0		35% without piped water; rely on wells and rain water
Chittagong (Bangladesh)	43.3	17.0	250	40% without piped water; rely on tubewells and ponds
Chonburi (Thailand)	79.8	0.0		Utility claims 89% coverage; those not served rely on tubewells and rain water
Colombo (Sri Lanka)	31.2	29.2	150	42% without piped water; rely on tubewells and dug wells
Davao (Philippines)	52.0	0.0		48% without piped water; rely on tubewells and rain collectors
Delhi (India)	65.8			Circa 11,000 public taps that are not metered and circa 7500 known unauthorized connections
Dhaka (Bangladesh)	35.6	6.7	500	58% without piped water; rely on tubewells and other sources
Faisalabad (Pakistan)	31.1	5.6	100	40% without piped water; rely mostly on tubewells
Hanoi (Vietnam)	70.8	4.9	116	24% without piped water; rely on wells, ponds and rain water
Ho Chi Minh City (Vietnam)	50.0	0.1	1270	48% without piped water; most rely on tubewells
Hong Kong (China)	99.6	0.3	89	
Jakarta (Indonesia)	20.5	6.7	300	73% without piped water; most use tubewells, dug wells and rain collectors
Johor Bahru (Malaysia)	99.9	0.0		
Karachi (Pakistan)	50.5	8.7	100	30% without piped water; rely on tubewells and dug wells
Kathmandu (Nepal)	69.3	6.0	42	Utility claims 81% coverage; those unserved use tubewells, dug wells and ponds
Kuala Lumpur (Malaysia)	45.9	0.0		Utility claims 100% coverage
Lahore (Pakistan)	81.5	2.3	100	16% without piped water; using tubewells with handpumps
Mandalay (Myanmar)	36.6	0.4	50	Utility claims 80% coverage; those without piped water use tubewells or rivers

Table 1.4 *continued*

Manila (Philippines)	38.0	5.7	357	33% without piped water; most depend on wells
Medan (Indonesia)	57.1	5.7	60	37% without piped water; most use tubewells and shallow wells
Mumbai (India)	99.9	0.0		Many people registered as having house connection clearly do not
Penang (Malaysia)	100.0	0.1	50	
Phnom Penh (Cambodia)	83.1	0.0		17% without piped water; rely on wells and ponds
Rarotonga (Cook Islands)	100.0	0.0		
Seoul (South Korea)	99.9	0.0		
Shanghai (China)	68.4	0.5	80	100% coverage claimed by utility
Singapore	100.0	0.0		
Suva (Fiji)	98.6	0.0		
Taipei (China)	100.0	0.0		
Tashkent (Uzbekistan)	37.3	24.1	100	Others connections are bulk supply to residential areas
Thimphu (Bhutan)	93.8	0.0		7% without piped water; rely on water from streams
Tianjin (China)	94.6	2.2	150	
Ulaanbaatar (Mongolia)	6.6	59.3	10,846	Includes bulk supply to housing and apartments and to water service centres where tankers draw water for delivery to water kiosks
Ulsan (South Korea)	83.7	0.0		16% without piped water; using ponds, streams and tubewells
Vientiane (Laos)	54.2	0.1	16.25	Utility claims 92% coverage; those not covered use wells, rivers and rainfall
Yangon (Myanmar)	56.4	11.8	180	40% without piped supplies, relying on tubewells, ponds and rain collectors

Source: McIntosh, Arthur C and Cesar E Yñiguez (1997), *Second Water Utilities Data Book*, Asian Development Bank, Manila, 210 pages.

another way, the line drawn onto Figure 1.1 to divide the urban population into those with improved provision and those without would be put in very different places, which also means very different implications in terms of the extent to which the 'improved' provision reduces the risk of faecal–oral diseases.

Comparing the figures in Table 1.3 with those in Table 1.4 and Box 1.2, it is clear that the proportions of the urban populations in Bangladesh, India, Indonesia, Myanmar, Pakistan, the Philippines, Sri Lanka and Vietnam with 'adequate' or 'safe and sufficient' water and sanitation provision are very much lower than the proportions with 'improved' provision. This may also be the case for many other nations. Thus, by 2000, 93 per cent of Asia's urban population may have had access to improved water supplies, and 78 per cent may have had access to improved sanitation, but a much lower proportion had access to adequate provision.

Taking water supply first, Table 1.4 and the case studies in Box 1.2 suggest that tens of millions of Asian households with access to improved provision for water have access only to public taps – to which it is difficult to get access (there are often 200 or more persons per tap) – or water from tubewells or shallow wells. For instance, Table 1.3 shows that 99 per cent of Bangladesh's urban population had access to improved water supplies in 2000. Studies drawn from individual cities within Bangladesh show that the proportion with safe and sufficient provision is much smaller. For instance, in Dhaka, the capital and much the largest city, the head of the water supply and sewerage authority estimated that there were

2.5 million people in Dhaka's slums in 2002, and most had very inadequate water and sanitation provision. Tens of thousands of children die each year in Dhaka because of water-borne diseases and polluted water.[23] Table 1.4 shows that in the mid-1990s, 58 per cent of Dhaka's population were not connected to piped water supplies, while 6.7 per cent had access only to public taps with, on average, 500 persons per tap. Many other studies have shown the inadequacies in provision for water in Dhaka.[24]

Similarly, Table 1.3 shows that 92 per cent of the urban population in India had improved water supplies in 2000, but descriptions of water provision in many city case studies suggest that a much smaller proportion have access to safe, sufficient provision; some of these case studies are summarized in Box 1.2. Indeed, these suggest that there may be no Indian city where 92 per cent of the population have safe and sufficient water supplies. Mumbai appears to be an exception: in the mid-1990s, 100 per cent of its population were said to have water piped into their homes, but the water utility there reported that there were 43.5 persons per house connection, which implies a rather different concept of household connection than that which operates in most other cities.[25] It is also clear from many studies of informal settlements in Mumbai that very large sections of the population do not have individual house connections (see Box 1.3). There are also some surprising examples in Box 1.2 – for instance, showing how much of the population in Bangalore suffer from very inadequate provision, despite this city's remarkable economic success.

In Pakistan, 96 per cent of the urban population may have had improved water supplies by 2000, but descriptions of conditions in Karachi and Faisalabad, as summarized in Box 1.2 and Table 1.4, suggest that a much smaller proportion have safe, sufficient provision. Very large gaps between the proportions of urban populations with improved supplies and those with safe and sufficient supplies are also evident in the Philippines (see, for instance, the descriptions of provision in Manila, Cebu and Davao, the

Ahmedabad (India)

In this city, with 2.9 million inhabitants within municipal boundaries in 1991, in the slums (which contained a quarter of all households) only 23 per cent of households had individual piped water connections and only 26 per cent had individual sanitation. Most slum households only had access to shared piped water or sanitation – for instance, through standpipes, with an average of 50 shelters per standpipe. Water is only available intermittently; in 1998, supplies were available for two hours in the morning and half an hour in the evening. 16 per cent had no access to piped water and 28 per cent had no sanitation facility. Water provision was better in the non-slum area, where 87 per cent had individual water connections and 73 per cent had individual toilets. Regarding sewers, only the old city and 60 per cent of the new incorporated area in East Ahmedabad is connected to an underground sewerage network. Around three-fifths of the population have sewer connections to their home. Official figures show that 550,000 people use public toilets but there is widespread dissatisfaction with their cleanliness and quality. A sample survey of members of the Self-Employed Women's Association (SEWA) found that 63 per cent of 1200 respondents used community public toilets, and of these, 75 per cent were dissatisfied because of a lack of cleanliness and unusable conditions because of no water connection. Many households also face very inadequate provision in terms of shared toilets. An estimated half a million people defecate in the open. A 1998 survey of 7512 slum households on the river banks found that 80 per cent had no water connection and 93 per cent had no toilet facility of their own. However, an upgrading initiative called the Slum Networking Project is underway, which aims to greatly improve water and sanitation provision.[29]

Bandung (Indonesia)

In 1995, only 31 per cent of the population of 2.25 million had house connections, with 10 per cent reliant on public taps (an average of 100 persons per tap) and 58 per cent not connected (mostly relying on tubewells and dug wells). Average water availability was only six hours per day. However, the number of connections had increased significantly between 1991 and 1995, and the hope was to reach 80 per cent coverage by 2000.[30]

Bangalore

In this city of close to 6 million inhabitants, a baseline survey covering 2923 households in 2000 found that 73 per cent of households in the municipal corporation area have access to water from the official network within the house or compound. But only 36 per cent have individual connections; 36 per cent share a connection with others, such as a landlord, other tenants or other users in an apartment and commercial complex. 27 per cent of the population do not have access to the piped water network. 29 per cent of all households (and a large proportion of low-income households) draw water from some 18,000 water fountains (although a much smaller proportion rely only on these); it is common for women to spend two hours collecting water from these fountains. A study of public fountains found that many were located in unhygienic surroundings: 45 per cent had wastewater stagnation in the surrounding area, 31 per cent had solid waste dumps in the immediate vicinity, and 24 per cent had evidence of defecation in the surrounding areas. Wastewater drainage was only found in 48 per cent of standpipes. In two-thirds of the standpipes, water is available on alternate days and when it is supplied, it is available on average for six hours a day. The household survey found that two-thirds of households in the city of Bangalore reported the presence of a toilet within the premises, but less than half of these have a tap in the toilet and only 4 per cent have a flush tank. 28 per cent share a toilet with other households and one-fifth of households who share a toilet report problems with the arrangement – such as too many people per toilet, problems of blockages, poor maintenance and lack of cleaning. 4 per cent use public toilets and many users complain that they are dirty, not cleaned regularly and lack lights. 1 per cent reported that they defecate in the open. Only one-third of poor households in the city have access to satisfactory sanitation facilities.[31] In a study of five slums, two had no water supply, one was supplied by borewells and two had to depend on public fountains, where between one and two borewells and one tap served a population of between 800 and 900. Residents of the four slums had to walk distances of between 20 metres and 1 kilometre to fetch water. In regard to sanitation, 113,000 households are reported to have no latrine at all. In a study of 22 slums, nine (with a total population of 35,400) had no latrine facilities. In another ten, there were 19 public latrines serving 102,000 people. Defecation in the open is common.[32]

Baroda (India)

A survey in 1991 found that only 70 per cent of households had access to adequate drinking water, with 53 per cent having individual bathrooms and 60 per cent having individual toilets. One-third of households were not connected to sewers.[33] A 1992 survey of 400 households drawn from different slums found that almost all had water available to them but only 12 per cent had an independent source. In all but one slum, most households depended on taps and handpumps provided by the municipality. Only 9 per cent had their own latrines. In many localities, community toilets had been provided by the municipality but people did not use them because they were not regularly cleaned or there was no water supply. Drainage facilities were equally poor: 87 per cent of the households in 12 slums reported that there was no provision.[34]

Calcutta (India)

In the Calcutta Municipal Corporation, only around 25 per cent of the population are served by single tap connections in their homes. About half the population of the slums or squatter colonies collect water from standposts. The rest of the population do not have access to the municipal water supply and have to make their own arrangements – for instance, relying on handpumps drawing from tube wells. 70 per cent of the population (and 50 per cent of the area) have sewerage and drainage facilities. Of the larger Calcutta Metropolitan Area population, only half have sewer connections and drainage facilities.[35]

Cebu (Philippines)

In 1990, only 15 per cent of households had their own individual household connection to a piped water supply, with another 24 per cent relying on a shared tap. Most others rely on wells (often shared) or buy water from vendors. Only 45 per cent of households had access to water-sealed toilets (and many of these shared such toilets), with 18 per cent relying on pit latrines and 36 per cent having no toilets. There is a lot of open defecation (wrap and throw).[36] In Metro Cebu in 1995, only 23 per cent of the population were served; 47 per cent got water from wells and 30 per cent from water vendors.[37]

Chittagong (Bangladesh)

In the mid-1990s, around one-quarter of the population of 1.6 million were served by individual house connections, 200,000 were served by 588 street hydrants and the rest collected water from other sources, such as natural springs, canals, ponds and rain water catchments.[38] In terms of sanitation, a 1993 survey found that nearly three-quarters of the metropolitan slum population relied on buckets or pit latrines.[39] A survey undertaken in the mid-1990s found that 62 per cent of those interviewed had experienced water service interruption in the month preceding the interview.[40]

Colombo (Sri Lanka)

In Colombo City, virtually all permanent residents have access to piped water but some 30 per cent rely on public taps, with 40–50 persons per tap on average. There is low pressure, and supplies in some areas are irregular. Two different figures are given for the proportion of residents served by the city sewerage system: 60 per cent and 78 per cent. A 1994 demographic survey showed that 46 per cent of the housing units in Colombo either share toilets or have no access to toilets. Open defecation is common. A high proportion of the population live in places with 50 or more persons per toilet. There are serious problems with flooding, linked to inadequate drainage in many parts of the city, in part because many waterways are not maintained adequately and so debris builds up, blocking the free flow of water. Poor drainage is also a major cause of filariasis, of which there are 700–2000 cases annually.[41] In Greater Colombo in 1995, only 58 per cent of the 2.8 million inhabitants had connections to piped water supplies (including several hundred thousand who shared public taps, with an average of 150 persons per tap). The rest were reliant on tubewells and dug wells.[42]

nation's three largest cities, in Table 1.4, and the description of provision in Cebu in Box 1.2). Similar gaps are evident in Myanmar, Indonesia, Sri Lanka and Vietnam.

However, most of the cities in Table 1.4 and Box 1.2 are large cities, so perhaps they are unrepresentative of conditions in all urban centres. Might it be that provision is better in smaller urban centres? But analyses of provision for water drawn from demographic and health surveys with sample sizes large enough to enable us to compare coverage in urban centres of different sizes suggest that provision for water is worse in smaller urban centres than in the larger cities,[26] and this is also confirmed by the (relatively few) studies of provision for water in smaller urban centres.

The data in Table 1.4 are drawn from a survey in 1995, while some of the figures in Box 1.2 are drawn from census data from the late 1980s or early 1990s. When census data from the censuses held in 2000 and 2001 become available they may show that provision has improved in many nations, but it is unlikely that the very large gaps between those with improved provision and those with safe and sufficient provision will have diminished much.

A comparable gap (between the proportion of urban dwellers whom international statistics show to have improved provision and those with adequate provision) is evident for sanitation. Detailed city studies show that a large proportion of the population with improved sanitation do not have safe, convenient sanitation. Table 1.3 shows that 82 per cent of Bangladesh's urban population had improved sanitation by 2000, but a much smaller proportion had adequate sanitation: 70–80 per cent of Dhaka's population have no connection to a sewer.[27] A survey in 1995 found that 42 per cent of the urban poor used a pit or open latrine, 2 per cent had no fixed arrangement, and 2.7 per cent defecated in the open (see Box 1.2). Provision for sanitation appears to be no better in Chittagong, the second-largest city. In India, 73 per cent of the urban population may have had improved sanitation by 2000, but the data on Indian cities in Box 1.2 and Table 1.4 suggest that the proportion with safe, convenient provision is much smaller.

It is also clear from various case studies that a large section of the population in many large Indian cities defecate in the open, either because there is no provision for sanitation, or because the only provision available to them is 'pay' toilets that they cannot afford or public toilets that are so dirty that open defecation is preferred. Many public toilets in India charge one rupee (R) per use, which would mean an expenditure of around R180 a month for a family of six if each family member used the toilet just once a day. This would represent a significant proportion of the income of any low-income household. In many Indian cities, large sections of the population live in settlements where the only provision for sanitation consists of government-provided public toilets, which are of such poor quality and so poorly maintained and irregularly cleaned that most people try to avoid using them.

In a few Indian cities remarkable progress has been made, including innovative programmes in Pune and Mumbai to greatly improve provision for sanitation in low-income areas through community-constructed and -managed public toilets, which are described in Chapter 7. These serve as a reminder of how far provision can be improved, given the political will and governmental capacity to work with community-based organizations (CBOs).

Box 1.3 presents some summaries of water and sanitation provision by people living in Dharavi, a large and densely populated informal settlement in Mumbai with around 1 million inhabitants. These are drawn from a larger programme of interviews with low-income inhabitants of Indian cities, which gave the interviewees the chance to talk about their needs and priorities and how conditions have changed.[28] Chapter 2 includes extracts from other interviews – from the Indian city of Pune – to highlight women's concerns about water and sanitation. They give some insights into the daily difficulties faced by low-income groups.

It is worth remembering, as one reads the accounts of the very poor quality provision in Box 1.3, that all the people in Dharavi are probably officially considered to have improved

Davao (Philippines)

In 1995, only 52 per cent of the population of close to 1 million were served by the piped water system; most of those not served relied on tubewells and rain collectors.[43]

Dhaka (Bangladesh)

According to a 1995 study of urban poverty in Bangladesh, 99 per cent of poor households in urban Bangladesh had access to safe drinking water. However, if 'access' is defined as the availability of water within 100 metres, the proportion counted as having access is much lower.[44] In 2002, the head of Dhaka's water supply and sewerage authority estimated that there were 2.5 million people in Dhaka's slums, and most have very inadequate water and sanitation provision. 70 per cent of the population have no sewers. Tens of thousands of children die each year in Dhaka because of water-borne diseases and polluted water.[45] A survey found that for half the population in slum areas, it takes more than 30 minutes to collect water.[46] In regard to sanitation, 13 per cent of the poor had a connection to a sewerage system, 13 per cent used a septic tank, 19 per cent had a sanitary/latrine, and 42 per cent a pit or open latrine. 2 per cent of the urban poor had no fixed arrangement, and 2.7 per cent used an open field.[47] Another source suggested that over 90 per cent of the slum population in Metro Dhaka rely on pit latrines or bucket/'hanging' latrines, which also served 35 per cent of the non-slum population.[48]

Faisalabad (Pakistan)

Some two-thirds of the city's 2 million inhabitants live in largely unserviced areas. Over half have no piped water supply and less than one-third have sewers.[49] Service coverage for water supply was said to be 60 per cent in 1995, with water available for, on average, seven hours a day, but this included those served by public taps with an average of 100 persons per tap.[50]

Jakarta (Indonesia)

In 1995, most of the city's population was still getting its water from tubewells, dug wells and rain collectors; the corporation in charge of water supply and sewerage suggested that 38 per cent of the population were connected to the water system, with other estimates suggesting a lower coverage. This coverage includes several hundred thousand people served only by public taps.[51] Residents face a great variety of problems in regard to water, sanitation and drainage. Microbial contamination of household water supplies is pervasive; almost nobody drinks unboiled tap or well water voluntarily. A household survey drawing on five households from each of 211 census areas found that the government's piped drinking water supply system reached only 18 per cent of households. Private wells were the primary source of drinking water for 48 per cent of households, with 22 per cent using water vendors (who charged about ten times the price of the piped water tariff). Many of those using wells faced problems; the salination of groundwater, possibly fuelled by excessive abstraction, has rendered water from wells in the northern part of the city undrinkable even after boiling. Many residents face supply interruptions – for instance, 9 per cent of respondents had suffered from periods of at least a week in the past year when there were regular interruptions to their drinking water supply. Regarding sanitation, the city has no sewer system. 73 per cent of households had private lavatories in their homes that they did not have to share, while 16 per cent had shared private toilets and 12 per cent used public toilets. There were high levels of dissatisfaction among those who used public toilets: the most common complaint was the long waiting times, although many households complained of dirt, damage or problems with flushing. Of the 851 household toilets observed, more than half had no hand-washing basin in the vicinity. One-third of respondents reported that some people in their neighbourhood sometimes defecated outside the toilet; this was mostly done by children, and the most common sites were drains and gutters. Problems of flooding are common in many parts of the city, and accumulations of water provide breeding grounds for insect vectors, including the dengue-bearing mosquito.[52]

Kabul (Afghanistan)

The most common type of toilet used in both planned and unplanned housing is the raised drop latrine. It consists of a raised squatting slab, often of wood and mud, built over a box structure (usually built of stone or concrete) with a base approximately at street level. This box has a small outlet that leads directly to the street. In two- or three-storey buildings, sewage from higher floors reaches the outlet box by means of a drop chute. Some sections of the community separate the urine and the faeces, with the faeces passing through to the receptacle and the urine down a tube to the outside of the house. This causes a pile of fresh faeces to build up under the slab until somebody removes it. In many areas there is no way to mechanically collect the faeces due to the steep terrain and narrow streets. When the latrine is not manually emptied, fresh faeces pass out into the street. Defecation in the open is also common practice. Kabul has an extensive network of surface drains for carrying rain water, but the municipality cannot afford to maintain them. Refuse and night soil are often dumped into the drains, forming blockages that restrict the water flow. This results in the formation of hundreds of large pools of standing water, forming breeding sites for disease vectors. In the rainy season, this inadequate drainage leads to flooding and the formation of large pools of sewage in the flatter areas, where the water collects and mixes with the excreta from the latrines.[53]

Karachi (Pakistan)

More than half of the city's 12 million inhabitants live in *katchi abadis* [informal settlements]. A survey covering 334 of the 539 *katchi abadis* in the city found that 71 per cent have water supply lines. Half of these were laid by people through self-help, and half were laid by government agencies. But only one-third of households get piped water, with the rest purchasing water from vendors or resorting to their own wells. The survey found that 84 per cent of households in the *katchi abadis* have sewer systems, of which 62 per cent were laid by self-help and 38 per cent by government agencies. In the remaining 16 per cent of households, people have invested in soakpits or open drains.[54]

Madras/Chennai (India)

With a metropolitan population of about 5 million, Madras has the lowest per capita supply of any metropolitan centre in India – an average of 70 litres per day. A household survey in 1996 found that 42 per cent of households in the city and 70 per cent of households in the rest of the metropolitan area were not connected to the piped water supplies. For the whole metropolitan population, 18 per cent of households had no water source on the premises, while 29 per cent relied on shallow wells. Statistics for 1991 suggested that the sewerage system serves 31 per cent of the metropolitan population, and raw sewage flows freely into the metropolitan area's natural watercourses at many points.[55] In 1995, water was available for four hours a day.[56]

Manila (Philippines)

In Metro Manila in 1995, 67 per cent of the population had piped water, although this included several hundred thousand who had access only to public taps, with an average of 357 persons per tap. The other third relied mostly on wells.[57]

Visakhapatnam (India)

The Water Supply Department claims that 90 per cent of the city's population have access to clean drinking water, although other sources suggest it is between 60 and 70 per cent. Official figures suggest that 48 per cent of residents have piped water supplies to their home, while 42 per cent rely on public fountains with an average of 150 residents to each fountain.[58] A 1996 case study on 170 slums in Visakhapatnam reported that few slum households in the city have private tap water, and only half of the slums have public tap water.[59] The water is supplied twice a day, for one and a half hours in the morning and one hour in the evening. In terms of sanitation, the underground sewerage system covers only one block. Close to two-thirds of slum dwellers have private toilets linked to septic tanks. A large section of the slum population have to rely on public toilets.[60] As a result, large sections of the population defecate in the open.[61]

Yangon (Myanmar)

In 1995, 60 per cent of the population of 3.3 million were connected to the piped water supply, and several hundred thousand of these had access to a public tap only (with on average 180 persons per tap). The rest of the population were reliant on tubewells, ponds and rain collectors.[62]

water and sanitation provision. Table 1.4 shows the official statistics for Mumbai, which state that 99.9 per cent of the population have house taps.

Among the points worth highlighting in these interviews are:

- the number of people who have to pay to use toilets (in Dharavi, as in many low-income areas in Indian cities, most houses do not have toilets), the high costs of doing so, and the complaints about the dirtiness of the public toilets;

- the queues at the public toilets, the difficulties of having to queue and the pressure from others in the queue to hurry up;

- the difficulties in getting water, and how common it is for the most accessible water sources to be of poor quality;

- the widespread practice of defecating in the open, but only doing so at night; and

- the fact that most households have problems with mosquitoes and with drainage.

The same gap between the proportion of urban populations with improved sanitation and the proportion with safe, convenient sanitation is also evident in Pakistan and the Philippines – and probably in many other Asian nations. But here too, there are local examples that show how far provision can be improved. In the case of Pakistan, there is the world's largest community-managed sewer construction programme, which was stimulated and supported by the local NGO, the Orangi Pilot Project. This has greatly improved provision for sanitation for hundreds of thousands of urban households in Pakistan (see Chapter 7 for more details).

The Asian Development Bank survey of provision for water supply on which Tables 1.4 and 1.5 draw was unusual in that it also collected information on the volume of water used per person, the quality of the water, the regularity of the supply and the price.

Many cities have very low levels of water consumption per person – for instance

Box 1.3 Provision for water and sanitation in Mumbai; interviews with inhabitants of Dharavi in July 2002

Chandrakala Macchinder Nausuke

There is a problem with water and toilets. During the rains there are a lot of mosquitoes and water comes into the house. We have to stay up all night. We have to get water from a place 15–20 minutes away. We went to a tap in the *chawl* [tenement] outside and we would pay Rs50 per month for the water. People living close by sometimes do not give water to people from the slums. That is why we had to go elsewhere. Sometimes from the highway, from the *chawl*. Even now we take water from here and there, maybe from a broken municipal pipe. There is no tap. We did not try for water because we felt that since we would be shifting to a building soon [it would not be worth it,] so we kept quiet. We have to go far for the toilets. We have to pay Rs1 per day. Every day we spend at least Rs2–3 on the toilet. There is water in the toilet but it is not clean. It is very dirty. The water containers are broken and dirty. It takes us ten minutes to reach the toilet, and once there it is very crowded. Children also go to the toilet after paying for it. There is only one toilet near the road crossing.

S Punnamal and Valiamma

The toilet was very dirty earlier, so the children used to squat in the drains. Now they have built better toilets but the kids still squat in the drains. We have to ask for the drains to be covered. Even schoolchildren defecate in the drain opposite my house. They don't listen. Four or five years back they built toilets for us, 10–12 for the ladies and separate ones for the gents. Before that we used to go to the *chawl* and squat. Everybody went there and dirtied the place. There is no problem about water. There is a tap in each house. Before that there was a tap in front of the Bank. We had to go there for water. It took a very long time, [there were] so many people and

there used to be fights.

We have water in the evenings for 2–3 hours, and a little in the morning. Before that, a man would shout 'water is here' and everybody would run to fill [containers]. This was 25 years ago. Then gradually taps came. We had meetings and everybody signed forms and went to the office, then each *gulli* (lane) was given a tap. [There was] one tap [shared] between 10 or 15 houses. It was a problem. [The water came out in] a very thin stream and [was only available] from time to time [in the] mornings and evenings. We had to stand in a queue and fight. Now there is a tap in each house. [The water is] metered. We had to pay Rs3000–5000; before that it was Rs2000–3000, but I was one of the last ones to take a tap four years ago, and I had to pay Rs5000.

Safikunnissa

I have been here for 40 years. For water we used to come to the municipal tap in Kalyanwadi. There were fights at the tap. We used to stand in line and get maybe one or two *handaa* [an urn that can hold 10–12 litres of water], and that after fights. Then we got taps for ourselves. 10–12 people took the taps, so the total cost came to about Rs35,000. Each house paid about Rs2000–2500. Then the bills came: Rs2000, Rs1500, Rs1000. Then we would collect the money to pay the bills. Our pay was Rs2000–2500 a month; what to eat and what to spend! There was a lot of waterlogging during rains, sea water also used to come in. We had to raise the floor of our hut every year. In this manner we passed 30 years. Now we have some relief because this building was built. We came here four months ago. Before that they moved us to the colony.

Sahin Bano

I have been here for seven or eight years. In the beginning it was very dirty, there was no place to walk. We had to go to the toilet in the

company compound. The municipal toilet was very dirty. If we went there we wanted to vomit. The toilet in the company compound was not far, just two minutes away. Water was a big problem. The tap was in a trench. We had to fill water [containers] by the number system – whatever we could get – two, four or six *handaa* [containers], depending on the amount of water in the trench. We had to take water from outside also. We did not pay for water. We would ask somebody for water, and if they had water they would give it.

Asmaa Bano

I have been here for ten years. [Before that] I lived in a village and came here occasionally. The village was much better. [Before the recent improvements] even the children did not like it here. It was so dirty here and there were mosquitoes. My village is Pratapgarh, and there each house has a tap. We had to go into the fields in the night to defecate. Here we had to go to the toilet like everybody else. Rains were a problem when walking along because of waterlogging. The children would fall sick because of the mosquitoes. The room would get waterlogged and every year we would raise the floor level. We never had enough drinking water because it was such a big *chawl*. Then the children would scrounge around and [find] water. We did not have to pay for water since the people around us would allow us to take some. Two years back we got taps in the house, and then we moved to the colony. There was no problem with the toilets and water in the colony, but the people were not good. We were not together. We were given houses when they were available. Now we are in the building, we are OK, although there are still some problems with light and water.

Bhagwati

I have been here for the past 18 years. 18 years ago we had to go to the Ganesh temple for water. We went at 4am and stood in line until 6am, and got two *handaa* of water. We had to leave the children at home. My child once fell into the drain and I thought he had died, but the neighbours picked him up and bathed him and he was OK. Five years back we put in a tap, but when they put in the borewell they broke the pipe. Now the water is dirty and we can only wash clothes in it. We have to go here and there for drinking water. The building *walas* [inhabitants] don't give us water. We can't complain because the boring is for our own building. For a toilet, we use the roadside. We have to pay Rs30 every month. Every time you go you have to pay Rs1. It is a problem. In the morning you have to send the children to school and your husband to the office. I have to cook, and if you have to go to the toilet at the same time, there is a queue. Even if we go at 5.30am then your turn comes after four people. Once you manage to go in then people shout at you to hurry up. If it rains, the water from the drain does not soak away.

Kalyani

I have been here for the past 39 years, since I got married. I came here before the highway was built. There was no toilet, no drains. There was no water. We had to go and beg for water. There was no path. There were stones here and we had to jump over them. We could get just four or six *handaa* of water. We would not bathe because there was no water. If we had to go to the toilet there were just two

toilets, one for men and one for women. Once we went in [the other people in the queue] would shout and we had to come out in two minutes. At night we would go across the road. When they dug the road all the mud came into our huts. We have a tap but the water is dirty. We have to get drinking water [from elsewhere]. We have to take water stealthily from the building. They would not give it to us openly. If somebody gives water [to us], somebody else will shout at them and tell them not to give water away. The toilet is also far off. It is a problem.

Lakshmi

I have lived here since childhood. We used to get water from Poonawana Chawl or from the temple. We have to queue up there also. I had seven or eight brothers and sisters, and we used to carry water along with my mother. [After that] it became better, but people broke the pipe when boring. Now the water is very slow. Sometimes it is OK, sometimes it stinks so that you can't even touch it, as if it has been mixed with drain water. Now sometimes I have to go to my mother's house for water. When it rains water comes into the house. There is no exit for the drain water. There is a drain just outside my house [and] even mosquitoes. You can't sit outside, even in the morning. We use mosquito coils all the time. We pay Rs1 to go to the toilet. Earlier there was a municipal toilet and we went there, but that has been demolished

[while they] construct a building. At night we have to go across the road with men on one side and women on the other! It is embarrassing. During the day we can't go there and we have to spend money. The toilet is five minutes away at least. We have to walk there, and if we are desperate we have to run, but when we get there we have to wait. Our turn comes, but if another woman is in a hurry she tells us to hurry up. Others say 'Where have you all sprung up from?' We have to listen to some [unpleasant] things [just so that we can go to the] toilet! There are a lot of problems.

Paliniamma

I have been here for 15–20 years. We have a lot of problems. There is no outlet for the drains. We dig holes near our houses and collect our *mori* water [washing water] in it. The building people say that no water should come out on the path, so we collect the dirty water in drums and then we take the drums and throw the water in the drain along the road. Children ask us when we will get the house. The other day I filled some containers with water and it was stinking. I couldn't drink any water at night after my food.

Source: This is drawn from a series of interviews undertaken by the NGO SPARC (Society for the Promotion of Area Resource Centres) in various Indian cities in 2002 that are to be published in the October 2003 issue of *Environment and Urbanization*. Further extracts from these interviews are included in Box 2.5 in Chapter 2.

Phnom Penh (32 litres per person per day), Hanoi (45), Yangon (67), and several others where the daily per-person usage is less than 100 litres (Nuku'alofa, Kathmandu, Thimphu, Dhaka and Beijing). Given that these are averages for whole city populations, and that the groups that have water piped to their home will have much higher consumption levels than those who draw on public taps or other sources, these average figures hide large disparities, and it is possible that significant proportions of each city's population use less

than 20 litres per person per day. It is difficult to put a specific figure on an 'adequate' volume of water, but in most circumstances, at least 20 litres per person per day is essential, and 60 litres per person per day is needed to allow sufficient water for such domestic needs as washing, food preparation, cooking, cleaning, laundry and personal hygiene. (More would be needed if flush toilets were being used.) This suggests that a large section of Asia's urban population does not get sufficient supplies.

Table 1.5 also shows the irregularity of supplies for many cities. Only 26 out of 50 utilities report that they provide a 24-hour water supply, and some provide water for only a few hours a day. A consumer survey in each of the cities listed in Table 1.4 drawn from 100 randomly selected consumers suggested that supplies were more irregular than was stated by the utilities. In only four cities did consumers confirm a 100 per cent 24-hour supply.

Provision for water and sanitation in urban areas of Africa

Sub-Saharan Africa's urban population probably has the world's worst provision for urban water and sanitation. There are a few cities that have relatively good provision. In most small urban centres, there is little or no public provision. South Africa is an exception in that a relatively high proportion of its urban population have adequate water and sanitation provision. Most nations in North Africa also have relatively good levels of provision.

Table 1.6 shows the proportion of the urban population in African nations with access to improved water supply and sanitation in 2000, while Tables 1.7 and 1.8 show the water and sanitation provision in the largest cities of most African nations. Box 1.4 gives short summaries of the extent of water and sanitation provision in different cities.

This gap between the proportion of urban dwellers with improved provision and the proportion with safe, sufficient provision is as evident in most African nations as it is in most Asian nations – perhaps even more so. Tables 1.7 and 1.8 and the case studies summarized in Box 1.4 suggest that a very large proportion of sub-Saharan Africa's urban population have very inadequate water and sanitation provision. Yet the data in these tables and box are mostly from the largest and most important cities, where the proportion of people with adequate provision is likely to be higher than in smaller cities and urban centres. The data in Table 1.6 could be used to test the association between per capita incomes and the extent of improved provision for urban

Table 1.5 Water availability and cost in Asian cities, mid-1990s

City	Water availability (number of hours per day)	Average tariff (US$ per cubic metre)	Per cent of unaccounted- for water
Almaty	24	0.056	13
Bandung	6	0.369	43
Bangkok	24	0.313	38
Beijing	24	0.061	8
Bishkek	24	0.027	42
Calcutta	10	0.011	50
Cebu	18	0.663	38
Chennai	4	0.247	20
Chiangmai	20	0.299	35
Chittagong	15	0.119	35
Chonburi	16	0.461	37
Colombo	22	0.144	35
Davao	24	0.271	31
Delhi	3.5	0.034	26
Dhaka	17	0.093	51
Faisalabad	7	0.034	30
Hanoi	18	0.113	63
Ho Chi Minh City	24	0.131	34
Hong Kong	24	0.555	36
Jakarta	18	0.611	53
Johor Bahru	24	0.186	21
Karachi	1–4	0.091	30
Kathmandu	6	0.141	40
Kuala Lumpur	24	0.131	36
Lahore	17	0.197	40
Mandalay	24	1.201	60
Manila	17	0.232	44
Medan	24	0.266	27
Mumbai	5	0.058	18
Penang	24	0.208	20
Phnom Penh	12	0.150	61
Rarotonga	24		
Seoul	24	0.281	34
Shanghai	24	0.068	14
Singapore	24	0.553	6
Suva	24	0.223	43
Taipei	24	0.388	26
Tashkent	24	0.022	14
Thimphu	12	0.052	37
Tianjin	24	0.059	11
Ulaanbaatar	21	0.102	49
Ulsan	24	0.396	33
Vientiane	24	0.081	33
Yangon	12	0.456	60

Source: McIntosh, Arthur C and Cesar E Yñiguez (1997), *Second Water Utilities Data Book*, Asian Development Bank, Manila, 210 pages.

Table 1.6 Proportion of the urban population in African nations with access to improved water supply and sanitation, 2000

Country	Percentage of urban population with improved coverage for	
	Water supply	Sanitation
Algeria	98	90
Angola	34	70
Benin	74	46
Botswana	100	
Burkina Faso	84	88
Burundi	96	79
Cameroon	82	99
Central African Republic	80	43
Chad	31	81
Congo	71	14
Côte d'Ivoire	90	
Democratic Republic of Congo	89	53
Egypt	96	98
Eritrea	63	66
Ethiopia	77	58
Gabon	73	25
Gambia	80	41
Ghana	87	62
Guinea	72	94
Guinea Bissau	29	88
Kenya	87	96
Lesotho	98	93
Libyan Arab Jamahiriya	72	97
Madagascar	85	70
Malawi	95	96
Mali	74	93
Mauritania	34	44
Mauritius	100	100
Morocco	100	100
Mozambique	86	69
Namibia	100	96
Niger	70	79
Nigeria	81	85
Rwanda	60	12
Senegal	92	94
Sierra Leone	23	23
South Africa	92	99
Sudan	86	87
Togo	82	71
Tunisia*	94	97
Uganda	80	96
United Republic of Tanzania	80	98
Zambia	88	99
Zimbabwe	100	99

Note: The table only includes nations with 1 million plus inhabitants in 2000 for which data were available.
Sources: WHO and UNICEF (2000), *Global Water Supply and Sanitation Assessment 2000 Report*, World Health Organization, UNICEF and Water Supply and Sanitation Collaborative Council, Geneva, 80 pages. * Data on Tunisia from Saghir, Jamal Manuel Schiffler and Mathewos Woldu (2000), *Urban Water and Sanitation in the Middle East and North Africa Region: The Way Forward*, Middle East and North Africa Region Infrastructure Development Group, The World Bank, Washington, DC.

populations. Certainly, some of those nations in which very low proportions of the urban population have improved water are among the poorest – Guinea Bissau, Chad, Mauritania. For other nations with low proportions such as Angola and Sierra Leone, this must partly be the result of the civil conflicts that so disrupted all aspects of life for much of their population in recent years. But what is surprising in Table 1.6 is the very high proportion of the urban population with improved water and sanitation in many low-income nations (including some that have had little or no economic growth in recent years, such as Burundi, Rwanda and Zambia). Might this suggest that good water and sanitation provision for urban populations is achievable with low per capita incomes and little economic growth? Are some sub-Saharan African nations considerable success stories for water and sanitation provision? With datasets such as these, it is tempting to examine the extent of the association between their performance in water and sanitation provision in urban areas and their per capita income or their economic performance over the last 10–20 years. But comparing the figures in Table 1.6 with findings from city case studies in Box 1.4 and the more detailed statistics for particular cities in Tables 1.7 and 1.8 suggests that the variations in Table 1.6 are better explained by different government interpretations of what constitutes 'improved' water and sanitation. For instance, although there are still grounds for improvement in provision for water in many urban areas in South Africa, its urban populations are generally much better served with water than urban citizens in Burundi, Malawi and Zimbabwe – even if the figures in Table 1.6 could be used to suggest otherwise.[63]

One puzzle in Table 1.6 is the number of nations in which a higher proportion of the urban population has improved sanitation than improved water. In general, provision for sanitation lags behind provision for water. This is almost certainly explained by the fact that pit latrines are counted as improved provision, and households can construct these at their own initiative without relying on any government programme. In most urban areas, individual household solutions for water are more difficult, or there is no local water source that each individual household can tap, or all local water sources are contaminated.

The case studies in Box 1.4 highlight how water and sanitation provision is very inadequate for large sections of the African urban populations that are classified as having 'improved provision' in Table 1.6. For instance, 87 per cent of Kenya's urban population may have had improved water supplies by the year 2000, but detailed studies in Kenya's two largest cities, Nairobi and Mombasa (summarized in Box 1.4) show that a much smaller proportion have safe, sufficient provision. The fact that 96 per cent of Kenya's urban population had improved sanitation is only possible because shared latrines were counted as 'improved'. The inhabitants of informal settlements such as Kibera in Nairobi, who compete with hundreds of other people for access to latrines, are counted as having 'improved provision'. Box 1.5 describes water and sanitation provision in Huruma, a settlement in Nairobi with around 6500 inhabitants. On average, there are 500 persons to each toilet. A study based on a representative sample of households in Nairobi's informal settlements (which house around half the city's population) suggested that 'the high proportion of slum residents who report access to pit latrines conceals the fact that most toilets in the slums are filthy and unusable because they are shared by a large number of households.'[64] This study found that more than 8 per cent of the population of these informal settlements defecate outside. It also found that 31 per cent of children under three years of age in Nairobi's informal settlements had diarrhoea in the two weeks prior to the survey, with 11 per cent of children having diarrhoea with blood which signifies serious systemic infection.[65] A study in Mukuru Kwa Reuben, another low-income informal settlement in Nairobi, found that the 10,000 inhabitants had only 215 toilets, which were on the settlement's periphery. Even these could not be used at night because it was unsafe to walk around the settlement.[66] And this is in a country which reports that 96 per cent of its urban population has improved sanitation.

Box 1.4 Examples of the inadequacies in cities' water supply and sanitation in Africa

Abidjan (Côte d'Ivoire)
In 1997, the official distribution network supplied 180,000 customers, less than half of all households (the city has some 3 million inhabitants). Most other households obtain water from standpipes or water re-sellers. In 1998, around one-fifth of households were connected to sewers.[74]

Accra (Ghana)
Interviews with 1000 households undertaken in 1991 found that only 35 per cent had water piped into their houses. Most of the rest relied on private or community standpipes or vendors, although a small percentage have to rely on open waterways, rain water collection and wells. Over 80 per cent of the lowest income quintile had to fetch their water, compared to 10 per cent of the wealthiest group.[75] The water distribution system to low-income areas is more vulnerable to contamination, and the water quality in low-income areas is generally worse than in those areas with indoor plumbing.[76] A survey of 558 households in 1997 found that only 45 per cent had drinking water from an inside tap.[77] For sanitation, 36 per cent of the 1000 households interviewed in 1991 had flush toilets, with 41 per cent using pit latrines, 20 per cent using pan or bucket latrines and about 4 per cent having no access to toilet facilities. Nearly three-quarters of the lowest income quintile shared toilet facilities with more than ten people.[78] Users of public toilets generally find them unsatisfactory in regard to cleanliness, convenience and privacy. Those using public toilets pay the equivalent of around US$1 per head per month. Those with pit latrines in the house paid about US$4 monthly to a private individual for emptying. There is a sewer system in Accra's central business district, but only 1 per cent of the city's population are connected.[79] Open defecation is a common practice, with people using various means including wrapping human excreta in polythene bags (commonly referred to as 'precious packages') for disposal. With no usable toilets in the home or conveniently located nearby, many Accra residents have no choice but to defecate along beaches, watercourses and drains.[80]

Addis Ababa (Ethiopia)
Around 30 per cent of residential dwellings in Addis Ababa use open fields for defecation. In peri-urban and urban centres outside Addis Ababa, about 46 per cent of families have no sanitary facilities.[81]

Benin City (Nigeria)
Families in the informal housing sector in Benin City normally use pit latrines. A 1995 survey found that 74 per cent of households relied on these, and most were of questionable quality. Household water is mainly piped from outside the housing premises (from another compound, the street or other neighbourhoods) or obtained from a water vendor or from a rain-harvester underground tank.[82]

Conakry (Guinea)
Around 45 per cent of the population are connected to water mains. Residents of unplanned and planned settlements that are not connected to the water network get water from those who have connections (32 per cent of households), from standpipes (7 per cent) and from handcarts (2 per cent). Conakry's sanitation network, built in 1954, is not operational due to the lack of maintenance and renovation of the facilities. A minute, antiquated sewer system services the city centre. Independent mini-systems are also in service in some areas.[83]

Cotonou (Benin)
This city of around 1 million inhabitants has no sewer system. For water, more than half the population depend on water re-sellers or handcart vendors. Many low-income areas are prone to flooding.[84]

Dar es Salaam (Tanzania)
According to a survey of 660 households drawn from all income levels in 1986–1987, 47 per cent had no piped water supply either inside or immediately outside their houses, while 32 per cent had a shared piped water supply. Of the households without piped water, 67 per cent bought water from neighbours while 26 per cent drew water from public kiosks or standpipes. The

average water consumption was only 23.6 litres a day. Of the 660 households, 89 per cent had simple pit latrines (and most of Dar es Salaam continues to rely on pit latrines). Only 4.5 per cent had toilets connected to septic tanks or sewers. Most households have to share sanitary facilities. Over-flowing latrines are a serious problem, especially in the rainy season, and provision for empty-ing septic tanks and latrines is very inadequate.[85] A study conducted during 1997–1998 in six low-income wards found that in most sites, water supplies were sporadic and often unsafe and expensive, and the sole water source was vendors. Where people had access to water from government wells, the wells were generally poorly managed. In some instances, pumps were stolen within weeks of being installed. In all the areas visited, pit latrines were the only form of sanitation.[86]

Gaborone (Botswana)
There is generally only one standpipe per 20 plots in self-help housing areas. Over 95 per cent of tenants renting a room in Gaborone have to share a communal toilet (usually a pit latrine) with their landlords and other tenant households on the plot. Cleaning the toilet is often a point of dispute, while in some cases there are so many households on one plot that one communal toilet is insufficient for their needs.[87]

Ibadan (Nigeria)
Only 22 per cent of the population are served by the municipal water supply system. The city has no sewer system. City inhabitants rely on pit latrines and latrines connected to septic tanks.[88]

Johannesburg (South Africa)
By 1995, 80 per cent of households had a water supply piped to their house or flat; 18 per cent had a tap on the plot and 2 per cent relied on public taps, kiosks or boreholes. The legacy of apartheid can be seen in the fact that nearly all households that had a tap on the plot or relied on public taps, kiosks or boreholes were Black. Most of those reliant on public taps, kiosks or boreholes lived in informal dwellings. Sewers cover almost 80 per cent of the metropoli-tan area. 70 per cent of households have a flush toilet within the dwelling, with another 23 per cent having one on site. But only half the Black population have a flush toilet within the dwelling (with another 38 per cent having a flush toilet on site). Virtually all households with toilets not connected to sewers (including pit, chemical and bucket toilets) are within Black households. Also, one cannot assume that a flush toilet on site means adequate provision, since landlords may not let tenants use it, and in hostels many households have to share a toilet. Provision for sanitation remains very inadequate in many settlements. For instance, a survey of informal settlements found that 39 per cent of households used pit latrines, 13 per cent buckets, 38 per cent portable latrines and 7 per cent flush toilets, while 2 per cent had no toilet.[89]

Kampala (Uganda)
Only inhabitants of affluent and middle-income districts in central and residen-tial areas have private connections serviced by the National Water and Sewerage Corporation. Water truckers supplement the corporation by supply-ing the non-serviced areas. The low-income population are supplied by private operators, standpipe vendors and connected customers who re-sell the water in densely populated and poor areas that are serviced by water mains or its extensions, and by bicycle water vendors outside the serviced areas. Only afflu-ent families are connected to sewers (which serve 9 per cent of households) or septic tanks (10 per cent).[90]

Khartoum (The Sudan)
A report in 1989 described how the systems of water supply and sewage disposal were inadequate both in coverage and in maintenance of the service. For water supply, coverage was poor, with low-income groups in squatter settlements paying the most for water, often bought from vendors. Breakdowns and cuts in the supply system were common. The municipal sewerage system served only about 5 per cent of the Khartoum urban area. Even that system was susceptible to breakdowns during which waste was discharged either directly into the river or onto open land. For most people in the low-income areas, there was no system of sewage disposal.[91]

Table 1.6 suggests that four out of five urban dwellers in Nigeria have improved water and sanitation. But, as illustrated in the case studies of Owerri, Benin City, Zaria and Ibadan in Box 1.4, water in piped systems is often contaminated, irregular and difficult to get because so many persons compete for access to each tap. Most of Nigeria's urban popula-tion have no access to toilets connected to sewers or septic tanks.

Table 1.6 suggests that four out of five urban dwellers in Tanzania have improved water and virtually all have improved sanita-tion. This is difficult to reconcile with detailed studies in informal settlements in Dar es Salaam (see Box 1.4) and data from other Tanzanian cities. More than 60 per cent of Dar es Salaam's population live in areas with minimal or no infrastructure for water supply, sanitation and drainage.[67] Only a small propor-tion of the population of Tanzania's largest cities such as Dar es Salaam, Arusha, Tanga and Tabora have sewerage connections.[68] 83 per cent of households in Dar es Salaam use pit latrines; 10 per cent have septic tanks and 6–7 per cent have sewers. The sewerage network covers only the central part of Dar es Salaam and a small section outside the city centre. The system is old and unreliable, owing to deferred maintenance.[69] Many cities in Tanzania have water for only a few hours a day on average – including Dodoma (seven hours), Shinyanga (six hours), Sumbawanga (five hours), Mtwara and Lindi (four hours) and Singida (two hours).[70] Official statistics may suggest that only 2 per cent of the urban population in Tanzania lack improved provision for sanitation and only 20 per cent lack improved provision for water, but a far larger proportion lack adequate provision.

Changes in provision for water and sanitation in urban areas of East Africa
For a range of urban sites in Kenya, Uganda and Tanzania, there are comparable data on water use for the late 1960s and the late 1990s which allow some insight into trends over time.[71] These showed the following trends.

Declining water use for those with piped supplies

For households with piped water, average per capita use declined from 124 litres a day in 1967 to 64 litres a day in 1997. In the 14 sites with piped water supplies covered by the research, all but three had much lower consumption levels in 1997 compared to 1967. In some the decline was dramatic, as in Iganga (Uganda) – from 79 to 34 litres per day – and in Moshi (Tanzania) – from 95 to 41 litres per day. Although the more affluent study sites – such as Parklands in Nairobi and Oyster Bay and Upanga in Dar es Salaam – experienced decreases in water-use levels, the mean daily water use in 1997 still remained well above the average, while for those with relatively low household incomes, water use was well below it. Many low-income households had such unreliable piped water supplies that their water use had fallen to levels similar to many households that did not have piped supplies.

Reduced reliance on 'improved' water sources used by households without piped supplies

In 1997, a smaller proportion of households that did not have piped supplies drew on protected or improved sources (wells, standpipes and hydrants) than had been the case in 1967. In 1967, more than three-quarters of unpiped sample households obtained water from protected or improved sources – with almost 100 per cent of households drawing from these in Mathare Valley (one of the largest informal settlements in Nairobi) and in the towns of Moshi and Dodoma in Tanzania. Thirty years later, only 56 per cent of unpiped households used protected or improved sources. In part this is because more are serviced by private vendors and kiosks, and these are particularly important in Mathare Valley and in Moshi and Dodoma where over half the sampled unpiped households view these as their primary source of water. Many households also use more than one water source – and by 1997, some 60 per cent of unpiped households regularly use a secondary source that is some distance from their home for water.

Kinshasa (Congo)

A report in 1989 noted that there is no sewerage system in Kinshasa. Around half the urban population (some 1.5 million people) were not served by a piped water network. High-income areas were often 100 per cent connected while many other areas had 20–30 per cent of houses connected – essentially those along the main roads. The sale of water flourished in areas far from the network – in these areas water was usually obtained from wells, the river or deep wells.[92]

Kumasi (Ghana)

Three-quarters of the population are served with piped water, but large numbers only have access through shared taps or standpipes and long waits and queues are common. Only 10 per cent of households have indoor plumbing. Even when an area has a piped network, water pressure is often inadequate and the service is not continuous. Those who depend on vendors have to pay high prices. Water provision is particularly poor on the urban periphery where there is rapid urban growth. For sanitation, only 30 per cent of households have satisfactory arrangements in their homes. 15 per cent of the population rely on bucket latrines, 7 per cent on pit latrines, 8 per cent on open defecation, 25 per cent on toilets and septic tanks and 7 per cent on sewers. Nearly 40 per cent rely on 400 public latrines scattered around city: long waits are common and most such latrines are poorly maintained. In Atoinsu, for example, there are only two public toilets with 14 squat holes each to serve 10,000 inhabitants. Many people relieve themselves in plastic bags, which are put into the community refuse skips or disposed of indiscriminately. There is no comprehensive storm drainage system, and flooding – with related building damage and loss of property – is a common occurrence during the rainy season. Usually the poor are affected most because they have settled the least desirable locations in low-lying areas adjacent to drains and watercourses.[93]

Luanda (Angola)

Of a population estimated at over 3.2 million, only 17 per cent of households report a domestic water connection and only 10 per cent have an internal water supply. Most of the population rely on water purchased from those with tanks who get their water from tanker lorries.[94] More than three-quarters of the city population have no access to sewers and, until 1989, on-site sanitation was discouraged, even though this was the only possible way to provide sanitation for much of the city population. A 1996 study in one of the municipalities in Luanda (Sambizanga) found that only half of all families had on-site sanitation.[95] A more recent review suggested that the proportion of families with on-site sanitation is dropping, as newly arrived migrants are less likely to be able to afford to construct a latrine.[96]

Mombasa (Kenya)

Although the majority of households are said to have access to piped water, a 1993 estimate suggested that only 29 per cent had their own connection. Very few parts of the city receive a continuous supply and some have had no water in their pipes for several years. On average, water is available for only 2.9 hours a day. In a sample-survey of 182 poor households in 1986, 92 per cent experienced water shortages – about half all the time, and half occasionally. Regarding sanitation, the 1989 census showed that only 10 per cent of Mombasa's households were served by a conventional sewerage system. The great majority of households (68 per cent in the mid-1990s and 81 per cent of poor households) use pit latrines. Shortages of water and capital funds have delayed extensions to the sewerage system and repairs to the non-functioning treatment works, with the result that untreated sewage runs into the sea. Those lacking sewers face particular problems disposing of their domestic wastewater (grey water).[97]

Nairobi (Kenya)

More than half the population depend on standpipe vendors for access to water; around 30 per cent of the population have a connection to the official network, with the rest relying on trucks or private operators. 10 per cent of the population are served by sewers, 20 per cent with septic tanks and 70 per cent with manually cleaned latrines. There are 260 latrines in Pumwani, with an average of 450 persons per latrine.[98] A report in 1994 described how 55 per cent of Nairobi's population lived in informal settlements, which are squeezed onto less than 6 per cent of the city's land area. Only 12 per cent of plots in these settlements have piped supplies. Most people have to obtain water from kiosks. Water shortages are common, with pipes often running dry; a survey found that 80 per cent of households complained of water shortages and pipes often running dry. In regard to sanitation, this same survey suggested that 94 per cent of the inhabitants of informal settlements do not have access to adequate sanitation. Only a minority of dwellings have toilets. Significant proportions of the total population have no access to showers and baths, and in most areas drainage is inadequate.[99] Kibera is the largest low-income urban area in Nairobi, covering an area of 225 hectares and with an estimated population of 470,000. Traditional pit latrines are the only excreta disposal system available, and a high proportion of households have no toilet within or close to their home. There are often up to 200 persons per pit latrine. Pits fill up quickly and emptying is a problem due to difficult access. Space to dig new pits is often not available.[100]

Ouagadougou (Burkina Faso)

23 per cent of households have water connections from the official water and sanitation agency; most others depend on getting water from standpipe vendors or handcarts. 8 per cent of the population are served by sewers, with 2 per cent served by septic tanks and 90 per cent served by traditional latrines. The sewer system is still in the embryonic stage.[101] A 1991 study covering 600 households found that 38 per cent were connected to the municipal water supply, although only one-third of these had indoor plumbing (the rest had yard taps). Most other households obtained water at higher costs from public standpoints, vendors or neighbours.[102] Around 75 per cent of the sample households were dissatisfied with existing arrangements for water supply. The average monthly household expenditure (exclusive of rent for tenant households) was FCFA45,000 (about US$200). Among the 600 households, 70 per cent used traditional pit latrines, 18 per cent used vault latrines and 5 per cent used septic tanks. About 7 per cent of the population were without any facility and defecated in the open. A public latrine existed in the Central Market but no respondent reported using a public latrine on a regular basis. About 57 per cent of the households were dissatisfied with current sanitation arrangements, including the odour and inconvenience.[103]

Owerri (Nigeria)

A 1995 study found that 83 per cent of the sampled residents had access to a piped water supply; the rest relied on other sources, which were often contaminated. More than half of those with access to piped water did not have private connections in their homes; they either shared with neighbours or used public taps near their houses. In regard to regularity, 45 per cent of respondents only received free flowing water for a few hours a day while 15 per cent had water flowing every alternate day, 2.5 per cent had water once a week, and 8.5 per cent rarely had water. When tap water was not available, most households used water from streams. 27 per cent of respondents had a bathroom in the home, 67 per cent had one in the compound and 6.5 per cent had no bathroom at all. For sanitation, water closets were the most common means (69 per cent) followed by pit latrines (15 per cent). 16 per cent of respondents had no toilet at all.[104]

Zaria (Nigeria)

A 1995 household survey found that most buildings in the core area did not have individual water connections, and relied on public connections. 83 per cent of the sample had access to piped water. Water supplies were irregular for much of the population, including 11 per cent who received water one day in two, 4 per cent who received it once a week or once a fortnight and 12 per cent who rarely or never received water. The most common type of toilet was the earth or pit latrine, used by 73 per cent of respondents. The remaining 27 per cent reported using a modern water-closet system.[105]

Reduced reliability of piped supplies

Different factors contribute to this reduced reliability, including a lack of system maintenance and the stress on existing network capacity from increasing urban populations. In 1967, virtually all the households interviewed who had piped supplies received 24-hour service; by 1997, only 56 per cent did so, with around one-fifth receiving only one to five hours of service a day. Again, the more affluent sites were generally the ones which had the most reliable water supplies. There had been a huge increase in the proportion of households storing water at home – from 3 per cent in 1967 to 90 per cent in 1997. In some sites, all those interviewed in 1997 collected water from various sources and stored it at home to ensure adequate supplies because the piped system is so unreliable. The single most important change in the nature of secondary water supplies is the introduction of private sources such as kiosks and vendors. By 1997, these were used by almost 40 per cent of piped sample households. Private sources are particularly important in many low-income areas such as Changombe and Temeke[72] in Dar es Salaam (Tanzania) and in Iganga (Uganda), where over 60 per cent of piped households use vendors as their primary source. By 1997, private water vending through kiosks or vendors had become a booming business in many of the low- and middle-income study sites, despite the fact that the water they sell frequently costs considerably more per litre than the public supplies. Researchers encountered several instances of public supplies being sabotaged.

The increase in the time taken to obtain water

The average distance that unpiped household members walked to obtain their water did not change much between 1967 (222 metres) and 1997 (204 metres), but distances to unprotected water sources had increased. The number of trips to collect water had increased from an average of 2.6 a day in 1967 to 4 in 1997. On average, unpiped urban household members were walking 1 kilometre each day to and from water sources (up from 0.6 kilometres a day in 1967). But the total time spent collecting water each day increased more than threefold, from an average of 28 minutes in the late 1960s to an average of 92 minutes in 1997. Households using private sources such as kiosks report the largest amount of time spent collecting water. By 1997, on average, those

Box 1.5 Provision for water and sanitation in Huruma in Nairobi

The Huruma informal settlements are situated in the Starehe division of Nairobi city and consist of six villages. The settlements have been in existence for as long as 28 years. The 3.8-hectare site occupied by these settlements is public land under the trusteeship of the Nairobi City Council, which has agreed to delineate this land and set it aside for the purpose of upgrading the area for the benefit of the residents.

An enumeration and mapping exercise in five of the settlements, undertaken by the residents with the support of Pamoja Trust and the City Council in 2001, found that these settlements have 2309 households and a total population of 6569 people. There are 1105 tenants and 1002 'structure owners' in these settlements. The average household income is Ksh5000 (Kenyan shillings) and the main areas of daily expenditure are food, transport, water and the use of toilet facilities.

In all instances, toilet facilities were perceived to be most insufficient. All the residents used the few public or community toilets or the so-called 'flying toilets' (which refers to the practice of wrapping excreta in plastic bags or waste paper and throwing it away).

- In Kambi Moto, no households have toilets of their own. There is one pit latrine and the Nairobi City Council toilets, which have three units for men and three for women. The cost is Ksh2 per visit.
- In Mahira, there is one self-help toilet with ten units – ten toilets and two bathrooms for a settlement with 332 houses and 1500 inhabitants. However, the toilets are not connected to the sewer line. The cost per visit is Ksh2. The respondents said that 80 per cent of excreta is disposed of in flying toilets.
- In Redeemed, there is a commercial toilet with six units. It is connected to the sewer line and costs Ksh2 per visit. The flying toilets are also prevalent in the settlement.
- In Ghetto, there is a self-help commercial toilet that is not connected to the sewer lines and costs Ksh2 per visit.
- In Gitathuru, the respondents indicate that there is no public toilet facility. The riverside was identified as the main place where residents go to the toilet.

Toilet facilities in all the settlements were perceived to be inadequate, with an average toilet-to-person ratio of 1:500 or more.

All the settlements draw their water from privately operated water points at Ksh2 per 20 litres of water; 45 water points were mapped within the five settlements. The only other water source is a river that passes Gitathuru, but this is extremely polluted as it is a major waste-dumping site.

The residents of Huruma are unanimous in seeing security of their homes and land as their biggest need. This comes against a backdrop of numerous evictions in other informal settlements or irregular allocations that benefit non-residents. Although upgrading the housing, sanitation and health facilities is considered vital, there is a rational fear that without tenure regularization the benefits of these other developments may not accrue to the residents, especially the tenants.

Source: Pamoja Trust (2001), *Huruma Informal Settlements – Planning Survey Report*, Pamoja Trust, Nairobi. This was based on an enumeration and mapping exercise undertaken between May and October 2001 by the Nairobi City Council in conjunction with the Pamoja Trust and the residents of five of the villages (Kambi Moto, Mahiira, Redeemed, Ghetto and Gitathuru), which was carried out as a first step towards the regularization of these settlements. The data collection in all instances was carried out by the residents of Huruma.

using kiosks were spending almost two hours a day collecting water.

The higher cost of water

In 1997, piped supplies were less than one-quarter of the cost per litre of supplies from vendors (the only other water source that delivers to the household). Water from kiosks was nearly twice the cost of piped supplies, but as noted above, getting this water was also time consuming. Getting water from a neighbour or from a protected or improved source was less costly than kiosks but more costly than piped supplies.

Provision for water in Africa's larger cities

Tables 1.7 and 1.8 provide more detail regarding the quality of water and sanitation provision in the largest city within each African nation. Drawing from Table 1.7, the following points can be noted:

- The number of cities where one-third or more of the entire population was unserved by public water supply systems in 2000 and relied on wells, vendors or other water sources; Luanda, Bangui, N'Djamena, Brazzaville, Accra, Conakry,

City	House connections (%)	Yard taps (%)	Public standpipes (%)	Boreholes with handpumps (%)	Other (%)	Unserved (%)
Abidjan (Côte d'Ivoire)	43					
Accra (Ghana)	25	20			50 (vendors)	5
Addis Ababa (Ethiopia)	4	48	45	0.7		2
Algiers (Algeria)	84				19	
Antananarivo (Madagascar)		22	35			43
Asmara (Eritrea)	47	12			40 (tanker trucks)	
Bamako (Mali)	20		36			
Bangui (Central African Republic)		12	11	0.6		75
Bissau (Guinea Bissau)	20	12				71
Blantyre (Malawi)	41		25			34
Brazzaville (Congo)		63			14 (vendors)	23
Bujumbura (Burundi)		55	35		8	2
Conakry (Guinea)	33	0.8	3		0.4	63
Dakar (Senegal)	63	15				22
Dar es Salaam (Tanzania)	7	13	17	15	8	39
Freetown (Sierra Leone)	2	8	0.4	0.2	24 (wells)	
Gaborone (Botswana)	43	2	56			
Harare (Zimbabwe)	8					
Kampala (Uganda)	42	8	13			
Kigali (Rwanda)	16	13	23			
Kinshasa (Democratic Republic of Congo)	70				15 (wells)	13
Libreville (Gabon)	31	23	39		7 (wells, surface water)	
Lome (Togo)		55	12			33
Luanda (Angola)	18	4	28			50
Lusaka (Zambia)		26	55			19
Malabo (Equatorial Guinea)	38	3		44	9	6
Maputo (Mozambique)	22	28	27	14	9	1
Maseru (Lesotho)		26	9			64
Mbane (Swaziland)	37	37				24
N'Djamena (Chad)	7	13	8	1	71 (wells)	
Nairobi (Kenya)	78		15	1	7 (wells)	
Niamey (Niger)	33		28	2	36 (vendors)	
Nouakchott (Mauritania)	30		70			
Ouagadougou (Burkina Faso)	27	48	5			20
Port Louis (Mauritius)	48	39	0.7		2 (wells)	
Windhoek (Namibia)	84		17			

Table 1.7 Africa: provision for water in the largest cities within each nation, 2000

Source: WHO (2001), *Water Supply and Sanitation Sector Assessment 2000; Africa Region Part 2; Country Profiles*, World Health Organization Regional Office for Africa, Harare, 287 pages.

Bissau, Maseru, Antananarivo, Blantyre, Niamey, Dar es Salaam and Lome. The list would be longer if there was complete information about all nations' largest cities. It is also likely that most urban centres in each of these nations had higher proportions of their population unserved by public water supply systems than in these cities.

- The low proportion of households with house connections in most cities; very few cities have as many as half of all households with house connections.
- The dependence of so many households on public standpipes – for instance, more than one-quarter of the city population in Luanda, Gaborone, Bujumbura, Addis Ababa, Libreville, Antananarivo,

Table 1.8 Africa: provision for sanitation in the largest cities within each nation, 2000

City	Sewer (%)	Septic tank (%)	Wet latrine (%)	VIP latrine and simple latrine (%)	Other (%)	Unserved (%)
Abidjan[**]	0	67		23		
Addis Ababa	0.01	2	2	12		
Algiers	82	10			11	
Antananarivo	0		13	39		45
Asmara	0	0	64	12	23	
Bamako	1.5	32		66		
Bissau	0.8	2	69			12
Blantyre	6	50 (septic tank and all kinds of pit latrine)				44
Brazzaville	0	7	0.3	71	1	21
Bujumbura	7	20		58		15
Casablanca[*]	70					
Conakry	7	63 (septic tanks and all forms of latrine)				28
Cotonou	0.3	14	62		6	18
Dakar	26	47		5		22
Dar es Salaam	5	30	63			2
Freetown	0	18	12		12	
Gaborone	32	1	3	60	3	1
Harare	6					
Kampala	11	6		83		
Kigali	0	10	10	90		
Kinshasa	1	6	1	44	15	
Libreville	0	27	67	6		
Lome	1		24	56		20
Luanda	17	25		20		38
Lusaka	41					
Maputo	25			71		4
Maseru	6	5		79		11
Mbane	47			50		2
Moroni	0	69	20	11		
N'Djamena	0	6		60	33	
Nairobi	30	16	11	43		1
Niamey	0	5		85	10	
Nouakchott	5	95[*]				
Ouagadougou	0	13		81	6	
Port Louis	15	3	0.7	3	59 (pail)	
Sao Tome	5					
Tunis[*]	70					
Windhoek	83				17 (communal)	

Note: VIP latrine stands for 'ventilated improved pit latrine'.
Sources: WHO (2001), *Water Supply and Sanitation Sector Assessment 2000; Africa Region Part 2; Country Profiles*, World Health Organization Regional Office for Africa, Harare, 287 pages, except for those cities marked * where the data are from Saghir, Jamal Manuel Schiffler and Mathewos Woldu (2000), *Urban Water and Sanitation in the Middle East and North Africa Region: The Way Forward*, Middle East and North Africa Region Infrastructure Development Group, The World Bank, Washington, DC. ** Another source suggests that a significant proportion of households that are connected to the water system are also connected to sewers or the wastewater system.

Bamako, Nouakchott, Niamey, Maputo and Lusaka. While well maintained and sufficient public standpipes can provide adequate water for good health, in most African urban areas it is rare for them to be well maintained, for water supplies to be regular and for water to be of good quality. It is also rare for there to be enough public standpipes relative to the population.

In the 43 African cities for which information on water and sanitation provision was collected, 31 per cent of the population was unserved, with only 43 per cent having a house connection or yard tap and 21 per cent relying on public taps. Thus, if the definition of 'adequate provision for water' is a house connection or yard tap, then more than half the population in these cities have inadequate provision. But this is not a representative sample of urban areas in the region. The largest city within each nation is generally the national capital and generally has higher levels of water and sanitation provision than other cities. Reviews of the findings from demographic and health surveys, which are based on representative samples of national populations with a sufficient sample size to allow comparisons between cities of different sizes, show that in general, the smaller the city, the larger the proportion of the population with inadequate provision.[73] So perhaps as few as one-quarter of sub-Saharan Africa's urban population have house connections for water.

Provision for sanitation in Africa's larger cities

The following points can be highlighted, drawing on Table 1.8:

- The only provision for sanitation for most of the population in the cities listed is latrines that households dig themselves, or public latrines which are often dirty and difficult to access.
- More than 90 per cent of the population in the following cities live in homes with no connection to a sewer: Addis Ababa, Antananarivo, Asmara, Bamako, Bissau, Blantyre, Brazzaville, Bujumbura, Conakry, Cotonou, Dar es Salaam, Freetown, Harare, Kigali, Kinshasa, Libreville, Lome, Maseru, Moroni, N'Djamena, Niamey, Nouakchott, Ouagadougou and Sao Tome. Good quality pit latrines or toilets connected to septic tanks can provide adequate quality alternatives – but the case studies summarized in Box 1.4 suggest that they do not do so for the majority of sub-Saharan Africa's urban population.
- Between 10 and 45 per cent of the population in many of the cities listed are classified as 'unserved'.

Provision for sanitation is so poor in many African cities that significant proportions of their populations resort to open defecation or to defecation in waste material (such as waste paper or plastic bags) – this is termed 'flying toilets' in Nairobi.[106] Studies of many individual cities, including Accra, Addis Ababa, Kumasi, Luanda, Nairobi and Ouagadougou, have found open defecation to be common.[107] A research project on on-site sanitation included interviews with 1843 households in Vijayawada (India), Maputo (Mozambique) and Accra, Cape Coast and Tamale (Ghana). The districts where the interviews were held included those where collaborating agencies had a history of community-based work; districts with mixed physical site conditions, mixed density housing and varying household plot sizes; and districts with a mix of formally and informally developed areas and areas where pit emptying practices could be found and observed. 29 per cent of households had no domestic sanitation facilities within their plots; the majority of cases were from Ghana (84 per cent).[108]

The WHO/UNICEF Assessment 2000's statistics for sanitation for 43 cities that are the largest in their country show that 19 per cent of the population are unserved. Of the people in these 43 cities, only 18 per cent have toilets connected to sewers. This very low proportion is confirmed by an analysis of demographic and health surveys, which suggests that 25 per cent of Africa's urban population have access to toilets connected to sewers.[109] As later chapters will discuss, on-site sanitation (ie, sanitation that does not require sewers) can provide good quality provision, and in many urban settings in sub-Saharan Africa it is more appropriate than sewer-based systems, especially where per capita incomes are very low, most housing is one-storey and water supplies are very inadequate (so flush toilets cannot work well). But most governments do not support on-site sanitation. Governments that have not ensured the installation of sewers have generally not supported household investment in good quality on-site sanitation and the support services it needs (for instance, regular pit-emptying services). Thus, it is unlikely that more than one-third of sub-Saharan Africa's urban population have access to sanitation that is adequate in terms of convenience and the safe disposal of human excreta.

The absence of provision for drainage and the collection of household wastes within most low-income settlements also contributes to the likelihood of faecal contamination of the environment and the large disease burden this brings. Most informal settlements in urban areas of Africa have no service to collect solid waste. In many African cities, only 10–30 per cent of all urban households' solid wastes are collected, and services are inevitably most deficient in informal settlements.[110] Uncollected garbage, along with human faeces, is often disposed of in drainage ditches, which can quickly become clogged. When waste-water and storm water cannot be easily drained, flooding spreads waste (including faecal matter) through the surrounding area. Standing water can also be contaminated by blocked sewers and over-flowing septic tanks, and pathogens are then spread quickly to everything else. Drainage is an especially serious concern for the many urban communities on steep or swampy land.[111] Organically polluted water also becomes a productive breeding place for certain disease vectors, ie, *Culex quinquefasciatus* mosquitoes, which in East Africa transmit lymphatic filariasis. But even where these mosquitoes do not transmit diseases, their biting is a constant and unpleasant nuisance that also causes loss of sleep – and many low-income households end up spending up to 5 per cent of their incomes on mosquito coils or other measures to protect themselves against this problem.

Provision for water and sanitation in urban areas of Latin America and the Caribbean[112]

Table 1.9 shows the proportion of the urban population in Latin American and Caribbean nations with improved water supply and sanitation in 2000. For water supply, this is divided into those with house connections and those with what is termed 'easy access' (usually access to water through public stand-

pipes within 400 metres[113]). One wonders at the validity of describing as 'easy access' water in a public standpipe 400 metres from the home (at which, in any dense urban settlement, there is likely to be a long queue).

If comparisons are to be made with provision for national urban populations in Africa and Asia, the proportion of urban inhabitants with house connections plus those with easy access in Table 1.9 would be equivalent to those with improved provision in earlier tables. The data on sanitation in Table 1.10 distinguish between those with connections to sewers and 'in situ' sanitation. Table 1.10 shows the provision of water and sanitation for 41 cities[114] while Box 1.6 gives short summaries of the extent of water and sanitation provision in selected cities or national urban populations.

For the region as a whole, only 7 per cent of the urban population lack improved provision for water and only 13 per cent lack improved provision for sanitation.[115] As in Asia and Africa, it is clear that there are very large variations in the quality and extent of water and sanitation provision between nations and between cities. At one extreme there is Haiti, with a small minority of its urban population with water piped to the home and none with sewer connections; at the other is Chile, with nine out of ten urban residents with water piped to their homes and sewer connections. In some nations, less than 2 per cent of the urban population is without improved provision for water (household connections or easy access), while in several 10–15 per cent are without improved provision (including Argentina, Panama, Paraguay and Venezuela). In Ecuador this figure is 19 per cent, in Paraguay 30 per cent and in Haiti 51 per cent.

For sanitation, in close to half the nations listed in Table 1.9 more than 10 per cent of the urban population have no sanitation service. In Ecuador and Venezuela more than a quarter of the urban population have no sanitation service, and in Haiti it is more than a half.

Although global assessments of water and sanitation provision may need to use the same assessment criteria for all nations, clearly, standards of provision (and the criteria

Table 1.9 Proportion of the urban population in nations in Latin America and the Caribbean with access to 'improved' water supply and sanitation, 2000

Country	Water supply; percentage of urban households with:			Sanitation; percentage of urban households with:		
	Household connection	No household connection but with 'easy' access	No service	Connection to sewers	No sewage connection but 'in situ' sanitation	Unserved
Argentina	72	13	15	55	34	11
Bolivia	87	6	7	45	37	18
Brazil	91	5	4	59	35	6
Chile	95	4	1	90	4	7
Colombia	89	9	2	79	18	3
Costa Rica	100			47	41	11
Cuba	84	15	2	48	49	3
Dominican Republic	62	35	4	31	64	4
Ecuador	77	5	19	61	9	30
El Salvador	86	6	8	64	22	14
Guatemala	87	11	1	93	2	5
Haiti	15	34	51	0	46	54
Honduras	89	5	6	55	39	6
Jamaica	59	39	2	30	60	10
Mexico	93	1	6	75	12	13
Nicaragua	88	7	5	32	61	7
Panama	87	14	12	64	35	1
Paraguay	69	1	30	13	72	15
Peru	76	11	13	67	23	10
Puerto Rico	100			60	40	0
Trinidad and Tobago	66	20	14	19	80	0
Uruguay	94	5	2	51	45	5
Venezuela	84	1	15	62	9	29

Note: The table only includes nations with 1 million plus inhabitants in 2000 for which data were available.
Source: PAHO and WHO (2001), *Water Supply and Sanitation: Current Status and Prospects, Regional Report on the Evaluation 2000 in the Region of the Americas,* Pan American Health Organization and World Health Organization, Washington, DC, 81 pages.

used to assess them) should be better in urban areas in Latin American nations with relatively high per capita incomes than in low-income nations (or in the very low-income Asian and African nations). If higher standards are set than those used to define 'improved provision', the proportion of the population inadequately served in Latin America and the Caribbean increases substantially. For instance, in Jamaica, Haiti, the Dominican Republic and Trinidad and Tobago, between 20 and 39 per cent of the urban population have improved provision but not house connections. Similarly, only 72 per cent of Argentina's urban population are served with house connections compared to 85 per cent with improved provision; in Cuba, Guatemala, Panama and Peru more than 10 per cent of the urban population have improved provision but lack house connections.

Similarly, in most nations, a large part of the urban population who have improved sanitation do not have connections to sewers. Only in Chile and Guatemala do official statistics suggest that more than 90 per cent of the urban population have connections to sewers. In most nations in the region with more than 1 million inhabitants, more than one-third of the urban population have in situ sanitation.

In Belize, only 39 per cent of the urban population had a connection to a public sewer in 2000; in Costa Rica this figure was 47 per cent, in Cuba 48 per cent, in Nicaragua 32 per cent, in the Dominican Republic 31 per cent, in Paraguay 13 per cent and in Haiti 0 per cent. The point that we made earlier – that 'in situ' sanitation can be good quality but also very poor quality – needs to be repeated. A very large proportion of in situ sanitation in urban areas in the region is not of good quality – in part because official agencies do little or nothing to support good quality in situ sanitation. In Argentina, only 55 per cent of the urban population had connections to sewers in 2000, compared to 89 per cent with improved sanitation. Within Brazil's urban population, 94 per cent may have had improved sanitation by 2000 but only 56 per cent had connections to sewer systems and nearly half of all municipalities in the nation have no sewers.[116] More than half the urban populations in the Dominican Republic, Nicaragua, Jamaica, Paraguay and Trinidad and Tobago have in situ sanitation. In all Latin American and Caribbean cities, less than half the urban population have conventional sewer connections, so a very large part of the urban households classified as having improved sanitation have only pit latrines or (less commonly) toilets connected to septic tanks. Around 10 per cent of urban households have no provision for sanitation.

The case studies of specific cities in Box 1.6 give further evidence that a large number of those with improved provision still have very inadequate provision. A large part of the urban population in Jamaica would be surprised to learn that they are officially classified as having improved provision for water and sanitation: it does not tally with local reports of the inadequacies in provision in the two largest cities, Kingston and Montego Bay (see Box 1.6). In Ecuador, 81 per cent of the urban population may have improved water and 70 per cent may have improved sanitation, but in Guayaquil, the nation's largest and richest city, only 60 per cent of the population are connected to piped water networks and only 50 per cent are connected to sewers (see also Box 1.6). In Honduras, 97 per cent of the urban population may have improved water provision but – as the description of provision for water in Tegucigalpa (its capital and largest city) in Box 1.6 shows – a very large proportion of its population have very inadequate provision. Table 1.9 suggests that only a minority of

---

Box 1.6 Examples of the inadequacies in cities' water supply and sanitation in Latin America and the Caribbean

Cochabamba (Bolivia)

Only 60 per cent of the urban area and 53 per cent of the population are connected to water systems either inside or outside the home, and only 23 per cent of those connected receive a 24-hour supply of water. The water network provided by SEMAPA (Servicio Municipal de Agua Potable y Alcantarillado) has not been able to keep up with the growth of the city, and it is estimated that 100,000 people are not connected to the system. Industrial, commercial and wealthier residential areas have the highest rates of connection, reaching 99 per cent in Casco Viejo. Yet half the homes in Cochabamba are located in the northern and southern suburbs, and in some districts in these areas, 1992 data indicate that less than 4 per cent of homes had potable water connections; 18 per cent had access to water outside the house; and 80–90 per cent obtained water supplies from cistern trucks. Only 46 per cent of the population have a connection to a sewerage network. There is insufficient water provision to meet existing levels of demand.[123]

Guayaquil (Ecuador)

35 per cent of the population of 1.6 million dwellers do not have access to adequate and reliable water supplies and the whole city suffers from chronic and absolute water shortages. The sewerage system is on the verge of collapse. Approximately 400 tankers service 35 per cent of the total urban population; these water merchants buy the water at a highly subsidized price and can charge up to 400 times the price per litre paid by consumers who receive water from the public water utility. There is sufficient supply available to be able to reach each inhabitant with an average daily consumption of 220 litres. In 1990, average daily consumption ranged from 307 litres per inhabitant in the well-to-do parts of the city to less than 25 litres per inhabitant for those supplied by the private water sellers. Compared with the internationally accepted standard of 150 litres per person per day, Guayaquil is in the position to provide every citizen with a sufficient supply of potable water. The problem is thus clearly one of distribution.[124]

Kingston (Jamaica)

Official estimates suggest that 35–40 per cent of the population in Kingston Metropolitan Area are served by sewers. Other estimates suggest that only 18 per cent are served by sewers with 27 per cent having soakaway pits, 47 per cent using pit latrines and 8 per cent with no facilities at all. The sewers in the inner city are very old and often blocked. 'A significant percentage of the Kingston Metropolitan Area population, especially in low-income communities, defecate in open lots, in abandoned buildings or in plastic shopping bags which are then thrown into gully courses to be washed down into the city.'[125]

La Paz (Bolivia)

The La Paz–El Alto metropolitan area has a population of over 1.3 million. As in many Latin American cities, public services in the poorer, often newer, neighbourhoods on the outskirts of the metropolitan area lag behind services in the wealthier and older central area. In-house water and sewer connections are much more common in central and southern La Paz than in El Alto. Between 83 and 93 per cent of El Alto and La Paz residents have access to some form of piped water service: either an in-house water connection or a public tap near their homes. Households without in-house water connections or access to public standposts get water from a combination of water vendors, municipal water delivery services, neighbours with water service, rain water collection, private household wells and nearby streams. An estimated 66 per cent of La Paz homes and between 30 and 45 per cent of El Alto homes have sewer connections. For households without sewers, septic tanks offer an alternative, but in 1992, only a small number of households had septic tanks: 4 per cent of households in El Alto and 21 per cent in La Paz. Households without septic tanks or sewer connections use stream beds, latrines, public toilets and toilets in other private homes.[126]

Lima (Peru)

According to a 1996 article, almost 2 million of Lima's inhabitants have no water supply, and 30 per cent of those who do receive water of dubious quality. The aquifer that provides a third of Lima's water is due to run out by 2005 because of over-abstraction.[127]

Montego Bay (Jamaica)

Over 90 per cent of households have access to good quality piped water for drinking, but in informal settlements a much smaller percentage have connections to their house. Two-thirds of the population (many in informal settlements) rely on pit latrines or septic tank systems or have no sanitation. The densest settlements often have only a few pit latrines to serve residents. Pit latrines are often little more than holes in the ground about 1–1.5 metres deep. Possibly 5 or even 10 per cent of those living in informal settlements put their faeces in plastic bags and throw these into nearby gullies or bushes.[128]

Port-au-Prince (Haiti)

Although local groundwater around Port-au-Prince is more than sufficient to supply all 2 million of the city residents with water, only 10 per cent of families have water connections in the home. The public water service, CAMEP, is heavily in debt and has stopped maintaining many of the city's standpoints (public water taps). A vast clandestine system of water distribution has sprung up to meet the needs of 90 per cent of the city's population. The operators of this system rely on private wells and distribution trucks that provide water to private tank owners. The tank owners then sell small amounts of water to individuals and families at prices that range from US$3–5 per cubic metre, compared to the 50 cents per cubic metre that CAMEP charges its customers. Residents in slums not only paid the highest prices for water, they also carried it for long distances in areas with no paved roads.[129]

Santo Domingo de los Colorados (Ecuador)

70 per cent of the water entering the supply system is tapped illegally (compared with 30–40 per cent for most South American cities). Approximately 60–80 per cent of households receive running water, but only for a few hours a day.[130]

Tegucigalpa (Honduras)

The water shortage in the city is particularly acute as there is not even enough water to supply consumers who are already connected to the municipal system, much less those who are outside the distribution network. Of the total urban population, it is estimated that 32 per cent receive their water from sources other than house connections and public taps. This includes 200,000 people in the *barrios marginales*. Many inhabitants of the *barrios marginales* receive their water from unregulated water vendors who sell 55-gallon barrels of water to the *barrios* for US$1.75. While water use differs between households (depending on factors such as family size and income), it is estimated that in the early 1990s the total cost to all households in the *barrios marginales* who buy water from vendors is collectively US$11–13 million a year. The price people pay in the *barrios* is estimated to be 34 times higher than the official government rate charged to the better-off families who are connected to the town system. If even a fraction of the total annual cost of water paid by people in the peripheral areas could be allocated to an urban system, the same level of service could be provided at a fraction of the cost.[131] (There is a programme underway to install water systems in all the city's legalized peri-urban communities.)

urban dwellers in Bolivia lack improved water and sanitation, but the descriptions of water and sanitation provision in La Paz (including El Alto) and Cochabamba in Box 1.6 make clear that a high proportion of their populations have very inadequate water and sanitation provision.

Different sources also give very different statistics for the extent of water and sanitation provision, probably because they are based on different definitions of 'adequate'. In Paraguay, a study by CEPAL suggests that 76 per cent of the urban population lived in

housing without access to sanitation in 1996[117] – compared to a figure of 15 per cent in the Assessment 2000.

The water coverage statistics in Tables 1.9 and 1.10 say nothing about the regularity of supply or the quality of the water within the piped systems. Available statistics from the Pan American Health Organization (PAHO)/WHO assessment suggest that in many cities, the typical number of hours per day in which water is available is 22–24, although for Lima it was 13 hours and for Port-au-Prince it was only 4 hours. For national urban populations, the number of hours per day during which drinking water was available was 14 in Peru, 6 in Haiti and Honduras and 6–12 in Guatemala.[118] There were no data for many of the nations with the largest urban populations in the region, including Brazil and Mexico. In addition, official statistics often over-state the regularity of supply. One estimate suggested that 60 per cent of the population served through household connections in the region are served by operationally intermittent water supply systems. In the capital of Honduras, Tegucigalpa, there are serious water shortages, which means that there is not enough water to supply consumers who are already connected to the municipal system, much less those who are outside the distribution network. Most urban networks provide only intermittent service (six hours a day on average).[119]

In reviewing the region, one commentator suggested that:

> Urban services [and especially water and sanitation provision] in Latin America show a common set of central problems: insufficient coverage that excludes an important proportion of the population; deficient quality that has a direct impact on quality of life ... [and] serious environmental impacts derived from the fact that the growth of needs has increased persistently quicker than the assigned financial resources and the capacity for provision, planning and regulation.[120]

Box 1.7 Struggles for water and sanitation in Latin American cities

Huaycan (Peru)

In July 1984, the settlement of Huaycan was created by the invasion of a vacant plot of land by a group of low-income households organized in an association. Having successfully occupied the land, a plan that had already been prepared before the invasion was put into effect: the householders set up housing groups measuring 1 hectare each on average, with 60 housing plots and space for streets, parks and communal premises. The first task was to protect the settlement from eviction and from the guerrilla groups that sought to take power. They also sought to get recognition from their own government. Promises from the government of electricity and water were not fulfilled, so in 1987, the inhabitants marched downtown to demand this. The electricity grid was then extended to Huaycan but no action was taken to provide water. A second march was organized in 1988 and this led to some improvement in provision for water. Titles to the land were also negotiated by many households. Many community leaders in Huaycan were threatened by guerrillas and several were killed, so the inhabitants sought to establish a police station. In the early 1990s, other projects were negotiated including a drainage system and a mother and child centre.[136]

Quilmes (Buenos Aires)

In late 1981, some 20,000 people invaded 211 hectares of abandoned private land in two outer districts of Buenos Aires. At first, the only official response was to try to bulldoze them or to set a cordon around them to stop supplies and people going in. The inhabitants developed six settlements, organized so that there was room for access roads and infrastructure. A representative community organization negotiated with external agencies, albeit with little success. The local government refused to pave streets, install sewers and drains or

provide health care. Illegal connections were made to water mains and to electricity pylons; the electricity company agreed to supply them but the police kept them out. In the run-up to democratic elections in 1984, each political party made promises to the inhabitants, and the democratic government elected in 1984 was more sympathetic to their needs, but by the late 1980s no infrastructure had been provided.[137]

Barrio San Jorge (Buenos Aires)

This settlement was originally founded in 1961 when the government resettled 60 families here. Despite the lack of infrastructure and services, other families moved in, attracted by the vacant land and the low risk of eviction. After 1979, the settlement expanded into a new section when the municipal authorities evicted some 200 families from a nearby site. After 30 years of settlement, in 1990 there was no sewer system and most households relied on public standpipes for water. There were no paved roads or drains and most inhabitants had no garbage collection service. Conditions have improved since then through self-help projects and some externally funded work (providing water supplies and small-bore sewers).[138]

Puertas del Sol IV (Cali, Colombia)

This settlement had 7152 inhabitants in 2001. It was formed in 1994 by families living in a squatter settlement in another part of Cali who were provided with plots on which they could build. The settlers underwent a lengthy negotiation to get the land: their former settlement had been built on hill sides that were at high risk of landslides. When they moved to the new site, there was no provision for water, sanitation or drainage. They had to ask the inhabitants of neighbouring settlements for water, but this was made difficult because the neighbours did not welcome the new

settlers. Some residents installed a community tap. Many tapped into nearby water pipes and ran hoses to their plots. During the first winter there were serious floods due to the lack of sewers and drains, and water and mud poured into the houses. A sewer has been built but it does not work very well, and in 1998 there was another serious flood which damaged several houses. Negotiations and lobbying have produced some infrastructure – a telephone in 1995, paved roads (which also meant public transport services) and garbage collection services. But the problem of sewers remains unresolved, and solving this is costly because it would mean rebuilding and repaving all the roads.[139]

El Vergel (Cali, Colombia)

The settlement of El Vergel had some 7400 inhabitants in 1999. It was formed initially by an invasion in 1980: the invaders cleared the land and marked off their house sites with rope. They had to defend their plots from the army and a militia hired by the landowner. Shacks were hastily assembled using bamboo, plastic, metal sheets and cardboard. There was no provision for water, sanitation, electricity, roads, health care or schools. Initially, water was obtained from small streams that ran through the plot, but these were insufficient and became contaminated. The settlers began to purchase buckets of water from a neighbouring settlement as well as more distant settlements, but this was expensive and inconvenient. El Vergel, like many illegal settlements, developed next to a legal neighbourhood because of the proximity to existing water and sewer mains and electricity supplies. The settlers managed to negotiate the right to stay, piped water supplies were extended and now most dwellings have piped water. However, there are serious flooding problems and rivers of sewage run through the community during periods of heavy rainfall.[140]

Table 1.10 Provision for water to households in selected Latin American cities

Nation	City	Water supply							
		Connected to network		Not connected to network					
		Total population	%	Total population	%	Public tap (%)	Well with pump (%)	Well without pump (%)	Other water sources* (%)
Argentina	Buenos Aires	7,483,000	78.1						
Bolivia	La Paz	775,000	95.9	33,000	4.1	3.8			0.24
	Santa Cruz de la Sierra	761,000	72.5	228,000	21.7				21.7
	El Alto	578,000	74.8	59,000	7.6	2.1			5.6
Brazil	Belem	792,000	50.2	148,000	9.4				9.4
	Belo Horizonte	3,715,000	95.2	148,000	3.8				3.8
	Curitiba	2,237,000	90.9	220,000	8.9				8.9
	Fortaleza	2,004,000	75.3	309,000	11.6				11.6
	Porto Alegre	2,983,000	90.9	285,000	8.7				8.7
	Recife	2,791,000	90.8	176,000	5.7				5.7
	Rio de Janeiro	9,247,000	89.8	992,000	9.6				9.6
	Salvador	2,560,000	92.6	106,000	3.8				3.8
	São Paulo	16,532,000	99.1	289,000	1.7				1.7
Chile	Gran Santiago	4,554,700	99.4						
Colombia	Barranquilla	974,970	81.2						
	Bogotá	5,566,320	91.1						
	Cali	1,884,440	91.5						
	Medellín	1,813,79	93.7						
Costa Rica	Región Metropolitana	430,870	30.1						
Dominican	Santo Domingo	1,582,000	62.2	960,300	27.8	13.8			24.0
Republic	Santiago	522,000	89.2	63,000	10.8	2.2			9.9
Ecuador	Guayaquil	1,284,500	60.6	200,000	9.4				9.4
Guatemala	Area Metropolitana	1,680,000	93.3	120,000	6.7	6.7			
Haiti	Port-au-Prince[141]	700,000	41.2	250,000		5.9			8.2
Honduras	San Pedro Sula	313,600	60.2	179,500	34.4				34.4
Mexico	Distrito Federal (Mexico City)	8,185,000	96.4	304,000	3.6	0.8			2.8
	Guadalajara	2,919,000	92.1	249,000	7.9	1.4			6.5
	Heroica Puebla de Zaragoza	1,001,000	86.4	157,000	13.6	1.5			12.1
	León Guanajuato	863,000	91.6	79,000	8.4	1.4			7.0
	Monterrey	2,752,000	94.8	151,000	5.2	1.5			3.8
Nicaragua	Managua	836,000	92.0	72,700	8.0	1.0			7.0
Panamá	Panamá	969,040	96.1	39,110	3.8				3.9
Paraguay	Asunción	525,185	92.2	44,668	7.8	3.8	3.1	0.9	
Peru	Lima Metropolitana	5,367,000	74.3	549,000		7.6			
Puerto Rico	San Juan	138,000	30.3	318,000	69.7				
Dominican	Santo Domingo	1,582,000	62.2	960,300	37.8	13.8			24.0
Republic	Santiago	522,000	89.2	63,000	10.8	2.2			9.9
Venezuela	Caracas	2,8551,000	90.3	305,000	9.7	4.9	1.8		0.7
	Maracaibo	1,068,000	56.0	840,000	44.0				
	Valencia	1,149,000	88.3	153,000	11.8				
	Maracay	928,000	88.3	123,000	11.7				

* Other water sources include rain water, river water, water fountains and purchased water jugs.
Source: Centro Panamericano de Ingenieria Sanitaria y Ciencias del Ambiente, *Evaluacion de los Servicios de Agua Potable y Saneamiento 2000 en las America*, www.cepis.ops-oms.org.

Table 1.11 Provision for sanitation to households in selected Latin American cities

Country	City	Connected to city sewer system		Not connected to city sewer system							
		Total population	%	Total population	%	Small-bore sewer connection (%)	Well/septic tank connection (%)	Latrine with water drainage (%)	Dry latrine (%)	Simple pit latrine (%)	Other (%)
Argentina	Buenos Aires	980,000	10.2	4600	0.05						
Bolivia	La Paz	611,000	75.6	30,000	3.7		1.7				2.0
	Santa Cruz de la Sierra	294,000	28.0	139,000	13.2		13.2				
	El Alto	308,000	39.8	136,000	17.6		3.0				14.6
Brazil	Belem	339,000	21.5	581,000	36.8		30.6				6.1
	Belo Horizonte	2,980,000	76.4	874,000	22.4		15.7				6.7
	Curitiba	1,409,000	57.3	999,000	40.6		36.1				4.5
	Fortaleza	643,000	24.2	1,822,000	68.5		66.8				1.7
	Porto Alegre	2,497,000	76.1	727,000	22.1		20.9				2.2
	Recife	1,123,000	36.5	1,794,000	58.3		51.7				6.6
	Rio de Janeiro	8,637,000	83.9	1,599,000	15.5		8.3				7.3
	Salvador	1,589,000	57.5	1,033,000	37.4		24.7				12.7
	São Paulo	14,837,000	88.9	2,005,000	12.0		7.7				4.4
Chile	Gran Santiago	4,518,400	98.6	36,300	0.8		0.8				
Colombia	Barranquilla	995,810	82.9								
	Bogotá	4,999,320	81.8								
	Cali	1,823,650	88.5								
	Medellín	1,837,680	95.0								
Costa Rica	Región Metropolitana	720,000	50.3	445,000	31.1		31.1				
Dominican	Santo Domingo	686,400	27.0	1,855,900	73.0						
Republic	Santiago	437,000	74.7	148,000	25.3	8.6	11.6				5.1
Ecuador	Guayaquil	1,055,000	49.8	250,000	11.8		9.4	1.7	0.7		
Guatemala	Guatemala City Metropolitan Area		71.9								
Haiti	Port-au-Prince			882,000	51.8		16.9	5.0	10.0	20.0	48.2
Honduras	San Pedro Sula	373,800	71.7	140,020	26.9		8.4	5.5	11.7	1.4	
Mexico	Mexico City (Distrito Federal)	7,651,000	90.1	838,000	9.87		5.2				5.7
	Guadalajara	284,000	89.7	328,000	10.4	5.7					4.6
	Heroica Puebla de Zaragoza	1,026,000	88.6	132,000	11.4		3.5				7.9
	León Guanajuato	877,000	93.1	65,000	7.0		4.1				2.8
	Monterrey	2,674,000	92.1	229,000	7.8						
Nicaragua	Managua	492,900	54.2	416,100	45.8					38.8	7.0
Panamá	Panamá	707,390	70.2	300,760	29.8		13.4		16.4		
Paraguay	Asunción	291,480	51.2	278,378	48.9		40.9			1.4	4.9
Peru	Lima Metropolitana	5,163,000	71.5	1,191,000	16.49		16.5				
Puerto Rico	San Juan	122,00'	26.8	334,000	73.3						
Dominican	Santo Domingo	686,400	27.0	1,855,900	73.0						
Republic	Santiago	437,000	74.7	148,000	25.3	8.6	11.6				5.1
Uruguay	Montevideo	948,490	70.5	396,350	29.5	24.4					5.1
Venezuela	Caracas	2,919,000	92.5	237,000	7.5						
	Maracaibo	694,850	36.4	1,213,150	63.6						
	Valencia	1,099,000	84.4	203,000	15.5						
	Maracay	730,000	69.5	321,000	30.5						

Source: Centro Panamericano de Ingenieria Sanitaria y Ciencias del Ambiente, *Evaluacion de los Servicios de Agua Potable y Saneamiento 2000 en las America*, www.cepis.ops-oms.org.

The political conflicts in various Latin American cities over water and sanitation also suggest that there are more problems than those implied by the statistics on who has improved provision. For instance, Table 1.9 suggests that most of the populations of Bolivian and Mexican cities are served with water, but there have been serious conflicts in various cities around issues of access, quality, distribution and price. The case of Cochabamba is one of the best known and best documented. In Mexico, there have been various widespread popular protests – for instance between the city of Monterrey and the Bajo Rio San Juan Tamaulipas settlers, and amongst people in Aguascalientes and Mexico City. In the Valley of Mexico, the social struggle took different forms: people withheld payment of water bills, complained that the amounts charged were excessive, destroyed the water meters, kidnapped water sellers or made violent attacks on the water utilities.[121]

> *The modernization policies which in many respects involve the expropriation of rights and further exclusion for large sectors of the population have been answered back not only with defensive actions from those being excluded, but also with initiatives directed at expanding the scope and depth of the rights of the people.*[122]

Despite the inadequacies in provision for both water and sanitation that affect large sections of the urban populations in most nations, it is also clear that the proportion of people reached by improved provision (and with good quality provision) has increased very considerably over the last few decades. The PAHO/WHO 2000 assessment only has figures for how coverage changed for total populations: in 1960 just 33 per cent of the region's population had water piped to their homes or easy access; by 2000 it was 85 per cent. In 1960, just 14 per cent of the population had connection to sewers; by 2000, 49 per cent had connections (and obviously most of those with sewage connections were in urban areas). It is also likely that, in general, most urban dwellers have more reliable and safer water supplies than was the case in 1960 – in part

spurred by the attention given to improving water quality and sanitation during the 1990s in response to the cholera epidemic that began in 1991.[132] However, the 1990s also brought a smaller drop in the proportion of the urban population with improved provision than in previous decades, which may be the result of a re-orientation in priorities towards improvements in water quality, disinfection and sanitation at the expense of increasing coverage.[133] One report suggests that the proportion of urban housing without sanitation increased considerably in Paraguay between 1990 and 1996 (from 64 to 76 per cent) while it did not diminish in Venezuela between 1990 and 1997 (sticking at 25 per cent).[134]

It is also difficult to gauge the overall impact of privatization on the quality of provision and coverage, although – as in other regions of the world – the proportion of the urban population served by large-scale, formal private enterprises is low (see Chapter 5 for more details).

No analysis of available statistics can bring out the years (or decades) of struggle by urban dwellers to get official water and sanitation provision. Box 1.7 gives some examples. Of course, the problem is, in part, related to the fact that large sections of the population in most cities live in informal or illegal settlements. Obviously, municipal or state water and sanitation agencies (or private companies that own or manage water and sanitation provision) may be reluctant to extend official water and sanitation provision to illegal settlements, because it implies official endorsement of their land occupation, or it is illegal for them to do so. However, as will be discussed in more detail in Chapter 2, in most cities there is a more complex story than this: some illegal settlements are well served, some are partly served and some are not served by official providers. In many cities, the extent of official water and sanitation provision in illegal settlements relates more to political structures and decisions and the competence, capacity and attitude of the utilities than to settlements' legal status. In addition, provision for infrastructure to illegal settlements is almost always ad hoc and bit by bit – so after negotiation and lobbying, they get roads paved one year (often just before elections!), perhaps a piped water supply some years later and (more unusually) sewer connections some years later. This also means that the whole process is more costly, as the different agencies responsible for different forms of infrastructure do not work together. In the case of Puertas del Sol IV in Box 1.7, the inhabitants finally got their roads paved but no provision for sewers and drains, and now the cost of putting in sewers and drains is much higher because it would mean repaving all the roads.[135]

In conclusion, it is clear that much of the urban population in this region are better served with water and sanitation than are the urban populations in Africa and Asia; it is also clear that considerable progress has been made in expanding and extending provision over the last few decades (although the momentum for improving provision slowed during the 1990s). However, it is also clear that a significant proportion of the region's urban populations still lack adequate water and sanitation provision – much more than the 7 per cent who lack improved provision for water and the 13 per cent who lack improved provision for sanitation highlighted in the 2000 assessment. Most of those with inadequate provision are in the poorer nations, or in the smaller cities and urban centres in the middle-income nations.

The special problems of smaller cities and towns in low-income countries

There is far more documentation of water and sanitation provision in large cities than in smaller cities or in the urban centres that are too small to be considered cities.[142] But most of the world's urban dwellers do not live in large cities. For instance, by 2000, less than 4 per cent of the world's population and less than 8 per cent of its urban population lived in the 16 mega-cities of 10 million or more inhabitants. But there is a much larger literature on the water and sanitation problems of mega-cities than on those of the tens of thousands of urban centres with under half a million inhabitants, which have more than six times as many people in total (and more than half the

world's urban population). Table 1.12 gives the proportion of people living in cities in different size categories in each region of the world.

In Africa (and Europe) in 2000, more than three-fifths of the urban population lived in urban centres with less than half a million inhabitants and this included a large proportion in urban centres with less than 20,000 inhabitants. In Latin America and the Caribbean and Asia, close to half the urban population lived in urban centres with less than half a million population. Even in Latin America, where a high proportion of urban dwellers live in mega-cities, there were still more than three times as many people in urban centres with less than half a million inhabitants, than in mega-cities.

All urban centres (whether large or small cities or urban centres too small to be called cities) need:

- water supply systems drawing from protected water sources, ensuring that uncontaminated water is easily available to all households (preferably through connections to homes or yards, and if not to nearby standpipes); and
- provision for the disposal of household and human wastes (including excreta, household wastewater, storm and surface run-off and solid wastes).

Provision for water and sanitation

The limited range of available statistics suggest that in general, within low- and middle-income nations, the larger the city, the higher the proportion of the population with water piped to their home or yard and connection to sewers – although, as noted earlier, many cities in Africa and Asia have no sewers. This was shown by an analysis of service provision in urban areas of 43 low- and middle-income nations drawn from demographic and health surveys (see Box 1.8). The variations in provision between urban centres of different size classes is less dramatic for water in the home (Figure 1.2) than for flush toilets (Figure 1.3), and in sub-Saharan Africa and Asia, in

Table 1.12 The distribution of the urban population between different size urban centres, 2000

Region	Urban population (millions)	Percentage of the urban population in urban centres with		
		10 million + inhabitants	500,000–9.99 million inhabitants	Under 500,000 inhabitants
World	2862	7.9	39.6	52.5
Africa	295	0	38.6	61.4
Asia	1376	9.9	40.3	49.8
Europe	534	0.0	35.7	64.3
Latin America and the Caribbean	391	15.0	36.9	48.1
Northern America	243	12.3	48.6	39.1
Oceania	23	0.0	54.2	45.8

Source: statistics drawn or derived from United Nations (2002), *World Urbanization Prospects; The 2001 Revision; Data Tables and Highlights*, Population Division, Department of Economic and Social Affairs, United Nations Secretariat, ESA/P/WP/173, New York, 181 pages.

urban centres with fewer than 100,000 inhabitants a greater proportion of the population apparently have water in the home than in the largest cities. For flush toilets, in all regions, urban centres with less than 100,000 inhabitants serve the lowest proportion of the population. Drawing from all the studies, less than two-fifths of the inhabitants of urban centres with less than 100,000 inhabitants have flush toilets, compared to 70 per cent for cities with 1–5 million inhabitants and more than 80 per cent for cities with 5 million plus inhabitants. Figure 1.3 is also a reminder of how small a proportion of the urban population in Africa has access to flush toilets.

In many nations, especially those where there have been improvements in water and sanitation provision in recent years, smaller urban centres in wealthier regions may have better provision than larger urban centres in poorer regions. Box 1.9 shows how water and sanitation provision varies by the size of urban centre in Brazil. This shows how within each region in Brazil, provision generally improves as the size of the city increases, but there are smaller differences between provision in large and small urban centres in the wealthier regions.

Detailed case studies of water and sanitation in small urban centres confirm that provision is generally very inadequate – although there are relatively few such case studies, especially in relation to the number of small urban centres in low- and middle-income nations. Box 1.10 provides some examples of

provision in different urban centres in Africa, and also illustrates the lack of any capacity among local authorities to ensure adequate water and sanitation provision. A review of provision for water in small towns in Africa highlighted that these generally have several different coexisting water supply systems, which sometimes compete with each other – for instance mechanized supplies (generally boreholes with motorized pumps supplying water to elevated storage tanks attached to a limited distribution system of public tapstands, sometimes coupled with cattle troughs and individual house connections) and water drawn from tapped and protected springs or other (often distant) sources.[143]

Note how few of the people (or in some instances none of them) had access to a piped water system in Mbandjock, Aliade, Igugh, Ugba, the smaller towns in Mwanza Province and two of the three towns in Benin. In Kumi and Wobulenzi in Uganda, most of the population have access to a piped supply but only through water kiosks, where the water is expensive. In 47 small towns in the Matam department in Senegal, with between 2000 and 15,000 inhabitants, that are part of a water management support programme, the typical water supply system is a borehole with motorized pump and a piped network with between 5 and 20 standposts and one or two cattle troughs.[144] A review of 25 small urban centres in two districts of northern Darfur in the Sudan pointed to comparable systems: boreholes equipped with diesel-powered pumps supplying

Box 1.8 The availability of water in the home and flush toilets in rural areas and urban areas by size class

The demographic and health surveys have limited data on geographic identifiers, but it was possible to analyse their data on service provision grouped within five categories: rural areas and four categories of urban areas (under 100,000 inhabitants, 100,000–499,999, 500,000–1 million, 1–5 million and above 5 million). Figure 1.2 shows the variation in water piped to people's homes, and Figure 1.3 shows the variation in the availability of a flush toilet.

Figure 1.2 Water in the home for different size classes of cities

Figure 1.3 Flush toilet for different size classes of cities

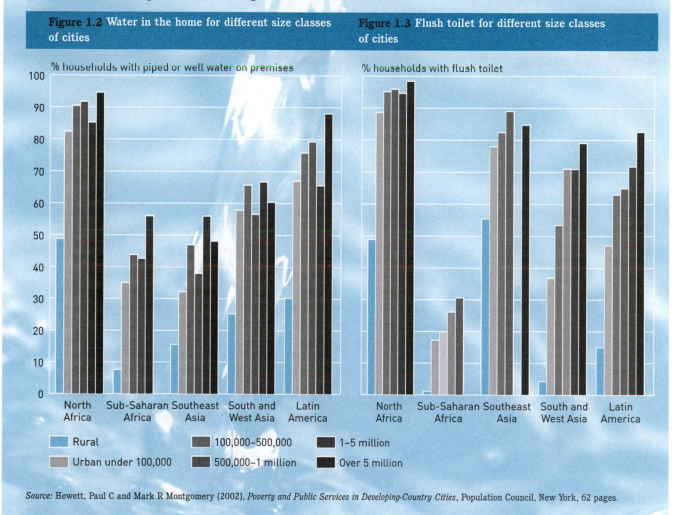

Source: Hewett, Paul C and Mark R Montgomery (2002), *Poverty and Public Services in Developing-Country Cities*, Population Council, New York, 62 pages.

water to elevated storage tanks with a limited distribution system of standpipes.[145]

Most small cities and urban centres in Africa have no public provision for sanitation. This does not just mean that there is no sewer system, but also that there is no public system to serve a population reliant on pit latrines – for instance, no service to advise on pit-latrine construction (so they function effectively and do not pollute groundwater) and no equipment to empty them. It is also clear from the case studies summarized in Box 1.10 that it is common for a significant proportion of households to have no latrine. What the case studies of such centres make clear is local authorities'

lack of any investment capacity for installing or expanding basic infrastructure, and the inadequacy of the basic infrastructure and equipment. Even when some capital investment has taken place, the capacity to manage or maintain it is often very limited. For instance, even though two of the smaller towns in the Mwanza region in Tanzania had a network of pipes in place and functioning pumping stations, water was rarely delivered to the network because the fuel allocation could only meet the requirements of a few weeks' operation per year.[146]

Given that some of the studies reported in Box 1.10 were undertaken ten or more

Box 1.9 Differences in provision for water and sanitation by the population size of the urban centre in Brazil

In general, the larger the city population, the higher the proportion of households with piped water and the greater the likelihood that the water is treated. Only 46 per cent of households in municipalities with under 20,000 inhabitants have access to the general water network system, and smaller municipalities are also less likely to have water treatment plants. 14 per cent of Brazil's population live in municipalities with fewer than 20,000 inhabitants.

The larger a city's population, the larger the proportion of households with connections to sewers, although in the wealthier regions, the disparities between large and small cities is much smaller. 48 per cent of municipalities in Brazil have no sewers, and there is a clear pattern of disadvantage in the poorer regions and the smaller urban centres. On average, in municipalities with more than 300,000 inhabitants, the proportion of households connected to sewers is three times greater than in municipalities with fewer than 20,000 inhabitants. In the southeast, 59 per cent of households in municipalities of

300,000 or more inhabitants have sewer connections, compared to 42 per cent of households in municipalities with fewer than 20,000 inhabitants. In the northeast, in municipalities with 300,000 or more inhabitants, the proportion of households with sewer connections is 3.4 times greater than in municipalities with fewer than 20,000 inhabitants; in the centre west there is a twenty-fold difference.

Source: Jacobi, Pedro (2002), *Management of Urban Water and Sanitation in Brazil*, Background Paper prepared for UN-HABITAT, Nairobi.

years ago, conditions may have improved since then. But one cannot assume this is the case. The section on Africa included details of how provision for water had got worse in many urban sites in East Africa over the last 30 years. Box 1.11 presents an example of this from a small urban centre in Uganda.

In Asia, there is far more documentation of the problems with water and sanitation in large cities than in small urban centres. In part, this is because census data about the extent of provision for water, sanitation and drainage are never published (or made available) for individual urban centres. It is usually independent research studies that provide evidence of the inadequacies in provision, as in Box 1.12, which gives examples from smaller cities in India. These examples also illustrate a problem which appears to be particularly common in smaller urban centres in Africa and Asia – the high proportion of low-income households that have no provision for sanitation and so defecate in open spaces.

For three urban centres in Box 1.12 the study focused on the slums, and in two of them, Bhilwara and Sambalpur, most slum households had no water source within the home and no toilet. In the study of Chertala, which covered the whole population, 25 per cent of households were without toilets. The study of Chertala and Ponani also showed how most households lacked household connections; in Chertala there were 238 household connec-

tions but around 43,000 inhabitants; in Ponani, 845 household connections and 51,770 inhabitants.

The 1999 *State of India's Environment* report produced by the Centre for Science and Environment[157] reports on environmental problems in smaller cities and urban centres. It reported studies in four industrial towns (Ludhiana, Jetpur, Tiruppur and Rourkela) and four non-industrial urban centres (Aligarh, Bhagalpur, Kottayam and Jaisalmet), which highlighted the very poor state of these urban centres' environments ranging from the inadequacies in provision for water, sanitation, drainage and garbage collection to failures to control industrial pollution. They also highlighted the absence of any organized civic effort to address this.

Box 1.13 reports on the findings of studies in three small urban centres in China.[158] The study from which these descriptions are drawn chose small towns from different areas: one is in the poor northwestern province, one is in a traditional (far from affluent) province and one is in a more prosperous coastal province. In each urban centre, 133 household interviews took place. The absence of any public provision for sanitation other than a few public latrines, and the absence of households with piped water supplies to the home, is particularly notable in Neiguan and Yantan. Of course, general conclusions cannot be drawn from these

Box 1.10 Examples of provision for water and sanitation in small African urban centres

Kumi (Uganda)

Kumi Town is the capital of Kumi district and has a population estimated at 17,000 inhabitants in 2000. Kumi town council is responsible for water and sanitation services. The town's water supply comes from boreholes and pumps plus overhead tanks feeding a piped distribution network, with public kiosks (at the time of the study there were 15 kiosks but two were closed from lack of operation) and a few household connections. In February 2000, water was available for two hours a day. Lakes that are 10 and 16 kilometres away could be tapped, but this would require external funding. In Kumi, virtually all households are reliant on water kiosks or water vendors. A family with an income equivalent to the average daily wage and consuming 24 litres per person per day would be spending 15 per cent of its income on water; if it relied on vendors, it would be 45 per cent of its income. Around 60 per cent of households have pit latrines and there are two public pit latrines in the town – one near the bus park, the other near the market – and these are free. They should be available during daylight hours but the latrine near the market was locked when visited by researchers in 2000. According to the market traders, the keyholder is often absent. A third public toilet with a septic tank was built beside the new market but was never completed, and the water had not been connected. Men who collect water are mostly vendors, and they bully women and children so that they can get priority, even when women have been queuing for as long as two hours. Children have lower priority in the queues than the women.[147]

Wobulenzi (Uganda)

The town's population was estimated at 12,000 in 2000. The town council is responsible for water and sanitation but has delegated responsibility to a water-users' association. Around 70 per cent of households have latrines.

There are also three public latrines, but the number of users is low because of a high charge (100 Ugandan shillings per use). A piped water network covers most of the town and feeds 31 kiosks, 64 private connections and 6 institutions.[148]

Kabale (Uganda)

With 27,905 inhabitants in 1991, this is a market town in an extremely fertile and high-density rural area. There were just 217 connections to the piped water system and, on average, water was supplied for four hours in the morning and two hours in the evening. Estimates suggest that less than 16 per cent of the population had access to water from this system. Provision for sanitation was also very deficient. Refuse collection relied on one working tractor and trailer, which collected wastes from 20 areas marked with signposts where refuse was deposited by the public. It is estimated that around 10–20 per cent of the daily refuse was collected.[149]

Matam department, northeast Senegal

Among 47 small towns with between 2000 and 15,000 inhabitants that are part of a water management support programme, the typical water supply system is a borehole with a motorized pump, and a piped network with between 5 and 20 standposts and one or two cattle troughs. For larger settlements, the number of private connections becomes significant (eg up to 200 connections in towns of 10,000 inhabitants). In towns of 5000 or more, the uncontrolled expansion of the original network causes water pressure imbalances and leaks.[150]

Northern Darfur (Sudan)

25 urban centres in two districts of northern Darfur were included in a water, sanitation and hygiene education project from 1987–1990. They ranged in size from 3000 to 10,000 inhabitants. 15 had mechanized water systems (that the project sought to rehabilitate) while ten were to have

new water suppliers. In all cases, deep boreholes equipped with diesel-powered pumps, supplying water to elevated storage tanks, were used. A limited distribution system of stand-pipes, troughs for watering livestock and a tank-filling outlet was provided in each town.[151]

Mbandjock (Cameroon)

Only about 20 per cent of the population (estimated at 20,000 in 1996) have access to piped water; the rest rely on wells and springs for their water supply, but tests found that all spring and well waters presented evidence of faecal contamination of human and/or animal origin. Data from the city hospital show that gastro-intestinal and diarrhoeal diseases are amongst the most prevalent in the community (after malaria and onchocerciasis). The city has no sewer system and the only methods of sewage disposal are pit latrines and septic tanks.[152]

Mwanza province (Tanzania)

According to the 1988 census, over 90 per cent of households in Mwanza Town used a piped water supply for drinking, but the situation in smaller towns nearby was much worse. Only 20–30 per cent of households in the other two towns on the lakeshore had piped drinking water, and in the inland towns this fell to just 1–5 per cent. The main problems in providing piped supplies in urban areas were the maintenance and installation of infrastructure, and obtaining fuel for pumping (the over-riding problem for smaller towns). Even though two of the smaller towns in the Mwanza region had networks of pipes in place and functioning pumping stations, water was rarely delivered to the networks because the fuel allocation could only meet the requirements of a few weeks' operation per year. In the smaller towns, virtually all households that report using piped water supplies are dependent on public standpipes. In Mwanza Town, around 20 per cent of households have water piped into the home or their yard, and 10 per cent have full plumbing facilities including flush toilets. In urban Mwanza, on average, migrant people had to walk 750 metres, and resident people 600 metres, to obtain water.[153]

Aliade, Igugh and Ugba (Nigeria)

Each of these urban centres had a population estimated at between 6000 and 8000 in 1980. Two of them have no piped water system, and in the third, only a small number of households have access to treated water (from the state rural water supply scheme). Most households obtain water from compound wells, which are the responsibility of the compound owner; the next most common sources of water are streams, ponds and rivers. The state water boards in Nigeria are responsible for providing water supplies to urban centres, but piped water schemes are rarely available to small urban centres. There is no public provision for sanitation; most households use pit latrines, although some households have no access to a latrine. About half of the households using such latrines share them. Refuse collection and disposal is in theory a local government responsibility, but 67 per cent of households dump refuse in their backyards while most of the rest burn or bury it. Only in one of the three urban centres was there neighbourhood collection and disposal, and this was organized on a small scale.[154]

Benin City (Nigeria)

Families in the informal housing sector in Benin City normally use pit latrines. A 1995 survey found that 74 per cent of households relied on these, and most were of questionable quality. Household water is mainly piped from outside the housing premises (from another compound, the street or other neighbourhoods) or obtained from a water vendor or from a rain harvester underground tank.[155]

Small cities in Benin

A study of three secondary cities in Benin found that in two of them, the vast majority of the population lacked running water and latrines, so most people defecated in the bush.[156]

statistics; there are 20,000 such *zhen* [small urban centres] in China. But the study from which these examples are drawn does highlight how a significant proportion of China's urban population live in small urban centres, so the quality and extent of water and sanitation provision in urban areas of China is much influenced by the quality and extent of provision in these small urban centres.

Vaclav Smil suggests that the problems with water quality found in most urban areas of China are especially serious in rural towns and medium-size cities.[159]

Box 1.11 The deterioration in the quality of municipal water supplies in Iganga (Uganda)

A study of domestic water supplies in Iganga in 1967 found that all sample households received adequate supplies of water 24 hours a day. A study in 1997 which returned to the same sites found that for the households interviewed, the municipal water system had deteriorated to the point that only 13 per cent of them received piped water, and even in these cases water only trickled out of pipes for a few hours each day. Some households reported being without piped water for up to three years. One respondent explained:

During the 1960s and early 1970s the situation was good, but from the late 1970s [onwards], the supply of water began to deteriorate. The situation worsened in the 1980s when water pumps and most of the distribution lines broke down. Of the four pumps operating in the 1960s, only one was still working by 1980.

The water storage tanks and the distribution lines were also rusty and leaking. One urban water officer reported that:

most of the revenue collected from water bills is spent on repairing the pipes and pumps. Moreover, since the water pumps run off electricity that is subject to frequent power cuts, the water supply is unreliable. It is really beyond our control.

By the late 1980s, in an attempt to compensate for these problems, alternative sources were developed. Private individuals began to drill boreholes and establish their own water kiosks. In 1998, these private sources were supplemented with kiosks built by the Iganga town council.

Per capita water use had increased for unpiped households, although not by very much – from an average of 15 litres per person per day in 1967 to 24 in 1997.

Source: Thompson, John, Ina T Porras, Elisabeth Wood, James K Tumwine, Mark R Mujwahuzi, Munguti Katui-Katua and Nick Johnstone (2000), 'Waiting at the tap: changes in urban water use in East Africa over three decades', *Environment and Urbanization*, Vol 12, No 2, October; and White, Gilbert F, David J Bradley and Anne U White (1972), *Drawers of Water*, University of Chicago Press, Chicago and London.

Box 1.12 Examples of water and sanitation provision in smaller urban centres in India

Chertala

With around 43,000 inhabitants in 2000, there is an abundance of water and a high incidence of mosquito-related disease, especially malaria and filariasis. The water supply is operated by the state water authority. The main water supply comes from tubewells and is distributed untreated to 437 standposts (around 1 per 100 people) and 238 house connections. The piped supply is inadequate and commonly regarded as unfit to drink. There is strong dissatisfaction among the town dwellers with the state agency, and there are plans to develop municipal water supplies in each ward. Estimates suggest that 70–80 per cent of households have latrines. There are three pay-and-use toilets – at the hospital, bus station and market place. Two further toilet complexes are planned. Officials regard these as facilities for busy public places, not for residential areas.

Ponani (Kerala)

With a population of 51,770 in 2000, this is one of the poorest towns in the state. Most of the poor live in ten coastal wards and rely on fishing for their livelihoods; the coastal wards have saline groundwater for six months of the year and poor drainage. The piped water system has 845 house connections (serving roughly 12 per cent of all households), 75 non-household connections and 488 standpipes. Most taps deliver water for 8–12 hours a day. Officials estimate that all houses will have latrines by 2001.

Bharatpur (Rajasthan)

With around 200,000 inhabitants in 2000, 61 per cent of households have legal household connections to the piped water supplies. The rest rely on standposts or other water sources. Water supplies in the piped system are intermittent and at risk of contamination. There are no sewers; 52 per cent of the population rely on toilets connected to septic tanks, 15 per cent use twin-pit pour-flush latrines and 33 per cent have no latrine or use a 'service latrine' (a simple dry latrine in which faeces are deposited on the ground beneath a squatting hole and removed each day by a 'sweeper'). There are also problems with flooding, especially for poorer groups who live in the most flood-prone areas.

A survey of 400 households drawn from different slums in each of three cities found the following.

Bhilwara

Most households surveyed had access to water through taps and handpumps, but many mentioned their distance from a water source as a major problem. Only 25 per cent had water sources inside their houses, and the proportion of households with water inside their houses rose with income – from 10 per cent for those with monthly incomes of less than R500 to 48 per cent for those with incomes above R2000. Three-quarters of surveyed households had no toilets, and most defecated in open spaces or nearby fields. There were no public or community toilets.

Sambalpur

95 per cent of the households surveyed depended on a community water source, and in most slums the number of such sources was inadequate. Only 56 per cent had access to a municipal piped water supply, and the supply was irregular. In four of the 12 sample slums there were no sources of piped water at all. Most of the slums had grown up around a tank or a pond which had initially been a major source of water, but these became unusable because they were not kept clean and many of them had dried up completely. The municipality does not take responsibility for cleaning these ponds. More than three-quarters of the 400 households reported that they had no provision for any type of toilet facility and no drainage facility around the house. Of the 24 per cent of households reporting any type of drainage, 43 per cent said that these were not cleaned regularly.

Siliguri

Half the households surveyed had independent water sources while the rest used common sources. Most houses had water supplies nearby, 87 per cent thought that the water was fit for drinking and nearly all of them were satisfied with the supply. Three-quarters of the houses had independent toilets (mostly built by the municipalities against a deposit of R150 by the beneficiary) and 18 per cent used communal toilets. Two-fifths of the households had no provision for drainage, and the rest had open drains that were rarely cleaned.

Source: For the first two studies, Colin, Jeremy and Joy Morgan (2000), *Provision of Water and Sanitation Services to Small Towns; Part B: Case Studies in Uganda and India*, Well Studies in Water, Sanitation and Environmental Health Task 323, WELL, Loughborough and London, 53 pages. For the study on Bharatpur, WSP (2000), *Urban Environmental Sanitation Planning; Lessons from Bharatpur, Rajasthan, India*, Field Note, Water and Sanitation Program, South Asia Region, New Delhi, 8 pages. This report also describes a programme to provide improved water and sanitation provision. For the studies on slums, Ghosh, A, S S Ahmad and Shipra Maitra (1994), *Basic Services for Urban Poor: A Study of Baroda, Bhilwara, Sambalpur and Siliguri*, Urban Studies Series No 3, Institute of Social Sciences and Concept Publishing Company, New Delhi, 305 pages.

In Latin America, there are also some case studies of smaller cities. Most highlight the inadequacies in water and sanitation provision. Box 1.9 on Brazil showed that by 2000, only 46 per cent of households in municipalities with under 20,000 inhabitants had access to the general water network system, and close to half of all municipalities had no sewer

Box 1.13 Provision for water and sanitation in three small urban centres in China

Neiguan

The town had 10,500 inhabitants in 1993. A piped water supply became available in 1992 for the first time; prior to this, residents relied on wells and river water. The town faces a serious water shortage, in part due to progressive reductions in river flow and over-exploitation of groundwater, and in part because of a series of low rainfall years. In a survey, only 20 per cent of households had access to tap water – in part because installation costs were very high. Half of the households relied on wells for their water. The town government has set up a dozen or so water stations, and it is estimated that around 2000 people use these. Among surveyed households, there was no wastewater plumbing. Over 90 per cent of surveyed households possessed their own latrines; members of other households used public toilets. 'The public toilets in factories and government offices were poorly maintained and usually extremely dirty due to the shortage of water for flushing' (page 53).

Yantan

This had 31,000 inhabitants in 1992, and around 50,000 by the mid-1990s if the floating population is included. 90 per cent of surveyed households used earth closet latrines, while the rest used public toilets; none were connected to sewers. Close to 75 per cent of the households surveyed obtained water from wells while most of the rest used pond or stream water. Only one household in the survey had piped water.

Shengze

By the mid-1990s, there were 32,000 urban residents – but if unregistered and temporarily permitted migrants were included it would be much higher. Over 60 per cent of households in a survey had connections to sewers and 94 per cent had tap water, although many complained about the quality (and there were worries about increasing numbers of typhoid cases).

Source: Kirky, Richard, Ian Bradbury and Guanbao Shen (2000), *Small Town China; Governance, Economy, Environment and Lifestyle in Three Zhen*, Ashgate, Basingstoke.

systems (the smaller municipalities and those in poorer regions were the least likely to have sewers).[160]

Table 1.13 shows potable water and sewer coverage in five 'secondary cities' in Nicaragua; the four smaller urban centres had below-average figures in regard to the proportion of the urban population with potable water, and sewage services.

The 2000 assessment of water and sanitation provision in Latin America included some data on smaller cities – see Table 1.14. This shows that the quality and extent of water and sanitation provision can be high, as in the three cities in Chile. The proportion of the population served with piped connections is also very high in Santa Clara (Cuba) and in the other Cuban and Venezuelan cities – indeed, higher than some of the large Latin American cities (see Table 1.10). However, in general, apart from the cities in Chile, provision for sanitation is much less extensive.

Other case studies of smaller cities mention the serious inadequacies in provision. For instance, a case study of Chimbote in Peru, while describing the innovative Local Agenda 21 developed by a coalition of groups, also noted that two-fifths of the population lacked piped water and connection to sewers – as well as the lack of a regular garbage collection system in most residential areas and the many informal settlements at high risk from floods.[161]

Virtually all the examples of water and sanitation provision so far in this section come from well-established urban centres. A study of the new urban centres that have grown up in the agricultural/forest frontier in Brazil[162] highlighted the lack of water and sanitation provision in these too:

* A survey of 419 households in Rolim de Moura (with a population of around 30,000 in 1990) found that 44 per cent had informal water supplies (either a private well without a pump or water carried from the local river) and 67 per cent had informal sanitation (lacking a septic tank or connection to a sewer and relying on outhouses or defecation outside).

* A survey of 208 households in Santa Luiza d'Oeste (with a population estimated at 6000 in 1990) found that 52 per cent relied on informal water supplies and 80 per cent relied on informal sanitation.

Table 1.13 Coverage of basic services in five 'secondary cities' in Nicaragua, 1995

City	Urban population	% average coverage of basic services per city				
		Potable water	Sewage	Streets	Electricity	Garbage collection
León	123,865	90	60	70	85	75
Chinandega	97,387	74	38	75	75	51
Estelí	71,550	78	35	15	75	55
Somoto	14,218	72	43	60	85	30
Ocotal	25,264	80	10	45	78	65
Average coverage in all urban areas		90	44	37	93	78

Source: PRODEL (1997), *Proyecto de la Segunda Fase*, PRODEL, Managua, and reports from the municipalities served by PRODEL; the Social Action Ministry (1995), *Medición de la Pobreza en Nicaragua* [Measurement of Poverty in Nicaragua], MAS/UNDP, Managua, reproduced in Stein, Alfredo (2001), *Participation and Sustainability in Social Projects: The Experience of the Local Development Programme (PRODEL) in Nicaragua*, IIED Working Paper 3 on Poverty Reduction in Urban Areas, IIED, London.

- A survey of 410 households in Xinguara found that 72 per cent relied on informal water supplies and 86 per cent on informal sanitation.
- A survey of 320 households in Tucumã found that 69 per cent relied on informal water supplies and 86 per cent on informal sanitation.
- A survey of 173 households in Ourilândia do Norte, which had 10,893 inhabitants in 1991, found that 95 per cent relied on informal water supplies and informal sanitation (typically outhouses or defecating outdoors).

Thus, it is not only in the smaller urban centres in the lower-income nations of Latin America and the Caribbean that there are serious problems, as examples from Argentina and Brazil show. Indeed, a substantial proportion of the population in some of the wealthiest smaller urban centres may still have serious problems, as illustrated by the case of San Carlos de Bariloche. This is a very successful tourist city with 81,000 inhabitants in 1991, located within an area of exceptional natural beauty. But in 1991, 19 per cent of households still lacked water piped into their home and 11 per cent lacked access to public water networks. A considerable proportion lacked adequate provision for sanitation; however, there had been considerable progress in reducing the proportion of the population with unmet basic needs between 1980 and 1991.[163]

In conclusion, we are faced with remarkably little detailed information on water and sanitation provision in urban centres other than the larger and more politically important cities. Yet there are tens of thousands of these urban centres, and they include a large proportion of the world's urban (and total) population. This section has drawn information from case studies of around 50 urban centres, which vary from small market towns to cities with several hundred thousand inhabitants. Most of these show the large inadequacies in water and sanitation provision, especially those from low-income nations in Africa and Asia. There is no reason to suspect that the case studies of smaller African urban centres in Box 1.10 or of smaller urban centres in India in Box 1.12 are untypical, or that the studies of these urban centres deliberately chose urban centres where water and sanitation provision was particularly inadequate.

There is also one final example worth mentioning: the city of Ilo in Peru. This is not a wealthy or large city; it had around 60,000 inhabitants by 2000 and had grown rapidly. Yet it had managed to increase the proportion of its population with drinking water connections from 40 to 85 per cent between 1981 and 1998, as well as increasing the regularity of the supply (along with many other improvements in living conditions). Much of the improvement was due to a consistent policy followed by the local government of supporting projects undertaken by community-level management committees during this period. It

Table 1.14 Provision for water and sanitation in selected smaller cities in Latin America

Nation	City	Population	% with piped connections	% with public sources	Other (%)
Chile	Arica	178,600	99.8		
	Osorno	130,200	98.6		
	Antofagasta	247,700	99.2		
Cuba	Camaguey	318,100	75.3	15.7 (well with pump)	4.8
	Pinar del Rio	138,100	79.3	5.3	7.2
	Santa Clara	201,080	97.3	1.6 (well with pump)	1.2
French Guyana	Saint Laurent du Maroni	19,200	46.8	26.0 (public sources)	26.0
Venezuela	Guanare	132,000	89.4		10.6
	San Cristobal	436,000	81.2		18.8

Nation	City	Population	% with sewer connections	% with connection to septic tank/soakaway	% with simple latrine	Other (%)
Chile	Arica	178,600	98.6	1.2		
	Osorno	130,200	93.3	5.3		
	Antofagasta	247,700	96.8	2.4		
Cuba	Camaguey	318,100	48.5	11.3	31.4	1.5
	Pinar del Rio	138,100	60.0	18.1	21.9	
	Santa Clara	201,080	44.1	36.7	3.2	16.3
French Guyana	Saint Laurent du Maroni	19,200	26.0	15.6		5.1
Venezuela	Guanare	132,000	79.6	18.9	1.5	
	San Cristobal	436,000	64.0	36.0 (without connection)		

Source: Centro Panamericano de Ingenieria Sanitaria y Ciencias del Ambiente, *Evaluacion de los Servicios de Agua Potable y Saneamiento 2000 en las America,* www.cepis.ops-oms.org.

also owed much to the succession of elected mayors from 1982 onwards.[164] It is a reminder that there is often scope for improving water and sanitation provision in smaller urban centres, if solutions are based on making the best use of local resources – including the willingness and capacity of the inhabitants to work with local authorities. This is a point to which this book will return in Chapter 7.

 Rural versus urban areas

This book underlines the need for governments and international agencies to give more attention to improving water and sanitation provision in urban areas. This chapter has presented the evidence to justify this. This might be taken as a demand for resources to be diverted from rural areas for this purpose. That is not our intention. The WHO/UNICEF Assessment 2000 makes clear the very large number of rural dwellers who lack improved provision for water and sanitation; in 2000,

only 47 per cent of Africa's rural population had improved water supplies; in Asia it was 75 per cent, in Latin America and the Caribbean it was 62 per cent. In all three of these regions, less than half the rural population had improved sanitation.[165]

The figures from this assessment might be taken to justify less attention to water and sanitation in urban areas because far more people in rural areas lack improved provision. For instance, in 2000, the number of rural dwellers lacking improved provision for water and for sanitation was around five times that in urban areas. But if the number of urban dwellers lacking adequate provision is three to four times more than those measured as having improved provision, then the difference in the proportion of the population lacking adequate provision between rural and urban areas diminishes a lot. However, there are also grounds for questioning whether the figures for the unserved rural population fully reflect the scale of need: the censuses or household surveys from which they draw also fail to measure whether provision is adequate.

The debate about the relative priority that should be accorded to rural populations versus urban populations has been one of the central debates in development policy for the last 30 years. Certainly, one of the most important changes in development policy that arose in the late 1960s and early 1970s was the recognition that most poor rural dwellers were being bypassed by most development programmes – although there is not much evidence that poor urban dwellers were doing much better, especially those who lived outside capital cities (which is the majority of urban dwellers). Most international agencies gave a higher priority to reaching rural populations and supporting smallholder farmers and pastoralists. However, since the mid-1970s many international agencies have been reluctant to support urban investments. Since this recognition that most of the rural poor were being bypassed by development assistance, many agencies have continually emphasized that rural needs are much larger than urban needs. For instance, in the 1996 Human Development Report, the figures for the provision of safe water and sanitation for rural and urban areas were presented in a way which emphasized that rural problems were much more serious than urban problems.[166]

But this and most other assessments of water and sanitation provision fail to recognize differences between rural and urban contexts. One limitation of all national statistics (and thus of the global statistics on which these are based) is their failure to recognize differences in context between (most) rural and (most) urban areas. The same criteria for improved provision cannot be used in all settings. A water source within 100 metres of all households is not the same in a village of 200 persons with 50 persons per tap as it is in a squatter settlement with 100,000 persons (and 500 persons per tap). Protecting a well from human excreta and wastewater is not the same in a village of 200 persons as it is in a squatter settlement of 100,000 persons (where there is 500 times more human excreta and household wastewater to dispose of). Defecation in the open is obviously less

hazardous in most rural areas because there is more open space and care can be taken that the areas where open defecation happens are not close to water sources or homes (although problems with hand-washing and harassment for women may be comparable). The Assessment 2000 suggests that 'reasonable access' for water should be broadly defined as 'the availability of at least 20 litres per person per day from a source within 1 kilometre of the user's dwelling.'[167] For most urban settings, this is an inappropriate standard. In large, dense urban settlements, the availability of a water source within 1 kilometre will mean long queues; the persons responsible for fetching and carrying water may be spending hours a day doing this. The appropriateness of the standard may also be questioned for both rural and urban contexts, since having to carry water for 1 kilometre (or even only 100 metres) is an arduous task – and usually households with distant water sources will not collect enough to ensure plentiful water supplies for washing (including washing children after defecation), laundry, food preparation and keeping the house and household utensils clean. Having a water tap within 1 kilometre does not mean that there is a regular supply in the tap, and problems of access and time spent queuing are often much increased as water is only available for a few hours a day (as shown by many of the examples given earlier). The water in the tap may not be safe, especially if the supply is intermittent. Having a tap within 1 kilometre does not mean that the supply is free or reasonably priced. It may be that this water supply is managed or controlled by a company or individuals who charge high prices for it.

Two other points have relevance to the rural versus urban issue. First, the relative sizes of the rural and urban populations within low- and middle-income nations have changed significantly since the debates about urban bias began (perhaps rather more than the debate itself). Since 1975, the urban population in low- and middle-income countries has nearly tripled; the rural population has increased by a third.[168] Among the nations classified by the United Nations as the least developed, the urban population has more than quadrupled since 1975 while the rural population increased by around 75 per cent. This is not to claim that urban need is greater than rural need, nor to pretend that urban populations outnumber rural populations among low-income nations (although they do in many middle-income nations). But this book does seek to highlight that there are very serious deficiencies in water and sanitation provision for large sections of the urban population in Africa, Asia and Latin America and the Caribbean, and that the needs of poor urban dwellers also need to be taken into account by governments and international agencies. Three-fifths of Africa's population may still be in rural areas, but the two-fifths in urban areas mean that it has more urban citizens and twice as many urban children as North America. This is a population that deserves more attention to its needs for water and sanitation.

The second point is that a large part of the investment in improving provision in urban areas can come from the better management of water and sanitation utilities and better governance, so that it need not draw on scarce national or international development funds. This is the main theme of this book's final chapter.

Notes and references

1. See for instance levels of provision in Porto Alegre in Brazil described in Menegat, Rualdo (2002), 'Participatory democracy and sustainable development: integrated urban environmental management in Porto Alegre, Brazil', *Environment and Urbanization*, Vol 14, No 2, pages 181–206.

2. See McIntosh, Arthur C and Cesar E Yñiguez (1997), *Second Water Utilities Data Book*, Asian Development Bank, Manila, 210 pages.

3. WHO and UNICEF (2000), *Global Water Supply and Sanitation Assessment 2000 Report*, World Health Organization, UNICEF and Water Supply and Sanitation Collaborative Council, Geneva, 80 pages.

4. Saghir, Jamal, Manuel Schiffler and Mathewos Woldu (2000), *Urban Water and Sanitation in the Middle East and North Africa Region: The Way Forward*, Middle East and North Africa Region Infrastructure Development Group, The World Bank, Washington, DC; Khatim, Kherraz (2002), *Water Supply and Sewage in Cities of Algeria*, Background Paper, UN-Habitat, Nairobi.

5. WHO and UNICEF 2000, op cit.

6. See Hewett, Paul C and Mark R Montgomery (2002), *Poverty and Public Services in Developing-Country Cities*, Population Council, New York, 62 pages.

7. Benneh, George, Jacob Songsore, John S Nabila, A T Amuzu, K A Tutu, Yvon Yangyuoro and Gordon McGranahan (1993), *Environmental Problems and the Urban Household in the Greater Accra Metropolitan Area (GAMA) Ghana*, Stockholm Environment Institute, Stockholm, 126 pages.

8. See Hewett and Montgomery 2002, op cit.

9. Data supplied by Perween Rahman from the Orangi Pilot Project – Research and Training Institute. See also Orangi Pilot Project – Research and Training Institute (2002), *Katchi Abadis of Karachi: Documentation of Sewerage, Water Supply Lines, Clinics, Schools and Thallas Volume 1: The First 100 Katchi Abadis Surveyed*, OPP-RTI, Karachi, 507 pages.

10. The WHO/UNICEF Joint Monitoring Programme for Water Supply and Sanitation intends to support and draw on new primary data sources – see www.who.int/water_sanitation_health/Globassessment/GlobalTOC.htm.

11. WHO and UNICEF 2000, op cit.

12. WHO and UNICEF 2000, op cit, page 23.

13. Bairoch, Paul (1988), *Cities and Economic Development: From the Dawn of History to the Present*, Mansell, London, 574 pages.

14. Hasan, Arif (2001), *Working with Communities*, City Press, Karachi, 200 pages.

15. Cotton, Andrew and Darren Saywell (2001), *On-plot Sanitation in Low-income Urban Communities; Guidelines for Selection*, Water, Engineering and Development Centre (WEDC), Loughborough University, Loughborough.

16. WHO and UNICEF 2000, op cit, page 77.

17. WHO and UNICEF 2000, op cit, page 77.

18. WHO and UNICEF 2000, op cit, page 78.

19. UNDP (2001), *Human Development Report 2001: Making New Technologies Work for Human Development*, Oxford University Press, Oxford and New York, 264 pages.

20. World Bank (2001), *World Development Report 2000/2001: Attacking Poverty*, Oxford University Press, Oxford and New York, see pages 276 and 290.

21. World Bank 2001, op cit, see page 321.

22. These were documented in detail in a background paper prepared for this volume by Micheline Duruz.

23. Vidal, John (2002), 'Water of strife', *The Guardian; Society*, March 27, pages 8–9.

24. See for instance Hanchett, Suzanne, Shireen Akhter and Mohidul Hoque Khan (2003), 'Water, sanitation and hygiene in Bangladesh slums: a summary of WaterAid's Bangladesh Urban Programme Evaluation', *Environment and Urbanization*, Vol 15, No 2; see Chapter 3 for more details.

25. McIntosh and Yñiguez 1997, op cit.

26. Hewett and Montgomery 2002, op cit.

27. Different sources give different figures although all show that most of Dhaka's population do not have connections to sewers. See Nawaz, Tanweer (2002), 'Dhaka city and possible slum resettlements programme', *CUS Bulletin on Urbanization and Development*, No 42, January–June, pages 36–39. See also Hanchett et al 2003, op cit.

28. For more details, see the paper by SPARC in *Environment and Urbanization* Vol 15, No 2, October 2003.

29. Dutta, Shyam and Richard Batley (2000), *Urban Governance, Partnership and Poverty: Ahmedabad*, Urban Governance, Partnership and Poverty Working Paper 16, International Development Department, University of Birmingham, Birmingham; and Dutta, Shyam S (2000), 'Partnerships in urban development: a review of Ahmedabad's experience', *Environment and Urbanization*, Vol 12, No 1, pages 13–26.

30. McIntosh and Yñiguez 1997, op cit.

31. Sinclair Knight Merz and Egis Consulting Australia in association with Brisbane City Enterprises and Feedback HSSI – STUP Consultants – Taru Leading Edge (2002), *Bangalore Water Supply and Environmental Sanitation Masterplan Project: Overview Report on Services to Urban Poor Stage 2*, AusAid, Canberra, March.

32. Benjamin, Solomon (2000), 'Governance, economic settings and poverty in Bangalore', *Environment and Urbanization*, Vol 12, No 1, pages 35–56; Benjamin, Solomon and R Bhuvaneshari (1999), *Urban Governance and Poverty: A Livelihood Perspective from Bangalore*, University of Birmingham. The data on the study of five slums come from Achar, K T V, B Bhaskara Rao and A de Bruijne (2001), 'Organization and management of water needs in slums', in Hans Schenk (ed), *Living in India's Slums: A Case Study of Bangalore*, IDPAD, Manohar, New Delhi, pages 161–186. The data on sanitation in the 22 slums come from Schenk-

Sandbergen, Loes (2001), 'Women, water and sanitation in the slums of Bangalore: a case study of action research', in Hans Schenk (ed), *Living in India's Slums: A Case Study of Bangalore*, IDPAD, Manohar, New Delhi, pages 187–216.

33. United Way of Vadodara quoted in Ghosh, A, S S Ahmad and Shipra Maitra (1994), *Basic Services for Urban Poor: A Study of Baroda, Bhilwara, Sambalpur and Siliguri*, Urban Studies Series No 3, Institute of Social Sciences and Concept Publishing Company, New Delhi, 305 pages.

34. Ghosh, A, S S Ahmad and Shipra Maitra (1994), *Basic Services for Urban Poor: A Study of Baroda, Bhilwara, Sambalpur and Siliguri*, Urban Studies Series No 3, Institute of Social Sciences and Concept Publishing Company, New Delhi, 305 pages.

35. Hasan, Samiul and M Adil Khan (1999), 'Community-based environmental management in a megacity, considering Calcutta', *Cities*, Vol 16, No 2, pages 103–110.

36. Cebu – National Statistical Office, 1990 Census on Population and Housing, quoted in Etemadi, Felisa (2000), *Urban Governance, Partnership and Poverty: Cebu*, Urban Governance, Partnership and Poverty Working Paper 13, International Development Department, University of Birmingham, Birmingham, 127 pages plus annexes.

37. McIntosh and Yñiguez 1997, op cit.

38. Kaneez Hasna, Mahbuba (1995), 'Street hydrant project in Chittagong low-income settlement', *Environment and Urbanization* Vol 7, No 2, October, pages 207–218.

39. Bangladesh Bureau of Statistics, Ministry of Planning, Government of the People's Republic of Bangladesh (with assistance from UNICEF) (1996), *Progotir Pathey Achieving the Mid Decade goals for Children in Bangladesh*, Dhaka, January.

40. McIntosh and Yñiguez 1997, op cit.

41. Fernando, Austin, Steven Russell, Anoushka Wilson and Elizabeth Vidler (2000), *Urban Governance, Partnership and Poverty: Colombo*, Urban Governance, Partnership and Poverty Working Paper 9, International Development Department, University of Birmingham, Birmingham.

42. McIntosh and Yñiguez 1997, op cit.

43. McIntosh and Yñiguez 1997, op cit.

44. Islam, Nazrul, Nurul Huda, Francis B Narayan and Pradumna B Rana (eds) (1997), *Addressing the Urban Poverty Agenda in Bangladesh, Critical Issues and the 1995 Survey Findings*, The University Press Limited, Dhaka, 323 pages.

45. Vidal 2002, op cit.

46. Survey by the International Centre for Diarrhoeal Disease Research, cited in UNICEF et al (1997), *The Dancing Horizon Human Development Prospects for Bangladesh*, UNICEF, Dhaka.

47. Islam, Huda, Narayan and Rana 1997, op cit.

48. Bangladesh Bureau of Statistics, Ministry of Planning, Government of the People's Republic of Bangladesh (with assistance from UNICEF) 1996, op cit.

49. Alimuddin, Salim, Arif Hasan and Asiya Sadiq (2000), *The Work of the Anjuman Samaji Behbood and the Larger Faisalabad Context*, IIED Working Paper, IIED, London.

50. McIntosh and Yñiguez 1997, op cit.

51. McIntosh and Yñiguez 1997, op cit.

52. Surjadi, Charles, L Padhmasutra, D Wahyuninsih, G McGranahan and M Kjellén (1994), *Household Environmental Problems in Jakarta*, Stockholm Environment Institute, Stockholm, 64 pages.

53. Safi, Mohammed Afzal (1998), 'An integrated approach to sanitation and health in Kabul', in John Pickford (ed), *Sanitation and Water for All*, Proceedings of the 24th WEDC Conference, WEDC, Islamabad, Pakistan.

54. Orangi Pilot Project – Research and Training Institute 2002, op cit, with additional data supplied by Perween Rahman.

55. Anand, P B (1999), 'Waste management in Madras revisited', *Environment and Urbanization*, Vol 11, No 2, pages 161–176.

56. McIntosh and Yñiguez 1997, op cit.

57. McIntosh and Yñiguez 1997, op cit.

58. Kumar, Sashi with Philip Amis (1999), *Urban Governance, Partnership and Poverty in Visakapatnam*, Urban Governance, Partnership and Poverty Working Paper, International Development Department, University of Birmingham, Birmingham, 47 pages; and Amis, Philip and Sashi Kumar (2000), 'Urban economic growth, infrastructure and poverty in India: lessons from Visakhapatnam', *Environment and Urbanization*, Vol 12, No 1, pages 185–197.

59. Abelson, Peter (1996), 'Evaluation of slum improvements: case study in Visakhapatnam, India', *Third World Planning Review*, Vol 13, No 2, pages 97–108.

60. Kumar with Amis 1999, and Amis and Kumar 2000, op cit.

61. UNICEF, 'Multi Indicator Cluster Surveys in India 1995–96', *Urban Slums*, UNICEF; NFHS: National Family Health Survey, 1992–93 cited in this source.

62. McIntosh and Yñiguez 1997, op cit.

63. Of course, strictly speaking, the figures in Table 1.6 do not say this; they only say that a higher proportion of the urban population in Burundi, Malawi and Zimbabwe have 'improved' provision than in South Africa and this says nothing about the quality of provision above 'improved'.

64. Wasao, Samson (2002), 'Characteristics of households and respondents', in APHRC, *Population and Health Dynamics in Nairobi's Informal Settlements*, African Population and Health Research Center, Nairobi, page 16.

65. Magadi, Monica A (2002), 'Maternal and child health', in APHRC, *Population and Health Dynamics in Nairobi's Informal Settlements*, African Population and Health Research Center, Nairobi, pages 95–118.

66. Musyimi, Jennifer (2002), 'When nature calls – the sanitation case at Mukuru', *Vijijini*, Newsletter of the Nairobi Informal Settlements Coordination Committee, Nairobi.

67. Mazwile, Margaret (2000), 'Involvement of women and community in "watsan" activities', paper presented at the 19th AWEC Conference, AWEC, Arusha, pages 131–135; and Mosha, J P N (2000), 'Small scale independent providers in provision of water and sanitation services', papers presented at the 19th AWEC Conference, AWEC, Arusha, pages 136–144.

68. Shayo Temu, Sylvia (2000), 'Cost recovery in urban water supply and sewerage services', paper presented at the 19th AWEC Conference, AWEC, Arusha, pages 12–20, quoting Urban Water Supply and Sewerage Division (2000), *Annual Report for UWSAs for 1998/1999*, and Arusha UWSA (2000), *Annual Report for the Year 1999/2000*, Arusha.

69. Mosha 2000, op cit; Ndezi, Timothy P (2000), 'Willingness and ability to pay for water and sanitation within low income communities in Dar es Salaam', paper presented at the 19th AWEC Conference, AWEC, Arusha, pages 109–116.

70. Njau, B E (2000), 'Demand management consideration in preparation of urban water supply programmes', paper presented at the 19th AWEC Conference, AWEC, Arusha, pages 55–65.

71. White, Gilbert F, David J Bradley and Anne U White (1972), *Drawers of Water: Domestic Water Use in East Africa*, University of Chicago Press, Chicago; and Thompson, John, Ina T Porras, Elisabeth Wood, James K Tumwine, Mark R Mujwahuzi, Munguti Katui-Katua and Nick Johnstone (2000), 'Waiting at the tap: changes in urban water use in East Africa over three decades', *Environment and Urbanization*, Vol 12, No 2, October.

72. Temeke is a municipality within Dar es Salaam with some 1.3 million inhabitants,

and most of its population lives in informal and underserviced settlements.

73. Hewett and Montgomery 2002, op cit.

74. Champetier, Séverine, Amadou Diallo and Jean Marie Sie Kouadio (2000), *Independent Water and Sanitation Providers in Africa: Abidjan, Côte d'Ivoire*, Case Study 3, Water and Sanitation Program – East and Southern Africa, Nairobi, 6 pages.

75. Songsore, Jacob and Gordon McGranahan (1993), 'Environment, wealth and health: towards an analysis of intra-urban differentials within Greater Accra Metropolitan Area, Ghana', *Environment and Urbanization*, Vol 5, No 2, October, pages 10–24.

76. Amuzu, A T and Josef Leitmann (1994), 'Accra urban environmental profile', *Cities*, Vol 11, No 1, pages 5–9.

77. Morris, Saul S, Carol Levin, Margaret Armar-Klemesu, Daniel Maxwell and Marie T Ruel (1999), *Does Geographic Targeting of Nutrition Interventions Make Sense in Cities? Evidence from Abidjan and Accra*, FCND Discussion Paper No 61, IFPRI, Washington, DC.

78. Songsore, Jacob and Gordon McGranahan 1993, op cit.

79. Amuzu and Leitmann 1994, op cit.

80. Bogrebon Allan, J (1997), 'Household demand for improved sanitation', in John Pickford et al (eds), *Water and Sanitation for All Partnership and Innovations*, Proceedings of the 23rd WEDC Conference, Durban, South Africa.

81. Yared, Tadesse, Ministry of Health (1996), 'Solid waste management in peri-urban areas of Ethiopia', *Water and Sanitation News*, Vol 3 (September–December), page 5. (A newsletter of NETWAS International, Network for Water and Sanitation International, Nairobi.)

82. Ogu, Vincent I (1998), 'The dynamics of informal housing in a traditional West African city: the Benin City example', *Third World Planning Review*, Vol 20, No 4, pages 419–439.

83. Champetier, Séverine and Amadou Diallo (2000), *Independent Water and Sanitation Providers in Africa: Conakry, Guinea, Case Study 4*, Water and Sanitation Program – East and Southern Africa, Nairobi, 8 pages.

84. Champetier, Séverine and Jean Eudes Okoundé (2000), *Independent Water and Sanitation Providers in Africa: Cotonou, Benin, Case Study 1*, Water and Sanitation Program – East and Southern Africa, Nairobi, 8 pages.

85. Kulaba, Saitiel (1989), 'Local government and the management of urban services in Tanzania' in Stren, Richard E and Rodney R White (eds), *African Cities in Crisis*, Westview Press, Connecticut, pages 203–245.

86. CARE Tanzania (1998), *Dar-es-Salaam Urban Livelihood Security Assessment*, Summary Report, June, CARE-Tanzania, Dar-es-Salaam.

87. Datta, Kavita (1996), 'The organization and performance of a low-income rental market: the case of Gabarone, Botswana', *Cities*, Vol 13, No 4, pages 237–245.

88. UNICEF (1997), *Profile of the Urban Local Governments of Ibadan, Planning Baseline Data*, Oyo State Government and UNICEF Zonal Office, Ibadan.

89. Beall, Jo, Owen Crankshaw and Susan Parnell (2000), *Urban Governance, Partnership and Poverty: Johannesburg, Urban Governance*, Partnership and Poverty Working Paper 12, International Development Department, University of Birmingham, Birmingham, 233 pages. The data on the study of informal settlements came from CASE (1998), *Investigating Water and Sanitation in Informal Settlements in Gauteng*, Report prepared for Rand Water, Johannesburg.

90. Champetier, Séverine and Bill Wandera (2000), *Independent Water and Sanitation Providers in Africa: Kampala, Uganda, Case Study 8*, Water and Sanitation Program – East and Southern Africa, Nairobi, 6 pages.

91. El Sammani, Mohamed O, Mohamed El Hadi Abu Sin, M Talha, B M El Hassan and Ian Haywood (1989), 'Management problems of Greater Khartoum', in Stren, Richard E and Rodney R White (eds), *African Cities in Crisis*, Westview Press, Boulder, USA, pages 246–275.

92. Mbuyi, Kankonde (1989), 'Kinshasa: problems of land management, infrastructure and food supply', in Stren, Richard E and Rodney R White (eds), *African Cities in Crisis*, Westview Press, Boulder, USA, pages 148–175.

93. Devas, Nick and David Korboe (2000), 'City governance and poverty: the case of Kumasi', *Environment and Urbanization*, Vol 12, No 1; also Korboe, David, Kofi Diaw and Nick Devas (2000), *Urban Governance, Partnership and Poverty: Kumasi*, Urban Governance, Partnership and Poverty Working Paper 10, International Development Department, University of Birmingham, Birmingham. Information on flooding is drawn from a 1996 World Bank staff appraisal report.

94. Cain, Allan, Mary Daly and Paul Robson (2002), *Basic Service Provision for the Urban Poor; The Experience of Development Workshop in Angola*, IIED Working Paper 8 on Poverty Reduction in Urban Areas, IIED, London, 40 pages.

95. Development Workshop (1999), *Community Based Solid Waste Management in Luanda's Musseques: A Case Study*, Development Workshop, Guelph, 41 pages.

96. Cain, Daly and Robson 2002, op cit.

97. Rakodi, Carole, Rose Gatabaki-Kamau and Nick Devas (2000), 'Poverty and political conflict in Mombasa', *Environment and Urbanization*, Vol 12, No 1, pages 153–170. The 1993 estimate was from UNCHS (1997), *Analysis of Data and Global Urban Indicators Database 1993*, UNCHS Urban Indicators Programme, Phase 1: 1994–6, Nairobi. The results of the household survey came from African Medical Relief Fund (AMREF) and Office of the Vice-President/Ministry of Planning and National Development (1997), *The Second Participatory Assessment Study – Kenya Vol 1*, Government of Kenya, Nairobi. As part of the national study, Mombasa district was selected for in-depth assessment as an example of an urban district. Other data drawn from Gibb (Eastern Africa) Ltd (1995), *Sewerage, Drainage and Sanitation Studies Strategy Study, Appendix E, Sanitation Options and Strategies*, report for the National Water Conservation and Pipeline Corporation as part of the Second Mombasa and Coastal Water Supply Engineering and Rehabilitation Project, Nairobi, page E/2.

98. Champetier, Séverine and Mohamed Farid (2000), *Independent Water and Sanitation Providers in Africa: Nairobi, Kenya, Case Study 5*, Water and Sanitation Program – East and Southern Africa, Nairobi, 8 pages.

99. Alder, Graham (1995), 'Tackling poverty in Nairobi's informal settlements: developing an institutional strategy', *Environment and Urbanization*, Vol 7, No 2, October, pages 85–107.

100. IRC (1996), *Water Newsletter* (developments in water, sanitation and environment), No 245, November, page 2, published by IRC, International Water and Sanitation Centre, WHO Collaborating Center.

101. Champetier, Séverine and Mahamane Wanki Cissé (2000), *Independent Water and Sanitation Providers in Africa: Ouagadougou, Burkina Faso, Case Study 2*, Water and Sanitation Program – East and Southern Africa, Nairobi, 8 pages.

102. Ouayoro, Eustache (1995), 'Ouagadougou low-cost sanitation and public information programme', in Serageldin, Ismail, Michael A Cohen and K C Sivaramakrishnan (eds), *The Human Face of the Urban Environment*, Environmentally Sustainable Development Proceedings Series No 6, World Bank, Washington, DC, pages 154–159.

103. Altaf, Mir Anjum and Jeffrey A Hughes (1994), 'Measuring the demand for improved water and sanitation services: results from a contingent valuation study in Ouagadougou, Burkina Faso', *Urban Studies*, Vol 31, No 10, pages 1763–1776.

104. Centre for African Settlement Studies and Development (CASSAD) (1995), *Urban Poverty in Nigeria: Case Study of Zaria and Owerri*, Cassad, Ibadan, 110 pages.

105. Ibid.

106. Pamoja Trust (2001), 'Huruma informal settlements-planning survey report', Pamoja Trust, Nairobi.

107. Hardoy, Jorge E, Diana Mitlin and David Satterthwaite (2001), *Environmental Problems in an Urbanizing World: Finding Solutions for Cities in Africa, Asia and Latin America*, Earthscan Publications, London, 470 pages; for Nairobi, APHRC (2002), *Population and Health Dynamics in Nairobi's Informal Settlements*, African Population and Health Research Center, April, 256 pages; for Angola, Cain, Daly and Robson 2002, op cit.

108. Cotton and Saywell 2001, op cit.

109. Hewitt and Montgomery 2002, op cit.

110. Hardoy, Mitlin and Satterthwaite 2001, op cit.

111. Cairncross, S and E A R Ouano (1990), *Surface Water Drainage In Low-Income Communities*, World Health Organization, Geneva.

112. This section draws on a background paper prepared by staff at IIED–America Latina in Buenos Aires.

113. As noted earlier, the WHO definition of 'improved' provision is water available within 1 km; the PAHO/WHO Report for Latin America and the Caribbean notes that most nations have defined 'easy' access as water within 200 or 400 metres with 40–50 litres per person per day. See PAHO and WHO (2001), *Water Supply and Sanitation: Current Status and Prospects, Regional Report on the Evaluation 2000 in the Region of the Americas*, Pan American Health Organization (PAHO) and World Health Organization (WHO), Washington, DC, 81 pages, for more discussion of this.

114. CEPIS Pan American Center for Sanitary Engineering and Environmental Sciences. Database on the situation and prospects of the Drinking Water and Sanitation Sector in the Region of the Americas (www.cepis.ops-oms.org).

115. WHO and UNICEF 2000, op cit.

116. Background paper prepared by Pedro Jacobi; note that many households in Brazil have a flush toilet that discharges directly to the drain or into municipally constructed sewers that are not registered with the official water and sanitation agencies.

117. MacDonald, Joan and Danieala Simioni (1999), *Consensos Urbanos. Aportes del Plan de Accion Regional De America Latina y el Caribe Sobre Asentamientos Humanos*, Serie

Medio Ambiente y Desarrollo No 21, CEPAL, Santiago de Chile.

118. Table 10 of PAHO/WHO 2001, op cit.

119. CEPIS 2000, op cit.

120. Duhau, 1991, page 87 quoted in Pirez, P (2000) *Servicios urbanos y equidad en America Latin: Un panorama con base en algunos casos*, CEPAL, Santiago de Chile, page 12.

121. Jose Esteban Castro (2002), *Urban Water and the Politics of Citizenship: The Case of the Mexico City Metropolitan Area (1980s–1990s)*, University of Oxford, Oxford.

122. Duhau, Emilio (1991) 'Gestion de los servicios urbanos en Mexico: alternativas y tendencias' in Schteingart, M and L d'Andrea (eds) *Servicios Urbanos, Gestion Local y Medio Ambiente*, El Colegio de Mexico, CERFE, Mexico, quoted in Pirez 2000, op cit.

123. Marvin, Simon and Nina Laurie (1999), 'An emerging logic of urban water management, Cochabamba, Bolivia', *Urban Studies*, Vol 36, No 2, pages 341–257.

124. Swyngedouw, Erik A (1995), 'The contradictions of urban water provision a study of Guayaquil, Ecuador', *Third World Planning Review*, Vol 17, No 4, pages 387–405.

125. Robotham, Don (1994), 'Redefining urban health policy in a developing country: the Jamaica case', in S Atkinson, J Songsore and W Werna (eds), *Urban Health Research in Developing Countries: Implications for Policy*, CAB International, Wallingford, pages 31–42. The quote is from page 39.

126. Kristin Komives (1999), *Designing Pro-Poor Water and Sewer Concessions: Early Lessons from Bolivia*, World Bank Policy Research Working Paper 2243, World Bank, Washington, DC.

127. Clapham, David (1996), 'Water and sanitation problems in Lima, Peru', *Water & Health*, No 19/96, North West Water Ltd, Warrington, UK.

128. Ferguson, Bruce (1996), 'The environmental impacts and public costs of unguided informal settlement: the case of Montego Bay', *Environment and Urbanization*, Vol 8, No 2, October, pages 171–193.

129. Constance, Paul (1999), 'What price for water? Why people in some of the poorest communities would rather pay more', *IDBAMÉRICA*, July–August, pages 3–5. Also gives details of scheme to reach poorest groups with improved provision by the French NGO GRET.

130. Ferguson, Bruce and Crescencia Maurer (1996), 'Urban management for environmental quality in South America', *Third World Planning Review*, Vol 18, No 2, pages 117–154.

131. Choguill, C L (1994), 'Implementing urban development projects: a search for criteria for success', *Third World Planning Review*, Vol 16, No 1.

132. PAHO/WHO 2001, op cit.

133. PAHO/WHO 2001, op cit.

134. MacDonald and Simioni 1999, op cit.

135. Asociación Arte y Cultura (ASOARTE), Asociación Mision Mixta (AMM), Fundación Grupo Experimental de Alternativas Culturales (GEAC) and Asociación Mujeres Activas por un Futuro Mejor (MAFUM) (2002), 'Exploring youth and community relations in Cali, Colombia', *Environment and Urbanization*, Vol 14, No 2, pages 149–156.

136. Arévalo, Pedro, T (1997), 'May hope be realized: Huaycan self-managing urban community in Lima', *Environment and Urbanization*, Vol 9, No 1, April, pages 59–79.

137. Cuenya, Beatriz, Hector Almada, Diego Armus, Julia Castells, Maria di Loreto and Susana Penalva (1990), 'Housing and health problems in Buenos Aires: the case of Barrio San Martin', in Cairncross, Sandy, Jorge E Hardoy and David Satterthwaite (eds), *The Poor Die Young: Housing and Health in Third World Cities*, Earthscan Publications, London.

138. Schusterman, Ricardo and Ana Hardoy (1997), 'Reconstructing social capital in a poor urban settlement: the Integrated Improvement Programme, Barrio San Jorge', *Environment and Urbanization*, Vol 9, No 1, April, pages 91–119.

139. This is drawn from one of four reports prepared by youth groups on their neighbourhoods in Cali; the findings of these reports were summarized in Asociación Arte y Cultura (ASOARTE), Asociación Mision Mixta (AMM), Fundación Grupo Experimental de Alternativas Culturales (GEAC) and Asociación Mujeres Activas por un Futuro Mejor 2002, op cit.

140. Ibid.

141. The figures drawn from the CEPIS-OMS database do not necessarily add up to 100 per cent.

142. The proportion of people living in cities is also considerably less than the proportion living in urban centres, as a significant proportion of the urban population lives in urban centres too small to be called cities (because they lack the size and the economic, administrative or political status that being a city implies). There is no agreement as to what characteristics an urban centre should have to be classified as a city.

143. Moriarty, P B, G Patricot, T Bastemeijer, J Smet and C Van der Voorden (2002), *Between Rural and Urban: Towards Sustainable Management of Water Supply Systems in Small Towns in Africa*, International Water and Sanitation Centre, Delft.

144. Information sheet in Water and Sanitation Program (2000), *Independent Water and Sanitation Providers in Africa: Beyond Facts and Figures*, WSP Africa Regional Office, World Bank, Nairobi.

145. Livingstone, A J (1994), 'Community management of small urban water supplies in Sudan and Ghana', in WHO and WSSCC Working Group on Operation and Maintainance, *Operations and Maintenance of Water Supply and Sanitation Systems: Case Studies*, World Health Organization, Geneva, pages 44–56.

146. Zaba, Basia and Ndalahwa Madulu (1998), 'A drop to drink; population and water resources; illustrations from Northern Tanzania', in de Sherbinin, Alex and Victoria Dompka (eds), *Water and Population Dynamics: Case Studies and Policy Implications*, American Association for the Advancement of Science (AAAS), Washington, DC, pages 49–86.

147. Colin, Jeremy and Joy Morgan (2000), *Provision of Water and Sanitation Services to Small Towns; Part B: Case Studies in Uganda and India*, Well Studies in Water, Sanitation and Environmental Health Task 323, WELL, Loughborough and London, 53 pages.

148. Ibid.

149. Amis, Philip (1992), *Urban Management in Uganda: Survival Under Stress*, The Institutional Framework of Urban Government: Case Study No 5, Development Administration Group, INLOGOV, University of Birmingham, Birmingham, 110 pages.

150. Estienne, C (2000), *The PAGE Water Supply Management Support Programme*, case study submitted to the Small Towns Water and Sanitation: Third Electronic Conference.

151. Livingstone 1994, op cit.

152. Tchounwou, P B, D M Lantum, A Monkiedje, I Takougang and P H Barbazan (1997), 'The urgent need for environmental sanitation and safe drinking water in Mbandjock, Cameroon', *Archives of Environmental Contamination and Toxicology*, Vol 33, No 1, pages 17–22.

153. Zaba and Madulu 1998, op cit.

154. Meekyaa, Ude James and Carole Rakodi (1990), 'The neglected small towns of Nigeria', *Third World Planning Review*, Vol 12, No 1, February, pages 21–40.

155. Ogu, Vincent I (1998), 'The dynamics of informal housing in a traditional West African City: the Benin City example', *Third World Planning Review*, Vol 20, No 4, pages 419–439.

156. Yacoob, May and Margo Kelly (1999), *Secondary Cities in West Africa: The Challenge of Environmental Health and Prevention*, Occasional Paper Series: Comparative Urban Studies, No 21, Woodrow Wilson International Center for Scholars, Washington, DC, 27 pages.

157. Agarwal, Anil, Sunita Narain and Srabani Sen (eds) (1999), *State of India's Environment: The Citizens' Fifth Report*, Centre for Science and Environment, New Delhi, 440 pages.

158. Kirkby, Richard, Ian Bradbury and Guanbao Shen (2000), *Small Town China: Governance, Economy, Environment and Lifestyle in Three Zhen*, Ashgate Publishing Ltd, Aldershot, 168 pages.

159. Smil, Vaclav (1995), *Environmental Problems in China: Estimates of Economic Costs*, East–West Center Special Report No 5, East–West Center, Honolulu.

160. Jacobi 2002, op cit.

161. Foronda, F Maria Elena (1998), 'Chimbote's Local Agenda 21: initiatives to support its development and implementation', *Environment and Urbanization*, Vol 10, No 2, October, pages 129–147.

162. Browder, John D and Brian J Godfrey (1997), *Rainforest Cities: Urbanization, Development and Globalization of the Brazilian Amazon*, Columbia University Press, New York and Chichester, 429 pages.

163. Abaleron, Carlos Alberto (1995), 'Marginal urban space and unsatisfied basic needs: the case of San Carlos de Bariloche, Argentina', *Environment and Urbanization*, Vol 7, No 1, April, pages 97–115.

164. López Follegatti, Jose Luis (1999), 'Ilo: a city in transformation', *Environment and Urbanization*, Vol 11, No 2, October, pages 181–202.

165. WHO and UNICEF 2000, op cit.

166. UNDP (1996), *Human Development Report 1996*, Oxford University Press, Oxford, 228 pages.

167. WHO and UNICEF 2000, op cit, pages 77–78.

168. United Nations (2002), *World Urbanization Prospects; The 2001 Revision; Data Tables and Highlights*, Population Division, Department of Economic and Social Affairs, United Nations Secretariat, ESA/P/WP/173, New York, 181 pages.

The Impacts of Deficient Provision

 Introduction

Chapter 1 described the inadequacies in water and sanitation provision for hundreds of millions of urban dwellers; how water sources are often distant, difficult to access, contaminated and intermittent; and how provision for sanitation does not fulfil its primary task – ensuring the safe disposal of human excreta and wastewater. This chapter focuses on the impact of these inadequacies. This includes the health burdens and the other costs to people, such as high monetary costs and the time and effort needed to get water. It also discusses who is most affected: overwhelmingly this is low-income households, but within these households the burdens of inadequate provision often fall especially heavily on women and girls (who typically end up doing most of the water collection and managing the disposal of wastes) and children (who typically suffer most from the diseases associated with inadequate water supplies and sanitation). To add insult to injury, while low-income dwellers often pay high prices for water, wealthier households nearby often have piped connections providing water that is heavily subsidized, because the price is well below the unit cost of providing it. This chapter also discusses the large economic costs of inadequate provision, for households, cities and nations.

This chapter focuses on urban areas in low- and middle-income nations because, as Chapter 1 made clear, this is where the deficiencies in water and sanitation provision are heavily concentrated.

 The health impacts of inadequate provision for water and sanitation

Overall impacts

There are two reasons why urban areas should have better health than rural areas, and should also be better served with water and sanitation provision, without a bias favouring provision there. The first is that urban areas provide significant economies of scale and proximity for the delivery of piped water and provision for good quality sanitation and drainage, so unit costs should be lower. Unit costs are also lower for many other services that improve health or reduce disease burdens – including good quality health care (with special provision for infants, children and pregnant mothers), emergency services (including those that rapidly treat health-threatening water-related diseases) and schools (and their links to improving knowledge of health-enhancing behaviours, including those related to hygiene). The second is that many cities have a more prosperous economic base than rural areas, providing higher average incomes for large sections of the population (and thus greater capacity to pay for good quality provision) and greater possibilities for governments (or private utilities) to raise revenues to fund such provision and to get costs back from user charges (from businesses as well as households). But making use of potential urban advantages depends on competent, effective local governments and/or water and sanitation utilities. In the absence of such institutions – and with the resulting lack of investment in infrastructure, services

Table 2.1 Examples of water- and sanitation-related diseases and the aspects of inadequacy that are linked to them

Disease	Strength of the link					
	Water quality	Water quantity or convenience	Personal and domestic hygiene	Wastewater disposal or drainage	Excreta disposal	Food sanitation/ hygiene
Diarrhoea						
Viral diarrhoea	Medium	High	High	–	Medium	Medium
Bacterial diarrhoea	Medium	High	High	–	Medium	Medium
Protozoal diarrhoea	Low	High	High	–	Medium	Medium
Poliomyelitis and hepatitis A	Low	High	High	–	Medium	Medium
Worm infections						
Ascaris, trichuris	Low	Low	Low	Low	High	Medium
Hookworm	Low	Low	Low	–	High	–
Pinworm, dwarf tapeworm	–	High	High	–	Medium	Low
Other tapeworms	–	Low	Low	–	High	High
Schistosomiasis	Low	Low	–	Low	High	–
Guinea-worm	High	High	–	–	Medium	
Other worms with aquatic hosts	High	–	–	Medium	Medium	High
Skin infections	–	High	High	–	–	–
Eye infections	Low	High	High	Low	Medium[+]	–
Insect-transmitted						
Malaria	–	–	–	Low	–	–
Urban yellow fever, dengue	–	–	Low[*]	Medium	–	–
Bancroftian filariasis	–	–	–	High	High	–
Onchocerciasis	–	–	–	–	–	–

Note: The degree of importance of each intervention for each particular disease is ranked as high, medium or low; a dash means that it has negligible importance.
* Vectors breed in water-storage containers.
+ Flies which transmit infection breed in scattered human faeces.
Source: This table draws on WHO (1983), *Maximizing Benefits to Health: An Appraisal Methodology for Water Supply and Sanitation Projects*, unpublished WHO Report ETS/83.7, WHO, Geneva, quoted in WHO (1986), *Intersectoral Action for Health – The Role of Intersectoral Cooperation in National Strategies for Health for All*, Background Document for Technical Discussions, 39th World Health Assembly, May, Geneva, updated and modified by Sandy Cairncross from the London School of Hygiene and Tropical Medicine.

and waste management – an urban concentration becomes a serious health disadvantage. Urban areas are not only concentrations of people and enterprises but also concentrations of their wastes – of which human excreta is a particularly dangerous example. As the WHO has recognized, when infrastructure and services are lacking, urban areas are among the world's most life-threatening human environments.[1]

Many diseases are associated with inadequate water, sanitation and hygiene. At any one time, close to half the urban population in Africa, Asia and Latin America are suffering from one or more of the main diseases associated with inadequate water and sanitation provision.[2] Some are associated primarily with poor water quality while others are more associated with the inadequate quantity of water available to households, or with inadequate hygiene or unhygienic food preparation practices; others are associated with inadequate provision for excreta disposal or wastewater disposal or drainage – including a group of diseases for which water or wastewater provides a habitat for disease vectors or hosts (see Table 2.1).

Water-related diseases can be classified into four categories, according to the environmental pathways by which infection takes place: faecal–oral, water-washed, water-based and water-related insect vector.[3]

Faecal–oral diseases, mostly diarrhoeal diseases, are the most common and account for a high proportion of infant, child and adult illnesses – and for most water-related infant and child deaths.[4] Diarrhoeal diseases cause 6000 deaths a day, mostly among children under five.[5] The micro-organisms which cause these diseases can be water-borne, or transmitted by other faecal–oral routes by which faecal matter can enter the mouth. Where water supplies and provision for sanitation are inadequate for much of a city's population, faecal–oral disease can be among the most serious health problems for the whole city.[6] Over-crowding and inadequate food hygiene exacerbate the risks from contaminated water and poor sanitation;[7] it is common for there to be three persons per room in tenements, cheap boarding houses and informal settlements where most low-income urban dwellers live in Africa, Asia and Latin America. There are also intestinal worms whose eggs are found in excreta. These can cause severe pain and undermine the nutritional status of hundreds of millions of urban dwellers (especially children), but only a small proportion of those infected will die of them.[8] Many case studies in low-income settlements show that a high proportion of the population have debilitating intestinal worm burdens.[9]

Water-washed diseases are associated with a lack of water supplies for washing, and include various skin and eye infections such as scabies and trachoma (from which millions become blind). The number of people who can be affected and the extent to which lower-income groups face greater problems (largely because of poorer quality provision for water) is illustrated by a study of 1103 primary school students in the urban district of Bamako (Mali's capital and largest city). This found the overall prevalence of scabies among the pupils to be 4 per cent, ranging from 1.8 per cent at the school with the highest socio-economic level to 5 per cent at primary schools serving poorer areas.[10] Most water-borne diseases are also water-washed, as their incidence is associated with inadequate water supplies as well as with contaminated water.

The two most significant water-based diseases are bilharzia (or schistosomiasis) and guinea-worm. Most of the 200 million people world-wide infected with bilharzia live in rural areas, since infection generally takes place as people work in irrigated fields or walk in streams and ponds. But it may be a serious health problem in urban areas too, as many people infected in rural areas have moved to urban areas, and there may be water bodies in urban areas that have the aquatic snails which house the vectors through which this disease is transmitted. Guinea-worm is also primarily rural and its incidence has been much reduced recently by the eradication initiative, but it has occurred in epidemic form in small urban centres when piped water systems break down.

Diseases spread by water-related insect vectors are among the most pressing environmental problems in many cities. Malaria, often considered a rural disease, is now among the main causes of illness and death among children and adults in many urban areas. In South Asia it is related to drinking water storage on rooftops (so-called overhead tanks), to which the malarial mosquito *Anopheles stephensi* has adapted its breeding habits; in Africa and Latin America it is more often associated with poorly drained locations where the *Anopheles* mosquitoes breed in clear standing water.[11] Some infrastructure works also contribute substantially to urban anopheline breeding, and in some South Asian cities, the cellars of buildings whose construction remains unfinished for reasons of investment and speculation become extensive breeding places during the rainy season. In some cities, a gradient has been observed where malaria transmission declines towards the city centre, with pollution of open water being the key determinant. *Aedes* mosquitoes, which transmit a number of viral diseases including dengue fever, dengue haemorrhagic fever and yellow fever, breed in small water collections and containers. These are related to poor drainage or to solid waste (car tyre dumps are notorious) and also small domestic water collectors. The latter may be the result of inadequate or intermittent water supplies, which force people to keep drinking water containers in their homes.[12]

Lymphatic filariasis, a parasitic worm infection that in its most dramatic forms becomes elephantiasis, mostly affects urban populations in East Africa, coastal Brazil and South and Southeast Asia.[13] The vectors of lymphatic filariasis (*Culex* spp) breed in organically polluted waters, including open sewage canals. Many other disease vectors thrive where there is poor drainage and inadequate provision for rubbish collection, sanitation and piped water – including house flies, fleas, lice and cockroaches.[14]

Box 2.1 reports on work by the WHO that estimates the burden of disease from water, sanitation and hygiene globally. This disease burden is measured in disability adjusted life years (DALYs), which means that account is taken not only of life years lost from premature death but also the loss of healthy life years from non-fatal illness or injury.[15] It suggests that the burden of inadequate water, sanitation and hygiene is at least 2.2 million deaths and 82.2 million DALYs each year; this is 4 per cent of all deaths and 5.7 per cent of all DALYs. But as the authors of this work stress, this includes no consideration of the role of inadequate water in constraining food production and its contribution to malnutrition (which causes several million deaths each year and more than twice as many DALYs as diseases from water, sanitation and hygiene). Diseases where water has some role in their transmission, such as malaria, account for another 1.6 million deaths a year and an additional 67.5 million DALYs – and a significant part of these should be added to the health burden related to inadequate water, sanitation and hygiene. Diarrhoea and many water-related diseases often combine with under-nutrition and, together, so weaken the defences of infants or young children that diseases such as measles and pneumonia become major causes of death; these two diseases are among the leading causes of infant and child death world-wide.[16] WHO estimates that the provision of a piped, well regulated water supply and full sanitation would lead to a 70 per cent reduction in cases of diarrhoea as well as reductions in other water-, sanitation- and hygiene-related diseases.[17]

The health burden linked to inadequate water, sanitation and hygiene is, not surpris-ingly, heavily concentrated in low- and middle-income nations; Figure 2.1 shows the very large differentials between regions in the scale of the health burden from diarrhoeal diseases.

Infectious diarrhoea is probably the largest contributor to the disease burden from water, sanitation and hygiene – although it is also transmitted through food and air. Disease burdens from diarrhoeal diseases in children younger than five can be up to 240 times higher in low-income nations than high-income nations. And if data were available for how diarrhoeal disease burdens varied between different income groups (or between those living in informal settlements and those in good quality housing), the differentials could be even larger. For instance, the prevalence of diarrhoea among children under three in many of Nairobi's informal settlements was found to be twice the national average (and the rural average) while the prevalence of diarrhoea with blood (which signifies serious systemic infection) was often three to four times the national average (and rural average).[18] Mortality due to diarrhoea recorded in Sambizanga *municipio* in Luanda (Angola) before a project to improve water supply was ten times greater than that in urban Luanda; in Cazenga it was 24 times greater.[19] Although diarrhoeal diseases are still common in high-income nations and in high-income areas of cities in low- and middle-income nations, their health impact is much smaller and very rarely do they cause death or seriously impair children's physical development.

Most of the studies that show the health impact of water-related diseases focus on their contribution to infant and child death or disease and are summarized in a later section. However, some studies show the scale of the impact on urban populations. A study in Peru's capital noted that

...water-borne and water-related diseases are a major cause of morbidity and mortality especially in the poorer neighbourhoods of Lima. The medical costs and lost wages from such diseases were a high part of household income for the poor, 27 per cent by one estimate.[20]

Box 2.1 The global burden of disease from water, sanitation and hygiene

The Global Burden of Disease study covered 107 major diseases and ten risk factors, and produced estimates as to the contribution of different diseases or disease clusters to people's health, using DALYs, which combined mortality and morbidity. The information on disease burdens was related to risk factors rather than to diseases; this is likely to be more relevant to policy because it may allow action to be directly targeted to modify exposure. WHO is now assessing the disease burden of about 20 risk factors; six focus on environmental and occupational health concerns.

The original estimate for 1990 suggested that world-wide, risk factors for water, sanitation and hygiene in terms of diarrhoeal and selected parasitic diseases accounted for 5.3 per cent of all deaths and 6.8 per cent of all DALYs. Other communicable diseases and non-communicable diseases associated with water were not considered (including typhoid, hepatitis A, schistosomiasis and arsenicosis).

Water, sanitation and hygiene risk factors are a number of interrelated transmission pathways composed of competing or complementing events for causing disease. Faecal–oral diseases account for an important part of this disease burden. Their transmission routes are complex; human and animal excreta can affect human health directly through drinking water, sewage, indirect contact and food, through various pathways. We assume risk factors for water, sanitation and hygiene to include the following transmission pathways:

- transmission through ingestion of water such as drinking water and to some extent bathing (includes diseases from faecal–oral pathogens and diseases from toxic chemicals);
- transmission caused by lack of water linked to inadequate personal hygiene (including trachoma and scabies);
- transmission caused by poor personal, domestic or agricultural hygiene (includes person-to-person transmission of faecal–oral pathogens, food-borne transmission of faecal–oral pathogens as a result of poor hygiene, or use of contaminated water for irrigation or cleaning);
- transmission through contact with water (through bathing or wading) containing organisms such as schistosoma;
- to a certain extent, transmission through vectors proliferating in water reservoirs or other stagnant waters or certain agricultural practices (eg malaria, lymphatic filariasis); and
- transmission through contaminated aerosols from poorly managed water resources (eg legionellosis).

There are also water-related injuries that could be prevented by appropriate water management, but these were not considered in this analysis.

This analysis suggested that there are 2.2 million deaths and 82.2 million DALYs lost; about 4 per cent of all deaths and 5.7 per cent of DALYs. This exceeds the disease burden of many major diseases (including malaria and tuberculosis). They disproportionately affect poorer members of society. The estimate is likely to be conservative because exposure data do not account for all routes, and because numerous diseases are not currently quantifiable, particularly those relating to water resource management and agricultural methods involving disease vectors. In addition, we based the estimate predominantly on risk information from intervention studies in water, sanitation and hygiene, and intervention studies tend to underestimate attributable risk because an intervention needs to be implemented at the community level in order to eliminate related disease burdens.

Diseases with as-yet unknown fractions due to water including malaria add up to 1.609 million deaths and 67.5 million DALYs; a significant fraction of this burden should probably be added to the fraction presented here. An additional factor is malnutrition related to water scarcity, which alone accounts for a burden more than double that reported here.

Source: Prüss, Annette, David Kay, Lorna Fewtrell and Jamie Bartram (2002), 'Estimating the burden of disease from water, sanitation and hygiene at a global level', *Environmental Health Perspectives*, Vol 110, No 5, May, pages 537–542.

16 per cent of all deaths in one Kathmandu hospital between 1992 and 1998 were due to water-related diseases.[21] Diarrhoeal diseases and malaria are the two main killers in Luanda.[22] For the urban population as a whole, there are large potential reductions in morbidity from many diseases as a result of improvements in water supply and sanitation (see Table 2.2).

 ## Reinforcing inequality, poverty and destitution

The section above concentrated on the direct health impacts of inadequate provision for water, sanitation and hygiene. But there are many other impacts that need to be considered, including:

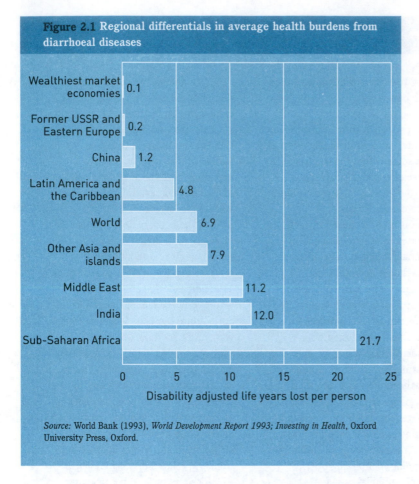

Figure 2.1 Regional differentials in average health burdens from diarrhoeal diseases

Wealthiest market economies: 0.1
Former USSR and Eastern Europe: 0.2
China: 1.2
Latin America and the Caribbean: 4.8
World: 6.9
Other Asia and islands: 7.9
Middle East: 11.2
India: 12.0
Sub-Saharan Africa: 21.7

Disability adjusted life years lost per person

Source: World Bank (1993), *World Development Report 1993; Investing in Health*, Oxford University Press, Oxford.

provision, including the conflicts that often arise in queues, the indignities of having to defecate in the open, the sexual harassment suffered by women and girls as a result of having to do so, the reluctance of children and women to visit public toilets after dark because streets are not safe; and

- the lack of sleep and large physical discomfort due to the constant mosquito nuisance at night.

These impacts are usually most evident among particular sections of the population in cities in low- and middle-income nations. These sections of the population can be characterized by their low incomes or by the particular settlements in which they live (for instance, tenements and illegal settlements). Chapter 1 highlighted the large differences between cities in the proportions of the population that face particularly serious problems with water and sanitation.

Table 2.3 lists different aspects of inadequacies in water and sanitation provision and the indicators commonly used to measure them. In well governed cities, there are no inequalities between low- and high-income groups in most of these aspects, as all (or virtually all) low-income households have the same quality water from the same piped system (delivered 24 hours a day) as high-income groups; their toilets are also connected to the same sewers and they are (generally) as well defended against floods.

For most of these variables, the differentials between high- and low-income groups become apparent as the data from high-income areas of a city are compared to the data from low-income areas. But this is less precise than

- the high costs of water to many low-income groups and how this affects household incomes;
- the high economic costs for those who fall ill from diseases related to inadequate water and sanitation, including the cost of treatment and of income forgone;
- the huge physical efforts needed to fetch and carry water – and often the hours needed to queue for it and the inconvenience of having to get up very early to get to water points before queues become too long;
- the stress and other difficulties faced by those having to cope with inadequate

Table 2.2 Potential reductions in morbidity for different diseases as a result of improvements in water supply and sanitation

Diseases	Projected reduction in morbidity (%)
Cholera, typhoid, leptospirosis, scabies, guinea-worm infection	80–100
Trachoma, conjunctivitis, yaws, schistosomiasis	60–70
Tularaemia, paratyphoid, bacillary dysentery, amoebic dysentery, gastro-enteritis, lice-borne diseases, diarrhoeal diseases, ascariasis, skin infections	40–50

Source: WHO (1986), *Intersectoral Action for Health*, World Health Organization, Geneva.

Table 2.3 Aspects of inequality in provision for water and sanitation

Nature of inequality	Typical measure	Differentials
Water supply		
Volume of water available	Litres per person per day	Within most low- and middle-income nations, there are very large differentials within cities where sections of the population lack access to piped supplies
Quality of water	Coliform count and many other measures	
Accessibility	Time spent each day collecting water Distance from tap Number of persons per standpipe	From households with internal piped connections who spend no time getting water to households where one or more people have to spend one to three hours a day queuing, fetching and carrying
Reliability	Hours a day or week that water is available	Varies from 24 hours a day to one or two hours a day, or in some instances a few hours every few days; low-income areas often get more water cuts than higher-income areas
Cost per unit volume	Price per cubic metre or per litre	Often high ratios (10–15:1) between the cost of water from vendors or kiosks and the cost of water from piped supplies to the home
Cost of connection to piped water supplies	Price per connection	Connection charges are often too expensive for low-income households
Sanitation		
Infrastructure to remove toilet wastes (sewers)	Sewer connection	Many cities and most smaller urban centres in Africa and Asia have no sewers; in most cities in low- and middle-income nations that have sewers, large sections of the population are unconnected
Risk of faecal contamination of water supplies	Coliform count	Very large differentials between households in most urban centres; the risks are particularly high for households who have to store water or use unprotected sources. Piped systems with intermittent supplies often become contaminated
Time taken to access toilets	Distance to toilet Time spent queuing	Households with their own toilets spend very little time waiting to use them; households that rely on public toilets often spend a significant amount of time each day queuing
Infrastructure to support drainage	House connected to a drainage network within settlement connected to wider drainage system	Many urban districts with little or no provision for drains; many have drains that are ineffective because of poor maintenance and blockages from solid wastes
Sewerage connection charges	Price per connection	High charges for new connections
Solid waste collection	Extent to which settlement or neighbourhood has regular service to collect household wastes	Within many urban centres, large sections of the population (typically those living in informal settlements) have no public service to remove household wastes, or the quality of the service is very inadequate. Where provision for sanitation is inadequate, household wastes often contain excreta so a regular waste collection service helps dispose of these safely
Citizen rights	Accountability to citizens of water and sanitation provider	Middle- and upper-income groups likely to have more possibilities of holding water and sanitation providers to account than low-income groups

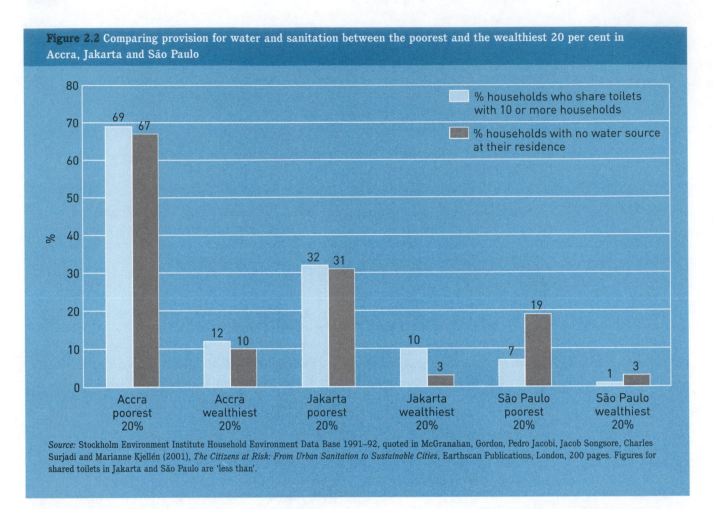

Figure 2.2 Comparing provision for water and sanitation between the poorest and the wealthiest 20 per cent in Accra, Jakarta and São Paulo

Source: Stockholm Environment Institute Household Environment Data Base 1991–92, quoted in McGranahan, Gordon, Pedro Jacobi, Jacob Songsore, Charles Surjadi and Marianne Kjellén (2001), *The Citizens at Risk: From Urban Sanitation to Sustainable Cities*, Earthscan Publications, London, 200 pages. Figures for shared toilets in Jakarta and São Paulo are 'less than'.

comparisons between income groups, since virtually all districts have some mix of income groups. The size of the differential between high- and low-income groups is also masked when data are only available to compare provision between populations of relatively large areas – for instance, for the municipalities which make up a major city. Most data on the quality and extent of service provision or on health outcomes for particular low-income districts are also only available as averages for the whole district's population, which can obscure the more serious health problems suffered by the poorer groups within that district. This was demonstrated by a study in a low-income settlement in Khulna (Bangladesh), which showed the sharp differentials in work days lost to illness or injury among the inhabitants when comparing the (within the context of the settlement) wealthier households to poorer households. It also showed how in the poorer households, such illness or injury often meant growing indebtedness and under-nutrition for all family members.[23]

Three studies are drawn on here to show the kinds of differentials in water and sanitation provision that occur between income groups. The first involved household surveys covering 1000 households in Accra, Jakarta and São Paulo, and the findings are summarized in Figure 2.2.

This study shows the dramatic differences in provision for water and reliance on shared toilets between the poorest and the richest 20 per cent of households, especially in Accra (which has the lowest per capita income of the three cities). In Accra, two-thirds of the poorest households had no water source in their residence, compared to 10 per cent for the wealthiest households. Similarly, two-thirds of the poorest households had to share toilets with ten or more households, compared to 12 per cent for the wealthiest households. The differentials are also large for the other two cities, although a lower proportion of the poorest and richest households have no water source in their residence and have to share toilets with ten or more households.

Table 2.4 Provision for water and sanitation among different socio-economic classes in Bangalore

Characteristics	Percentage of the population with access by socio-economic category:						
	Total	SEC-A	SEC-B	SEC-C	SEC-D	SEC-E	Slums*
Within Bangalore Municipal Corporation							
Proportion of all households	100	16	20	27	20	17	17
Individual connection to official water network	36	60	45	35	23	19	25
Shared connection to official water network	36	32	40	40	36	30	29
Any public fountain	29	5	11	27	15	55	61
Toilet at home	66	96	85	69	50	32	34
Shared toilet outside home	28	4	14	28	43	52	44
Public toilet	4			3	6	12	19
Defecate in open	1				1	5	5
Tap in toilet**	47	73	58	39	23	14	9
Carry water to toilet**	45	14	32	56	71	81	86
Drainage connection to municipal sewers***	81	91	89	83	73	70	75
Household collection of solid wastes	34	45	45	35	25	20	12
Conurbation							
Toilet at home	47		66	56	39	26	
Shared toilet outside home	19		11	27	20	14	
Open area	35		23	18	40	62	

Note: Based on a survey of 3937 households: 2923 in the municipal corporation, 310 in the conurbation and 704 in the green belt areas. Using the characteristics of education and occupation of the chief wage earner, households were divided into upper income (SEC-A), middle-income (SEC-B and C) and low-income (SEC-D and E).

* NB: many poor households are found in other settlements of the city; these are the settlements that are officially designated as slums.

** For the 1877 households having an Indian toilet.

*** For the 2818 households that have drainage outlets in their home.

Source: Sinclair Knight Merz and Egis Consulting Australia in association with Brisbane City Enterprises and Feedback HSSI – STUP Consultants – Taru Leading Edge (2002), *Bangalore Water Supply and Environmental Sanitation Masterplan Project; Overview Report on Services to Urban Poor Stage 2*, AusAid, Canberra.

The second study was of the quality of water and sanitation provision in the city of Bangalore and its surrounds. Drawing on household interviews, this examined not only the differentials between geographic areas but also differentials according to socio-economic category (which were defined based on the education and the occupation of the chief income earner) (see Table 2.4). In general, all indicators relating to the quality of water and sanitation provision decline as one moves from the highest to the lowest socio-economic category. For instance, 60 per cent of households in the highest socio-economic category have individual connections to the official water network, compared to 19 per cent of households in the lowest. Virtually all households in the highest socio-economic category (96 per cent) have toilets in their home, compared to 32 per cent of households in the lowest.

The third study to highlight differentials between income groups is an analysis of demographic and health surveys from 43 low- and middle-income nations, which compared water and sanitation provision for urban poor and urban non-poor households. Households were allocated to 'poor' and 'non-poor' based on data on consumer durables and housing quality; this study pointed out that most datasets on public services and demographic behaviour have no data on household incomes and consumption. The analysis allowed a prediction of the proportion of households with water on the premises (piped or well) and a flush toilet (see Table 2.5). This highlights what might be expected: the proportion of poor households with water on their premises and flush toilets is much lower than the proportion of non-poor households. (It should also be recalled that such an exercise in urban areas

Table 2.5 Predicted percentage of households with access to water on the premises and flush toilets by relative poverty status

Countries in region	Water on premises	Flush toilet	Electricity	Lack all three services
North Africa				
Urban poor	0.75	0.88	0.86	0.08
Urban non-poor	0.92	0.97	0.97	0.02
Sub-Saharan Africa				
Urban poor	0.31	0.20	0.26	0.57
Urban non-poor	0.46	0.32	0.52	0.34
Southeast Asia				
Urban poor	0.36	0.67	0.77	0.12
Urban non-poor	0.50	0.88	0.97	0.01
South, Central, West Asia				
Urban poor	0.59	0.48	0.71	0.22
Urban non-poor	0.74	0.60	0.92	0.06
Latin America				
Urban poor	0.59	0.44	0.84	0.12
Urban non-poor	0.74	0.67	0.98	0.02

Source: Hewett, Paul C and Mark R Montgomery (2002), *Poverty and Public Services in Developing-Country Cities*, Population Council, New York, 62 pages.

of high-income nations would find little or no difference between poor and non-poor households.) The figures also show the very large number of non-poor households lacking adequate provision – ie, half of the urban non-poor in Southeast Asia and more than half the urban non-poor in sub-Saharan Africa do not have water on their premises.

Water consumption

Where there are statistics for water consumption per person, they often reveal large differentials between richer and poorer areas of a city which are linked to the quality of provision for the water (see Box 2.2).

Monetary costs of water and sanitation

The monetary costs of water vary greatly from city to city. This can be seen in the data on the average water tariff in different Asian cities in the mid-1990s (see Figure 2.3).

For water, the cost per litre to urban consumers around the world varies by a factor of at least 10,000! At one extreme, there are instances where the cost of water is the equiv-

alent of US$0.00001 per litre (for instance, the cost of water in Calcutta's piped supply from a 1995 survey) while at the other extreme, there are urban households who pay water vendors the equivalent of $0.1 or more per litre[24] (although as Tables 2.6 and 2.7 show, most water from vendors is a lot less than this). Table 2.6 and Figure 2.4 highlight this. Of course, bottled water can cost far more than this.

However, in some ways the data in the above figures and tables are misleading, in that the differentials in price for water are evident within cities as much as between cities. Most urban poor groups not only pay a higher proportion of their total incomes for water and sanitation than higher-income groups, but they often pay much higher prices per litre for water and for access to sanitation – and this is so even when provision is much worse than for richer groups. Tables 2.7 and 2.8 show differentials within cities in the cost of water. Water costs were particularly high for most of those that used water vendors, with the price for water from vendors going from 10 to 100 times the unit price for house connections. As the Asian Development Bank survey highlights, the unit cost of water from

Box 2.2 Examples of differentials in water volumes used

Accra (Ghana)

In the high-class residential areas with water piped to the home and water closets for sanitation, water consumption per capita is likely to be well in excess of the recommended figure of 200 litres per person per day. In slum neighbourhoods such as Nima-Maamobi and Ashiaman, where buying water from vendors is common, the water consumption is about 60 litres per capita per day.[25] A survey of 1000 households in 1991–1992 found that the average water consumption among the wealthiest 20 per cent was 90 litres per capita per day, while it was 33 litres per capita per day for the poorest 20 per cent.[26]

Dar es Salaam

A 1997 study of domestic water use in four sites, all with piped supplies, found large differentials in water use and reliability. The average per capita water use for households interviewed in Oyster Bay (a high-income area) was 164 litres a day. It was much less among households in two lower-income areas: in Changombe it was 44 litres a day and in Temeke, 64 litres a day. 70 per cent of the households interviewed in Oyster Bay received a 24-hour supply, compared to 10 per cent of households in Temeke and 11 per cent in Changombe. The unreliability of the piped water supplies in Changombe and Temeke meant that more than 60 per cent of the interviewed households with piped supplies use vendors as their primary source, despite the higher costs.[27]

Guayaquil (Ecuador)

In 1990, average daily consumption ranged from 307 litres per inhabitant in the well-to-do parts of the city to less than 25 litres per inhabitant for those supplied by the private water sellers.[28]

Nairobi (Kenya)

Average daily water consumption varies between 20 and over 200 litres per person per day, depending on the quality of provision for water.[29]

---

public taps may also be much higher than from house connections; in its survey, this was the case in several cities, including Hanoi, Chennai, Kathmandu and Karachi.

It is also difficult to separate the discussion of the costs of provision (or the prices charged) from the inadequacies of provision, because they are related. One key reason why so many urban dwellers defecate in the open is because they have no toilets in their homes and regular use of pay toilets is too expensive. Low-income groups often use poor quality water because it is more easily accessed and much cheaper than good quality water. So data on how much low-income households pay for water or for toilets may be misleading, because they are incurring high costs in other forms to save money (eg, long queues, fetching and carrying water from long distances, living with the economic and health costs that arise from inadequate provision).

Fifteen years ago, John Briscoe estimated that water vendors probably serve between 20 and 30 per cent of the urban population in low- and middle-income nations;[30] the proportion has probably fallen world-wide but the number of people who rely on vendors may have gone up (the urban population in Africa, Asia and Latin America has grown by over 700 million in the last 15 years).[31] And in particular cases, the proportion of urban dwellers that rely on vendors has gone up, as described in Chapter 1 for many urban centres in East Africa. Most households will purchase water from vendors for use only in cooking and drinking and rely on poorer quality but cheaper water sources for, for instance, washing and laundry. However, water from vendors often costs US$1–5 per cubic metre and sometimes far more than this (see Tables 2.6, 2.7 and 2.8).

Some studies have examined what proportion of household income goes on water and sanitation. It should be noted that in most low- and middle-income nations, there is an assumption that water and sanitation provision does not cost much, since the income at which poverty lines are set makes no explicit provision for the cost of water and sanitation. In fact, low-income households that have to rely on water vendors in major cities often spend 5–10 per cent of their total income on water. There are examples of low-income households paying a much higher proportion than this: in Nouakchott, the purchase of water is estimated to absorb 14–20 per cent of the budget for most low-income households,[32] while a case study in Karton Kassala

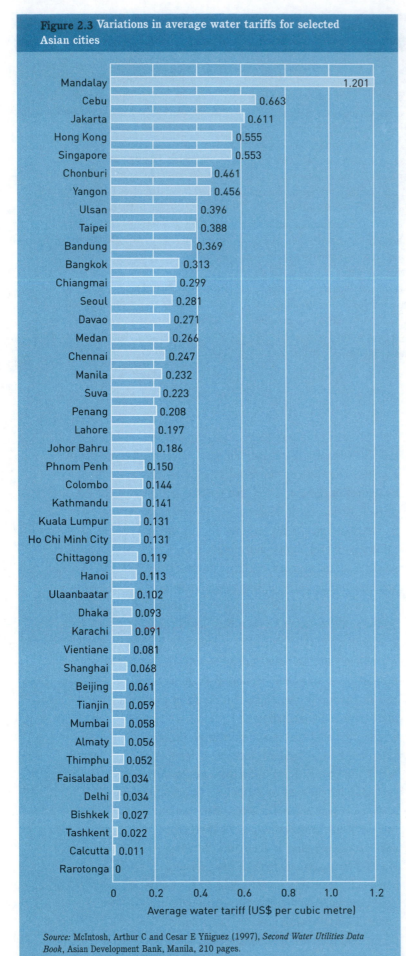

Figure 2.3 Variations in average water tariffs for selected Asian cities

City	Average water tariff (US$ per cubic metre)
Mandalay	1.201
Cebu	0.663
Jakarta	0.611
Hong Kong	0.555
Singapore	0.553
Chonburi	0.461
Yangon	0.456
Ulsan	0.396
Taipei	0.388
Bandung	0.369
Bangkok	0.313
Chiangmai	0.299
Seoul	0.281
Davao	0.271
Medan	0.266
Chennai	0.247
Manila	0.232
Suva	0.223
Penang	0.208
Lahore	0.197
Johor Bahru	0.186
Phnom Penh	0.150
Colombo	0.144
Kathmandu	0.141
Kuala Lumpur	0.131
Ho Chi Minh City	0.131
Chittagong	0.119
Hanoi	0.113
Ulaanbaatar	0.102
Dhaka	0.093
Karachi	0.091
Vientiane	0.081
Shanghai	0.068
Beijing	0.061
Tianjin	0.059
Mumbai	0.058
Almaty	0.056
Thimphu	0.052
Faisalabad	0.034
Delhi	0.034
Bishkek	0.027
Tashkent	0.022
Calcutta	0.011
Rarotonga	0

Source: McIntosh, Arthur C and Cesar E Yñiguez (1997), *Second Water Utilities Data Book*, Asian Development Bank, Manila, 210 pages.

(Khartoum) found that 35 per cent of household income went on payments to water vendors.[33] As this Khartoum case study noted, payments for water come out of the household's food budget, exacerbating the prevalence of malnutrition and so contributing to high levels of child mortality.

Table 2.9 shows the average monthly expenditure on water for a sample of just over 6000 low-income Namibian households living in informal settlements, backyard shacks and isolated dwellings. 61 per cent of these households have municipal supplies. The figures show the significance of water-related expenditures as an item of household income. On average, 8 per cent of household income went on water – although in certain locations, the proportion was as high as 15–20 per cent.

In many of the cases of communities dependent on truckers or vendors, getting 150 litres per household per day would cost more than US$1 a day. Thus, many households would be paying more than a dollar a day if they used 150 litres a day (ie generally 20–30 litres per person per day), but this volume is not generally sufficient for good hygiene. If they were to get enough for good hygiene – say 600 litres per household per day – the cost would be several US dollars per day, which for most low-income households is far more than their total income. Obviously no low-income household uses 600 litres a day when the only water they can get is from expensive vendors. But this is a reminder that the price of water is also a major constraint on allowing many urban households to get safe, adequate supplies of water. However, households served by vendors would generally be even worse off without these supplies, and vendors usually operate in a competitive market where the high cost of the water they supply reflects the high costs they face in obtaining the water and/or in travelling with the water to supply the low-income households.

Households that have no toilets in their homes may be spending considerable sums on using public toilets. In Kumasi, Ghana's second largest city, the use of public toilets just once a day by each family member can use up 10–15 per cent of the main income earner's wages.[34] In many Indian cities, low-income

Table 2.6 The very large variations in the cost of water in cities

	Price paid per litre (US$)	Price of 150 litres per day (US$)	Price of 600 litres per day (US$)
Water tariff in Cairo[35]	0.00004	0.006	0.024
Cooperative in Santa Cruz[36]	0.00025–0.00055	0.04–0.08	0.15–0.33
Public tap in Bandung[37]	0.00026	0.04	0.16
Utility in Lima[38]	0.00028	0.042	0.17
Independent water provider in Asuncion[39]	0.00035	0.05	0.2
House connection in Bandung[40]	0.00038	0.06	0.23
Price of water from a standpipe in Ouagadougou[41]	0.00048	0.072	0.29
Water tariff in Amman[42]	0.00061	0.09	0.37
Water vendor in Dhaka (1995)[43]	0.00084	0.13	0.5
Price paid for water to standpipe operators in Nairobi[44]	0.001–0.025	0.15–0.38	0.6–1.5
Average paid by urban households in East Africa with piped water connection (1997)[45]	0.001	0.15	0.6
Water tariff in Ramallah[46]	0.00111	0.17	0.67
Water from water point in Huruma (Nairobi)[47]	0.0013	0.195	0.78
Kiosks in Kampala[48]	0.0015–0.007	0.23–1.1	0.9–4.2
Standpipes in Dar es Salaam drawing water from mains[49]	0.0015	0.23	0.9
Average paid by urban households in East Africa that lack piped water[50]	0.002	0.3	1.2
Average price paid to vendors by low-income groups living in salinated areas in Jakarta (1991)[51]	0.002	0.3	1.2
Water trucker in Lima[52]	0.0024	0.36	1.44
Handcarts delivering to homes in Dar es Salaam[53]	0.0035–0.0075	0.53–1.13	2.1–4.5
Water vendor in Bandung (1995)[54]	0.0036	0.54	2.16
Price of water from tankers in Luanda in 1998[55]	0.004–0.02	0.6–3.0	2.4–12.0
Price of water from a handcart in Conakry[56]	0.004	0.6	2.4
Average price paid to vendors in East African urban areas (1997)[57]	0.0045	0.7	2.7
Bicycle water vendor in Kampala, delivering to non-serviced area[58]	0.0054–0.0108	0.81–1.6	3.24–6.5
Water from public tap in Lae (Papua New Guinea)[59]	0.00596	0.9	3.6
Water from vendor in Kibera (Nairobi)[60]	0.0065	0.97	3.9
Those purchasing 55 gallon barrels of water from vendors in Tegucigalpa (US$1.75 per barrel)[61]	0.0072	1.08	4.3
Vendor in Malé (1995)[62]	0.011	1.7	6.6
Vendor in Kibera (Nairobi) during local water shortages[63]	0.013	1.95	7.8
Water from a tanker in Luanda for those in areas distant from water sources[64]	0.02	3.0	12.0

people defecate in the open because they cannot afford to use public toilets.[65]

Even where public facilities are provided with every attempt to keep down costs, many households still face difficulties paying. Chapter 1 included a box about Huruma in Nairobi. The average household income is Ksh5000 a month and the main areas of daily expenditure are food, transport, water and the use of toilet facilities. The costs of water and sanitation do not appear high; 20 litres of water costs Ksh2. But a household that used 100 litres a day would be spending around Ksh300 a month on water; a visit to the toilet is Ksh2–3, so even if each family member only used the toilet once a day, in a five-member household that is Ksh10–15 a day or Ksh300–450 a month. So a very minimum level of water and sanitation provision would be taking up more than 10 per cent of the income for those with average incomes. In Dhaka, families who have to purchase their water by the pot pay 50 *paise* per 20-litre pot; this does not seem expensive since this is

Figure 2.4 The very large variations in the cost of water from different providers in different cities

Provider	Price (US$ per litre)
Water from a tanker in Luanda for those in areas distant from water sources	0.02
Vendor in Kibera (Nairobi) during water shortage	0.013
Vendor in Malé	0.011
Vendors in Tegucigalpa	0.0072
Vendor in Kibera (Nairobi)	0.0065
Public tap in Lae	0.00596
Bicycle water vendor in Kampala	0.0054
Handcart in Conakry	0.004
Tankers in Luanda	0.004
Vendor in Bandung	0.0036
Handcarts delivering to homes in Dar es Salaam	0.0035
Water trucker in Lima	0.0024
Vendors in salinated areas in Jakarta	0.002
Standpipes in Dar es Salaam drawing water from mains	0.0015
Kiosks in Kampala	0.0015
Water point in Huruma (Nairobi)	0.0013
House connection in Ramallah	0.00111
Standpipe operators in Nairobi	0.001
Water vendor in Dhaka	0.00084
House connection in Amman	0.00061
Standpipe in Ouagadougou	0.00048
House connection in Bandung	0.00038
House connection, independent water provider in Asuncion	0.00035
House connection in Lima	0.00028
Public tap in Bandung	0.00026
House connection, cooperative in Santa Cruz (cheapest)	0.00025
Tariff in Cairo	0.00004

Price of water (US$ per litre)

Sources: See Table 2.6

US$0.01. But to get 100 litres a day would represent a significant proportion of the income of the poorest families. The cost of access to adequate water and to toilets is about 8 per cent of the poorest families' monthly budget, but can only be afforded by reducing essential food consumption.[66]

Connection charges for water are often a major barrier to low-income households getting better provision. In Lima, when the contracts for privatization were being prepared, connection charges were estimated to be US$850; this sum would be repaid over five years with an interest charge of 1.2 per cent a month. Figures suggested that costs for a minimum consumption of 22 cubic metres a month would be about US$5 or 2.5–3 per cent of income for the 43 per cent of Lima's residents who fell into the lowest income category. When the connection charge was included, it was estimated that water costs would rise to 16 per cent of income. Privatization did not take place and, when discussing reasons for the lack of interest in greater private sector involvement in Peru, Alcazar, Xu and Zuluaga suggest that '...the higher tariffs combined with connection charges would make water unaffordable to many unconnected poor consumers, even compared to water from vendors.'[67]

Collignon and Vezina compare household connection fees in ten East and West African cities with gross domestic product (GDP) per capita. The results provide a powerful summary of how unattainable piped water may be for the poor. In Guinea and Côte d'Ivoire, per capita GDP equalled or exceeded the cost of connecting to piped water supplies. In Benin, Burkina Faso, Kenya, Mauritania and Uganda, the costs exceeded GDP per capita by the following ratios: 5:1, 1.3:1, 4:1, 2.5:1 and 4:1. Connections are unaffordable for most.[68] A study in Bangalore found that the cost of connection charges to piped water supplies was one of the main constraints on extending the provision of piped supplies.[69]

Even those with access to piped water may have major problems with their supply. In Lima, 48 per cent of those who are connected receive water services for less than 12 hours a day. (75 per cent of the population have a water connection.) Many families cannot afford the investment required for a water storage tank.[70] In the study of water and sanitation provision in Bangalore mentioned earlier in this chapter, not surprisingly, higher-income groups had much greater provision for water storage within their homes, allowing them to have sufficient water when piped supplies were cut.[71]

Time spent getting water

Households connected to reliable piped water systems spend no time at all fetching and carrying water. Households that have no water piped to their home or yard often have one or more persons who spend one to two hours each day getting water. The time that has to be spent queuing and then filling the water containers is a particularly unwanted extra burden, especially since low-income people often work very long hours. Queuing for water when long waits are necessary and supplies are uncertain is also a source of tension and can precipitate fights.[72] Queuing at a tap and carrying water from the tap to the home takes away from time that could be used in earning an income. In some communities, people have to queue for hours each day – for instance in Shajahmal within the Indian city of Aligarh, where the only water available is from a municipal tubewell.[73] Interviews with a range of households in 16 sites in nine urban areas in Kenya, Uganda and Tanzania in 1997 found that those without piped supplies spent an average of 92 minutes each day collecting water.[74] This represents a more than threefold increase compared to the late 1960s, when the average time collecting water in these same sites had been 28 minutes a day.[75] In 1997, those using kiosks were spending almost two hours a day collecting water.

The persons within a household who are allocated the responsibility of collecting water (generally women or children) often have to get up very early to make sure there is water available in the morning. Water is also very heavy to carry any distance and requires much physical effort, so the amount of water used will be influenced by the distance that it has to be carried. If a household keeps its water

Table 2.7 Examples of differentials in the price of water within cities

	Price of water (US$)	
	150 litres	600 litres
Kampala[76]		
Kiosks	0.23–1.1	0.9–4.2
Bicycle water vendors	0.81–1.6	3.24–6.5
Lima[77]		
Water trucker	0.36	1.44
Utility	0.042	0.17
Average price in East African urban areas[78]		
Vendors	0.7	2.7
Households that lack piped water	0.3	1.2
Households with piped connection	0.15	0.6
Dar es Salaam[79]		
Standpipes drawing from mains	0.23	0.9
Handcarts delivering to homes	0.5–1.13	2.1–4.5

Table 2.8 The cost of water from house connections, public taps and water vendors in Asian cities

City	Cost of water per cubic metre (US$)		
	House connections	Public tap	Water vendor
Bandung	0.38	0.26	3.60
Bangkok	0.30	–	28.94
Chennai	0.30	0.58	–
Chonburi	0.38	–	19.33
Colombo	0.04	0.02	–
Dhaka	–	0.08	0.84
Hanoi	0.09	0.55	0
Karachi	0.10		1.14
Kathmandu	0.18	0.24	2.61
Lae	2.20	5.96	–
Malé	5.08	–	11.20
Manila	0.29	–	2.15
Mumbai	0.07	0.07	0.50
Phnom Penh	0.13	–	0.96
Port Vila	0.42	0.86	8.77
Seoul	0.25	14.13	21.32
Shanghai	0.08	0.06	–
Tashkent	0.01	0.02	–
Thimphu	0.03	0.05	–

Source: Consumer surveys from each city undertaken by the Asian Development Bank and reported in McIntosh, Arthur C and Cesar E Yñiguez (1997), *Second Water Utilities Data Book*, Asian Development Bank, Manila, 210 pages. Note that some of these cities with very high costs for vendors actually have a very small proportions of their population served by vendors (eg Seoul).

Table 2.9 Monthly expenditure on water: shack dwellers in Namibia

	Average (mean) monthly income in Namibian dollars (Na$)	Average (median) monthly income (Na$)	Average (mean) expenditure on water (Na$)	Average (median) expenditure on water (Na$)	Mean % of income on water	Median % of income on water	Number of households in survey*
Malthahohe	334	250	20.3	15.0	6.1	6.0	84
Mariental	421	300	24.4	15.0	5.8	5.0	321
Gibeon	300	200	25.9	31.5	8.6	15.8	140
Keetmanshoop	580	500	80.6	50.0	13.9	10.0	217
Windhoek	744	611	18.7	12.5	2.5	2.05	2592
Dordabis	486	310	–	–	0	0	65
Okahandja	447	300	71.2	50.0	15.9	16.7	211
Otjiwarongo	462	300	9.6	12.0	2.1	4.0	560
Karibib	626	600	20.5	20.0	3.3	3.3	199
Usakos	421	300	53.0	50.0	12.6	16.7	91
Swakopmund	631	500	114.9	100.0	18.2	20.0	266
Walvis Bay	1221	1000	146.5	150.0	12.0	15.0	549
Tsumeb	411	300	49.3	40.0	12.0	13.3	249
Oshakati	794	500	33.1	18.0	4.2	3.6	368
Rundu	436	400	41.0	25.0	9.4	6.3	374
Average	554.3	310	47.3	25.0	8.5	8.1	

* Average household size is 4.5 persons.
Source: Namibia Housing Action Group (2000), information collected in 15 urban areas in Namibia by the Shack Dwellers Federation of Namibia.

consumption down to only 150 litres a day (and many use more than this) this still means that the equivalent of 8–12 full buckets of water have to be collected each day. This means carrying a total weight of 150 kilos of water each day from the standpipe, well or kiosk to the home. This often means having to lift this weight high to allow it to be poured into a water tank. Not surprisingly, those who have to fetch and carry water (usually women) often suffer severe back problems. Limited quantities of water mean inadequate supplies for washing and personal hygiene – and for washing food, cooking utensils and clothes – with all the implications that this has for disease, as described earlier.

One of the most easily measured (and dramatic) indicators of the time and effort needed to get water is the number of persons per tap. Figure 2.5 shows how it is common for those who are reliant on public taps in Asian cities to have at least 200 other people competing for access; these are city averages, so much higher numbers of people per tap are likely in the lowest-income areas. In Nouakchott, just 179 standpipes were installed

to cover the entire urban area, which meant an average of only one standpipe for around 2500 inhabitants.[80] In many areas of Luanda, there is one standpost for 600–1000 persons.[81]

The time needed to collect water is often made all the worse by the irregularity of supply. So not only does each household have to share a standpipe with dozens of other households, but water is only available intermittently at the standpipe. Chapter 1 gave many examples of cities where water was only available in piped systems for a few hours a day.

Time and money lost to water-borne and other water-related diseases

It is obvious that where water and sanitation provision is inadequate, there are likely to be large costs relating to the time and money lost to faecal–oral and other water-related diseases. There is surprisingly little detailed research on this. A study of Lima mentioned earlier suggested that the medical costs and lost wages from water-related diseases 'were a

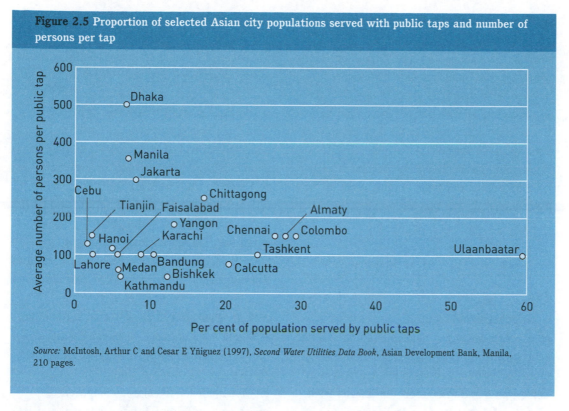

Figure 2.5 Proportion of selected Asian city populations served with public taps and number of persons per tap

Source: McIntosh, Arthur C and Cesar E Yñiguez (1997), *Second Water Utilities Data Book*, Asian Development Bank, Manila, 210 pages.

high part of household income for the poor, 27 per cent by one estimate.'[82] The study in an inner city *bustee* [slum] in Khulna (Bangladesh), also mentioned earlier, showed that 24 per cent of households had lost labour days due to an illness or accident in the month prior to the interview, and the average number of labour days lost was ten per month. In general, the poorest households within this *bustee* lost most work days to illness and injury and also most income and much the highest proportion of their income. The presence of an incapacitated principal income earner in a household was a significant risk factor for severe under-nutrition among young children in the household.[83] While this study was looking at all forms of adult ill-health (including many that were not related to water and sanitation) it is a reminder of the very large economic impact of the health burdens associated with very poor living conditions and working conditions.

Impacts on infants and children[84]

Children bear much the greatest burden of ill-health and premature death from diseases related to inadequate water and sanitation.

They also represent around half the urban population in the regions where water and sanitation provision is worst. But it is rare for their needs and priorities to be given much consideration. This section seeks to remedy this.

Thousands of small children still die every day from preventable diseases related to the inadequate provision of water and sanitation in urban and rural areas. Many more live with repeated bouts of diarrhoea, worm infestations, skin infections, malnutrition and chronically challenged immune systems as a result of unsanitary living environments. The effects are often long term, and may include both physical and mental stunting. This violates the rights of millions of children – to survival and health, to optimal development and to a decent standard of living. This section looks at the practical realities of inadequate provision for young children and their caregivers, and reviews current knowledge of the implications for children's health and general development.

Around 1 billion children live in urban areas – close to half the children in the world – and over 80 per cent of the world's urban children live in Africa, Asia and Latin America.[85] Africa, one of the least urbanized regions, already has more than twice as many urban children as North America.[86] It is common for between 45 and 55 per cent of the urban population in low- and middle-income nations to be under 18 years of age. In most sub-Saharan African nations more than half the urban population is in this age group, and surveys in Yemen (1991), Zambia (1996), Niger (1998) and Chad (1996) found more than 55 per cent. Within nations, smaller cities generally have higher proportions of 0–18 year olds than large cities.[87]

Health burden for children

Although infant and child mortality rates have come down significantly in most nations in recent decades, 1.5–2 million children still die each year from water- and sanitation-related diseases,[88] and many more are debilitated by illness, pain and discomfort – primarily from diarrhoeal diseases, intestinal worms, and from various eye and skin diseases and infections related to insufficient water for washing. Although insufficient and unsafe water supplies and sanitation affect people of all ages, children's health and well-being is particularly compromised. Approximately 84 per cent of the global burden of diarrhoeal disease is experienced by children under five; 74 per cent of the health burden from helminth (worm) infections affects children between 5 and 14.[89]

In cities well served by piped water, sanitation, drainage, waste removal and a good health care system, child mortality rates are generally around 10 per 1000 live births and few if any child deaths are the result of water-related diseases. In cities or neighbourhoods with inadequate provision, it is common for infant and child mortality rates to be 10 to 20 times higher. Many low-income countries still have urban under-five mortality rates of between 100 and 200 per 1000 live births – including Chad (190 in 1996), Malawi (194 in 1992), Mali (172 in 1995), Mozambique (169 in 1997), Zambia (174 in 1996) and Haiti (135 in 1994). For some nations for which data from surveys were available for different years, under-five mortality rates in urban areas increased – for instance in Madagascar when

comparing 1992 to 1997, in Mali when comparing 1987 and 1995, in Zambia when comparing 1992 and 1996 and in Zimbabwe when comparing 1988 and 1992.[90]

Many middle-income nations still have urban child mortality rates of 50 to 100.[91] These are average figures for entire urban populations, and as such obscure the higher child mortality rates within the lower-income settlements. In a well managed city, the difference in mortality rates for children between the lowest and highest income areas is not very large; in a badly managed city they can vary by a factor of 10, 20 or more. Surveys in seven settlements in Karachi found that infant mortality rates varied from 33 to 209 per 1000 live births.[92] Table 2.10 shows how infant and under-five mortality rates varied in Nairobi between various informal settlements (where around half the entire city's population lives) and compared to averages for Nairobi, urban centres in general and rural populations. In some of the informal settlements, under-five mortality rates were three or four times the average for Nairobi (and likely to be 10–30 times the rates in high-income areas).

There are differences of opinion regarding the contribution of water supply and sanitation to death and disease. City-level data from Global Urban Indicators show child mortality rates to be generally more highly correlated with a lack of access to potable water and sewerage connections than with other variables commonly cited, such as the number of households below poverty lines or the availability of health services.[93] Some studies have established tight links between environment and health even when socio-economic variables are held constant.[94] On the other hand, it is clear that the influence of water and sanitation is related in complex ways to these other factors, and that this relationship can vary from place to place. An analysis of demographic and health survey (DHS) data from Ghana, Egypt, Brazil and Thailand, for instance, demonstrates that although socio-economic status, access to health services and levels of provision are interrelated in their effects on the health and survival of urban children, the relative importance of these

Table 2.10 Mortality rates for infants and young children in the informal settlements of Nairobi

Location	Neonatal mortality rate	Post-neonatal mortality rate	Infant mortality	Under-five mortality rate	Prevalence of diarrhoea*	Prevalence of diarrhoea with blood*
Nairobi informal settlements (average)	30.4	60.9	91.3	150.6	30.8	11.3
Nairobi informal settlements in:						
Central	24.5	43.5	68.0	123.1	34.6	13.6
Makadara	34.1	52.2	86.3	142.7	20.4	10.0
Kasarani	19.2	58.2	77.4	124.5	30.8	9.2
Embakasi	111.1	52.5	163.6	254.1	27.6	9.1
Pumwani	16.3	56.3	72.6	134.6	26.7	12.5
Westlands	23.1	79.9	103.0	195.4	30.4	12.2
Dagoretti	0.0	35.0	35.0	100.3	26.0	10.5
Kibera	35.1	71.1	106.2	186.5	36.9	9.8
National**	28.4	45.3	73.7	111.5	17.1	3.0
Rural**	30.3	45.7	75.9	113.0	17.1	3.1
Nairobi**	21.8	16.9	38.7	61.5	12.9	3.4
Other urban**	16.9	39.8	56.6	83.9	19.4	1.7

* Per cent of children under three years of age with watery diarrhoea and diarrhoea with blood during the two weeks preceding the survey.
** Based on the 1998 Kenya Demographic and Health Survey.
Source: APHRC (2002), *Population and Health Dynamics in Nairobi's Informal Settlements*, African Population and Health Research Center, Nairobi, 256 pages.

factors varies from one site to another. In Ghana, for instance, environmental differentials in diarrhoea prevalence are modest after socio-economic status is controlled for – probably a reflection of the fact that provision is relatively poor throughout urban areas and falls below the threshold at which exposure to infection begins to decline; other income-related factors are more significant here in the relative effects they have for children. In Thailand, inequalities in environmental conditions are strongly correlated to diarrhoea prevalence, but not to mortality – probably because of widespread access to and use of health services.[95]

Regardless of differences from place to place, however, it is clear that, where water and sanitation provision is inadequate, children have higher rates and intensity of diarrhoeal illness, worm infestations, skin infections and malnutrition, and that improved provision (including increases in the amounts of water used) contribute to reductions in morbidity and mortality.[96]

Diarrhoeal diseases are still a primary cause of infant and child death for large sections of the world's urban population. The health burden for children under five that arises from diarrhoeal diseases linked to inadequate water, sanitation and hygiene is up to 240 times higher in Africa than in high-income nations.[97] As noted above, the impact of diarrhoeal diseases on infant and child deaths can be considerably under-estimated since, when combined with under-nutrition, they can so weaken the body's defences that diseases such as measles and pneumonia become major causes of child death.[98] Intestinal worms also cause severe pain to tens of millions of urban children and undermine their nutritional status, retard their physical development and contribute to poor school attendance and performance.[99] Many case studies in low-income settlements have shown the high proportion of children who have debilitating intestinal worm burdens.[100] The prevalence among children of various skin and eye infections, such as scabies and trachoma, that are associated with a lack of water supplies for washing is also particularly high among those living in poor quality homes and neighbourhoods.[101]

Diarrhoea and intestinal parasites contribute much to malnutrition in children.[102] These links are complex and reciprocal: malnutrition weakens the body's defences and causes children to be more vulnerable to disease. But at the same time, diarrhoeal disease and intestinal parasites contribute to malnutrition by causing decreased food intake, impaired nutrient absorption and direct nutrient losses.[103] Even a relatively mild infestation of intestinal parasites, for instance, can consume 10 per cent of a child's total energy intake, as well as interfering with digestion and absorption.[104] Unsanitary environments also contribute to malnutrition by challenging children's immune systems; nutrients that would otherwise support growth instead go towards supporting the immune response.[105] Data from 84 countries indicate that the best predictor of nutritional status, next to sufficient funds for food, is the level of access to water.[106]

The case is often made that the effect of infection or diarrhoea on growth is transient, and that children generally catch up quickly. This seems to be true if they have stretches of diarrhoea-free time.[107] But for many children living in adverse conditions, diarrhoea in the early years may be too severe or too frequent to allow for catch-up growth, and it is associated with continued low weight or substantial shortfalls in growth when children are older.[108] Long-term impacts for children are not restricted to health; research in poor urban settlements in Brazil has related early diarrhoeal disease in children to impaired cognitive functioning several years later.[109]

Poor provision can affect growth in other ways too; when water is at a distance, this can contribute to heavy workloads for older children, causing them to burn calories that they depend on for adequate nutrition. Carrying overly heavy containers can even contribute to deformities in bone growth.[110]

Children's vulnerabilities

Children's vulnerability to pathogens is related to both their exposure and their level of immunity. The less effective immune systems of infants and younger children are somewhat compensated for by their relative protection from exposure to pathogens, especially for those children being breast-fed. The greater mobility of children after infancy increases their exposure, but their acquired immunity provides some protection.[111] Bottle-fed infants are at especially high risk where there is inadequate water and sanitation provision. Without clean water and hygienic conditions, bottles cannot be sterilized and formula milk cannot be safely mixed. A survey of the milk being fed to 149 children of between 6 and 24 months in a slum settlement in Varanasi, India found that 53.7 per cent of the samples were contaminated by bacteria. The odds of contamination were 25 times as high when feeding utensils were not properly cleaned.[112] Although HIV positive mothers are warned about the possibility of transmitting the disease to their infants through breast-feeding, the reality is that many of these infants, if bottle-fed in environments that do not support adequate hygiene, are at even higher risk of death from diarrhoeal disease than from AIDS.[113]

Children being weaned from the breast are also at high risk, as they first encounter the pathogens in a contaminated environment. A prospective study of urban Filipino infants found that feeding even small amounts of contaminated water supplements to breast-fed infants nearly doubled their risk of diarrhoea.[114]

Children in child care centres and other institutions may also be more vulnerable. Possibilities for disease transmission are always higher when a number of children are together, and several studies from urban areas in Latin America have shown higher rates of diarrhoea for children in day care centres.[115] Inadequate toilets or hand-washing facilities may allow parasites or disease to spread quickly from child to child, and from there through the community.

It is common for schools to have little or no provision for toilets. Schools with several hundred (or even thousand) children and often with very over-crowded facilities often have a few poorly maintained pit latrines. Even where facilities are technically present, they may be poorly adapted to the use of children.[116]

The impacts for mental and social development

Research in urban Brazil and Peru has demonstrated strong connections between infection with diarrhoeal pathogens in the first two years of life and cognitive functioning when children are between six and nine. One study controlled for current nutritional status; the other for socio-economic status and amount of schooling children had received.[117] More generally, malnutrition and stunting have been found in numerous studies to be related to children's mental and social development, both in the short and longer term. Children who have suffered from early malnutrition have lower IQ levels and school achievement, and more behavioural problems later on.[118] Some of these studies have found these effects independent of schooling or socio-economic status; others have pointed to the fact that stunted children tend to receive significantly less schooling than non-stunted children.[119] For those children attending school, parasitic infestations continue to take a toll, in part as a result of the cognitive effects of anaemia associated with worms. A study in Java, for instance, found that infection with hookworms had a significant adverse effect on children's working memory, with consequences for their reasoning ability and reading comprehension. This association increased with age.[120]

The effects of malnutrition on children's capacity to learn are not well understood, but it is hypothesized that, because stunted children are more listless and slower to develop and move around, they are less involved in interaction with both their social and physical environment, and experience lower levels of the stimulation that promotes cognitive development.[121] Some research has found higher levels of physiologic arousal in stunted children, along with more inhibition, anxiety and inattention than in non-stunted children from the same poor neighbourhoods. It is hypothesized that higher cortisol levels in these children may be linked to poor cognitive performance as well as to their decreased functional immunity.[122]

No research was found that has established a direct relationship between access to water and sanitation and children's cognitive functioning. Any number of variables and complications would presumably mediate and confound such a connection. Given the intermediate links that have been established, however, between provision and disease, disease and malnutrition, and malnutrition and psycho-social performance, it makes sense for all practical purposes to acknowledge the possibility and even likelihood of such a relationship in considering the impacts of poor provision.

The quality of provision is also linked to children's psycho-social development through the direct impact that these services (or their absence) may have on opportunities for play and learning. Healthy children are driven by curiosity, energy and a desire for competence to explore the world around them. Through their engagement with their surroundings, they gain important information about the properties of objects, about cause and effect, about their own capacity to make things happen. Through active play, they learn to use their bodies and to understand physical laws and spatial relationships. Through the diversity and repetition of activities, they gain a range of skills and a growing sense of competence and assurance. A stimulating physical environment is a basic support for this active learning, and has been recognized by many major theorists as fundamental for development.[123] A contaminated environment is not necessarily less stimulating, but it can require caregivers to make difficult choices between protecting their children's health and allowing them free access to play.

Poor provision can limit opportunities for older children too, in part by limiting the availability of open space for recreation, but also through the impacts that it can have on their time. Many children, most often girls, spend hours each day collecting water, and this can interfere with school attendance.[124] Girls' attendance can also be affected by the quality of sanitation facilities in school, especially once they have started to menstruate.[125] As described above, many urban (and rural) schools have inadequate and poorly maintained facilities, and in some cases none.

What matters for children with regard to water and sanitation?

Quantity and accessibility versus quality

Safe supplies of uncontaminated water are vital, but there is a general consensus that water quantity is as or even more important than quality, especially for maintaining children's health.[126] Water quality may be more critical for the health of children under three years of age, while water quantity becomes a crucial health determinant above the age of three.[127] Contaminated water contributes to outbreaks of disease, but too little water makes it difficult to maintain the sanitary conditions that prevent contamination, and that are essential for controlling the endemic disease that contributes so heavily to the death and repeated illness of many children.[128] Studies from urban areas in Bangladesh and Niger, for instance, find that faecal contamination leading to diarrhoeal disease and intestinal parasites is more highly correlated to dirty hands (a good indicator of the accessibility of water supplies) than it is to the quality of drinking water.[129]

Too little attention is generally given to this important aspect, and distance to water points, regularity of supply, and time spent waiting are serious concerns – especially for caregivers dealing with young children. Although 20 litres per person per day is currently the standard for household water consumption,[130] it has been estimated that 30 to 40 litres a day are the minimum needed per person if drinking, cooking, laundry and basic hygiene are all taken into consideration.[131] When water is at a distance and needs to be carried (or when it needs to be purchased from vendors), many households with young children who technically have access to water make do on far less than they really need. Hands, food, utensils, floors, cooking surfaces and children are all less likely to be kept clean when water must be carried any distance. Even 100 metres, a distance that has frequently been used to define adequate provision, fails to guarantee optimal use. In Malawi it was found that water supply had to be brought to within a few yards of the house in order for the amounts of water used by caregivers to be significantly increased.[132]

The effects for child health can be dramatic. In an urban settlement in Papua New Guinea, the presence of a standpipe within the compound was associated with a 56 per cent reduction in diarrhoeal morbidity for children under five.[133] In Burkino Faso, mothers with access to a tap in their yard were three times as likely to use safe hygiene practices as those fetching water from wells outside their compound.[134] In a study in Porto Alegre (Brazil), infants were four times as likely to die in households using public standpipes as in those with water piped to the house.[135]

Storing water

Ease of access is not the only issue here. There is also the matter of storage. No matter how close the source is, when water is not piped directly into a house or yard, it needs to be stored in containers. Even when water is piped to the house, it will have to be stored if the flow is not regular. This can provide a number of opportunities for contamination. It is a particular problem in households with young children, who may dip dirty hands into a storage bucket, or leave water scoops on the floor, contributing to contamination and disease.[136] The prevalence of diarrhoea for small boys in Ethiopia, for instance, was found to be significantly associated with drinking water obtained by dipping from storage containers; by contrast, the water source and the amount of water consumed were not significant risk factors.[137] In a poor neighbourhood of Abidjan, Côte d'Ivoire, where drinking water is stored in most households, E. coli was found in only 1 per cent of source water samples, but in 41 per cent of stored water samples.[138] In a slum settlement in Nairobi, uncovered water containers were found to be the most significant factor influencing children's recovery from diarrhoea.[139] In peri-urban Peru, children in households with water stored in containers without a tap were twice as likely to have a high incidence of diarrhoea (more than seven episodes a year) as those who used containers with taps.[140] An intervention trial in a refugee camp in Malawi found that, when water was stored in containers with a cover and a spout, there was a 69 per cent reduction in faecal coliform levels in the water, and 31 per cent less diarrhoea in children under five.[141] One of the appealing features of water piped directly and regularly into the house is the fact that there is no need for a storage tank, and that those using the water cannot contaminate the supply.

Sanitation

Sanitation-related illnesses affect young children most heavily, in part because of their lower immunity to pathogens, but also because of their behaviour. Small children have a drive to play and explore, they are in closer contact with the ground and they have less appreciation of hygiene. This means that they are more likely to come into contact with excreta, the primary source of diarrhoeal disease and intestinal parasites, as well as other pathogens. Where children are concerned, the only safe sanitation methods are those that eliminate all possibility for contact with excreta. Safe stool disposal is far more effective as a safeguard against disease than any amount of hand-washing.[142] Yet more than half of the world's urban households lack a sanitary means for disposing of human waste.

Chapter 1 described how many low-income urban settlements are served by public latrines that are filthy, foul smelling, crowded, and distant from many of the dwellings they serve, causing many people to defecate in the open. Such arrangements are particularly challenging for young children and their caregivers. Taking a young child any distance for toileting is impractical, especially when there is likely to be a queue at the latrine. The WHO/UNICEF Assessment 2000 standards do not consider such public latrines to constitute adequate coverage. Yet even shared toilets, which are defined as 'improved provision', can present problems for young children. When facilities are shared, maintenance frequently becomes an issue:[143] neighbours resent it when children leave things dirty, and children themselves are at higher risk of faecal contact than they would be with private facilities. Pit latrines present a particular problem. The darkness, smelliness and large openings of most latrines make their use unpleasant and

even frightening for young children. Reports from Malawi, Nepal, Burkina Faso and India point out that children rarely use latrines before they are six or eight because of the risk that they might fall into the pit.[144] A survey conducted by UNICEF's India office found that only 1 per cent of children under six use latrines, that the stools of an additional 5 per cent are thrown into latrines, and that the remainder end up in drains, streets or yards, increasing the likelihood of contamination.[145] Considering the numbers of young children in any poor settlement, it is no wonder that the surroundings quickly become fouled even in situations where provision meets international criteria for improved coverage.

Strong links have been found in many urban communities between the quality of sanitary provision and rates of diarrhoea. In urban Brazil, the risk factor most significantly associated with incidence of diarrhoea, next to the age of the child (under two), was the lack of sanitation facilities.[146] In Pakistan, infants born in households with soakpits were 60 per cent more likely to die than those with toilets connected to underground sewers.[147] In Sri Lanka and Cebu, the Philippines, unsanitary disposal of children's faeces (linked to the absence of adequate provision) was associated with a higher incidence of diarrhoea in young children, relative to children in households that followed sanitary practices.[148] The higher incidence of intestinal parasites in urban children, similarly, has been repeatedly associated with shared toilets or a lack of connection to city sewer systems.[149] Multi-country research in 1996 explored whether incremental improvements in water and sanitation conditions resulted in incremental health effects for diarrhoea and nutritional status. The effects of improved provision were found to be greater for urban than for rural dwellers. Improvements in sanitation had more of an impact than did improvements in water provision; in fact the benefits from improved water only occurred when sanitation was also improved.[150] Other research, looking at the benefits of partial coverage, has had mixed findings. Work in urban Africa found that the provision of improved water and sanitation to a small number of households in an area may

Box 2.3 Managing children's faeces in Lima

Research in Lima, Peru looked at the various ways that small children's faeces were dealt with in a densely populated shanty town, where water for the most part was purchased from tankers, and where only some households had latrines.

Almost all children under one year were kept in diapers, which were washed daily because of limited stocks and rinsed at least three times to avoid diaper rash. The costs in terms of both water and time were a strong motivation for getting children out of diapers as soon as possible. Potties were considered the most hygienic solution at this point, and in some cases training began as early as six months. But because mothers were busy, potty training was generally inconsistent, and it was common for children to defecate in their clothes – a transgression most commonly greeted with shouting or slaps. As in the case of diapers, faeces from potties were emptied into latrines in those households that had them, but otherwise onto a rubbish dump or a nearby hillside commonly used for defecation. Most mothers felt that potties should be emptied and washed as soon as possible – but acknowledged that they were generally too busy to do this.

Because of the time commitment involved in training children and keeping potties clean, only 20 per cent of small children actually used potties, and in most cases mothers simply allowed them to defecate directly onto the ground – although defecation away from the home area, and especially near a neighbour's home, was considered unacceptable. Faeces were sometimes left on the ground, and sometimes scooped up and disposed of in latrine or dump. Although children were generally cleaned up with paper, 30 per cent were found to retain some faecal matter on their clothes or bodies.

Latrines were considered an unrealistic solution for children under the age of four because of flies and bad odours, but also because of the large openings and the need for small children to be accompanied. Although some learned to manage latrines independently over time, most children over three used the hill side, looking for a spot that was free of faeces and trash.

Source: Huttly, S R A, C F Lanata et al (1998), 'Feces, flies, and fetor: findings from a Peruvian shanty town', *Revista Panamerican de Salud Publica*, Vol 4, No 2, pages 75–9; Yeager, B A C, S R A Huttly, R Bartolini, M Rojas, C F Lanata et al (1999), 'Defecation practices of young children in a Peruvian shanty town', *Social Science and Medicine*, Vol 49, No 4, pages 531–54.

not actually protect even those families from infection when the overall level of faecal contamination in the environment is high.[151] But other research points to the flip-side of this phenomenon, indicating that even partial coverage reduces overall faecal contamination and lowers contact between susceptible children and opportunities for infection.[152] Clearly, it is important for improved provision to reach a critical 'tipping point' for things to change substantially.

Drainage and waste collection

Inadequate drainage and waste collection pose particular problems for children, who tend to play wherever there is open land or interesting opportunities for exploration, and who may be drawn to wade or play in standing water and in drainage ditches, or to scavenge in piles of garbage. In many communities, it is impossible for children to play outdoors and to avoid these hazards (see Box 2.4). Children between 5 and 14 years old, for instance, are disproportionately affected by helminths and by such water-based diseases as bilharzia.[153]

The quality of care and hygienic practices

Poor provision also affects children through the time burdens that it imposes on their caregivers. Managing water supplies, keeping children clean and safe, dealing with waste and excreta in the absence of adequate services, and handling food and utensils hygienically can take more hours than there are in a day – and these challenges are often handled on top of 'real' work. The sheer drudgery resulting from inadequate provision takes its toll not only on the capacity of caregivers to provide care, but also on the capacity of families to function optimally. Improving provision for water can not only greatly increase the amount of water used for child hygiene but it can also increase the time mothers spend on child care, including feeding and hygiene.[154]

The key to children's environmental health problems is often assumed to lie in the education of caregivers in hygiene and other protective measures. Not only is health education perceived as a more affordable solution than investment in infrastructure, but experience has also indicated that, in the absence of hygienic behaviour, improvements in provision may have a minimal effect on health.

Hygienic practices such as hand-washing have been demonstrated to result in impressive reductions in disease.[155] However, it still remains unclear how changes in health behaviour are best brought about. A number of studies have demonstrated that information does not reliably change behaviour, and that efforts to improve hygiene solely through health education may have little effect in the absence of supportive provision. In a shanty town in Lima, Peru, for instance, where knowledge of the importance of hand-washing and other hygiene practices was high, only 13 per cent of faecal contamination episodes were found to be interrupted by washing. Researchers concluded that, where water is scarce, education is unlikely to change hygiene practices.[156] In Burkina Faso, research into factors affecting hygiene behaviour found that the location of water sources was more important than health education, income, maternal education or culture.[157] In Sri Lanka, a case control study of environmental and behavioural risk factors for unsafe disposal of children's excreta concluded that latrine ownership may be a necessary condition for improving safe stool disposal.[158]

Unhygienic practices in some cases are determined by beliefs that run counter to formal biomedical knowledge, and these situations are likely to be quite resistant to change. In urban Karachi, for instance, infant diarrhoea is frequently considered to be related to teething or the weather, and so is considered a 'normal' event.[159] Curtis and colleagues point out that simply telling people about the likely health benefits of a given behaviour is unlikely to provide enough motivation to change lifelong habits. When mothers believe that diarrhoea results from teething or from sitting on damp ground, explanations involving microbes are unlikely to have a great impact.[160] But non-compliance with hygienic practice is not always a question of conflicting beliefs. It may be a matter of time and energy – as in Malawi, for instance, where water use increased signifi-

cantly only when supplies were brought very close to the house,[161] or in the Dominican Republic, where mothers revealed that in many cases they were simply 'too tired to boil water'.[162]

In their Assessment 2000, WHO and UNICEF remind us that 'the simple act of washing hands with soap and water can reduce diarrhoeal disease transmission by one-third.'[163] Such statements are undoubtedly true for much of the population. But they tend to overlook the fact that keeping two- and three-year-olds clean in a contaminated environment is far from 'simple'. On the contrary, it can call for constant vigilance and even for unrealistic restrictions on children's play and socialization (see Box 2.4).

Another critical consideration is the fact that caregivers seldom face these problems one at a time. Environmental risk factors generally exist in clusters. It might be possible for caregivers to respond effectively to any one of them, but coping hygienically with daily challenges in the absence of reasonable provision is likely to mean a number of time consuming tasks:

- obtaining sufficient supplies of water for hygienic living;
- ensuring that stored water does not become contaminated;
- washing potties or diapers, and/or disposing safely of small children's stools (often loose stools, and often those of more than one child);
- ensuring that latrines are kept clean;
- ensuring that hands (and often the body) are washed every time a small child defecates or eats; and
- keeping small children away from local sources of contamination as they play. In addition, other measures must be taken to avoid the contamination of food.

When these challenges are compounded by crowded and unfinished housing, an absence of safe play space, long distances to work and services and a lack of child care, the difficulties can become overwhelming and unmanageable. It becomes far-fetched to assume in these complex situations that

Box 2.4 The informal settlement of Banshighat in Kathmandu

The informal settlement of Banshighat in Kathmandu, Nepal, is criss-crossed by foul-smelling open drains which run down to the river nearby, carrying wastewater from other parts of the city as well as from this community. Because there is no provision here for waste removal, all local garbage is also dumped into these drains. Plastic bags, orange rinds and broken glass litter the banks. Although most people in the community use the river bank for defecation, some households have latrines on the way down to the river, and these also empty into the drains. Small children in Banshighat do not use latrines, however, and they are not allowed down by the river. Caregivers throw their excreta into the drains – the simplest way to keep the narrow walkways clean. This means that faecal matter is present in the drains at every point in the community.

Parents are well aware of the health hazard that these drains present, but their awareness is no match for their children's energy and drive to play. Even the most vigilant caregivers have trouble protecting children from their contaminated environment. One mother described to a researcher all the measures she took to ensure that her children did not touch water from the drains. While she spoke, her son dropped his ball into the drain behind her. He jumped right in, retrieved the ball, and continued throwing it back and forth to other children. Another small boy was observed driving his 'car' – a small slab of wood – down to the edge of the drain, through the water, and out the other side while his mother washed clothes nearby.

The drains are especially hazardous for children just learning to walk. Everyone watches these little ones carefully, said one mother, but inevitably they trip and fall in at some point. They are scolded or beaten when they fall in, in an attempt to impress on them the importance of avoiding the drains. Children who are not yet mobile are at lower risk – but for those between about one and five years, the drains and the generally dirty conditions present a constant threat to health. Diarrhoea, worm infestations, skin problems and eye infections are a routine part of life for most small children in Banshighat.

Source: Save the Children Norway (2002), 'Banshighat: preparatory research for ECD programming', unpublished report, Kathmandu.

children's health can reasonably be protected by health information in the absence of appropriate provision.

 ## Vulnerability and susceptibility[164]

The presence of a disease-causing agent (for instance, one that causes diarrhoeal disease) does not necessarily mean that it will harm someone. This also depends on the characteristics of the individual, household or social group exposed to it. Certain individual or group characteristics can also influence the severity of the health impact.

Certain people or households are more at risk from the diseases associated with inadequate water and sanitation provision because they are:

- less able to avoid them (eg, living in a settlement lacking provision for protected water, sanitation and drainage);
- more affected by them (eg, infants are at much greater risk of death from diarrhoeal diseases than older groups); or

- less able to cope with the illness (eg, persons who cannot afford to go to a doctor or pay for medicine; households whose incomes and asset bases are so low that the temporary illness and incapacity of a household member means too little money is available to buy sufficient food and meet other necessities).

Such individuals or households are generally termed vulnerable. But to ensure a more precise understanding (from which more appropriate responses can be developed), it is worth distinguishing between susceptibility (where the increased risk is related to endogenous factors such as a person's nutritional status, the state of their immune system or their genetic makeup) and vulnerability (where it is external social, economic or cultural conditions that increase the risk – for instance, through an increased likelihood of exposure to excreta or less capacity to cope with or adapt to any illness that such exposure causes).[165]

Weak body defences (in turn influenced by age and nutritional status) make people more susceptible to the diseases related to inadequate water and sanitation, while a considerable variety of factors influence their vulnerability to these diseases, including:

- income and assets, which influence the individual's or household's ability to afford good quality housing with good provision for water, sanitation and drainage, health care and emergency responses including purchasing the most effective medicines, and taking time off to recuperate when sick or injured;
- economic or social roles, which can increase the exposure to hazards (for instance, particular occupations such as picking through excreta-contaminated garbage or particular tasks such as being responsible for disposing of human excreta within a household);
- the extent of public, private and community provision for health care, including emergency response to acute diseases; and
- individual, household or community coping mechanisms for when disease occurs, for instance, knowing what to do, who to visit and how to rearrange individual/household survival strategies.[166]

The key role that assets have in helping low-income individuals or households to avoid deprivation is now more widely recognized. However, this discussion generally concentrates on those assets that are important for generating or maintaining income, or for helping low-income people to cope with economic stresses or shocks. Too little attention has been given to the role of good quality housing, infrastructure and services in reducing low-income groups' vulnerability by reducing exposure to diseases, and the role of health care services and emergency services in reducing their health impact. In this sense, it is the quality of housing and the provision for water, sanitation and drainage that is the asset – regardless of whether the house is owned, rented or borrowed. The discussions of housing as an asset tend to concentrate on its capital value or its potential income-earning possibilities (through providing space for income-earning activities or for renting out) rather than its potential role in helping its

inhabitants avoid disease burdens (and other hazards associated with poor quality housing). The income-enhancing potential of improved water and sanitation provision is also often forgotten. Providing an accessible piped water supply to city neighbourhoods where the inhabitants previously relied on expensive water from vendors can increase the income available for food and other necessities. Providing house or yard connections to households who previously relied on public standpipes with long queues provides great savings in time and physical effort. As Chapter 7 will describe, community-built and -managed public toilets in Mumbai and Pune greatly reduced the cost of using public toilets. Better water and sanitation provision can also mean much less income lost because income earners are unable to work (because they are sick or nursing other sick family members) or because of the need to pay for treatment and medicines.

In any city population, there are particular groups within the low-income population that face particularly high levels of risk from the environmental hazards associated with inadequate water and sanitation. For instance, there are particular groups who face the most difficulty getting access to water and washing and bathing facilities, such as pavement dwellers or those who sleep in open spaces, parks and graveyards. Street children who have been abandoned by their families (or have run away from home)[167] generally have very poor quality accommodation (often sleeping in the open or in public places) and great difficulty in finding places to wash, defecate and obtain drinking water and health services. There are also other children in especially difficult circumstances who face particular difficulties in getting provision; for instance, a study by the Indian NGO SPARC in Bombay/Mumbai identified children of pavement dwellers and construction workers and 'hotel boys' as particularly vulnerable, along with street children.[168] The children of construction workers who live on-site lack access to schools, day care, health facilities, water and sanitation. There is also a need to consider the particular problems faced by the elderly and those with physical disabilities, who inevitably face much greater difficulties in fetching and carrying water. There are also those groups within the population of any city that face discrimination in obtaining access to good quality housing and environmental services because of their ethnicity, skin colour, caste, sex or the fact that they are immigrants.

The particular difficulties faced by two groups in getting better water and sanitation provision or in suffering from the impacts of inadequate provision are discussed here: women and renters.

 Women

A disproportionate share of the labour and health burden of household and neighbourhood water and sanitation inadequacies falls on women. It is typically women who collect water from public standpipes, often queuing for long periods in the process and often having to get up very early or go late at night to get the water. It was noted earlier just how heavy water is to fetch and carry. It is typically women who have to make do with often inadequate water supplies to clean the home, prepare the food, wash the utensils and do the laundry. It is also women who typically care for the infants and children (including bathing them), both when they are well and when they are ill. It is important not to under-estimate this side of the water burden. There are no compelling international statistics, comparable to the health statistics, document-ing the labour burdens of inadequate water. Box 2.5 presents extracts from the accounts of women in low-income settlements in Pune (India) about the difficulties they face (or used to face) getting water and sanitation. It is very difficult for those who have never had to rely on public taps and public toilets to appre-ciate just how tiresome, tiring, stressful and inconvenient this can be. It is also difficult for research to capture this – especially since most research on water and sanitation is trying to quantify the inadequacies in provi-sion. This box provides some insights into qualitative aspects that often go unrecorded. These reveal many difficulties that women face in getting water and accessing toilets that rarely come out in quantitative studies, some of which are discussed below.

The opposition of those living in a settlement to 'outsiders' coming to use 'their' public taps

> *When we went to get water (from a neigh-bouring building because there were no supplies in our settlement), when we put the* handaa *[water container] under the tap, some women would spit from above, or they would shut off the tap, or taunt us. We had to be thick-skinned to get our water. When we went there again they would say things again, curse us, call us beggars, call us all kind of things, saying that these are dirty people, they dirty up the whole ground. They should not be given water.*

Some interviewees mentioned the need to go at night to other settlements to get water because the inhabitants would not like them using 'their' taps. 'There is a Hanuman Temple a little way away from the settlement which had a tap. But the people there did not want us to go there because we lived in a slum. We would go at night, at 1am, 1.30am, 2am, when the tap was free and take water.'

The pressure placed on those at the public standpipe not to take too much, or too long, by those waiting in the queue behind them

> *If somebody had a lot of vessels then until they had finished filling them, they would not allow other people to fetch water. This was how a lot of fights got started.*
>
> *Nothing could be done without fights. Until you fought and heard swear words you did not get water!... There was just one tap and there were 200–250 houses in the settle-ment; maybe more.*

In other instances, there are community limits on how much water can be taken – but this means that it is difficult to draw enough water for all household tasks. Of course, this problem is much exacerbated if there is low pressure in the system (and so a slow flow of water from the standpipes), or water is only available in the pipe for a few hours a day.

The scramble to get water among those living in settlements dependent on water tankers

Frequently, daughters are kept out of school to make sure that water can be obtained when the tanker comes.

The difficulties of getting to public toilets

We have no toilets: we use two toilets in Ambedkar Nagar. It is outside our settlement, five minutes away. People from two settlements use the four toilets – two for men and two for women. We have to stand in a queue for half an hour. That is why the men all go under the bridge and only the women use the toilets. Children also go out in the open.

How disgusting it is to use public toilets that are not well maintained

Even now, insects climb up our legs. They do not clean the toilets properly.

If you go to see the toilets, they are so dirty that a person cannot put a foot in them, but we have no choice and we have to go there. The children squat in the road, to the extent that you cannot walk along the road.

The toilets are very dirty. The cleaner does not come regularly. For two or three days or more, they do not clean. Rags and cloths accumulate inside. Men have better toilets.

Though we have a toilet, built by the corporator, it does not have water, or electricity, and it is not cleaned. It is always very dirty. There is a lot of dirty graffiti on the walls, and the filth brings insects and animals, and the children fall sick. It is dark, there is no light there, and there are mosquitoes.

Blaming others for the dirty toilets, especially tenants and outsiders

The same people who dirty the toilets can also make a complaint about the dirtiness. It is not always possible to know who dirties the toilets. They are people from within the settlement who are outsiders.

They live on rent. Everyone eats, they have to use the toilet. The outsiders who come here for a short time vandalise and steal, and the rest of the settlement gets a bad name.

Conflicts for those who defecate in the open

Just today, there was a fight between the women from 6am till 9am. Somebody had dirtied the drain. They throw garbage in the drains. And if we go to tell them not to, they say 'You are not our leader. Take care of your own house and wastes!' It is not only the women who say this: my husband said 'Don't you have any other work? Cook lunch for the children.' I said 'OK, I'll leave it, it's a big fight, they are swearing...' Somebody had defecated in the drain today. I took two mugs of water from my house and threw them on it. They said 'Why do you want to wash it away? We are fighting about it.' I said, 'Don't fight: I will pour water on it', and I asked them if they wanted me to sweep it away. But they said 'You are not a sweeper.' I told them to go ahead and fight. The fight is probably still going on.

The difficulties in managing shared stand-pipes and toilets

Such difficulties include raising the funds to get them, getting the relevant authority to install them, allocating payments among users, collecting payments, taking responsibility for getting the taps mended and keeping the shared toilets clean.

The box below illustrates in some detail why women are more vulnerable than men to many environmental hazards associated with inadequate water and sanitation provision, because of gender relations (ie, as a result of the particular social and economic roles that women have in regard to water and sanitation, determined by social, economic and political structures). They are also particularly susceptible to many environmental hazards when pregnant, since the reproductive system is particularly sensitive to adverse environmental conditions. The diseases linked to inadequate water and sanitation provision (and their role in malnutrition) contribute to many of the

Box 2.5 Women from Pune talk about the difficulties they face with water and sanitation

This box reproduces extracts from interviews undertaken in some of the 21 informal settlements in Pune surveyed during 2002. More than 750,000 people live in informal settlements or slums. The settlements were distributed throughout the city and represented a variety of situations: settlements in the central part of the city had ample water supplies while settlements in outer zones had less than adequate supplies. Some settlements are close to a river or canal and some are not; some are on level ground and some on slopes; some are recognized by the government as slums (meaning that the government accepts some responsibility for providing services) and some are not. Some of the interviewees mention the improvements in provision for public toilets since the municipal corporation introduced a major programme to support the building of toilets by community organizations and NGOs. Some also mention Mahila Milan, savings groups formed by the inhabitants of informal settlements, which also lobbies for improved services.

Jyoti R S Bhende

I live in Jaibhavani Nagar on the hill side and I am near the top of the hill. My settlement had a problem since there was no water anywhere in it. There were just three taps near the toilet, and the canal at the bottom. If we went to the canal and it was not dry, we had to get down the whole hill and then climb up again. Before that there was no water in our settlement. We had to get it from near the public toilets. If the men had to go the toilet, they would fill their cans from that tap and we had to fill from that same tap.

Once it happened that the toilet was blocked, but nobody paid attention to it. The floor was broken and water gathered there from the outside urinals, and mixed with the small children's shit. There were insects which flew outside and all of those insects fell into our *handaas* [water containers]. I get up in the morning

and get two *handaas* of water first… There is no drainage in our area because it is on the hill. There is no road even now. When my children were very small, and if I left early then my children would follow me one by one and walk in the drain. I would go forward to fill my *handaa* and on coming back people would tell me to hurry because the children were drinking from the drain. So half my mind was on the water and half on the children. And on top of that there was the hurry to go to work.

If I went to the other side (to draw water from the tap in the men's toilet) then all the men sitting there to bathe would soap themselves … we would say 'Brother, please move a bit'. They would not listen. 'Wait, we are getting late.' So much, we would cry! People would be telling me that my children were jumping in the drain, and here were these men with soap suds. All this, and they used to use such dirty words when we were waiting for water. We would stand in line for the tap and put out our *handaas*, and they would say such dirty things that I used to cry. I thought that after the elections we would get water… They [politicians] canvass for the elections, and don't come back! [A politician] was elected, but did not come back to meet us. Then Mahila Milan came to our settlement. All us women came together. We explained to everybody how we would benefit. That was when we were told that taps would come to our settlement. The pipes and taps were laid for the past three years. But when will the water come out of them? When we opened the stopcock and water came out with [sufficient] pressure, all the children and women were under the pipe!

Manda Hadvalaya

I live at Chandrama Nagar near the mental hospital. In my settlement before 1997 there were a lot of problems regarding water. Some of us went to Panchsheela Nagar (a neighbouring settlement which had a public

tap). When we went to get water (from a neighbouring building because there were no supplies in our settlement), when we put the *handaa* under the tap, some women would spit from above, or they would shut off the tap, or taunt us. We had to be thick-skinned to get our water. When we went there again they would say things again, curse us, call us beggars, call us all kind of things, saying that these are dirty people, they dirty up the whole ground. They should not be given water. Even if it was a government tap, they would say that it was not our right and that they would not give us water. They would say 'The slum people are dirty, why should we give them water.' They would scold us. We would still go there. The whole day would be taken up in fetching water. We would go at 8am or 8.30am… and we would go back at 12 noon. Later we would have to go again. Even then we did not get enough water. We had to go round looking for water.

Sangita Chavhan

I live in the Patil Estate slum. Previously, I used to get water from the court in *handaas*. There were no taps in our slum. We used to go to the toilet near the river side. The insects used to climb up our legs. I used to go to the toilet in the bungalow where I worked. We went to defecate under the bushes. When we got water from the court, then we went to the toilet with water. It would take us two to three hours to get a *handaa* of water. Then, in the elections, Qazi Saheb [a local politician] came and arranged for taps. Each house had a tap, but there was no provision for toilets. Even today the toilets are as they are. It takes one to one-and-a-half hours to use the toilet. And even now, insects climb our legs. They do not clean the toilets properly. They made open drains, but all the children defecate in them. And people throw wastes into them. If we sit in our doorway, the stink of the drain reaches us. We can't sit there and eat. The children have to sit inside and study. They have made a road, but it is not proper. Everything is thrown into the road. Women come back from work and wash their faces there, and that is where they all throw their dirt. People fall sick, coughing and so on. The children get diarrhoea. When they come to take the garbage away, all the dirt flies up onto the doors. They throw all the dirt at the door. Even the water in the drain does not flow properly.

Padma Gore
I live in Dattawadi, Vighnaharta Nagar. I work for Mahila Milan in my settlement, and have done so since 1997. My settlement lies along the river. It runs almost into the water, rather than stopping at the river banks. We are afraid, because if extra water flows into the river it carries off our houses. In 1997, our houses were carried off by the waters, and then, within fifteen days, Mahila Milan came to our settlement. Mahila Milan told us about themselves, about savings and so on, and we began working with them.

Previously, I used to pay Rs50 per month for water to a person called Pawar. We did not have drinking water and electricity in our settlement. We used to fill 10 or 15 *handaas*. For the rest – washing clothes or utensils – we used water from the river. Later, after Mahila Milan came to us, we got one tap – between 28 houses. We got electricity in the same way. Before Mahila Milan came to our settlement we did not have steps to come down the slope, but they built some. Then they got us a streetlight, and now we go to and fro in that light. Mahila Milan [did these things] for us: later on the municipal authorities also helped, but Mahila Milan began the process.

We have no toilets: we use two toilets in Ambedkar Nagar. It is outside our settlement, five minutes away. People from two settlements use the four toilets – two for men and two for women. We have to stand in a queue for half an hour. That is why the men all go under the bridge and only the women use the toilets.

Children also go out in the open. We live near the river, so children go near the river.

Fatima Abdul Khan
I live in Patil Estate, Gulli Number 3, near the river. There were a lot of problems regarding water earlier on, but now it is a bit easier. Those who have water taps would leave them running and not shut them off. If we told them, they would run after us and start a fight. Before that, we had just one tap. We would dig a hole in the ground and collect subsoil water. That was what we drank. We used to strain it. We used to get one *handaa* and one bucket. We did not get a third *handaa*. We went through so much difficulty. Now our corporator has given us a line and a tap, but the women do not maintain the cleanliness around the tap.

We have a lot of problems with the toilet. Previously we used to go to the toilet on the river bank – one side for the men and the other for the women. Even now [some people continue to do this]: those who are sensible understand, and others don't. The toilets are very dirty! They clean them once a week or once a month. Insects come out of them. The toilet building is five minutes away. In the ladies' toilets there are six seats, and in the men's there are also six. We stand in lines.

Sukubai Dengle
I live in Kamgarputla Vasahat. I have had water since the beginning, ever since I came to live here. The water is close to us. That is why there is no problem about water. Our difficulty was with toilets, but ever since Mahila Milan built toilets we have not had any tension. This year all the toilets have been completed, and now we do not have to queue. Even the water is properly arranged. Before this, I had to get up very early. Using the toilet was a source of tension. There would be a queue of 10 or 20 women; sometimes there were even 30. Sometimes, a woman would defecate on the steps if the wait was too long. If you have diarrhoea, you

can't hold it back. How can you stop it? That is why the primary problem was toilets! Now Mahila Milan has made such a nice arrangement that we do not have to stand in queues, and there is no tension about the toilet. There is water in the toilet 24 hours a day, and they are very ordered and clean. Once I sit down in the toilet, I don't feel like getting up for a couple of hours! Really, I have a toilet at home yet I like that toilet so much that I go and sit in it. Mahila Milan has made such nice toilets for us that they feel like a bungalow. Ever since the organization built the toilets there has been less sickness. The small children now don't fall sick at all. I know it for sure. Previously, my father-in-law, husband and children would go to the doctor regularly. But ever since the toilets have been built there is no dirt, and that is why there is no sickness. Sickness happened because of the toilets. They would get blocked, insects would come out of the chambers. Some would tell children to defecate outside the toilets, or inside, and sometimes over the drains. But now there is such a good arrangement for the small children that they go happily to the toilet. The toilets make a big difference in my settlement. And the environment is much cleaner for the children. The condition is so good.

Surya Kaborkar
I come from Sanjay Park, Vimandarshan, Lohegaon Road. There are about 280 houses here. There has been a branch of Mahila Milan here for the past four months. About 80 of us women save with Mahila Milan. In four months we have deposited Rs22–23,000... We have just one problem – the settlement is on military land. That is why there can be no amenities (including piped water) and no drains. Mahila Milan has now built toilets. The toilets are clean. But cleanliness alone is of no use, because the drains are very dirty. The military does not allow any amenity and that is why there are lots of problems. There are toilets but there is no water in the toilets. We have to get a tanker and fill the

overhead tanks above the toilets. We get only two tankers a day. They do not provide enough for all the houses. Two tankers come from the corporation. We are near a disused quarry, so in many homes the men and children go to the quarry for a bath. In some houses the clothes and even vessels are taken to the quarry for washing. We take only bath water for the women, drinking water and water for the utensils from the tankers. That is why we need five to seven *handaas*. We do not have any arrangement except for the tanker. The tanker comes sometimes at 11am or 12 noon, or at 1pm. We do not know when it will come.

Chhaya Waghmare

I live in Sanjay Park. The tankers come right in the middle of the settlement. People on this side put their vessels on this side and people on the other side put their vessels on the other side. When the tanker comes, everybody knows about it. All the women and children gather there. We put the vessels there earlier, in the morning, and leave them there till the tanker comes. Everybody has their specific place in the queue but only their vessels will be there. Everyone has a pipe, and when the tanker comes the pipe has to be put into the tanker. One person is needed to go on top of the tanker to put their pipe into the tanker. One person is needed below to suck out the water by mouth, and then everybody fills their *handaas*. Sometimes people do not get water. I have a small sister who used to go to school. She studied till the second or third standard, but we have kept her at home to fill the water whenever the tankers arrived, since I have to go out to work. That is why her schooling was abandoned. For 22 years we have been getting tanker water. Previously there was just one tanker, but now, because there were fights, there is another one.

Sona Vaitale

I live at Wadar Basti, Yerawada. Five or six years ago there was a municipal connection, with two taps where we used to get water. But [the supply was intermittent:] water would come one day and not the next… We did not have enough water for several years. There were a lot of fights; everyday there would be fights, people would throw each other's *handaa* away etc. The water came from the pipe from the toilet. That water we would fill for drinking and for washing. In our area the system was that the vessels were put in place in the morning; *handaas* and so on were left at the tap, and once water came to the tap, we would fight and fill out containers. Sometimes someone's *handaa* would be stolen, and sometimes there would be fist fights. This is what happened. Our relations with each other would be spoiled because of the conflicts over water…

Though we have a toilet, built by the corporator, it does not have water, or electricity, and it is not cleaned. It is always very dirty. There is a lot of dirty graffiti on the walls, and the filth brings insects and animals, and the children fall sick. It is dark, there is no light there, and there are mosquitoes. The day before yesterday two girls were admitted [to the hospital]: one is three months and the other is nine months. They had vomiting and diarrhoea.

Chhaya Raju Gaikwad

I live in Dattawadi … there used to be two taps between 45 houses. It was so crowded that we could not get any water. Even at 11–12pm, we could not get water. We used to fill our containers in the evening. At the end of 1997, we got houses, and in 1998 we got taps; we had to pay R275 and we got a tap in the house. The river is close to us, so when we got water it was OK if we just had enough for baths and to clean the house. We used to wash the utensils and clothes at the river… We have a toilet. It was built three years ago, and there are just three toilets between 45 houses. Men also go there, and we have to go out in the open also. In some areas they have to go out in the open too.

Rehana Azim Sheikh

I live in Netaji Nagar, Survey number 8. I have been living in the settlement for the past 15 years. Water is not a problem, now there are taps in each house. Five years ago there were a lot of problems; there were no taps in the house. We had to bring water from outside. We did not have to go far. There was a municipal tap which was very crowded. We had to get up at 4am to fill our containers. There was a queue till 10am…

The toilets are very dirty. The cleaner does not come regularly. For two or three days or more, they do not clean. Rags and cloths accumulate inside. Men have better toilets. We have to pay Rs20 per month. The toilets have been built by the corporation. Avinash Savle, [a politician] who was elected, got new toilets built for the men. Women do not have a new toilet. Already, three or four doors to the toilets are broken and they are not clean; it is dirty all the time. They don't come to clean them, sometimes even for a week.

There used to be fights. Nothing could be done without fights. Until you fought and heard swear words you did not get water!… There was just one tap and there were 200–250 houses in the settlement; maybe more. There was another tap, but it was very far away, it took us half an hour to go there. We would get between four and ten *handaas* of water… We would go to the tap at night, at 12 midnight or 1am. If our man was in the house we would get him to fetch the water, or we would do it ourselves. The tap was free at night. We could not get to it during the day. Now they have given us water; one tap between five houses. Previously, water would be available from 4am to 9am. After 9am the water would stop… We had to pay R500 each [for the new tap]. The water is free.

Suman Babban Pande

I live on 214 Dandekar Street, opposite Lokmanya Nagar. Previously, we had such a problem with water that we had to get up at 5am. If we went to the tap later than that, then the other women would put our vessels aside and put their own vessels under the tap instead. If you wanted to fight, you could fight every day. I did not fight, I would sit quietly: 'OK, if you want to put aside my vessels, do it'. Sometimes I had to take drinking water from Dattawadi. There was no provision for bathing. They had made *moris* [small enclosures for bathing] along the road, but the corporation demolished them. Then we made *moris* in the houses. We would dig holes, have a bath and then fill buckets and throw the water on the other side. This is the convenience we had. Then Vandana Tai was elected and she gave us taps in the houses. She cleaned the open drains outside our doors and closed them. These are the good things she did for us. For water we had to go here and there; I fell down several times. We had to get up at 5am. Sometimes, if it was late and I was in a hurry and worried about whether I would get water or not, I would slip and fall down. There was a lot of tension about water. We would fill the drums at night and fetch water until 12 at night. And then in the morning again we had to get up at 5am for water. There were many taps but we had to queue up. And the [other women] would not give me water until they had fetched their washing water and drinking water.

Helen Babban Mayekar

I live on Ram Takri, near the Blind School, Survey number 109, Hadapsar area. I have been here for six months. There used to be a lot of problems regarding water in my settlement. There was only one tap and water was sold: one *handaa-kalsi* [container] cost 25 paise (a quarter of a rupee). If a woman wanted extra, she was allowed only four *handaas* and the rest would have to be filled later. People used to fight. Then I got a tap in my own house. My husband is a TV mechanic and I have studied till the tenth standard in English. But I did not get a job and now I sell vegetables. There were so many problems, and I have given 25 paise for one *handaa* of water before now... There is

a big problem with the drains. Just today, there was a fight between the women from 6am till 9am. Somebody had dirtied the drain. They throw garbage in the drains. And if we go to tell them not to, they say 'You are not our leader. Take care of your own house and wastes!' It is not only the women who say this: my husband said 'Don't you have any other work? Cook lunch for the children.' I said 'OK, I'll leave it, it's a big fight, they are swearing...' Somebody had defecated in the drain today. I took two mugs of water from my house and threw them on it. They said 'Why do you want to wash it away? We are fighting about it.' I said, 'Don't fight: I will pour water on it', and I asked them if they wanted me to sweep it away. But they said 'You are not a sweeper.' I told them to go ahead and fight. The fight is probably still going on. We also have a problem with water. There is a lot of water but [the pressure is too low and] it does not come to our level, and we have to buy it instead. Today there was no water in the taps.

Neelam Sathe

I live in Yeshwant Nagar in Yerawada. There used to be a huge problem in our area. About 10–15 years back we had to fetch water from the bathroom in the men's toilet block; there was also a toilet for women but there was no tap there. We fetched our water from there, for drinking and for other things. Apart from this the men would have their baths there. While they had their baths we had to wait outside. Once their baths were over we went inside and fetched water. Some of the boys were so bad that only when the girls came and wanted water would they go and have a bath. When they saw the girls waiting, they would rub on more soap and bathe for longer. They would not move at all and they were shameless. Many days were wasted like this. Then a corporator came, he was not elected then. He saw that all the women had to fetch water from the bathroom, they even had to fetch drinking water from there, so he got us two taps outside. We used to fetch water from there.

The water came in the morning at 3am or 4am. There were 15–20 houses at that time. There were lots of fights, because the water was not there for the whole day and it would stop at 9am. Everybody wanted a lot of water. They would fetch water in whatever vessels they had. They would get up early in the morning and put the vessels in a line. They would stand in a queue and wait for their turn to fill their vessels. If somebody had a lot of vessels then until they had finished filling them, they would not allow other people to fetch water. This is how a lot of fights got started.

Noorshah Salim Sheikh

I live on Harris Bridge, Gandhi Nagar. My slum is on the Bombay–Poona Road. This settlement is 20–25 years old. Previously, there were few houses and there were a lot of problems regarding water. There was a pipeline running under the bridge and the water used to leak from it. People would stand with a vessel on their head to catch the water as it fell. There was no other water to be had. There is a Hanuman Temple a short distance away from the settlement which had a tap, but the people there did not want us to use it because we lived in a slum. We would go at night at 1am, 1.30am, 2 am when the tap was free and fetch water... Toilets were built and a woman from our organization was asked to take care of it. But because some people dirtied the place so much, the woman got a bad name – people claimed that she did not maintain cleanliness. Some people would pay her on time and some would not. She was removed... Now there is another caretaker there. The same people who dirty the toilets can also make a complaint about the dirtiness. It is not always possible to know who dirties the toilets. They are people from within the settlement who are outsiders. They live on rent. Everyone eats, they have to use the toilet. The outsiders who come here for a short time vandalise and steal, and the older settlement gets a bad name.

Bhamabai Laxman Jagtap

I live in Gandhi Nagar, Pimpri. Mahila Milan has been in our area for the past one-and-a-half years. For 10–15 years we had lots of problems with water, electricity and so on, but then we got water taps, one or two in each lane. Even then there were long queues for water. It was not convenient for us all to queue at one tap... Those who lived nearby could stand in the queue, but those who lived far away could not get water. In my lane, I got the women together. There were 20–25 women and I told them: 'We have this problem with water, and we have to get our own tap'... I collected R25 from each woman, and with that we put in a pipe, and we wrote to the municipality and told them that we needed water here, and we are ready to pay for it. They gave us a tap in our lane immediately...

Each settlement also has toilets, but they are not clean. The one up the hill is not OK. We have even taken photos of that one, because there have been explosions there. It is so dirty, and there is no [ventilation to allow] the foul air to go out, and explosions occur. If you go to see the toilets, they are so dirty that a person cannot put a foot in them, but we have no choice and we have to go there. The children squat in the road, to the extent that you cannot walk along the road.

Tabassum Sheikh

I am from Sangam Wadi and live on the upper side. I came here in 1987 and there was a (municipal) corporation toilet, which was at the top. On the wall of the toilet there was a tap from which everybody took water. Almost 50 families took water from there. There were two women in the settlement who were fighters. If they did not get any water they would break the tap. Once the tap was broken, the others could not get water either... Then [someone proposed a] scheme to provide one tap between every five families, and many people who had money [joined the scheme]. Others contributed, and wrote a letter to the corporation, and got the tap a little lower down the hill and now we fetch water from there. Now water is provided properly.

Toilet facilities are also provided, but the children's toilet is not good. It is just a small drain which has been placed in an empty space. Children squat in the drain. Once a boy was squatting there when some officers came. They called his father and fined him Rs50. My son also used to squat there, but his father picked him up and brought him into the house. He did not want to have to pay the Rs50 fine. Because there is no children's toilet, small children of three or four years have nowhere to go. They sit in the drain.

Source: SPARC water and sanitation study in Pune. A more detailed account of this will be published in *Environment and Urbanization*, Vol 15, No 2, October 2003.

serious health problems faced by mothers and thus also to their capacity to cope with difficulties during pregnancy, childbirth and the post-partum period, to produce a strong healthy baby and to breast-feed and care for it.[169] They also have a role in the very high maternal mortality rates evident in most low- and middle-income nations (although the absence or very poor quality of health services for childbearing women is the main cause).[170]

Women are generally far more severely affected than men by poor quality and overcrowded housing conditions and by the inadequate provision of water, sanitation and health care (and also schools and nurseries) because they take most responsibility for looking after infants and children, caring for sick family members and managing the household.[171] It is generally women who are responsible for the disposal of human wastes when provision for sanitation is inadequate, and this exposes them to diseases associated with contact with human excreta. The fact that women take most responsibility for child care means that they also have to cope with most of the illnesses and injuries from which infants and children suffer (including those relating to inadequate water and sanitation). Caring for the sick and handling and laundering soiled clothes are particularly hazardous tasks when water supplies and sanitation and washing facilities are inadequate.

The people within a household who are responsible for water collection and its use for laundry, cooking and domestic hygiene also suffer most if supplies are contaminated and difficult to obtain – and these people are generally women or girls. Women often suffer more than men from chronic back pain, because they have to collect water from wells or public standpipes.

A study of household environmental management in Accra noted that:

Household and neighbourhood level environmental problems do not receive the attention they deserve in environmental debates and this probably reflects, at least in part, a form of gender discrimination: once the water has left the tap, the fuels have been purchased, and more generally the environmental problems have entered the home, they are considered less important 'private' problems. But since 'private' environmental problems tend also to be 'women's' problems, the seemingly rational emphasis on 'public' problems can easily mask a lack of concern for women's problems.[172]

These gender-related or sex-related differentials are obviously related to the discrimination that women face in many sectors. For instance, one of the reasons that women have difficulty finding better quality housing with adequate water and sanitation provision is the discrimination they face in obtaining employment, in what they are paid when they do find work, in purchasing or renting housing and in obtaining credit.

Renters

Whilst much of the discussion about access to water and to sanitation refers to which houses and settlements obtain provision, there are also issues about who receives provision within houses and settlements. An estimated 29 per cent of the population of Kathmandu are renters who negotiate provision for water with their landlords. 'Unlike many South Asian cities, many of the poor live in socially heterogeneous communities rather than in well bounded slum and squatter areas. Despite this, their access to water services is not comparable to that of their wealthier neighbours.'[173] Experiences from elsewhere suggest that these experiences are perhaps more common than this quote implies. In South Africa, renters normally also have to negotiate their access to water and sanitation provision with their landlords, and it is common for landlords to restrict access; for example, to an outside tap. Tenants in Cochabamba (Bolivia) also face particular problems with water and sanitation.[174] 'There's no water' complained one tenant; 'The lack of cleanliness – nobody cleans, especially not in the toilet' said another. In low-income areas of Dhaka, tenants are not 'allowed' to own tubewells,

latrines or other facilities; non-tenant resident and absentee landlords made decisions about local facilities, with tenants being given responsibility for keeping facilities clean.[175]

In Mukuru Kwa Reuben, a low-income squatter community in Nairobi, the residents have been denied access to toilet facilities by landlords wishing to maximize their rental income. As a consequence, 215 toilets were placed on the periphery of the settlement of 10,000 people. At night, when it is unsafe to walk about the settlement, residents relieve themselves in the areas outside their shacks. The lack of facilities explains the presence of 'flying toilets', in which people wrap the excreta in plastic bags or newspaper and throw it away. The houses are built close together with some pathways only 40cm wide. As a consequence of the lack of facilities, these pathways become drainage channels and often are blocked with stagnant water and garbage. The toilets consist of just cloth or sack walls and very shallow pits. The toilets fill up very fast, and when it rains they overflow and the settlement is covered with human excreta. Subsequently there are frequent outbreaks of sanitation-related diseases such as typhoid, cholera and dysentery. As one resident puts it: 'The waste comes into our houses and in the morning we just scoop it out and life goes on.'[176]

Restricting economic development

The discussion of the costs of inadequate water and sanitation provision in this chapter have concentrated on the costs to those who are most directly affected. Other costs need to be considered, including the impact on labour productivity, and the ability of cities and nations to attract private investment.

Table 2.11 illustrates this by considering the losses in Peru in 1991 as a result of the cholera epidemic. The appearance of cholera in Latin American cities came as a shock to the region; it had not been seen for decades and it had been assumed that improvements in water, sanitation, sewerage treatment and food safety had eliminated the

Table 2.11 Loss in the time of cholera; Peru, 1991

Item	US$ thousand
Exports	27,972
Imports	233
Tourism	147,120
Subtotal; external market losses	175,325
Internal fisheries	32,568
Street food vendors	15,850
Cholera patient care	29,053
Absence from work due to illness	17,586
Absence from work due to death	8292
Future absence from work due to death (post-1991)	233,764
Subtotal: internal market losses	337,112
Total losses	**512,437**
Benefits:	
Pharmaceutical industry	(5534)
International donations	(11,602)
Total benefits	**(17,136)**
Total net loss	**495,301**

Note: Net loss in 1991: US$232 million, approximately 1 per cent of Peru's GDP.
Compare this with the cost of providing standpost water supplies for Peru's 5.9 million
unserved population; at a mean cost of US$41 per head = US$242 million.
Source: This table was drawn from a presentation by Sandy Cairncross. The statistics
come from Petrera, M and A Montoya (1992), *PAHO Epidemiological Bulletin*, Vol 13,
No 3, pages 9–11; the costs of providing standpipe supplies comes from WHO and
UNICEF (2000), *Global Water Supply and Sanitation Assessment 2000 Report*, World
Health Organization, Geneva.

It is also obvious that a city's capacity to attract new investment (perhaps especially foreign investment) is influenced by the quality of provision for water, sanitation and drainage. Cities with intermittent water supplies must impose a heavy burden on all businesses that need regular supplies – although the cost may be in the extra provisions that businesses have to make to ensure regular supplies (for instance, large storage tanks or tapping other water sources) rather than in production lost when water is not available in the pipe. However, it may only be influenced by the quality of provision for the factory or office in which the investment is made and/or for the housing of senior staff. One can point to the success of Porto Alegre or Singapore in attracting foreign investment and argue that this must in part be due to the high quality of these cities' environmental infrastructure: all or virtually all businesses and households have their own piped water supplies and sanitation. But there are other examples such as Bangalore (see Chapter 1), with its great success in attracting high technology industries in a city where provision for water, sanitation and drainage is very inadequate for much of the population. Or, in the Philippines, the success of Cebu in attracting foreign investment, despite very inadequate water and sanitation provision for much of the population.[178]

Improved provision for water and sanitation and poverty reduction

The question of how much improved water and sanitation provision contributes to poverty reduction will be discussed in more detail in Chapter 6. But certain points from the sections above need highlighting. Good quality water and sanitation provision not only brings major health benefits but also:

- for income earners, increased income from less time off work because of illness or the need to nurse sick family members, and less expenditure on medicines and health care;

disease, just as they had in Europe and North America in the late 19th and early 20th century.[177]

Apart from the thousands of deaths and the much larger number of people who were seriously ill, there was also the devastating economic impact. A study by Petrera and Montoya showed the very large losses to the Peruvian economy in 1992 as a result of the epidemic – some US$28 million from lost exports and US$147 million from loss in tourism earnings – with other high costs such as patient care, the losses to those who earned a living as street food vendors and from fisheries, and the losses due to death and absence from work. The net loss to the Peruvian economy was around US$232 million in just this one year, which is about the same as the cost of providing standpost water supplies for Peru's unserved population.

- support for household enterprises that need water and that are important for income earning;
- better nutrition (eg, less food lost to diarrhoeal diseases and intestinal worms);
- less time and physical effort needed by those collecting water;

- lower overall costs for those who, prior to improved supplies, had to rely on expensive water vendors; and
- a reduced risk of floods that can damage and destroy housing, which is often a low-income household's main capital asset and also where they store other assets. Protection from flooding also often leads to investment in improving and extending housing.

Notes and references

1. WHO (1999), 'Creating healthy cities in the 21st century', Chapter 6 in David Satterthwaite (ed), *The Earthscan Reader on Sustainable Cities*, Earthscan Publications, London, 472 pages.
2. Ibid.
3. Classification developed by David Bradley; see Cairncross, Sandy and Richard G Feachem (1993), *Environmental Health Engineering in the Tropics: An Introductory Text* (second edition), John Wiley and Sons, Chichester (UK), 306 pages.
4. See for instance Songsore, Jacob and Gordon McGranahan (1993), 'Environment, wealth and health: towards an analysis of intra-urban differentials within Greater Accra Metropolitan Area, Ghana', *Environment and Urbanization*, Vol 5, No 2, October, pages 10–24; Misra, Harikesh (1990), 'Housing and health problems in three squatter settlements in Allahabad, India', in Sandy Cairncross, Jorge E Hardoy and David Satterthwaite (eds), *The Poor Die Young: Housing and Health in Third World Cities*, Earthscan Publications, London; Adedoyin, M and S Watts (1989), 'Child health and child care in Okele: an indigenous area of the city of Ilorin, Nigeria', *Social Science and Medicine*, Vol 29, No 12, pages 1333–1341.
5. WHO (2002), 'Water for promoting and protecting health', the World Health Organization's chapter in the *World Water Development Report* to be published by UNESCO in 2003.
6. See for instance Songsore and McGranahan 1993, op cit, and Surjadi, Charles (1988), *Health of the Urban Poor in Indonesia*, Urban Health Problems Study Group Paper No 29, Atma Jaya Research Centre, Jakarta, 45 pages.
7. Rossi-Espagnet, A, G B Goldstein and I Tabibzadeh (1991), 'Urbanization and health in developing countries: a challenge for health for all', *World Health Statistical Quarterly*, Vol 44, No 4, pages 186–244.
8. WHO (1990), *Environmental Health in Urban Development*, Report of a WHO Expert Committee, World Health Organization, Geneva, 65 pages.
9. Many of these are summarized in Bradley, David, Carolyn Stephens, Sandy Cairncross and Trudy Harpham (1991), *A Review of Environmental Health Impacts in Developing Country Cities*, Urban Management Program Discussion Paper No 6, The World Bank, UNDP and UNCHS (Habitat), Washington, DC, 58 pages. See also Mahfouz, A A, H el-Morshedy, A Farghaly and S Khalil (1997), 'Ecological determinants of intestinal parasitic infections among pre-schoolchildren in an urban squatter settlement of Egypt', *Journal of Tropical Paediatrics*, Vol 43, No 6, pages 341–344, and Misra 1990, op cit.
10. Landwehr, D, S M Keita, J M Ponnighaus and C Tounkara (1998), 'Epidemiological aspects of scabies in Mali, Malawi, and Cambodia', *International Journal of Dermatology*, Vol 37, No 8, pages 588–590.
11. WHO (1999), *World Health Report: 1999 Database*, World Health Organization, Geneva.
12. Cairncross and Feachem 1993, op cit.
13. WHO 2002, op cit.
14. Satterthwaite, David, Roger Hart, Caren Levy, Diana Mitlin, David Ross, Jac Smit and Carolyn Stephens (1996), *The Environment for Children*, Earthscan Publications and UNICEF, London and New York, 284 pages.
15. For more details, see World Bank (1993), *World Development Report 1993: Investing in Health*, Oxford University Press, Oxford.
16. WHO (1992), *Our Planet, Our Health: Report of the WHO Commission on Health and Environment*, World Health Organization, Geneva, 282 pages.

17. WHO 2002, op cit.

18. Magadi, Monica A (2002), 'Maternal and child health', in APHRC, *Population and Health Dynamics in Nairobi's Informal Settlements*, African Population and Health Research Center, Nairobi, pages 95–118; more details from this study are presented later in this chapter.

19. Cain, Allan, Mary Daly and Paul Robson (2002), 'Basic service provision for the urban poor: the experience of development workshop in Angola', IIED Working Paper 8 on Poverty Reduction in Urban Areas, IIED, London, 40 pages.

20. Alcazar, Lorena, Lixin Colin Xu and Ana Maria Zuluaga (2000), 'Institutions, politics and contracts: the attempt to privatise the water and sanitation utility of Lima, Peru', Policy Research Working Paper, WPS 2478, World Bank, Washington, DC, reporting on an earlier World Bank study.

21. Etherington, Alan, James Wicken and Dinesh Bajracharya (2002), *Preparing for Private Sector Management of Kathmandu Urban Water Supply*, WaterAid, Nepal.

22. Cain, Daly and Robson 2002, op cit.

23. Pryer, Jane (1989), 'When breadwinners fall ill: preliminary findings from a case study in Bangladesh', in *Vulnerability: How the Poor Cope, IDS Bulletin*, Vol 20, No 2, April, pages 49–57; Pryer, Jane (1993), 'The impact of adult ill-health on household income and nutrition in Khulna, Bangladesh', *Environment and Urbanization*, Vol 5, No 2, October, pages 35–49.

24. Bottled water is often even more expensive than this – for instance, in a restaurant in high-income nations, it is common to spend US$5 on one litre of mineral water, which means $5000 per cubic metre.

25. Songsore, Jacob (1992), *Review of Household Environmental Problems in the Accra Metropolitan Area, Ghana*, Working Paper, Stockholm Environment Institute, Stockholm, 21 pages.

26. McGranahan, G, P Jacobi, J Songsore, C Surjadi and M Kjellén (2001), *Citizens at Risk: From Urban Sanitation to Sustainable Cities*, Earthscan Publications, London.

27. Thompson, John, Ina T Porras, Elisabeth Wood, James K Tumwine, Mark R Mujwahuzi, Munguti Katui-Katua and Nick Johnstone (2000), 'Waiting at the tap: changes in urban water use in East Africa over three decades', *Environment and Urbanization*, Vol 12, No 2, pages 37–52.

28. Swyngedouw, Erik A (1995), 'The contradictions of urban water provision a study of Guayaquil, Ecuador', *Third World Planning Review*, Vol 17, No 4, pages 387–405.

29. Lamba, Davinder (1994), 'The forgotten half: environmental health in Nairobi's poverty areas', *Environment and Urbanization*, Vol 6, No 1, April, pages 164–173.

30. Briscoe, John (1986), 'Selected primary health care revisited', in Joe Tulchin (ed), *Health, Habitat, and Development*, Lynne Reinner Publishers, Boulder, pages 105–124.

31. See Chapter 3 for more details.

32. Azandossessi, A (2000), 'The struggle for water in urban poor areas of Nouakchott, Mauritania', *Waterfront*, Issue 13, January, UNICEF, New York.

33. Cairncross, Sandy (1990), 'Water supply and the urban poor', in Jorge E Hardoy, Sandy Cairncross and David Satterthwaite (eds), *The Poor Die Young: Housing and Health in Third World Cities*, Earthscan Publications, London, pages 109–126.

34. Korboe, David, Kofi Diaw and Nick Devas (2000), *Urban Governance, Partnership and Poverty: Kumasi*, Urban Governance, Partnership and Poverty Working Paper 10, International Development Department, University of Birmingham, Birmingham.

35. Saghir, Jamal, Manuel Schiffler and Mathewos Woldu (2000), *Urban Water and Sanitation in the Middle East and North Africa Region: The Way Forward*, Middle East and North Africa Region Infrastructure Development Group, The World Bank, Washington, DC.

36. Solo, Tova Maria (2000), *Independent Water Entrepreneurs in Latin America: The Other Private Sector in Water Services* (draft), World Bank, Washington, DC.

37. McIntosh, Arthur C and Cesar E Yñiguez (1997), *Second Water Utilities Data Book*, Asian Development Bank, Manila, 210 pages.

38. Solo 2000, op cit.

39. Ibid.

40. McIntosh and Yñiguez 1997, op cit.

41. Information sheet on standpipe operators in Ouagadougou in Water and Sanitation Program (2000), *Independent Water and Sanitation Providers in Africa: Beyond Facts and Figures*, WSP Africa Regional Office, World Bank, Nairobi.

42. Saghir, Schiffler and Woldu 2000, op cit.

43. McIntosh and Yñiguez 1997, op cit.

44. Champetier, Séverine and Mohamed Farid (2000), *Independent Water and Sanitation Providers in Africa: Nairobi, Kenya, Case Study 5*, Water and Sanitation Program – East and Southern Africa, Nairobi, 8 pages.

45. Thompson, Porras, Wood et al 2000, op cit.

46. Saghir, Schiffler and Woldu 2000, op cit.

47. Pamoja Trust (2001), *Huruma Informal Settlements: Planning Survey Report*, Pamoja Trust, Nairobi.

48. Champetier, Séverine and Bill Wandera (2000), *Independent Water and Sanitation Providers in Africa: Kampala, Uganda, Case Study 8*, Water and Sanitation Program – East and Southern Africa, Nairobi, 6 pages.

49. Thompson, Porras, Wood et al 2000, op cit.

50. Ibid.

51. McGranahan, Jacobi, Songsore et al 2001, op cit.

52. Solo 2000, op cit.

53. Champetier, Séverine, Adam Sykes and Bill Wandera (2000), *Independent Water and Sanitation Providers in Africa: Dar es Salaam, Tanzania, Case Study 10*, Water and Sanitation Program – East and Southern Africa, Nairobi, 6 pages.

54. McIntosh and Yñiguez 1997, op cit.

55. Cain, Daly and Robson 2002, op cit.

56. Manager of handcarts for water resale in information sheet on Conakry, in Water and Sanitation Program 2000, op cit.

57. Thompson, Porras, Wood et al 2000, op cit.

58. Champetier and Wandera 2000, op cit.

59. McIntosh and Yñiguez 1997, op cit.

60. Katui-Katua, Munguti and Gordon McGranahan (2002), *Small Enterprises and Water Provision in Kibera, Nairobi: Public Private Partnerships and the Poor*, Water, Engineering and Development Centre (WEDC), Loughborough, 38 pages.

61. Solo 2000, op cit.

62. McIntosh and Yñiguez 1997, op cit.

63. Katui-Katua and McGranahan 2002, op cit.

64. Cain, Daly and Robson 2002, op cit.

65. Burra, Sundar and Sheela Patel (2002), 'Community toilets in Pune and other Indian cities', *PLA Notes*, 44; Special Issue on Local Government and Participation, IIED, London, pages 43–45.

66. Hanchett, Suzanne, Shireen Akhter and Mohidul Hoque Khan (2003), 'Water, sanitation and hygiene in Bangladesh slums: a summary of WaterAid's Bangladesh Urban Programme Evaluation', *Environment and Urbanization*, Vol 15, No 2; see Chapter 3 for more details.

67. Alcazar, Xu and Zuluaga 2000, op cit.

68. Collignon, B and M Vezina (2000), *Independent Water And Sanitation Providers In African Cities*, UNDP-World Bank Water and Sanitation Program.

69. Sinclair Knight Merz and Egis Consulting Australia in association with Brisbane City Enterprises and Feedback HSSI – STUP Consultants – Taru Leading Edge (2002), *Bangalore Water Supply and Environmental Sanitation Masterplan Project; Overview Report on Services to Urban Poor Stage 2*, AusAid, Canberra.

70. Alcazar, Xu and Zuluaga 2000, op cit.

71. Sinclair Knight Merz et al 2002, op cit.

72. Moser, Caroline O N, personal communication.

73. Agarwal, Anil, Sunita Narain and Srabani Sen (eds) (1999), *State of India's Environment: The Citizens' Fifth Report*, Centre for Science and Environment, New Delhi, 440 pages.

74. Thompson, Porras, Wood et al 2000, op cit.

75. Ibid; White, G F, D J Bradley and A U White (1972), *Drawers of Water: Domestic Water Use in East Africa*, University of Chicago Press, Chicago.

76. Champetier and Wandera 2000, op cit.

77. Solo 2000, op cit.

78. Thompson, Porras, Wood et al 2000, op cit.

79. Champetier, Sykes and Wandera 2000, op cit.

80. Azandossessi 2000, op cit.

81. Development Workshop (1995), *Water Supply and Sanitation and its Urban Constraints: Beneficiary Assessment for Luanda*, Development Workshop, Luanda, 35 pages plus many annexes.

82. Quoted in Alcazar, Xu and Zuluaga 2000, op cit.

83. Pryer 1993, op cit.

84. This draws on a background paper written by Sheridan Bartlett which will be published in *Environment and Urbanization*, Vol 15, No 2, October 2003.

85. UNICEF (2002), *Poverty and Exclusion among Urban Children*, Innocenti Centre, Florence.

86. By 2000, Africa had an urban population of 297.1 million while Northern America had 239 million; Africa also has around twice as many children within its population as Northern America – see United Nations (2000), *World Urbanization Prospects: The 1999 Revision*, Population Division, Department of Economic and Social Affairs, ESA/P/WP.161, United Nations, New York, 128 pages; United Nations (2001), *World Population Prospects: The 2000 Revision (Highlights)*, Population Division, Department of Economic and Social Affairs, United Nations Secretariat, ESA/P/WP.165, United Nations, New York, 69 pages.

87. UNICEF 2002, op cit. These figures are drawn from an analysis of 86 demographic and health surveys held in 53 different nations between 1986 and 1998 by Mark Montgomery of the Population Council.

88. Official figures vary. Global burden of disease figures for 2000 show 1.3 million annual deaths for children under five from diarrhoeal disease – Murray, C J, A D Lopez, C D Mathers and C Stein (2001), *The Global Burden of Disease 2000 Project: Aims, Methods and Data Sources*, Global Programme on Evidence for Health Policy Discussion Paper

No 36, World Health Organization, Geneva. The WHO 1999 figures indicate 1.85 million deaths for children under five from diarrhoeal disease, and another 0.13 million for children from 5–14 – *World Health Report, 1999 Data Base*, World Health Organization. In addition, there are the deaths related to parasites and to malnutrition. In 1990 there were an estimated 3 million deaths annually for children under five from diarrhoeal disease.

89. WHO 1999, op cit. Also Murray, C J and A D Lopez (1996), *The Global Burden of Disease: A Comprehensive Assessment of Mortality and Disability from Diseases, Injuries and Risk Factors in 1990 and Projected to 2020*, Harvard University Press, Boston.

90. These figures are drawn from an analysis by Mark Montgomery (Population Council) in 2002 of 86 demographic and health surveys held in 53 different nations between 1986 and 1998.

91. Montgomery 2002, op cit.

92. Surveys undertaken by the Community Health Department of the Aga Khan University quoted in Hasan, Arif (1999), *Understanding Karachi: Planning and Reform for the Future*, City Press, Karachi, 171 pages.

93. Shi, A (2000), *How Access to Urban Potable Water and Sewerage Connections Affects Child Mortality*, World Bank Development Research Group, Washington, DC.

94. For instance, Victoria, C G et al (1988), 'Water supply, sanitation and housing in relation to the risk of infant mortality from diarrhoea', *International Journal of Epidemiology*, Vol 17, No 3, pages 651–654; Woldemicael, G (2000), 'The effects of water supply and sanitation on childhood mortality in urban Eritrea', *Journal of Biosocial Science*, Vol 32, No 2, pages 207–227.

95. Timaeus, I M and L Lush (1995), 'Intra-urban differentials in child health', *Health Transition Review*, Vol 5, pages 163–190.

96. Bradley, Stephens, Cairncross and Harpham 1991, op cit; Curtale, F, M Y Shamy, A Zaki, M Abdel Fattah and G Rocchi (1998), 'Different patterns of intestinal helminth infection among young workers in urban and rural areas of Alexandria Governorate, Egypt', *Parassitologia*, Vol 40, No 3, pages 251–4; Ludwig, K, F Frei, F Alvares-Filho and J T Ribeiro-Paes (1999), 'Correlation between sanitation conditions and intestinal parasitosis in the population of Assis, State of Sao Paulo' (in Polish), *Revista da Sociedade Brasileira de Medicina Tropical*, Vol 32, No 5, pages 547–555; Mahfouz, el-Morshedy, Farghaly and Khalil 1997, op cit; Shi 2000, op cit; and Timaeus and Lush 1995, op cit.

97. Prüss, Annette, David Kay, Lorna Fewtrell and Jamie Bartram (2002), 'Estimating the burden of disease from water, sanitation and hygiene at a global level', *Environmental Health Perspectives*, Vol 110, No 5, May, pages 537–542.

98. WHO 1992, op cit.

99. WHO 2002, op cit.

100. Bradley, Stephens, Cairncross and Harpham 1991, op cit.

101. See for instance Landwehr, Keita, Ponnighaus and Tounkara 1998, op cit.

102. Rice, A L, L Sacco, A Hyder and R E Black (2000), 'Malnutrition as an underlying cause of childhood deaths associated with infectious diseases in developing countries', *Bulletin of the World Health Organization*, Vol 78, No 10, pages 1207–1221.

103. Stephenson, C B (1999), 'Burden of infection on growth failure', *Journal of Nutrition*, Vol 129 (2S Supplement), pages 534S–538S.

104. Satterthwaite, Hart, Levy et al 1996, op cit.

105. Solomon, N W, M Mazariegos, K H Brown and K Klasing (1993), 'The underprivileged developing country child: environmental contamination and growth failure revisited', *Nutrition Reviews*, Vol 51, No 11, pages 327–332.

106. Lechtig, A and B Doyle (1996), 'The impact of water and sanitation on malnutrition and under 5 mortality rates', *Waterfront*, Vol 8, pages 5–19.

107. Wierzba, T, R El-Yazeed, S J Savarino, A S Mourad et al (2001), 'The interrelationship of malnutrition and diarrhea in a periurban area outside Alexandria, Egypt', *Journal of Pediatrics Gastroenterology and Nutrition*, Vol 32, No 2, pages 189–96.

108. Molbak, K, M Andersen et al (1997), 'Cryptosporidium infection in infancy as a cause of malnutrition: a community study from Guinea-Bissau, West Africa', *American Journal of Clinical Nutrition*, Vol 65, No 1, pages 149–52; Moore, S R, A A Lima, M R Conoway, J B Schorling et al (2001), 'Early childhood diarrhoea and helminthiases associated with long-term linear growth faltering', *International Journal of Epidemiology*, Vol 30, No 6, pages 1457–1464.

109. Guerrant, D I, S R Moore, A A Lima, P D Patrick, J B Schorling and R L Guerrant (1999), 'Association of early childhood diarrhea and cryptosporidiosis with impaired physical fitness and cognitive function four–seven years later in a poor urban community in northeast Brazil', *American Journal of Tropical Medicine and Hygiene*, Vol 61, No 5, pages 707–713.

110. Lechtig and Doyle 1996, op cit; Nicol, A

(1998), *Carrying the Can: Children and their Water Environments*, Save the Children-UK, London.

111. Al-Eissa, Y A, S A Assuhaimi, A M A Abdullah, A M Abobakr, M A Al-Husain et al (1995), 'Prevalence of intestinal parasites in Saudi children: a community-based study', *Journal of Tropical Pediatrics*, Vol 41, pages 47–49; Agha, S (2000), 'The determinants of infant mortality in Pakistan', *Social Science and Medicine*, Vol 51, pages 199–208; Woldemicael 2000, op cit.

112. Ray, G, G Nath and D C Reddy (2000), 'Extents of contamination of top milk and their determinants in an urban slum of Varanasi, India', *Indian Journal of Public Health*, Vol 44, No 4, pages 111–117.

113. UNICEF (1998), *The State of the World's Children 1998*, Oxford University Press, New York.

114. VanDerslice, J, B Popkin and J Briscoe (1994), 'Drinking-water quality, sanitation, and breast-feeding: their interactive effects on infant health', *Bulletin of the World Health Organization*, Vol 72, No 4, pages 589–601.

115. Barros, A J, D A Ross, W V Fonseca, L A Williams and D C Moreira-Filho (1999), 'Preventing acute respiratory infections and diarrhoea in child care centres', *Acta Paediatrica*, Vol 88, No 10, pages 1113–1118; Hillis, S D, C M Miranda et al (1992), 'Day care center attendance and diarrheal morbidity in Colombia', *Pediatrics*, Vol 90, No 4, pages 582–588; Sempertegui, F, B Estrella et al (1995), 'Risk of diarrheal disease in Ecuadorian day-care centers', *Pediatric Infectious Disease Journal*, Vol 14, No 7, pages 606–612.

116. In Vietnam schools, the standard for drinking water availability was 1 litre of boiled water for every three students in summer, and for every ten students in winter, and only 10 per cent of schools met this standard. 30 per cent of schools had no latrines, 80 per cent had insufficient latrines, 75 per cent had latrines in bad condition (Laugeri, L (1993), *Hygiene Education And Environmental Sanitation In Schools In Vietnam*, WHO, Hanoi); throughout Latin America, facilities were also found to be lacking or inadequate (Burgers, L, M Simpson-Hebert, L Laugeri and L Clark (1993), *School Sanitation And Hygiene Education in Latin America: Summary Report of a Workshop on Problems and Options for Improvement*, PAHO, WHO and IRC, Cali, Colombia).

117. Guerrant, Moore, Lima et al 1999, op cit; Berkman, D S, A G Lescano, R H Gilman, S L Lopez and M M Black (2002), 'Effects of stunting, diarrhoeal disease, and parasitic

infection during infancy on cognition in late childhood: a follow-up study', *Lancet*, Vol 359 (9306), pages 564–571.

118. Grantham-McGregor, S (1995), 'A review of studies of the effect of severe malnutrition on mental development', *The Journal of Nutrition*, Vol 125, No 8 (Suppl) pages 2233S–2238S; Grantham-McGregor, S M and L C Fernald (1997), 'Nutritional deficiencies and subsequent effects on mental and behavioral development in children', *Southeast Asian Journal of Tropical Medicine and Public Health*, Vol 28 (Suppl 2), pages 50–68; Mendez, M A and L S Adair (1999), 'Severity and timing of stunting in the first two years of life affect performance on cognitive tests in late childhood', *The Journal of Nutrition*, Vol 129, No 88, pages 1555–1562.

119. Brown, J and E Pollitt (1996), 'Malnutrition, poverty and intellectual development', *Scientific American*, Vol 274, No 2, pages 38–43; Mendez and Adair 1999, op cit.

120. Sakti, H, C Nokes, W S Hertanto, S Hendratno et al (1999), 'Evidence for an association between hookworm infection and cognitive function in Indonesian school children', *Tropical Medicine & International Health*, Vol 4, No 5, pages 322–334.

121. Engle, P (1996), 'Combating malnutrition in the developing world' in S C Carr and J F Schumaker (eds), *Psychology and the Developing World*, Praeger, Westport, Connecticut; Gardner, J M, S M Grantham-McGregor, J Himes and S Chang (1999), 'Behaviour and development of stunted and nonstunted Jamaican children', *Journal of Child Psychology and Psychiatry and Allied Disciplines*, Vol 40, No 5, pages 819–827.

122. Fernald, L C and S M Grantham-McGregor (1998), 'Stress response in school-age children who have been growth retarded since early childhood', *American Journal of Clinical Nutrition*, Vol 68, No 3, pages 691–698.

123. For example, Piaget, J (1952), *The Origins Of Intelligence In Children*, International Universities Press, New York; Montessori, M (1965), *Spontaneous Activity In Education*, Schocken, New York; Wohlwill, J and H Heft (1987), 'The physical environment and the development of the child' in D Stokols and I Altman (eds), *Handbook of Environmental Psychology*, Wiley, New York.

124. Nicol 1998, op cit.

125. Doyle, B (1995), 'Increasing education and other opportunities for girls and women with water, sanitation and hygiene', *Waterfront*, UNICEF NY special issue, August.

126. Cairncross, S (1990), 'Water supply and the urban poor' in J Hardoy, S Cairncross and D

Satterthwaite (eds), *The Poor Die Young: Housing and Health in Third World Cities*, Earthscan, London; WHO and UNICEF (2000), *Global Water Supply and Sanitation Assessment 2000 Report*, World Health Organization, Geneva.

127. WHO 2002, op cit.

128. A review of epidemiological studies found that increases in water quantity were associated with a 20 per cent reduction in diarrhoea, while provision of safe water was associated with a 15 per cent reduction – Esrey, S, J Potash et al (1991), 'Effects of improved water supply and sanitation on ascariasis, diarrhoea, dracunculiasis, hookworm infection, schistosomiasis and trachoma', *Bulletin of the World Health Organization*, Vol 69, No 5, pages 609–621. See also Cairncross 1990, op cit.

129. Henry, F J and Z Rahim (1990), 'Transmission of diarrhoea in two crowded areas with different sanitary facilities in Dhaka, Bangladesh', *Journal of Tropical Medicine and Hygiene*, Vol 93, No 2, pages 121–126; Julvez, J, M A Bade et al (1998), 'Intestinal parasitic diseases in an urban environment in Sahel: a study in a district of Niamey, Niger', *Bulletin de la Societe de Pathologie Exotique*, Vol 91, No 5, pages 424–427.

130. WHO/UNICEF 2000, op cit.

131. Godin, L (1987), *Preparation des Projets Urbains d'Amenagement*, World Bank, Washington, DC.

132. Lindskog, P and J Lundqvist (1998), *Why Poor Children Stay Sick: The Human Ecology of Child Health and Welfare in Rural Malawi*, Scandinavian Institute of African Studies, Uppsala.

133. Bukenya, G B and N Nwokolo (1991), 'Compound hygiene, presence of standpipes and the risk of childhood diarrhoea in an urban settlement of Papua New Guinea', *International Journal of Epidemiology*, Vol 20, No 2, pages 534–539.

134. Curtis, V, B Kanki et al (1997), 'Dirt and diarrhoea: formative research in hygiene promotion programmes', *Health Policy and Planning*, Vol 12, No 2, pages 122–131.

135. Victoria et al 1988, op cit.

136. Lindskog and Lundqvist 1998, op cit; Roberts, L, Y Chartier et al (2001), 'Keeping water clean in a Malawi refugee camp: a randomized intervention trial', *Bulletin of the World Health Organization*, Vol 79, No 4, pages 280–7.

137. Teklemariam, S, T Getaneh et al (2000), 'Environmental determinants of diarrheal morbidity in under-five children, Keffa-Sheka zone, south west Ethiopia', *Ethiopian Medical Journal*, Vol 38, No 1, pages 27–34.

138. Dunne, E F, H Angoran-Benie et al (2001), 'Is drinking water in Abidjan, Cote d'Ivoire, safe for infant formula?', *Journal of Acquired Immune Deficiency Syndrome*, Vol 28, No 4, pages 393–398.

139. Mirza, N M, L E Caulfield et al (1997), 'Risk factors for diarrheal duration', *American Journal of Epidemiology*, Vol 146, No 9, pages 776–785.

140. Yeager, B A C, S R A Huttly, R Bartolini, M Rojas, C F Lanata et al (1999), 'Defecation practices of young children in a Peruvian shanty town', *Social Science and Medicine*, Vol 49, No 4, pages 531–554.

141. Roberts, Chartier et al 2001, op cit.

142. Curtis, V, S Cairncross et al (2000), 'Domestic hygiene and diarrhea: pinpointing the problem', *Tropical Medicine & International Health*, Vol 5, No 1, pages 22–32.

143. Grimason, A M, K Davison et al (2000), 'Problems associated with the use of pit latrines in Blantyre, Republic of Malawi', *Journal of the Royal Society of Health*, Vol 120, No 3, pages 175–82.

144. Curtis, V, B Kanki et al (1995), 'Potties, pits and pipes: explaining hygiene behaviour in Burkina Faso', *Social Science and Medicine*, Vol 41, No 3, pages 383–393; Lindskog and Lundqvist 1998, op cit; National Shack Dwellers Federation, Mahila Milan, SPARC (1997), *Toilet Talk*, No 1, SPARC, Bombay, December; *Urban Basic Services, A Community Profile*, prepared for Biratnagar Municipality, Ministry of Local Development, HMG/Nepal and UNICEF, Biratnagar, Nepal.

145. UNICEF (2000), *Multiple Indicator Survey*, UNICEF, Delhi.

146. Vasquez, M L, M Mosquera et al (1999), 'Incidence and risk factors for diarrhoea and acute respiratory infections in urban communities of Pernambuco, Brazil', *Cad Saude Publica*, Vol 15, No 1, pages 163–171.

147. Agha, S (2000), 'The determinants of infant mortality in Pakistan', *Social Science and Medicine*, Vol 51, pages 199–208.

148. Mertens, T E, S Jaffar et al (1992), 'Excreta disposal behaviour and latrine ownership in relation to the risk of childhood diarrhoea in Sri Lanka', *International Journal of Epidemiology*, Vol 21, No 6, pages 1157–1164; Baltazar, J C and F S Solon (1989), 'Disposal of faeces of children under two years old and diarrhoea incidence: a case-control study', *International Journal of Epidemiology*, Vol 18, No 4, pages S16–S19.

149. Mahfouz, el-Morshedy et al 1997, op cit; Ludwig, Frei et al 1999, op cit.

150. Esrey, S A (1996), 'Water, waste, and well-being: a multicountry study', *American Journal*

of Epidemiology, Vol 143, No 6, pages 608–623.

151. Feacham, R, M Guy et al (1983), 'Excreta disposal facilities and intestinal parasitism in urban Africa: preliminary studies in Botswana, Ghana and Zambia', Transactions of the Royal Society of Tropical Medicine and Hygiene, Vol 77, No 4, pages 515–521.

152. Root, G P (2001), 'Sanitation, community environments, and childhood diarrhoea in rural Zimbabwe', Journal of Health, Population and Nutrition, Vol 19, No 2, pages 73–82.

153. Satterthwaite et al 1996, op cit.

154. Prost, A and A D Négrel (1989), 'Water, trachoma and conjunctivitis', Bulletin of the World Health Organization, Vol 67, No 1, pages 9–18.

155. See for instance Curtis, Cairncross and Yonli 2000, op cit; Vaz, L and P Jha (2001), 'Note on the health impact of water and sanitation services', CMH Working Paper Series, No WG5, Commission on Macroeconomics and Health, Geneva; Victoria et al 1988, op cit.

156. Gilman, R H, G S Marquis, G Ventura, M Campos et al (1993), 'Water cost and availability: key determinants of family hygiene in a Peruvian shantytown', American Journal of Public Health, Vol 83, No 11, pages 1554–1558.

157. Curtis, Kanki, Mertens et al 1995, op cit.

158. Mertens, T E, S Jaffar, M A Fernando, S N Cousens and R G Feacham (1992), 'Excreta disposal behaviour and latrine ownership in relation to the risk of childhood diarrhoea in Sri Lanka', International Journal of Epidemiology, Vol 21, No 6, pages 1157–1164.

159. Qureshi, A F and M A Lobo (1994), 'Socio-anthropological determinants and home management in childhood diarrhoea in a squatter settlement of Karachi, Pakistan', Journal of Tropical Pediatrics, Vol 40, December, pages 378–380.

160. Curtis, Kanki, Cousens et al 1997, op cit.

161. Lindskog and Lundqvist 1998, op cit.

162. Mclennan, J D (2000), 'To boil or not: drinking water for children in a periurban barrio', Social Science and Medicine, Vol 51, No 8, pages 1211–1220.

163. WHO and UNICEF 2000, op cit.

164. This section draws on Hardoy, Jorge E, Diana Mitlin and David Satterthwaite (2001), Environmental Problems in an Urbanizing World: Finding Solutions for Cities in Africa, Asia and Latin America, Earthscan Publications, London, 470 pages.

165. Tony McMichael at the London School of Hygiene and Tropical Medicine helped develop this distinction.

166. This list draws from Chambers, Robert (1989), 'Editorial introduction: vulnerability, coping and policy', in Vulnerability: How the Poor Cope, IDS Bulletin, Vol 20, No 2, April, pages 1–7; Corbett, Jane (1989), 'Poverty and sickness: the high costs of ill-health', in Vulnerability: How the Poor Cope, IDS Bulletin, Vol 20, No 2, April, pages 58–62; and Pryer 1989, op cit. The literature on rural poverty was the first to develop a detailed under-standing of what underpins vulnerability for poorer groups, but this encouraged urban researchers to also develop vulnerability frameworks – see for instance Moser, Caroline O N (1996), 'Confronting crisis: a summary of household responses to poverty and vulnera-bility in four poor urban communities', Environmentally Sustainable Development Studies and Monographs Series, No 7, The World Bank, Washington, DC, 19 pages; and Moser, Caroline O N (1998), 'The asset vulnerability framework: reassessing urban poverty reduction strategies', World Development, Vol 26, pages 1–19.

167. It is useful to distinguish between children who work in the street but live in a stable home, usually with their parents, and children who live and work on the streets. UNICEF has suggested three categories. The first is 'children on the street', which is much the largest category of 'street children'; these are children who work on the streets but have strong family connections, may attend school and, in most cases, return home at the end of the day. The second category is 'children of the street'; these see the street as their home and seek shelter, food and a sense of commu-nity among their companions there. But ties to their families exist, even if they are remote and they only visit their families infrequently. The third category is 'abandoned children'; these are difficult to distinguish from children of the street since they undertake similar activities and live in similar ways. However, these children have no ties with their families and are entirely on their own.

168. Patel, Sheela (1990), 'Street children, hotels boys and children of pavement dwellers and construction workers in Bombay: how they meet their daily needs', Environment and Urbanization, Vol 2, No 2, October, pages 9–26.

169. World Bank (1990), World Development Report 1990; Poverty, Oxford University Press, Oxford.

170. Germain, Adrienne, Sia Nowrojee and Hnin Hnin Pyne (1994), 'Setting a new agenda: sexual and reproductive health and rights', Environment and Urbanization, Vol 6, No 2, October, pages 133–154.

171. See for instance Beall, Jo and Caren Levy (1994), 'Moving towards the gendered city', overview paper prepared for the Preparatory Committee for Habitat II, Geneva; Lee-Smith, Diana and Catalina Hinchey Trujillo (1992), 'The struggle to legitimize subsistence: women and sustainable development', *Environment and Urbanization*, Vol 4, No 1, April, pages 77–84. See also Songsore, Jacob and Gordon McGranahan (1998), 'The political economy of household environmental management: gender, environment and epidemiology in the Greater Accra Metropolitan Area', *World Development*, Vol 26, No 3, pages 395–412 for a detailed analysis of this for Accra.

172. Songsore and McGranahan 1998, op cit, page 409.

173. Etherington, Wicken and Bajracharya 2002, op cit, page 24.

174. Richmond, Pattie (1997), 'From tenants to owners: experiences with a revolving fund for social housing', *Environment and Urbanization*, Vol 9, No 2, October, pages 119–139.

175. Hanchett, Suzanne, Mohidul Hoque Khan and Shireen Akhter (2001), *WaterAid Bangladesh Urban Programme Evaluation*, Planning Alternatives for Change and Pathway Ltd, Dhaka, page 47. A condensed version of this report will be published in the October 2003 issue of *Environment and Urbanization*.

176. Musyimi, Jennifer (2002), 'When nature calls: the sanitation case at Mukuru Vijijini', *Newsletter of the Nairobi Informal Settlements Coordination Committee*, page 10.

177. WHO 1992, op cit.

178. Etemadi, Felisa U (2000), 'Civil society participation in city governance in Cebu City', *Environment and Urbanization*, Vol 12, No 1, pages 57–72.

Explaining Deficiencies in Urban Water and Sanitation Provision

 Introduction

Many factors contribute to the inadequacies in water and sanitation provision that are described in Chapter 1, and to the very serious implications that these have for health and well-being described in Chapter 2. These factors act at every level from the most local to the international. Figure 3.1 illustrates this by highlighting some of the factors that can contribute to contaminated water causing high levels of diarrhoeal disease in a squatter settlement, from the most immediate or 'proximate' cause (such as the inhabitants' use of drinking water that is contaminated with human faeces) through various contributory causes (poor quality water and sanitation provision, in part because of the settlement's illegal status) and underlying causes (weak and ineffective local government, lack of investment by national government and low priorities given to water and sanitation by many international agencies).

If the goal is to reduce the health burden from people's infection through contaminated water, with so many contributing factors it is difficult to know where limited resources should be focused. There has been a tendency among many governments and international agencies to focus on relieving the symptoms – for instance, on ensuring the availability of oral rehydration salts for the rapid treatment of diarrhoeal diseases – rather than addressing the causes. There are good reasons for doing so and the wider availability of oral rehydration salts and the knowledge of how to use them has contributed to a substantial reduction in the deaths and disease burdens caused

by diarrhoeal diseases (and at low unit costs). Indeed, there are various examples of cities where good quality community-level health care services have contributed much to reducing infant and child mortality, and rapid treatment for water-borne diseases has played a key role.[1] But rapid and effective health care when someone falls sick (or is injured) does not address the causes of the illnesses or injuries. Rapid treatment may save the lives of many infants and children, but without addressing the causes the very high risk of infection remains unchanged. Curative responses, effective as they are, do not prevent re-infection. Nor do they eliminate days lost to illness. As far as children are concerned, curative responses do not address the accompanying setbacks to their overall health and development.

Focusing on medical solutions to water- and sanitation-related health problems also ignores the many non-health implications of poor provision that were described in Chapter 2 – the time burdens and physical efforts for those who collect water, the high prices paid to vendors or to those managing taps (which for most low-income households come out of funds that would otherwise have been spent on food), the constraints on play for children in contaminated environments, and so on. Finally, while oral rehydration salts can be given at home, many health care responses to water-related diseases require the intervention of trained medical personnel and the supply of medicines, and present a continual burden on already over-taxed health services. In many

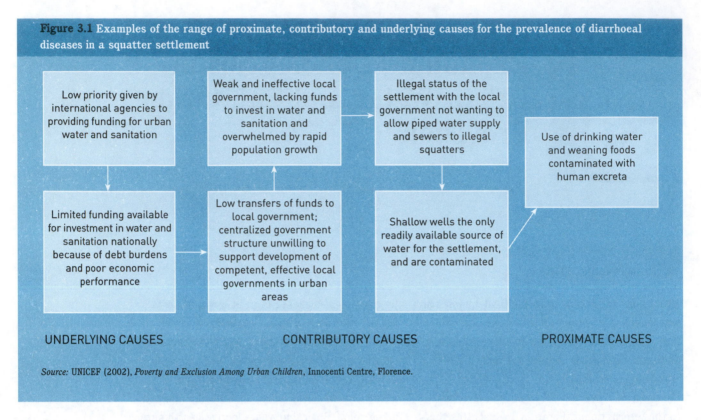

Figure 3.1 Examples of the range of proximate, contributory and underlying causes for the prevalence of diarrhoeal diseases in a squatter settlement

Low priority given by international agencies to providing funding for urban water and sanitation

Weak and ineffective local government, lacking funds to invest in water and sanitation and overwhelmed by rapid population growth

Illegal status of the settlement with the local government not wanting to allow piped water supply and sewers to illegal squatters

Use of drinking water and weaning foods contaminated with human excreta

Limited funding available for investment in water and sanitation nationally because of debt burdens and poor economic performance

Low transfers of funds to local government; centralized government structure unwilling to support development of competent, effective local governments in urban areas

Shallow wells the only readily available source of water for the settlement, and are contaminated

UNDERLYING CAUSES   CONTRIBUTORY CAUSES   PROXIMATE CAUSES

Source: UNICEF (2002), *Poverty and Exclusion Among Urban Children*, Innocenti Centre, Florence.

locations, the need for health care services exceeds the capacity to deliver – which usually results in long queues for those seeking treatment (and many people being discouraged from seeking treatment) and inadequate supplies of medicines. Adequate water and sanitation provision, by preventing a significant proportion of the disease burden in low-income settlements, would increase the capacity of health services to manage other pressing health problems.

One reason why most national governments and international agencies have focused on addressing symptoms rather than causes is that this is much simpler (and may appear cheaper). For large cities, it is often very expensive to install good quality systems for water and sanitation because there is so little existing infrastructure, or the infrastructure that exists is in need of replacement or substantial upgrading; the costs per person served may not be high, but when water and sanitation systems have to be installed to serve several hundred thousand (or several million) people, the total costs are high. In many urban contexts, the disadvantage of high costs is countered by a high willingness to pay among unserved or poorly served populations, so the issue is not so much the high cost but the financial system that supports the invest-

ment and the institutional structure needed to collect user charges to allow the investment capital to be repaid. Very often, these institutional structures and financial systems are lacking.

Even where the focus is on improving provision for low-income households, cost-recovery may be possible. As Chapters 6 and 7 will describe, there are many examples of projects or programmes that greatly improved water and sanitation provision for low-income households where costs were fully recovered. They show that in many circumstances, the cost of improved provision is not the problem. But the constraint is the existence of a local organization (whether public, private commercial, private non-profit, NGO or CBO based) that can develop the solutions that are most appropriate to that locality and its inhabitants, build efficiently (so unit costs are kept down and the gap between cost and capacity to pay is minimized), and set up and manage a cost-recovery system so that users can and will pay. This is the crux of the problem in most cities. It is also not helped by private sector provision, where the expansion of coverage is influenced by whether a rapid return on any investments can be made rather than a longer-term view which accepts that the costs of extending provision can be funded by user

Table 3.1 The range of causes contributing to inadequate water and sanitation in urban areas

Underlying causes acting at the regional, national and international level	Contributory causes acting at the city or municipal level	Proximate causes acting at the household and neighbourhood level
National governments not providing support (political choice, debt burden, etc)	Water shortages	Limited household capacity to pay
	Rapid population growth overwhelming agencies or utilities responsible for provision	Illegal status of many settlements
International agencies not providing support	Ineffective local institutions (including city and municipal government)	Constraints on 'do-it-yourself' provision for households or communities (including absence of water locally)
	Refusal of water and sanitation agencies to work in informal settlements	

charges but with a longer time horizon and less orientation to profit.

Addressing the lack of any local organization able to do this is often politically controversial, especially if it requires changes in the distribution of power, authority and resources between different levels of government and changes in the quality of local government's 'governance' in terms of its responsiveness, accountability, transparency and engagement with civil society. It can be particularly difficult, or impossible, if the background conditions are unfavourable – for instance, economic recession (depleting both the capacity to invest by providers and the capacity to pay by users), impossible debt burdens (depleting investment capacity) or political conflict or war (making better local governance impossible).

Many other explanations are put forward for the inadequacies in water and sanitation provision in cities. One of the most common is that there are shortages of fresh water which constrain improved provision, in part because cities have polluted or over-used local resources. But as this chapter will outline and Chapter 4 will develop in more detail, this is not a good general explanation because water and sanitation provision is very inadequate in many cities with plenty of fresh water – including some of the world's largest cities. There also appears to be no association between areas facing water stress and the proportion of people with inadequate water

and sanitation provision in urban areas (see Chapter 4).

Another common explanation for the inadequacies in water and sanitation provision is cities' very rapid population growth, which overwhelms any local capacity to improve and extend provision. This is certainly a valid reason in many places but it is a poor general explanation, because water and sanitation provision is very good in many cities that have grown very rapidly and very inadequate in many cities and smaller urban centres which have grown very slowly, or have stopped growing, or even have declining populations. As a later section in this chapter describes, a city's rapid growth usually reflects its growing prosperity; many rapidly growing cities have managed to develop the institutions to improve water and sanitation provision, in part because it is easier to do so with an expanding economy, in part because maintaining their economic success depended on them doing so. Chapter 1 also described how water and sanitation provision is often very poor in smaller urban centres, including those that are not growing rapidly.

Table 3.1 lists the range of causes that will be the focus of the rest of this chapter: the proximate causes that act in the settlement itself at household or neighbourhood level, the contributory causes that act at the city or municipal level, and the underlying causes acting at the regional, national and international level.

Proximate causes

This section will focus on the causes of inadequate provision at community and household level, and examine how poverty, the pressure to settle in water- and/or sanitation-deficient areas, rapid population growth and unresponsive utilities combine to create water and sanitation deficiencies.

Illegal status of many settlements

It is common in cities in Africa, Asia and Latin America for between a quarter and a half of the population to live in informal or illegal settlements, meaning that some aspect of the occupation of the land or its development for housing is illegal.[2] This has considerable importance for water and sanitation provision since public or official private water and sanitation providers may be forbidden by law from operating in such settlements. Alternatively, the preconditions necessary for them to operate there may not be present (for instance, house plots may not have formal addresses, inhabitants may lack legal documents that allow them to become registered, or householders may lack documents that show where plot boundaries are and who owns each plot).

For instance, in Jamaica, informal neighbourhoods with insecure tenure suffer from particularly bad supplies because the National Water Commission of Jamaica requires proof of landownership before installing a connection. The law is being changed so that those squatting on public land can receive water; for households squatting on private land it will be sufficient to have verbal permission from the private landowner.[3] In many cities in India, a large proportion of the poor live in slums on private lands or as tenants in areas that have not been officially recognized as slums, and they cannot get an individual connection because the water and sanitation authority provides individual connections only where households can provide proof of ownership of property and a recent receipt for payment of property tax.[4] In Central America, contractual rights can be transferred between properties but not between persons, so public utility companies do not want to extend service contracts to squatters for fear that they will face legal action from the owner.[5] In Cordoba (Argentina) the lack of land title is a major reason for non-connection; 5 per cent of the 14 per cent of households that are not connected to the main network in that city are occupying private and state land without titles.[6] Government officials working for the Dhaka Water Supply and Sewerage Authority are also reluctant 'to legitimize slums by providing them with public facilities (water points)', although after long negotiations there has been some willingness to achieve a compromise.[7]

The absence of land titling is also a problem in those cases where private sector involvement has been sought as the best means to extend supply.[8] The lack of a legal title may mean that there is no legal requirement for the concessionaire to extend the service to these families. For instance, in Cartagena (Colombia), while the World Bank suggested that one-third of residents did not have running water and sanitation in 1999, the concessionaire argued that over 90 per cent of residents were served by the water network as it excluded squatters from its calculations.[9] In Greater Buenos Aires, a study showed how the majority of requests for sanitation services from those living in informal settlements had been refused by the private utility, primarily due to the lack of land tenure, but also because of:

- the distance between informal settlements and existing sewer networks;
- the irregular urban layout that characterizes many of the settlements;
- the cost of construction in zones below the water table restriction (many low-income settlements in Buenos Aires are on low-lying land, at risk of flooding); and
- the utility's lack of confidence that costs would be recovered and regular payments for services made by inhabitants.[10]

However, there are many degrees of illegality, and water and sanitation agencies may have no difficulties in working in many illegal settlements. For instance, they may routinely support water and sanitation provision in 'illegal sub-divisions', where the land is not occupied illegally but no official permission was obtained to develop the land for housing. In some cities, most of the informal settlements consist of homes developed on illegal sub-divisions. The homes never received official approval, but the occupation of the land is legal, so water and sanitation companies have fewer worries about investing in them, especially when many middle- and upper-income groups live in illegal sub-divisions. Companies may routinely provide services if those living in an illegal settlement have reached an agreement with the authorities or with the water and sanitation agency. In many cities, illegal settlements develop with the tolerance, approval or even support of local governments, and here again the risks of eviction are reduced. In some cities, there is a long tradition of illegal land occupation and development and an accepted (if often long and inefficient) process by which the inhabitants lobby for basic infrastructure, as described in the section on Latin America in Chapter 1. So although it is clear that the illegal or informal nature of many settlements in cities does inhibit improved water and sanitation provision by the official (public or private) providers, the extent to which it does so varies greatly between cities and between settlements within cities. In addition, small-scale providers may be less reluctant to invest in informal settlements, and people who develop their own homes in illegal settlements may also invest in better provision if they are confident that they will not be evicted.

One important constraint on improving provision in many illegal settlements is the complexity of moving from illegal to legal status, and the many public agencies whose agreement is needed to do so. This was highlighted in a study in Buenos Aires.[11] Here, there is a legal basis for providing legal tenure to illegal settlements but the process is complicated, expensive and needs many different agencies to agree to it. For the inhabitants of

an illegal settlement, it requires a long process of negotiation, journeys to the office where the registry is located, familiarity with provincial government processes and knowledge of how to complete the process. For local governments, it requires professional support (for instance lawyers and surveyors) which they often lack. There are often complicated or conflictual relations between politicians and civil servants. If the illegal settlement arose from the illegal occupation of private land, this adds a further complication because the transfer of the land from the private owner needs to be negotiated and compensation agreed (which is often expensive) or the process of expropriation gone through. Part of the problem is that official standards for sub-divisions for housing are too high: if smaller lot sizes were permitted, it would allow more legal sub-divisions; if smaller frontages were permitted, it would reduce unit costs for infrastructure. The study in Buenos Aires also highlights the fact that the private utilities were not prevented from extending provision to illegal settlements in most instances and it was more these utilities' unwillingness to do so that explained the lack of provision – because the possibilities of profit were less certain.

Community capacity to develop autonomous solutions

Later chapters include many case studies of remarkable community action that has improved water and sanitation provision in low-income areas. But it should be recognized that there are many constraints on this. It is no easy task to get agreement from all those in large settlements with diverse populations to cooperate in planning, installing, funding and managing a piped water supply, sewers and drains. There may be no readily available local water source to tap, so negotiations are needed to get access to other sources – for instance, to water mains. It also requires considerable technical expertise to design and install systems that will work properly and will not need constant maintenance. It is also more difficult to install water and sanitation systems in settlements that lack clearly demarcated plots, regular plot layouts, and access roads and paths to each house; it is tricky to make drainage and sewage networks operate in settlements lacking regular solid waste collection services and having high silt-loads in surface run-off. And if the settlement is at risk of eviction – which is often the case – no household will want to invest its limited resources in a water and sanitation system when the members might be evicted at any time.

There are also the difficulties posed by the differing interests of tenants and owners in many settlements, especially if many of the landowners do not live in the settlement. Chapter 2 noted the difficulties that tenants often face in informal settlements or tenements in getting access to water and sanitation, even if piped water is available. Tenants face particular problems, especially if (as is frequently the case) landlords are reluctant to allow them to organize. In many cities too, the political system hardly encourages local organizations to develop.

Finally, there are the difficulties that international agencies face in supporting community-based systems. All the official aid agencies and development banks have, by their very structure, to work with and through national governments. No national government is going to view with any favour an international agency steering funds direct to CBOs. There are instances where official agencies have steered support direct to community-directed schemes for water and sanitation with considerable success, and various international NGOs have also supported community-based provision, as Chapter 6 will describe. But these are the exceptions, and current international funding systems do not lend themselves to a large expansion of this. There are also grounds for questioning whether focusing on supporting improved community provision does not simply avoid the more fundamental problem that needs addressing – the weakness of official water and sanitation providers – although as Chapters 6 and 7 will describe, effective community provision has often helped change the approach of municipal authorities, and on occasion has been the result of municipal authorities' own support.

Household capacity to pay

There is an obvious justification for seeking cost-recovery when improving water and sanitation provision, because if improved provision can pay for itself this means that the quality of provision can be maintained and there are no constraints on expanding provision. Achieving cost-recovery is particularly important for CBO- or NGO-based provision, because getting a constant subsidy from an external source is difficult or impossible. There are also many case studies showing how provision has been improved and costs recovered, as described in Chapters 6 and 7. But the difficulty in getting full cost-recovery in very low-income settlements should not be underestimated. It is common for large sections of the population of cities in Africa, Asia and Latin America to have incomes that are so low that they cannot afford sufficient food. One of the key reasons why so many people live in informal settlements is because they cannot afford to spend much (if anything) on housing. The main reason why so many low-income households use poor quality water sources is – again – that these are much cheaper or free. It is worth recalling various examples from Chapter 2: the women in Pune who had to use a canal to do their laundry to save money; the households that refrained from using pay toilets and defecated in the open to save money. External specialists may consider it reasonable to expect low-income households to spend 5 per cent of their income on water and sanitation, but for many low-income groups this is a heavy financial burden. Box 3.1 describes the difficulties of reaching the poor in Bangladesh's two largest cities, Dhaka and Chittagong. A total of 1130 households were interviewed in 146 low-income areas, including a mix of 'beneficiary' households (those within the project areas) and non-beneficiary households. Here, even with improved provision through water points provided by non-profit institutions, it was still difficult to reach the very poor within programmes that achieve cost-recovery. The survey found that a third of households had monthly incomes of less than US$50, while the poorest had monthly incomes below US$10.

Box 3.1 Reaching the poor in urban areas of Bangladesh

The WaterAid Bangladesh Urban Project was initiated in 1996 with a pilot project in collaboration with one local NGO, Dushtha Shasthya Kendra. The programme has since expanded to include activities with six additional NGO partners working in 168 low-income settlements. The services provided are hygiene education and the construction of water and sanitation facilities (water points connected to the city supply network, tubewells, household latrines, sanitation blocks for small groups of households and community latrines).

Of the 168 settlements in which the project is active, 160 are in Dhaka and eight are in Chittagong. These settlements are home to an estimated 92,000 households. The programme has sought to improve water and sanitation provision with cost-recovery, as the only way in which the interventions can reach large numbers of households. But this is a challenge, given the very low incomes of many households. A third of house-holds in the slums have monthly incomes of less than US$50; some have monthly incomes of less than US$10. The emphasis placed on cost-recovery within the programme has tended to encourage NGOs to imple-ment the programme in the more stable settlements, in which at least a proportion of the population can afford to pay for services.

An assessment of the programme surveyed 1130 households: roughly half were programme beneficiaries and half non-beneficiaries. More than 98 per cent of the beneficiaries have access to water in their settlements compared to 77 per cent in non-beneficiary areas. In regard to

addressing the needs of the poorest, the frequency of payment differs. Some projects are based on charges collected each month while others charge per pot of water. It is evident that some people do not earn suffi-cient income to take part; one NGO staff member suggested that this percentage was as high as 40 per cent in some of the areas in which they worked.

Generally it is felt that some water should be offered to the very poor on a charitable basis, but access may be restricted in some cases and the quantity made available is likely to be small. Some of those unable to afford water can be employed as caretakers for the project. Public water hydrants providing free water are an alternative source but there are often long queues for these, and access is often difficult as they are placed on the edges of slum areas.

Paying for water by the pot as it is collected is likely to be more expen-sive than a single monthly payment. On current rates it is estimated that roughly US$2 will be required for a family of four using the minimum amount of safe water for drinking, cooking, bathing and laundry. About 20 per cent of this charge is the cost of the water, which has to be paid to the Dhaka Water and Sanitation Agency. This charge is about 8 per cent of the poorest families' monthly budget and can only be afforded by reducing essential food consumption.

Community latrines, toilet blocks and individual latrines have improved provision in the low-income settle-ments. However, 'the great majority of slum dwellers continue to practise open defecation near water bodies or

to use semi-enclosed "hang latrines" that drain into ditches or water bodies…' The survey found that among beneficiary households, 24 per cent used hang latrines, 8 per cent used slabs over water, 3 per cent used slabs over drains and 0.4 per cent used open spaces. In non-beneficiary households, 39 per cent used hang latrines, 4 per cent used slabs over water, 4 per cent used slabs over drains and 2 per cent used open spaces. A latrine for each household is considered to be the best solution but there are many areas in which there is simply insufficient space, or where households cannot afford it. Households pay the full cost of such latrines, generally over a two-year period.

The community management committees function alongside local 'muscle men', who are widely used by government agencies and NGO projects to support water and sanita-tion projects. A difficult issue is how to manage these individuals. They may seek to prevent improvements or influence the operation. The agencies that WaterAid supports to implement this programme all seek to establish or strengthen local committees. All the agencies recognize that commit-tees play a vital role but acknowledge that it is hard to ensure that they work effectively. Generally, the poorest are not involved in committees and hence their perspectives and interests may be under-represented in decision-making.

Source: Hanchett, Suzanne, Shireen Akhter and Mohidul Hoque Khan (2003), 'Water, sanitation and hygiene in Bangladesh slums; a summary of WaterAid's Bangladesh Urban Programme Evaluation', *Environment and Urbanization*, Vol 15, No 2.

 ## Contributory causes

This section will focus on what contributes to inadequate water and sanitation provision at the level of the town or city.

The weakness/incapacity of local utilities

One important change in the perception of the problem of water and sanitation provision in urban areas over the last ten years has been the increased recognition of the poor performance of companies or utilities with responsibility for water (and usually sanitation). This is best illustrated by the two *Water Utilities Data Books* produced by the Asian Development Bank for the Asian and Pacific Region – the first in 1993, the second in 1997.[12] The second of these reviewed the performance of 50 water utilities in 31 nations (the section on Asia in Chapter 1 drew much on this review). It highlighted not only the inadequacies in the performance of many utilities (including low proportions of city populations served and intermittent services), but also inadequacies in management (poor billing arrangements, water prices well below the costs of provision, over-staffed utilities and high proportions of unaccounted-for water). There were cities where utility performance was good and where the consumer survey showed high consumer satisfaction, but these were the exceptions rather than the rule.[13]

In regard to finance for capital investment, many utilities were dependent on grant financing, including ten that were 100 per cent dependent on grant financing. However, utilities in nine of the cities reviewed had resorted to commercial financing, with four (Chonburi, Chiangmai, Tianjin and Manila) using local authority bonds.

This review also highlighted the difficulty of balancing the need to keep down prices while ensuring sufficient revenues to allow good quality provision and coverage. However, it also stressed that good management limits this trade-off; many of the utilities with the highest water prices were also those with poor quality management (including high ratios of staff to the number of connections and high levels of unaccounted-for water). The WHO/UNICEF Assessment 2000 identified inadequate cost-recovery and inadequate operation and maintenance as two of the principal constraints on the development of water supply and sanitation – and both are largely the result of the weakness or incapacity of water and sanitation agencies.[14]

Rapid population growth

It might be expected that water and sanitation provision in urban areas is worst in nations that have experienced the most rapid increases in their urban population as a proportion of their total population (ie, urbanization levels), but this is not so. Indeed, some of the regions with the largest increases in urbanization levels have achieved much better levels of provision than some regions with smaller increases. It might be expected that water and sanitation provision is particularly bad in very rapidly growing cities, but this is only partly so. Many of the world's most rapidly growing cities over the last 50 years have very good water and sanitation provision, and many much slower growing cities or smaller urban centres have very poor provision. It might be expected that it is the very large cities that face insurmountable problems in acquiring fresh water. Many of the world's largest cities today are 50–200 times larger than they were 100 years ago – and since per capita water use has also gone up dramatically, this can mean total fresh water use of 200–1000 times more than 100 years ago. While many of the world's largest cities face serious problems with obtaining sufficient fresh water, this is often more due to poor water management. What is more surprising is the number of large cities that do not face serious water shortages. The question is thus: Why, when cities have grown so much, have they not run out of water?

This section reviews the scale of urban change world-wide over the last 50 years and considers where rapid urban growth is an important factor in explaining inadequate water and sanitation provision.

The expansion of urban and city populations[15]

Between 1950 and 2000, the world's urban population increased more than fourfold and now, close to 50 per cent of the world's population live in urban centres. Many aspects of urban change in the last 50 years are unprecedented, including not only the level of urbanization and the size of the world's urban population but also the number of countries becoming more urbanized and the size and number of very large cities.[16]

Just two centuries ago there were only two 'million-cities' world-wide (ie, cities with 1 million or more inhabitants): London and Beijing (then called Peking). By 1950, there were 85; by 2000, 388 (see Table 3.2). A large (and increasing) proportion of these million-cities are in Africa, Asia and Latin America. Some have populations that grew more than twentyfold between 1950 and 2000, including Abidjan, Dar es Salaam, Dhaka, Kampala, Kinshasa, Nairobi, Lagos, Lusaka, Riyadh, Tijuana, Ulsan and Yaounde. Many others grew more than tenfold, including Amman, Bhopal, Campinas, Curitiba, Douala, Faisalabad, Harare, Khartoum, Khulna, Luanda, Maputo, Santa Cruz, Surat and many Chinese cities. Brasilia, the federal capital of Brazil, did not exist in 1950 and now has more than 2 million inhabitants. However, very rapid city growth is not only a feature of low- and middle-income nations. Several cities in the USA had spectacular growth rates: the populations of Las Vegas and Fort Lauderdale have grown more than twentyfold in the last 50 years, and those of Orlando, West Palm Beach, Phoenix and Riverside-San Bernardino have grown more than tenfold.

What is even more spectacular is the multiplication in size since 1900. Many of today's large cities were so small in 1900 that their population has multiplied by between one-hundredfold and three-hundredfold. In some cases, no such calculation is possible because the cities did not exist in 1900. If we take only urban centres that already had 10,000 or more inhabitants in 1900, many of their populations have multiplied more than one-hundredfold during the 20th century, including Belo Horizonte (now with more than 300 times its 1900 population), Pusan, Lagos, San Diego, Casablanca, Chittagong, Riyadh, Dhaka, Luanda, Los Angeles, Tampa-St Petersburg, Bandung, Dar es Salaam and Dakar. There are very large variations in the quality and extent of water and sanitation provision among the cities on this list; some have very high levels of provision – not only those in high-income nations (the USA and Saudi Arabia) but also Belo Horizonte and, in comparison to most cities in its region, Dakar. Cities such as Porto Alegre and São Paulo (Brazil) and Seoul (South Korea) and, within high-income nations, Houston, San José,

Dallas-Forth Worth and Vancouver are among those whose populations increased by between fiftyfold and one-hundredfold, and all (or close to all) their inhabitants have piped water supplies. This is not to say that very rapid growth does not pose problems for the public or private companies responsible for water and sanitation, but often they have not proved insuperable.

Large cities never figure in the list of cities with the most rapid growth rates, although they obviously did when they were smaller. The larger a city's population at the beginning of any period for which growth rates are being calculated, the larger the denominator used to divide the increment in the city's population to calculate the growth rate. In any nation undergoing rapid urbanization, an analysis of inter-census population growth rates for all urban centres usually highlights some small urban centres with population growth rates of between 7 and 15 per cent a year. It is very rare for any city with a million or more inhabitants to achieve population growth rates of 7 per cent a year; within the UN's dataset of city populations, all the cities that had a million or more inhabitants in 1990 had population growth rates of less than 7 per cent a year during the 1990s, and most had annual average growth rates of less than 3 per cent a year, while some had shrinking populations (showing up as negative growth rates).

However, for water and sanitation utilities, the absolute number of people added to a city's population each year is probably a more relevant indicator of growth. Using this indicator, many of the largest cities figure prominently. Dhaka, Delhi and Mumbai grew by more than 300,000 persons a year during the 1990s. Even Mexico City and São Paulo – both with low population growth rates (below 2 per cent a year) and more people moving out than in during the 1990s – had very large annual average increments to their populations during the 1990s (around 250,000 persons a year). (Again, just to avoid an assumption that this is a phenomenon only in low- and middle-income nations, metropolitan Los Angeles grew by around 200,000 inhabitants a year during the 1990s.)

Table 3.2 The distribution of the world's urban population by region, 1950–2010

Region	1950	1970	1990	2000	Projection for 2010
Urban population (millions of inhabitants)					
World	751	1357	2286	2862	3514
Africa	32	82	197	295	426
Asia	244	501	1023	1376	1784
Europe	287	424	521	534	536
Latin America and the Caribbean	70	164	313	391	470
Northern America	110	171	213	243	273
Oceania	8	14	19	23	26
Percentage of population living in urban areas					
World	29.8	36.8	43.5	47.2	51.5
Africa	14.7	23.1	31.8	37.2	42.7
Asia	17.4	23.4	32.2	37.5	43.0
Europe	52.4	64.6	72.1	73.4	75.1
Latin America and the Caribbean	41.9	57.6	71.1	75.4	79.0
Northern America	63.9	73.8	75.4	77.4	79.8
Oceania	61.6	71.2	70.8	74.1	75.7
Percentage of the world's urban population living in:					
World	100	100	100	100	100
Africa	4.3	6.1	8.6	10.3	12.1
Asia	32.5	37.0	44.8	48.1	50.8
Europe	38.3	31.3	22.8	18.7	15.3
Latin America and the Caribbean	9.3	12.1	13.7	13.7	13.4
Northern America	14.6	12.6	9.3	8.5	7.8
Oceania	1.0	1.0	0.8	0.8	0.8

Note: Many of the figures for 2000 draw on national censuses held in 1999, 2000 or 2001, but some are based on estimates or projections from statistics drawn from censuses held around 1990. There is also a group of countries (mostly in Africa) for which there are no census data since the 1970s or early 1980s so all figures for their urban (and rural) populations are based on estimates and projections.
Source: Statistics drawn or derived from United Nations (2002), *World Urbanization Prospects; The 2001 Revision; Data Tables and Highlights*, Population Division, Department of Economic and Social Affairs, United Nations Secretariat, ESA/P/WP/173, United Nations, New York, 181 pages.

The average size of the world's largest cities has also increased dramatically. In 2000, the average size of the world's 100 largest cities was around 6.2 million inhabitants. This compares to 2.1 million inhabitants in 1950, around 725,000 in 1900 and just under 200,000 in 1800.[17] While there are various examples of cities over the last two millennia that had populations of 1 million or more inhabitants, the city or metropolitan area with several million inhabitants is a relatively new phenomenon: London was the first to reach this size in the second half of the 19th century.[18] By 2000, there were 39 cities with more than 5 million inhabitants. However, a review of the quality and extent of water and sanitation provision in the world's largest cities also shows no obvious tendency for these

to be particularly poor. Indeed, as described in Chapter 1, most of the world's largest cities have relatively good provision in comparison to other cities and smaller urban centres in the same country.

Patterns of growth and change in the distribution of the world's urban population

Most of the world's urban population is now outside Europe and North America (Table 3.2). Asia alone contains close to half the world's urban population, even if more than three-fifths of its people still live in rural areas. Africa, which is generally perceived as overwhelmingly rural, now has a larger urban population than North America or Western Europe. The urban population of Africa, Asia and Latin America and the Caribbean is now nearly three times the size of the urban population of the rest of the world. UN projections also suggest that urban populations are growing so much faster than rural populations that 85 per cent of the growth in the world's population between 2000 and 2010 will be in urban areas, and virtually all this growth will be in Africa, Asia and Latin America.

Levels of urbanization in certain regions increased dramatically between 1950 and 2000 (Table 3.2); for instance, from 15 to 37 per cent in Africa and from 17 to 37 per cent in Asia. Particular sub-regions had even larger changes – for instance, 27 to 65 per cent in Western Asia and 39 to 68 per cent in Eastern Europe. However, the growth rates of urban populations and the rates of increase in levels of urbanization are not unprecedented; many countries in Western Europe, the USA and Japan had periods when their levels of urbanization increased as rapidly.[19]

However, certain points regarding urban change need emphasis, as outlined below.

Smaller and fewer large cities than expected

Recent censuses show that the world today is also less urbanized and less dominated by large cities than had been anticipated. For instance, Mexico City had 18 million people in 2000,[20] not the 31 million people predicted 25 years ago.[21] Calcutta had around 13 million by 2000, not the 40–50 million that had been predicted during the 1970s.[22] São Paulo, Rio de Janeiro, Seoul, Chennai (formerly Madras) and Cairo are among the many other large cities which by 2000 had several million inhabitants fewer than had been predicted in the late 1970s and early 1980s. In addition, the actual number of mega-cities with more than 10 million inhabitants in 2000 is much smaller than had been expected.[23]

Lower levels of urbanization

The world's urban population in 2000 was 270 million fewer than had been predicted 20 years previously,[24] and the date on which the world's urban population is expected to exceed its rural population has also been delayed; this transition had been expected in the late 1990s but now it is predicted to

happen around 2007. Many nations had much slower urban population growth rates than anticipated during the 1980s and 1990s, in part because of serious economic problems. For most nations, urban population growth rates also fell because of falling fertility rates. For some, it was also because of rising mortality rates. By the late 1990s, this included high and increasing levels of mortality from HIV/AIDS. This is particularly apparent in certain sub-Saharan African nations with high levels of infection and the absence of drugs to control it, and this is reshaping urban trends in many nations.[25]

An economic logic to city growth and urban change

The association between a nation's per capita income and its level of urbanization is well known – ie, in general, the higher the per capita income, the higher the level of urbanization. Most of the nations with the most rapid increase in their level of urbanization between 1960 and 1990 also had the most rapid economic growth,[26] and this is unlikely to have changed during the 1990s.[27] In 2000, the world's five largest economies (the USA, China, Japan, India and Germany) had 9 of the world's 16 mega-cities and 46 per cent of its million-cities. By 2000, all but two of the world's 16 mega-cities and more than two-thirds of its million-cities were in the 20 largest economies. Similarly, within each of the world's regions, most of the largest cities are concentrated in the largest economies – for instance, Brazil and Mexico in Latin America, and China, India, Indonesia and South Korea in Asia. One of the main reasons why the world is less urbanized in 2000 than expected is the slow economic growth (or economic decline) that many low- and middle-income nations experienced for much of the period since 1980. This helps explain slower population growth rates for many cities in Africa and Latin America. Part of this is also related to structural adjustment policies, which brought declines in employment, falling real incomes and declining urban welfare, and which proved to be less successful than hoped in stimulating economic growth.[28]

What role for water within urban change?

The size of the population in each of the 50,000 or so urban centres in the world[29] and each urban centre's rate of change are influenced by external factors and by factors related to each centre's own particular local context – including its site, location, natural resource endowment (of which fresh water availability is particularly important), demographic structure, existing economy and infrastructure (the legacy of past decisions and investments) and the quality and capacity of its public institutions. External influences range from the natural resource endowments in its surrounds to trends within the regional and national economy, and decisions made by national governments and the 30,000 or so global corporations who control a significant share of the world's economy.

Although this book includes details of many cities facing serious water shortages, it also needs to consider why the problems are not more serious. For instance, why was it possible for the largest cities in Latin America (Mexico City, São Paulo, Buenos Aires) to grow to sizes that are hundreds of times the size that their founders could have envisaged, with fresh water uses that must be thousands of times greater than those of the early cities, without running out of water? When these colonial cities were founded during the 16th century, a city with 50,000 inhabitants was a big city in Europe. The same question can be asked for most major cities in Latin America; a careful review of provision for water in Latin America's largest cities called *Thirsty Cities* highlights not so much serious water shortages as inadequacies in management and inefficient use of existing resources. The same question can be asked of the large Asian and African cities. Again, there are cities with very serious water shortages, but such shortages are not evident in many of the largest cities. In addition, there is no clear association between the availability of fresh water per person and the quality and extent of provision for piped water; indeed, many cities with the worst provision for piped water have plentiful fresh water supplies available locally.

Part of the reason for large cities not running out of water is that most of the world's large cities today were founded in areas with rich agricultural potential, which also means plentiful fresh water availability. Most were founded and grew to be important cities before motorized transport, so no major city could be too far from its main sources of fresh food. Most of the world's largest cities today have long histories as cities. Most of the largest urban centres in Europe, Latin America, Asia and North Africa today have been important urban centres for centuries. Of the 388 million-cities worldwide in 2000, more than three-fifths were already urban centres 200 years ago, while more than a quarter have been urban centres for at least 500 years.[30] One key reason why the Spanish founded Mexico City was because of the fertile soil and good water availability that were already serving one of the world's largest cities at that time, the Aztec city of Tenochtitlan.[31] The founders of Buenos Aires were influenced by its excellent farming potential, easy maritime access, good land communications and practically unlimited volumes of water.[32] Although there is still a tendency to discuss 'rural' and 'urban' separately or to see 'agricultural' and 'urban' as somehow in opposition, competing for resources, many major cities today owe their initial prosperity to being service centres for prosperous agriculture and prosperous farmers.[33] The fact that so many of the world's largest cities are old cities also means that many are located on large, navigable rivers, because these were the main transport arteries when they were founded. There is also the obvious point that industries that need water do not choose cities where they cannot get water – whether from a piped water system or direct from ground or surface water sources. So water availability has long influenced the location of industries (and thus where urban centres grow).

There are circumstances that encourage the foundation and early development of cities where water resources are more limited. For instance, the location of many sub-Saharan African cities was determined by colonial regimes, which avoided river valleys because of the problems of malaria or other insect-borne diseases. Such sites may have had plentiful water for small colonial cities (which colonial regimes kept small by apartheid-like controls on the rights of non-colonials to live in urban areas) but have now grown too large for local sources to supply. Many of the world's largest cities are also sea ports, and while some are beside large fresh water rivers, others are not and suffer from limited local groundwater resources and the need to go far inland to tap new resources.

War and civil conflict

Wars and civil conflicts are a key part of the explanation of why water and sanitation provision (and much else besides) is so inadequate, especially in sub-Saharan Africa. For instance, millions of people fled to urban areas in Angola, Mozambique and the Sudan during civil wars there during the 1980s and 1990s, just as they had done in Zimbabwe/Rhodesia during the liberation struggle of the 1970s.[34] It is difficult to know the exact dimensions of these movements – for instance, Angola has had no full census since 1970.[35] Yet during the 1980s, there were huge population displacements in Angola, as many rural areas were insecure and people fled to small towns and inland cities as well as main cities near the Atlantic coast. The post-election war from 1992 to 2002 affected the inland cities more, so displaced populations headed to the cities on the Atlantic coast.[36] The number of international refugees in Africa and Europe rose to unprecedented levels during the 1990s and a considerable proportion came to live in cities, for refuge or seeking new bases for their livelihoods.[37] Famines have also influenced urban trends in many African nations over the last 50 years, especially where urban centres provide rural populations with a greater chance of survival.

Weak city and municipal government

Inadequate city government generally has two aspects: local government structures and institutions that are weak, under-funded and often unrepresentative (including water and sanitation utilities with little or no investment capacity as described earlier); and higher levels of government that are unwilling to allow local institutions the resources and revenue-raising powers they need to become more effective. This section looks at the critical role that local government has in development in general, including the provision of adequate water and sanitation, whether or not a government agency is actually responsible for provision. The discussion is focused more on the political and institutional framework for ensuring good water and sanitation provision than on the performance of water and sanitation agencies (which was discussed earlier).

The developmental role of local government

Within Europe and North America (and in high-income nations elsewhere), urban populations have become so used to the web of local institutions that serve, support and protect them that they forget their importance. They assume that they will have water of drinking quality piped to their homes, sanitation and electricity 24 hours a day, that their garbage will be collected regularly and that the costs will represent a very small part of their income. There are schools and health centres to which even the lowest-income households have access. There are emergency services available to all. There are local politicians on whom demands can be made and to whom grievances can be voiced. Legislation and courts protect people from eviction, discrimination, exploitation and pollution. There are safety nets for those who lose their jobs or fall sick, and pensions to support those who retire. There are lawyers, ombudsmen, consumer groups and watchdogs to whom people can turn if they feel that they have been cheated. There are also legal systems and police forces that may not have eliminated corruption but have limited its influence over access to basic services and livelihoods. All of this is possible because of local government institutions overseen by democratic structures. Even if some services are provided by private companies, non-profit institutions or national or provincial public agencies, the framework for provision and quality control is provided by local governments or local offices of national or provincial governments. While coverage for some services may be sub-standard and some groups ill-served, the broad web of provision adequately serves the vast majority of the population.

This is not the case for most of the urban (and rural) population living in low- and most middle-income nations. The basic structure of government agencies, supervised by elected politicians who are able to meet their responsibilities, is at best only partially present and at worst non-existent. Local governments are also often rooted in undemocratic structures that favour local elites, patron–client relationships that limit the capacity of low-income groups to demand their rights, and corruption. Perhaps the most pressing issue for improving water and sanitation in urban areas is the development of accountable, effective local governments – or if this is impossible, other local institutions that are accountable and responsible to those lacking adequate water and sanitation provision. Local institutions are also critical for many other aspects related to water and sanitation – the investments and good management needed upstream of the water pipes in acquiring sufficient fresh water and ensuring its quality, and downstream of sewage and drainage systems to protect water quality and water users. Local institutions need to provide the rule of law through which the rights and entitlements of all groups (including low-income groups) and the public good are protected – which includes the right of low-income (or other) groups to organize and to demand better provision. Local institutions need to provide the web of health services that help reduce the health and economic impact of water-related diseases. They need to provide schools and day care services which help promote good personal and environmental hygiene. If local government agencies are not themselves the providers of water and sanitation, it falls on them to provide the framework within which provision is guaranteed, standards ensured and, for services that are natural monopolies, prices controlled among the private, NGO or CBO

groups that are important providers of some of these. The quality of service provided by all these institutions will also depend on whether they are overseen by robust, effective democratic processes, including the values this implies such as each institution's accountability to citizens and transparency in the generation, allocation and use of public resources. Local governments (or local offices of regional or national governments) also have a critical role in protecting water quality from pollution by local commercial and industrial establishments, and ensuring that enterprises do not contravene environmental regulations.

Much of the discussion among international agencies of the 'big' issues – such as greater equity, greater justice (and protecting human rights), protecting key resources, achieving greater democracy and reducing poverty – takes place without discussing the local institutions needed to ensure progress in these areas. The discussion about improving water and sanitation provision is no exception.

The weaknesses in local authorities

Assessing the quality of local governments is difficult. Many aspects are not easily measured, such as accountability, transparency and commitment to ensuring that all citizens are served by the rule of law. Statistics can show the number or proportion of people with piped water supplies, but as Chapter 1 discussed, very rarely are there statistics on the quality of the water, the regularity of supply and other key qualitative aspects. It is also difficult to compare the cities by the size of their revenue base and the scale of their investments in infrastructure without knowing precisely what role their governments have in infrastructure provision; low investments per person may simply reflect the fact that it is regional authorities or other providers who supply most investment for water and sanitation, rather than weak local government. In addition, given its importance for development, there is remarkably little international research on the quality of local government and on the quality of its relationship with civil society (local governance).

A research initiative in the early 1990s sought to collect comparable statistics from a

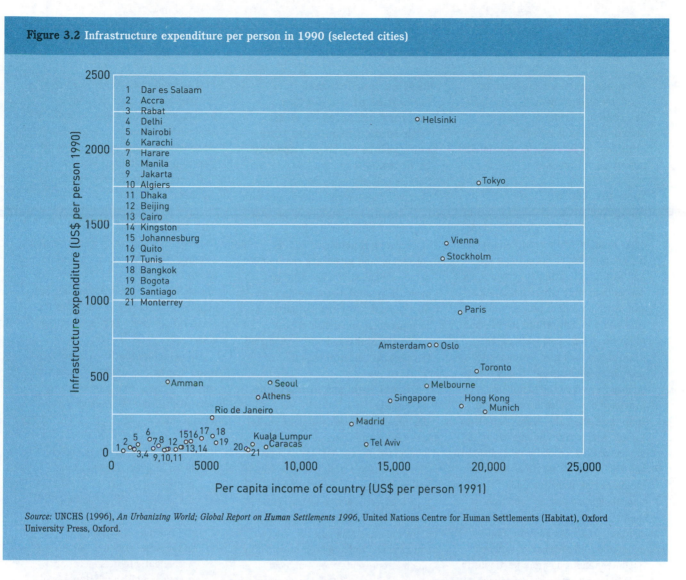

Figure 3.2 Infrastructure expenditure per person in 1990 (selected cities)

1 Dar es Salaam
2 Accra
3 Rabat
4 Delhi
5 Nairobi
6 Karachi
7 Harare
8 Manila
9 Jakarta
10 Algiers
11 Dhaka
12 Beijing
13 Cairo
14 Kingston
15 Johannesburg
16 Quito
17 Tunis
18 Bangkok
19 Bogota
20 Santiago
21 Monterrey

Source: UNCHS (1996), *An Urbanizing World; Global Report on Human Settlements 1996*, United Nations Centre for Human Settlements (Habitat), Oxford University Press, Oxford.

range of cities on housing and basic service provision, and this included figures for a range of cities on the expenditure per person on water supply, sanitation, garbage collection and other forms of infrastructure and services (see Figure 3.2). This shows the dramatic differences between cities in high-, middle- and low-income nations. For many cities, infrastructure expenditure per person per year is the equivalent of US$1 or US$2 – compared to cities such as Stockholm, Vienna, Tokyo and Helsinki, which have expenditures of US$1000–$2200 per person. It must also be remembered that most cities in Figure 3.2 are capital cities or the largest and most prosperous cities in their nation, and so probably have among the highest infrastructure expenditures per person of any city in their nation. Other sources confirm the very low capital expenditures made by local governments in low- and most middle-income nations.[38]

The inadequacies of urban government structures in low- and middle-income nations have also meant that many water issues other than those directly related to water and sanitation provision have been ignored or poorly managed. Existing fresh water resources remain unprotected and are often continuously degraded or depleted. Surface water sources are often polluted because there is so little regulation of commercial and industrial enterprises; very few cities in Africa, Asia and Latin America have rivers flowing through them that are not heavily polluted, and much the same applies to nearby lakes, estuaries and seas.[39] Watersheds remain unprotected and are often being degraded as there are few effective controls on industrial and urban developments there. Although most nations have the environmental legislation in place to limit water pollution, it is rarely enforced.[40] It is also common for urban expansion to take

Box 3.2 The constraints on extending water and sanitation in Bangalore

Water and sanitation provision in Bangalore has many deficiencies, as described in Chapter 1. A recent review of the problems the city faced identified the following constraints on improving provision.

Insecure tenure

A large proportion of the poor live in unrecognized slums on private lands or as tenants. They cannot get individual connections because the water and sanitation authority provides such connections only where households can provide proof of property ownership and a recent receipt for payment of property tax. Residents of recognized slums may also be unable to provide such documentation if responsibility for water and sanitation provision has not been transferred from the Karnataka Slum Clearance Board (which takes on upgrading in slums that are officially recognized) to the municipal corporation. In settlements at risk from eviction, households are discouraged from making the significant investments required to access an individual connection. High tenancy rates with absentee landlords are a particularly difficult impediment to household investments in improvements.

Limited ability of poor households to pay for both the one-off connection charge and the monthly user charges

Connection charges are increased by road cutting charges and by other charges levied by the plumbers responsible for providing the connection.

Limited institutional capacities of the service delivery agencies to work with communities, and time constraints on their capacity to do so

Service delivery agencies are dominated by technical personnel with little expertise in working in partnership with CBOs. Community mobilization is perceived as time consuming and something that cannot be accomplished in a short project cycle. In general, there are also few institutional capacities for participatory planning and delivery, both within the utility and within communities seeking better provision.

Political interest in business as usual

The provision of free water has historically been an important means by which leaders win popular support. The city of Bangalore has over 15,000 public fountains, connected to the piped network, where water is free to users, although the utility records show only half this number; the rest are assumed to have been provided by elected representatives and local leaders. About 4500 public fountains are located in the slums, with most of the rest in low- and middle-income residential areas. The water taken from the unregistered public fountains represents a significant part of unaccounted-for water.

Limited financial and institutional resources

This refers not only to very limited financial resources but also to the incapacity of institutions to work in an integrated manner, leading to duplication of efforts and wasteful expenditures. Much more could be achieved with existing resources if government institutions worked with NGOs, communities and elected members.

The high cost of water

The city draws much of its water from a source 94 kilometres away, and it has to be pumped up to the city (due to its elevated location), which brings high costs. Energy costs account for about 60 per cent of the cost of the water.

The factors that constrain households from taking a water connection with the official government utility were identified in a baseline survey, and include:

- the fact that tenure is unrecognized in many slums (12 per cent);
- the high cost of connection (20 per cent);
- the absence of the water network in the area, which is particularly problematic in peripheral areas and urban villages (30 per cent); and
- access to alternative sources such as groundwater, illegal connections and public fountains (29 per cent).

Source: Sinclair Knight Merz and Egis Consulting Australia in association with Brisbane City Enterprises and Feedback HSSI – STUP Consultants – Taru Leading Edge (2002), *Bangalore Water Supply and Environmental Sanitation Masterplan Project; Overview Report on Services to Urban Poor Stage 2*, AusAid, Canberra.

place over ecologically important areas such as wetlands and mangroves. Meanwhile, for many large cities, powerful industrial and commercial interests allied to the higher-income groups that have piped water can appropriate fresh water resources from other watersheds when local resources are depleted or degraded, often drawing on them from large distances with negative consequences for the ecology and water users in these areas.

One reason for the weakness of many urban governments might be the emergence of so many new cities where the institutions of government have to be built from scratch. If new cities are mushrooming everywhere, this might explain the weakness in government.

But as noted earlier in this chapter, most of the world's largest cities today were already urban centres 200 years ago. The two regions that stand out as having the most new cities are North America and sub-Saharan Africa; these regions have most of the cities that now have more than 1 million inhabitants but had not been founded or did not exist as urban centres in 1800.[41]

What is often a more serious problem is new local government units within expanding cities that are particularly weak. Large cities often have local government structures formed by many municipal governments, and there are very large differences between these municipal governments in terms of their competence, capacity and the size of their revenue base. For instance, richer areas of large cities – such as central districts and middle- and upper-income group suburbs – often have more effective and much better funded local governments than elsewhere. Meanwhile, there are often particular municipalities within large cities that have high concentrations of low-income households and much weaker revenue bases. These often include some municipalities on parts of the urban periphery where there is a particularly rapid growth in illegal settlements. The overall population of many large cities may be growing slowly, but there are often parts within cities with rapidly expanding populations, and these are often in areas with weak and under-funded local governments. This problem may also arise as cities expand over their official boundaries, and much of the overspill takes place in areas where the local government has little capacity to manage it.

Box 3.2 is included here as an example of the many contributory and proximate causes that help explain the inadequacies in water and sanitation provision in a particular city – in this case, Bangalore. This provides an example of many of the points discussed above, such as the limited household capacity to pay, the illegal status of many settlements (and the refusal of water and sanitation agencies to work there), water shortages and rapid population growth.

 ## Underlying causes

It is worth recalling how long it took for cities in high-income countries to develop the government structures that ensured universal water and sanitation provision, how ridden with conflict this process was, and how reluctant national governments were to support it, as it implied a considerable loss of power for them. It is not possible to discuss why water and sanitation provision is so poor in low- and middle-income countries without considering broader issues of national government and economic circumstances.

For many nations, perhaps most notably in sub-Saharan Africa, conditions have not favoured the development of competent, effective city authorities. The colonial governments gave very little priority to developing local government structures, so there was little to build on at independence in the 1950s, 1960s or 1970s. The newly independent governments then had to cope with explosive urban change, as the restrictions on the rights of citizens to live and work in urban areas were removed (virtually all the European colonial powers had kept down urban populations by imposing apartheid-like restrictions on the rights of their national populations to live and work in urban centres).[42] In most cities, colonial governments had done little to put in place the local government systems that would allow good water and sanitation provision for city populations. So at independence, the local government systems for urban areas and the legislative base they needed were generally very weak. Then the newly independent national governments did not give priority to building this capacity, not least because nation-building was seen as a priority and there were worries regarding the separatist tendencies that can arise from strong local governments. Add to this the difficulties that many sub-Saharan African nations have had in developing robust and prosperous economies, and the fact that many have suffered from wars or civil conflicts, and it is hardly surprising that water and sanitation provision is so poor in most urban centres.

The lack of international funding for investment in water and sanitation in urban areas

Perhaps not surprisingly, funding limitations are often mentioned as a key cause of inadequacy in water and sanitation provision. This includes the lack of funding from most international agencies, which is linked to the low priority that most choose to give to water and sanitation in urban areas.

But it is difficult to assess the scale of funding from international agencies for water and sanitation in urban areas, and its relative importance in regard to total investments in water and sanitation. Most international agencies do not report on the division between rural and urban areas of their investments in water and sanitation. In addition, official statistics on the priority given to water and sanitation in urban areas under-report the scale of their investments because projects or programmes with important water and sanitation components – such as slum and squatter upgrading, or serviced site schemes – are not included in funding for water and sanitation. For instance, in the case of the World Bank, the proportion of its total funding flows to urban water and sanitation during the 1980s and 1990s increases significantly if the upgrading, serviced site schemes and core housing schemes that included provision for water and/or sanitation are included.[43] The World Bank has also supported many housing finance schemes over the last 20 years; where these helped lower-income groups to obtain credit to buy, build or improve their homes, it probably contributed to improving water and sanitation provision. The World Bank and some other international agencies have also given strong support to local government reform over the last 10–15 years and this would never be included under 'water and sanitation' even if, as this book emphasizes, stronger, more effective, more accountable local governments have great importance for improving and extending provision.

However, most international agencies do not have major urban programmes, which helps explain why so few of them publish figures on the proportion of their funding that goes to urban areas. Many agencies have deliberately avoided supporting urban programmes on the assumption that urban populations were privileged over rural populations, or that meeting urban populations' needs was too expensive.[44] Of those agencies that do publish figures about urban programmes, the proportion of their funding going to urban projects is usually between 2 and 12 per cent[45] – and only a proportion of this goes to urban water and sanitation. Available data suggest that it is rare for urban water and sanitation projects to receive as much as 4 per cent of total funding, and most agencies are likely to allocate much less than this.[46] In addition, few international agencies allocate much to projects that may help improve water and sanitation provision but are not classified as such – for instance, upgrading projects, serviced site schemes or housing finance schemes that enable lower-income households to buy or build better quality homes.[47] However, there is a growing interest among many bilateral agencies in urban development, both within individual agencies (for instance, changes in the late 1990s in the Swedish International Development Cooperation Agency (Sida) as it developed an urban strategy and an urban division) and collectively (as in the support many bilateral agencies gave to the World Bank/UN/Habitat Urban Management Programme, or the fact that most of the large bilateral agencies are members of the Cities Alliance).[48] There is a growing awareness among international agencies of the need for:

- more urban investments;
- more recognition of the economic importance for nations of well functioning urban centres and systems; and
- better coordination among the international agencies in the urban investments they make.[49]

Reviewing the estimates presented in the Assessment 2000, external support provided on average US$3.6 billion a year between 1990 and 2000 for urban water supplies and US$716 million a year for sanitation (see Figure 3.3). More than half the external support for urban water supply went to Africa. External support also accounts for nearly half of all investments made in urban water supplies in Africa, Asia and Latin America and the Caribbean between 1990 and 2000. Its role was particularly noticeable in Africa, where external support was almost twice the value of national investments. In Asia, external support accounted for around a third of all investments in urban water supplies; in Latin America and the Caribbean it represented only a quarter. Africa received most investment, Latin America the least. But as this assessment notes, the investments made by households that were independent of government aid (for instance, the construction of their own latrine) are unlikely to have been included in the figures.[50]

Some of these figures may be too high. It is difficult to believe that US$21 billion of external funding was invested in urban water supplies in Africa during the 1990s to so little effect – unless these investments were heavily concentrated in South Africa and North Africa, where the quality and extent of provision is well above average for the region. Given that there were around 295 million urban dwellers in Africa by 2000, an external investment of US$21 billion over this ten-year period is equivalent to US$71 per person, or several hundred dollars per urban household. Asia, with an urban population of 1376 million in 2000, is reported to have received US$10.17 billion in external support for urban water supplies over this decade, which is the equivalent of only US$7.40 per person.

The figures for sanitation suggest that external agencies give it little importance. Total investment from external agencies in urban sanitation over the decade was one-fifth of the investment in urban water supply and, here, most investment was in Latin America and the Caribbean. One suspects that this was due to the greater possibilities of funding urban sanitation in this region through non-concessional loans (for instance, those provided by the World Bank and the Inter-American Development Bank). It may also be that a considerable proportion of this is for sewage treatment plants in middle-income nations, rather than improving and extending

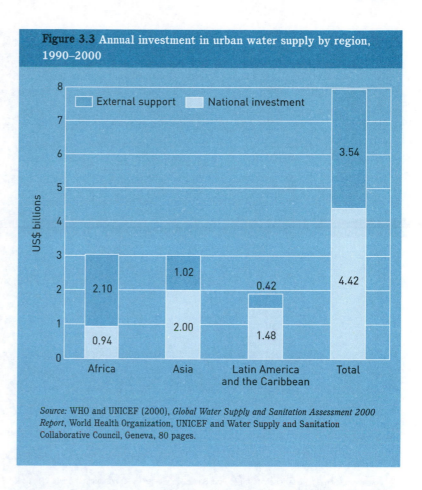

Figure 3.3 Annual investment in urban water supply by region, 1990–2000

Source: WHO and UNICEF (2000), *Global Water Supply and Sanitation Assessment 2000 Report*, World Health Organization, UNICEF and Water Supply and Sanitation Collaborative Council, Geneva, 80 pages.

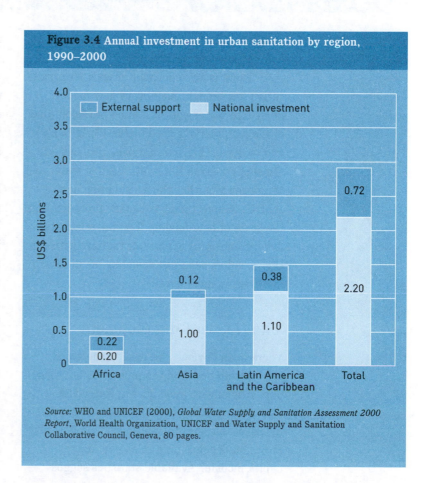

Figure 3.4 Annual investment in urban sanitation by region, 1990–2000

Source: WHO and UNICEF (2000), *Global Water Supply and Sanitation Assessment 2000 Report*, World Health Organization, UNICEF and Water Supply and Sanitation Collaborative Council, Geneva, 80 pages.

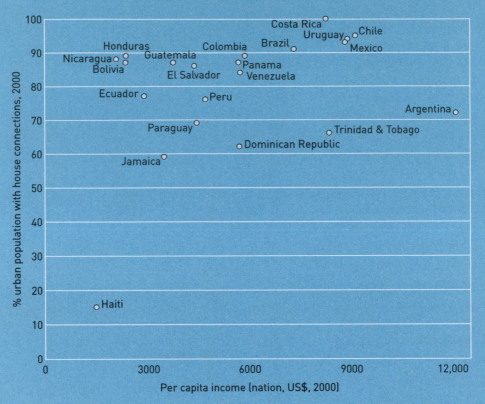

Figure 3.5 The percentage of urban populations in Latin American nations with house taps in relation to their national per capita incomes, 2000

Source: Centro Panamericano de Ingenieria Sanitaria y Ciencias del Ambiente, *Evaluacion de los Servicios de Agua Potable y Saneamiento 2000 en las America*, www.cepis.ops-oms.org.

provision for sanitation among urban households in low-income nations.

There is also the issue of whether privatization has brought significant new funding flows into water and sanitation provision. One of the justifications used by the World Bank and various other international agencies for the support given to privatization of water and sanitation was that this would bring new sources of investment to expand provision. But the scale of new funding from the relatively few international companies that are active in this area has been disappointing, as Chapter 5 discusses in more detail.

The 'lack of development'

There is an obvious and easily understood relationship between the proportion of urban populations with good quality water and sanitation provision and nations' per capita incomes. But does this mean that good quality provision depends on a relatively high per capita income? Available statistics suggest

not, for two reasons: because of the very large variations in the proportion of urban dwellers with 'improved' or 'adequate' provision among nations with comparable per capita incomes; and because in some nations with relatively low per capita incomes, relatively high proportions of the urban population have adequate provision. Here we look at this in more detail. Figure 3.5 shows the proportion of urban populations in Latin American nations with house taps compared with their per capita incomes, while Figure 3.6 shows the proportion with connection to sewers. These indicators provide a stronger basis for inter-country comparison, given that the statistics on improved provision encompass such a large range of possible improvements (see Chapter 1). In effect, the proportion of the population with house taps and with connection to sewers is a relevant measure of the extent to which households are served with provision by external agencies, since both depend on external piped systems and sewer systems. This is not to say that these are the only means to get

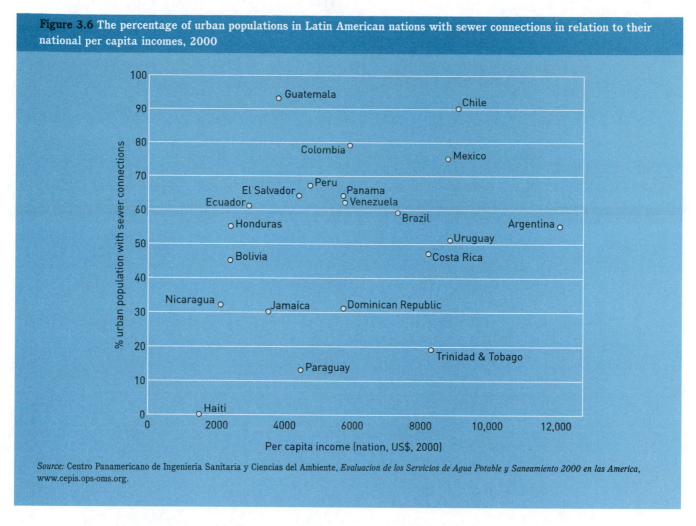

Figure 3.6 The percentage of urban populations in Latin American nations with sewer connections in relation to their national per capita incomes, 2000

Source: Centro Panamericano de Ingenieria Sanitaria y Ciencias del Ambiente, *Evaluacion de los Servicios de Agua Potable y Saneamiento 2000 en las America*, www.cepis.ops-oms.org.

adequate water and sanitation, but they are valid measures of the extent to which urban populations are served by external systems.

Both Figures 3.5 and 3.6 show the expected association between per capita income and proportion of the urban population with house taps and sewer connections. But Figure 3.5 shows that many nations with relatively low per capita incomes (Nicaragua, Honduras, Guatemala, Ecuador) have as high a proportion of their urban population with house taps as much wealthier nations. Argentina's poor performance relative to its per capita income is also notable. In Figure 3.6, the proportion of urban populations served by sewers obviously reflects policies and investment plans over the last few decades; the lack of provision in Haiti is obviously linked not only to its very low per capita income but also to decisions made by the dictatorship that controlled it, and the political instability it has suffered since this ended. Again, there is a group of relatively low-

income nations that perform as well or better than some relatively high-income nations.

Figure 3.7 shows the proportion of people with household connections for water in various Asian cities (most of which are the capital and/or largest city in their nation) plotted against the per capita income of the nation in 2000. Again, there is the expected association between higher per capita income and higher coverage. But in some cities in relatively low-income nations, high proportions of the population have household connections (Suva, Beijing, Tianjin, Mumbai and Thimphu) – although, at least for Mumbai, this must in part be explained by rather loose definitions of what constitutes a household connection.[51] In others, such as Cebu, small percentages of the households have connections relative to the nation's per capita income – and in the case of Cebu, given its economic success, relative to its own per capita income.

Figure 3.8 shows the proportion of people with household water connections in various

Figure 3.7 The percentage of households in selected Asian cities with household connections for water (circa 1995) in relation to their nations' per capita income, 2000

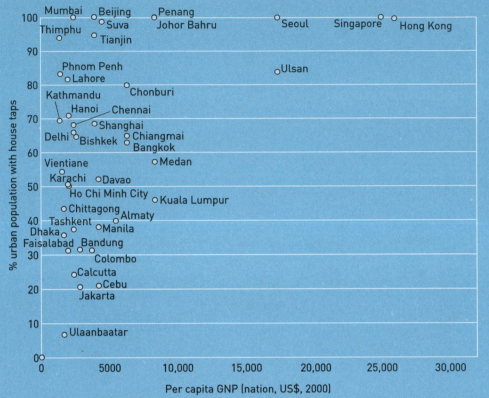

Source: Data on household connections from McIntosh, Arthur C and Cesar E Yñiguez (1997), *Second Water Utilities Data Book*, Asian Development Bank, Manila, 210 pages.

African cities (most of which are the capital and/or largest city in their nation) plotted against the per capita income of the nation in 2000. Here too, there is the expected association between higher per capita income and higher proportions of city households with house connections. There is the expected cluster of cities in countries with very low per capita incomes where very low proportions of the population have house connections – Addis Ababa, Dar es Salaam, Freetown and N'Djamena. But there are also high levels of variation between cities in nations with comparable levels of per capita income. In some cities, surprisingly low proportions of households have water connections, given the national per capita income (Port Louis in Mauritius, Gaborone in Botswana, Libreville in Gabon, Malabo in Equatorial Guinea and Harare in Zimbabwe). In others, relatively high proportions of households have house

connections compared to the nation's per capita income (Windhoek in Namibia, Algiers in Algeria, Dakar in Senegal, Nairobi in Kenya and Kinshasa in the Democratic Republic of Congo) although one wonders at the accuracy of these statistics, at least for Nairobi and Kinshasa.

The reasons for the above average or below average performance in water and sanitation provision among urban populations in different cities or different nations needs a more careful analysis than that provided here, and one would also need to check the accuracy of the statistics, especially for low-income nations or cities in low-income nations with far above average performance. But these figures are presented here as a reminder that relatively good levels of water and sanitation provision are possible in urban areas even with relatively low levels of national per capita income.

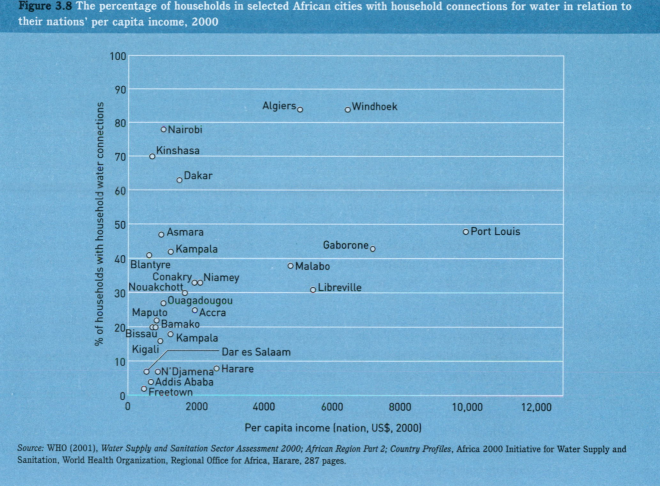

Figure 3.8 The percentage of households in selected African cities with household connections for water in relation to their nations' per capita income, 2000

Source: WHO (2001), *Water Supply and Sanitation Sector Assessment 2000; African Region Part 2; Country Profiles*, Africa 2000 Initiative for Water Supply and Sanitation, World Health Organization, Regional Office for Africa, Harare, 287 pages.

The political under-pinning of good provision for water and sanitation

Both this chapter and the previous two chapters have presented many examples of the political and institutional failures or shortcomings that explain inadequate water and sanitation provision. There are many factors constraining the development of more effective government structures, especially where these increase costs and limit choices for politically powerful enterprises and populations. Middle- and upper-income groups who have long received piped water supplies at lower than the cost price may be able to pay more realistic prices, but it does not mean that they will be happy to do so. Good water management means limits on where industries can locate and developers can build; also on what local water sources they can tap and what wastes they can dispose of. But in cities where most industries have been used to operating outside any such management framework and have

been saving money by doing so, they will not welcome such changes.

It is relatively easy to point to rational and cost-effective ways to improve water and sanitation provision in most urban areas. But what is more difficult is to understand why these have not been implemented. If significant improvements can be made for which lower-income groups are able and willing to pay, why haven't they been done? Why haven't politicians promoted such solutions?

One obvious problem is political systems in which the politicization of water pricing gives water utilities no incentive to improve or extend provision because they cannot recover the costs of doing so – and may not be able to cut off non-payers. Politicians often prevent rises in water prices, but this results in low revenues and the water utilities' inability to invest in maintenance and system expansion. And if it is largely middle- and upper-income groups and businesses that are connected, these benefit from low prices while those lacking connections suffer from the inability of the utility to expand. Public sector water and sanitation provision 'is prone to government opportunism, triggering a downward spiral of low prices, low investment, low quality, low coverage and high levels of corruption'.[52] For instance, in Lima, the water utility had little interest in extending the system as the tariff did not cover operating costs and it was unable to take sanctions against non-payers.[53] In Buenos Aires, an analysis of how provision has changed over the last 100 years showed the strong influence of political changes in the quality and extent of provision to the point where much of the population was better served in the 1930s than they were in the 1980s or 1990s.[54]

Although there are strong examples of good quality water and sanitation provision by public sector utilities, the widespread failure of national and local governments to support the development of efficient public utilities in most low- and middle-income countries helps explain the enthusiasm for seeking private sector solutions. The hope was that a private sector company could have the autonomy to set prices that allowed sufficient revenues to ensure better services, better maintenance and expanding coverage. As they were no longer run by unaccountable and untransparent government institutions, the private sector operations would respond to consumer demand. But the shift to privatization was also in part because of the new conventional wisdom during the 1990s that was espoused by many governments and most international agencies. This was that governments must cut their involvement and there should be strict financial constraints applied to their capacity to invest – which then encouraged them to pass on their responsibilities.[55] For example, the importance of reducing the fiscal burden on provincial government in Argentina was one reason for the decision to privatize water services.[56]

Privatization also seems to have been driven by the financial rewards it can bring to elites and the improved provision it gives to those who are already connected to the system. For instance, in Buenos Aires, the privatization of the water sector can be seen as the culmination of a pattern of inequitable development. 'Power relations shifted dramatically within Buenos Aires in the 1990s and the water concession was a contributory force. Elite international and national groups have gained, whilst poor groups have lost.'[57] Between 1989 and 1993, the government privatized the Buenos Aires water and sewerage network. The deficiencies in the public network were evident, but no alternative to privatization was considered – for instance, the obvious need for changes in the government agency responsible for provision to make it more directly accountable to city populations.[58] Offering opportunities for private investment and profit was seen as the only solution. Collignon and Vezina observe that 'the way in which privatization has been carried out indicates that the underlying perspective is commercial rather than service orientated since any notion of a competitive market is absent from concession and leasing contracts.'[59]

In more recent times, questions have been raised about powerful economic interests wining large contracts with bids and conditions that they had no intention of meeting. Once these contracts were secured, these powerful economic interests sought to use multiple strategies to ensure that the outcomes of the regulatory process were in their favour.[60]

However, it should not be assumed that the political process is necessarily in favour of privatization. In Mexico City, the PRI, which had been the leading party for a long time before the recent elections, sought a solution that strengthened its political support. The reduction of the role of patronage in determining access to water might reduce support for the local politicians that were themselves part of their complex system of securing political hegemony.[61] Private sector involvement did not take place in Lima despite initial widespread support for privatization, an economic crisis and a president (Fujimori) who at that time was committed to enhancing the role of private capital. Fujimori became reluctant to continue with the process because the urban poor were an important source of political support and there was growing concern about price rises (estimated to be from US$0.30 to US$0.45 per cubic metre under the concession as drafted).[62] Prices were particularly high because of water supply shortages and the need for expensive investments in order to increase coverage of the supply network.

 Conclusions

The cause of the inadequacies in water and sanitation provision is not a lack of knowledge about how to address these problems – although many city and municipal governments may lack trained personnel with this knowledge. The evidence presented in this chapter suggests that the root of the problem is that in most cities and smaller urban centres, government structures have not developed to efficiently and equitably address these problems and resolve the trade-offs that inevitably arise. As Chapter 7 will discuss in more detail, good government for water and sanitation implies not only frameworks to ensure provision but also regulations (to protect water sources and to protect and promote health) and revenue-raising (to pay for the system's functioning, maintenance and expansion).

In low- and many middle-income nations, there are serious difficulties in raising the funds for the major investments needed from local, national or international sources. Large and fast-growing cities in low-income nations face particularly serious problems. Not only is there a large backlog of households and businesses in need of better provision, but there is also a rapid growth in need as the population and economic base continues to grow rapidly. But even here, there are many examples of local innovation showing how water and sanitation provision (and wastewater management) can be much improved. The last 30 years have produced many innovations to show how good quality water, sanitation and drainage is financially feasible in low-income cities or low-income areas of cities. In discussions about improving water and sanitation provision, perhaps too much stress is placed on the need for additional international funding. Without improved local government (and better local governance), additional resources may bring few benefits to low-income groups and little improvement in overall water management.

 Notes and references

1.   See, for instance, the health care system developed in Cebu in the Philippines described in Etemadi, Felisa U (2000), 'Civil society participation in city governance in Cebu City', *Environment and Urbanization*, Vol 12, No 1, pages 57–72; and Fuentes, Patricio and Reiko Niimi (2002), 'Motivating municipal action for children: the municipal seal of approval in Ceará, Brazil', *Environment and Urbanization*, Vol 14, No 2, pages 123–133.

2.   Hardoy, Jorge E and David Satterthwaite (1989), *Squatter Citizen: Life in the Urban Third World*, Earthscan Publications, London, 388 pages; UNCHS (Habitat) (1996), *An Urbanizing World: Global Report on Human Settlements, 1996*, Oxford University Press, Oxford and New York.

3.   As noted by Ferguson, Bruce (1996), 'The environmental impacts and public costs of unguided informal settlement: the case of Montego Bay', *Environment and Urbanization*, Vol 8, No 2, October, pages 171–193.

4.   Sinclair Knight Merz and Egis Consulting Australia in association with Brisbane City Enterprises and Feedback HSSI – STUP Consultants – Taru Leading Edge (2002), *Bangalore Water Supply and Environmental Sanitation Masterplan Project; Overview Report on Services to Urban Poor Stage 2*, AusAid, Canberra.

5.   Walker, Ian, Max Velasquez, Fidel Ordonez and Florencia Maria Rodriguez (1999), 'Reform efforts and low-level equilibrium in the Honduran water sector' in Savedoff, W D and P T Spiller (eds), *Spilled Water: An Institutional Commitment of the Provision of Water Services*, Inter-American Development Bank, Washington, DC, pages 35–88.

6.   Nickson, Andrew (2001), *The Córdoba Water Concession in Argentina*, Working Paper, Building Municipal Capacity for Private Sector Participation Series, GHK International, London.

7. Hanchett, Suzanne, Mohidul Hoque Khan and Shireen Akhter (2001), *WaterAid Bangladesh Urban Programme Evaluation*, Planning Alternatives for Change and Pathway Ltd, Dhaka, page 47. A condensed version of this report will be published in the October 2003 issue of *Environment and Urbanization*.

8. Nickson 2001, op cit.

9. Nickson, Andrew (2001), *Establishing and Implementing a Joint Venture: Water and Sanitation Services in Cartagena, Colombia*, Working Paper 442 03, Building Municipal Capacity for Private Sector Participation Series, GHK International, London, 37 pages.

10. Almansi, Florencia, Ana Hardoy, Gaston Pendiella, Ricardo Schusterman and Gastón Urquiza (2002), *The Problem of Land Tenure in the Expansion of Potable Water and Sanitation Services to Informal Settlements*, Paper prepared for WaterAid, IIED-América Latina, Buenos Aires.

11. Almansi, Hardoy, Pendiella et al 2002, op cit.

12. McIntosh, Arthur C and Cesar E Yñiguez (1997), *Second Water Utilities Data Book*, Asian Development Bank, Manila, 210 pages.

13. Ibid; see the comments, city by city, on pages 8–12.

14. WHO and UNICEF (2000), *Global Water Supply and Sanitation Assessment 2000 Report*, World Health Organization, UNICEF and Water Supply and Sanitation Collaborative Council, Geneva, 80 pages.

15. This section draws most of its statistics from United Nations (2002), *World Urbanization Prospects; The 2001 Revision; Data Tables and Highlights*, Population Division, Department of Economic and Social Affairs, United Nations Secretariat, ESA/P/WP/173, United Nations, New York, 181 pages; much of the analysis comes from Satterthwaite, David (2002), *Coping with Rapid Urban Growth*, RICS International Paper Series, Royal Institution of Chartered Surveyors, London.

16. Satterthwaite 2002, op cit.

17. This redoes the analysis in Satterthwaite, David (1996), *The Scale and Nature of Urban Change in the South*, IIED Working Paper, IIED, London, 29 pages, drawing on UN 2002, op cit.

18. Chandler, Tertius and Gerald Fox (1974), *3000 Years of Urban Growth*, Academic Press, New York and London.

19. Preston, Samuel H (1979), 'Urban growth in developing countries: a demographic reappraisal', *Population and Development Review*, Vol 5, No 2, pages 195–215; Satterthwaite 1996, op cit.

20. Garza, Gustavo (2002), *Urbanization of Mexico During the Twentieth Century*, Urban Change Working Paper 7, IIED, London.

21. United Nations (1975), *Trends and Prospects in the Population of Urban Agglomerations, As Assessed In 1973–75*, Population Division, Department of International Economic and Social Affairs, ESA/P/WP.58, United Nations, New York.

22. Brown, Lester (1974), *In the Human Interest*, W W Norton and Co, New York.

23. The United Nations Population Division had predicted that there would be 27 mega-cities by the year 2000 in its 1973–1975 assessment (United Nations 1975, op cit) and 23 in its 1984–1985 assessment – United Nations (1987), *The Prospects of World Urbanization Revised as of 1984–5*, Population Studies No 101, ST/ESA/SER.A/101, United Nations, New York.

24. United Nations (1980), *Urban, Rural and City Population, 1950–2000, As Assessed in 1978*, ESA/P/WP.66, June, United Nations, New York, 38 pages and United Nations 2002, op cit.

25. Potts, Deborah (2001), *Urban Growth and Urban Economies in Eastern and Southern Africa: An Overview*, Paper presented at a workshop on African Urban Economies: Viability, Vitality of Vitiation of Major Cities in East and Southern Africa, Netherlands, 9–11 November, 19 pages plus annex, to be published in D Bryceson and D Potts (eds), *African Urban Economies: Viability, Vitality or Vitiation of Major Cities in East and Southern Africa*.

26. UNCHS (1996), *An Urbanizing World: Global Report on Human Settlements, 1996*, Oxford University Press, Oxford and New York.

27. There is insufficient census data available from the censuses held around 2000 for this analysis to be undertaken yet.

28. For sub-Saharan Africa, see Potts 2001, op cit.

29. This figure of 50,000 urban centres in the world is a very rough estimate, based on an extrapolation from various censuses that gave the total number of urban centres in a particular country. For instance, Colombia in its 1993 census had over 1000 urban centres; India had over 4000 in its 1991 census; Brazil over 8000 in its 1990 census. Of course, the number of urban centres in any nation depends not only on the level of urbanization and the spatial distribution of the urban population but also on the official definition of an urban centre. India would have tens of thousands of urban centres if it changed its urban definition to settlements of 2500 or more inhabitants. The figure of 50,000 urban centres is given only to stress the very large

number of urban centres worldwide, each of which will have its own unique pattern of growth (or decline).

30. These statistics almost certainly considerably under-state the extent to which the world's largest cities today have long been important urban centres. This is related to the incompleteness of historic records for city populations, despite the efforts of scholars such as Tertius Chandler and Paul Bairoch to fill this gap.

31. Hardoy, Jorge E (1999), *Ciudades Precolombinas*, Ediciones Infinito, Buenos Aires, 498 pages.

32. Anton, Danilo J (1993), *Thirsty Cities: Urban Environments and Water Supply in Latin America*, IDRC, Ottawa, 197 pages.

33. See Chapter 9 of Hardoy, Jorge E and David Satterthwaite (1989), *Squatter Citizen: Life in the Urban Third World*, Earthscan Publications, London, 388 pages.

34. Potts, Deborah (1995), 'Shall we go home? increasing urban poverty in African cities and migration processes', *The Geographical Journal*, Vol 161, Part 3, pages 245–264.

35. Cain, Allan, Mary Daly and Paul Robson (2002), *Basic Service Provision for the Urban Poor; The Experience of Development Workshop in Angola*, IIED Working Paper 8 on Poverty Reduction in Urban Areas, IIED, London, 40 pages.

36. Cain et al 2002, op cit.

37. Castles, Stephen and Mark J Miller (1993), *The Age of Migration: International Population Movements in the Modern World*, MacMillan, London and Basingstoke, 306 pages.

38. UNCHS 1996, op cit.

39. Hardoy, Jorge E, Diana Mitlin and David Satterthwaite (2001), *Environmental Problems in an Urbanizing World: Finding Solutions for Cities in Africa, Asia and Latin America*, Earthscan Publications, London, 470 pages.

40. Hardoy, Mitlin and Satterthwaite 2001, op cit.

41. Satterthwaite 2002, op cit.

42. Potts 1995, op cit.

43. Satterthwaite, David (2001), 'Reducing urban poverty: constraints on the effectiveness of aid agencies and development banks and some suggestions for change', *Environment and Urbanization*, Vol 13, No 1, pages 137–157.

44. Hardoy, Mitlin and Satterthwaite 2001, op cit; UNCHS (Habitat) (2001), *Cities in a Globalizing World*, Earthscan Publications, London, 330 pages.

45. Milbert, Isabelle and Vanessa Peat (1999), *What Future for Urban Cooperation? Assessment of Post Habitat II Strategies*, Swiss Agency for Development and Cooperation, Berne, 341 pages.

46. Hardoy, Mitlin and Satterthwaite 2001, op cit, and UNCHS 2001, op cit.

47. Ibid.

48. See www.citiesalliance.org.

49. OECD (2000), *Shaping the Urban Environment in the 21st Century: From Understanding to Action*, A DAC Reference Manual on Urban Environmental Policy, OECD, Paris, 32 pages.

50. WHO and UNICEF 2000, op cit.

51. Mumbai claims that 100 per cent of its population have household connections, but it is clear that a large proportion of households only have access to shared taps; the official statistics show that there are 43.5 persons per household connection whereas in most other cities, there are 3–6 persons per household connection. See McIntosh and Yñiguez 1997, op cit.

52. Spiller, Pablo T and William D Savedoff (1999), 'Government opportunism and the provision of water' in Savedoff, W D and P T Spiller (eds), *Spilled Water: An Institutional Commitment of the Provision of Water Services*, Inter-American Development Bank, Washington, DC, pages 1–34.

53. Alcazar, Lorena, Lixin Colin Xu and Ana Maria Zuluaga (2000), *Institutions, Politics and Contracts: The Attempt to Privatise the Water and Sanitation Utility of Lima, Peru*, Policy Research Working Paper, WPS 2478, The World Bank, Washington, DC.

54. Pirez, Pedro (1998), 'The management of urban services in the city of Buenos Aires', *Environment and Urbanization*, Vol 10, No 2, pages 209–222.

55. Manor, James (1999), *The Political Economy of Democratic Decentralization*, The World Bank, Washington, DC.

56. Chisari, Omar, Antonia Estache and Carlos Romero (1999), 'Winners and losers from the privatisation and regulation of utilities: lessons from a general equilibrium model of Argentina', *World Bank Economic Review*, Vol 13, No 2, pages 357–378.

57. Loftus, Alexander J and David A McDonald (2001), 'Of liquid dreams: a political ecology of water privatization in Buenos Aires', *Environment and Urbanization*, Vol 13, No 2, pages 180–181.

58. Pirez 1998, op cit.

59. Collignon, B and M Vezina (2000), *Independent Water And Sanitation Providers In African Cities*, UNDP-World Bank Water and Sanitation Program, Nairobi, page 10.

60. Esguerra, Jude (2002), *The Corporate Muddle of Manila's Water Concessions: How the World's Biggest and Most Successful*

Privatisation turned into a Failure, WaterAid, London, page 2.

61. Haggarty, Luke, Penelope Brook and Ana Maria Zuluaga (2000), *Thirst for Reform? Private Sector Participation in Mexico City's Water Sector*, Policy Research Working Paper WPS 2311, The World Bank, Washington, DC.

62. Alcazar, Xu and Zuluaga 2000, op cit.

CHAPTER

4

Increasing Water Stress and How it Relates to Urban Water and Sanitation Provision

 Introduction

At the International Conference on Freshwater in Bonn in December 2001, water scarcity was attributed to growing demand, and increased pollution and waste. It was emphasized that scarcity could be avoided if water resources were properly managed. This chapter supports these conclusions, in particular when water scarcity (or water stress) is defined at the scale of the watershed or nation. It is important, however, not to confuse the water scarcity faced by individuals and households with water resource scarcity at the scale of watersheds and nations.

In cities where an appreciable share of urban residents face difficulties obtaining adequate water and sanitation, water resource problems can make matters worse. Urban growth and development often contribute to water resource problems. Global trends indicate that water resource scarcity is increasing as populations and per capita water demands grow. However, the amounts of water required to meet basic human needs are relatively modest, water resource scarcity is only one aspect of the water resource problems cities face, and water resource problems do not make a major contribution to the inadequate urban water and sanitation provision in most low-income cities. Addressing water resource scarcity, particularly at the global, national or river basin scale, will not address more than a small share of the household- and neighbourhood-level water and sanitation problems described in previous chapters. Indeed, well intentioned but ill-conceived measures to reduce water stress can

actually undermine attempts to improve water and sanitation provision. In low-income cities where water resources are scarce, one of the major challenges is to address water stress in a manner that improves, rather than undermines, water and sanitation provision. This requires careful attention to the local physical and socio-economic context, and highlights the importance of locally driven approaches. Related issues arise in relation to 'natural' disasters.

 Global trends and increasing water stress

Recent trends have raised fears of a global water crisis driven by increasing water demands in the face of limited supplies. Human activities have been altering the water cycle for many centuries. In urban centres, the scarcity of water for human consumption has been a concern since the first cities developed, often posing serious problems for governments as well as residents. Conflicting uses of water have also long been an issue, as when, in the 14th century, Ibn Khaldûn criticized North African rulers for being more concerned with securing water for their camels than for their urban residents – a factor he argued had contributed to the demise of a number of cities.[1] During the 19th and 20th centuries, cities that could afford to were inclined to address their water scarcities by drawing on increasingly distant supplies, contributing to the spatial expansion of interconnected water systems. Over the course of the 20th century, however, world population tripled, the use of water for human purposes multiplied sixfold, and water pollution also accelerated.[2] The scope for resolving local water scarcity by diverting water from areas of water 'surplus' has diminished greatly. Moreover, there is growing recognition that water diversions can have adverse ecological consequences.

In the coming century, climate change and the growing imbalance between fresh water supplies and consumption could alter the water cycle to an unprecedented degree. While many people are already living in regions facing water stress, characterized as having insufficient water of satisfactory quality and quantity to meet human and environmental needs, by 2025 it has been estimated that the share of the world's population living in water-stressed regions will increase to 35 per cent.[3] Urban water issues are increasingly being viewed in this global context. On the one hand, there is concern that growing water stress is having adverse impacts on cities and their residents, and on the other hand, that urban development is adding to water stress.

As described in later sections of this chapter, these concerns tend to be over-simplified in discussions of the global water crisis. Regional water stress is sometimes portrayed as the major determinant of households' access to adequate water and sanitation and of the prevalence of water-related diseases. Existing evidence suggests, however, that other factors noted in the previous chapter are currently far more important, and a narrow focus on water stress could actually undermine measures to improve urban water provision in deprived areas. Moreover, while urban areas do consume and pollute water, urbanization itself need not contribute to water stress, and much can be done to reduce the adverse impacts of urban development. Increasing water stress is an important issue in many parts of the world. Cities often contribute more than they should to water stress and urban residents already lacking access to adequate water supplies are likely to be the worst affected by certain forms of water stress. But crude international generalizations are in danger of misleading rather than informing water sector policy, particu-

larly in countries where international development assistance influences local policy.

Predicting a global crisis

Much of the literature on the global water crisis is, in effect, a call to action. At its simplest, the message is that the world is running out of water, and must change its ways:

> As populations grow and water use per person rises, demand for fresh water is soaring. Yet the supply of fresh water is finite and threatened by pollution. To avoid a crisis, many countries must conserve water, pollute less, manage supply and demand, and slow population growth.[4]

> Around the world, there are now numerous signs that human water use exceeds sustainable levels. Groundwater depletion, low or non-existent river flows, and worsening pollution levels are among the more obvious indicators of water stress... Satisfying the increased demands for food, water, and material goods of a growing global population while at the same time protecting the ecological services provided by natural water ecosystems requires new approaches to using and managing fresh water.[5]

> [M]any countries, especially developing and newly industrialized regions in the Middle East, Africa, Asia and South America will be vulnerable to lack of water... [T]his will affect health, mortality and the prospects for peace if nothing is done to correct the imbalance between supply and demand... [S]carcity is largely the result of poor water management and ... with the implementation of proven methods of raising the efficiency of water withdrawal, use and consumption on the one hand, and of more efficient and integrated water supply on the other, the problem could be solved.[6]

The problems of urban areas, and especially mega-cities,[7] are sometimes presented in even more strident terms, as in the following example:

Mega-cities, ie cities with more than 10 million residents are growing fast... Water-related problems in these cities are already enormous, and further degradation is expected. Water shortage is a growing problem and delivery of safe drinking water cannot be assured... Solution of this mega-problem of mega-cities requires efficient regulations and actions to stop further population growth and, in the water sector, to develop novel environmentally friendly and economically efficient methods of water conservation and treatment.... Technological change must be accompanied by basic changes in all sectors, social and central structures, educational and research programmes, and in lifestyle.[8]

Numerous projections have been made of global water availability and use, often by region.[9] There is considerable debate about data, definitions and techniques. The analysis is inevitably somewhat confounded by the fact that water is not so much 'used up' as diverted or transformed, making it at least temporarily less useful, and having ecological conse-quences. Nevertheless, whatever techniques and definitions are applied, the central message is almost invariably that water problems are already serious in many parts of the world, and that unless people change their ways, they are going to get worse. What varies is when and where these problems are expected to be most severe.

The models (and arguments) used to predict large-scale water deficiencies typically rely on some form of supply–demand balanc-ing, with sustainable supplies compared to demands[10] and problems assumed to become increasingly severe as demand approaches the available supply. Since water problems do undoubtedly exist in many parts of the world, and since water consumption is estimated to have increased by a factor of six over the course of the 20th century, it is hardly surprising that such models predict serious problems.

Indicators of regional water stress

One of the simplest and most common indicators of national water stress is the Falkenmark indicator – renewable water resources per capita per year – named for the Swedish water researcher Malin Falkenmark.[11] When this indicator is applied, a value of less than 1700 cubic metres per capita per year is taken to indicate water stress, and a value of less than 1000 cubic metres per capita is taken to indicate severe water stress (or water scarcity). From a supply–demand balancing perspective, this indicator implicitly assumes that demand is directly proportional to population.

The Falkenmark indicator lends itself to population-based projections. The authors of a report published by the Population Information Program of the Johns Hopkins School of Public Health used estimates of national fresh water availability and United Nations population projections to estimate the population living in countries with less water than the Falkenmark threshold in 1995 and 2025.[12] The results indicate that about 460 million people lived in water-stressed (or water-scarce) countries in 1995, and that the number would be expected to reach about 2.8 billion – about 35 per cent of the world's population – by 2025. Having presented these projections, the report proceeds to summarize the 'health dimension' by giving details on morbidity and mortality from all water-related diseases.

No water expert would ever claim that the Falkenmark indicator is precise. At their best, such projections can help draw attention to certain types of water issues, provide heuristic tools through which these issues can be better understood, and create a useful framework within which to situate more detailed understandings of specific problems in particular places. At their worst, however, they create misunderstandings about the actual nature of water issues, and support misguided actions. This can easily arise in relation to urban water issues, where the spatial dimensions of water scarcity are particularly critical. In any case, the quantity of renewable water resources is a crude indicator of water availability and the number of people is a crude indicator of the demands placed on those resources. Moreover, when applying the Falkenmark indicator at a national level, there are a number of inadequacies which should be kept in mind, including those outlined below.

Local variation and boundary issues

National boundaries often cut across a number of drainage basins, making it difficult to assign renewable water resources unambiguously to individual countries. Perhaps more importantly, problems of water stress can vary enormously within a country, with different problems arising at different scales, and often extending unevenly over space. From an urban perspective the scale issues are particularly acute, since cities concentrate certain water-related pressures and demands, accessible supplies depend heavily on location, and radically different levels of water stress are often evident in different cities within a single country. But local variation can also be very important in rural areas, particularly in countries without the infrastructure to divert water to sites of demand. Alternatively, cities and even countries can import water-intensive products, displacing water demands beyond their boundaries.

Temporal variation and seasonal issues

Variations in water availability across seasons and years can be critical to water stress, so averages can be deceiving – a lack of water in one season is hardly compensated for by floods in another. Seasonal variations tend to be greater in tropical countries, and some parts of the world are more prone to long-term variations. Anthropogenic climate change may also shift the patterns of water stress appreciably.

Adaptability and comparability issues

To some degree, both ecosystems and human systems can adapt to, as well as alter, the prevailing water regime, but adaptation requires time as well as capacity. Where water availability has been high historically, a decline to a lower level can lead to considerably more water problems than where water availability has historically been at that lower level. Thus, if Tanzania were to face a 50 per cent decline in all of its renewable water

resources, the effects would undoubtedly be devastating, although it would still have more renewable water resources available per capita than Morocco.

Accessibility and economic capacity issues

There can be a great deal of variation in how accessible a country's renewable water resources are, and what level of investment can be made to achieve better access. Thus a poor country, or one with comparatively inaccessible water resources, is likely to face more severe problems than a wealthy country with accessible water resources, even if according to the Falkenmark index their water stress levels are the same. A poor country is also likely to face greater problems adapting to changes in water availability, although this relationship is less straightforward.

Unaccounted-for water

Estimates of fresh water availability include neither stocks of water, nor what has come to be termed 'green water': the share of rainfall that is stored in the soil and eventually evaporates from it. Such water resources can make a large difference to the water resource problems a country faces.

Several more recent indicators of water stress attempt to correct at least some of these problems, though not altogether successfully. Different attempts to improve upon the Falkenmark indicator can have very different consequences for where water stress is identified. Two variants are described in the following paragraphs. The first tends to identify more water stress in affluent countries (where water withdrawals are high). The second tends to identify more water stress in poor countries (where the economic capacity to access more water is lacking, and population is growing quickly).

The WaterGAP model, employed in the Water Visions exercise, employs what is termed the 'criticality ratio': withdrawals for human use divided by renewable water resources.[13] This indicator is sensitive to variations in water use per capita (though it does not distinguish between usage that prevents re-use and that which does not). It also applies this indicator to

Figure 4.1 World map of projected water scarcity in 2025

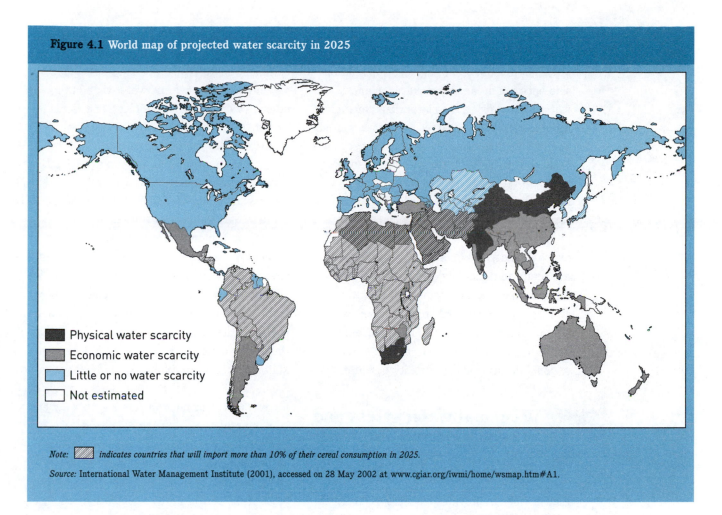

Physical water scarcity

Economic water scarcity

Little or no water scarcity

Not estimated

Note: indicates countries that will import more than 10% of their cereal consumption in 2025.

Source: International Water Management Institute (2001), accessed on 28 May 2002 at www.cgiar.org/iwmi/home/wsmap.htm#A1.

basins rather than countries, avoiding at least some of the boundary problems that arise with national indicators. The results indicate high water stress in areas with high withdrawals, including large parts of the USA and other affluent countries not identified as water-stressed by the Falkenmark indicator. Not surprisingly, the 'business as usual' scenario indicates increasing water stress, and is used to argue for radical changes in water management.

Taking a somewhat different approach, researchers at the International Water Management Institute have projected water demands forward to the year 2025, and attempt to identify both absolute (or physical) and economic water scarcity.[14] A country is assumed to face an absolute water scarcity if projected demand exceeds renewable fresh water availability, while a country is assumed to face economic water scarcity if the estimated increases in water withdrawals required to meet projected demands are deemed to require economically excessive investments. As indicated in Figure 4.1, this procedure assigns economic water scarcity to most low-income

countries, but leaves North America, Europe and Japan with little or no water scarcity.

These adapted indicators, projections and scenarios still contain numerous crude assumptions. At the global level they are informative, provided the user and audience understands at least roughly what they are based upon. Unfortunately, in order to create a simple and powerful message, it is all too tempting to ignore uncertainties in the projections and complexities in actual and emerging water problems, and use the results to promote a narrative in which the increasing scarcity of water resources is the driving force.

Given the numerous uncertainties, it important not to assume that existing deficiencies in urban water and sanitation provision are the outcome of national or even city-level water stress. More specifically, it is important to avoid the tendency to present water stress statistics, statistics on the population with safe or improved access to water and sanitation, and statistics on water-related diseases, as if presenting a sequence of causally linked problems.

The following section examines the consequences of water stress for urban water provision in more detail, but also the relationship between urban water provision and water-related diseases. The national availability of fresh water resources per capita is used as the principal indicator of water stress, not because it is the best, but because it is widely used and relatively easy to interpret. Estimates based on watershed boundaries rather than national boundaries would be preferable, but cannot be compared with the available statistics on access to water, which are compiled nationally. Alternatively, including economic status in indicators of water stress would be misleading, since economic status is clearly a factor affecting access to water in ways that are independent of the regional or city-wide availability of water.

Regional water stress and its consequences for urban water and sanitation provision and health

As described in previous chapters, the regional availability of fresh water resources per capita is only one factor determining whether urban households have access to adequate water and sanitation. Cities in regions with plentiful fresh water resources may be situated in water-scarce localities, while cities in water-stressed regions may be located near plentiful supplies. Affluent cities can afford to tap more distant supplies, and compete more aggressively with other users. Perhaps more importantly, especially in less affluent cities, plentiful fresh water resources for the city as a whole are no guarantee that all residents will have access to adequate water and sanitation. There are many examples of cities well endowed with natural fresh water resources where a large share of the population have to fetch water of dubious quality from locations far from their homes, or pay high prices for water from itinerant vendors. And there are cities that are far less well endowed with fresh water where a far greater share of households have adequate water and sanitation. A comparative analysis of the water situation in Accra (Ghana), Harare (Zimbabwe) and Gabarone

(Botswana), for example, found that 'the country where water is not considered extremely scarce (Ghana) supplies its capital-city citizens with far less water than in the other two cities'.[15] Nevertheless, one would expect that on average urban residents in countries facing water stress would be less likely to have adequate access to water and perhaps even sanitary facilities. Problems of water scarcity do appear to be particularly acute in the many urban centres in relatively arid areas. Hundreds of urban centres which developed in relatively arid areas have grown beyond the point where adequate supplies can be tapped from local or even regional sources.

A review of urban water and sanitation in the Middle East and North Africa found that there were serious water shortages in Kuwait, Malta, United Arab Emirates, Qatar, Libya, Saudi Arabia, Yemen, Bahrain, Jordan and Israel, and constraints on meeting water needs in many other nations such as Algeria, Tunisia, Egypt and Oman.[16] Periodic droughts in the region can mean a decline in surface water supplies to about half the average level. Most of the region's urban population has piped supplies but intermittent supplies are common, especially during the summer.

For instance, in Algeria, the lack of rain during the last ten years with particular severity during 2000–2002 has cut water availability and affects most urban centres.[17] 86 per cent of the urban population is connected to the water network but the availability of water has declined – from several hours a day to several hours every two, three or even four days. This is despite the large investments made by the Algerian government since 1962 to mobilize ground- and surface-water resources – including the construction of 48 large dams. But many of the dams have reservoirs with water levels far below their intended capacity and some are close to empty. The problem of water shortages has been compounded by 20 years of under-investment in maintenance and management, which results in high levels of water loss to leaks and under-pricing, which in turn has meant that revenues were unable to cover the costs. Water prices were increased in the 1990s but the institutions

Box 4.1 Guadalajara's water crisis

Guadalajara is the second largest city in Mexico, with around 3.5 million inhabitants in 2000. It is the capital of the state of Jalisco and also the motor of its economy, which, by 1999, generated 7 per cent of Mexico's GNP. The city faces a very serious water shortage because the lake of Chapala from which it draws more than half its fresh water supply is drying up. This is largely the result of a long history of poor water management of the Lerma-Santiago Basin to which Chapala Lake belongs.

Chapala Lake is the largest lake in Mexico. Its water level has been dropping steadily for years and is at its lowest level for 100 years, with only some 23 per cent of its capacity in 2001; it is estimated that the level will decline to 19 per cent in 2002. As the lake becomes increasingly shallow, the temperature of the water increases and so too does the rate of evaporation. If the lake dries up, the city of Guadalajara will have great difficulty meeting the demand for water (already some rationing is taking place), and it will also affect the livelihoods of thousands of families who depend on it – for instance through tourism, fishing and water sports. Chapala Lake is also a natural regulator of the extended region's weather and if it dries up, it is likely to bring a decrease in rainfall.

The city of Guadalajara is seeking to cut the volume of water drawn from the lake. For example, the city will cut its withdrawals from the lake by 21 per cent during 2002, according to the most recent agreements of the basin's council, and eight different projects are being evaluated that would tap water from other sources, although all options mean going further and imply heavy investments.

Addressing this problem depends on concerted policies and actions in many states. Chapala Lake is fed by the Lerma River, which, because of water withdrawals upriver, now has decreasing flows. There are several dams upstream and heavy use of the river's water for agriculture. Urban, industrial and agricultural wastes also pollute the Lerma River as it crosses four states before arriving at the lake. The water resource problem is also not confined to Guadalajara, since the Santiago River (the lake's natural drainage) is heavily polluted by untreated industrial and urban wastewater as it flows through Guadalajara, affecting the possibilities for its use by other cities, smaller towns and farmers in the 547 kilometres it passes through before reaching the Pacific Ocean.

In part, this crisis is a result of too little attention given to water resource management (especially pollution control) over the last few decades, during which there have been rapid urban growth and increased industrialization. In the last decade, there have been important innovations within Mexico in regard to a stronger legal and institutional base for controlling pollution and managing water basins, but many city and state authorities have yet to act on these. In Guadalajara, a major project to address the water problems developed in 1998–1999 with external funding, but did not come to fruition because of political fights between the two main parties.

Awareness of the problem with Chapala Lake has increased at a regional, national and international level. The lake was chosen at the World Summit on Sustainable Development as a candidate 'on test' for a year to be part of the Living Lakes Association, in order to support projects for the recovery of the lake. However, as yet, the government has no projects in place to treat Guadalajara's urban wastewater.

Source: von Bertrab, E (2002), *Reconciling the Brown and the Green Agendas in an Urban and Regional Water Crisis; The Case of Guadalajara, Mexico*, Development Planning Unit, University College London, London.

were too weak to address 20 years of underinvestment in maintenance and management. Many new initiatives and investments are now underway to address these problems and to improve water management.

Many urban centres in other dryland areas in Africa also face particularly serious problems because of a combination of rapid growth in demand for water and unusually low rainfall in recent years, with the consequent dwindling of local fresh water resources. These and many other cities face problems in financing the expansion of supplies to keep up with demand – as the cheapest and most easily tapped water sources have been tapped or

polluted, and drawing on newer sources implies much higher costs per unit volume of water.[18] In Dakar (Senegal), as in many other cities, water supplies have to be drawn from ever more distant sources; this is because local groundwater supplies are fully used (and polluted) and local aquifers are over-pumped, resulting in saltwater intrusion; a substantial proportion of the city's water has to be brought in from the Lac de Guiers, 200 kilometres away.[19]

In Latin America, many of the coastal cities in Peru (including Lima), La Rioja and Catamarca in Argentina and also various cities in Northern Mexico are among the many cities

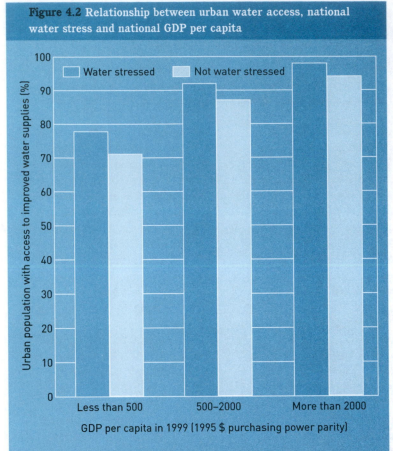

Figure 4.2 Relationship between urban water access, national water stress and national GDP per capita

Note: The figures include all countries for which there are estimates for renewable water resources per capita, GDP per capita and the share of urban households with access to improved water supplies. The shares presented weight the shares for each country equally regardless of population. Countries are defined as water stressed if their internal renewable water resources per capita are less than 1700 cubic metres.
Source: The estimates are based on data drawn from the Data Compendium of the United Nations Environment Programme (2002), *Global Environment Outlook 3*, UNEP and Earthscan, London.

with severe constraints on expanding fresh water supplies. Box 4.1 summarizes the water resource situation in Guadalajara, where there is an emerging water crisis as the result of increasing water stress and a lack of water resource management.

Despite these examples, it is important to question generalizations about the relationship between water stress and access to water and sanitation in urban centres. The following subsection employs internationally published data to explore the relationship between national fresh water availability per capita (a rough indicator of water stress) and the national share of urban population with access to 'safe', or more accurately 'improved', water supplies (see Chapter 1 for a discussion of recent revisions in international water access statistics, and an explanation for why 'improved' is now the preferred term). Past

studies indicate that the share of a country's population with access to 'improved' water supplies increases with rising per capita income.[20] The hypothesis implicit (and sometimes explicit) in the global water crisis literature is that access to safe water declines with rising water stress.

Comparing statistics on water stress and water access

Figure 4.2 summarizes the urban water access statistics for over 100 countries, with data on water stress, GDP per capita and the share of the urban population with access to improved water supplies. The results do not bear out the claim that water stress is contributing to inadequate access to water among urban populations. For both water-stressed and non-water-stressed countries, the average share of the population with access to improved water supplies increases with per capita income. However, at each of the three income levels, the average share among countries facing water stress is actually higher than among those countries not facing water stress. The differences between water-stressed and non-water-stressed countries within each income category are barely significant statistically, but these figures are difficult to reconcile with the claim that water stress is making an appreciable contribution to the difficulties people face in gaining access to improved water supplies.

A statistical analysis based on earlier estimates of access to water supplies provided similar results.[21] For both urban and rural populations, the statistical analysis found a significant and positive relationship between income and access to water, but again found that access to water was actually higher in countries facing water stress.

That water access statistics are surprisingly high in water-scarce countries has long been remarked upon, and explained in terms of the priority given to securing 'protected' or 'improved' water supplies where water is scarce. In countries where water is more plentiful, households may be more likely to rely on 'unimproved' sources (eg surface water), as these are more readily available.

Similarly, governments may not make the same effort to ensure that improved water supplies are made widely available. If unimproved sources truly are unsafe, such factors could create a situation where more plentiful supplies are associated with less safe household water supplies.

Not having access to an improved source would, however, be expected to impose more of a health and welfare burden where water resources are scarce. Thus, the implicit assumption that unimproved sources are equally unsafe and improved sources are equally safe, could lead to a relative under-estimate of the water-related burdens households face in water-scarce countries and cities. Even within a city, differences in water stress can make an appreciable difference. In Jakarta, for example, shallow well water is considered unsafe for human consumption, although a large share of the population relies on it for washing and often for drinking as well. However, the hardship and risks of not having access to improved (ie, piped) supplies are far greater in North Jakarta, where the groundwater is saline, than in South Jakarta. The statistics may look better in North Jakarta than in South Jakarta, with an estimated 33 per cent rather than 9 per cent having piped water connections in 1991. However, those without piped supplies in North Jakarta were forced to buy extremely expensive drinking water from itinerant vendors, and often had to wash with salinated water. In South Jakarta, on the other hand, the residents themselves generally consider the well water adequate for all purposes (drinking water is always boiled in Jakarta, whether from wells or piped supplies). These sorts of differences might also be expected to arise when comparing more and less water-stressed cities.

The difficulties that urban populations face in coping with increasing water stress must also be viewed in terms of the more general tendency to ignore the water-related problems of disadvantaged groups, in terms of both statistics and policy responses (see Chapter 1). Just as the problems some urban households face getting adequate water and sanitation tend to be under-represented in the statistics, any additional difficulties related to water stress – such as falling water tables – will also tend to be ignored when they affect only economically and politically disadvantaged groups. Moreover, in many cities in Asia, Africa and Latin America, an appreciable share of households rely on multiple water sources, not just for different uses, but because their supplies are unreliable: piped supplies are inter-rupted, wells dry up, vendor prices change. Increasing water resource scarcity can further decrease the reliability of at least some of the water supplies, including piped water supplies when these are not well managed.

The gender dimensions of water stress can also be important, as it is often women who have to respond to water stress at the household level, and their difficulties can be hidden behind household statistics and policies that target households. More generally, the manner in which increasing water stress at a regional level translates into changes at city and neighbourhood levels depends very much on the social and economic as well as physical context.

Water stress, sanitation and health

In over-simplified accounts, increasing global water stress is not only blamed for the inade-quate access to water in many urban centres, but for inadequate sanitation and water-related diseases. If the relationship between water stress and access to water is not as direct as is sometimes claimed, bringing in sanitation and health makes the relationships even less straightforward, and further empha-sizes the importance of the local context.

Just as it is sometimes suggested that water stress is the major factor preventing urban residents from being able to access adequate water, it is sometimes suggested that the ingestion of water contaminated with faecal material is the main cause of illness in low-income countries. In the plan of action (Agenda 21) that emerged from the United Nations Conference on Environment and Development, for example, it was stated that 'An estimated 80 per cent of all diseases and over one third of deaths in developing countries are caused by the consumption of contaminated water'. This statement contrasts strongly with the discussion of water and health in Chapter 2. It is not only an extreme over-statement of the relative importance of water-borne diseases, but a misleading portrayal of how and why such diseases spread.[22] The water-related diseases described in Chapter 2 relate to water in many different ways. More importantly, the responses that will be effective vary. The extent of this variation is hidden by references to unsafe or contaminated water.

Even for diarrhoeal diseases, contaminated water is typically only one of many (faecal–oral) transmission routes. A wide range of pathogens, including various bacteria and viruses, can cause diarrhoea. Diarrhoeal diseases are often classified as water-borne because most of these pathogens can be transmitted through drinking water. The term 'water-borne' is misleading inasmuch as it can seem to imply that these diseases are always (or predominantly) transmitted in water. Almost all diseases that can be acquired by drinking contaminated water can also be acquired by eating contaminated food, through personal contact with infected people, and through direct exposure to faecal material.[23] As such, a lack of water for washing, poor food and personal hygiene practices and inadequate sanitation can also facilitate their spread. The favoured routes vary depending on the nature of the pathogen (eg, the infective dose, the existence of non-human hosts, the latency period and the ability of the pathogen to persist and multiply outside of a host), and of course on local conditions. The majority of cases of diarrhoea are not a straightforward effect of inadequate access to clean drinking water supplies. Where sanitation is very poor or hygiene behaviour does not change, improving access to water is unlikely to have an appreciable affect on health.[24]

For most other water-related diseases, water resource scarcity and the availability of clean drinking water are typically even less central. Most urban malaria is contracted from mosquitoes breeding in accumulations of relatively clean water – water stress caused by pollution or even scarcity can actually reduce malaria transmission. The mosquitoes that spread dengue fever favour different breeding sites, often including small water containers[25] more likely to be found in households with irregular or distant water supplies (and hence using more water containers). Trachoma is associated with insufficient face washing, and depends more on having access to water than on the quality of that water.[26] The eggs of intestinal worms (helminths) are generally excreted in faeces, and can be transported in water, but the parasites more typically enter the body by other means than water. Schistosomes (the flatworms that cause schistosomiasis, which is sometimes called bilharzia) enter the body through contact with infested surface water, and may be contracted while collecting drinking water in peri-urban areas, but not usually from ingesting the water.

In short, while these health problems do relate to cities' water resource problems, they can take a variety of different forms. One can be confident that in a healthy city or neighbourhood, people are getting sufficient water and disposing of faeces safely, but the important water-related risks in unhealthy cities and neighbourhoods can range from groundwater contaminated by local latrines, to falling water tables, to sewage entering the water pipes, to unhygienic behaviour, to the presence of breeding sites for malarial mosquitoes, to polluted waterways, to high water prices, and any number of other possible conditions. Increasing population and competing water demands are likely to exacerbate a number of water-related health risks, but a great deal depends not only on the local context but also on the local response to the increasing water stress.

Both inadequate water provision in poor neighbourhoods and water stress in urban regions are often critical problems demanding urgent attention. In principle, they could be addressed in tandem, with measures to reduce water stress also being used to secure better access to water for low-income households. If water stress is not the cause of inadequate water access, however, this complementarity will not be achieved automatically or without conflicts of interest. Water freed up by conservation measures, for example, is unlikely to flow to those without piped water connections unless the reasons for their deprivation are addressed directly. Any attempt to address these problems must also come to terms with the political, economic and institutional aspects of water use and distribution. Indeed, the obvious explanation for the lack of relation between national water stress and household water scarcity is that the human-made water supply and distribution systems are not responding to the needs of the urban (and rural) poor.

Institutional issues are addressed in more detail in later chapters. The following section turns instead to the other side of the relationship between water stress and urban water and sanitation systems: the ways in which urban development itself can contribute to water stress.

Urban development and its contribution to water stress

Cities transform the water environments and landscapes not only within the built-up area but also for considerable distances around. This includes environmental impacts in the region around the city, which usually includes large areas defined as (or considered) rural. The more populous the city and the richer its inhabitants, the greater the demand on resources and, in general, the larger the area from which these are drawn. Water use and pollution are also critically influenced by the nature of a city's productive activities and its land use patterns. From a water perspective, 'the boundaries drawn on a map have little relationship to an urban area's true boundaries, which are defined more correctly by water extraction and disposal'.[27] Moreover, urban consumption and production can make indirect demands on even more distant water systems through the use of what has come to be termed 'virtual water'.

Virtual water refers to the water used to produce food crops, electric power and other commodities that are traded internationally.[28] For example, use of virtual water has helped to achieve national food security in Egypt

through imports of wheat and maize.[29] Use of virtual water rather than actual water in cities can reduce urban water demand and the consequent effects of this demand on the region, without compromising city commodity security. If virtual water is considered, the ecological footprint of a city in terms of water use can extend far beyond the local watershed. The principal focus of this section, however, is on the more direct impacts of urban development on water stress in the region where the city is located.

The inhabitants, environment and natural resource base of the region in which an urban area is located are usually affected by:

- the demand from city-based enterprises, households and institutions for the products of forests, rangelands, farmlands, watersheds or aquatic ecosystems that are outside its boundaries (including, for example, hydroelectricity);
- the solid, liquid and air-borne wastes generated within the city and transferred to the region around it which have environmental impacts, especially on water bodies in which liquid wastes are disposed of or storm and surface run-off ends up without adequate treatment; and
- the expansion of the built-up area and the transformations this brings – for instance, as land surfaces are reshaped, valleys and swamps filled, large volumes of clay, sand, gravel and crushed rock extracted and moved, water sources tapped and rivers and streams channelled.[30]

From a water perspective, these three broad groupings of environmental impacts can be narrowed down to issues of urban water demand, urban water pollution and the effects of urban structural transformations on water systems. Each is discussed in turn below. However, it is important to bear in mind that many of the other environmental consequences of urban development, such as the demand for forest products and urban air pollution, can also affect water systems. Moreover, while this section concentrates on the environmental costs, urban-based demand for rural resources

Table 4.1 Water withdrawals by sector and region (combines various recent years)

Region	Water withdrawals (cubic kilometres per annum)	Agriculture (%)	Industry (%)	Domestic (%)
Africa	152	85	6	9
Asia and Pacific	1850	86	8	6
Europe	456	36	49	15
Latin America and Caribbean	263	73	9	18
North America	512	39	47	13
West Asia	84	90	4	6
Total	3317	71	20	10

Source: United Nations Environment Programme (2002), *Global Environment Outlook 3* (Data Compendium), UNEP and Earthscan, London.

is also an important (and often the most important) basis for rural incomes and livelihoods. Such rural incomes produced by urban demand may form the basis for prosperous, well managed farms, fisheries, forests and water management. A focus on cities' water-related burdens is useful for identifying challenges that need to be addressed, but should not be interpreted as a comprehensive or balanced account of how urban development alters water systems.

Urban water demand

Table 4.1 provides a summary of water withdrawals by sector for different regions of the world. Statistics distinguishing between urban and rural uses are not available, but one would expect urban uses to account for a small share of agriculture, and a large share of industry and domestic uses (which include household water use, but also other municipal uses). With about 70 per cent of global water withdrawals for agriculture, the share of withdrawals accounted for by urban water use

would appear to be less than a quarter, with even smaller shares in Africa, Asia and the Pacific where agriculture accounts for about 85 per cent of water withdrawals.

Table 4.2 provides a breakdown of global water withdrawals and consumption (1995 estimates). Judging by these estimates, urban water use is even less significant when measured in terms of consumption (which only includes water withdrawals that result in evaporation or incorporation into products or organisms). This is because a large share of industrial and municipal water use is returned to local water bodies in the form of wastewater. This water may or may not be available for re-use, depending on how it is used and whether it is treated prior to release. Polluted wastewater may render large additional quantities of water unusable. But from a narrow supply–demand balance perspective, urban water consumption is not a major global issue. Far more important is how urban centres use and abuse water.

Along with pollution (see following subsection), the spatial concentration of urban

Table 4.2 Global water withdrawals and consumption by sector

	Total (cubic kilometres per annum)	Agriculture (%)	Industries (%)	Municipalities (%)	Reservoirs* (%)
Water withdrawals	3800	66	20	9	5
Water consumption	2100	83	4	2	10

Note: * = evaporation.
Source: Shiklomanov, I A (2000), 'Appraisal and assessment of world water resources', *Water International*, Vol 25, No 1, 2000, pages 11–32, cited in Cosgrove, W J and F R Rijsberman, *World Water Vision: Making Water Everybody's Business*, Earthscan, London.

water demands can have important implications for the broader water environment. On the one hand, concentrated and growing urban demands may require the delivery of water from increasingly distant locations or lead to the over-abstraction of groundwater resources. On the other hand, many cities are purposefully located on or near rivers or lakes (not only to facilitate withdrawals of water for urban uses but also for reasons of transport and communications), making urban demands easier to meet than if those same households and industries were dispersed in the rural landscape. Much depends on the specific situation of individual cities, and it is difficult to generalize about urban contributions to water stress.

While the use of more distant water resources requires infrastructure investment and is more common in affluent regions, changes are evident in low-income countries. Research on changing water demand in African urban areas, for example, reveals that in the early 1970s, many used groundwater supplies such as springs, wells and boreholes as their primary sources of water. Only North African and Saharan locations were reported to use distant groundwater supplies. However, in the 1990s, urban areas relied more on inter-basin water transfers, and moved from depending on groundwater to river water. Many African urban areas increased the number of rivers they tapped, and also relied increasingly on rivers further than 25 kilometres away.[31]

The economic or demographic growth of cities in poor water locations can create special challenges. Much of Hong Kong's water supply is transferred over from the East River (Dongjiang) basin in mainland China,[32] and Mexico City receives a quarter of its water supply, or around 16 cubic metres per second, from an aqueduct importing water from the neighbouring Lerma and Cutzamala basins.

Often cities face very significant choices about how to increase their water supplies. Beijing is currently facing such a choice. Water shortages in the North China plain and the cities of Beijing and Tianjing could be eased by the proposed 'middle route project' of south to north water transfer. This project is 1230 kilometres long and consists of the Danjiangkou dam and canal system, which will transport 15 billion cubic metres of water from the Danjiangkou reservoir, where a water surplus exists, to the provinces of Henan and Hebei.[33] However, one of the reasons for the lack of usable water in Beijing is the land use patterns and industrial pollution in upstream Hebei province. An alternative approach would be to invest in ecological improvements upstream. To date, pressures from Beijing have contributed to the degradation of the upstream ecology, siltation and the pollution of water flowing down towards Beijing. This is not a physical necessity, however, and mechanisms to link Beijing's demand for water to improvements upstream are also being explored (see discussion of integrated water resource management in Chapter 6).

Demand for hydroelectric power has also increased the water demand associated with urban development. Hydroelectric power is a major source of electricity for 26 countries from the Sahel to Southern Africa, and a secondary source for a further 13.[34] The Chinese government has favoured large water engineering projects for many years, as illustrated by the Three Gorges Dam project, which is the largest hydro-development in the world.[35]

Water withdrawal for direct or indirect urban use can cause several regional environmental problems. Subsidence as a result of aquifer over-exploitation is a common problem and has been documented in the Po Valley of Northern Italy,[36] the Valley of Mexico in which Mexico City is located, Bangkok and a number of other cities. The central part of Mexico City has subsided an average of 7.5 metres over the last 100 years. This in turn has exacerbated flood problems, and in order to confine storm water, dykes have had to be built and pumping has been required to lift drainage water that used to flow by gravity. Because subsidence rates vary, many structures (including sewers) have been weakened, and some buildings lean dangerously, a phenomenon which is made more serious by frequent seismic activity. Since the 1950s, when many wells in the city centre were closed, the subsidence rate in the central area has stabilized at around 6 centimetres per year, but in other areas sinking velocity can be up to 40 centimetres per year. In other cities, land subsidence has required the transportation of water over long distances at enormous costs.[37]

Aquifer over-exploitation also leads to falling water tables, spring cessation, decreasing river flows, the enlargement of dry root zones in soils, increased pollution vulnerability and (for coastal cities) sea water intrusion. For example, wetland drying, subsidence, piezometric level decline and decreased river flow have been observed in the Toluca Aquifer, which supplies urban and industrial water to Mexico City.[38] The total abstraction from Mexico City's aquifer is over 55 cubic metres per second (of which 42 are used for the city, and the rest for agriculture), and many local springs have dried up as a result.

While poorly managed urban development can lead to various forms of water stress, it is important to recognize that this depends very much on planning decisions (or the lack thereof). Perhaps more importantly from the perspective of water and sanitation provision, the water required to meet basic health needs is not a source of significant water stress globally or even, with a few exceptions, locally. Supplying everyone in the world (including both rural and urban dwellers) with the 60–100 or so litres a day considered necessary for health would require roughly 220 cubic kilometres of water a year, or about 6 per cent of total withdrawals. Supplying the urban population alone would account for about half of this, amounting to roughly a third of current municipal water use.[39] Of course, a large share of the world's urban dwellers already use more than 100 litres a day. Assuming half of the world's urban dwellers need an average of 30 more litres of water a day, municipal water use would only need to increase by about 5 per cent to meet the 100 litre target. Even given the extremely rough nature of such estimates, it seems reasonable to conclude that supplying people with adequate water to meet basic needs does not contribute seriously to the threat of water stress, unless it is done in a way that also encourages additional uses of water by other users or pollutes large amounts of additional water.

Water pollution

Urban development can contribute to water stress in other ways than just through the redistribution and use of water. Water needed for industrial processes, for supplying residential and commercial buildings, for transporting sewage and for other uses is then returned to rivers, lakes or the sea at a far lower quality than that originally supplied. The effects of cities on the rural environment through agro-environmental demands such as deforestation and vegetation removal, wetland transformation, monocultural crop production, agro-chemical inputs, concentrated animal production, over-grazing and irrigation also raise the pollution levels of associated water bodies and affect both soil water quantity and quality.[40] Cities pollute groundwater supplies, aquifers and coastal areas, and air pollutants generated by city-based enterprises or consumers are often transferred to the surrounding region through acid rain and can affect water bodies at considerable distances from the pollution source. Thus regional and global water cycles can be affected by urban development, the consequences of which can be felt amongst urban residents themselves, the surrounding region and the wider global environment.

Liquid wastes from city activities often have environmental impacts stretching beyond the immediate hinterland. It is common for fisheries to be damaged or destroyed by liquid effluents from city-based industries, with hundreds or even thousands of people losing their livelihoods as a result. River pollution from city-based industries and untreated sewage can lead to serious health problems in settlements downstream. The *Fifth Citizen's Report on the State of India's Environment* documents in considerable detail the high levels of river pollution in many major Indian rivers coming from industries, industrial or mining complexes or cities, which then affect the health and livelihoods of those living downstream.[41] Rivers that are heavily contaminated as they pass through cities may become unusable for agriculture downstream, or particular contaminants in the water may damage crops or pose risks to human health. For instance, cadmium and lead concentrations in rivers are particular problems downstream from certain industries, and if the water is used for growing crops like rice, those regularly eating that rice can easily exceed the WHO-defined acceptable daily intake.[42] For instance, the Damodar river in India is so polluted by industries on its banks that its water becomes unfit even for agriculture, let alone for human consumption. Yet the river remains the main source of drinking water for numerous rural and urban centres that are located along its banks downstream of the industries.[43]

Contaminated aquifers are expensive and difficult, if not impossible, to purify. 53 per cent of Africa's land surface has no discharge to the sea, which means contaminants in aquifers are likely to persist.[44] Aquifer contamination occurs due to pollution from industry and also household waste. For example, groundwater nitrate levels have risen in the central valley of Costa Rica due to unsewered sanitation systems.[45] Excessive pollution can pose a major constraint to development, as illustrated in Tianjin City in China's Huaihe Basin, one of the most polluted and water-scarce river basins in the country.[46]

Storm and surface run-off can be particularly high in pollutants. It collects large pollution loads as it flows through cities, especially where there is inadequate provision for solid waste collection. Faecally polluted urban run-off in combination with inadequately treated wastewater effluents from Bloemfontein, South Africa, overcame the assimilation capacity of the Renoster Spruit beside the city to the extent that downstream water posed an infection risk for potential users for considerable distances.[47] Urban storm water can be up to ten times more polluted than dry weather wastewater owing to wash-off from roads and open spaces, pollution gathered during percolation through the soil, and resuspension of deposits accumulated in sewers and drains.[48] This results in pollution surges. For example, studies of storm water run-off in developing and developed urban areas in South Africa revealed that pollution levels exceeded safety margins in guidelines for recreational water quality. This run-off was then a major source of faecal river pollution for river catchments downstream that were used for human consumption and recreation.[49]

In cities on or close to coasts, untreated sewage and industrial effluents often flow into the sea with little or no provision to pipe them out far enough to protect the beaches and inshore waters. Most coastal cities in low- and middle-income nations have serious problems with dirty, contaminated beaches, and sea water can be a major health risk to bathers. Oil pollution often adds to existing problems of sewage and industrial effluents. Pollution may be so severe that many beaches have to be closed to the public. It is usually the most accessible beaches that are most polluted and, in many cities, these are the beaches most widely used by lower-income groups. Richer households suffer much less, as those with automobiles can reach more distant, less accessible and less polluted beaches.[50]

The contamination of rivers, lakes, sea shores and coastal waters is often an example of government negligence in controlling pollution and managing surface and wastewater flows. This can lead to serious health problems for large numbers of people whose water supply is drawn from these water sources. The possibilities for improvement vary greatly. In many of the largest cities in Europe and North America that are located on rivers or by lakes, great improvements have been achieved in reducing water pollution – mostly through stricter controls on industrial emissions and more sophisticated and comprehensive treatment of sewage and water run-off collected in drains. Rather less success has been achieved in reducing polluting discharges to the sea. In most cities in low- and middle-income nations, the problems are not so easily addressed as they have much more serious 'non-point' sources of water pollution because of the lack of sewers and drains in many city districts and peripheral areas, and the inadequate collection of solid wastes.

Structural transformations

The construction of urban infrastructure usually involves reshaping land surfaces and altering natural water systems. Swamps may be filled and lakes drained. For example, Mexico City has gradually overtaken numerous former lakebeds, progressively drained since colonial times. The Valley of Mexico, originally a closed basin, was also artificially opened in the 1700s in order to control flooding. This has enabled Mexico City to remove its effluents from the basin. Without this, or some alternative form of displacement, Mexico City's aquifer would have been destroyed by pollution long ago.[51] Urban areas also tap and channel water sources. It has been estimated that 'at least 90 per cent of total water discharge from US rivers is strongly affected by channel fragmentation from dams, reservoirs, inter-basin diversions, and irrigation'.[52] Structures to store water in dams and reservoirs for city use have been constructed in greater numbers over the years. For example, research on changing water demand in African urban areas shows that less than one-third of locations studied stored water for collective use in the 1970s, whereas 46 per cent of locations made efforts to collect water in the 1990s. Many of these storage facilities were for the provision of hydroelectric power,[53] which is often erroneously thought to have a neutral effect on water resources because evaporation from water reservoirs is not taken into account.[54]

In most low- and middle-income nations, in the absence of any effective land use plan or other means to guide and control new developments, cities generally expand haphazardly – determined by where different households, residential areas, enterprises and public sector activities locate, legally and illegally. Uncontrolled physical growth impacts most on what might be termed the immediate hinterland around a city, much of which cannot be described as urban and yet is no longer rural. Within this area, agriculture may disappear or decline as land is bought up by people or companies in anticipation of the increases in land value accompanying changes from agricultural to urban use. There is usually a lack of effective public control of such land use changes or on the profits that can be made from them, even when it is public investment (for instance the expansion of road networks) that creates much of the increment in land value.[55]

In most low- and middle-income nations, unplanned and uncontrolled city expansion produces a patchwork of different developments, including businesses, industry and many high-density residential settlements, interspersed with land that remains undeveloped in anticipation of speculative gain. Development occurs through legal and illegal action by various landowners, builders, developers and real estate firms in an ad hoc way. There are usually many legal sub-divisions in this hinterland for houses or commercial and industrial buildings which have been approved without reference to any city-wide plan. Many cities have a considerable range of new factories and other businesses developing in surrounding 'rural' areas although their functioning and markets are intimately tied to the city.[56] In more prosperous cities, many new low-density, high-income residential neighbourhoods may also develop here, along with some commercial developments and leisure facilities for higher-income groups (for instance, country clubs and golf courses). In many cities, especially those with high levels of crime and violence, there are often many residential developments enclosed within walls around the cities (usually close to major highways) which are protected by private security firms – the 'walled cities' or *barrios cerrados*. There are usually many unauthorized sub-divisions as well and where regulation is lax, these may cater for middle- and upper-income developments too. There are usually illegal squatter communities too, who originally located there because the inaccessibility, lack of infrastructure and poor quality of the site gave more chance of not being evicted. In many cities (including Buenos Aires, Delhi, Santiago, Seoul and Manila), this hinterland also contains settlements formed when their inhabitants were dumped there after being evicted from their homes by slum or squatter clearance.[57]

The uncontrolled and unregulated physical expansion of a city's built-up area usually has serious social and environmental consequences. This includes the segregation of low-income groups in the worst located and often the most dangerous areas, to which it is difficult and expensive to provide water, sanitation and drainage. The haphazard expansion of settlements generally builds into the urban fabric greatly increased costs for providing basic infrastructure as new developments that need connection to networks of water mains and sewerage and drainage systems spring up far from existing networks. Illegal or informal settlements are often concentrated on land sites already subject to flooding, or at risk from landslides or other natural hazards, especially where these offer well-located sites on which low-income settlers have the best chance of establishing a home and/or avoiding eviction. But these are also land sites to which it is more difficult and expensive to extend basic infrastructure.[58] Most illegal settlements also have layouts and other site characteristics – such as unclear plot boundaries, unstable soils and lack of public rights of way – which greatly increase the costs of infrastructure provision.[59] In addition, as discussed in Chapter 3, the agencies or companies whose responsibility it is to provide piped water and provision for sanitation and drainage may be reluctant to install the needed infrastructure in illegal settlements or may be prohibited from doing so.

It is not only around the major cities that uncontrolled urban expansion produces these kinds of serious social and ecological impacts. For instance, in Bamenda in Cameroon, settlements expanded up the steep hill slopes of the Bamenda escarpment with no public provisions to ensure that the more unstable areas were avoided or to minimize soil erosion when sites were cleared. Flooding has become a particular problem, as land-clearance-induced erosion contributes to the silting of stream beds or other drains and more rapid water run-off. The impact of the floods is made more serious by the expansion of settlements over flood plains and the inadequate provision for drainage, along with the expansion of paved or otherwise impervious surfaces.[60]

Other water problems related to uncontrolled city expansion include:

- The difficulties in protecting water sources and moderating storm flows as new urban developments occur within watersheds and surface water sources become polluted. The lack of control of new development may mean a rapid expansion of new settlements and enterprises around water reservoirs, which also dispose of their wastes into the reservoirs. Drainage systems are often damaged by uncontrolled developments, including land clearance and deforestation, which greatly increase silt loads that clog drainage channels. In general, as small towns grow into cities, urban run-off increases and reaches water bodies faster and with greater force – which also often means heavier sediment loads.[61]

- The increase in wastewater flows (including storm and surface run-off) with the expansion of impermeable surfaces and the extraction, use and disposal of available water sources, which often brings much increased risks of flooding and reduces the infiltration and recharge of aquifers.[62]

- The new possibilities for disease vectors. The expansion of the built-up area, the construction of roads, water reservoirs and drains together with land clearance and deforestation can effect drastic changes to the local ecology. Natural foci for disease vectors may become entrapped within the suburban extension and new ecological niches for the animal reservoirs may be created. Within urban conurbations, disease vectors may adapt to new habitats and introduce new infections to spread among the urban population.

- The impact on peri-urban agriculture. Most major cities grew within fertile agricultural areas, and expanding new urban developments often cover high-quality agricultural land, while water demand from urban-based enterprises or consumers can pre-empt water previously used by farmers.

Disasters and water and sanitation

All cities face risks from a range of disasters such as extreme weather events, fires, epidemics, transport and industrial accidents. Many cities are also in areas at risk of earthquakes. Floods are obviously the disaster most connected to water and sanitation, in that the infrastructure for getting rid of wastewater is usually also the infrastructure for getting rid of storm water (for instance, when sewers are also used as storm drains or surface drains also serve as sewers). Water management systems for supplying fresh water also generally have important roles in controlling floods – or should have. Changes that affect water flows beyond a city's boundaries can also affect the likelihood of floods. Thus flooding can also be made worse by changing rural land use patterns and inadequate watershed management.

Most cities face risks from floods, in part because so many cities are located on coasts or in river valleys, and in part because cities by their very nature have large areas that are built over and thus impervious so that rain, flood water and wastewater do not drain into the ground. Heavy rain falling on large urban areas produces large and rapidly flowing volumes of water, which are very dangerous if the drainage network cannot cope with them. When floods occur, the fact that buildings and infrastructure stand in the way of flood waters can lead to large and rapidly flowing flood water channels, which can be particularly destructive.

There are many links between good provision for water and sanitation, and disaster prevention and preparedness. For instance, a city with a good sewerage, drainage and garbage collection system is also a city much better able to reduce the risk of flooding. Good quality housing and infrastructure reduces risks of collapse if flooding occurs. A good emergency service that exists to respond to daily non-disaster accidents and acute illnesses can also serve as the basis for rapid and effective emergency responses when disasters occur.

Floods

Floods in cities occur when the volume of water (from whatever source) overwhelms the natural and human-constructed systems of drainage; well designed and managed sewers, drains and natural or artificially created water bodies are a key part of removing or reducing the risks that these pose. Most floods arise from natural causes – heavy rainfall or snowmelt, exceptionally high tides and storm surges[63] – but most of the deaths, injuries and loss of property they cause in urban areas are human-induced, both because protective measures were not taken (so no provision was made to safely channel or store abnormally high volumes of water) and because of inaction in flood warning, flood preparation and post-disaster response. In cities where flooding is common, it is generally low-income people who are most affected as they have settled on floodplains or the banks of rivers, drains or other areas most at risk of flooding.

During the decade 1991–2000, floods were the most commonly reported form of 'natural' disaster world-wide.[64] Of the 2557 natural disasters recorded, 35 per cent were floods, 29 per cent windstorms, 9 per cent droughts/famines and 8 per cent earthquakes. (There were almost as many non-natural disasters as natural disasters during this decade, most of them the result of transport accidents.) Floods were also the (natural and non-natural) disaster type that affected most people and caused most damage; a total of 1.44 million people were affected by flood disasters during the period 1991–2000, with estimated damage totalling US$273 million. But floods were behind droughts/famines and windstorms in terms of the number of people reported killed; 97,747 people were reported killed during the decade by floods, with droughts/famines disasters killing 280,007 and windstorm disasters killing 205,635 (see Table 4.3).

All disasters that disrupt provision for water and sanitation bring a risk of disease epidemics. Floods can contaminate all available water supplies and be associated with epidemics of dysentery or other water-borne and water-washed diseases. Outbreaks of

Table 4.3 The impact of flood disasters by region and by human development score

Region	Number of flood disasters	Number of people killed by flood disasters	Number of people affected	Total amount of estimated damage (US$m)
Africa	174	8163	16,267	591
Americas	214	35,687	9593	37,051
Asia	342	52,437	1,413,095	125,392
Europe	134	1438	3335	108,861
Oceania	24	22	230	923
High human development countries	199	2121	5819	65,340
Medium human development countries	496	82,566	1,344,397	184,401
Low human development countries	193	13,060	92,306	23,078
Total	888	97,747	1,442,521	272,819

Note: For these statistics, a 'disaster' is defined as a situation or event in which at least one of the following criteria are fulfilled:
• ten or more people killed;
• 100 people reported affected (ie, requiring immediate assistance during a period of emergency – requiring basic survival tools such as food, water, shelter, sanitation and immediate medical assistance);
• call for international assistance; and/or
• declaration of state of emergency.

Source: Drawn from tables in the International Federation of Red Cross and Red Crescent Societies (2001), *World Disasters Report: Focus on Recovery*, Kumarian Press, Bloomfield, USA. The figures are based on data drawn from the Emergency Events Database maintained by the Centre for Research on the Epidemiology of Disasters.

leptospirosis (usually caused by drinking water infected by rat urine) have been associated with floods in Rio de Janeiro and São Paulo, and those living in poor-quality settlements at risk of flooding with high levels of over-crowding and inadequate provision for garbage collection (or living close to garbage dumps) are particularly at risk.[65] Leptospirosis is recognized as a serious environmental health problem in many areas in India, including its two largest cities, Delhi and Mumbai.[66]

Table 4.3 also shows how most of those who were killed or seriously affected by floods during the 1990s lived in low and medium human development countries. As with most disasters, the economic costs of floods may be high in the wealthier nations, but they kill or seriously affect far fewer people. Most people in wealthier nations have insurance to cover the costs of losses to property, and relatively few lose their livelihoods. This is generally not the case in floods in low- and middle-income nations, where there is a huge (and usually uncounted) cost that goes beyond those killed or injured by the floods. It includes the often devastating loss of homes, property and means of earning an income for many low-income groups, which may not add up to much in terms of economic value but still includes most

or all of these groups' asset bases and livelihood sources. And these groups have no insurance. Floods often bring particularly serious problems of water contamination for those without piped water supplies and for those reliant on pit latrines, as these over-flow and human excreta is spread everywhere. Without rapid and effective emergency responses, large sections of the population are often forced to rely on contaminated water sources. Food prices often rise dramatically after disasters. Those whose homes and neighbourhoods have been destroyed are often moved to temporary shelters or relief camps, which are far from the locations where they previously earned their income. These are the kinds of costs that often do not get counted, or that are given a monetary value which bears almost no relation to the devastation caused to large numbers of people.

However, the catastrophic floods affecting large areas of Europe in August 2002 demonstrate that even the wealthiest nations may not have made provision to cope with exceptional conditions – and here there was a significant loss of life, although this was small compared to the loss of life from major floods in most cities in low- and middle-income nations.

It is not possible to provide a rural–urban breakdown for the figures in the above table, and a very large part of the deaths, injuries and loss of livelihoods from floods occur in rural areas. But a large and probably increasing proportion of the people and businesses affected by floods are in urban areas. In part, this is because an increasing proportion of the population and economic activity are in urban areas in most nations. In part, this is because many urban areas concentrate people and economic activities in ways that greatly increase their vulnerability to flooding – rather than reducing it, which is what should happen in any well governed city. Box 4.2 gives the example of flooding in Vargas in Venezuela, which killed over 30,000 people in 1999, seriously affected another 100,000 and devastated the state's economy. Although the trigger for the floods and landslides was exceptionally heavy rainfall, the main reason for the scale of this devastation was the large numbers of houses and businesses that had developed with little control to limit the risk from flooding and avoid the development of land sites most at risk. The point made in Chapter 1 about the multiple linkages between rural and urban areas also needs stressing here; floods in rural areas usually also flood the network of market towns and administrative and service centres that meet rural-based demand for goods and services, and the devastation that floods bring to rural livelihoods also brings devastation to those (rural and urban) businesses that rely on their produce or their demand.

Other kinds of disaster

Floods are not the only disaster of concern for water and sanitation. Most disasters have the potential to disrupt, damage or destroy the systems used by households, neighbourhoods, cities or city regions for water and sanitation, or to pollute water supplies and thus bring very large risks, including risks of epidemics from water-borne diseases. So there is an obvious need for understanding disaster risks in each city and taking measures to reduce the vulnerability of water and sanitation systems to them. Consideration also needs to be given

to non-flood disasters that arise from the failure to manage wastewater flows – including the landslides or mudslides that so often claim dozens or even hundreds of lives in cities around the world and, like floods, leave a far larger number of people homeless and without livelihoods, and cause serious damage to schools, health centres and other urban buildings. Landslides can take the form of mudflows, rockfalls or avalanches. They are often triggered by storms, waterlogged soils or heavy construction (although they may also be triggered by earthquakes or volcanic eruptions). Many major cities and thousands of smaller urban centres have high concentrations of people living on or below steep slopes and cliffs. Most are low-income households with limited possibilities of finding land for housing elsewhere and limited means to make their shelters safer.

High winds (including cyclones) often occur with heavy rainfall (which in turn may cause flooding, landslides and mudflows) and, in low-lying coastal areas, storm-surge flooding. The urban areas most at risk are heavily concentrated in coastal areas in the tropics, where there are thousands of urban centres, including many of the world's large cities.

Effective fire-fighting services usually need large volumes of water locally available throughout a city. Generally, this requires water mains available in all parts of a city at high pressure. Historically, many of the greatest urban disasters have been caused by fires, although with modern materials and urban designs and fire-fighting responses, this is no longer the case. Measures to limit the risk of large-scale fires were also among the first examples of disaster prevention. Many disasters set off numerous accidental fires – for instance, the fires in ruptured gas pipes in the 1995 Kobe earthquake.

Global warming will increase the frequency and severity of many floods and other 'natural' disasters in urban areas. For instance, the threat of flooding will be particularly serious for many port cities because of the rise in sea level and the increased frequency and severity of storms. Rising sea levels and the increased scale and frequency of floods will also bring disruption to sewers and

Box 4.2 Floods and landslides in Vargas, Venezuela

In Vargas state, landslides destroyed 5500 homes and apartments, damaged another 25,000 and wrecked roads, hospitals, and water, sanitation and communications infrastructure; between 80,000 and 100,000 people were affected and up to 30,000 died. Along a 52-kilometre strip, whole neighbourhoods were washed away or buried by walls of water, mud and boulders 15–20 metres high. Unusually high rainfall linked to La Niña triggered this; in the first fortnight of December 1999, it rained eight times harder than normal. Mudslides washed away topsoil and vegetation and rockslides followed; huge trees were also washed down slopes by flood waters. Floods and mudslides hit eight states in Venezuela, but Vargas experienced 80 per cent of the damage and 99 per cent of the death toll.

This disaster cannot be blamed on deforestation upstream since the Avila mountain range is a protected area free from extensive deforestation and inappropriate land use – but slopes that were stable 30–40 years ago have become unstable over time. Vargas is heavily urbanized, a narrow strip of land squeezed between the Caribbean coast and the mountains. It has 37 rivers and 42 canyons, and over 200 inhabitants per square kilometre. It has grown rapidly, especially after a fast highway linking it to nearby Caracas made it a popular weekend resort. Rich and poor households alike settled there and built with little control. Squatter settlements sprang up on slopes and near ravines, while upmarket high rises and summer villas crowded onto floodplains and close to river banks.

Landslides destroyed 70 per cent of Vargas's sewerage system and badly damaged the state's water supply. There was rapid provision for emergency shelter for those affected, but the longer-term plans were ill-conceived. The government wanted to relocate those who had been displaced to aid development in sparsely populated rural areas to the south. Many of those who were relocated lacked jobs; the houses were incomplete and schools were lacking. People in Vargas had had a sophisticated urban culture, social networks and ways of life centred around service industries on the coastal strip. Unhappy settlers staged demonstrations about the lack of jobs in remote locations. Houses often had no sewers and salty tap water. Many who were relocated trickled back to rebuild their old homes, although without clear land use regulations, this was simply rebuilding vulnerability. But as a coordinator in one of the 37 shelters in Vargas stated, 'To rebuild Vargas should not entail kicking us out.' An association of *damnificados* [those affected by the disaster] representing 1076 families is making demands, seeking self-help solutions and developing its own plans.

Source: International Federation of Red Cross and Red Crescent Societies (2001), *World Disasters Report: Focus on Recovery*, Kumarian Press, Bloomfield, USA.

drains, and may undermine buildings and increase the risk of sea water intrusion into fresh water aquifers. Changes in rainfall regimes may reduce the availability of fresh water resources or bring an increased risk of floods and landslides. Many cities are located below mountains, or close enough to mountains to be at risk from the large volumes of storm run-off flowing onto the flat lands below.

Defining disasters

Disasters are considered to be exceptional or unusual events that suddenly result in large numbers of people killed or injured, or large economic losses. As such, they are distinguished from everyday hazards, such as the deaths and other impacts that arise from inadequate provision for water and sanitation (described in Chapter 2). Large numbers of flood-related deaths in urban and rural areas go unrecorded in disaster statistics because the incidents are too small to be classified as disasters. Floods are only recorded as disasters, and therefore included in the statistics in Table 4.3, if ten or more people are killed; 100 people reported affected; there is a call for international assistance; or there is a declaration of state of emergency. It may have become so common for 'a few people' to die from floods that these remain unreported in all but the local press. This is especially so if the deaths occur in informal or illegal settlements. If it were possible to record all deaths from floods, it is likely that the annual total from 'non-disaster' floods would be greater than the total from 'disaster' floods. Official statistics suggest that landslides cause far fewer deaths and injuries than floods, cyclones and earthquakes, but as with floods, this may be because of the under-estimate of deaths from landslides, which have become so common that they are not considered disasters, or because most deaths from landslides occur in events too small to be recorded in disaster statistics. 'Non-disaster' fires probably have a greater impact in terms of loss of life, serious injury and loss of property than 'disaster' fires in many cities, especially those in which a significant proportion of the population live in informal settlements lacking water mains and electricity, have houses made of flammable materials (wood, cardboard and so on), and make widespread use of kerosene lamps (or candles), open fires, or wood, coal or kerosene stoves.

There is an assumption that disasters are unusual events that need special agencies to respond to them. However, there is a growing recognition that poorly managed urban development exposes people not only to the health and other risks described in Chapter 2, but also to risks from disasters. Or to put it another way, urban development can result in increasing levels of risk from disasters to increasing numbers of people – rather than reducing levels of risk for increasing numbers of people (which is what would be expected in a well governed city).

Causes of disasters

It is now widely accepted that the root causes of the deaths, injuries and damage caused by floods (and other disasters) in cities are the political and institutional failures to prevent them or limit the damage that they cause. Floods in cities are not 'natural', because all cities should have provision to prevent them – or to make sure that very unusual natural events (such as unusually high rainfall or an unusually large tidal surge) are managed without loss of life and with minimum damage to property. A disaster does not consist of the event itself (ie, the flood, earthquake or hurricane) but the effects that it has on society.[67] There has to be a vulnerable population for a natural event to become a disaster. Social scientists have been linking disasters with inadequately managed development processes for many years; researchers have also identified the 'risk accumulation processes' inherent in poorly managed urban development. For instance, urban areas expand over floodplains

and up potentially unstable slopes; natural drainage channels are built over or blocked; drainage systems become less effective because of deposits of silt and urban wastes; and growing built-up or paved areas reduce water infiltration into the soil. This means an increase in both hazard levels and vulnerability levels. But most national governments and international agencies have neglected this link and concentrated only on the effects of disasters, not the causes. Building an efficient system to respond to disasters can give the impression that disasters are being managed, when in reality, the population's vulnerability remains the same or even gets worse as urban development leaves more people and their homes, neighbourhoods and infrastructure at risk.

Understanding disaster risks in cities

The processes by which cities develop can increase risks from disasters, or reduce them. In well governed cities, there are many economies of scale and proximity for the kinds of infrastructure and planning measures that limit risk, and the kinds of services that ensure disaster preparedness. In addition, cities generally have average incomes well above the national average and larger revenue bases per person, which should allow more investments to be made by local governments. If local populations recognize high levels of risk, they will be more willing to contribute to the costs of lessening such risks if they are confident that local agencies will be effective in doing so. However, in poorly governed cities, the concentration of people and production (and usually their large volumes of waste-waters) in the absence of appropriate investments increases all forms of environmental risk, including risk of disaster.

There are two particular problems that are evident in many cities. The first is the development of settlements on land in or close to cities that are on hazardous sites – for instance, floodplains or hill sides that are at risk from mudflows, rockfalls or avalanches, or areas around unstable waste dumps. The vast majority of those who live on such hazardous sites are low-income people who choose these sites because their location and low monetary cost meets their most immediate needs. Hazardous sites are often the only places where they can build their homes or find rental accommodation close to employment opportunities. To the hazards inherent in the site are added those linked to a lack of investment in infrastructure and services, especially drainage infrastructure for the removal of storm and surface water and households' liquid wastes. It is also common for such settlements to combine high densities, shelters built with flammable materials and the widespread use of open fires, kerosene stoves/lamps or candles, which mean high risks of accidental fires – and usually little provision for effective fire-fighting (for instance, a guaranteed supply of water from the mains) and for emergency services that provide rapid treatment on-site and transport to hospitals for those who are burnt. Such settlements – with their poor quality housing, high densities, often large sizes (some have hundreds of thousands of inhabitants) and limited infrastructure – are also particularly at risk from extreme weather events.

The second problem is urban expansion that takes place without any effective governance system to ensure that environmental risks (of all kinds) are kept to a minimum. The devastating impact of the floods in Vargas that were described in Box 4.2 was largely the result of rapid urban development that took place without an appropriate government system – in this instance, one that supported the new economic activities that were developing and the need for housing for the growing population, but in ways that prevented development on the most dangerous sites. Cities expand as enterprises concentrate there for the advantages that accrue to their owners or shareholders; migration flows respond to their concentration of economic opportunity and services. In the absence of good governance, watersheds go unprotected and land developments (and their environmental impacts) go uncontrolled, while little or no investment is made in drainage and flood control. If investments are made, they concentrate on limiting flood risks or damage in business districts and

wealthier residential areas. City development involves very large modifications to natural sites, including reshaping hill slopes, extracting groundwater and (usually) filling valleys and swamps.[68] Streams are canalized and land is paved over (for houses, industries, offices, commercial centres, roads, highways, etc), increasing the speed and volume of storm and surface run-off. The extraction of groundwater, perhaps combined with the compaction of soil, may increase the risk of floods and seriously interfere with drainage systems. The exposure of soil during the building of new residential, commercial or industrial developments often leads to the erosion of surface soil, which then increases silt loads of streams by as much as 50–100 times, blocking drains and raising the bed of rivers and streams, greatly exacerbating the scale of floods.[69]

The growing number of water-related disasters

Disaster records show that although it is generally low-income groups that suffer most, in cities with inadequate governance systems middle- and upper-income groups are also affected. The landslides in Caracas in 1999 and the floods in Buenos Aires in 1997 showed that relatively wealthy neighbourhoods were also at risk due to a combination of factors that included government neglect, people's misperceptions of risk, infrastructure problems, the lack of services and obsolete land zoning codes.

As far as floods are concerned, a common response has been to treat the emergency and reconstruct property without modifying the vulnerability patterns of the city. However, at least in Latin America, recent disasters that affected the region (the El Niño event of 1997–1998, La Niña in 1999–2000, the earthquake in Armenia, Colombia in 1998, Hurricanes George and Mitch in 1998 and the floods in Venezuela in 1999) have helped to change this view.[70] National governments and international aid and donor agencies have begun to realize the need to take into account the causes of vulnerability and reduce risk levels, integrating hazard management into development processes. But this needs careful analyses in each location on the relation between disasters, development processes and environmental degradation.[71] The greater recognition – that disasters in cities are part of a wider set of problems that have to do with poorly managed urban expansion, social vulnerability and environmental degradation – has yet to lead to the actions needed to mitigate or prevent disasters in most cities, or the local analyses on which these should be built.[72]

Keeping track of urban disasters in Latin America and the Caribbean

Latin America and the Caribbean is a region prone to disasters. According to the Office of Foreign Disaster Assistance of the US Agency for International Development (USAID), 250 disasters were recorded there between 1990 and 1999. The International Federation of Red Cross and Red Crescent Societies has recorded twice as many disasters in the same period – the difference depends on the definition of disasters used, though both consider events that need outside assistance and have caused severe human and economic losses. However, if one looks into small- and medium-scale disasters, the number of events that occurred in the region rises dramatically. For instance, during the 1999–2000 rainy season in Colombia, 707 'small' disasters were registered by the Red Cross, affecting 500,000 people in 769 different local government areas. In Caracas, every rainy season brings mudslides that claim dozens of lives, livelihoods and homes.[73] Between 1984 and 1999, just one municipality in Caracas recorded 674 floods and landslides affecting 11,265 families.[74] So the number of people affected by disasters is greatly influenced by the criteria used to define 'disaster'.

To address the lack of information on local risk and 'smaller' disasters, data were collected in eight nations on large-, medium- and small-scale events by a network of research centres (the LA RED de Estudios Sociales en Prevencion de Desastres en America Latina – the Network of Social Studies in the Prevention of Disasters in Latin America). Using the same computer software (DESINVENTAR), data were collected from Mexico, Guatemala, El Salvador, Costa Rica, Colombia, Peru, Argentina and Panama. Because of the lack of continuous official disaster records in these countries, this research reviewed disasters that had been reported in national newspapers (while recognizing that these are likely to have a bias towards capital cities and larger urban centres, and to have under-reported events in small urban centres). For the years between 1990 and 1998, the DESINVENTAR database shows 20,000 events in the eight countries surveyed. The difference in the number of cases registered with USAID and the International Federation of Red Cross and Red Crescent Societies mentioned above is the result of including any event that has caused losses to the population, the economy or the infrastructure of the place.[75] The DESINVENTAR database varies from country to country in terms of continuity of registers and period covered. Of the different disaster categories analysed in the database, hydro-meteorological associated events (especially floods) are reported the most, and are responsible for most of the damages and losses in the countries analysed.[76] In the Dominican Republic during Hurricane George in 1998, many lives were lost and houses destroyed as rivers flooded entire neighbourhoods. The worst damages were felt in the poorest provinces: San Juan de Maguana, Azua, Bahoruco and Barahona. The losses in the Dominican Republic, compared with losses in other islands affected by the same hurricane, showed how little the national government had done to prevent disasters and reduce risks.[77]

After Hurricane Mitch in 1999, 30 per cent of the central district of Honduras, which includes the cities of Tegucigalpa and Comayaguela, was destroyed. Most of the damage was concentrated around the four rivers that cross the city. Obsolete and inadequate infrastructure (especially for water and sanitation), the lack of zoning codes, the concentration of services and infrastructure in just a few centres, the lack of official prevention and mitigation strategies, and the inappropriate management of river basins, combined to create high levels of vulnerability.[78]

Government offices are often not aware of the magnitude of the problem, and there seems to be a tendency for society to forget past events.[79] It may happen also that the risk scenarios and risk maps used as the basis for measures to prevent disasters cannot anticipate many disaster situations, because risks change. Lavell suggests that the conventional risk maps now used need to be continuously updated and that it is important to involve the local community at risk in doing so.[80] The losses that occurred in Peru in the region of Piura and Tumbes during the El Niño event in 1997–1998 illustrate this.[81] In this case, prevention measures were not enough, in part because the disaster scenario used to prepare prevention measures was based on the 1982–1983 El Niño event and proved too optimistic. Prevention measures in the north of Peru included clearing river channels, building dykes and river defences, cleaning or constructing water drains in the cities and strengthening bridges. The measures taken only proved appropriate in some cases. In Piura and Tumbes, rivers over flowed several times and city drains collapsed and flooded surrounding areas. The use of water pumps also had limitations. National and local governments did not take full account of the disaster possibilities. There are cases of state-financed housing projects located in low-lying areas in which flood waters came up to the first floors of houses. Some other investments showed their limitations. In the case of the city of Sullen, a gorge divides the city in two and the old riverbed was canalized after the floods of 1982–1983, but the work was never finished and in 1997 it was receiving water from the city and all its surrounding area. With heavy rains, the river over flowed and many houses were lost.

In Honduras and Nicaragua, the governments' response was slow and inefficient after Hurricane Mitch. Most help came from local NGOs and the population. 20,000 people were reported dead or missing in the region, indicating that in many places the early warning and evacuation systems were inappropriate.[82]

The city of Buenos Aires has experienced many floods in neighbourhoods of different income levels. According to DESINVENTAR

registers, between 1990 and 1998, 24 flood events occurred. These floods were the result of obsolete drainage and sewer systems that cannot evacuate heavy rains, and of *sudestadas* [local winds coming from the southeast] which make the River de la Plata rise and flood low-lying areas. Drainage systems in the city are old and designed for a city with many vacant plots and open areas that no longer exist. They were designed to serve a city with less than half of its present population. The necessary investments in infrastructure works have not been made and the culverted streams that cross the city still await the construction of over-flow channels. At the same time, there is little coordination among the 26 municipalities that, with the federal district, make up the metropolitan region of Buenos Aires. There is no unified policy for managing the region's river basin, urban expansion, infrastructure works and services, or flood management. Government officials have not done much to deal with this situation.[83] The inhabitants of the Villa Devoto, Villa Real and Versailles neighbourhoods have been demanding action against a rising water table that floods basements. The water table used to be 2 metres below the ground but is now only 50 centimetres below. Government officials lack definite studies but claim that it is the result of more rains, a greater area of paved surfaces and the lack of sufficient sewerage systems in the suburbs. In recent years, the privatized water company has extended the piped water system without an equal extension of the sewerage system.[84] The recent expansion towards the peri-urban areas to serve the *barrios cerrados* [gated communities] increasingly favoured by middle- and upper-income groups has only heightened the flood risks in Buenos Aires. Land sites are reshaped, low-lying areas filled and drainage networks installed for these rich *barrios* without taking into account the impact on flood risk in the surrounding neighbourhoods.[85]

The city of Pergamino, also in Argentina, has a history of floods due to the over-flow of the Pergamino and Chu-Chu rivers. One of the worst cases registered is the floods of 1995, when 80 per cent of the city was flooded. The magnitude of the floods was a result not only of heavy rains concentrated in a short period of time but of the lack of a regional river basin management plan, appropriate infrastructure (flood alleviation channels) and sewer and drainage systems. Now, most of the city gets flooded when it rains hard, even without the over-flowing of the city's rivers, whereas previously, only certain areas of Pergamino were flooded when the Pergamino over-flowed. The public works undertaken in the city can be seen as both a problem and a solution. Roads, railway lines, pavements and landfills act as barriers to the water's natural flow and have altered the area's infiltration capacity. A natural system of lagoons that previously mitigated floods has been filled and built on. The city has grown without a proper urban expansion plan and has hardly invested in drainage and sewer systems. The Chu-Chu receives most of the city's wastewaters and has become an open-air waste dump, which dramatically reduces its natural drainage capacity. Since 1990, the Pergamino has flooded at least 15 times, of which eight have had serious effects mostly in terms of material losses and severe cuts in basic services, especially piped water.[86]

The city of Quito is another example of how poor environmental management and the lack of appropriate urban plans increases risks.[87] Quito is situated at the foot of the Pichincha Volcano, on very steep slopes. In the last 30 years the city's population has increased fourfold. This population growth combined with economic crisis and debt problems led to both legal and illegal occupation and development on the slopes. Because the city is situated on steep hills the costs of providing infrastructure and services is very high, especially to many irregular settlements. The lack of sewers and drainage systems increases the risk of floods, and many have been recorded in recent years. Another problem is that only a small proportion of household wastes are collected; the rest are left in gorges and ravines, blocking the normal water flow and increasing the risk of floods and landslides. While, as described in Chapter 6, new mechanisms are being developed to help prevent upstream activities from causing water-related problems in Quito, measures taken in and around the city will also be necessary if flooding is to be avoided.

Notes and references

1. Khaldûn, I (1981), *The Muqaddimah: An Introduction to History*, Bollingen Series, Princeton, New Jersey.

2. Shiklomanov, I A (1997), *Assessment of Water Resources and Water Availability in the World*, World Meteorological Institute and Stockholm Environment Institute, Stockholm.

3. Hinrichsen, D, B Robey and U D Upadhyay (1998), *Solutions for a Water-Short World*, Johns Hopkins University School of Public Health, Baltimore, Maryland.

4. Ibid.

5. Postel, S L (2000), 'Entering an era of water scarcity: the challenges ahead,' *Ecological Apageslications*, Vol 10, No 4, pages 941–948.

6. Stikker, A (1998), 'Water today and tomorrow: prospects for overcoming scarcity,' *Futures*, Vol 30, No 1, pages 43–62.

7. See Chapter 3 for details of how there are fewer mega-cities than expected and how many of them are not growing fast.

8. Niemczynowicz, J (1996), 'Megacities from a water perspective,' *Water International*, Vol 21, No 4, pages 198–205.

9. Gleick, P H (2000), *The World's Water 2000–2001: The Biennial Report on Freshwater Resources*, Island Press, Washington, DC.

10. Demand is being used here in a very loose sense. In more rigorous analysis, water demand, withdrawal, use and consumption are defined differently, with water consumption referring specifically to water use that results in evaporation or incorporation into products and organisms.

11. Falkenmark, M, J Lundqvist and C Widstrand (1989), 'Macro-scale water scarcity requires micro-scale approaches: aspects of vulnerability in semi-arid development,' *Natural Resources Forum*, Vol 13, No 4, pages 258–267.

12. Hinrichsen 1998, op cit.

13. Cosgrove, W J and F R Rijsberman (2000), *World Water Vision: Making Water Everybody's Business*, Earthscan, London.

14. Seckler, D, R Barker and U Amarasinghe (1999), 'Water scarcity in the twenty-first century,' *International Journal of Water Resources Development*, Vol 15, No 1, pages 29–42.

15. Porter, R C, L B Yiadom Jr, A Mafusire and B O Tsheko (2002), *The Economics of Water and Waste in Three African Capitals*, Ashgate, Aldershot.

16. Saghir, J, M Schiffler and M Woldu (2000), *Urban Water and Sanitation in the Middle East and North Africa Region: The Way Forward*, Middle East and North Africa Region Infrastructure Development Group, The World Bank, Washington, DC.

17. Khatim, K (2002), *Water Supply and Sewage in Cities of Algeria*, Background Paper to this report, UN-HABITAT, Nairobi.

18. Bartone, C, J Bernstein, J Leitmann and J Eigen (1994), *Towards Environmental Strategies for Cities; Policy Considerations for Urban Environmental Management in Developing Countries*, UNDP/UNCHS/World Bank Urban Management Program, World Bank, Washington, DC.

19. White, R R (1992), 'The international transfer of urban technology: does the North have anything to offer for the global environmental crisis?', *Environment and Urbanization*, Vol 4, No 2, October, pages 109–120.

20. Shafik, N T (1995), 'Economic development and environmental quality: an econometric analysis', *Oxford Economic Papers*, Vol 46, pages 757–773; and Torras, M (1998), 'Income, equality and pollution: a reassessment of the environmental Kuznets curve', *Ecological Economics*, Vol 25, No 2, pages 147–160.

21. McGranahan, G (2002), *Demand-Side Water Strategies and the Urban Poor*, International Institute for Environment and Development, London; and Mahmud, M (2002), *Explaining the Poor Access to Water in Low-income Countries*, Environmental Economics Unit, Department of Economics, Göteborg University, Göteborg.

22. McGranahan 2002, op cit.

23. Cairncross, S and R G Feachem (1993), *Environmental Health Engineering in the Tropics: An Introductory Text* (second edition), John Wiley & Sons, Chichester, 306 pages.

24. Bateman, O M, S Smith and P Roark (1993), *A Comparison of the Health Effects of Water Supply and Sanitation in Urban and Rural Areas of Five African Countries*, Water and Sanitation for Health Project, WASH Operations Center, Arlington, VA; and WELL (1998), *Guidance Manual on Water Supply and Sanitation Programmes*, Department for International Development, London.

25. Lane, R P and R W Crosskey (1993), *Medical Insects and Arachnids*, Chapman & Hall, London.

26. Cairncross and Feachem 1993, op cit.

27. Showers, K B (2002), 'Water scarcity and urban Africa: an overview of urban–rural water linkages', *World Development*, Vol 30, No 4, pages 621–648.

28. Bouwer, H (2000), 'Integrated water management: emerging issues and challenges', *Agricultural Water Management*, Vol 45, No 3, pages 217–228.

29. Wichelns, D (2001), 'The role of "virtual water" in efforts to achieve food security and other national goals, with an example from Egypt', *Agricultural Water Management*, Vol 49, No 2, pages 131–151.

30. Douglas, Ian (1983), *The Urban Environment*, Edward Arnold, London, 229 pages; Douglas, Ian (1986), 'Urban geomorphology', in P G Fookes and P R Vaughan (eds), *A Handbook of Engineering Geomorphology*, Surrey University Press (Blackie and Son), Glasgow, pages 270–283.

31. Showers 2002, op cit.

32. Chen, Y D (2001), 'Sustainable development and management of water resources for urban water supply in Hong Kong', *Water International*, Vol 26, No 1, pages 119–128.

33. Wang, L S and C Ma (1999), 'A study on the environmental geology of the middle route project of the south–north water transfer', *Engineering Geology*, Vol 51, No 3, pages 153–165.

34. Showers 2002, op cit.

35. McCormack, G (2001), 'Water margins: competing paradigms in China', *Critical Asian Studies*, Vol 33, No 1, pages 5–30.

36. Martinelli, G, A Minissale and C Verrucchi (1998), 'Geochemistry of heavily exploited aquifers in the Emilia-Romagna region (Po Valley, northern Italy)', *Environmental Geology*, Vol 36, No 3–4, pages 195–206.

37. Ramachandraiah, C (1997), 'Weather and water in urban areas', *Economic and Political Weekly*, Vol 32, No 43, pages 2797–2800.

38. Esteller, M V and C Diaz-Delgado (2002), 'Environmental effects of aquifer overexploitation: a case study in the highlands of Mexico', *Environmental Management*, Vol 29, No 2, pages 266–278.

39. Shiklomanov 1997, op cit.

40. Tonderski, A (1996), 'Landuse-based nonpoint source pollution: a threat to water resources in developing countries', *Water Science and Technology*, Vol 33, No 4–5, pages 53–61.

41. Agarwal, A, S Narain and S Sen (1999), *State of India's Environment: The Citizens' Fifth Report*, Centre for Science and Environment, New Delhi.

42. Conway, G R and J H Pretty (1991), *Unwelcome Harvest*, Earthscan, London, 645 pages.

43. Agarwal et al 1999, op cit.

44. Showers 2002, op cit.

45. Rodriguezestrada, H and H Lloiciga (1995), 'Planning urban growth in ground water recharge areas: Central Valley, Costa Rica', *Ground Water Monitoring and Remediation*, Vol 15, No 3, pages 144–148.

46. Bai, X M and H Imura (2001), 'Towards sustainable urban water resource management: a case study in Tianjin, China', *Sustainable Development*, Vol 9, No 1, pages 24–35.

47. Griesel, M and P Jagals (2002), 'Faecal indicator organisms in the Renoster Spruit system of the Modder-Riet River catchment and implications for human users of the water', *Water SA*, Vol 28, No 2, pages 227–234.

48. Roche, Pierre-Alain, Francois Valiron, René Coulomb and Daniel Villessot (2001), 'Infrastructure integration issues', in Cedo Maksimovic and José Alberto Tejada-Guibert (eds), *Frontiers in Urban Water Management: Deadlock or Hope*, IWA Publishers, London, pages 143–228.

49. Jagals, P (1997), 'Stormwater runoff from typical developed and developing South African urban developments: definitely not for swimming', *Water Science and Technology*, Vol 35, No 11–12, pages 133–140.

50. Hardoy, Jorge E, Diana Mitlin and David Satterthwaite (2001), *Environmental Problems in an Urbanizing World: Finding Solutions for Cities in Africa, Asia and Latin America*, Earthscan Publications, London, 470 pages.

51. Kjellén, M and G McGranahan (1997), *Urban Water: Towards Health and Sustainability*, Stockholm Environment Institute, Stockholm.

52. Jackson, R B, S R Carpenter, C N Dahm, D M McKnight, R J Naiman, S L Postel and S W Running (2001), 'Water in a changing world', *Ecological Applications*, Vol 11, No 4, pages 1027–1045.

53. Showers 2002, op cit.

54. Calder, I R (1999), *The Blue Revolution*, Earthscan, London, page 3.

55. Hardoy, Mitlin and Satterthwaite 2001, op cit.

56. Jones, G W (1983), 'Structural change and prospects for urbanization in Asian countries', *Papers of the East West Population Institute No 88*, East–West Center, Hawaii, 46 pages; McGee, T G (1987), 'Urbanization or Kotadesasi: the emergence of new regions of economic interaction in Asia', working paper, Environment and Policy Institute, East West Center, Honolulu, June.

57. Hardoy, Mitlin and Satterthwaite 2001, op cit.

58. Ibid.

59. Roche et al 2001, op cit. However, this is not always the case and some illegal settlements or illegal sub-divisions develop with careful attention to site layouts that allow for future infrastructure installation.

60. Acho-Chi (1998), 'Human interference and environmental instability: addressing the environmental consequences of rapid urban growth in Bamenda, Cameroon', *Environment and Urbanization*, Vol 10, No 2, pages 161–174.

61. Vlachos, Evan and Benedito Braga (2001), 'The challenge of urban water management', in Cedo Maksimovic and José Alberto Tejada-Guibert (eds), *Frontiers in Urban Water Management: Deadlock or Hope*, IWA Publishing, London, pages 1–36.

62. Rodda, John C (2002), 'The state of the resource', Background paper prepared for the World Water Development Report, UNESCO, Paris, 12 pages.

63. Human-induced climate change as a result of greenhouse gas emissions may come to contribute much to flooding because of its impact on sea level rise and on the frequency and severity of extreme weather events.

64. This section draws its global statistics from International Federation of Red Cross and Red Crescent Societies (2001), *World Disasters Report: Focus on Recovery*, Kumarian Press, Bloomfield, USA.

65. WHO (1992), *Our Planet, Our Health*, Report of the WHO Commission on Health and Environment, World Health Organization, Geneva, 282 pages.

66. *Down to Earth* (2000), 'The curse of poor sanitation', 15 September, pages 14–15.

67. Lavell, A (1999*)*, *Un Encuentro con la Verdad: Los Desastres en América Latina Durante 1998* in *Anuario Político y Social de América Latina*, No 2, FLACSO, San Jose, Costa Rica.

68. Douglas, Ian (1983), *The Urban Environment*, Edward Arnold, London, 229 pages.

69. Douglas, Ian (1986), 'Urban geomorphology', in P G Fookes and P R Vaughan (eds), *A Handbook, of Engineering Geomorphology*, Surrey University Press (Blackie and Son), Glasgow, pages 270–283.

70. Lavell 1999, op cit; Lavell, A (2000), 'Desastres urbanos: una visión global' in the seminar on *El Impacto de los Desastres Naturales en Areas Urbanas y en la Salud Publica Urbana en Centro América y el Caribe*, ASIES, Guatemala; Clarke, C (2000), 'El rol de las instituciones internacionales de financiamiento en la gestión del riesgo de desastres en areas urbanas: una perspectiva del Banco Interamericano de Desarrollo' from the seminar on *El Impacto de los Desastres*

Naturales en Areas Urbanas y en la Salud Publica Urbana en Centro América y el Caribe, ASIES, Guatemala.

71. Lavell 1999, op cit.

72. Gellert, G (2000), 'Iniciativas urbanas locales para construir comunidades sostenibles' in the seminar on *El Impacto de los Desastres Naturales en Areas Urbanas y en la Salud Publica Urbana en Centro América y el Caribe'*, ASIES, Guatemala.

73. Jimenez Diaz, Virginia (1992), 'Landslides in the squatter settlements of Caracas: towards a better understanding of causative factors', *Environment and Urbanization*, Vol 4, No 2, October, pages 80–89.

74. International Federation of Red Cross and Red Crescent Societies 2001, op cit.

75. See Lavell 2000, op cit.

76. Velázquez, Andrés and Rosales Cristina (1999), *Escudriñando en los Desastres a Todas las Escalas. Concepción, Metodología y Análisis de Desastres en América Latina Utilizando DesInventar*, OSSO/LA RED/ITDG, see www.desenredando.org.

77. Meyreles, Lourdes (2000), 'Huracán Georges en la República Dominicana: sociedad civil y participación local', from the seminar on *El Impacto de los Desastres Naturales en Areas Urbanas y en la Salud Publica Urbana en Centro América y el Caribe*, ASIES, Guatemala.

78. Mejía, Fanny Y (2000), 'Construyendo una ciudad mas saludable y sostenible ambiental-mente; estrategia municipal para la superación de condiciones de vulnerabilidad del distrito central, capital de Honduras' from the seminar on *El Impacto de los Desastres Naturales en Areas Urbanas y en la Salud Publica Urbana en Centro América y el Caribe*, ASIES, Guatemala.

79. Franco, Temple Eduardo (1999) *¿El Niño 1997–1998 o 'El Desastre' 1997*? ITDG/LA, www.desenredando.org.

80. Lavell 2000, op cit.

81. Franco 1999, op cit.

82. Lavell 2000, op cit, page 24.

83. Herzer, Hilda and Nora Clichevsky (2001), 'Perspectiva histórica: las inundaciones en Buenos Aires', in Kreimer Alcira et al (eds), *Inundaciones en el Area Metropolitana de Buenos Aires*, World Bank, Washington, DC.

84. *La Nación* (2002), 22 July.

85. Herzer, Hilda and Nora Clichevsky (2001), 'El impacto ambiental de las inundaciones', in Kreimer Alcira et al (eds), *Inundaciones en el Area Metropolitana de Buenos Aires*, World Bank, Washington, DC.

86. Herzer, Hilda et al (2001), 'Grandes inundaciones en la ciudad de Pergamino: extraordinarias, pero recurrentes, análisis de un proceso de vulnerabilidad progresiva', *Realidad Económica*, No 175, pages 92–116.

87. Zevallos Moreno, Othon (1996), 'Ocupación de laderas: incremento del riesgo por degradación ambiental urbana en Quito, Ecuador' in M A Fernández (ed), *Ciudades en Riesgo; Degradación Ambiental, Riesgos Urbanos y Desastres*, La Red, Peru.

Changing Perspectives and Roles in Urban Water and Sanitation Provision: Privatization and Beyond

Introduction

Despite the localized and site-specific nature of many water and sanitation problems, the need for reform in the water and sanitation sector is widespread, and has fostered a search for generic prescriptions. Three directions for water and sanitation management commonly advocated in the international policy arena in the 1990s were:

1   Develop more integrated water resource management at the river basin level and manage water demand more effectively (rather than simply withdrawing more and more water to meet the growing demands).
2   Rely more heavily on private sector enterprises and market mechanisms to provide water and sanitation (rather than depending on the public sector).
3   Devolve responsibilities for water and sanitation management to the lowest appropriate level (rather than keeping all decision-making centralized).

These reflect broader tendencies in international development discussions: to take environmental issues more seriously, to favour markets over government provisioning, and to favour decentralized over centralized governance.

The influence of these tendencies has been mixed. The dangers of a global water crisis have been widely discussed in the international arena, but relatively few urban centres have made substantial adjustments as a result. Private sector participation in water and sanitation provision has increased in a number of countries, but has been hotly debated and has only rarely achieved the benefits anticipated. Government decentralization has been occurring in many countries, but again not always successfully, and not always accompanied by decentralized control over water and sanitation provision.

All of these shifts have created obstacles as well as opportunities for improving water and sanitation provision in deprived urban areas. Moreover, in each case, the local context, the timing and sequencing of these shifts, and how they have been implemented at the local level, can make an enormous difference. In the long run, better water resource management may be critical to achieving sustainable improvements in urban water and sanitation provision. However, policies designed only with a view to conserving and managing water resources can also make it unnecessarily difficult to extend adequate water and sanitation provision to those currently deprived. In the right circumstances, water markets and private sector participation may be able to help improve efficiency and increase the financial resources available for improving water and sanitation services. However, attempts to increase private sector participation for its own sake can create new regulatory and corruption problems, direct finance to urban centres and neighbourhoods that are already comparatively well served, and further polarize the politics of water and sanitation provision. The decentralization of responsibilities for water and sanitation management may have the potential to stimulate locally driven initiatives for improving water and sanitation and increase the accountability and transparency of local utilities. However, decentralizing responsibilities, without a decentralization of power and revenue-generating mechanisms, can further undermine the financial basis of water and sanitation services and reinforce regional inequalities.

Increasing private sector participation in water and sanitation utilities has been the most controversial approach to improving provision in recent years, and it receives most attention in this chapter. The overall conclusion is that increasing private sector participation, at least as it has been promoted in recent years, is not going to resolve the problems of inadequate water and sanitation provision found in most urban centres in Africa, Asia and Latin America. Many of the current obstacles to improved provision have little to do with whether or not private enterprises are playing a major role in water utilities. While tenure problems can inhibit public utilities from extending provision to low-income communities, they can just as surely inhibit privately operated utilities. While pervasive corruption problems can undermine public utilities, they can just as easily undermine privately operated utilities. Conversely, most of the 'pro-poor' measures now being promoted in relation to privately operated utilities are equally relevant in relation to public utilities. Similarly, while inadequate regulatory environments can undermine privately operated utilities, they can just as easily undermine public utilities. In any case, the large water and sanitation companies that have attracted so much attention in recent years have shown little interest in extending their markets to include the smaller, low-income cities and towns where a large share of those without adequate water and sanitation now live.

Before reviewing the debates and experiences surrounding private sector participation, a brief overview of changing international perspectives on water and sanitation is provided. This helps to situate the discussion of private sector participation within the broader context of water resource management. Following the discussion of private sector participation in water and sanitation utilities are sections on small-scale providers and civil society organizations (CSOs), both of which often play very different roles in water and sanitation provision to the formal utilities, be they public or privately operated.

Evolving international perspectives on water and sanitation

Many of the perspectives on water and sanitation, still viewed as 'conventional', originated in the sanitary reforms that were initiated in European and North American cities in the 19th century. At the time, most of the economically successful industrializing cities were extremely unhealthy to live in, with death rates considerably higher than the surrounding countryside. Epidemics were common. Crowded and unsanitary living conditions were often blamed, with sanitation defined broadly to include a wide range of local environmental hazards. While germ theories of disease did not gain ascendancy until the last decades of the century, competing theories – such as that diseases were contracted from exposure to 'miasmas' that could rise up from urban filth – also motivated improvements in water and sanitation provision. During the second half of the 19th century, water and sanitation emerged as a major public issue, with piped water and water-flushed toilets and sewers the principal urban solutions.

During the 20th century, efforts to improve public water and sanitation provision were institutionalized in cities around the world. By the second half of the 20th century, indoor piped water and water closets had become widely accepted goals of development, espoused by governments of a wide range of political persuasions and in diverse social and physical settings. Networked public water and sewerage systems were widely assumed to be the model for the future, although in much of the world a substantial share of urban dwellers still had no access to piped water or sewered toilets. Demand-side management, whether for health or conservation, was not a major policy concern. Even more so than in the earlier sanitary movement, the urban sanitary revolution came to be seen as a question of infrastructure provision.

As noted in Chapter 1, the International Drinking Water and Sanitation Decade (the 1980s) was driven by the goal of achieving universal 'safe' water supplies and sanitation, if possible by the end of the decade. Rural areas were found to be particularly poorly served, and received much of the attention. Sanitation was found to be lagging behind water provision, and was the cause of particular problems in urban areas.

The decade also heralded a significant change in the treatment of urban water issues, however. One of the challenges recognized at the start of the decade was to 'embrace lower-tech alternatives, and to convince engineers and planners to include them in master plans for developing country contexts'.[1] During the course of the decade there was also an increasing emphasis on institutional rather than technical improvement, with community participation and gender awareness gaining prominence. More importantly, though perhaps more subtly, environmental and free market viewpoints were becoming more prevalent in international development debates. These both had a profound influence on international policy statements in the water sector in the 1990s.

Contemporary environmentalists view water and sanitation very differently from the early sanitary reformers who helped form many of the ideas about urban water and sanitation that are now considered conventional. Environmental issues were central to 19th century sanitary reforms. However, where sanitary reformers emphasized getting more water to cities, contemporary environmentalists emphasize managing water resources. Where sanitary reformers emphasized managing water demand to improve cleanliness and health, contemporary environmentalists emphasize managing water demand to prevent excessive use. Where sanitary reformers emphasized getting human excreta out of cities (often using water), contemporary environmentalists emphasize avoiding water pollution and recycling human wastes (and are

often very critical of water-borne sewerage systems). Thus, bringing the new set of environmental concerns into international policy discussions on water and sanitation required a significant shift in emphasis, and did not, at least initially, sit well with goals and targets framed exclusively in terms of improving access to clean water and healthy sanitation.

Contemporary views on the appropriate roles for the private and public sectors are also very different from the early sanitary reforms. Private sector participation was also widely debated in 19th century Europe and North America, and the free market viewpoint was very prevalent in many of the countries undergoing sanitary reform. However, the early sanitary reformers typically faced private sector failures (such as the failure of London water companies to provide uninterrupted water supplies), and called for more public sector involvement to achieve reforms and, increasingly, to deliver water and sanitation services. By way of contrast, modern reformers typically face public sector failures, and many have called for more private sector involvement.

By the end of the Water and Sanitation Decade, while the targets were still far from met, a new consensus appeared to be emerging among a number of international actors within the water sector. The 'Dublin Principles' – set out at the International Conference on Water and the Environment held in 1992 – illustrate this new perspective, and are reproduced in Box 5.1.

These four principles apply four development dicta of the 1990s to the water sector: care for the environment, increase the participation of non-governmental stakeholders, be sensitive to gender issues, and increase the role of markets. In this sense, they are unexceptional, even if, as in the broader development arena, it remains far from clear how such principles are to be combined and implemented, and whether they are really supported by a broad-based consensus. What is striking, however, is that the need to treat water as a finite and vulnerable resource is explicit in the first principle, while the need to ensure adequate water and sanitation provision is

> **Box 5.1** The Dublin Principles
>
> **1 Fresh water is a finite and vulnerable resource, essential to sustain life, development and the environment**
> Since water sustains life, the effective management of water resources demands a holistic approach, linking social and economic development with protection of natural ecosystems. Effective management links land and water uses across the whole of a catchment area or aquifer.
>
> **2 Water development and management should be based on a participatory approach, involving users, planners and policy-makers at all levels**
> The participatory approach involves raising awareness of the importance of water among policy-makers and the general public. It means that decisions are taken at the lowest appropriate level, with full public consultation and involvement of the users in the planning and implementation of projects.
>
> **3 Women play a central part in the provision, management and safeguarding of water**
> The pivotal role of women as providers and users of water and guardians of the living environment has seldom been reflected in institutional arrangements for the development and management of water resources. Acceptance and implementation of this principle requires positive policies to address women's specific needs and to equip and empower women to participate at all levels in water resources programmes, including decision-making and implementation, in ways defined by them.
>
> **4 Water has an economic value in all its competing uses and should be recognized as an economic good**
> Within this principle, it is vital to recognize first the basic right of all human beings to have access to clean water and sanitation at an affordable price. Past failure to recognize the economic value of water has led to wasteful and environmentally damaging uses of the resource. Managing water as an economic good is an important way of achieving efficient and equitable use, and of encouraging conservation and protection of water resources.
>
> *Source:* WMO (1992), *International Conference on Water and the Environment: Development Issues for the 21st Century: The Dublin Statement and Report of the Conference*, World Meteorological Organization, Geneva.

embedded in a principle relating to the treatment of water as an economic good. At least superficially, this represents a major shift in priorities from the Water and Sanitation Decade, which treated the universal provision of adequate water and sanitation as the overarching goal. Statements from the major international meetings that have taken place since 1992 have tended to give more prominence to water and sanitation provision. The sense of urgency in the water sector, however, has continued to be driven by concerns about water resource management and water economics.

In the wake of Dublin, many international organizations realigned their position in the water sector, and a series of new water sector organizations and institutions emerged.[2] The World Bank came to play a central role in developing and promoting new approaches consistent with their interpretation of the Dublin Principles, and in particular the treatment of water as an economic good. The two most visible NGOs set up in the wake of the Dublin Conference are the Global Water Partnership and the World Water Council.

These two organizations were intended to help articulate the new water sector challenges and facilitate international and regional responses. The Global Water Partnership, established in 1996, was designed to work with a large grouping of partners to help translate the perceived consensus in the international water sector into new institutional arrangements for integrated water resource management, and to help coordinate the policies and programmes of different international agencies, governments and other stakeholders. The World Water Council, also established in 1996, was intended more as a think tank, devoted to the study of global long-term water policies and the advocacy of better management of the world's water resources. Both still promote a similar perspective on water and its management, at least roughly in line with the Dublin Principles.

At the Millennium Summit in September 2000, the states of the United Nations agreed on a set of Millennium Development Goals, which addressed water issues in the context of 'ensuring environmental sustainability'. Two of the four indicators identified were:

1   the proportion of population with sustainable access to an improved water source; and

2   the proportion of population with access to improved sanitation (for current definitions of these indicators, see Chapter 1).

One of the two specific targets identified was to halve the proportion of people without sustainable access to safe drinking water by 2015. At the World Summit on Sustainable Development in September 2002, another relevant target was set: halving the proportion of people without access to adequate sanitation by 2015.

One of the major challenges facing international development strategies for urban water and sanitation is to address the growing water resource concerns and the increasing role of the private sector in water and sanitation provision, while meeting development goals articulated in terms of access to water and sanitation. For reasons outlined in Chapter 4, addressing issues of water stress will not, in itself, remove the major obstacles to improving water and sanitation provision in deprived urban neighbourhoods. For reasons outlined below, increasing private sector participation is also not going to remove these obstacles. Nor will the continuing efforts of small-scale providers and CSOs. Ultimately, as described in the following chapters, addressing this challenge will require a significant departure from recent trends.

The increasing role of the private sector in water and sanitation utilities

The degree of private sector participation in different utility sectors, of which the water and sanitation sector is just one, has increased significantly since the 1980s, especially so between 1990 and 2000.[3] The expansion of private sector involvement in water and sanitation provision has been more controversial than in other utility sectors. The aim of this section is to summarize the debate and the issues arising from private sector participation in water and sanitation services, with a focus on urban centres in low- and middle-

income countries where services are often absent or inadequate. The summary starts with a review of some of the definitional and conceptual issues, continues with a discussion of the issues and options surrounding private sector participation in water and sanitation utilities, and ends with a brief summary of recent trends in private sector participation in water and sanitation utilities and specific pro-poor initiatives.

A number of issues addressed in this summary have relevance beyond the narrow question of whether or not increasing private sector participation is a good thing. Many of the problems that have been encountered with privatization can also arise with public utilities, while many of the strengths of private sector participation can also be achieved by reforming public sector utilities. In the 1990s, many proponents of privatization considered rapid transitions necessary, so as to avoid protracted periods of uncertainty and institutional conflict, during which the opportunity to implement radical reforms might be lost. Rapid transitions involving radical shifts in responsibilities are inherently risky, however. There is little time for consultation and stakeholder engagement. If radical reforms do not actually address the underlying problems, they can make matters worse. Thus, the failures of the rapid approach to the privatization of state enterprises in some east and central European countries is often compared unfavourably with the more gradualist approach in China. More specifically, if the failings of a public utility reflect governance problems, these governance problems are likely to persist and undermine water and sanitation provision, regardless of whether more responsibilities are given to the private sector.

Defining privatization, private sector participation and public–private partnership

The terms 'privatization', 'private sector participation' and 'public–private partnership' are widely used, but not in a consistent fashion.[4] 'Privatization' is sometimes used as a generic term to refer to increasing private sector involvement, but at other times is used to refer to the model of full privatization (divestiture) adopted in the UK. Similarly, 'private sector participation' tends to refer to the participation of formal (and often large-scale) private companies, although most small-scale and informal operators can be considered to be part of the private sector. CSOs are also sometimes considered part of the private sector when they engage in the provision of water and sanitation services.

In this book, 'privatization' refers to processes that increase the participation of formal private enterprises in water and sanitation provision, but do not necessarily involve the transfer of assets to the private sector. Most references to 'private sector participation' refer to formal private enterprises operating (or participating in) water and/or sanitation utilities. It is recognized, however, that small-scale and informal operators as well as CSOs can play an important role in water and sanitation provision, particularly in low-income areas, and these roles are examined in later sections of this chapter.

The term 'public–private partnership' (PPP) is rarely defined explicitly, despite a growing literature on the topic. It is often used to refer to situations where a public agency works with one or more private enterprises to provide goods or services previously provided by the public sector. In the water and sanitation sector it tends to be used to refer to arrangements based upon contracts in which the private sector assumes greater responsibility and/or risk, in particular through concession contracts.

The term 'partnership', however, is often taken to imply that the parties involved have mutually shared objectives and working arrangements that go beyond the fulfilment of any contractual agreement. Given the difficulties of defining the term and ascertaining whether any given arrangement is a true partnership, the term is only used in this report as a label of convenience when the parties involved describe their collaboration as a PPP.

In applying these terms, it is important to recognize that private utilities are not just driven by market pressures (even if they are trying to maximize profits), and public utilities are not just driven by government plans. Private water and sanitation utilities are always regulated. Some public utilities are run on commercial principles. Thus while there is clearly an association between privatization and increasing reliance on market mechanisms, in practice there is a great deal of variation in how utilities respond to market pressures, and not all of this variation depends on the level of private sector participation. Similarly, while the case for public utilities is often associated with a planning approach to water and sanitation provision, in practice there is a great deal of variation in the extent to which utilities respond directly to national development goals, again regardless of the level of private sector participation.

Conceptual issues in the privatization debates: public goods, economic goods, natural monopolies and human rights

In debating whether water and sanitation should be provided by the public sector, the private sector or through collaborative arrangements, numerous attempts have been made to argue that, given the innate characteristics of water and sanitation systems, one or other form of provision is inherently superior. In practice, shifting international opinions regarding the appropriate roles of the public and private sectors in water and sanitation provision respond to broad political trends far more closely than they respond to evidence emerging from experiences in the water and sanitation sector. This is unfortunate. Politically driven shifts in international opinion are a poor basis for addressing local water and sanitation problems.

Moreover, dwelling on the public–private dichotomy can divert attention from the important roles often played by NGOs and CBOs, and lumps together very diverse actors and agencies in both the private sector (eg, informal vendors and multinational corporations) and the public sector (eg, public utilities, regulators, local authorities and national ministries). A large public utility, for example, has far more in common with a large private utility than either has in common with neighbourhood water associations or small-scale water vendors.

Nevertheless, the conceptual debates have thrown up a number of interesting issues. They have not come up with any clear guidance on the most appropriate roles for the public and private sectors, let alone the many organizations and actors that do not fall neatly into this sectoral divide. They have, however, identified concerns that need to be addressed if water and sanitation provision is to be improved.

Public goods and the case for public provisioning

Private enterprises supplying market demands fail to provide some goods because, once these goods are produced, they benefit the public at large and cannot be sold to or used up by individuals. Such 'public' goods are usually taken to include territorial protection from threats such as floods, ambient pollution, epidemics or military attack. It is often argued that since such goods will not be provided by the private sector, they must be provided for free by the public sector.

Urban water, drainage and sanitation systems are not pure public goods, but they can provide important public benefits, including some public protection from infectious diseases, floods and even fires. Such public benefits dominate in the cases of drainage and sanitation. When people dispose of their wastewater or human waste carelessly, it is other people who bear the burden, and once a drainage or sanitation system is in place it is uneconomic to exclude people who are not willing to pay. Thus some combination of regulation, subsidized provision and obligatory fees is likely to be necessary to achieve adequate provision.

Water provision clearly provides private benefits to the receiving household, and it is technically possible to charge people for water on the basis of how much they choose to use. However, if people are unwilling or unable to purchase enough water (or water of a sufficient quality) to protect their own health, and contract infectious diseases as a result, then the health of others is also put at risk. Moreover, a water network provides protection

against fires, with clear public benefits. To a first approximation, the public benefits of water provision only really become significant when the private benefits are insufficient to finance adequate provision. This is more likely to arise in low-income areas, or when people are unaware of the private health benefits.

When the appropriate roles of the private and public sectors are being debated, the case for a more active public sector role is strengthened by evidence of important public benefits, while the case for a greater private sector role is strengthened by evidence of important private benefits. Thus, proponents of more private sector involvement in water provisioning are inclined to emphasize the relatively high prices that even low-income households are willing to pay for water, while proponents of public provisioning are inclined to emphasize the public health burdens of inadequate provision.

It can be very misleading, however, to argue the case for more or less private sector involvement on the basis of abstract arguments about the extent to which water, drainage and sanitation provide public versus private benefits. The public benefits of having adequate water, drainage and sanitation provision do not necessarily imply that these should be provided by the public sector, even when they do have implications for the appropriate payment arrangements. Depending on the local circumstances, it may be more appropriate to rely on regulated private provision, and perhaps to use public funds to pay for additional private provision. Alternatively, even if people are willing to pay the full cost of adequate provision, there may be other reasons that make it appropriate for the water and sanitation utility to be publicly owned (rather than, for example, to be owned by a foreign corporation).

Moreover, whether water, drainage and sanitation services are to be provided by the public or private operators (or for that matter by CBOs or NGOs), it is critical for governments to have reliable information on their public benefits and on how much people are willing to pay for the services. An otherwise sensible decision to create a private concession for water provision (for reasons of efficiency, for example) can go seriously wrong if it is based on an over-estimation of how much low-income households are willing to pay for water services. Yet when claims concerning willingness to pay and public health get bound up with heated debates over whether or not to privatize water or sanitation, it can become very difficult to ensure that these claims are not being exaggerated, particularly when they are based on evidence provided by parties actively engaged in the debates.

Economic goods and the case for private provisioning

When the public sector provides scarce goods for free (or at subsidized prices), they tend to be over-used: people have an incentive to consume them even when the benefits they receive are less than the costs of providing more of the good. However, the goods that most economists argue are efficiently supplied by private enterprises operating in a competitive market are not just scarce: their full costs of production are borne by the producer, and their full benefits accrue to the purchaser. Economics suggests that such goods should generally be priced at their 'marginal cost': the cost of providing an additional unit of the good, taking into account the opportunity cost of not providing it to another purchaser. This is also the price that economic theory indicates will result given a free and competitive market.

In debating the appropriate role of the private and public sectors, recognizing water as an economic good can seem to support a strong private sector role. This is not strictly correct, and depends on how the term 'economic good' – which is not widely used in economics – is interpreted. If 'economic goods' are taken to mean the sort of goods idealized in economic theories of perfect markets, then the case for private provision of economic goods is strong, but urban water services are not economic goods in this sense (and in any case, as noted below, water utilities rarely operate in a competitive market). Alternatively, if economic goods are simply taken to be goods that have an economic value, and to which economic principles apply, then this would also apply to public goods and

is largely irrelevant to the case for private provisioning. In any case, water is not always and everywhere an economic good in this sense, but only in specific circumstances.

In many circumstances, water is scarce or prone to over-use. However, like drainage and sanitation services, water is not an ideal good for private provisioning, any more than it is a pure public good. Not only does water provide public benefits in some circumstances, but, as environmentalists are fond of pointing out, withdrawing water from natural water sources often imposes environmental costs over and above those that a private operator is likely to incur. Moreover, people may be unaware of the costs and benefits of their water use and, if they have piped water, are unlikely to know more than roughly how much water they are using for different purposes. All of these factors can interfere with the role of market mechanisms in allocating water efficiently.

In short, while economic issues are central to defining appropriate roles for the public and private sectors, these issues are merely confused by semantic debates over whether or not water is an economic good. Historically, many public water utilities have undoubtedly been under pressure to keep water prices low, even when this leads to excessive water use among connected households (and in some cases removes a potentially important source of finance for expanding the water network to unconnected households). Commercial pressures can undoubtedly play a positive role in driving efficiency improvements. However, privately run utilities also respond to political pressures, and may have little incentive to improve efficiency (it depends on the nature of their contract and how it is regulated). Even if a privately operated utility is more likely to favour high water prices, this is not the same as taking the environmental costs of water withdrawals into account (which depends on how and from where water is withdrawn, and not just how much is withdrawn). Moreover, a privately run utility that succeeds in improving efficiency may end up reducing prices, driving up water demand and thereby increasing the pressure on water resources. Like drainage and sanitation, water provision raises a number of economic and governance issues that cannot simply be resolved by bringing in private operators, any more than they were resolved in the past by bringing in public operators.

Natural monopolies and the case for regulation

In comparison with firms operating in a competitive market, monopolists have an incentive to over-price and under-produce, thereby realizing 'excess' profits (ie, profits greater than the normal rate in competitive markets). In most circumstances over-pricing and under-production go together, since it is by restricting production that the typical monopolist achieves higher prices (if a firm in a competitive market restricts production it simply reduces its market share, and has no effect on the market price). Natural monopolies can be said to exist if total costs are lower when a single enterprise produces the entire output for a given market than when any collection of two or more enterprises divide the production amongst themselves. The most common explanation for natural monopolies is increasing returns to scale: the larger the producer, the lower the average costs. Economics suggests that natural monopolies will generally require some form of public regulation to prevent over-pricing, and this has at times been used to justify public ownership and operation.

Piped water and sewerage networks approximate natural monopolies. Multiple networks competing for the same consumers will have higher infrastructure costs than a single network. A 'natural' outcome of market competition would, therefore, be for one network owner to buy out its competitors and become a monopolist. For some networked services, such as telecommunications, attempts have been made to 'unbundle' the system, and develop a regulatory system that promotes competition where feasible (eg, regulations preventing firms from excluding competitors by purposefully adopting technologies that their competitors cannot connect to). In the energy sector, for example, electricity generation, transmission and distribution can be unbundled. For water and sewerage

networks, however, unbundling has proved difficult, and competition is generally restricted to competition *for* the market rather than competition *within* the market. In competing for the right to supply a given market for a specified period, bidders can be required to specify the prices they will charge. This requires public sector involvement, but at least in principle this form of competition can eliminate excess profits.[5]

Network monopolists do not actually have the same unambiguous incentive to restrict production as other monopolists, and when pricing and investment behaviour are only lightly regulated this may work to the advantage of residents who are not yet connected. While a conventional monopolist raises prices by restricting output, a network monopolist with a marketable product (eg, water) can adopt a dual strategy of raising prices for existing users while expanding output by extending the network to new users at a low connection fee. Excess profits from existing users can, again in principle, provide the finance necessary to expand the network rapidly.

Such pricing and investment strategies may lead to more rapid improvements in water provision than the more common public utility practice of charging low water prices but not investing in expansion. Indeed, it has been argued that where under-investment is the most critical problem, unregulated private monopolies could be beneficial.[6] Perhaps more seriously, given the host of other problems that unregulated private monopolies can bring, this demonstrates the importance of taking local conditions and priorities seriously, recognizing that different regulatory strategies can serve different interests, and not assuming that the same regulatory strategy is appropriate in every setting.

The extent to which urban water and sanitation provision are natural monopolies should not be exaggerated, since even limited competition within an urban area can be an important means of preventing the abuse of monopoly powers. In particular, purposeful measures designed to create exclusive monopolies should not be confused with the existence of a natural monopoly. With a true natural monopoly, concession contracts would not have to grant exclusivity to the concession holder: it would emerge 'naturally'. In practice, alternatives to piped water supplies (eg, wells) and alternatives to formal utilities (eg, informal vendors) can fill gaps in a utility's services, and also force the utility to compete more actively for customers. When, as in colonial Beira for example, a water utility convinces public authorities to fill in wells, this can have serious long-term consequences for public health.

Moreover, while private monopolies raise a number of regulatory issues, so do public sector monopolies. Efficient and equitable regulation may involve different challenges when there is more private sector participation, but regulatory questions merge with governance issues and are critical, whatever form the urban water and sanitation system takes.

Finally, the monopolization of individual networks is in many respects less of a concern than the level of concentration in the industry internationally. A small number of transnational corporations are involved in a large share of the more significant private sector participation initiatives. Especially in countries where the need for improved water provision is the greatest, national and local governments typically have far less experience in negotiating contracts and addressing regulatory issues than the companies they must negotiate with. Given this imbalance, it is far more difficult than it might otherwise be to set in place effective regulatory structures to deal with the local natural monopoly issues.

Human rights and the case for public accountability

Various human rights have been recognized in international declarations, covenants and conventions, and are supported by international legal instruments. The right to adequate water and sanitation is not central to any of these agreements, but is implicit in several, and the right to clean drinking water is explicit in the Convention on the Rights of the Child.[7] As indicated above, the right to access clean water and sanitation at an affordable price is also acknowledged in the Dublin Principles, as well as in a number of other international statements in the water sector.

Recognition that adequate water and sanitation are human rights does not in itself imply that the public sector must be the provider of water and sanitation services. The International Covenant on Economic, Social and Cultural Rights, which sets out the basis of state responsibilities towards the realization of the rights to health and to an adequate standard of living (either of which could be taken to imply a right to adequate water and sanitation), does not rule out a central role for private enterprises. However, it does require states to 'take the necessary steps towards the progressive achievement of the right of everyone to an adequate standard of living, including access to water and sanitation'.[8]

In effect, only through a critical examination of private sector participation can it be determined whether private sector participation is helping or hindering the realization of a state's obligations to the achievement of human rights. Since human rights have an international dimension, at least some of these obligations extend beyond the borders of countries where there is inadequate access to water and sanitation, to, for example, aid donors that are promoting private sector participation in recipient countries.

The language of human rights is very different from the language of economics that is typically used to justify increased private sector participation. At the very least, the recognition of water and sanitation as a human right implies that, whether or not water is considered an economic good, economic values as conventionally measured do not provide a sufficient basis for judging water sector policies and practices.[9] From a narrow economic perspective, the fact that infants, young children and women bear a disproportionate share of the burden of inadequate water and sanitation is incidental. From a human rights perspective, such facts are crucial. More generally, a human rights approach tends to emphasize legal frameworks and issues of discrimination, participation and accountability, while a narrow economic approach tends to emphasize institutional structures and issues of choice, efficiency and mutual gain. However, in human rights as in economics, there is considerable room for debate and interpretation. Some human rights approaches are more accepting of economic principles than others, just as some economic perspectives are more amenable to a human rights approach (see, for example, the work of Amartya Sen).[10]

The view that human rights are violated by privatization is often based on the assumption that privatization is accompanied by full cost-recovery through user fees – an interpretation that is consistent with the emphasis given to cost-recovery in many attempts to promote private sector participation. A recent report to the Commission on Human Rights on 'adequate housing as a component of the right to an adequate standard of living' takes this line and is very critical of privatization:

> *Privatization by its nature is increasingly forcing central and local authorities to become profit-seeking in the provision of essential services. In a context where a large portion of the population lives in poverty, many groups cannot absorb the costs of providing a market rate of return to the investor for services provided through market mechanisms. Unless some costs are subsidized for these groups, as called for by general obligations of human rights instruments, they are likely to be excluded from receiving the services they need.[11]*

The report also raises other concerns regarding privatization and cost-recovery, the accountability of private service operators, and public sector underwriting of private investment risks.

Yet again, however, the key issues centre on how privatization is implemented, to what extent and in what context. There is no inherent contradiction between private sector participation and the achievement of human rights, but contradictions will arise in particular circumstances. A human rights perspective provides universal principles that can be applied when private sector participation is being debated, even if it does not support universal conclusions. As described in the following section, even among the standard forms of private sector participation, there is sufficient variation to make generalizations extremely difficult.

Different forms of private sector participation in water and sanitation utilities

Urban water and sanitation utilities are virtually never sold off to private enterprises to use as they see fit. Only in exceptional cases – such as privatization in England and Wales in the 1980s – are private companies granted ownership of a utility's assets indefinitely. There are several models of private sector participation and numerous variations, depending on the legal and regulatory frameworks, the nature of the company and the type of contract. In all of these models, regardless of the level of private sector involvement, the public sector role and the regulatory environment are critical. Moreover, while this section focuses on the different contractual arrangements through which private enterprises can participate in water and sanitation utilities, it should be kept in mind that the timing, phasing, contractual details and regulatory procedures for private sector involvement can be at least as important as the model selected.

Brief descriptions of typical forms of private sector involvement in water and sanitation utilities are provided below. They are ordered in terms of the extent of private sector responsibility. Table 5.1 summarizes the allocations of responsibilities. As one moves from left to right across the table, the level of responsibility allocated to the private sector increases. Two further options, which are also summarized briefly in the text but do fit within this scheme, are when the public sector or cooperative owns all or part of the utility but sets up as a private company, and when a private company runs more than one utility (eg, water and electricity).

Table 5.1 Allocation of key responsibilities for private participation options

Increasing private participation →

	Service contract	Management contract	Affermage contract	Lease contract	Concession contract	Build-own-transfer (BOT) contract	Divestiture
Asset ownership	Public	Public	Public	Public	Public	Private/public	Private
Capital investment	Public	Public	Public	Public	Private	Private	Private
Commercial risk	Public	Public	Shared	Shared	Private	Private	Private
Operations/ maintenance	Private/ public	Private	Private	Private	Private	Private	Private
Contract duration	1–2 years	3–5 years	8–15 years	8–15 years	25–30 years	20–30 years	Indefinite

Source: Adapted from Walter Stottman (2000), 'The role of the private sector in the provision of water and wastewater services in urban areas', in J J Uitto and A K Biswas, *Water for Urban Areas*, United Nations University Press, Tokyo.

Service contract[12]

Service contracts are usually short-term agreements whereby a private contractor takes responsibility for a specific task, such as installing meters, repairing pipes or collecting bills. Fees are usually fixed or per unit, and are agreed in advance. This type of contract allocates the least responsibility to the private sector, as it is only responsible for specified tasks. Examples can be found in Mexico City and Uganda.[13]

Management contract

Under a management contract, the government transfers the responsibility for the operation and maintenance of the water and/or sewerage network to a private company. The public sector retains responsibility for investment and expansion. Sometimes the public sector will choose to keep control of certain management aspects, such as billing and revenue collection. Payment is either fixed or performance-related. Management contracts are often used in countries and cities that the private sector considers too risky to invest in. They are sometimes also used as entry points for private companies, who wish to test the water before committing themselves further, and can lead on to concession contracts. These contracts typically run for approximately five years. Examples can be found in Johannesburg, Monagas State (Venezuela) and the Gambia.

Affermage contract

This type of contract is similar to a management contract, but the private operator takes responsibility for all operation and maintenance functions (technical and commercial). Although the contractor collects the tariff revenue, this goes into a fund from which the contractor is paid an agreed-upon affermage fee for each unit of water produced and distributed. There is a risk of commercial loss to the contractor if its operation and maintenance costs are higher than the affermage fee. On the other hand, the contractor does not need to be directly concerned with the water tariff, provided the government can guarantee that the fund will cover the affermage fee. Examples can be found in Côte d'Ivoire, Senegal and Guinea.[14]

Lease contract

The lease contract is similar to the affermage contract. The difference is that the revenue is determined solely by tariffs. The contractor collects tariffs in the same way as the affermage contract, pays the lease fee to the public sector, and retains the difference. Mozambique provides an example.

Concession contract

Under concession contracts, the private contractor manages the whole utility at its own commercial risk. It is also required to invest in the maintenance and expansion of the system. The key difference is that the company takes commercial risks in operational and investment activities, although many studies point to the fact that risks are minimized as much as possible both in the contracts and in subsequent renegotiations once the contract is underway.[15] Such contracts have terms of between 25 and 30 years to allow the operator to recoup expended capital, and at the end of the contract the assets are transferred back to the state or a further concession is granted. The role of government in concession contracts is predominantly regulatory. Examples can be found in Buenos Aires, Manila, La Paz, Córdoba (Argentina) and Nelspruit (South Africa).

BOT (build-own-transfer) contracts[16]
These contracts are similar to concession contracts with the difference that they are usually used for greenfield projects, where the private contractor is responsible for constructing the infrastructure from scratch. They are also different in that they are usually used for water purification and sewage treatment plants rather than distribution networks (as the latter rarely have to be built from scratch). The private partner then manages the infrastructure, with the government purchasing the supply. At the end of the contract, the assets may either remain indefinitely with the private company or be transferred back to the government, sometimes at a pre-determined fee. Examples can be found in San José (Costa Rica), São Paulo, Cancún, urban areas in Malaysia and rural areas in South Africa.

Full privatization (divestiture)
This model has only been adopted in England and Wales, apart from a few small and isolated instances. The private company purchases the assets from the government and takes over their operation and maintenance as a business on a permanent basis, but under strict commercial rules. In England and Wales, private water companies are subject to regulations that do not apply to other public limited companies. For instance, water companies are very unlikely to be allowed to file for bankruptcy.[17] The government only maintains a regulatory role, although this can be very strong, as in England and Wales.[18]

Joint ventures, public water PLCs and cooperatives
A joint venture is not a contract, but rather an arrangement whereby a private company forms a company, with the public sector with the participation of private investors, which then takes a contract for utility management. Examples can be found in Colombia (eg, Cartagena), the Czech Republic, Hungary and Poland.[19]

Similarly, the public water public limited company (PLC) model is an arrangement whereby a PLC is formed, subject to the same rules and regulations as other PLCs, and run on a commercial profit-making basis, but whose shares are owned by local, provincial or national governments. This model then combines operation in accordance with business principles with a degree of public control through government shareholding.[20] Examples can be found in the Netherlands, Germany, Poland and Chile.

Bolivia runs some of its water utilities under a cooperative model. The cooperative is set up as a limited company, and domestic customers are members who elect the administrative board, which in turn appoints the general manager and approves tariffs. Customers also elect a separate supervisory board that monitors the performance of the administrative board. While the cooperative model is uncommon, the Saguapac cooperative in Santa Cruz is said to be one of the best-run water utilities in Latin America. Examples can be found in Santa Cruz, Tarija and Trinidad (Bolivia).[21]

Multi-utility contracts
This is an arrangement whereby a private company runs more than one different type of utility. This practice is more common among other utilities (notably gas, electricity and telecommunications) than with water. In the few cases in which water has been bundled with another utility, it has been done with electricity. The attraction of bundling water and electricity is that the greater revenue

from electricity can offset the higher costs of water. In Gabon, for example, revenue from electricity provision in the capital, Libreville, and principal port, Port-Gentil, enable cross-subsidization for supplying water to the same areas.[22] Combining utilities can also make it easier to apply sanctions (eg, by cutting off electricity supplies) to ensure payment, and saves on billing costs. Examples can be found in Gabon, Mali, Chad and Honduras (water and electricity).[23]

What drives the public sector to involve private enterprises?

Finance is usually the paramount consideration driving governments to involve the private sector in water and sanitation utilities. The failure of public utilities to deliver efficient and adequate water and sanitation services may be a concern. Arguments and evidence favouring private sector participation may be influential. Political shifts can make a difference. In recent years, however, public sector decisions to radically increase the involvement of private enterprises are almost always related to the need for finance, even when undertaken by pro-private-sector governments. The divestiture of water and sanitation utilities in England and Wales undertaken in the 1970s, for example, was spurred by the need to reduce state expenditure on services and avoid having to use public funds for the substantial investments required to meet European Union quality and environmental protection standards.[24]

The most immediate external driver in indebted low-income countries is conditionality from multilateral development agencies, in particular in relation to loans. This has been the case since the implementation of structural adjustment policies in the 1980s, under which the reduction of state spending was aggressively promoted. While the policies of bilateral development agencies are not so forceful, many promote private sector participation in their recipient countries.

The use of international development finance to promote private sector participation in water and sanitation utilities can create local resistance, however, further polarizing policy debates. There are only a small number of multinational companies vying for new (large) contracts, and local companies in heavily indebted countries rarely have the capacity to compete except as minority partners. Under such circumstances, applying pressure by withholding development finance is inevitably perceived by some as a means of pursuing the interests of donor countries rather than those of the recipients. The fact that some donors are promoting private sector participation in countries where they have not traditionally been active amplifies these concerns.[25]

Financial pressures can also interfere with reforms that may be needed prior to significant private sector involvement (or even in the absence of private sector involvement). While extreme financial pressures may convince a government of the need to involve the private sector, they are not conducive to well conceived and consultative processes of privatization.[26]

What drives the private sector to participate?

The private sector has its own criteria regarding what it considers to be viable opportunities, and these criteria have little to do with water and sanitation targets as defined by the international development community. Companies may develop their own strategies in the water and sanitation sector, but these strategies must be consistent with the demands of their funders and the market conditions.

The most important aspect for private companies and their financial partners is the potential profit or rate of return. A key consideration is scale. Bankers and multinational water companies are looking for large-scale projects, with values of US$100 million upwards, in population centres with at least 1 million inhabitants. Smaller urban centres are unlikely to be attractive unless they are high-income areas, such as Riberão Preto in South Brazil, or they can be bundled with other locations or other utilities.[27]

Project opportunities must also have acceptable levels of financial and political risk.

Ideally, companies are looking for BOT-type projects or large concessions, as these can provide the greatest returns – management and lease/affermage contracts are often less attractive. Companies will avoid locations with very weak economies and/or unstable governments. Sub-Saharan Africa is generally regarded as a risky region for investment. The selection of attractive locations by private operators is termed 'cherry picking', and occurs at all scales: regions (those with large or growing economies), countries (those with larger economies and larger populations), cities (the more populous and richer the better, and preferably not including sparsely populated peri-urban zones[28]), and within cities (more affluent neighbourhoods that are already connected to the network).

This is not to say that companies will not engage in poorer countries, cities or neighbourhoods – they will do so, at a price that is high enough to outweigh the potential risks, and backed by a series of safety clauses in the contracts. However, it is to be expected that financially oriented companies seek out the best possible opportunities for investment and profit-making; to complain about this is pointless.[29]

Water provision is comparatively straightforward and more inherently attractive to private companies than sewerage provision, which is complex and unprofitable unless it is either subsidized or backed up by government regulations that require people to connect and pay specified fees. Nevertheless, many of the larger contracts, and certainly concessions, are for both water and sewerage services. This is because governments often insist on the private sector taking on both services. By contrast, management and lease/affermage contracts tend to be for water only. When contracts for water only are awarded to private operators, state utilities usually retain responsibility for sanitation, as in the case of Córdoba in Argentina.[30] Often, however, wastewater management is not coordinated with increasing water provision, and this can lead to environmental and public health problems.

The bidding process and renegotiations for large contracts

The first phase in most of the significant private sector participation initiatives starts with the development of a strategy that defines the direction of the restructuring exercise, typically with the help of an advisory team. Time constraints usually lead to a focus on the core technical, financial and legal issues necessary to create the basis for private sector participation, with issues specifically related to the improvement of water and sanitation provision in deprived areas treated secondarily, if at all.

The bidding process for large contracts typically starts with the government making the decision to privatize, and then having its team of legal, financial and technical consultants develop the bid documents, prescribing how potential bidders should present their offers. Interested private operators assemble, and their teams start doing their own assessments of the local context (eg, state of the utilities, current tariffs, extent of coverage, nature of government). Companies then submit bids in accordance with the bid documents, based on models and estimations of both the current situation and expected targets. In line with the bid documents, bids rarely focus specifically on addressing the obstacles to improving services in low-income areas. Once companies have won a bid and are in place, they carry out more detailed assessments to assess the situation, which in some cases can be worse than they had expected. In these cases, companies usually try to renegotiate relevant terms of the contract.

Companies may also submit bids with a view towards under-bidding the competition, even if the financial viability of the bid is doubtful – a practice known as 'dive bidding'. Given the substantial costs to the private company of preparing a bid (US$3–5 million for a large concession), this is an attractive strategy so long as renegotiation is possible at an early stage. In Manila, one of the companies submitted a bid for one of the city's two concessions with a tariff substantially lower than the nearest competitor: 26 per cent of existing tariffs, as opposed to 57 per cent of existing tariffs bid by another company.[31] The lower tariff should have been flagged by the government consultants (hired from international institutions, including the International Finance Corporation) as unfeasible and rejected on that basis. As things transpired, once in operation, neither company was able to provide the service for the tariff level they had quoted. Both set out to renegotiate at an early stage with the regulator, and despite initial resistance, tariff increases were approved, saving the private operator from bankruptcy.[32]

With several companies now employing this strategy, some companies have started to collude on projects, rather than compete. They do this by agreeing to submit a joint bid for a project, dividing the functions between them (according to expertise and ability), and then bidding for the next contract in the same way. In this way, companies are content to settle for an acceptable percentage of a project in the knowledge that they will also gain a share of the next contract. These are all sound financial strategies, but are not necessarily best for the utility customers, and undermine the purpose of competitive bidding.

Such strategies are more common when the bidding process is poorly organized. They are far more likely to arise when the privatization process is being rushed, the government is unfamiliar with the sorts of contracts being negotiated, the public utility is poorly run, the companies are unfamiliar with local conditions, and local governance is weak: in short, the sort of conditions likely to hold where water and sanitation services are in greatest need of improvement. The difficulties involved in orchestrating a competitive bidding process that can provide the basis for efficient utility management also tend to divert attention away from the need for consultation with local stakeholders and other mechanisms that might ensure that private participation works to the advantage of deprived groups.

Private participation and finance

One of the justifications for private sector participation in urban services in low- and middle-income countries is that public funds and development assistance cannot finance the level of investment required to expand water and sanitation services to all of those currently lacking adequate provision. Without foreign private finance it is difficult to see how the required investments can be made. Unfortunately, the level of foreign private finance has been disappointing, even in projects involving private sector participation. Most finance for investment in water and sewerage services in the cities of low- and middle-income countries continues to come from development loans, equity finance and the public sector, with comparatively little investment from international corporations.[33] Unfortunately, statistics on investment in projects involving private sector participation do not distinguish between difference sources of finance, and can even give the false impression that all of the investment is privately financed.

Private companies prefer to obtain most of their finance from equity finance (shareholders) rather than loans or bonds, because equity finance reduces the risk to the company and also helps attract lenders. Confidence needs to be generated before investors will buy shares, however. Multilateral finance can be either in the form of loans or equity, where the development institution invests as a shareholder, as in the case of La Paz, Bolivia.[34] In some cases, governments receive development loans that they use to pay the private companies for non-investment contracts (the governments thereby assume the risk for the loan). In other cases, non-concessionary loans are given directly to private companies by international financial institutions.

Most loan finance has come from (multilateral and bilateral) international financial institution development loans, rather than loans from commercial banks. Commercial banks often consider water and sanitation projects too risky and insufficiently profitable. Most loans have been financed on a limited recourse basis – that is, with project cash flows as collateral as opposed to the assets of the parent company[35] (see for instance the example of Manila).[36] The other, little used, option is corporate financing, in which project finance comes from the company's own turnover, meaning that it assumes the risk for its investment.

Given the high levels of uncertainty in most water and sewerage ventures, especially in politically unstable settings, companies are anxious to protect themselves as much as possible from financial risk. Multinationals almost always form subsidiaries (usually consortia), partly to relieve the parent company of liability and partly because governments often insist on consortia involving local companies.[37] Many of the consortia created do not have strong enough balance sheets to raise debt and equity finance, and local bond and equity markets are often too weak to attract the scale of investment needed.[38]

The private sector is only required to invest under BOT-type, concession and joint venture projects, while service, management, lease and affermage contracts attract no investment at all from the private sector. Therefore, in regions where non-investment contracts dominate, such as sub-Saharan Africa, virtually all investment still comes via the public sector, almost entirely through development loans, with the government bearing the risk.[39] Where possible, governments want the private operator to take the risk for finance and investment, but companies – in particular multinationals, which have their own financial experts – are very wary of taking undue risks, and will not commit themselves where they consider the risks to be too high to justify the expected returns. When they do accept a moderate level of risk, they ensure that provisions are written into contracts for mitigating the impacts of risks. Alternatively, as indicated above, private operators may take on low-risk contracts such as management or lease contracts in order to assess whether it is feasible to undertake investment in the future. However, this can result in the government delaying public sector investments in the hope

that the private sector will eventually bring its own finance.

Regulation of private water and sanitation enterprises

Regulation is often seen as a way of controlling the private company to make sure that it does not abuse its monopoly position. The role of the regulator is to act as a referee between the operator, the consumers and the relevant government bodies, in order to determine what is reasonable.[40] The functions of a regulatory system are therefore usually wider than just protecting against market abuse, and comprise:

- ensuring that users receive an adequate level of service at reasonable price and protecting them from abuse by firms with substantial market power;
- ensuring that investors receive a reasonable return on capital and protecting them from arbitrary action by government; and
- monitoring and ensuring that other conditions and standards are met, that the operator complies with the conditions and provisions of the contract, setting or regulating prices, and regulating environmental standards.[41]

The information necessary for effective regulation is often difficult to obtain, frequently leading to problems of information asymmetry, in which the company is far better informed than the regulator. It is also often difficult to balance the rights and interests of the different groups. Tariffs are a particularly sensitive area for regulators. Keeping services affordable for lower-income groups is not always consistent with keeping utility prices high enough to provide private operators with reasonable returns, but it is difficult to assess what is affordable to households or sufficiently profitable for private operators. Tariffs may be set by the government (rather than by the regulator), but even so, information asymmetry can complicate the regulatory tasks.

In order to be objective and fair, the regulator should be both independent and strong enough to withstand pressures from both government and the private operator.[42] An independent regulator should have an arm's-length relationship with operators, government authorities and consumers. Some recommend that regulators should be autonomous organizations with (adequate) designated funding and independent salaries in order to avoid co-optation and corruption.[43] However, cases have arisen in which the regulator is accused of being biased in favour of the private operator. In Wales, the regulator (OFWAT) ruled that Welsh Water was within its rights to install pre-payment meters in the homes of low-income consumers, but this was reversed by a successful legal challenge by local governments.[44] In Manila, the regulator approved tariff increases for the two operators earlier than set out in the terms of their contracts. A citizens' group is now initiating legal proceedings against the regulator on the grounds that its actions were against regulatory procedures and unfairly favoured the concessionaires.[45] In Buenos Aires, the regulator (ETOSS) is independent, but that did not stop the government over-ruling its refusal to grant an unscheduled price increase requested by Aguas Argentinas to placate investors.[46]

The following measures have been suggested to avoid some of these problems:

- transparent decision-making processes;
- provision for appealing against the regulator's decisions;
- the use of external auditors or watchdogs; and
- mechanisms for the removal of the regulator in the event of poor performance.[47]

The degree of power and discretion that governments will want to give to regulators depends on the roles they are expected to play. Some will want to allow the regulator minimal discretion (especially over tariffs), and will therefore set up a rigid and/or restrictive regulatory framework. Others will want to give the regulator more responsibility, and will use more flexible mechanisms to ensure that the regulator acts in accordance with its mandate. While rigid regulatory systems tend

to be unresponsive in the face of unforeseen events, provisions can be – and often are – written into contracts to protect private operators from potential risks (such as local currency devaluation).[48] Alternatively, while giving the regulator more discretion may raise concerns about the transfer of political power, the regulator can also be subjected to close supervision by a political, judicial or administrative body.

Some experts recommend a low degree of regulation, especially when a large share of the population does not yet have access to the networks. Deregulation of tariffs can provide an incentive for investment in expanding the networks. If rules controlling market entry – especially for small-scale and/or informal service providers – are relaxed, these groups will be able to legally provide services to lower-income groups that do not have access to the networks, and in some cases provide market competition. Similarly, flexible prices and quality standards can, in some circumstances, allow provision to the poor and/or unserved populations to be improved more rapidly, especially when the existing standards set by contracts imply costs that are unaffordable to low-income groups. When a low degree of regulation is accompanied by inadequate monitoring and enforcement, however, an imbalance of power is likely to result, and can cause severe problems.

It is widely agreed that the regulator should be in place before the contract is implemented, although this is not always the case. First, it is important for the privatization process itself, because investors will want to see that firm rules are in place, especially regarding protection from political risk.[49] Second, an independent regulator can help to ensure the fairness of the contract bidding and award process. Third, the regulator should be party to contract negotiations to ensure the inclusion of pro-poor measures.[50] Regulators can help to incorporate specific pro-poor measures in the contracts, such as provision for low-cost technologies, alternative payment mechanisms and pro-poor tariff structures and/or subsidies. Insecure land tenure can become a barrier to the provision of services to informal neighbourhoods by private operators.

Aguas Cordobesas in Córdoba (Argentina) argued that no mention was made of the need to provide for settlements without legal titles in the contract,[51] indicating that this and similar issues need to be considered prior to the contract being drawn up, and then explicitly addressed in the contract documents. In order to build their capacity on pro-poor measures, regulators could also engage more with local communities and their representatives.

All regulators also need to be accountable for their actions, and to be regulated at a higher level. This is particularly important when regulators have been established recently or have a poor record. A mechanism needs to be in place to ensure that the regulator does not stray from its mandate or become inefficient, or even be coopted or engage in corruption. Regulatory bodies are often staffed by former public utility employees. Since the private sector is often brought in to salvage failing public utilities, this raises the question of whether former utility staff are necessarily more capable of regulating the system than they were of running it,[52] especially when the staff of the privately operated utility also include former public utility staff.

Regulation need not be restricted to privately operated utilities. Indeed, it is now often argued that regulatory systems should be developed for public utilities. This raises important issues of sequencing. For much of the 1990s, the conventional wisdom in international development circles was that privatization was the priority, and would provide the basis for second-order improvements. If, however, a good regulatory environment is necessary for privatization to succeed, and can also improve public sector operations, the more obvious sequencing is to concentrate first on regulatory improvement – which is closely related to issues of governance – and initiate privatization as and when it can proceed smoothly and with local support.

Privatization and measures for pro-poor provision

In general, there are few specific measures being implemented to improve water and sanitation provision to unserved low-income areas by private operators. Some cases that have been identified are listed below.[53]

- In Buenos Aires, Argentina, after a long struggle, several low-income settlements (*Barrios* San Jorge, San Martín, La Paz and Villa Zemira) successfully negotiated provision from the private operators, despite their lack of legal land titles. The successful negotiations were assisted by CSOs – either NGOs or CBOs – and, in some cases, support from the local mayor. Some residents even managed to negotiate individual bills, despite resistance from the operator.[54]
- In an informal low-income settlement in Cartagena, Colombia (*Barrio* Nelson Mandela), the private operator extended its service to the area in order to deter residents from using illegal connections. The community is being billed collectively through ten communal meters in order to develop a payment culture for the eventual installation of household connections.[55]
- In La Paz and El Alto, Bolivia, condominial sewerage and yard connections have been introduced for low-income households. Families contribute labour for installation in order to reduce costs, although if the costs of this free labour were included, the cost would actually be higher than paying for the installation of the conventional system.[56] The condominial system is criticized for being sub-standard as the narrow diameter pipes and the low consumption from yard taps lead to frequent blockages, and the pipes are laid too shallowly and often resurface and break: 'a poor quality solution for poor people'.[57]
- In South Africa, communal water facilities (standpipes) are often installed in low-income areas, despite research which shows that the health benefits from

improved water supply are greatest when yard or household connections are provided and accompanied by sanitation provision. This is also a politically sensitive issue: 'given the historical disparities between race groups in South Africa, it is not appropriate to provide inferior services to the disadvantaged populations'.[58]

- In some locations in South Africa, pre-payment cards were introduced for standpipes. This was a controversial measure. Forcing pre-payment meters on customers in England and Wales was declared unlawful.[59]
- In South Africa, a lifeline tariff of 6000 litres of free water per household per month was introduced in 2000 by the government. This has been received with hostility by private operators. For example, in Nelspruit, the private Greater Nelspruit Utility Company (already facing financial difficulties) argued that its contract did not include the provision of free water and continued its policy of disconnection for non-paying households. The company did concede, following a local campaign, but put its plans for water expansion to peri-urban areas on hold.[60]

While it is encouraging that some private operators are considering ways of addressing the needs of lower-income users, such initiatives are still rare. Moreover, some of the factors that have led private operators to take innovative measures to serve low-income settlements have been location-specific and difficult to replicate. In at least two cases (in Buenos Aires and Cartagena), private operators have sought out innovative ways of providing formal connections to low-income residents, at least in part to address the problems posed by illegal connections.[61] Generally one would expect the risk of illegal connections to reduce operators' incentives to extend the water network. If, however, the network is being extended, then the threat of illegal connections may convince the operator to facilitate legal connections so as to avoid water losses. Again, much depends on the

local circumstances. Various proposals have been put forward to help ensure that private sector participation is more pro-poor. These include:

- devoting more resources to consultation and participation at all stages in the privatization process;
- providing more information relating to current conditions in low-income areas, obstacles to improvement and targets for the future;
- giving more weight to pro-poor measures when evaluating bids (this could be made explicit in the tender documents);
- addressing the tenure problems that inhibit connections in low-income areas;
- reducing connection costs, even if this requires higher unit rates; and
- building indicators of coverage (or lack of access, such as the price charged by vendors) into the contract, so that the operator's profit depends on them.

Many of these measures are discussed in more detail in the following chapter, in the context of demand-side management and improving services to the urban poor. What is striking is that most of these could equally apply, in some cases with minor modifications, to public water and sanitation utilities.

Trends in private sector participation in water and sanitation utilities

In the utilities sector, private sector participation is concentrated in energy and telecommunications, while water and sanitation services have seen comparatively little privatization, especially in low-income countries.[62] The percentage of the world's population currently estimated to be served by formal private water providers and PPPs is still less than 10 per cent, although there are significant regional differences. In much of Africa, Asia and Latin America, a much higher share of households are served by informal and/or small-scale private water providers, and the share can rise as high as 70–80 per cent in some poorly served African cities, such

Table 5.2 Investment in water and sanitation infrastructure projects with private sector participation (US$ billions)

Year	Investment (US$ billions)	Year	Investment (US$ billions)
1990	0.0	1995	1.7
1991	0.1	1996	2.2
1992	1.9	1997	8.9
1993	7.5	1998	2.6
1994	0.7	1999	5.9

Note: These figures are from the World Bank's Private Participation in Infrastructure (PPI) database. 'Investment' refers to total investment, not private investment alone. Also, many small projects are omitted.
Source: Izaguirre, A K and G Rao (2000), 'Private infrastructure: private activity fell by 30 per cent in 1999', Private Sector Viewpoint Note 215, Public Policy for the Private Sector Series, the World Bank, Washington, DC.

as Bamako (Mali), Conraky (Guinea), Cotonou (Benin) and Dar es Salaam (Tanzania).[63] This section, however, is not concerned with these informal and small-scale water providers, which are discussed later in the chapter.

Prior to 1990 there were just a handful of large private initiatives in water and sanitation infrastructure and services. Privatization in the water and sanitation sector accelerated sharply in 1990, and peaked in 1997. Table 5.2 shows the pattern of investment in water and sanitation infrastructure projects with private participation. The investment figures in this and subsequent tables are not based on private investment (or private finance) alone, and should not be interpreted as additional to the investment that would have occurred in the absence of private sector participation. Indeed, given the importance often accorded to using private sector participation to attract private sector finance, it is surprisingly difficult to obtain statistics that would help to discern the role of private sector finance to date.

Following the Asian financial crisis, investors have been less confident about investing in the South in general, particularly in East Asia and Latin America.[64] In the water sector specifically, lenders and operators alike have realized that the water and sewerage sector is both more complex and less profitable than originally anticipated. Experiences of failed contracts, such as those in Cochabamba (Bolivia) and Tucumán (Argentina) – although generally viewed as isolated events – have also made investors and water companies more cautious. There is also a feeling that

there are fewer projects available that are 'bankable'. Many of the most attractive locations were either privatized during the 1990s, or show few signs of preparing to engage with the private sector. While there are still many viable locations, especially for concessions, the early expectations of continuous rapid growth in private sector participation are being revised downwards.

There are strong regional and national concentrations of private sector participation in the water and sanitation sector. Among low- and middle-income countries, the greatest number of projects, and the greatest proportion of investments, are both concentrated in Latin America and East Asia, as shown in Table 5.3.

Within Latin America and East Asia, six countries – Argentina, Mexico, Brazil, the Philippines, Malaysia and China – dominate in terms of total investment and number of projects (see Table 5.4), with Argentina, the Philippines and Malaysia accounting for 69 per cent of total investment in projects with private sector participation.[65] Generally speaking, the countries in which investment is concentrated all have larger economies and populations and are characterized by high percentages of urban population. These all relate to key attributes that make them attractive to the private sector. There are relatively few private sector water and sanitation projects in low-income countries, especially in sub-Saharan Africa.[66] More recently, some multinational water companies are concentrating on the USA and China as targets for market expansion.[67]

Table 5.3 Private water and sanitation projects in selected regions, 1990–1997

Region	Projects		Investment	
	Number	*%*	*1997 US$ millions*	*%*
Latin America and Caribbean	40	42	8225	48
East Asia and Pacific	30	31	11,913	33
Europe and Central Asia	15	15	1499	6
Sub-Saharan Africa	8	8	37	0
Middle East and North Africa	4	4	3275	13

Note: These figures are from the World Bank's Private Participation in Infrastructure (PPI) database. 'Investment' refers to total investment, not private investment alone. Also, many small projects are omitted.
Source: Silva, G, N Tynan and Y Yilmaz (1998), 'Private participation in the water and sanitation sector: recent trends', Private Sector Viewpoint Note 147, Public Policy for the Private Sector Series, the World Bank, Washington, DC.

However, there is only a weak relationship between the number of projects and the amount of investment, principally because the majority of projects only entail operation and maintenance, with no investment.[68] With a few exceptions in South Africa, there are almost no investment contracts in sub-Saharan Africa because the region is perceived as too risky, and this is exacerbated by the fact that previous projects there, such as the Mozambique concession, have encountered problems.[69] As of 1998, there were also no large-scale contracts in South Asia, but several BOT-type contracts are in place for water/wastewater treatment plants (eg, Tirupur, India), and there is keen interest in the larger South Asian cities, such as Bangalore, Chennai, Kathmandu and Karachi, among others.[70]

Table 5.5 presents the number of projects and levels of investment by contract type. Regional data indicate that there is a predominance of concession contracts in Latin America and Southeast Asia, BOT-type contracts in South Asia, and lease and management contracts in sub-Saharan Africa. Most of the larger water contracts include water supply and sanitation, although there are a few contracts for water supply only, such as in Córdoba.[71] There are also a few sanitation-only contracts, such as in Malaysia, but these are uncommon.

In some cases, water and sanitation projects have been bundled to create larger projects of a scale that is financially viable for the private operator. This can involve either multiple locations (eg, more than one city or town) or multiple utilities (eg, electricity as well as water and sanitation). In Mozambique, a concession was given for seven different cities,[72] and in Guinea, a contract was given for the capital, Conraky, and 16 other towns. National or regional utilities have been or are being privatized to serve the whole area in a number of other countries, such as Venezuela (Monagas and Zulia provinces) and Argentina (La Rioja, Corrientes and Salta provinces). This is being developed on a national scale in several African countries (Ghana, the Gambia, Chad, Burkina Faso) and also Paraguay, Trinidad and Tobago, and Puerto Rico. In the case of different utilities, water has only been bundled with

Table 5.4 Investment in water and sewerage projects in selected countries, 1990–1997

	Number of projects	Total investment in projects (1997 US$ millions)
Argentina	7	6183
Philippines	3	5820
Malaysia	6	5030
Turkey	2	1230
Mexico	12	597
Brazil	8	583
China	13	503
Czech Republic	6	25

Note: These figures are from the World Bank's Private Participation in Infrastructure (PPI) database. 'Investment' refers to total investment, not private investment alone. Also, many small projects are omitted.
Source: Silva, G, N Tynan and Y Yilmaz (1998), 'Private participation in the water and sanitation sector: recent trends', Private Sector Viewpoint Note 147, Public Policy for the Private Sector Series, the World Bank, Washington, DC.

Table 5.5 Contract types for water and sewerage projects 1990–1997 in low- and middle-income countries

Region	Projects		Investment	
	Number	%	1997 US$ millions	%
Concession	48	50	19,909	80
BOT-type (greenfield)	30	31	4037	16
Management/lease/affermage	13	13	n/a	0
Divestiture	6	6	997	4

Note: These figures are from the World Bank's Private Participation in Infrastructure (PPI) database. 'Investment' refers to total investment, not private invest-ment alone. Also, many small projects are omitted.
Source: Silva, G, N Tynan and Y Yilmaz (1998), 'Private participation in the water and sanitation sector: recent trends', Private Sector Viewpoint Note 147, Public Policy for the Private Sector Series, the World Bank, Washington, DC.

electricity, and this has been done in several countries in sub-Saharan Africa (Burundi, Cape Verde, Gabon, the Gambia, Guinea Bissau, Chad and Mali), but very rarely elsewhere.[73] Furthermore, although some of the water multi-nationals, especially Vivendi, operate in other utility sectors, they do not appear to be bundling utilities in the same location.

The water and sanitation sector, both world-wide and in the South, is dominated by a very small number of multinational utility companies: namely Vivendi, Ondeo, Thames and Saur. Together, these four companies control over 80 per cent of the privatized water and sewerage market.[74] Vivendi and Ondeo alone control between 50 per cent and 70 per cent of the market, and also own many of the water-related subsidiaries, such as water and sewerage pipe manufacturers.[75] Table 5.6 gives data on the main multinational companies active in the water and sewerage sector.

Judging from current trends, the future of privatization in urban water and sanitation utilities is very uncertain. The role of privati-zation in meeting the global challenge of ensuring that all urban dwellers have adequate access to affordable water and sanitation services is clearly limited. There are indications that the privatization process may be stalling, and yet it has hardly begun to make a significant impact on the urban

Table 5.6 Dominant private companies in the water and sewerage sector

	Number of projects 1990–1997	Investment (1997 US$ millions) 1990–1997	Water sales (€ millions)* 2001	World-wide customers (millions) 2001
Ondeo (SUEZ)	28	16,153	10,088	115
Vivendi	13	5275	13,640	110
Aguas de Barcelona	6	9072	n/a	n/a
Thames Water	6	1375	2746	37**
SAUR International	5	38	2494	36
Anglian	n/a	n/a	936	5
Cascal	n/a	n/a	181	6.7
International Water	n/a	n/a	100	10

Note: The investment figures are from the World Bank's Private Participation in Infrastructure (PPI) database. 'Investment' refers to total investment, not private investment alone. * In 2001, 1 euro (€) = approximately US$0.9.
** 'Thames' excludes those customers on shared contracts (eg Adelaide, Budapest, Berlin).
Source: Number of projects and investments are from Silva, G, N Tynan and Y Yilmaz (1998), 'Private participation in the water and sanitation sector: recent trends', Private Sector Viewpoint Note 147, Public Policy for the Private Sector Series, the World Bank, Washington, DC; water sales and numbers of customers are from Hall, D (2002), *The Water Multinationals 2002: Financial and Other Problems*, Public Services International Research Unit, University of Greenwich, London.

centres and neighbourhoods where water and sanitation problems are most severe. It would be a serious mistake to assume that PPPs, designed around principles of cost-recovery, will attract sufficient finance to play a major role in providing adequate water and sanitation to deprived neighbourhoods. There may well be scope for making private sector participation more pro-poor, as indicated in several recent reports.[76] However, many of the measures identified as important in making privately operated utilities more pro-poor could also be applied to public utilities, and could be pursued independently of any privatization process. Moreover, over-optimistic forecasts of private sector finance reduce pressure on the public sector to develop more sustainable financing systems. Furthermore, it is important not to neglect the roles of small-scale private providers, CBOs and NGOs, which continue to grow in many of the more water- and sanitation-deprived settlements – particularly in countries like Tanzania, where the public sector has been withdrawing from service provision but formal private sector participation has not developed.[77]

The role of small-scale providers

Most of those unserved or inadequately served by official systems of provision in urban areas rely on small-scale private providers or community provision for part or all of the water they use. Most low-income households without access to piped supplies will also use any available free water, such as local rivers, streams or shallow wells; but these are often not available in urban areas and if they are, their quality is poor, so households will still rely on water from vendors, kiosks or stand-pipes for drinking or cooking whenever possible. Small-scale providers or community organizations are also often important for sanitation, although the form of the service they provide varies greatly – from constructing and managing sewers or public toilets, to latrine construction, to services that remove human wastes (for instance septic tank or latrine emptying services). In many cities and smaller urban centres, there are also providers of water and sanitation services that are neither single, large public or private water and sanitation companies nor small-scale providers, such as cooperatives or private water networks that serve several hundred to several thousand households. Local or international NGOs also have important roles in many cities.

These forms of provision have importance for three reasons. The first is that they are providing water and sanitation services to a very large proportion of low-income urban households (and in many cities to large sections of middle- and upper-income groups too); without them, provision for water and sanitation would be much worse. They often serve populations living in areas that are difficult to serve with conventional water distribution and drainage networks.[78]

It is difficult to estimate how many people rely on them, but in many cities and smaller urban centres in sub-Saharan Africa and in low-income nations in Asia and Latin America, they are certainly far more important than large-scale private water companies both in terms of the number of people they reach and in terms of benefiting low-income households. Official statistics on provision for water and sanitation generally fail to highlight their importance. This is especially the case where independent providers are important for water piped to homes or sewers. For instance, the official statistics on provision for water in Asunción in Paraguay do not mention that a significant proportion of the households with water piped to their homes get this from small independent private water supply networks.[79] Nor is the key role of cooperatives in provision for water to households in Santa Cruz de la Sierra in Bolivia apparent in official statistical tables.

The second reason why it is important to consider the role of independent providers is that they are generally providing services with no subsidy and with prices and/or services that compare favourably with what official providers make available; if they did not, they would not be able to operate. Third, there is increasing evidence to suggest that in many locations, working with and through such independent providers can be a cheaper, more effective way of improving and extending provision for water and sanitation than conventional public sector provision or reliance on large-scale private (often international) utilities. But this evidence also shows how responses by local or national governments and international agencies need to be rooted in the specifics of each city or urban centre (or urban neighbourhood).[80] Once again, we return to the issue of effective, accountable local government structures that, where needed, encourage and support effective local action and innovation.

It is difficult to generalize about independent providers, since they take many forms (private for-profit, private non-profit, community, condominial, cooperative) and operate at many scales. A study in six Latin American cities highlighted the diversity in form and scale of independent providers for water and suggested a distinction between:

- individuals with push-carts selling water by the glass, bag or gallon, who can reach 100–200 persons daily;
- truckers who carry water from house to house, who serve between 70 and 350 households or 400–1500 persons a day; and
- independent water networks, which serve from 100 to several thousand households (with some beginning with as few as ten customers).[81]

A study of independent water and sanitation providers in cities in ten African nations highlighted the variety of providers. For instance, for water:

- hand-pushed carts that carry 100–200 litres of water;
- horse- or donkey-pulled carts with up to 500 litres (especially in cities of the Sahel, where draught animals are raised in abundance);
- water truckers who serve larger customers – for instance, filling water tanks in larger houses or offices; and
- various types of water re-sellers operating from fixed points of sale, including

standpipe vendors and, in some cities, mini-piped networks.

For sanitation:

- septic tank cleaners with suction trucks;
- manual latrine or septic tank cleaners who operate where roads are too narrow for trucks or septic tanks are not suited to mechanical cleaning;
- masons who build latrines; and
- public toilets and showers, often at train stations, markets, stadiums and universities.[82]

For many urban centres in Africa and Asia, water kiosks are particularly important (ie, standpipes run by private entrepreneurs, community organizations or non-profit organizations where water is sold).

Chapter 1 emphasized how large proportions of the population in most major cities in Africa and many in Asia do not have direct access to piped supplies, either through in-house connections or through access to standpipes supplied by pipes. The study of independent water and sanitation providers in African cities mentioned above showed how between 17 and 78 per cent of household water needs are met through the formal distribution network in ten cities, with the remainder being serviced by informal providers (or direct groundwater sources).[83] In Bamako, for example, only 18,000 households are served by the city water agency while 92,000 are served by independent providers. Of these independent providers, private wells serve 50,000 and standpipe operators serve 35,000, with the remaining households being served by carters and small network operators. The Drawers of Water II study mentioned in Chapter 1 suggests that private wells have become more important for residents in the nine East African urban centres it covered because of the unreliability and intermittent nature of supplies through the piped network.[84] It is also interesting to note the increasing private market in water. In 1967, more than 75 per cent of households with unpiped supplies used hydrants or standpipes, with the remaining sources being rain water and surface water. In 1997, rain water and surface water supplied less than 15 per cent of the water needs of those households without piped water; the private market had grown from zero to 24 per cent with hydrants or standpipes supplying 56 per cent of house-holds.[85]

It is perhaps surprising how long it has taken development assistance agencies (and the international discussions about how to improve provision for water and sanitation) to recognize the importance of small-scale independent water vendors, truckers and network operators and of those who offer sanitation services. As Tova Solo stresses, many are large scale and have been operating successfully for decades. The early stereotype of water vendors as highly exploitative in the prices they charge has been replaced with a recognition that the prices charged generally reflect real costs, because most vendors operate in highly competitive markets (if they are charging a high price, this is often related to the reluctance or refusal of official water supply systems to support them). Poorer groups may pay high prices to vendors but they would be much worse off without them.[86] If more had been known about the *aguateros* [small-scale water entrepreneurs] in Asunción (Paraguay), or the water cooperatives in Santa Cruz de la Sierra (Bolivia) or Córdoba (Argentina) in the 1980s, or the community-built sewers supported by Orangi Pilot Project in Karachi, or the many local NGO-supported programmes for standpipes, water kiosks and public toilets, when the World Bank and other agencies strongly promoted privatization of water and sanitation, perhaps it would have led to less promotion of the conventional large-scale privatizations involving international corporations. Perhaps one reason for this lack of attention is the reluctance of many inter-national agencies to work in urban areas – or even to acknowledge the scale of need in urban areas. Another obvious reason is the difficulties for large official external agencies of working with a multiplicity of small-scale providers, since these agencies were set up to work with and through national governments. Large centralized international agencies always have difficulties supporting diverse

local solutions involving many actors,[87] which is one reason why support for privatization in water and sanitation has tended to favour large companies.

Whilst there have long been suggestions of the need for a much greater recognition of the importance of informal water vendors,[88] there was relatively little official interest in this until the end of the 1990s. There was also little recognition of the extent to which their potential to improve and extend provision was being constrained by official policies, rules and regulations. For instance, households get far more convenient supplies and cheaper water per litre from private piped water networks than from vendors, but entrepreneurs will not invest in piped water systems if these may be expropriated or closed down by governments or official providers. In addition, the price charged by vendors is strongly influenced by how easily they can obtain water close to their customers – which is usually much influenced by official policies and attitudes to vendors. However, by the late 1990s, the importance of independent water and sanitation providers for low-income urban dwellers was gaining recog-nition – as can be seen by the research and publications of the Water and Sanitation Program, run by the World Bank and funded by many bilateral donor agencies.[89] By 1999, it was being suggested in a World Bank Viewpoint newsletter that those setting regulatory standards should ensure that there was a potential for small-scale private providers in order to open a range of service options for low-income households. It suggested that policy-makers '… need to refocus regulation on facilitating entry and monitoring quality and prices to end users'.[90]

The proportion of people purchasing water- and sanitation-related goods or services from independent providers, and the range of goods or services offered, obviously depend on the scale and nature of demand, the competition from official large providers and community initiatives, and the influence of government policy and practice. They are also likely to be influenced by local innovations that are seen to work and so expand and develop.[91] Albu and Njiru make a useful distinction between wholesale vendors (who may buy a tanker or even have a small network), distributing vendors (who sell directly to consumers door-to-door) and direct vendors (who sell to consumers who come to them).[92]

It has been suggested that where the very poor do not have formal infrastructure services, 'informal, private and community infrastructure solutions fill the gap for many households.'[93] In practice, it is not so clear that they only fill a gap, since the informal, private and community services may be cheaper than the formal services. For instance, it was only when the company with the concession for much of Buenos Aire, Aguas Argentinas, was competitive on price that people were prepared to change suppliers.[94] Households may restrict their use of water from formal suppliers and choose to use cheaper (poorer quality) informal supplies.

Tova Solo argues that such providers should not be seen simply as subsidiary to the public network. She suggests that:

> *Small-scale water and sanitation enterprises are not simply marginal peculiarities with limited replicability. In Guatemala City, over 200 independent operations are responsible for service provision to over half of the population of the metropolitan area. When allowed to flourish, the small-scale entrepreneurs are efficient, competitive and replicable – requiring no subsidies or monopolistic conditions.*[95]

Another study that is supportive of their role suggests that: '...perhaps the most difficult task facing the regulator is to ensure that positive aspects of the small-scale operators are preserved while ensuring that services are provided efficiently and do not generate externalities elsewhere.'[96] Solo notes that whilst prices may be higher, this is not universally the case and a review by the World Bank Water and Sanitation Program found that private provider charges varied between one-tenth and eight times those of public providers.[97]

A recent study of infrastructure coverage using a dataset of 55,000 households in 15 countries (World Bank Living Standards Measurement Study) included an assessment of water consumption.[98] Information on water vendors was available in the case of Côte d'Ivoire, Ghana, Pakistan and Nicaragua. Only 2.4 per cent of the sample depended on water vendors as a primary source of drinking water although 15 per cent of households in Côte d'Ivoire used water vendors. Perhaps surprisingly, less than 1 per cent of households using vendors were in the poorest decile of their countries, whilst 20 per cent were in the richest decile. Average expenditure for those using water vendors was generally not higher than the cost of in-house piped services (although the price per unit of water is higher).[99]

Collignon and Vezina note that, in general, they found little evidence of strongly competitive behaviour between the informal suppliers in ten East and West African towns. In some cases this may be because they come from the same geographical region or ethnic group, in others because they face similar difficulties and have frequent social contact.[100] However, they also cite examples from Nairobi of more aggressive and violent behaviour between water carriers and those laying a new community network.

The role of CSOs

The growing interest in small-scale private providers has also been accompanied by a growing awareness of the need to develop models of community-managed services that place considerable emphasis on self-regulation. Such models have become popular in the last ten years,[101] although these often build on much longer traditions of self-managed assets.[102] In part, this reflects a pragmatic response to the inadequacies of public provision – although it also reflects a much more widespread recognition of the importance of more participatory development models.[103]

In such models, users have a voice and choice in aspects such as technology, level of service, service provider, financing arrangements and management systems, in exchange for making contributions (in cash or in kind).[104] Such models often seek to engage community members from the beginning of the service delivery process, in order to build community ownership and strengthen their capacity to manage services. They are driven by the understanding that many communities are willing and able to develop their own water supply systems rather than wait for government provision, often because their costs will fall if they work together to improve on existing provision.[105] Community-managed systems vary from relatively unsophisticated systems such as large water tanks, from which the inhabitants can collect water,[106] to piped water supplies and sewers connecting all or virtually all households in a settlement.[107]

Community control is more likely to ensure access for the poorest, although it does not guarantee this – for instance, committees formed by local residents to manage new water points can also be exclusionary and discriminatory.[108] A study in Dhaka describes this when discussing the attempts of a local NGO to improve water supply. 'Access to scarce resources is a recurring source of conflict in a slum and often provides a power base for a distinct social leadership, which dictates the terms and conditions under which residents in a particular neighbourhood have to live.'[109] The NGO, Dushtha Sashthya Kendra, found its first community-managed initiative sabotaged by the local leader, who stole water to sell. In response, it spent more time creating and strengthening a community management team that was able to manage finance and staff. The study notes that '…the main emphasis was laid on capacity building in the community, and preparing them to operate a community service based on accountability and transparency'.[110]

An evaluation of a five-year programme by WaterAid in Bangladesh shows both the possibilities and the difficulties with community provision.[111] Box 3.1 in Chapter 3 described WaterAid's programme in Dhaka and Chittagong, supporting seven local NGOs that worked with local communities in squatter and slum areas to provide water points connected to the city supply network, or tubewells, individual latrines, community latrines and toilet blocks. Toilet blocks are connected to the piped water system and generally serve 100 households or more. Community latrines generally serve a smaller area of 10–50 households. It is clear that the programme has considerably improved provision of water and sanitation for a large number of households; unit costs have remained low and mechanisms for cost-recovery have been put in place. But generally it is difficult to completely hand over responsibility to the community because the NGO is held responsible for the water bills. However, in the case of water supply systems that draw from tubewells, it has proved possible. The evaluation found that, generally, committees were successfully managing tubewells but some had stopped collecting funds. Handover happens once the loan (to cover the cost of the installing the tubewell) has been repaid, and generally money management becomes more lax. Ledger accounts are only kept in one-third of cases, compared to 80 per cent of those not yet handed over. It appears that in a number of cases, strong individuals have taken over control of the water point and general access for the community has not been maintained. The same evaluation warns against the simple assumption that business-related sales can be simply added on to community provision. In a number of cases, sales to outsiders became more important than serving the needs of the immediate community.

It is not clear how financially viable community-managed systems can be, and perhaps it is inappropriate to generalize, given the differences in local circumstances – not least the differences in the costs of improved provision and what households can afford to pay. Certainly, there are examples showing how community-managed services have improved provision for water and sanitation with most or all the costs recovered. But a study of 88 community-managed systems in 12 countries, none of which had a subsidy, concluded that nearly half were failing to collect sufficient revenues to meet current operating costs.[112] However, they judged all but one to have a functional local management committee.

There is no single model for community-managed supplies. Generally, they are supported by an external agency, most probably a local NGO. The attitude to subsidy varies considerably, as does the actual division of responsibilities within any water supply or sanitation initiative. One of the best known

Box 5.2 Community-managed water provision: the politics and the pipes

Faisalabad is one of Pakistan's largest cities, with close to 2 million inhabitants in 1998. There has long been a large gap between the growing population's need for land for housing with provision for piped water, sanitation and drainage, and the capacity of the government agencies responsible for their provision. Two-thirds of the population live in areas with little or no official provision for services and most new housing and land developments take place without official approval. Less than half the population have piped water and less than one-third have connections to the sewer system.

A local welfare organization run by local residents, the Anjuman Samaji Bahbood, has demonstrated that it is possible for communities to build and finance piped water supplies and sewers in the informal settlements in which most of Faisalabad's population lives – but to achieve this on any scale requires support from the water and sanitation authority to allow the community systems to draw on the official piped water network and trunk sewers.

One settlement called Hasanpura was chosen as a pilot area because there was no potable water, although (saline) underground water from boreholes was used by residents for washing clothes and some other activities. The 1000 households in the settlement were spending considerable sums of money on water, with further costs incurred through purchasing soap (more was needed because of the saline water) and medical services due to high levels of disease. The

project sought to connect the settlement to a water main located around 110 metres away from the settlement, with individual lanes then laying pipes to connect households to mains water. Each household's share of the costs of the mains water pipe was R1300 (in 2000 there were around R55 to a US$, so this is was the equivalent of US$24). The cost of connection is an average of R600 (US$11) and the charge to connect to the public network is R1175 (US$21).

Initially, local authorities showed little interest in the work. Negotiating with the water and sewerage authority for permission to connect to its water supply network took a long time. One reason for this was the bureaucratic procedures necessary to get permission for the connection to cross a road. One official demanded a bribe to permit this. The community decided to do this portion of their work at night, confident that once it was completed they would be able to keep the pipe and pay a fine. Through a combination of clandestine activities and occasional bribes, the community completed the connection to the mains water supply. Their first successes were judged by some to be more of a threat than an achievement. One local politician sought to undermine their activities by promising households free connections if they stopped participating in the programme. The politician started to lay his own line but the work was sub-standard, and once this was evident the community lost interest.

In addition to a sceptical local authority, the CBO faced local house-

holds who were unwilling and unable to invest a large amount in water and sanitation. A grant from an NGO enabled the organization to construct secondary pipes, thereby establishing the beginnings of a network that families could connect to. Families were asked to pay the connection costs for their house to the lane sewer and repay their share of the cost of the secondary pipe, enabling further expansion of the network. Anjuman Samaji Bahbood found that families were willing to do this. External donor finance and local leaders were successful in catalysing a change in attitudes. More and more families became interested in taking part.

As the local authority began to see that families were willing to pay the cost of piped water, they also became interested. Nazir Wattoo, the leader of the organization, was invited to participate in a number of government activities. Within a few months, he had been offered state funds to carry on his work, extending activities to other settlements. At the same time, interaction increased between local staff of the water authority and Anjuman Samaji Bahbood activists. Anjuman Samaji Bahbood offered its own area plans to assist in state-financed improvements. It was asked to assist in monitoring private contractors on a state programme.

Source: Alimuddin, Salim, Arif Hasan and Asiya Sadiq (2000), *Community Driven Water And Sanitation: The Work Of The Anjuman Samaji Behbood And The Larger Faisalabad Context*, IIED Working Paper 7 on Poverty Reduction in Urban Areas, IIED, London, 84 pages.

examples of community-managed sanitation is the Pakistan NGO, Orangi Pilot Project, which has assisted more than 100,000 households in Karachi to install and manage lane-based sanitation schemes that have developed connections to the main sewer network. With the support of the Orangi Pilot Project, communities in Faisalabad have developed similar methodologies to provide themselves

with water and sanitation. Box 5.2 describes their work, and also demonstrates the continuing significance of political forces in such provision. But the description of Orangi Pilot Project's work in Karachi is kept for Chapter 7, since it is better seen not as autonomous community-level provision but as a partnership between local authorities, local utilities and community organizations. Chapter 7 will present many more examples of schemes for improved provision for water and sanitation that were led by CBOs or local NGOs (or both). These include: the housing programmes of the South African Homeless People's Federation and the Shack Dwellers' Federation of Namibia, through which low-income groups acquired good quality housing with provision for water and sanitation; the public standpost programme in Luanda, initiated by a local NGO that involved local water committees, the water company and local authorities; and the community toilets in Pune and Mumbai. Their importance is not so much as examples of autonomous community provision as examples of partnerships that community organizations forged with local authorities and/or utilities.

Box 5.3 describes an ambitious community-based development in El Mezquital (Guatemala City), but in this instance, external funding agencies also had an important role. This shows both the potential and the limitations of community-based, externally supported interventions that operate with little or no support from local government. After 15 years of struggle, the community organization had achieved much, including legalization of the land (underway), good provision for water and sanitation, electricity, and housing improvements. However, as Box 5.3 explains, there was a tendency by external agencies to view this as a one-off infrastructure project and not as a means to help develop the capacity of community organizations, and the role of local authorities in supporting this development.

Community-managed services may not fail simply because of political interference but because the tasks place further burdens on communities that are already struggling to address their multiple needs. This is illustrated by the difficulties faced by communal water associations in Cebu City in the Philippines.[113] These associations are provided with taps by the city council in order to improve water provision in a city in which only 41 per cent of residents have access to piped water. The study notes that many community water associations:

are beset with management problems … such as lack of active participation by members, undemocratic if not oppressive management style, irregular or no annual election resulting in monopoly of leadership, and a lack of financial transparency and accountability. It is not uncommon to hear that a communal water association official has disappeared with the association money to the dismay and consternation of the members.[114]

In conclusion, it is possible to point to community-initiated and community-managed systems that have improved provision for water and sanitation, including many which have done so very cheaply and some which have managed to do so based only on internally generated funding. If there was more documentation available of provision for water in informal settlements in cities or in smaller urban centres, this may well show many more examples of community-managed initiatives, including those undertaken by residents' committees. But one obvious characteristic of most urban residential areas is that they are part of a larger settlement, so it is difficult to develop autonomous solutions. In part, this is because there are regulations that inhibit this, in part because one settlement's solution may be another settlement's problem (for instance, as the wastewater of one settlement runs into a neighbouring settlement or pollutes their water supply). Another obvious characteristic of any urban centre is competition between the households and businesses for access to water and to infrastructure for wastewater removal – and in the absence of a system to manage this, the poorer groups will generally lose out to the richer groups. This is why one of the central themes of Chapter 7 is the possibilities for improved provision for water and sanitation presented by community initiatives that are supported by local governments.

Box 5.3 El Mezquital: a community's struggle for development

El Mezquital is a large informal settlement in Guatemala City with over 20,000 inhabitants. Externally funded, community-based programmes have brought considerable improvements in housing, infrastructure and services since its formation by a land invasion in 1984 by some 1500 families, who moved onto a 35-hectare site next to an existing residential settlement. They succeeded in resisting attempts by police and local residents to evict them, and this was the only successful land invasion in Guatemala City at the time. Many families who came to El Mezquital had also taken part in land occupations in 1982 or 1983 but had been evicted. When attempts to evict the invaders failed, the settlement attracted more settlers and expanded and consolidated, with community management boards set up in the different sub-divisions. Each management board had representatives on a settlement-wide association and there were various other community organizations for sectors, streets and micro-zones. The government provided no support and the settlers had to rely on illegal connections for water and electricity. Support was received from a range of national and international non-governmental groups, in part in response to a typhoid epidemic in 1985–1986. There were often tensions and conflicting goals between the many different community organizations within El Mezquital.

The settlement-wide community organization sought support from the government's National Reconstruction Committee to develop the first programme for urban improvement. Relatively little support was received and progress was slowed down by the dissatisfaction among many residents with what the government offered. The residents developed their own cooperative (COIVEES), which organized the construction of the first well and two large water tanks with support from UNICEF and the Swiss government. This cooperative also developed a piped water distribution system. The Catholic Church, which had supported many community initia-

tives, provided the land for the well and the tanks. In 1994, support was provided by the World Bank, UNICEF and the National Reconstruction Committee for a programme for the urban development of El Mezquital. This included:

- Infrastructure, including sewers and sewage treatment plants, rain water drains, pavements for pedestrians, the introduction of electricity and the creation and maintenance of green areas. Community members contributed to the implementation.
- Drinking water: to continue the COIVEES water project and to extend it to one of the unserved sub-divisions. This included sinking two new wells.
- Support for the construction of new houses and the improvement of existing houses, to be funded through a loan system.
- The relocation of families who lived in areas that impeded development to areas with similar conditions within the settlement. 350 families were selected for moving and two fully urbanized new sub-divisions were developed for them, and were integrated into the settlement.

After 15 years of community work, almost all the families in El Mezquital have access to good quality piped water supplies. The settlement's cooperative supplies a much better, cheaper and more reliable service than that provided in most residential areas in Guatemala City. 95 per cent of families have electricity in their homes and virtually all houses have sewers and drains. El Mezquital is also well known for its community-based integrated health programme. This was based on the work of elected community health workers, called *reproinsas*, within each micro-zone (each of which had around 50 families). They work part-time and were trained to provide basic health care, including immunization, oral rehydration for diarrhoeal diseases, health advice and support for groups

with particular health needs (including children and pregnant mothers). The *reproinsas* also supported other initiatives, including literacy programmes. This served as a community-based health care model that was expanded into other informal settlements in Guatemala City.

However, there are important limitations to these improvements. These include the incapacity or unwillingness of government agencies to respond to the needs of the community (for instance, the state water agency refused to supply water because the settlement was illegal) and their under-estimation of community capacity, which included opposition to the work of the community health workers. The support from international agencies and NGOs allowed considerable improvements in infrastructure and service provision. It also supported important processes of community empowerment, including greater status and possibilities for women. However, there were also limitations to most of the international support, including the limited scope provided by many international agencies for community participation, especially in project design. Most external agencies' strategies have been top–down and non-participatory, with no transparency in terms of how decisions were made and resources allocated. There are also the different perceptions of the external agencies, who regard their work as done because the project is finished, and the inhabitants, who still face many deprivations. In the absence of effective, accountable local government institutions able to provide continued support, the inhabitants feel abandoned. Seeing poverty reduction in terms of a single project-based intervention fails to recognize the importance of supporting long-term processes within low-income settlements that allow one success to stimulate and support others.

Source: Cabanas Díaz, Andrés, Emma Grant, Paula Irene del Cid Vargas and Verónica Sajbin Velásquez Díaz (2000), *El Mezquital: A Community's Struggle for Development*, IIED Working Paper 1 on Poverty Reduction in Urban Areas, IIED, London.

Notes and references

1. Black, M (1998), *Learning What Works: A 20 Year Retrospective View on International Water and Sanitation Cooperation*, UNDP-World Bank Water and Sanitation Program, Washington, DC.

2. Finger, M and J Allouche (2002), *Water Privatisation: Trans-national Corporations and the Re-regulation of the Water Industry*, Spon Press, London.

3. Bakker, K (2002 forthcoming), 'A political ecology of water privatization', *Studies in Political Economy*.

4. Budds, J (2000), *Public Private Partnership and the Poor in Water and Sanitation: An Interim Review of Documents*, WEDC, Loughborough University, Loughborough.

5. Edwin Chadwick, perhaps the foremost sanitary reformer of the 19th century, clearly articulated the case for this form of competition as a means of achieving competitive results in natural monopoly conditions in Chadwick, E (1859), 'Results of different principles of legislation and administration in Europe; of competition for the field, as compared with competition within the field of service', *Journal of the Royal Statistical Society of London*, 22. This did not prevent a later wave of nationalization in the face of persistent private sector failures, however.

6. Brook Cowen, P and T Cowen (1998), 'Deregulated private water supply: a policy option for developing countries', *The Cato Journal*, Vol 18, No 1, pages 21–41.

7. Gleick, P H (2000), *The World's Water 2000–2001: The Biennial Report on Freshwater Resources*, Island Press, Washington, DC.

8. Hausermann, J (1999), 'A human rights approach to development: some practical implications for WaterAid's work', The First WaterAid Lecture, WaterAid, London.

9. In economic terms, defining access to adequate water and sanitation as a human right could be taken to reflect the fact that humans place a high value on ensuring that everyone has such access. This would imply that access to adequate water and sanitation is a 'merit' good, and values could be assigned on that basis, as indication in Johnstone, N and L Wood (eds) (2001), *Private Firms and Public Water: Realising Social and Environmental Objectives in Developing Countries*, Edward Elgar, Cheltenham. This is not conventionally done in economic assessments of water and sanitation improvements, however.

10. Sen, A (1999), *Development as Freedom*, Oxford University Press, Oxford.

11. Kothari, M (2002), 'Economic, social and cultural rights: report of the Special Rapporteur on adequate housing as a component of the right to an adequate standard of living', E/CN.4/2002/59, United Nations Economic and Social Council, New York.

12. Also referred to as 'contracting out'.

13. See Hazin, L S (1997), 'Toward more efficient urban water management in Mexico', *Water International*, Vol 22, No 3; and WaterAid Uganda (2002), *The Paradoxes of Funding and Infrastructure Development in Uganda*, WaterAid, London.

14. See Trémolet, S (2002), 'Rural water service: is a private national operator a viable business model?', Private Sector Viewpoint Note 249, Public Policy for the Private Sector Series, PPIAF, Washington, DC; and Brook Cowen, P (1999), 'Lessons from the Guinea water lease', Private Sector Viewpoint Note No 78, Public Policy for the Private Sector Series, PPIAF, Washington, DC.

15. See, for example, the following accounts of the concessions in Buenos Aires and Manila: Loftus, A and D McDonald (2001), 'Of liquid dreams: a political ecology of water privatization in Buenos Aires', *Environment and Urbanization*, Vol 13, No 2, pages 179–199; Esguerra, J (2002), *The Corporate Muddle of Manila's Water Concessions: How the World's Biggest and Most Successful Privatisation turned into a Failure*, WaterAid and Tearfund, London.

16. Variations include: build own [operate] [train] [transfer] (BOO/BOOT/BOTT).

17. Rees, J (1998), 'Regulation and private participation in the water and sanitation sector', Technical Advisory Committee Background Paper No 1, Global Water Partnership, Stockholm.

18. See Bakker, K (2001), 'Paying for water: water pricing and equity in England and Wales', *Transactions of the Institute of British Geographers* (new series), No 26, pages 143–164; and Green, J (2002), *The England and Wales Water Industry Privatisation*, WaterAid and Tearfund, London.

19. See Lobina, E (2001b), *Water Privatisation and Restructuring in Central and Eastern Europe, 2001*, Public Services International Research Unit, University of Greenwich, London; and Nickson, A (2001), 'Establishing and implementing a joint venture: water and

sanitation services in Cartagena, Colombia', GHK Working Paper No 442 03, GHK, London.

20. Blokland, M, O Braadbaart and K Schwartz (eds) (1999), *Private Business, Public Owners: Government Shareholdings in Water Enterprises*, Netherlands Ministry of Housing, Spatial Planning and the Environment, The Hague.

21. Nickson, Andrew (1998), *A Water Co-operative for a Large City: Does it Work?* University of Birmingham, International Development Department, Birmingham.

22. Trémolet, S (2002), 'Multi-utilities and access: can private multi-utilities help expand service to rural areas?', Private Sector Viewpoint Note No 248, Public Policy for the Private Sector Series, PPIAF, Washington, DC.

23. Ibid.

24. Green 2002, op cit.

25. Schulpen, Lau and Peter Gibbon (2002), 'Private sector development: policies, practices and problems', *World Development*, Vol 30, No 1, pages 1–15.

26. WaterAid Tanzania (2002), *Water Utility Reform and Private Sector Participation in Dar es Salaam*, WaterAid and Tearfund, London.

27. Haarmeyer, D and A Mody (1998), 'Pooling water projects to move beyond project finance', Private Sector Viewpoint Note No 152, Public Policy for the Private Sector Series, PPIAF, Washington, DC.

28. For instance, the city of Manaus in the state of Amazonas in Brazil (1.2 million inhabitants) was offered separately to a private operator, while the rest of the sparsely populated state was to be served by the public provider.

29. Drakeford, M (2002), 'Providing water in Wales: is there a third way? The Welsh experience with public and private utilities and the emergence of the not-for-profit model', paper presented at PRINWASS Second Research Workshop, Oxford, 28 February.

30. Nickson, Andrew (2001), 'The Córdoba water concession in Argentina', GHK Working Paper No 442 05, GHK, London.

31. Esguerra 2002, op cit.

32. Ibid.

33. Gutierrez, E (2001), *Framework Document: A Survey of the Theoretical Issues on Private Sector Participation in Water and Sanitation*, WaterAid and Tearfund, London.

34. Crespo, C (2001), 'La concesión de La Paz a los cinco años: elementos para una evaluación', unpublished paper, University of Newcastle, Newcastle.

35. Haarmeyer, D and A Mody (1998), 'Financing water and sanitation projects – the unique risks', Private Sector Viewpoint Note No 151, Public Policy for the Private Sector Series, PPIAF, Washington, DC.

36. Esguerra 2002, op cit.

37. Gutierrez 2001, op cit.

38. Haarmeyer and Mody 1998, op cit.

39. Silva, G, N Tynan and Y Yilmaz (1998), 'Private participation in the water and sanitation sector: recent trends', Private Sector Viewpoint Note No 147, Public Policy for the Private Sector Series, PPIAF, Washington, DC.

40. Hay, W (2000), 'The regulator's perspective', paper presented to a meeting on Infrastructure for Development: Private Solutions and the Poor, London.

41. See Hay 2000, op cit; Rees 1998, op cit; and Smith, W (1997), 'Utility regulators: the independence debate', Private Sector Viewpoint Note No 127, Public Policy for the Private Sector Series, PPIAF, Washington, DC.

42. Hay 2000, op cit; Rees 1998, op cit.

43. Smith 1997, op cit.

44. Drakeford, M (1998), 'Water regulation and pre-payment meters', *Journal of Law and Society*, Vol 25, No 4, pages 558–602.

45. Esguerra 2002, op cit.

46. Loftus and McDonald 2001, op cit.

47. Smith 1997, op cit.

48. Ibid.

49. Ibid.

50. Hay 2000, op cit.

51. Nickson 2001, op cit.

52. Rees 1998, op cit.

53. Buenos Aires, La Paz/El Alto and Cartagena are all case study locations for the Business Partners in Development initiative's water and sanitation cluster. This initiative seeks to research innovative projects that serve the poor through a joint effort from the public, private and civil society sectors. Business Partners in Development is also active in Durban, South Africa. Examples of provision to low-income areas outside this initiative are rare, and private operators sometimes use these initiatives for public relations purposes, making it difficult to determine whether they are replicable.

54. See: Almansi, F, A Hardoy, G Pandiella, R Schusterman and G Urquiza (2002), *Everyday Water Struggles in Buenos Aires: The Problem of Land Tenure in the Expansion of Potable Water and Sanitation Service to Informal Settlements*, WaterAid and Tearfund, London; and Schusterman, R, F Almansi, A Hardoy, G McGranahan, I Oliverio, R Rozenszteijn and G Urquiza (2002), *Experiences with Water*

Provision in Four Low-income Barrios in Buenos Aires, WEDC, University of Loughborough, Loughborough.

55. Nickson, A (2001), 'Establishing and implementing a joint venture: water and sanitation services in Cartagena, Colombia', GHK Working Paper No 442 03, GHK, London.

56. Crespo 2001, op cit.

57. Crespo 2001, op cit, page 6.

58. Bond, P (1997), 'Privatisation, participation and protest in the restructuring of municipal services: grounds for opposing World Bank promotion of "public–private partnerships"', page 11, originally presented to the World Bank/NGO Dialogue on Privatisation, Washington, DC, reproduced for The Water Page, www.thewaterpage.com/ppp_debate1.htm.

59. Drakeford 1998, op cit.

60. Hall, D, K Bayliss and E Lobina (2002), *Water Privatisation in Africa*, Public Services International Research Unit, University of Greenwich, London.

61. Schusterman et al 2002, op cit; Nickson 2001, op cit.

62. Houskamp, M and N Tynan (2000), 'Private infrastructure: are the trends in low-income countries different?', Private Sector Viewpoint Note No 216, Public Policy for the Private Sector Series, PPIAF, Washington, DC.

63. Collignon, B and M Vézina (2000), *Independent Water and Sanitation Providers in African Cities: Full Report of a Ten-country Study*, Water and Sanitation Program, the World Bank, Washington, DC.

64. See Brocklehurst, C, B Evans and M Kariuki (2002), *New Designs for Water and Sanitation Transactions: Making Private Sector Participation Work for the Poor*, PPIAF and Water and Sanitation Programme, the World Bank, Washington, DC; Houskamp and Tynan 2000, op cit; and Izaguirre and Rao 2000, op cit.

65. Silva et al 1998, op cit.

66. Houskamp and Tynan 2000, op cit.

67. Hall, D (2002), *The Water Multinationals 2002 – Financial and Other Problems*, Public Services International Research Unit, University of Greenwich, London.

68. Silva et al 1998, op cit.

69. Hall 2002, op cit; Houskamp and Tynan 2000, op cit; Silva et al 1998, op cit.

70. Brocklehurst, Clarissa and Barbara Evans (2001), 'Serving poor consumers in South Asian cities: private sector participation in water and sanitation', overview paper, Water and Sanitation Program South Asia, New Delhi.

71. Nickson, A (2001), 'The Córdoba water concession in Argentina', GHK Working Paper No 442 05, GHK, London.

72. Maputo, Beira, Quelimane, Nampula, Pemba, Dondo and Matola.

73. See Hall, D, K Bayliss and E Lobina (2002), *Water Privatisation in Africa*, Public Services International Research Unit, University of Greenwich, London; and Sommer, D (2001), 'Multi-utilities: trends: blurring industry boundaries', Private Sector Viewpoint Note No 227, Public Policy for the Private Sector Series, PPIAF, Washington, DC.

74. Esguerra 2002, op cit; Silva et al 1998, op cit.

75. Hall 2002, op cit.

76. See Brocklehurst, C, B Evans and M Kariuki (2002), *New Designs for Water and Sanitation Transactions: Making Private Sector Participation Work for the Poor*, PPIAF and Water and Sanitation Programme, the World Bank, Washington, DC; and Halcrow Management Sciences (2002), *Public Private Partnerships and the Poor Strategy, Implementation, Regulation* (three volumes), WEDC, Loughborough University, Loughborough.

77. Semboja, J and O Therkildsen (eds) (1995), *Service Provision under Stress in East Africa*, Centre for Development Research, Copenhagen; and Kjellén, M (2002), 'Water provisioning in Dar-es-Salaam, Tanzania:from public pipes to private hands', paper submitted to *Urban Water*, University of Stockholm, Stockholm.

78. Collignon, B and M Vezina (2000), *Independent Water And Sanitation Providers In African Cities*, UNDP-World Bank Water and Sanitation Program, Nairobi.

79. Solo, Tova Maria (1999), 'Small scale entrepreneurs in the urban water and sanitation market', *Environment and Urbanization*, Vol 11, No 1, April, pages 117–131; Solo, Tova Maria (2000), *Independent Water Entrepreneurs in Latin America; The Other Private Sector in Water Services* (draft), the World Bank, Washington, DC.

80. Solo 2000, op cit.

81. Ibid.

82. Collignon and Vezina 2000, op cit.

83. Ibid.

84. Thompson, John, Ina T Porras, Elisabeth Wood, James K Tumwine, Mark R Mujwahuzi, Munguti Katui-Katua and Nick Johnstone (2000), 'Waiting at the tap: Changes in urban water use in East Africa over three decades', *Environment and Urbanization*, Vol 12, No 2, pages 37–52.

85. Ibid.

86. For an early discussion of this, see Cairncross, Sandy (1990), 'Water supply and the urban poor', in Jorge E Hardoy, Sandy Cairncross and David Satterthwaite (eds), *The Poor Die Young: Housing and Health in Third World Cities*, Earthscan Publications, London, pages 109–126.

87. See Satterthwaite, David (2001), 'Reducing urban poverty: constraints on the effectiveness of aid agencies and development banks and some suggestions for change', *Environment and Urbanization*, Vol 13, No 1, pages 137–157.

88. Lewis, M A and T R Miller (1987), 'Public private partnerships in water supply and sanitation in sub-Saharan Africa', *Health Policy and Planning*, Vol 2, No 1, pages 70–79; Cairncross 1990, op cit.

89. For more details, see www.wsp.org/english/index.html.

90. Brook, Penelope and Nicola Tynan (1999*), Reaching The Urban Poor With Private Infrastructure; Public Policy For The Private Sector*, Note No 188, Finance, Private Sector and Infrastructure Network, the World Bank, Washington, DC.

91. See Collignon and Vezina 2000, op cit, for several examples of entrepreneurs developing considerable businesses in different sub-Saharan African cities.

92. Albu, Mike and Cyrus Njiru (2002), 'The role of small-scale providers in urban areas', *Waterlines*, Vol 20, No 3, pages 16–18.

93. Komives, Kristin, Dale Whittington and Xun Wu (2001), *Infrastructure Coverage and the Poor: A Global Perspective*, University of North Carolina at Chapel Hill, page 3.

94. Solo, Tova Maria (1998), *Competition in Water and Sanitation: The Role of Small Scale Enterprises*, Public Policy for the Private Sector Note No 165, Finance, Private Sector and Infrastructure Network, the World Bank, Washington, DC.

95. Solo 1999, op cit, page 123.

96. Johnstone, Nick and Libby Wood (eds) (2001), *Private Firms and Public Water: Realising Social and Environmental Objectives in Development Countries*, Edward Edgar Publishing, Cheltenham, page 53.

97. Solo 1999, op cit.

98. Komives et al 2001, op cit, pages 2–3.

99. Komives et al 2001, op cit, pages 16–17.

100. Collignon and Vezina 2000, op cit.

101. Gross, Bruce, Christine van Wijk and Nilanjana Mukherjee (2001), *Linking Sustainability with Demand, Gender and Poverty*, Water and Sanitation Program, the World Bank, Washington, DC.

102. Lammerink, Marc P, Eveline Bolt, Dick de Jong and Tom Schouten (2001), 'Strengthening community water management', *PLA Notes: Community Water Management*, No 35, pages 21–28.

103. See for instance de Silva's review of community contracting: De Silva, Samantha (2000), *Community Based Contracting: A Review Of Stakeholder Experience*, the World Bank, Washington, DC.

104. Gross et al 2001, op cit.

105. See Rahardjo, Budi and Dan O'Brien (1994), 'Community self-financing of water and sanitation systems', *Waterlines*, Vol 12, No 3, pages 10–13 for an example in Indonesia.

106. See a discussion of community managed tanks in Ahmed, Noman and Muhammad Sohail (2003, forthcoming), 'Public–private partnership in water supply for the urban poor; an alternative model: case of Awami (people's) tanks in Orangi Town, Karachi', *Environment and Urbanization*, Vol 15, No 2, October.

107. See Díaz, Andrés Cabanas, Emma Grant, Paula Irene del Cid Vargas and Verónica Sajbin Velásquez (2000), *El Mezquital: A Community's Struggle for Development*, IIED Working Paper 1 on Poverty Reduction in Urban Areas, IIED, London; and Schusterman, Ricardo and Ana Hardoy (1997), 'Reconstructing social capital in a poor urban settlement: the Integrated Improvement Programme, Barrio San Jorge', *Environment and Urbanization*, Vol 9, No 1, pages 91–119.

108. Dikito-Wachtmeister, Mercy (2001), 'Social capital: the "missing link" in water resources management', *Waterlines*, Vol 20, No 2, pages 29–31.

109. Matin, Nilufar (1999), *Social Inter-mediation: Towards Gaining Access to Water for Squatter Communities in Dhaka*, Water and Sanitation Program – South Asia/Swiss Agency for Development and Cooperation/WaterAid/ Dushtha Shasthya Kendra, Dhaka, page 11.

110. Matin 1999, op cit, page 19.

111. Hanchett, Suzanne, Mohidul Hoque Khan and Shireen Akhter (2001), *WaterAid Bangladesh Urban Programme Evaluation*, Planning Alternatives for Change and Pathway Ltd, Dhaka, page 47. A condensed version of this report will be published in the October 2003 issue of *Environment and Urbanization*.

112. Gross et al 2001, op cit.

113. Etemadi, Felisa (2001), *Towards Inclusive Urban Governance in Cebu*, Urban Governance, Partnerships and Poverty Research Working Paper 25, University of Birmingham, Birmingham.

114. Etemadi 2001 op cit, page 96.

Improving Urban Water and Sanitation Provision as part of Integrated Water Resource Management

Introduction

The need to take an integrated approach to water management is central to many of the new tools and approaches being discussed at international water conferences. Integrated water resource management (IWRM)[1] is intended to overcome the many problems that can arise in a watershed area as a result of the uncoordinated use and abuse of increasingly scarce water resources. As described in Chapter 4, however, many of the reasons for inadequate urban water and sanitation provision have little to do with the mismanagement of water resources in the narrow sense. Better management of upstream water resources can be important to achieving sustainable urban water systems, but will only rarely improve access to water or sanitation among currently deprived residents, or result in the sort of health improvements that better water and sanitation provision allows. Similarly, avoiding urban water waste is important, but if urban water policies focus narrowly on saving water, the water that is saved is unlikely to find its way to the urban residents who need it most. Thus one of the principal purposes of this chapter is to make the case for explicitly addressing the need to improve water and sanitation provision for deprived urban residents within a framework of integrated water (and sanitation) management.

The next section of the chapter discusses the concept of IWRM and its relevance to urban centres. The Global Water Partnership has defined IWRM as a process which promotes the coordinated development and management of water, land and related resources in order to maximize the resultant economic and social welfare in an equitable manner without compromising the sustainability of vital ecosystems.[2] IWRM is intended to extend across whole watersheds and include consideration of inter-basin transfers. There have been a number of innovative attempts to enable downstream water users, including urban centres, to invest in upstream environmental improvements to help secure their own water supplies. IWRM should also ensure that urban water systems do not impose undue harm on their local water resources, or impose excessive costs on their downstream users. The aspect of IWRM with the most immediate relevance to urban water and sanitation management, however, is demand-side management (DSM). Urban DSM is often treated as a means of saving water without compromising on water services, and avoiding costly investments to create the infrastructure needed to bring additional water to urban centres. It also has the potential to improve water and sanitation provision, however.

The main body of the chapter examines a range of approaches to urban DSM, treating the conservation-oriented approach to DSM as one particular approach. The other approaches include a public health approach (which focuses on the potential to improve water and sanitation provision and use so as to reduce water-related diseases), an economic approach (which focuses on the use of price incentives to increase the efficiency of water provision and use) and a community action approach (which focuses on the role that community groups can play in improving water and sanitation provision). Each of these approaches is concerned with the demand side, and tends to be critical of the 'supply-fix' approach that has characterized the development of urban water and sanitation systems historically. Each, however, emphasizes different means and/or goals.

The chapter concludes by comparing the different approaches to DSM and exploring their compatibility. These approaches have different priorities, and these priorities are not equally relevant to all urban centres or even to all groups within an urban centre. If these different approaches are to be combined successfully, they must respond to local priorities in an equitable manner. In particular, in urban centres where a significant share of the population lacks adequate access to water and sanitation, ways must be found to ensure that the DSM strategies respond to these priorities.

IWRM

For an urban water utility, IWRM implies that the utility's water management will be an integral part of a broader regional or river basin management strategy. The integration of water resource management should ideally take place across a number of different dimensions. Upstream management should be integrated with downstream management, so as to ensure that downstream needs are considered when taking upstream decisions. Meeting one demand for water should be balanced against the opportunity costs of not meeting others, so as to ensure that water is allocated efficiently and equitably. The use of water to bear away wastes should be balanced against the impacts this may have on its capacity to meet other human and environmental demands. Managing supplies should be integrated with managing demands, so as to ensure that costly additions to supply are not undertaken when there are less costly opportunities to reduce demands. Environmental demands for water should be considered alongside human demands, so as to ensure ecological sustainability.

IWRM is spatially, temporally and administratively more extensive than traditional water project or utility management. Spatially,

it tries to work with water-relevant boundaries, such as watersheds and river basins, rather than political or property boundaries. Temporally, it tries to work with an environmental time horizon, rather than a project-based or political time horizon. Administratively, it tries to work across all water stakeholders, rather than focusing on a specific set of beneficiaries.

The underlying motivation for IWRM is that changes to one part of a water system have consequences for other parts, and these consequences must be taken into account to ensure that the water system is not abused. Neither the boundaries of private property nor those of government agencies are likely to internalize these consequences. One property owner may affect the water system to the detriment of other users. The water-related decisions of one ministry (eg, agriculture) can have adverse consequences for users outside of that ministry's traditional concerns (eg, residential and industrial users). Similarly, the water-related decisions in one planning district (or country) can have adverse consequences for people living in other districts (or countries). Historically, these cross-boundary impacts have been addressed in a piecemeal fashion, in response to emerging problems. IWRM is intended to treat water systems in a more holistic fashion, and introduce mechanisms (eg, markets for environmental services), institutions (eg, river basin authorities) or regulations (eg, pollution standards) that take these cross-boundary impacts into account.

The aspirations of IWRM could easily be taken to imply the need for strong central planning and regulation. In practice, however, the tools associated with IWRM are more in line with the Dublin Principles described in the previous chapter, and rely on economic instruments, stakeholder consultation and/or negotiation rather than central planning. There are no clear operating procedures or institutional forms universally appropriate to IWRM. Even within a single country, the need to adapt to local circumstances can be critical. Thus, for example, a review of five water utilities pioneering in integrated water resource planning in the USA found that it was important to adapt 'the process to the needs and circumstances of the particular localities engaged in integrated planning rather than assuming that "one size fits all".[3] If adaptability is important within the USA, it is doubly important in the international context, where geographical, economic and institutional differences are far more pronounced.

Most of the measures undertaken as part of IWRM are implemented in rural areas, but in some cases a large share of the beneficiaries may be urban. Upstream activities can make a major difference to urban water supplies and their sustainability. The relevant upstream activities relate not only to water withdrawals and pollution, but also land use patterns. For example, land use that results in erosion can cause siltation, which can in turn affect urban water reservoirs. Finding the means to balance upstream and downstream water-related priorities is a major challenge. Even committed and well organized national governments or river basin authorities will typically find it difficult to design and enforce regulations that can resolve upstream–downstream conflicts efficiently and equitably. Alternatively, without any institutional framework, urban centres find it difficult to influence upstream activities. Most legal systems have procedures that allow increasing urban water demands to be met through infrastructure investments that tap distant water sources, even if this imposes costs on rural residents and producers. Few, however, are well adapted to facilitating negotiations over the range of upstream activities that can undermine urban water supplies.

As a result, costly investments in water infrastructure are often undertaken when more cost-effective measures based on upstream improvements are forgone. Urban centres have, at least until recently, rarely considered investing in such upstream measures, partly because of the transaction costs involved. By providing an institutional framework that facilitates upstream–downstream negotiation, IWRM can work to reduce these transaction costs. Chapter 7 provides an example of an initiative in Ecuador to use a water conservation fund to support watershed protection, financed in part by urban water charges. This can be seen as one of a broader set of initia-

tives being designed in many parts of the world to create markets for environmental services.[4] It is too early to judge how significant this sort of initiative will be for helping to secure sustainable urban water supplies. It is already clear, however, that if they are to be successful, adapting to the local institutional and physical context will be critical.

Getting urban water utilities or authorities to invest in upstream activities that help secure their water supplies is only one element of integrated water management relevant to urban centres. Also, the notion that downstream water users should pay to prevent upstream land and water use practices that undermine their water supplies is itself open to question. It goes against the polluter-pays principle, for example, to have downstream users paying to reduce upstream pollution. IWRM not only involves developing institutional arrangements that allow negotiations between the different stakeholders in a river basin or smaller watershed area, but ensuring that these arrangements are considered equitable. Urban centres are themselves upstream of other water users, and it can be even more important to develop mechanisms to ensure that downstream needs are taken into account within urban water management. This is likely to involve restrictions on the uses to which water is put, and the pollution loads allowed in urban centres. It also raises a number of issues concerning the treatment of human waste, and the potential for ecological sanitation systems that can allow human wastes to be recycled locally.

From the perspective of improving water and sanitation provision in urban centres, urban DSM is a particularly critical element of IWRM. While the potential for supply-side measures is often very restricted within the boundaries of an urban centre, there is usually considerable scope for demand-side measures. Moreover, as indicated in Chapter 4, even residents of cities with plentiful water resources often have great difficulty accessing adequate water and sanitation. Here the importance of adapting to local conditions, and ensuring that those currently lacking adequate water and sanitation provision can influence the process, is particularly important. Moreover, as described in the following sections, it is critical to go beyond water-saving measures and extend DSM to areas where the problem is too little, rather than too much, water use. Similarly, it is important not to restrict the measures to those involving water supplies, and to incorporate sanitary improvements as part of the broader integration.

Urban demand-side water management as part of IWRM[5]

Demand-side water management is typically presented as part of an integrated approach to water resources management, correcting a historic tendency to over-emphasize supply-side investment. Somewhat ironically, demand-side water management itself has come to be associated with a narrow approach that emphasizes conservation and fails to address other demand-side issues, including the need for sanitary improvement. Especially in poor urban settlements, however, other demand-side approaches have been receiving increasing attention, and deserve to become part of IWRM.

DSM can be defined as a coordinated set of measures to improve service delivery by inducing changes at the point of consumption. It is usually taken to refer to attempts to meet increasing service demands without increasing water supplies or compromising on the quality of service delivery. In principle, however, it can include attempts to improve the quality of service delivery.

The term 'demand-side management' was coined in the USA in the 1980s, when world energy shortages were in the headlines, regional water scarcity was a growing concern and the country's urban infrastructure was beginning to fail. Both electric and water utilities were criticized for taking a supply-fix approach, assuming that increasing demands had to be met by increasing supplies. Advocates of DSM argued that what people wanted were services (eg lighting and washing). By increasing end-use efficiency and reducing waste, these services could be provided using less electricity or water. If only utilities would take a more balanced approach – went the argument – and demand-side

measures could be placed on an equal footing with supply-side measures, both utilities and their consumers could benefit financially and scarce resources could be conserved.

DSM did not prove to be as straightforward as some of its early proponents hoped, but the need for DSM is now widely accepted in international water policy debates. Concerns about the global water crisis, described in Chapter 4, have reinforced interest in DSM as an internationally relevant tool for improving water services. Summarizing the 'changing water paradigm', one of the world's leading water specialists recently wrote that:

> *A reliance on physical solutions continues to dominate traditional planning approaches, but these solutions are facing increasing opposition. At the same time, new methods are being developed to meet the demands of growing populations without requiring major new construction or new large-scale water transfers from one region to another. More and more water suppliers and planning agencies are beginning to shift their focus and explore efficiency improvements, implement options for managing demand, and reallocate water among users to reduce projected gaps and meet future needs.[6]*

The need to move away from a narrow supply-fix approach can be just as compelling in poor settings as in affluent ones. However, many of the insights, priorities and tools that have come to be associated with DSM are inappropriate to low-income settings: they derive from a conservation perspective, and ignore the health, economic and community development perspectives that tend to be critical in deprived urban areas. Similarly, they can lead to the neglect of sanitation, which is often a more critical problem in low-income settlements.

In order to bring together these different perspectives, more attention must be given to the following:

• Securing better access to water for the urban poor. DSM in high-income countries focuses on the wasteful and excessive consumption of water. Waste and excess also occur in the cities of low- and middle-income countries, but under-consumption is usually a more critical problem in deprived areas. As described in Chapters 1 and 2, many households do not consume sufficient water to meet their basic needs for health. It is impor-tant not only to prevent conservation-oriented measures from further reducing the water consumption of deprived house-holds, but also to implement demand-side measures that improve access to water, even if (and in some cases especially if) this increases their consumption.

- Promoting sanitation and the hygienic use of water. Especially in conditions of poverty, it is important that DSM takes account of needs for improved sanitation and hygiene behaviour, and access to sanitation facilities. Health is one of the major benefits that water and sanitation facilities can help to provide, but depends upon how the water is used and whether adequate sanitary facilities are also available and used. Users often lack a relevant knowledge of hygiene, and experts in DSM are often ignorant of both hygiene issues and of local condi-tions in low-income settlements. From a health perspective, better sanitary improvements can also be critical, but will be ignored if DSM focuses exclu-sively on water deficiencies. Taking health issues seriously will require a major shift in the approach to DSM, but can be seen as an extension of IWRM.

- Empowering deprived groups. One of the goals of DSM in low-income areas should be to give more influence to those currently deprived of water and sanita-tion. The supply-fix approach has often favoured affluent consumers over both future generations and the poor. Orthodox DSM attempts to address the concerns that are particularly relevant to future generations. Future generations cannot take an active part in designing and implementing demand management; the urban poor can. To assist deprived urban dwellers, DSM cannot simply rely

on finding better means to manipulate the demand for water, but must help ensure that the residents (especially women) gain more influence over water and sanitation provision and use.

In short, even in low-income settings there are good reasons to concentrate more on the demand side, but not to prioritize water conservation or rely on expert-led water management. Indeed, one of the goals of DSM in low-income areas could be to prevent conservation strategies from undermining residents' entitlements to adequate water and sanitation facilities to meet their basic health and welfare needs, and to increase the involve-ment of local residents in driving water and sanitation provision.

While this could be seen as adding new requirements to DSM, it can also be seen as bringing together different strands of a new demand-side approach to water and sanitation provision. Many of these strands have emerged independently of the conservation-oriented DSM prevalent in high-income countries. Health specialists often argue that the supply-fix approach of most water utilities neglects the importance of hygiene education and sanitation, and their potential role in helping people get the most out of their water supplies. Economists and local activists have been arguing that the supply-fix approach often fails because it is not sufficiently demand-responsive (though economists and local activists often have very different visions of what it means to respond to demand).

In addition to adding these new concerns to DSM, it is also important to reconsider the role of utilities and their planners in DSM. Early proponents of DSM tended to be over-optimistic about the extent to which utilities had an incentive to engage in DSM (some of the initial successes of DSM relied on a partic-ular combination of regulatory and economic circumstances that were constraining prices and increasing marginal costs). Adding new public health and equity goals to DSM is likely to further distance the goals of the utilities from those of DSM. Moreover, as described in Chapter 5, the water and sanitation sector has undergone considerable restructuring since the early 1980s: private sector involvement has been promoted widely and many public utilities have been made more responsive to commercial incentives. Commercially oriented utilities that get their revenue from selling water may favour higher prices, but they do not necessarily want their customers to find inexpensive ways to save water, achieve better health or otherwise improve their welfare by using water more effectively. In short, there is no reason to assume that utilities have an incentive to engage in DSM, and there may be good reasons to look for alternative organizational homes.

A basic premise of this chapter is that demand-side strategies should be able to accommodate multiple goals, and that – as with other aspects of IWRM – the relative importance of these goals needs to be location-specific. Some, mostly affluent, cities urgently need to conserve water, but have few water-related health problems. Some, mostly poor, cities have severe water-related health problems, including inadequate provision for sanitation, but abundant fresh water resources. In some cities the most critical demand-side improvements could be achieved by getting water markets and prices right, while in others the key is to help low-income communities organize to address their own water and sanitation problems or make appropriate demands of water and sanitation utilities. Unfortunately, most urban centres face a variety of water and sanitation problems, and their demand-side strategies need to reflect this. The institutional settings of different cities also vary, further complicating demand-side strategies.

Managing demand to save water without compromising on water services

DSM is often taken to refer to measures designed to reduce water demand without compromising water-related services. It is often simply assumed that a planner's purpose in managing water demand is to reduce waste and thereby avoid the need for expensive infrastructure investment and excessive water withdrawals. This stands in sharp contrast to the archetypal sanitary engineer during the heyday of sanitary reform, who may not have used the phrase 'demand-side management', but was certainly concerned with managing water demand – principally to improve public health.

DSM did not emerge in opposition to sanitary reform, however. As indicated above, it was a response to a more recent tendency to assume that the role of water sector planning was simply to meet water demands and handle the wastewater. A book on urban water-demand management and planning describes the challenges that contributed to the emergence of DSM in the USA as follows:

> *The broadening of water planners' perspectives to include demand management alternatives and other innovative solutions has been brought about by a number of new challenges that water planners must face today and in the future.*

- Untapped sources of water are becoming rarer, and the depletion and contamination of groundwater sources has further limited supplies.
- The increased frequency of droughts during the last decade has increased competition for water between urban and agricultural interests.
- Environmental concerns about increased water use have intensified during the last two decades to the point where the development of new supplies is politically infeasible, and the prospects for financing major construction programmes are discouraging for many water agencies.[7]

These challenges are not limited to the USA. Similar statements are often made about the water-related challenges faced in other countries around the world, from some of the poorest to the most affluent. Indeed, this could easily be a summary taken from an account of the global water crisis. However, as described in Chapter 4, it is important not to assume that the problems associated with inadequate water and sanitation provision in low-income settlements are the result of these emerging water scarcity problems.

Most of the early DSM programmes focused on technological improvements. Price incentives have since become an accepted part of DSM, but most proponents of demand-side conservation measures believe that pricing incentives are insufficient. Users are often unaware of the range of conservation technologies and measures available or how much water these measures will save. Often they have little idea how much water they are using, or for what purpose. This is almost inevitable with piped water and wastewater systems, where the water only appears for a moment, if at all, before it disappears down a drain. Thus, demand-side conservation programmes are particularly relevant where water is unmetered or heavily subsidized, but are also relevant more widely.

A systematically developed urban demand-side conservation programme in a relatively affluent city could be expected to include the following stages:[8]

1   Establishing programme goals and principles. The appropriate goals and principles depend on the local conditions of water supply and demand: eg, whether the most serious problems are short term or long term, involve inadequate aggregate supplies or inadequate distribution, are localized or system wide, are seasonal or not.

2   Assessing technical feasibility. In high-income countries there are now a large number of well documented technical measures that can reduce water demand without compromising service delivery. For household uses, they range from low-flush toilets and low-flow shower heads to water-efficient dishwashers and washing machines. For landscape uses, they range from soaker hoses to soil moisture sensors. For commercial industrial uses, they include such measures as the re-use of cooling and process water and reducing 'blowdown' on evaporative coolers, boilers and cooling towers. For all users, water audits can be a useful means of identifying the importance of different options, but can also be a conservation-promoting measure in its own right. Leakage reduction and changes in water pricing should also be considered (though whether leakage within the water distribution system should be considered DSM, is open to debate). An initial listing and screening of possible measures can help to determine which measures are likely to be applicable and technically feasible.

3   Assessing social acceptability. Social acceptability is critical, whether or not the measures are intended to be voluntary, although the means of assessment vary. Experiences from other locations can aid in assessing social acceptability, but focus group discussions, surveys and public forums can also be useful. The information collected at this stage can then be used to predict uptake and eventually estimate water savings.

4   Estimating potential water savings. The water savings can be estimated for those measures deemed technically feasible and socially acceptable. This can be done on the basis of assumptions about the coverage of the measures (eg, how many users are likely to adopt it) and the average reduction in water use for each adopter. For many measures, technical parameters are available for estimating water savings. Pilot programmes can provide more empirically grounded estimates.

5   Conducting benefit–cost analysis. Benefit–cost analysis or cost-effectiveness analysis can provide an additional means of screening possible water-saving measures. The distinction between these two approaches is that benefit–cost analysis estimates both the benefits and costs of a given measure, while cost-effectiveness analysis estimates the costs of achieving a specified effect (eg, reducing water demand by 1 cubic metre per day). In most cases, emphasis is placed on the cost estimation, and in particular the equipment and maintenance costs, although full costing and benefit assessment is clearly necessary if a ranking of alternative measures is desired. Benefit–cost analysis can become complex and controversial when

difficult-to-quantify social and environmental benefits and costs are involved, or when the benefits and costs are unevenly distributed. In principle, social benefit–cost analysis can attempt to incorporate all such considerations, but in practice it may be preferable to conduct a more limited analysis and be explicit about these limitations.

6   Developing an action plan. Benefit–cost analysis can be employed to help rank the measures, and this ranking can be used to develop a timed and costed action plan. However, some measures are likely to be incompatible (eg, the same water cannot be saved twice) while others may be complementary (eg, certain water-saving behaviours may facilitate the use of water-saving devices). Moreover, the value of saving water is likely to depend on the overall consumption levels, as well as other factors identified in developing the programme goals (eg, whether the water availability problems are localized or system-wide). As a result, the coherence and acceptability of the overall action plan also needs to be assessed, with the details of the plan open to modification.

7   Integrating the action plan into the water management strategy. If the demand management programme has an appreciable effect on water use, it will have implications for supply-side planning (indeed, this is the intention). Ideally, DSM should be an integral part of water resource management, in which case the label IWRM is appropriate.

For reasons outlined in previous chapters, the more deprived neighbourhoods of low-income settlements face very different water-related problems from those motivating this type of DSM. Where the water infrastructure is far less developed, it is important not to exaggerate the economic or environmental costs of supply-side expansion. Where people have to fetch water, getting the most out of small amounts of water is a major issue, but promoting awareness of the need to do so is not. Where hygiene is poor, focusing DSM on

conservation could be extremely hazardous. Moreover, many of the measures designed to conserve water in affluent settings are irrelevant in settlements where piped water is rare, flush toilets and the like are unaffordable luxuries, and where people need more water rather than less.

Even in low-income cities, there are often people who waste large quantities of water, particularly in the more affluent neighbourhoods. Water losses due to leakage are often far higher than in affluent cities. Leakage can affect water pressure and the infiltration of sewage, with serious repercussions for water provision. Moreover, many cities in low-income countries face serious problems getting enough raw water or treating enough water even for their limited supply systems, and economic constraints make it all the more important that cost-effective demand-side options do not lose out to more expensive supply-side investments. It would clearly be inappropriate to simply adopt the conservationist's perspective and assume that the goal of DSM is to save water. There is, however, an important role for demand-side water savings to play, even in low-income settlements, and a growing literature on the subject. Moreover, there have been various attempts to adapt the lessons of conservation-oriented demand-side water management to cities in low-income countries.

One of the key lessons learnt in the implementation of UN-HABITAT's Water for African Cities Programme is that the current water wastages in cities cannot be reduced by pricing, technical or regulatory measures alone. These measures are necessary, and must be pursued vigorously by water managers, but they are not sufficient by themselves. To be effective, they need to be complemented by advocacy, awareness raising and education initiatives. Water education in schools and communities can play an important role in bringing about a new water-use ethic in cities.

Education, particularly value-based education, is an important agent for behavioural and attitude changes in key actors in the urban water and sanitation scene (see Box 6.1). As noted by Professor Kader Asmal, South Africa's Minister of Education: 'Education is an impor-

Box 6.1 Value-based approach to water education

Value-based water education is an innovative approach to water education that not only seeks to impart information on water, sanitation and hygiene, but also inspires and motivates learners to change their behaviour and adopt attitudes that promote the wise and sustainable use of water. A value-based approach to water education seeks to bring out, emphasize and stress desirable human qualities which help us in making informed choices in water resources management. Nurturing such values as honesty, integrity, tolerance, responsibility, sharing and caring, particularly in children during the formative years, will contribute to caring and responsible adults in the future. They, in turn, will lay the groundwork for the character development of the generations following them.

The introduction of value-based water education in African cities followed a consensus recommendation of an Expert Group Meeting convened by UN-HABITAT in collaboration with the United Nations Environment Programme and the Stockholm International Water Institute in Johannesburg in 2001. This group noted that water education should aim to promote a better understanding of water as a key social, economic and environmental resource and

should facilitate the emergence of a new water management ethic on the continent. It observed that the introduction and implementation of value-based water education through formal, non-formal and informal channels of learning, especially the use of the curriculum, is a promising way to bring about a positive and lasting change in attitudes and behaviour towards water at all levels of society.

As a first step in implementing the group's recommendations, UN-HABITAT convened two sub-regional workshops to expose educators and those involved in the implementation of the project to the concept of value-based water education and its possible use through formal, non-formal and informal channels; and to develop country-level action plans for project implementation in the participating countries. The first sub-regional workshop, held in Ndola, Zambia, in July 2001, was attended by senior professionals from the education and water sectors in Ethiopia, Kenya, Tanzania, South Africa and Zambia. The second sub-regional workshop, held in Accra, Ghana, in August 2001, brought together senior professionals from the education and water sectors in Côte d'Ivoire, Ghana and Senegal.

After the two regional workshops, UN-HABITAT has supported

the development of teaching tools for pilot testing value-based water education in schools, covering pre-primary, primary and secondary levels. This included collecting and reviewing current school curricula, teacher training and learning resources from various countries and developing lesson plans covering pre-primary, primary and secondary levels. This was followed by five-day workshops on value-based water education in Abidjan, Accra, Dakar, Addis Ababa, Lusaka and Nairobi. The objective of the workshops was to train curriculum development specialists, inspectors of schools, subject specialists and non-formal education practitioners in value-based water education and in techniques for mainstreaming it in national education. The trainees would, in turn, impart training to primary and secondary level teachers and community groups in their respective countries. During the workshops, participants developed time-bound action plans detailing how they wished to proceed with implementation. The main post-workshop activities included training teachers in the pilot schools, pilot testing in pilot schools, continuous monitoring and evaluation, and mainstreaming value-based water education in the entire school curriculum by June 2003.

tant cornerstone to help conserve water and manage it in a wise manner so that future generations will not suffer from our mistakes of today.'[9] The need to change people's behaviour patterns through water education in schools and communities is also part of the recommendations of a technical report, *Defining and Mainstreaming Environmental Sustainability in Water Resources Management in Southern Africa*. This suggests that 'If communities become aware of the limitations in their water resources and of the impacts their activities have on the water resources, behaviour patterns and traditions may change to focus on conservation rather than utilization.'[10]

The UN-HABITAT's Water Education Initiative in African Cities[11] has brought together, for the first time, professionals from education, urban, and water and environment sectors to bring about a positive and lasting change in attitudes and behaviour towards water at all levels of society. The broad aim of water education is to facilitate changes in behaviour and personal attitudes among water consumers and to promote a better understanding of the environment in a water context. The main activities under the programme include:

- Development of a water-related environmental education strategy for African cities.
- Establishment of water classrooms.
- Schools water audit.
- Water quality education.
- Curriculum development and introducing water education in pilot schools.
- Non-formal education with community initiatives.
- Water health care education.
- Information exchange and North–South twinning arrangements.

Education is critical to long-term shifts in people's behaviour patterns, but in the short run, public awareness campaigns can be equally important and can help to provide a better basis for education programmes. The section below summarizes some of the lessons that have been learned from UN-HABITAT's work in seeking to raise awareness on water and sanitation issues through public campaigns in low- and middle-income countries. Two key lessons are that sanitation issues need to be destigmatized, and that public awareness campaigns need to take account of the diverse water and sanitation circumstances that often exist even within a single urban area. Both of these lessons relate to the importance of public health concerns, particularly in areas where existing water and sanitation services are severely deficient. As described in the following section, from a public health perspective, DSM can extend well beyond water conservation.

Raising awareness of water and sanitation through public campaigns[12]

In raising public awareness of water and sanitation issues, it is important to recognize the divergence in public perception between the two. Whilst the need to improve the access of low-income groups to clean water enjoys broad-based support, pro-poor sanitation has largely tended to be the domain of CBOs and NGOs working closely with affected communities. Most governments and development agencies will address and champion water issues, but the same is not always so for sanitation. As a result, sanitation is often relegated to the bottom of the agenda in most international fora, in the work plans of many development agencies, and in the development plans of many governments. There is a need to destigmatize sanitation and raise its profile in the arena of public debate.

The participation of city residents, the private and public sectors, NGOs, CBOs and all other stakeholders in the water and sanitation debate is imperative. Seeking synergies between water and sanitation awareness campaigns and linking the two at every available opportunity is one way of realizing tangible and sustainable long-term results in the provision of both water and sanitation for the poor.

Public awareness campaigns for water and sanitation need to take into account the different situations, needs and circumstances of discrete user categories. This necessitates the definition of existing user perceptions about the level and quality of service access for both water and sanitation, assessment of water and sanitation usage habits, establishment of major impediments to better access, and determination of practical and socially acceptable ways of overcoming such impediments to access. Only then can appropriate messages be designed that adequately address the role of each target group in improving access to water and sanitation for low-income groups.

Target audiences for campaigns
Even among low-income groups, there are differing levels of access to water and sanitation services. Different individuals, groups and organizations have varying and sometimes conflicting needs, habits, circumstances and priorities. To maximize the impact of public awareness campaigns, the user populations must be segmented into niches, with relevant messages being developed for each group that address their particular circumstances. Within the low-income category, the distinction between residents of formal and informal settlements must be recognized.

High-income water consumers

Many consumers in this category pay for their water, but due to the relatively low rates charged by many city water utilities and the more reliable and consistent supplies, they are insensitive to the need to conserve water. As a result of this insensitivity, their consumption habits tend to be profligate. In situations of shortage or drought, many high-income residential areas are excluded from rationing programmes, rendering residents oblivious to the water shortages and rationing that affect middle- and low-income consumers. Wasteful habits such as daily watering of gardens, washing cars using hose pipes, cleaning pavements with treated water and leaving swimming pools uncovered in high tempera-tures are commonplace. Encouraging high-income water consumers to adopt better usage habits offers the potential to free up considerable volumes of water that could be made available to unserved or under-served low-income groups in the same localities (although as noted elsewhere, there is no guarantee that these two aspects will be linked).

To raise awareness within this category, households should be challenged through public awareness campaigns to cap consump-tion voluntarily at fixed monthly levels. Messages for this category of consumers would be tailored to remind them of their monthly limits and why it is important for them to comply. In the medium to long term, more practical deterrents, such as the imposi-tion of steep tariff increases above the cap level, may be adopted to control wastage and encourage high-income consumers to adopt more prudent usage practices.

While most low-income groups struggle daily to have access to the minimum volumes of water necessary for survival, many high-income households use treated water to flush their toilets. Recycling water for this purpose is one way of making more of the treated water available to the poor.

Middle-income water consumers

In many cities, this category comprises the largest cluster of consumers. Although short-ages and rationing may affect many of them directly, good usage and conservation methods are rarely practised habitually. This is partly due to the low level of awareness about the value of water and the need to conserve it, and wasteful usage habits developed over a lifetime. Many of these habits have evolved as a result of government-subsidized city water supplies being priced far below cost, so that even those middle-income consumers who have to pay their own water bills have little or no incentive to adopt prudent consumption habits.

Low-income water and sanitation users

Low-income consumers who have to fetch and carry water from standpipes or other sources and/or purchase water from vendors exhibit few of the wasteful habits of middle- and upper-income consumers. However, communal or public water taps may not be managed effectively, which can result in water wastage.

Industrial water consumers

Given the current tariff structures in most cities, water bills are unlikely to account for more than 1 per cent of total operational costs, even for the largest industrial consumers. Industries often benefit from uninterrupted supplies that are guaranteed by their large-scale consumption and – sometimes – by their classification as essential services. Not many industrial consumers have felt a need to pay attention to the conservation of water through good usage practices.

The challenge is therefore to find innova-tive ways of securing their participation, because collectively, industrial users often consume a large percentage of the water resources in a city. Even marginal savings in this category may free up a considerable amount of water for domestic use in informal settlements. Whilst promoting the concept of participation as responsible corporate citizens is one way of achieving this objective, regula-tory mechanisms to curb profligate use may need to be considered in the longer term. Industrial consumers also need to be reminded that they have a vested interest in securing the long-term sustainability of water supplies for their cities.

Institutional and government consumers

Consumers in many institutions and government buildings do not pay directly for their water, which often results in wasteful consumption levels. Here, the focus may need to be on monitoring and documenting usage carefully with a view to taking corrective action for institutions where consumption levels are particularly high.

Politicians, civic leaders and administrative personnel

Being acknowledged formal leaders, this group of consumers has the potential to exert significant influence in mobilizing other categories of consumers to participate in water conservation and good usage practices. This group can also be a major force in facilitating a more practical, relevant, efficient and all-inclusive process for improving access to water and sanitation services for low-income groups. Because they are looked upon as opinion leaders, such people can play a critical role in conveying messages on good water and sanitation usage practices to groups of consumers, transcending the socio-economic spectrum with a great deal of credibility.

Messages targeting politicians and civic leaders should aim at inculcating a participatory sense of partnership in the improvement of water and sanitation services for the poor. Seminars and workshops could sensitize carefully selected representative groups to the need for a common approach to the problems of the poor, and through their practical involvement, accelerated awareness within a core group of influential advocates can be achieved, with the attendant trickle-down benefits.

NGOs, CBOs and city administrative authorities

Grassroots organizations that have well established and regular contacts with low-income groups in both formal and informal settlements have mechanisms in place for information dissemination and awareness creation. Residents' associations, churches, local administrations, local business groupings, women's groups, youth associations and other CSOs can provide effective and direct means of spreading the message. Many agencies and NGOs will also be involved in various community projects, particularly in low-income residential areas. Such organizations should be identified and partnerships forged with them to avoid wasteful and often counterproductive duplication of effort.

Employees of city utilities

The involvement, commitment and full participation of employees of city water and sanitation utilities are vital to the long-term sustainability of public awareness campaigns. This requires the establishment of regular fora for the dissemination of up-to-date information to all employees who are involved in the delivery of water and sanitation services. These fora also enable city managers to obtain first-hand feedback from employees on the opportunities and obstacles to the improvement of access to these services.

Development agencies

The long-term sustainability and success of the awareness campaigns depends on the development of appropriate capacity within cities. This must invariably go hand-in-hand with the creation of a critical mass of middle-level professionals conversant with and committed to the pro-poor provision of water and sanitation services.

A cross-section of development agencies is involved in funding various aspects of water and sanitation in many countries. By seeking synergies and areas of mutual cooperation, they can play a facilitating role in channelling existing and new funding into projects to improve the provision of water and sanitation. Separate messages addressing the development community and targeting as broad a cross-section of them as possible should therefore be an integral component of all awareness campaigns.

Campaign launch and duration
The objective

Besides the need to educate users and consumers on good usage practices, there is the more fundamental need to change attitudes to inculcate a participatory and solution-oriented mindset. A highly visible and intensive public awareness campaign is necessary to create an atmosphere in which low-income groups have a sense of ownership of the problem and its solutions. This can only happen if they have a clear understanding of their situation and, thus, a more objective understanding of the causal factors. The awareness campaigns therefore need to be ubiquitous, informative, educative and inspirational. The over-riding objective should be to goad stakeholders at all levels and across all categories into a sense of individual responsibility, and thereby inspire them to take immediate remedial action in areas within their immediate control. The willingness of low-income groups to participate actively in awareness campaigns is predicated upon their appreciation of the difference they can make as individuals.

Overcoming the scepticism with which low-income groups as well as some sections of the media may view various initiatives taken by city authorities, NGOs, CBOs and development agencies could well be the initial challenge in some cities. Demonstrable and tangible results must be delivered on a scale that convinces even the sceptics of the viability, sustainability and seriousness of these initiatives. The awareness campaigns can then leverage these initiatives by devising creative, relevant and cost-effective ways of drawing maximum public attention to the problem of improving access to water and sanitation for the poor, and their active participation in these initiatives.

The strategy

During the initial phase of the public awareness campaigns, dedicated and professional capacity must be built within city water and sanitation utilities. This requires the establishment of full-time campaign secretariats headed by qualified full-time communications professionals. As the central sources of all information pertaining to the various pro-poor initiatives for the provision of better access to water and sanitation, the secretariats should be the focal points of the public awareness campaigns. Stakeholders and other interested parties should be encouraged to obtain any information they require, make suggestions on

implementation, and offer feedback on the awareness campaigns to the secretariats. Creating ongoing dialogue between city water and sanitation utilities in their capacity as providers on the one hand, and the users of these services on the other, is imperative to the success of public awareness campaigns.

Media and private sector involvement

Support from various sections of the media is crucial in changing user perceptions and attitudes about existing situations. This is even more so in situations where the media are among the most virulent and sceptical critics of the city authorities' performance in the water and sanitation sector. Regular workshops, seminars and study tours for selected media representatives act as important tools for raising the level of awareness of pro-poor water and sanitation issues. These tools are then reinforced with the frequent distribution of media kits containing updated information on water and sanitation issues, conservation initiatives, good usage practices, success stories in other cities and practical problems or obstacles to the improvement of access.

The private sector has a vested interest in ensuring the sustainability of water supplies through conservation and good usage practices. Institutions such as hotels have a direct interest in managing demand. Efforts should therefore be made to co-opt them as active partners in all awareness campaigns.

Campaign duration

Ideally, once launched, the public awareness campaigns should be open-ended. Water conservation and improving access to clean water and better sanitation services are continuous processes rather than an exercise with a finite lifespan. However, due to resource limitations, intensive awareness campaigns can only be sustained for a limited period of time. The most viable approach is therefore to follow up launch campaigns with scaled-down public awareness campaigns managed within the city utilities that are sustainable on a long-term basis. The need to build in-house capacity to manage the campaigns after the initial launch period is thus an integral part of the public awareness strategy.

The launch phase of any campaign must however be sustained for a period that is sufficient to facilitate a critical evaluation of the content and direction of the campaign, and offers adequate opportunities for the objective assessment of its impact. Furthermore, to enable those dedicated to the subsequent management of the campaigns to attain a level of competence and comfort that will ensure seamless continuity, the launch campaigns need to run for a period of time ranging from six months to one year. The time frame required to build the requisite institutional capacity must also be taken into account.

Campaign evaluation

To establish an objective entry point, baseline customer attitude surveys should be carried out before launching any public awareness campaigns. The surveys should be structured to question user perceptions of aspects such as the level and quality of service delivery, ways to improve access, the perceived role of the poor in the process, and their overall impressions of the existing situation. At the end of the launch phase of the campaign the same survey should be repeated and the responses evaluated against those received in the first survey.

To effectively address the specific concerns of various user categories as established through the consumer attitude surveys, the public awareness campaigns must be intensive and high profile in order to draw and focus the attention and interest of even the most indifferent users. Those who may have accepted the status quo and have seemingly adjusted to it must be shaken out their state of lethargy with creative, imaginative, relevant and compelling messages.

Managing demand to improve public health

From a health perspective, the principal urban water problem is the enormous unexploited potential for using water more effectively to improve health. As described in Chapters 1 and 2, this potential lies primarily in the more deprived neighbourhoods of cities in Africa,

Asia and Latin America, where people do not have access to enough water of sufficient quality to meet their basic hygiene requirements, and sanitary facilities are inadequate. Superficially, at least, this sets the health agenda in direct opposition to the conservation agenda, which is looking for ways to reduce the use of water. However, as noted in Chapter 3, the quantity of water required to meet basic hygiene requirements is very small in the context of overall water demands. The health and conservation agendas may be pointing in different directions and using contradictory narratives to justify their own importance. But as long as supplies can be targeted, meeting basic hygiene requirements need not conflict with reducing water stress.

The most straightforward form of urban water demand management for health is to make potable water and sanitary facilities accessible and affordable to currently deprived households, thereby increasing demand where the health benefits will be greatest. This is, of course, more easily said than done, especially in the light of competing demands from other users with more economic and political power. But, equally importantly from a demand management perspective, access to adequate water is often not sufficient for health improvement. In most of the cases where health impact studies have found significant impacts associated with the provision of water supply or sanitation, this provision has been accompanied by improvements in hygiene and/or sanitation.[13] In short, much depends on how the water and sanitation facilities are used, and especially on what has come to be termed 'hygiene behaviour'.

The same supply-fix approach that conservationists criticize for wasting water resources, hygiene advocates criticize for wasting the potential health improvements that water can bring. In both cases, a demand-side approach requires a better understanding of what people actually want from water, and shifts attention from the relatively controlled arena of water engineering to the more unpredictable arena of human behaviour.

The list below includes a range of behaviours that could be expected to improve health in many poor communities. Many of these behaviours can be greatly facilitated by adequate water supplies and sanitation facilities. There is no guarantee, however, that people provided with better access to water and sanitary facilities will engage in these behaviours. Moreover, these behaviours are likely to be all the more important to health when sanitary conditions are inadequate. Well nourished people living in uncrowded conditions, who have indoor piped water of high quality and flush toilets, and who purchase food from supermarkets subject to regular food inspections, risk comparatively little when they ignore such hygiene recommendations. For poorly nourished people living in over-crowded conditions, with dubious water supplies, simple latrines and food of questionable quality, they can be a matter of life and death.

- Wash hands (preferably with soap) after defecation.
- Wash hands (preferably with soap) prior to food preparation.
- Wash food, especially vegetables, prior to preparation.
- Clean food utensils with water after use.
- Wash surfaces, especially in toilets and food areas.
- Store water in clean containers away from human contact.
- Boil water of doubtful quality before drinking.
- Wash sanitary facilities regularly.
- Site the toilet away from the kitchen (or well).
- Prevent insects from coming into contact with food.
- Ensure that children as well as adults use sanitary facilities.
- Dispose of infants' and small children's faeces safely (away from human contact).
- Wash body regularly – face first if re-using water while bathing.
- Wash grazes and cuts with soap and water.
- Avoid hand contact with water in water containers.
- In case of diarrhoea, administer oral rehydration therapy (a water-based solution).

- Avoid creating open containers of still water, especially in areas where dengue fever is a risk.

This indicates the need for a form of DSM, similar to that envisaged by the conservationist, but focusing on health. Superficially, health might seem to be a more straightforward goal for DSM than conservation. Hygiene promotion programmes have a long history. Human health is a less debatable and more self-motivating objective than resource conservation. And hygiene promotion should enable water (and sanitation facilities) to provide a better service, rather than simply maintain service levels while saving water. However, as for conservation, DSM for health cannot expect to succeed simply by undertaking objective assessments, presenting the results and then waiting for the recommended measures to be adopted.

One approach to reducing the health risks of improper water use and inadequate sanitation is to introduce standards. Standards are often developed for a range of water uses and sanitation conditions, including drinking water and irrigation water standards. In both of these cases, however, rigorous and strictly enforced standards can be counterproductive. Overly strict drinking water standards, for example, can force water utilities to focus on water quality, even where insufficient quantities of water are the principal health risk.[14] Similarly, overly strict irrigation water standards can undermine the livelihoods of many urban farmers and reduce urban food security.[15] In any case, regulatory approaches to DSM are extremely limited, and need to be situated within a broader strategy to be effective in improving health.

Again, the institutional setting and the relations between water (and sanitation) users and demand-side managers are critical. In the case of health, much depends on public attitudes towards the health establishment, and whether the demand-side managers are located in water and sanitation utilities, government departments, NGOs or health care establishments.

Hygiene promotion is complicated by the fact that it cannot be fully disengaged from other relations of power and authority, most of which work to the disadvantage of the urban poor. For example, many of the urban poor do not have legal rights to their homes, and unhealthy sanitation and hygiene practices are sometimes used to justify their eviction. Under such circumstances, residents are predisposed to view hygiene promotion programmes with suspicion. More generally, hygiene promotion can easily intrude on personal and social behaviours that people do not believe should be prescribed by outsiders, whether or not they have health expertise.

Even the best-intentioned hygiene promotion programmes face difficult decisions about which measures to promote and how to convey relevant knowledge to local residents. And even the best-informed and most receptive residents have good reason to be sceptical of some of the claims made in the name of hygiene. Identifying the most appropriate hygiene behaviour often depends upon having an intimate knowledge of local conditions, priorities and cultures, as well as health expertise. As indicated in earlier chapters, there is a great deal that environmental health specialists do not know about water-related health risks and their relative importance. Even if specialists know that local groundwater is faecally contaminated, for example, they are unlikely to know which wells are safe to use for which purposes. Health specialists are also typically unaware of the constraints on local behaviour, and misguided hygiene measures may create unanticipated health risks. Where fuels are costly, for example, boiling water to reduce exposure to waterborne pathogens may lead to reduced food consumption, and attendant problems of undernutrition (as well as exposure to indoor air pollution). Water itself may be so costly that following all the recommended hygiene behaviours could create poverty-induced health burdens.

Many practitioners perceive, however, that if they qualify or complicate their hygiene messages, people are less inclined to change their behaviour. The search for clear messages that are widely applicable can easily restrict hygiene recommendations to a few simple behaviours, such as hand-washing after defecating and before preparing food. Such measures are undoubtedly important, but do not reflect the full potential for water-related hygiene improvement in areas where potable water is scarce and decisions on how to use water are critical to health.

One of the lessons taken from past hygiene promotion campaigns is that health concerns alone are rarely sufficient to motivate the desired changes in water-related behaviour. This probably reflects local scepticism regarding health claims that they cannot verify, as well as the importance of other concerns. A common conclusion is that hygiene improvements also need to be grounded in more immediate concerns, such as convenience or social status. In situations where unhealthy habits and conditions are considered unpleasant or inconvenient, these aspects can be taken into account in developing recommendations and emphasized in their promotion. Where they are considered immoral or of lower status, these aspects too can be taken into account and emphasized. In focusing on the more immediate goals of local residents, the uncertainty of the health benefits becomes less critical.

Unfortunately, practices considered by health specialists to be unhygienic may also be supported by local social norms, cultural beliefs and practicalities. This inevitably complicates matters, particularly since the health benefits themselves are often uncertain. Historically, hygienic behaviour has often been promoted as socially and even morally superior to local practices, even in programmes ostensibly grounded in health sciences. (Yet again, there are parallels with conservation-oriented DSM, which also tends to have strong moral overtones.) Such moralizing is sometimes criticized for undermining the scientific credibility of hygiene promotion. If people perceive that hygiene programmes are moralizing, they may reject the advice. Equally important, moralizing can draw hygiene promotion more firmly into prevailing power relations that oppress the urban poor and undermine their legitimate claims for a say in their own development.

The moral dimensions of hygiene promotion were more explicit in the sanitary reforms of the 19th century than they are today. The expert-driven model prevalent during most of the 20th century has also been attenuated. Participation, partnership and empowerment are often presented as central to hygiene promotion. Even market mechanisms are being adapted to hygiene promotion, and a recent initiative has enlisted a number of soap manufacturers in Kerala and Ghana to promote hand-washing.[16]

Nevertheless, specialist knowledge is central to hygiene promotion, including health-oriented DSM. One of the key justifications for taking a health perspective is that social norms, developed through trial and error or normative reasoning, do not provide a sufficient basis for achieving the health benefits that water and sanitation can provide. Where water is piped into toilets and kitchens, and drained away from sinks and toilets, a few simple hygiene conventions may suffice. For most of the urban poor, identifying appropriate behaviours is more complicated, but the potential benefits are higher. The image of the expert prescribing local hygiene behaviour may be misguided. However, ensuring that the urban poor have access to water-related health expertise (as well as water itself) remains a central task.

Managing demand to increase economic efficiency and affordability

Market economists tend to focus on prices and the institutions through which prices are set rather than the practices that users ought to adopt. They are inclined to assume that consumers are rational and, if well informed, will demand and use a commodity in ways that best suit their budgets and needs. The price of a commodity provides an indicator of scarcity, which both suppliers and consumers can respond to, both serving their own interests and ensuring that the commodity only goes to uses that are valued at least as highly as their cost. The appropriate price is usually taken to be the marginal cost: the cost of providing an additional unit, ideally including resource depletion and other environmental costs. Facing this price, the consumer will, again ideally, use the commodity up to the point at which the marginal benefits from consuming an additional unit are equal to the marginal costs of providing it.

The problems with treating water as a normal economic good were outlined in Chapter 5 and are dealt with in some detail in other publications.[17] In summary, while in many circumstances economists favour marginal cost pricing, it is recognized that water often poses a number of difficulties. The environmental costs can be difficult to estimate. The public health benefits of water, of particular relevance in low-income settlements, are also difficult to estimate. Users may not even be aware of the health benefits. If water is metered at the point of use, there are more pricing options than with more conventional goods, since prices can comparatively easily be varied depending on the user and the amount they consume. Metering is costly, however, and water meters are prone to breakdown, especially when water supplies are intermittent. Moreover, even metered users are often unaware of how much water they are using for which purpose, making it difficult for them to respond efficiently to price signals.

Even ignoring such problems, defining and estimating the correct marginal cost can be extremely difficult. Urban water supply systems have high capital costs, and new projects often increase supplies on a very large scale. This means that pricing at the short-run marginal cost will typically induce demand to increase relatively rapidly up to a point at which the marginal cost increases dramatically (because only a large new investment will enable supplies to increase). The problems of price volatility alone make this undesirable. Water users could easily be induced to invest in water-intensive technologies and practices when water prices are low, only to find them uneconomical when prices suddenly rise. Thus economists have generally favoured long-run marginal cost pricing, on the grounds that in the long run additional water demand will require investments in supply infrastructure, and that a price that reflects these costs will provide more appropriate signals to users.

The very concept of long-run marginal cost is somewhat incoherent: how long is the long run, and where is its margin? The best one can realistically hope for is an estimate of marginal cost based on incremental operating costs and capital costs per unit of capacity expansion, averaged out over a period of time sufficient to avoid disruptive price changes. In any case, long-run marginal cost pricing is not equivalent to the clearing price in a perfect market. In practical terms, there are evident short-term inefficiencies if water prices are set to reflect the costs of building a new reservoir or canal, when the current ones are being only partially utilized.

Despite these and other complications, long-run marginal cost pricing is often taken as an appropriate rule of thumb. The long-run marginal cost may be difficult to define, let alone measure. However, water tariffs often diverge so strongly from any reasonable version of marginal cost pricing that such difficulties are irrelevant. Most often, prices are clearly below the marginal cost. Governments have tended to set piped water prices very low, particularly for households. Moreover, when users access water from natural sources they often get it for free (leaving aside time and labour costs), even when water use is depleting groundwater aquifers or diverting surface water from other users.

It is often argued that getting water prices right is an important part of DSM, and would go a long way towards solving problems of water stress. In the current literature on DSM, water pricing is typically seen as complementing the more technical approach that conservationists have traditionally taken. It is worth keeping in mind, however, that when the term 'demand-side management' was coined a few decades ago, proponents were openly critical of what they perceived as market economists' over-reliance on prices as a means of balancing supplies and demands. Without the appropriate technologies and demand-side programmes, they argued, price-induced savings would have to be achieved by reducing service levels rather than providing the same service levels with fewer resources. Economists tended to counter that it was prices that would provide the incentives for users and private enterprises to seek out the appropriate technologies and demand-side measures. This difference in perspectives is

still evident, even if conservationists are more inclined to accept pricing policy as an important tool of demand management, and economists are more inclined to accept that other tools of demand management can sometimes help price incentives to operate more efficiently.

Of more concern to the central issues of this book, higher water prices would hardly seem to be a response relevant to the water problems of the urban poor. As indicated in earlier chapters, the urban poor who lack piped water connections often have to pay far more than the official tariff for water, and purchase it in small quantities from informal water vendors. Alternatively, they may have to incur high costs in time and effort to collect water from a distant source. This is not so much because water resources are scarce, but because the infrastructure required to deliver water cheaply and conveniently is lacking. The notion that higher prices will help solve such problems would appear, at least superficially, to be absurd.

Market economics can also explain, however, how 'under-priced' piped water may actually contribute to 'over-priced' water and excessive collection costs in low-income neighbourhoods. Very briefly, if a utility depends on water sales to help meet costs and finance expansion, price controls that compel them to charge excessively low prices for piped water can inhibit the expansion of the water supply system. If the water network does not expand, low-income neighbourhoods will remain unconnected (even if residents would be willing to pay the full economic cost), and re-sale markets will be under-supplied, leading to higher prices in these secondary markets. Moreover, economics predicts that efforts to control secondary water markets by punishing vendors who sell at high prices are likely to reduce supplies still further, leading to still higher black market prices for the urban poor, or increasing collection costs.

While this may be an over-simplification, it at least bears a relation to some of the problems faced in many low-income cities. Water utilities are often required to sell water at prices well below those required to maintain the piped water system, let alone finance expansion. Subsidies rarely make up the difference, and these financially unviable utilities cannot attract private or, increasingly, international development bank finance.[18] There is under-investment in many piped water systems, particularly in low-income areas, which lack both political and financial clout, and are often bypassed by public water utilities whose funds are not sufficient to cover all areas. Partly as a result, the urban poor often pay exorbitant prices for water, restrict consumption, or both.[19] In North Jakarta, for example, a survey found that the poorest 20 per cent of households had to purchase potable water from vendors who often charged more than ten times the official piped water price, and ended up paying an average price more than twice that paid by the richest households, despite using saline well water for many purposes.[20] It is also common for households to be prohibited from re-selling water, although if a lack of competition is the reason for high vendor prices, this is likely to make things worse.[21] In some cities, no water vending is officially allowed, even though it is common, leading to widespread opportunities for corruption.

On the other hand, it is also important to recognize that long-run marginal cost pricing is not a very good rule of thumb for DSM in low-income urban settings, even from the perspective of market economics, and that without water meters it is infeasible in any case. At least two mutually reinforcing problems with setting water prices equal to the marginal cost have received a great deal of attention over the years, though they tend to be neglected in current water resource debates. The first relates to equity and is not strictly speaking a DSM issue: water for the urban poor should be subsidized so as to serve redistributive goals, which the market does not spontaneously address, but which are valued by society. The second relates to public health and clearly does involve DSM: water for the poor should be subsidized so as to reflect the public health benefits of adequate water (for example, the benefits that local residents receive from not being exposed to the infectious diseases their neighbours contract as a result of inadequate water supplies). These two reasons reinforce each other. Subsidizing

public goods for the poor can be an efficient means of achieving redistributive goals,[22] and while water itself is not a public good, some of the services it provides could be described as spatially localized public goods. To be efficient and equitable, it is critical, of course, that the finances for the subsidies themselves be raised efficiently and equitably, and are sufficient to ensure that enough water can be supplied at the desired price.

These are, unfortunately, some of the same reasons used to justify the low water prices that have often not been financed by appropriate subsidies, undermining the financial viability of the public utilities, and actually resulting in high water prices for the urban poor. In effect, policies adopted in the name of the poor have sometimes subsidized the better off, and left the poor unserved. This phenomenon is not peculiar to water, however. The interests of politically disadvantaged groups are often well represented in the early stages of policy formulation, and then lose out during implementation. There is no reason to believe that equitable and efficient policies are more difficult to implement in the water sector than in other policy arenas. Moreover, there is a great deal of variation in the equity and efficiency of urban water provision, and in most urban centres there is considerable room for improvement. Setting low water prices for all households is unlikely to be either efficient or equitable, particularly if it not matched by efficiently financed subsidies. But more targeted demand-side measures, assisting the least well-off, are not as difficult to design as they are to implement.

There are a number of pricing measures that can be taken to target the urban poor and their economic needs. Which measures are most suitable depends heavily on local circumstances. Indeed, the demand-side economics can be quite complex, even if superficially the pricing options are straightforward. Examples include:

Free public water taps

Free public water taps are sometimes provided in deprived areas. Water consumption per capita is likely to remain low unless the taps are actually located in house compounds.[23]

Moreover, where free water taps are scarce, long queues may develop, to the point where users are indifferent between the public taps and alternatives such as vended water. From the users' perspective, the queues can make the 'free' supplies as costly as vended water. Social norms and pressures can act to prevent excessive queuing, but may also lead to conflicts. Alternatively, more formal measures can be taken to prevent excessive queuing and similar rent-dissipating behaviour, ranging from tying buckets together to create proxy queues, to hiring tap attendants to charge for water. Generally, however, neither the utility nor the government is in a good position to regulate such behaviour, and much depends on the organization of the local communities. By providing more taps, the need for such controls is reduced, and though the quantity of water consumed may increase, it is unlikely to exceed the levels required to meet health needs. On the other hand, the users have little incentive to prevent wastage at the tap if the water is provided free.

Water hydrants for vended water

Water hydrants are sometimes provided with water at a relatively low tariff, for re-sale by water vendors. If the amount of water made available to water hydrant operators or vendors at this price is less than demand, then even if the market is competitive the re-sale price will rise until supply and demand are balanced, regardless of the price at which the vendors purchase water. Vendor competition to obtain a greater share of the water may ensure that the vendors themselves do not profit from the situation, but unless supplies can be increased, this will not reduce prices. Instead, vendors themselves will engage in queuing or other unproductive but competitive behaviour. Alternatively, water hydrant operators or vendors may collude with utility staff and share the rents (or utility staff may capture all of the rents). On the other hand, if the demand for hydrant water at the low tariff can be met by the utility, then competition between vendors (and, if they exist, between hydrant operators) can help to ensure that the re-sale mark-up only reflects the costs incurred by the vendors (and hydrant operators).

Lifeline tariffs

Water is sometimes provided free or at a very low price to residential users who are considered to be consuming quantities that are just sufficient to meet basic water needs. This works best when the urban poor have individual, metered water connections, but this is often considered too costly. In principle, minimal provision can also be supplied using water tanks or water connections that limit consumption through time-of-day or flow restrictors. Problems can develop when most poor households cannot even afford individual lifeline connections, since most lifeline tariff systems do not allow connection sharing, which can otherwise be a low-cost coping strategy.

Increasing block tariffs

Increasing block tariffs are often used, and justified on the grounds that they favour users who only consume small amounts of water. With an increasing block tariff, the first block (typically a specified number of cubic metres of water consumed in a given month) is charged at lower price than the subsequent block, which is in turn charged at a lower price than the next block, and so on. Ideally, the blocks would be sized and priced to take into account public health, redistributive, water resource and cost-recovery concerns, though these goals can rarely be reconciled perfectly. As a possible compromise, the size of first block could be set at the quantity of water required to meet water-related health requirements, and priced low to reflect the public health and redistributive benefits; the last block could be priced at the long-run marginal cost; and any intermediate blocks (and a fixed charge or rebate) could be sized and priced with a view towards cost-recovery and redistributive concerns.[24] In practice, this rarely comes even close to being achieved, and in many low-income cities the first block is well above minimal requirements, and may even be sufficiently large to cover the water consumption of the majority of households. In any case, as with the lifeline tariff, if increasing block tariffs are to assist the urban poor, care must be taken to ensure that very poor residents do not end up paying higher prices as the result of meter sharing, insufficient connections and high vendor prices. For instance, in Bangalore, it is middle- and upper-income groups that receive much of subsidy for water through the increasing block tariff pricing structure, because most low-income groups do not have an individual tap. However, a pilot project is underway to allow those who share a group tap to get the lowest block rate, as each household sharing the tap rather than the tap itself gets allocated a maximum volume of water which is available at the cheapest rate.[25]

Single volumetric rate with rebate

On the grounds that increasing block tariffs rarely serve either efficiency or equity goals, a two-part tariff has recently been proposed, consisting of a single volumetric charge combined with a fixed monthly credit or rebate.[26] The single water rate can be set at the long-run marginal cost (or some approximation thereof), while the rebate can help to ensure that purchasing small quantities of water is not a financial burden. A small minimum fee is also proposed to prevent abuse of the system. One of the main advantages of this system is its relative simplicity, though it does require metering, and does not address the problems of those without connections.

Reduced tariffs for low-income housing or deprived areas

If deprived areas or housing types can be identified, connections for these residents can be charged at preferential rates. Differentials can be applied to both metered and unmetered households, and even if the urban poor share connections, they can still receive the preferential rates. Area-based systems are more likely to be effective where residential areas are relatively homogenous. Housing-based systems are more likely to be effective where residential areas are mixed, but certain housing types are closely associated with poverty (in principle, low house values could be used as an indicator of poverty, though they may be too difficult to estimate). Such systems are more likely to be considered unfair by those who pay higher rates, since, unlike with the rising block tariff, households actually face different tariffs

(when different prices emerge from a single tariff this is less likely to be viewed as discriminatory, even when that is the intention). Moreover, at least some affluent people are likely to live in low-income housing or in deprived areas. It is also important to recognize that in a great many urban areas the poorest residents do not even have security of tenure, or the right to obtain water at the standard tariff, let alone access to preferential treatment. Nevertheless, in cities where there is the political will to improve services to the poor, this remains an option.

Reduced connection costs

Economics suggests that reduced connection costs may be more advantageous to low-income households than reduced water rates. The urban poor often find it difficult to make large lump-sum payments. They rarely have substantial savings and often face very high borrowing costs. In some circumstances, a utility is in a good position to provide the equivalent of low-interest loans to newly connected households, paid off through the water bills, or to cross-subsidize connection costs with water bills. This assumes that the billing system is operating efficiently, and that the utility has the capacity to meet the demand for new connections.

A choice of tariffs

Utilities can offer a choice of tariffs to individuals or communities, including some that are purposefully designed to assist low-income consumers. This may be administratively difficult, but can overcome the disadvantages of either assuming that one tariff suits all connections or having the utility or government decide who should be charged at which tariff.

Despite these and many other qualifications that economists have examined, the principal demand-side insight of market economics is typically taken to be that water should be priced at its full economic cost. In a well functioning market, this gives the user the incentive to avoid wasting water on uses that they do not value as much as the cost of providing the water, and give the suppliers the incentive to provide the water demanded. As indicated in the previous chapter, this is what is sometimes implied by the admonition to treat water as an economic good, even if water markets rarely function as well as this argument assumes.

On the other hand, the demand-side perspective of the market economist need not focus exclusively on resource issues. Public health issues, for example, can also be taken into account. More generally, how the water markets function, the scope for competition, the importance of non-market mechanisms of water access and distribution (whether based upon government intervention, the actions of user associations or social norms), and many other critical issues are all suitable topics for water economics, and influence both water demands and supplies.

Managing demand to empower deprived communities

For the grassroots activist, as for the market economist, the problem with supply-driven water planning is not so much that residents do not know about saving water or how to use it, but that they often have little control over water provision. Thus grassroots activists and provision-oriented market economists tend to agree on the need for what has come to be termed the 'demand-responsive' approach to water provision in low-income areas. The demand-responsive approach is based on a critique of supply-side approaches, whether adopted by public authorities or private monopolists. When the urban poor are more directly involved in water provision initiatives – so the argument goes – supplying them with water becomes less expensive, more efficient, more sustainable and better suited to local needs. Even from the grassroots perspective, part of the argument is typically based on the observation that if people are not making a substantial commitment to acquiring their 'improved' water supplies, it is not possible to ensure that they will value the water system and act to maintain it.

Grassroots activists and market economists tend to have different interpretations of what a demand-responsive approach entails, however. Grassroots activists tend to focus on local politics and community organizing, whereas market economists tend to focus on prices and economic competition. Thus from a (stereotypical) grassroots perspective, the relevant demands are those of communities, and the most obvious way of ensuring that those demands are articulated and acted upon is to help communities organize and participate in their own water provision. On the other hand, from an (equally stereotypical) market economics perspective, the relevant demands are those of individual consumers or households, and the most obvious way of responding to those demands is to ensure that the water tariffs are set correctly, and that suppliers have the incentive to meet any demand at the correct tariff.

The grassroots approach is often taken to be one of community participation, although 'community' and 'participation' are somewhat contentious terms, which are themselves subject to varying interpretations. 'Community' is sometimes used to refer to idealized social groupings, while at other times it is simply meant to indicate people living in a certain area, or having other characteristics that give them common interests and the possibility of acting together to pursue those interests. Participation implies some level of involvement, but there are genuine (as well as tactical) differences of opinion on the level and type of involvement that should qualify as 'participation'. Since strengthening community participation is being presented here as a form of DSM, it is worth taking these definitional issues seriously.

The use of the term 'community' by advocates of community participation is often taken by detractors to imply the existence of well bounded, non-hierarchical groups, living in harmony and capable of making consensual decisions. Few grassroots activists seriously believe that such communities exist, although some may be guilty of romanticizing communities in opposition to governments and markets (just as economists have been guilty of idealizing the perfect market, and planners have idealized the perfect plan). Many do believe, on the other hand, that better organized and better informed urban poor groups could do a great deal to address their water problems,

Table 6.1 A typology of participation in water and sanitation provision

Form of participation	Characteristics
Passive participation	Residents participate by being told about water and sanitation initiatives that are being planned or have already been decided upon, without any attempt to elicit local opinion or knowledge.
Participation through information (giving)	Residents are asked questions about their water and sanitation situation or needs through surveys or similar instruments. The information is fed anonymously into the decision-making process without feedback.
Participation through consultation	Residents are consulted as to what should be done to improve the local water and sanitation situation, and may discuss different options being proposed by sector professionals, but the professionals are not obliged to take residents' views into account.
Participation through contribution	Residents are asked to provide labour or financial contributions towards water and sanitation improvements, but do not choose what improvements are on offer.
Participation through collaboration	Resident groups and other key actors (eg, local government and a water and sanitation utility) agree to take responsibility for certain components of a negotiated water and sanitation improvement, with residents taking primary responsible for some well defined components.
Participation through partnership	Resident groups and other key actors share resources, knowledge and risks in pursuit of commonly agreed-upon water and sanitation improvements. 'Partnership' can be taken to imply a long-term, equitable relationship.
Participation through self-mobilization	Residents work together to demand and/or implement water and sanitation improvements. They develop contacts with external actors, some of whom may contribute organizational as well as technical skills, but resident groups retain control over how the resources are used.

Source: Adapted from Pretty, J, I Guijt, I Scoones and J Thompson (1995), *A Trainer's Guide for Participatory Learning and Action*, International Institute for Environment and Development, London, page 61.

and that conventional approaches to water provision do not respond to, and often undermine, this potential. This could be seen as a position on DSM, on the understanding that groups of users can be considered demand-side managers.

The varied use of 'participation' reflects both legitimate differences of opinion, and dubious attempts to present conventional projects as participatory (in order, for example, to secure donor finance). Unfortunately, it is often difficult to tell the difference, since what were once considered dubious definitions became conventional usage as the term became more popular. Table 6.1 provides a typology of participation in water and sanitation provision. It is doubtful whether 'passive participation', 'participation through consultation' or 'participation through contribution' should ever really justify labelling an initiative 'participatory'. Yet even these weak forms can make a difference where they have previously been absent.

International NGOs have helped to ensure that some form of community participation is adopted in most water and sanitation initiatives purposefully targeting low-income areas. Even water and sanitation engineers, economists, utilities and others not predisposed to take community-level organization seriously have come to accept the importance of engaging with local groups in deprived areas, and not treating water and sanitation as simply a service to be delivered or a product to be sold. In some cases, even telling local residents about a planned initiative is an improvement over previous practices. More active consultation undoubtedly helps. Many conventional project managers have found that if residents can be persuaded to contribute labour, land or finance to a project, that project is more likely to succeed. Even private water and sanitation companies have been exploring multi-sector, multi-stakeholder partnerships for water and sanitation provision.[27]

But from a grassroots activist's perspective, community participation ought to involve active collaboration at the very least, and ideally some level of self-mobilization on the part of the local residents. A large share of water and sanitation in poor urban areas is not provided through conventional projects, and in such circumstances the mobilization of local groups can be particularly important. Moreover, while from a conventional planning perspective a lack of community capacity may be seen as the principal obstacle to increasing community participation, from a grassroots perspective organized community groups may be seen to be needed to increase the capacity and capabilities of government institutions.

While the role of local groups has not always been recognized within the formal water and sanitation sector, it has long been central to provision in many deprived urban neighbourhoods. Where neither the private sector nor the government are providing water or sanitation (or where provision is very poor), local groups or local leaders often organize in the attempt to meet water and sanitation needs. The resulting systems vary in their efficiency, safety and equity, but they often involve very innovative measures, tailored to local conditions. Where piped water systems do not exist, local groups may organize well digging or drilling, or piping water from nearby surface water sources. Similarly, where there is no utility providing sanitation, local groups may organize the building of pit latrines, drains or even simple sewerage systems. Alternatively, local groups or leaders may organize to demand conventional services from utilities, which tend to be hesitant about providing water and sanitation services to low-income settlements, particularly when land tenure issues remain unresolved and the economic costs of distribution are high. Where piped systems supply adjoining neighbourhoods, but are not extended to low-income areas, local groups may also request access to the system, but provide for local distribution themselves. Local groups may also tap the piped system without (formal) permission, and local officials may implicitly condone this, and even demand (informal) payments. Such activities can take an enormous range of

institutional forms, and involve a wide array of technologies.

In most policy documents, community participation is assumed to mean that the community is participating in an initiative being organized by outsiders. Indeed, the term 'community participation' can be taken to suggest this: if, at one end of the spectrum, passive participation comes close to being a contradiction in terms, at the other end of the spectrum so does participation through self-mobilization. After all, if communities organize to drive their own water agenda, one could argue that they have ceased to be mere participants in the process. But this makes community participation a very limiting concept, and risks playing semantics with substantive disagreements over the role communities do or could play in water provision. Understanding the actual or potential importance of organized communities is a potentially critical part of a demand-side strategy, however community participation is defined. Moreover, mobilizing local residents is central to a number of grassroots approaches to water and sanitation provision.

The Orangi project in Karachi is probably the best known community-based sanitation project,[28] and its approach has since been extended to other urban services and centres, including water supply in Faisalabad.[29] In a recent summary of the lessons for working with communities taken from the experiences of the Orangi Pilot Project's Research and Training Institute, Arif Hasan's first point emphasizes the role of community organization in increasing the government's capacity:

Capacity and capability of government institutions can never be successfully built without pressure from organized and knowledgeable groups at the grassroots. Such groups can only be created by activists, who have to be identified, trained and supported financially. Formally trained professionals and technicians are not an alternative to such activists. The formation of such groups forces transparency in the functioning of government agencies.[30]

Thus, where many policy documents on community participation emphasize the need for governments to strengthen the capacity of communities (so as to enable them to participate), Hasan emphasizes the need for communities to become better organized in order to increase government capacities.

In practice, grassroots strategies must be rooted in local politics. Experiences in Pakistan cannot simply be applied to other urban settings, even where poverty is equally pervasive and water supplies are clearly inadequate. Just as the physical context heavily influences which conservation and health measures are appropriate, and the economic context heavily influences which pricing and market measures are appropriate, so the political context heavily influences which sorts of grassroots measures are likely to be appropriate. The claim that community organization must be created by activists, who have to be identified, trained and supported financially, for example, is based on political assumptions that may not always apply. On the other hand, the importance of organized and knowledgeable community groups for the effective functioning of government institutions is likely to be more widely applicable, and formally trained professionals and engineers will rarely have either the capacity or inclination to engage in community activism.

Poorly organized communities – and especially their more vulnerable members – are inherently at a disadvantage when natural water sources are scarce and degraded and individual water connections are not being provided. A lack of good governance, unresponsive public authorities, private monopolists, tenure insecurity, ethnic conflict and a range of other inter-related conditions very common in low-income settlements can easily compound this disadvantage. However, the manner in which communities are organized can also make a major difference, again particularly for vulnerable groups. If, for example, communities are organized in a way that allows a small number of powerful individuals to monopolize water or sanitation facilities, problems are almost certain to arise.

Advocates of privatization sometimes argue that by privatizing public utilities, water can be depoliticized, and in effect supplied like most other marketed commodities. As indicated in Chapter 5, there is little evidence for this, in relation to either international, national, city-wide or community politics. Indeed, both large water concessions and informal water vending are almost always politicized, and well organized communities are likely to be in a far better position to turn these politics to their advantage.

Early in the recent wave of privatization, the Buenos Aires water concession was often held up as a successful example, largely on the grounds of efficiency improvement. It was not especially successful in providing water to low-income areas.[31] Moreover, particularly in areas where tenure conflicts arise – and a large share of the urban poor live – provision remained inherently politicized, since the company was under no contractual obligation to provide water to unauthorized settlements, and without government support was unwilling to entertain their requests for water provision. When the private utility, Aguas Argentinas, did begin to extend water to low-income areas, this was done at the instigation of community groups (and an NGO), and only after the local government also lent its support.[32] While the manner in which these communities were organized may have been far from ideal, it did provide the impetus for improvement.

In low-income settlements where private vendors provide most of the water, community organization can also make a critical difference. In Kibera, the largest squatter settlement in Nairobi, privately owned water kiosks that get their water from the piped system provide a large share of the water.[33] The kiosks provide an important service, but also charge high prices, especially during periods of scarcity. Again, the situation is politically charged. A CBO supplying water in part of Kibera reportedly charges both lower and more stable prices. When a large water improvement project was initiated with international funding, some local stakeholders proposed that an association of water vendors be created to help ensure equitable and competitive water pricing (though some residents were concerned that any measures that might seriously reduce water-related profits could lead to retribution). Unfortunately, the project was stopped without consultation, or even much explanation, resulting in considerable disillusionment.

Even more than with the other approaches to DSM, the success of a grassroots approach is also likely to depend on who the demand-side managers are and where they are located institutionally: in a water utility, a government department, an NGO, a CBO or some combination.

A DSM group in a water and sanitation utility is unlikely to be competent in grassroots organizing, and would not want to mobilize communities to make costly water or sanitation-related demands on its own utility. At a minimum, however, it could consult with community groups regarding the type of service they would like, where the pipes are to be laid, where public water taps or latrines are to be located, the options for cost-recovery, and how the utility should relate to intermediaries (eg, vendors) that purchase water from the piped system. It could likewise make it easier for communities to organize around shared cost systems, whereby local residents, the utility and perhaps local government all make a contribution to extending water and sanitation services. It could also work with community groups to resolve some of the problems that utilities often encounter in low-income communities, including violence towards company employees, non-payment of bills and vandalism. And at the same time, it could actively respond to the problems that communities often encounter with the utilities, including inflexible regulations, prohibitions on water redistribution and extra-official charges. In some circumstances it may be easier for a utility to work with a well organized community group than with individual households even if, as noted above, this may lead to greater demands on the part of the communities.

Whether the utility is public or private can also make a difference, though this difference should not be exaggerated. Two purported strengths of private utilities are efficiency and political neutrality. Two purported strengths of public utilities are a concern for the public interest and political accountability. In practice, however, even private utilities must be regulated well if they are to operate efficiently, and as noted above privatization need not depoliticize water provision. Alternatively, public utilities are not inherently concerned with the public interest or politically accountable, and indeed are increasingly asked to become more commercial in orientation. Ultimately, the extent to which a utility can contribute to community-driven DSM must be determined locally, not in the abstract.

Combining demand-side strategies and serving the urban poor

The different approaches to DSM are summarized in Table 6.2. They are united primarily by their common aversion to the supply-fix approach to water problems. According to the conservationist, unless the technical opportunities to save water are implemented, water resources will be over-exploited (and capital will be invested in unnecessary infrastructure). According to the hygiene specialist, unless opportunities to use water and sanitation facilities more hygienically are seized, the health benefits of water and sanitation will not be realized (leading to unnecessary ill-health and hardship, especially in low-income areas). According to the market economist, the supply-fix approach has led to the underpricing of water (with the attendant misallocation of scarce water and resource depletion) and water systems that are unresponsive to the demands of individual users. And according to the grassroots activist, the failure to engage constructively with deprived groups has led to water and sanitation provisioning that is ill-suited to the needs of poor communities.

At least superficially, both the conservation and hygiene approaches to DSM have tended to be expert-driven. Thus, a key justification for DSM for conservation is that users are often unaware of how they could save water, while a key justification for hygiene interventions is that users are unaware of the health consequences of different water and

Table 6.2 Comparing different approaches to demand-side water management in the household sector

	The conservation argument	The hygiene argument	The marginal cost pricing argument*	The community action argument
Guiding concern	Water stress is a growing problem in most parts of the world, due to excessive water consumption	Water- and sanitation-related diseases still constitute a large share of the global burden of disease	Water is a scarce commodity, with an economic value in numerous alternative uses	Adequate water and sanitation is a basic need, without which people cannot live healthy and fulfilling lives
Key insight	There are numerous unexploited opportunities for saving water without reducing the services that water provides	Achieving health depends on how water and sanitation facilities are used as well as how much water (of adequate quality) is provided and whether sanitation facilities are available	Piped water is typically priced well below its (marginal) economic value	Disorganized (poor) communities are at a disadvantage in both addressing their own water and sanitation needs and negotiating with outsiders
Contributory factors	Householders using piped water often cannot tell how much of their water is going to which purposes, are not aware when they are wasting water, and do not have the means of judging water-conserving technologies	Householders cannot discern the health consequences of their water and sanitation practices, and often rely on social norms which, especially in crowded and generally hazardous living environments, may be unhealthy	Water is often treated as a social good, with provision organized as a non-commercial enterprise. Even commercial providers rarely bear the full (marginal) costs of water withdrawal and in any case do not operate in a competitive market	Water and sanitation utilities are not responsive to the needs and demands of low-income communities, especially if they are located in informal settlements. Local organization is often suppressed for political reasons
Demand-side consequences	Users are unaware and unconcerned about water conservation, and waste water unnecessarily	Users often fail to adopt safe water and sanitation practices, and do not achieve the potential health benefits even when they receive piped water	Consumers over-use water, either leading to resource problems and/or depriving others of valuable water	Residents receive inappropriate or inadequate water and sanitation services, or must rely on informal and often costly and inadequate water sources
Recommendation	Conservation education and promotion should become an integral part of piped water provision	Hygiene education and promotion should become an integral part of water provision	Piped water pricing should be based on long-run marginal costs, giving users the incentive to manage their own demand efficiently	Poor communities should mobilize (or be mobilized) around local water and sanitation issues, and providers should be responsive to community as well as individual demands

Note: * This column concentrates on the economic arguments for marginal cost pricing, and ignores the economic arguments more specific to low-income communities. It also ignores the potential supply-side consequences of under-pricing, including a lack of revenues for expansion.
Source: Adapted from McGranahan, G (2002), 'Demand-side water strategies for the urban poor', *Poverty, Inequality and Environment Series No 4*, International Institute for Environment and Development, London.

sanitation practices. In both cases, the dominant response has been to have experts identify opportunities for improvement, and then try to develop programmes to ensure that these improvements are implemented. By and large, cultural beliefs and practices are seen as obstacles to overcome. This took an extreme form in the early decades of the sanitary movement, but it remains a tendency in many hygiene and conservation programmes today.

The market-economic and grassroots approaches aspire to be user-driven, and conform to market and voluntary action approaches to water and sanitation provision. As noted in the section on urban DSM for economic efficiency, one of the most common assumptions of market economics is that individual users are in the best position to judge the value of water (and other goods), while the literature on participation and community action typically assumes that community groups are in the best position to articulate the needs of local residents. This clearly emerges in relation to DSM, with market economics focusing on individual (or household units) responding to prices, and the community action approach focusing on groups and collective action and negotiation.

In terms of physical priorities, the conservation and market-economic perspectives tend to emphasize the dangers of over-use and abuse, while the hygiene and grassroots approaches tend to emphasize the benefits of adequate and appropriate provision. This emphasis is inherent in the conservation and hygiene approaches, and somewhat contingent in the market-economic and grass-roots approaches. The logic of market economics, for example, can be used to make a case for low water prices in areas where public health is threatened by inadequate access to water, even if arguments for marginal cost pricing currently dominate, at least in policy arenas. Similarly, while the logic of collective action has been applied here to the community level, where environmental health problems tend to be central, it could also be applied to resource issues that arise at the watershed level. As presented here, the demand-side emphasis of the conservation and

market economic perspectives is on water, while the hygiene and grassroots perspectives extend to sanitation. Again, this is more related to the demand-side issues currently being debated than to any inherent bias: there are also conservation and economic issues relating to sanitation.

Despite all of their differences, it is possible to view these perspectives as supporting complementary rather than contradictory approaches to DSM. Serious contradictions arise primarily when one or other approach is taken to be *the* approach to DSM. Efforts to promote conservation, environmental health, market mechanisms or community participation are often grounded in simple, expansive narratives that leave little room for alternative perspectives. It is easy to mistake contradictions between these narratives for inherent conflicts between different demand-side processes and actions. At the local level, there are issues of institutional fitness and coordination – there is unlikely to be a single institution capable of implementing all the different forms of DSM – but this is precisely the sort of challenge IWRM is meant to address.

Different cities have different water conditions, institutions and political and economic settings. In any particular city, some or all of the arguments may not apply. The fact that supply-side approaches have often been adopted uncritically is no excuse for adopting demand-side approaches equally uncritically. Moreover, while a paradigm shift may indeed be required in order to remove a longstanding bias towards supply-side solutions, it is important to recognize that any new paradigm will have its own political and ideological content, which may be suitable in one part of the world and destructive in another. Indeed, the danger that the environmentalist paradigm that has generated much of the concern about a forthcoming 'global water crisis' is undermining the case for providing water to the urban poor has been a recurrent theme in this report.

The principal focus of this chapter has been the potential of demand-side approaches for water and sanitation management in poor urban neighbourhoods, where supply-side measures have often failed. In these neighbourhoods the main challenge is usually to get more water and better sanitation facilities to local residents, not to protect regional water resources. As indicated in the previous section, conservationists, health specialists, economists and grassroots activists all make convincing arguments for giving the demand-side more attention in urban water (and sanitation) management. Generally, the arguments of health specialists and grassroots activists are of more immediate relevance in most low-income contexts. Indeed, a narrow focus on ensuring that water prices reflect the full marginal cost of water, or on conserving water so as to protect raw water resources, could be detrimental to the welfare of urban poor groups. On the other hand, there are important insights in the conventional economic and conservation perspectives that should not be dismissed.

Even within a single city it is technically possible to get more water and better sanitation facilities to the urban poor, while also introducing water saving and waste recycling measures where wastage is a serious problem. Similarly, it is organizationally possible for communities to take more control of their own water and sanitation services, even as prices and markets are being reformed to serve conservation efficiency and public health goals. Indeed, if the alternative approaches could be combined effectively, water conservation in one part of the system could mean more water for the urban poor, hygiene education could help residents use water more efficiently, and better organized communities might even press for economically efficient price reforms.

There are also likely to be measures that can help provide a better basis for DSM generally. Housing insecurity and legal and political systems ill-suited to the needs of the informal city work against all forms of demand management in low-income settlements. Local residents do not trust outsiders, even those claiming to be working for their benefit, and better local organization is often perceived by the government as a threat rather than part of a solution. Under such conditions, the more technocratic approaches to DSM are unlikely

to make much headway on their own, and the politics of water and sanitation provision are highly dependent on the broader political setting. (This should not be taken to imply that improvements must await political improvement – in some circumstances, water system improvements in particular can help signal or cement political shifts.)

There are, in any case, conflicting priorities within DSM, as well as within the water and sanitation sector generally. The compromises that emerge are often based on very blunt approaches to DSM, and do not serve any of the interests represented in the declared goals. The classic example is water pricing, where the trade-off has conventionally been perceived to be between higher prices for water conservation and subsidized prices to keep water affordable for the poor. A typical compromise in low-income cities has been low water prices but minimal subsidies, leading to low water prices for the more affluent residents and scarce (and hence costly) water for the poor. Somewhat similar compromises can arise in relation to sanitation. Alternatively, in compromising over the extent to which local communities participate in water and sanitation initiatives, it is not uncommon for residents to be consulted and for their views to be subsequently ignored, adding to their frustrations and mistrust rather than their empowerment.

In short, sound DSM cannot replace water and sanitation politics, but can improve the basis for water and sanitation politics. Each individual approach to DSM contains part of the means for improving certain aspects of urban water and sanitation systems – as long as they are not interpreted dogmatically. By combining the different approaches, there is the potential for adapting DSM to diverse settings, and incorporating a concern for the urban poor as well as for the broader public and future generations. Moreover, by combining forces in the international arena, where water and sanitation policies and agendas are currently being debated, the potential for overcoming the deficiencies of the supply-fix approach could be greatly increased.

Notes and references

1.   Integrated water resource planning, sustainable water management and various other terms have been used to refer to approaches that would be considered integrated water resource management in the context of this discussion.

2.   GWP-TAC (Global Water Partnership – Technical Advisory Committee) (2000), *Integrated Water Resources Management*, TAC Background Papers No 4, Global Water Partnership, Stockholm, Sweden.

3.   Beecher, J A (1998), 'Integrated water supply and water demand management', in D D Baumann, J J Boland and W M Hanemann (eds), *Urban Water Demand Management and Planning*, McGraw-Hill, New York, pages 303–327.

4.   See Landell-Mills, N and I T Porras (2002), *Silver Bullet or Fools' Gold*, International Institute for Environment and Development, London; and Pagiola, S, J Bishop and N Landell-Mills (eds) (2002), *Selling Forest Environmental Services*, Earthscan, London.

5.   This section draws on McGranahan, G (2002), *Demand-side Water Strategies and the Urban Poor*, International Institute for Environment and Development, London.

6.   Gleick, P H (2000), 'The changing water paradigm: a look at twenty-first century water resources development', *Water International*, Vol 25, No 1, pages 127–138.

7.   Page 8 of Baumann, D D and J J Boland (1998), 'The case for managing urban water', in D D Baumann, J J Boland and W M Hanemann (eds), *Urban Water Demand Management and Planning*, McGraw-Hill, New York, pages 1–30.

8.   These stages are based on Opitz, E M and B Dziegielewski (1998), 'Demand management planning methods', in D D Baumann, J J Boland and W M Hanemann (eds), *Urban Water Demand Management and Planning*, McGraw-Hill, New York, pages 1–30.

9.   UN-HABITAT (2001), *Water Education in African Cities*, Report of an Expert Group Meeting held in Johannesburg, South Africa, 30 April.

10. Mujwahuzi, M R (2002), 'Community-based water resources management' in Hirji, R, P Maro and T Matiza Chiuta (eds), *Defining and Mainstreaming Environmental Sustainability in Water Resources Management in Southern Africa*, SADC, IUCN, SARDC, World Bank, Maseru/Harare/Washington, DC, page 255.

11. The Water Education Initiative is being implemented in six cities, namely: Abidjan (Côte d'Ivoire), Accra (Ghana), Addis Ababa (Ethiopia), Dakar (Senegal), Lusaka (Zambia) and Nairobi (Kenya).

12. This section is an edited version of a paper by James Ohayo.

13. WELL (1998), *Guidance Manual on Water Supply and Sanitation Programmes*, Department for International Development, London.

14. Cairncross, S (1990), 'Water supply and the urban poor', in J E Hardoy, S Cairncross and D Satterthwaite (eds), *The Poor Die Young*, Earthscan, London, pages 109–126.

15. See Conclusions and Recommendations of the International Water Management Institute – Resource Centre for Urban Agriculture and Forestry E-conference on Agricultural Use of Untreated Urban Wastewater in Low Income Countires, 24 June–5 July 2002: www.ruaf.org/conference/wastewater/.

16. The World Bank Water and Sanitation Programme, the London School of Hygiene and Tropical Medicine and the private sector, along with various other collaborators, have established a Global Public–Private Partnership to Promote Handwashing with Soap, and initiated pilot projects in Ghana and Kerala in 2001.

17. Johnstone, N and L Wood (2001), *Private Firms and Public Water: Realising Social and Environmental Objectives in Developing Countries*, Edward Elgar, Cheltenham.

18. In the water sector literature, price controls are often mislabelled 'subsidies'. A water subsidy is a financial transfer, typically to a water utility, designated as funding water supplies. Price controls set the price of water. In theory, price controls can be matched by subsidies, allowing the utility to meet demand at a reduced water price. If such subsidies are guaranteed, they should help to attract complementary private finance (though they may be difficult to justify for other reasons). Many of the water sector problems typically ascribed to subsidies are actually the result of price controls that are not accompanied by matching subsidies.

19. See Kjellén, M, A Bratt and G McGranahan (1996), *Water Supply and Sanitation in Low and Middle Income Cities: Comparing Accra, Jakarta and São Paulo*, Stockholm Environment Institute, Stockholm; and Swyngedouw, E A (1995), 'The contradictions of urban water provision: a study of Guayaquil, Ecuador', *Third World Planning Review*, Vol 17, No 4, pp 387–405.

20. Surjadi, C, L Padhmasutra, D Wahyuningsih, G McGranahan and M Kjellén (1994), *Household Environmental Problems in Jakarta*, Stockholm Environment Institute, Stockholm.

21. Crane, R (1994), 'Water markets, market reform and the urban poor: results from Jakarta, Indonesia', *World Development*, Vol 22, No 1, pages 71–83.

22. Dasgupta, P (1993), *An Inquiry into Well-being and Destitution*, Oxford University Press, Oxford.

23. Cairncross, S and R G Feachem (1993), *Environmental Health Engineering in the Tropics: An Introductory Text* (second edition), John Wiley & Sons, Chichester.

24. A simpler version sometimes proposed as a means for meeting cost-recovery and marginal cost pricing goals is a two-block structure with the second block priced at the marginal cost, and the first block designed to ensure that the utility breaks even. As long as all consumers face the marginal cost for some of their water consumption, the efficiency properties of marginal cost pricing are retained. In practice, even this is usually impossible to achieve, given the wide variety of consumption patterns.

25. This information was supplied by Rupa Mukerji from Taru Leading Edge; this came out of their work in Sinclair Knight Merz and Egis Consulting Australia in association with Brisbane City Enterprises and Feedback HSSI – STUP Consultants – Taru Leading Edge (2002), *Bangalore Water Supply and Environmental Sanitation Masterplan Project; Overview Report on Services to Urban Poor Stage 2*, AusAid, Canberra.

26. Boland, J J and Whittington, D (2000), 'The political economy of increasing block tariffs in developing countries: increasing block tariffs versus uniform price with rebate', in A Dinar (ed), *The Political Economy of Water Pricing Reforms*, Oxford University Press, New York, pages 215–236.

27. Caplan, K, S Heap, A Nicol, J Plummer, S Simpson and J Weiser (2001), *Flexibility by Design: Lessons from Multi-sector Partnerships in Water and Sanitation Projects*, BPD Water and Sanitation Cluster, London.

28. Hasan, A (1990), 'Development through partnership: the Orangi project in Karachi', in D Cadman and G Payne (eds), *The Living City: Towards a Sustainable Future*, Routledge, London, pages 221–226.

29. Alimuddin, S, A Hasan and A Sadiq (2002), *The Work of the Anjuman Samaji Behbood and the Larger Faisalabad Context*, International Institute for Environment and Development, London.

30. Hasan, A (2001), *Working with Communities*, City Press, Karachi.

31. Loftus, A J and D A McDonald (2001), 'Of liquid dreams: a political ecology of water privatization in Buenos Aires', *Environment and Urbanization*, Vol 13, No 2, pages 179–199.

32. Schusterman, R, F Almansi, A Hardoy, G McGranahan, I Oliverio, R Rozensztejn and G Urquiza (2002), *Public Private Partnerships and the Poor: Experiences with Water Provision in Four Low-income Barrios in Buenos Aires*, WEDC, Loughborough University, Loughborough.

33. Katui-Katua, M and G McGranahan (2002), *Public Private Partnerships and the Poor: Small Enterprises and Water Provision in Kibera, Nairobi*, WEDC, Loughborough University, Loughborough.

Governance for Good Water and Sanitation Provision: Getting the Best Out of Public, Private and Community Organizations

 Introduction

Local governance for water and sanitation must address the needs of low-income groups. It must seek the most appropriate way to achieve this, and this will be much influenced by local circumstances including local resource availabilities and local capacities (within government and civil society). Otherwise, the internationally agreed upon targets for water and sanitation will not be met. This may sound like a plea for high-cost public sector piped provision to each home, but low-income households also want reliable, sustainable systems, and high-cost systems that fail to generate the revenues needed to maintain them are not sustainable and are rarely reliable. Low-income groups also know that if there are water shortages in a network, their settlements are likely to be the ones that get cut off or get restricted supplies. They have a strong interest in well managed, well financed, well maintained systems. They also have the least resources to help them to manage when centralized water supply, sanitation or drainage systems break down.

Thus, what is sought is urban governments that get the best out of the public, private and community organizations within their jurisdiction. In some places, a water and sanitation system managed by a private company under contract to the local government may be the most appropriate solution; in others, there is a need for partnerships between public utilities and resident committees or community organizations. The examples given in this chapter are not replicable models of how to intervene, but

illustrations of how local solutions were developed to fit local circumstances.

 The role of city governments

The involvement of government institutions in water and sanitation in any city or smaller urban centre is both simple and complex. Simple because its goals are simple – to ensure adequate and sustainable water and sanitation provision for all. Complex because this requires not only complex and expensive infrastructure (water collection, treatment and distribution; wastewater collection, treatment and disposal) and mechanisms for quality control, but also coordination across many sectors (in which the cooperation of the roads, town planning and building control departments are particularly important) and cooperation from users (households, industries and other businesses, public institutions), including the willingness to pay. It obviously requires a financial system from which to draw funds for investment, and a revenue-generating system to allow it to cover its costs. Where formal private sector institutions have a role, it also requires institutions capable of encouraging their involvement, setting appropriate conditions and regulating their performance.

Adequate water and sanitation provision usually requires coordination between different local governments, as most cities' water supplies draw on water catchments outside their boundaries while the wastewaters flow into other jurisdictions. Ensuring adequate water and sanitation provision is also complex because within each locality, the institutional structure has to be developed to ensure this is achieved in ways that are accountable to local populations and that fit within other government institutions and tasks. It is also complex because of what is required upstream and downstream: water and sanitation require a good quality, protected, sustainable water supply at one end and a system to manage the wastewater (and human wastes) at the other end. Good water management locally requires the support of institutions at higher levels of government and appropriate legal frameworks and financial mechanisms.

From a water management perspective, very few cities develop guided by careful water and wastewater management. For cities that today have good water supplies and wastewater management, this was not a feature of the city's original growth but something that developed in response to the water and waste problems generated by growth. All cities grow beside or on top of a convenient water source but this does not imply that measures are taken to manage it or safeguard its quality or continuity. The very poor quality water and sanitation provision in so many cities and smaller urban centres in low- and middle-income nations was made apparent in Chapter 1 – but it was as bad in London or New York (or any urban centre in Europe and North America) only 150 years ago, and the risk of dying from water-related diseases was much greater then, because health care was extremely poor and people had little idea of what was causing these diseases. In these cities then, as in many cities today, city authorities gave little attention to water, so long as water scarcity was not constraining growth, and businesses, government offices and households did not protest.

The process by which water is obtained and wastewater disposed of in a rapidly growing city is often chaotic and poorly managed, as each business seeks the cheapest source of water, even if this means depleting groundwater sources or over-using or mismanaging surface water sources. Each business also seeks the most convenient (and cheapest) means to dispose of wastewaters –

which often means that their wastewaters contaminate water sources for their neighbours or for other groundwater users, or for those downstream. Households may also have little option but to contribute to land and water pollution for their neighbours, especially those that have no provision for drains to remove wastewater and no convenient provision for toilets, which means that they defecate in the open.

In general, the larger a city and its industrial base, the more complex water management becomes.[1] It involves not only ensuring a regular supply of good quality water for all households and businesses and the convenient removal of wastewater, but also giving attention to pollution control (especially from industries), the sustainable use of water sources (especially as city growth usually involves very rapid increases in water use) and wastewater management (including ensuring the safe disposal of human excreta and flood prevention). Wastewater management becomes all the more important if use is made of the wastewater – for instance, by farmers or by households for whom this is the most convenient and cheap source of water for household uses or urban agriculture (see Box 7.1). The importance of ensuring good water quality in rivers, lakes and beaches used for recreation, and of limiting ecological damage to the water bodies that receive wastewater and storm and surface run-off, has added considerably to the tasks of the responsible authorities. These tasks are also made more complex where the volume of wastewaters are particularly high or vary in volume – for instance, in cities with high rainfalls, especially when these are concentrated in short bursts. All these tasks require trained personnel and funding, and systems to collect charges from users. There must be systems to ensure accountability and transparency, control corruption and ensure that planning is based on local realities and local demands. And inevitably, there are the particular difficulties facing local authorities in cities with rapidly growing populations, or urban centres with weak economies and limited possibilities of raising funds for water management.

Box 7.1 The use of untreated urban wastewater in agriculture in low-income nations

The use of urban wastewater in agriculture is a widely established practice, especially in urban and peri-urban areas in arid or seasonally arid zones. Wastewater is also used to provide irrigation water, plant nutrients and trace elements, allowing farmers to reduce or even eliminate the purchase of chemical fertilizers. The importance of urban agriculture in the food supplies of cities and smaller urban centres and in the livelihoods of low-income urban dwellers is often not recognized by governments and international agencies.

Using untreated wastewater poses serious public health risks, as sewage has disease-causing agents from human excreta, including bacteria, viruses, protozoa and helminths (intestinal worms) that can cause human infection. Wastewater may also contain poisonous chemicals from industrial sources as well as

hazardous materials from hospital waste. Unregulated and continuous irrigation with sewage water may lead to problems such as soil structure deterioration, salination and phytotoxicity. These risks are not limited to 'official' wastewater and often apply to rivers and other water bodies.

The ideal solution is to ensure the full treatment of wastewater before use, to World Health Organization guidelines. But in practice, in most cities in low-income nations, there is not the capacity to treat more than a modest proportion of the wastewater produced. The rapid and unplanned growth of cities with multiple and dispersed wastewater sources makes wastewater management more complex.

However, it is possible to reduce the health risks associated with the use of untreated, partially treated or diluted wastewater in agriculture.

Rather than focusing on the end-of-pipe treatment of wastewater, one can focus on proper health risk management by the users of the untreated or partially treated wastewater, and strategies to prevent and reduce the industrial pollution of domestic sewage and of water and rivers that are used for irrigation. These include measures such as cropping restrictions, blending wastewater with fresh water, appropriate irrigation techniques, primary stabilization of other low-cost alternatives and pollution source management.

Source: This draws on the conclusions and recommendations that arose from an e-mail conference organized by the Resource Centre on Urban Agriculture and the International Water Management Institute on Agricultural Use of Untreated Urban Wastewater in Low-income Countries, held between 24 June and 5 July 2002. For more details, see www.ruaf.org and www.iwmi.org.

Few city governments in low- and middle-income nations can hope for anything like an ideal water and sanitation system. This means that difficult decisions and priorities must be negotiated, often using legal instruments, standards and institutional arrangements that are ill-suited to the changing local circumstances. Industries argue that strict pollution standards would drive them to bankruptcy. Downstream users argue that pollution is destroying their livelihoods. Households argue that curbing their use of wells or evicting them from water-sensitive locations would deprive them of their basic needs. Environmentalists point to declining water tables and the high costs of inappropriate settlement patterns. The water and sanitation utilities claim that they need more finance (or higher tariffs) to achieve the goals set for them. Critics argue that the utilities should not receive more finance (or be allowed higher tariffs) until they are reformed. Steering through the myriad of claims and counterclaims, it is rarely possible to fall back on unambiguous rules, procedures or precedents. But unless the government structures

provide an equitable basis for the negotiation and enforcement of regulations and agreements, it is likely to be the most deprived residents in the present, and water resources for future generations, that suffer.

In today's high-income nations and some middle-income nations, over time, cities acquired government structures that greatly improved water supply, sanitation and drainage (and all the national or provincial laws and financial systems to support this). In cities in high-income nations, it is taken for granted that there is a 24-hour water supply piped into each home or business that can be used for drinking as well as other tasks, and hygienic, easily cleaned toilets available to all (including one or more in each house or flat). If anyone falls seriously ill or dies because of contaminants in the water system, it is a scandal that gets widespread coverage in the press. Yet it was little more than 100 years ago that this began to be accepted as part of any city's water management. There are many examples of good water and sanitation provision in cities that go back 2000 or more years.

but these only served a small proportion of a city's population. Only in the late 19th century did it become accepted that all city dwellers should have safe, piped supplies and good sanitation, and only then did the necessary government structures develop.[2]

This acceptance by governments that everyone should have safe, sufficient water and provision for sanitation (in urban and rural areas) seems universal. In 1976, at the UN Conference on Human Settlements (Habitat), 132 governments formally committed themselves to a recommendation stating that 'safe water supply and hygienic disposal should receive priority with a view to achieving measurable qualitative and quantitative targets serving all the population by a certain date.'[3] In 1977, at the UN Water Conference, governments agreed that national plans should aim to provide safe drinking water and basic sanitation to all by 1990 if possible. But Chapter 1 showed how far from being met these targets are in urban areas, more than ten years after the target date.

The problem is not a lack of knowledge about how to address these problems – although many city and municipal governments lack personnel who have this knowledge. Knowledge about how to install and maintain piped water supplies and wastewater removal systems for cities has developed over the last 150 years. Over the last 30 years, additional knowledge about how to integrate this with a broader regional concern for sustainable water use (so that the demands on water sources do not deplete groundwater resources or over-tax surface sources) and minimize water pollution has come to light. In well governed cities, there is also careful provision for emergencies or unusual events – including water storage facilities to ensure a continued water supply during times of low rainfall, and sophisticated drainage and water storage systems to guard against floods during storms or periods with abnormally high rainfall. This does not completely eliminate all the risks, as can be seen by the catastrophic floods that occasionally hit large parts of Europe and the USA, and the fact that even wealthy cities can face supply constraints.[4] But systems are in place to ensure supplies

during times of low rainfall and to minimize loss of life when floods strike – and most of those who lose property or suffer damage to their goods are insured.

The root of the problem is that in most cities and smaller urban centres in low and middle-income nations, government structures have not developed to address these problems. National governments may have committed themselves to universal provision (in 1976, in 1977, reaffirmed in the Convention on the Rights of the Child in 1989) but most have not supported the development of local government structures capable of realizing this commitment. And good government for water and sanitation implies not only frameworks to ensure provision, but also regulations to protect water sources and protect and promote health, and revenue-raising to pay for the system's functioning, maintenance and expansion. Chapter 3 pointed to the many factors constraining the development of appropriate government structures, especially where these increase costs and limit choices for politically powerful enterprises and populations. Good water management means charging users for the water and wastewater management services they get. Government institutions must pay their water bills (which they often do not). Good water management (and flood protection) also requires a water-basin-wide perspective, but political or administrative boundaries are not set to serve good water-basin management; in most large cities, there are many different political divisions within the water basin, and local governments are often controlled by various political parties. Politicians may refuse to collaborate with their neighbours in ensuring an ecologically sound and fair regional water management system. In addition, as earlier chapters have described, there are powerful vested interests and money to be made from the lack of good governance for water. Many large water basins also encompass more than one nation, which brings obvious difficulties in regard to good management.

Obviously in low- and many middle-income nations, there are serious difficulties in raising the funds for the major investments needed. The large and fast-growing cities in low-income nations face particularly serious problems, as not only is there a large backlog of households and businesses in need of better provision, but the population and economic base continues to grow rapidly. As earlier chapters have noted, improving provision for sanitation is often more problematic than improving provision for water. But even here, there are many examples of local innovation showing how water and sanitation provision (and wastewater management) can be much improved, sometimes by drawing only on local resources. As the examples given in this and previous chapters show, the last 30 years have produced many innovations that show how good quality – or, at least, far superior – water, sanitation and drainage are financially feasible in low-income cities or areas within cities. Good government for water and sanitation is also about developing the most cost-effective solutions and not taking on unnecessarily large loans to improve water and sanitation provision, impoverishing the local government with debt repayments that it cannot afford.[5]

Inadequate city government generally has two components:

1   weak, under-funded local institutions (including water and sanitation utilities with little or no investment capacity), and weak and often unrepresentative urban government structures; and
2   higher levels of government that are unwilling to allow local institutions the resources and revenue-raising powers they need to become more effective.

Of course, the problem is made much more difficult by the low incomes of hundreds of millions of urban dwellers, yet this in itself is not a good explanation for inadequacies in water and sanitation provision. As Chapter 3 described, it is common for low-income groups to be paying 2–50 times more per litre for water than higher-income groups, because low-income groups have to purchase from vendors while higher-income groups are being under-charged for the water that is piped to their homes. In addition, there are many examples of low-income settlements with good quality water and sanitation provision and full cost-recovery from user charges, or users paying enough towards the overall costs to mean that they become affordable to existing city and municipal authorities. As far as a large section of the under-served urban population is concerned, conventional public utilities may lack the funding to extend piped water and sewer connections to each home; but the funding could be made available to greatly improve provision through community–municipal partnerships, or support for community provision or small-scale providers, or household investment in improved on-site sanitation. Similarly, where water and sanitation provision has been privatized, effective demand in lower-income areas of cities is rarely sufficient to motivate profit-seeking companies to extend good quality water and sanitation provision (although it can often support water supply alone), but there are often intermediate solutions that combine public, private and community investment in ways that greatly improve provision and can recover most or all costs.

The inadequacies in local governments' involvement in water and sanitation are usually part of a broader institutional failure to ensure that citizens' needs are met. What needs to be addressed in the cities and smaller urban centres in most of Africa and Asia and much of Latin America and the Caribbean is the fact that urban centres have developed without the public institutions needed to govern them. In these regions, it is common for between a third and a half of a city's population to live in illegal or informal settlements, which developed with little or no infrastructure in place for piped water, sanitation and drainage.[6] This is a process that has been taking place for decades, as large sections of the growing urban population had to occupy or purchase land illegally to get accommodation. Informal settlements have sprung up wherever lower-income groups had some hope of avoiding eviction; they usually chose to occupy poor quality or dangerous land, such as steep slopes or floodplains, because their homes would have been bulldozed if they had chosen more valuable, better quality, better located sites. Or they purchased land in areas that had been illegally sub-divided by landowners or developers, and that had little or no provision for water, sanitation and drainage. In effect, urban labour markets grew more rapidly than urban government structures – in part because higher levels of government were unwilling to allow urban authorities the revenue-raising powers and resources they needed.

In discussions about improving water and sanitation provision, perhaps too much stress is placed on the need for additional international funding. International funding often comes at a cost, especially if it is a loan that has to be repaid. It may encourage unnecessarily expensive systems. International funding can also shift decision-making away from local arenas, where it is (or should be) accountable to citizens and where it should draw on local resources and expertise. And without improved local governance, additional international resources may bring few benefits to low-income groups and little improvement in overall water management. Too little attention has also been given to developing local capacities to raise funds and tap local finance. However, even if more local funding is mobilized, in many nations, external funding will still be needed to help finance the city- and region-wide systems of pipes and drains that serve neighbourhoods. Neighbourhood water distribution systems generally require water mains from which to draw; neighbourhood sewers and/or drains require larger systems into which to feed. While it is inaccurate to characterize the problems of inadequate water and sanitation provision in cities as problems of inadequate investment alone, there is a need for significant amounts of extra finance, especially in cities and smaller urban centres where government structures have the capacity to make sure it is used well.

From improved government performance to good governance

Good government for water and sanitation can be considered to have four aspects:

1   good administration: being efficient in managing provision, or managing and supervising the companies, corporations or other bodies that are given responsibility for managing provision, and also ensuring that the providers are accountable to clients;

2   economically viable/cost effective: delivering good value services at an affordable price while also ensuring that revenues are sufficient to fund system management and expansion;

3   political support: water and sanitation management must be supported by the appropriate legal, financial and regulatory systems and accountable to an elected political system, while also being protected from political interference; and

4   technical competence: the competence and capacity to deliver good quality services within broader systems that ensure sustainable supplies and good wastewater management.

All four of the aspects outlined in Figure 7.1 are needed. A water utility may have competent administration and technical capacity but might not be allowed to charge a realistic tariff, which then undermines its capacity to maintain the system and expand provision. Or – as is the case in most smaller urban centres and many larger cities in low-income nations – there may be political support but not technical and administrative skills.

Good governance has the same focus, but adds the dimension of government–civil society interaction. Figure 7.2 shows how the elements of good management must be linked to the needs and priorities of citizens. All city dwellers (and businesses) want low prices, but also effective management (for instance, unambiguous bills), technical competence (regular good quality services) and a system that is accountable to democratic pressures (and with systems overseeing it that are accountable to citizens too).

Evaluations of good government centre on the performance of government institutions; evaluations of good governance are broader, because they also evaluate the quality of the relationship between government institutions and civil society – including citizens, community organizations, private enterprises and

Figure 7.1 Management of water and sanitation

Administration (efficiency, transparency, accountability)	Economically viable/ cost effective (low price and good cost-recovery)
Political support (level of accountability within wider system; level of support of or interference with management or prices; appropriate legal, financial and regulatory support)	Technical competence (quality and regularity of services; good management of wider system, eg with water basin)

Source: This is based on a framework suggested by Mario Vásconez from CIUDAD, Ecuador.

scope for neighbourhood-level or district-level initiatives undertaken by community organizations and NGOs. This is a recognition that both good government and good governance are needed if water and sanitation provision is to improve. In wealthier or better managed cities, this kind of direct involvement by citizen organizations with water and sanitation may not be necessary as city governments have the capacity to ensure adequate provision to all homes and households, and are accountable to citizens through representative political systems.

This shift from good government to good governance is not easy for any government institution. It means that government institutions must allow CSOs – especially representative organizations of the urban poor – a greater role in determining policies and projects. To some extent, this reduces the role and influence of elected politicians, which is why many of the innovations described in this chapter were opposed by some local politicians. Participatory budgeting in Brazil is often held up as an example of good governance, and in the cities where it has worked well, it has brought major benefits to low-income groups – but because it shifted power away from elected politicians to CSOs, it was

local NGOs. For cities or smaller urban centres with inadequate water and sanitation provision, good governance provides more scope for civil society involvement, including mechanisms to allow low-income households and their organizations more influence in decisions and resource allocations. It also provides more

Figure 7.2 Elements of good governance for water and sanitation

Management of water and sanitation		Citizen demands and priorities	
Administration (efficiency, transparency, accountability)	Economically viable/ cost effective (low price and good cost-recovery)	Effective management (clear bills, fair management)	Low price
Political support (level of accountability within wider system; level of support of or interference with management or prices; appropriate legal, financial and regulatory support)	Technical competence (quality and regularity of services; good management of wider system, eg with water basin)	Accountable to democratic pressures	Good quality services (regular, good quality service)

Source: This is based on a framework developed by Mario Vásconez from CIUDAD, Ecuador.

opposed by some local politicians.[7] Good governance has to ensure that there are explicit channels through which citizen displeasure can be channelled and responded to; it is easier for city governments to set up mechanisms to elicit citizen views than to act on what they hear.[8] In addition, it may be difficult for city governments to respond to many of the suggestions and requests voiced by their citizens because they require actions that lie outside their responsibilities, and fall within the jurisdiction of national or state/provincial agencies. But city governments that provide for involving their citizens and CSOs in governance get much in return. Suddenly, solutions appear to problems that previously seemed impossible or too expensive. Many of the examples given in this chapter illustrate improvements to water and sanitation provision that neither private not public agencies for water and sanitation could have achieved alone. In few cities in Africa, Asia and Latin America do most of the inhabitants have sufficient incomes to afford conventional water, sanitation and drainage services, whether provided by public or by private utilities.

Towards more effective approaches

This book has stressed how much local circumstances and citizen preferences influence the most effective means of improving provision. This makes it difficult to generalize about more effective approaches to water and wastewater governance when considering all the world's cities and smaller urban centres. Clearly, there is a very urgent need to improve provision for water, sanitation and hygiene in cities in low- and middle-income nations, but there is also a very urgent need to improve provision in small towns and rural areas, too. In most cities, there is a need for government systems that lessen the ecological disruption caused by water withdrawals and wastewater returns, and that make better use of existing water resources. For many, this includes shifts to systems that do not deplete groundwater resources. Most cities also need to invest in disaster avoidance – ie, systems that are better able to avoid flooding during and after

extreme weather events, and to ensure water supplies during periods of low rainfall – as well as disaster preparedness. For most cities, achieving all of these criteria generally necessitates coordinated action across administrative boundaries.

When government systems are weak or ineffective, it is easy for different water and sanitation goals to come into unnecessary conflict. City-wide water scarcity can become an excuse for delaying improvements in water and sanitation provision, even when these improvements would actually require very little water. Similarly, inadequate provision of water and sanitation can become an excuse for costly water withdrawals, even when the water never actually gets to the deprived settlements. As described in Chapter 4, oversimplified accounts of the global water crisis can reinforce the misleading notion that the water and sanitation problems in deprived neighbourhoods reflect city-wide or regional water scarcity, which is never the complete story, and in many cases is simply untrue. Perhaps the only generalization concerning improved water management that is valid across all the cities and smaller urban centres in low- and middle-income nations is the need for good local governance, as the most effective and appropriate solutions are always site-specific. As discussed above, this is more than effective government institutions since the term governance includes not only the political and administrative institutions of government (and their organization and inter-relationships) but also the relationships between government and civil society.[9] Better governance for water and sanitation means that all citizens' water needs are considered, and that the institutions responsible for water and wastewater management are accountable to them – whether they are public, private or community institutions. There is also an obvious need in most cities for a shift to system-wide management in which different sectors, agencies and administrative areas collaborate, and which integrates ecological concerns. This is easy to say, and easily justified. But it is difficult to achieve, especially in cities with weak, ineffective and undemocratic local governments and nations where higher

Box 7.2 Community toilets in Pune and other Indian cities

In Pune, a partnership between the municipal corporation, NGOs and CBOs has built more than 400 community toilet blocks. These have greatly improved sanitation for more than half a million people. They have also demonstrated the potential for municipal–community partnerships to improve conditions for low-income groups, and similar programmes are now being developed in other cities.

Pune has 2.8 million inhabitants, two-fifths of whom live in slums (there are over 500 in the city). Various local government bodies are meant to provide and maintain public toilets in these settlements, but provision is far below what is needed. In addition, in those settlements in which toilet blocks were built, there was no consultation with the inhabitants regarding the location, design and construction, and the agencies responsible for construction and maintenance had little accountability to the communities. The quality of toilet construction (undertaken by contractors) was often poor and the design often inappropriate – for instance, there were limited water supplies or no access to drainage. The municipal staff whose job it was to clean the toilets did not do so, the blocks often fell into disuse, and the space around them became used for open defecation and garbage dumping.

In 1999, Pune's municipal commissioner, Ratnakar Gaikwad, sought to greatly increase the scale of public toilet construction and ensure that more appropriate toilets got built by inviting NGOs to make bids for toilet construction. Between 1988 and 1998, only 22 toilet blocks had been constructed; the new programme planned to build 220 blocks during 1999–2000 and another 220 during 2000–2001. The contracts were not only for building toilets but also for maintenance. One of the NGOs that

received contracts, SPARC, had long had a partnership with two people's organizations, the National Slum Dwellers' Federation and Mahila Milan (a network of slum and pavement women's savings and credit groups). The three institutions had been working in Pune for five years prior to this, supporting a vibrant savings and credit movement among women slum dwellers. Now this alliance became one of the principal contractors and constructed 114 toilet blocks (with a total of more than 2000 adult toilet seats and 500 children's toilet seats). The alliance designed and costed the project, the city provided the capital costs and the communities developed the capacity for management and maintenance.

In many places, the inhabitants were involved in the design and construction of these toilets. Some women community leaders took on contracts themselves and managed the whole construction process, supported by engineers and architects from SPARC. The design of the toilet blocks introduced several innovations. Unlike the previous models, they were bright and well ventilated, with better quality construction (which also made cleaning and maintenance easier). They had large storage tanks to ensure that there was enough water to allow users to wash after defecation and keep the toilets clean. Each toilet block had separate entrances and facilities for men and women. A block of children's toilets were included, in part because children always lose out to adults when there are queues for a toilet (so they often defecate outside because they cannot wait), and in part because many young children are frightened to use conventional latrines. The children's toilets were specially designed for children's use, including such features as smaller squat plates, handles (to

prevent over-balancing when squatting) and no large pit openings. In many toilet blocks, there were also toilets designed for the elderly and the disabled. Toilet blocks also included a room where the caretaker and his or her family could live, which meant that lower wages could be paid for maintenance, thus reducing the running costs. In some toilet blocks, where there was sufficient space, a community hall was built; the small fees charged for its use could also help to cover maintenance costs, and the presence of a community hall right on top of the toilets also puts pressure on the caretaker to keep the complex clean. Despite these innovations, the cost of the toilet blocks was 5 per cent less than the municipal corporation's costing.

This programme was also unusual for India because of its transparency and accountability. There was constant communication between senior government officials and community leaders. Weekly meetings brought all stakeholders together to review progress and identify problems that needed to be addressed. All aspects of costing and financing were publicly available, and the access that community organizers had to senior officials also kept in check the petty corruption that characterizes so many communities' relationships with local government agencies.

The alliance of Mahila Milan, SPARC and the National Slum Dwellers' Federation is also managing a comparable large-scale, community-managed public toilet construction programme in Mumbai.

Source: Burra, Sundar and Sheela Patel (2002), 'Community toilets in Pune and other Indian Cities', PLA Notes 44: Special Issue on Local Government and Participation, IIED, London, pages 43–45; and Asian Coalition for Housing Rights and Slum/Shack Dwellers International (2003), *Community-Driven Water, Sanitation and Infrastructure*, ACHR, Bangkok.

levels of government retain powers and revenues that are needed by local governments.[10]

There are many examples of more effective approaches. They range from sophisticated water-basin-wide water governance systems that incorporate all stakeholders,[11] to simple innovations in individual squatter settlements that reduce water costs while greatly improving access. Several are described below. Their relevance to other cities lies not so much in what was built as in how it was done – how low-income groups developed their own sewers or community-managed toilets, and demonstrated their validity to local governments; how a new technology permitted the emptying of pit latrines in houses without road access in squatter settlements; how a city developed the capacity to use treated wastewater as a response to fresh water shortages; and so on. These examples are better seen as the application of good local governance, as local solutions were developed within particular local contexts, rather than as practices that are transferable to other cities. The community toilets built in Pune and Mumbai that are described in Box 7.2 are obviously not the most appropriate solution for cities where it is possible to provide good quality sanitation to each house or apartment. But what does have wider relevance is the way in which representative organizations of the urban poor, and the local NGOs that work with them, were able to work with local authorities in developing major improvements in sanitation that both the users and the government could afford. This is good local governance (or at least better local governance) in action.

Two different models can be highlighted:

1   Conventional agency model. Conventional formal agencies (public, private or cooperative) providing good quality provision for sanitation and piped water to each building, within broader systems for the good management of water going into the system and wastewater coming out of the system.
2   Support for bottom–up investments. Support for public, small-scale private,

NGO, community and household provision in each neighbourhood because of the incapacity of conventional formal agencies. Among local governments, there is a recognition of their limitations in being able to provide conventional city-wide solutions (or provide the environment for formal private sector providers to do so), so pragmatic support is given to initiatives within each neighbourhood to ensure adequate provision. Thus, particular neighbourhoods can draw from their own local water source (a tubewell, a river) and develop their own water supply distribution systems. Where incomes are very low, solutions are developed that represent the best compromise between cost and cost-recovery. Although water piped to each home or yard remains the best solution from a public health perspective (and is much preferred by virtually all households), it is unrealistic to suggest that this can be afforded in many cities and most smaller urban centres in low- and middle-income nations. Here, the goal is a regular, safe, affordable supply within easy reach of all households. This must be more comprehensive than the most common 'solution' – 250–500 persons per standpipe, and water supply systems that are irregular and often of poor quality. For sanitation, in most instances, support will be provided for households to develop their own toilets, although attention will be given to supporting good design and construction and ensuring good management of human excreta – for instance, through pit latrines supported by efficient and affordable latrine-emptying services, or neighbourhood sewer systems with local provision for treatment or connection to city networks. Small-scale water and sanitation providers can be particularly important within this system. It is worth recalling the point made earlier that the high prices charged by water vendors are usually the result of the difficulties that households and vendors face in getting water. So if all households have reliable

Table 7.1 Addressing the underlying, contributory and proximate causes of inadequate provision for water and sanitation in urban areas

Acting on the underlying causes of inadequate provision	Acting on the contributory causes of inadequate provision at the city or municipal level	Acting on the proximate causes of inadequate provision at the household and neighbourhood level
National and provincial governments providing support for more competent, effective, accountable local governance and financial support for improved provision, especially for less prosperous cities and smaller urban centres*	Good governance in each city and municipality that gets the best out of public, private and community organizations – where necessary, within a water-basin-wide governance system. Civil society institutions at the city level able to represent consumer interests	Reducing the gap between the cost of adequate provision and low-income households' capacity to pay through more efficient provision or innovations in the form of provision
International agencies with a long-term and consistent policy to support the above	Agreements developed between water and sanitation providers and the inhabitants of illegal settlements regarding how best to improve provision	Support for secure tenure for illegal settlements and for improved water and sanitation provision; also, credit to allow households to improve provision in their own homes or afford connection to wider systems; policy that supports low-income households in acquiring land for housing with water and sanitation provision
		Where appropriate, supporting individual, household and community investment in improved provision

Note: * Where urban governments are very weak, this might best be done by a provincial agency.

standpipes within 50 metres of the home and all vendors have easy access to good water sources, water vendor prices will be kept down. Community provision can also be very important both for solutions for each household (as in the sewer systems connected in Karachi supported by Orangi Pilot Project) and for communal facilities (as in the toilets designed, constructed and managed by the community- in Pune and Mumbai, described in Box 7.2).

In some wealthier cities with more competent and accountable governments, the first model may be the most appropriate one as the extension of piped water supplies and sewer connections to all homes by public or private utilities may be possible, within a commitment to better water basin and wastewater management. In water-scarce areas, this can include innovations to keep down water consumption and make good use of wastewater. This has been achieved in many cities in many middle-income nations (and virtually all urban areas in high-income nations), as noted in Chapter 1.

Support from national or provincial governments can help to ensure improved and extended provision in smaller urban centres or cities in less prosperous regions. The lessons of the last 20 years do not invalidate a strong government commitment to improving and extending water and sanitation provision in urban (and rural) areas. But what they do suggest is the need for competent, effective, accountable local government to ensure that it happens in each locality, and more attention to a robust financial base for water and sanitation utilities (which includes the need for efficient provision and realistic pricing). Table 3.1 in Chapter 3, which highlighted the underlying, contributory and proximate causes of inadequate water and sanitation provision, could be re-written to highlight what is needed (see Table 7.1).

Where there is the financial and institutional capacity and willingness to extend piped water and provision for sanitation to each household, special measures may be needed for low-income households or particular low-income settlements. Generalizations as to what should be done are inappropriate in that good local governance systems should work out the best means of achieving this. 'Lifeline' tariffs, which guarantee all connected households a minimum volume of water, or tariff structures that make this minimum volume of water cheaply available, are one possibility – although they are unpopular with water utilities. Another possibility is to have a good quality, easily accessed, well managed, universally available standpipe service in which the price of water is kept down (or no charge is made), and house connections where cost-recovery is sought. Many solutions lie beyond the water and sanitation providers – for instance, in programmes that help low-income households to buy or build their own homes with good water and sanitation provision (as examples given later in this chapter will show). It is often forgotten that one of the most effective ways of improving water and sanitation provision for low-income households is to support their efforts to acquire or build better quality housing with good water and sanitation provision. In many informal settlements, providing secure tenure and protection from flooding can trigger household investments in home improvements, including improved water and sanitation provision.

For many cities and smaller urban centres, the most appropriate approach will be a mix of models 1 and 2. Use will be made of conventional formal agencies (public, private or cooperative) that provide good quality provision for sanitation and piped water – to each building where possible (and where users can afford to pay the full cost of this and are made to do so), or to well managed, convenient public facilities. Support will be provided for public, private, NGO, community and household provision in neighbourhoods where this is not possible, within a long-term goal of extending services from formal agencies to all communities that desire them and have the capacity to pay for them.

The approach outlined in model 2 is the one most likely to deliver improved and extended provision in most cities and smaller urban centres in low-income nations, and in the less prosperous urban areas or urban districts in middle-income nations. The main

difficulty with this approach is that it also requires competent, effective, accountable local government to get the most out of it. However, if such governmental support does not exist, in effect, an ad hoc version of this system develops anyway, as each household, neighbourhood and business seeks its own solution to getting water and getting rid of wastewater. A myriad of formal and informal private enterprises and NGO and community initiatives develop in response to this. The key issue is how much more effective these different initiatives can be if supported by local government. Local government support and coordination can also ensure that many of the disadvantages of this approach can be avoided – for instance, by ensuring provision for wastewater removal and protecting groundwater resources.

Here, the example of the community-managed sewer-construction programme supported by the Pakistan NGO Orangi Pilot Project (OPP) – Research and Training Institute has much relevance.[12] Although this is normally applauded for being a large-scale, community-driven, self-financing solution to sanitation, its main relevance, as stressed by OPP staff, is its potential as a model partnership between communities and local government. Box 7.3 describes what was done. Also, the OPP example has demonstrated that low-income households can afford and will pay for good quality sewers, if prices are kept down (which means keeping down unit costs). If the local water and sanitation utilities are incapable of installing these, then they can concentrate on providing the trunk sewers and drains to which each community-developed neighbourhood system can connect. This can also be done with respect to water, with local water and sanitation utilities providing the water mains from which community organizations can draw, in developing and managing distribution systems.

There are obvious constraints on local governments developing frameworks to support community provision within each neighbourhood. Local engineers will dislike this and distrust the capacity of communities to develop sound technical solutions. Many local politicians may dislike it because they

Box 7.3 Beyond pilot projects: the work of Orangi Pilot Project

Orangi is a low-income settlement extending over 10,000 acres (or 4160 hectares) with some 1.2 million inhabitants. The informal settlement began in 1965, and now most of the 113 settlements within Orangi have been accepted by the government, and land titles have been granted. Most inhabitants built their own houses and none received official help in doing so. There was no public provision for sanitation as the settlement developed; most people used bucket latrines, which were emptied every few days, usually onto the unpaved lanes running between the houses. More affluent households constructed toilets connected to soakpits, but these soakpits filled up after a few years. Some households living near creeks constructed sewerage lines which emptied into the creeks. The effort of getting local government agencies to lay sewerage lines in Orangi was too much for local residents, who felt that these should be provided free. Believing that government should provide, they had little incentive to improve their situation.

A local organization called the Orangi Pilot Project (OPP), established in 1980 by Dr Akhtar Hameed Khan, was sure that if local residents were fully involved, a cheaper, more appropriate sanitation system could be installed. Research undertaken by OPP staff showed that the inhabitants were aware of the consequences of poor sanitation for their health and their property, but they could not afford conventional systems, and they did not have the technical or organizational skills to use alternative options. OPP organized meetings in lanes that comprised 20–25 adjacent houses, explained the benefits of improved sanitation and offered technical assistance. Where agreement was reached among the households in a lane, they elected their own leader who formally applied for technical help. Their site was surveyed, plans drawn up and cost estimates prepared. Local leaders kept their groups informed and collected money to pay for the work. The laying of sewers then proceeded, and the maintenance was also organized by local groups.

OPP's research concentrated on whether the cost of sanitary latrines and sewerage lines could be lowered to the point at which poor households could afford to pay for them. Simplified designs and standardized steel moulds reduced the cost of sanitary latrines and manholes to less than one-quarter of the contractors' rates. The cost of the sewerage line was also greatly reduced by eliminating the profits of the contractor. The average cost of the small-bore sewer system is no more than US$30 per house.

Technological and financial innovations were the easy part. The difficult part was convincing residents that they could and should invest in their own infrastructure, and changing the nature of local organizations so that they responded to these needs. OPP staff had to wait for six months before the inhabitants of one lane were prepared to organize themselves to develop their own sewerage system. Gradually, the residents of other lanes, after seeing the results achieved, also sought OPP's assistance. There were problems in some lanes, and money sometimes went missing or proved to be insufficient. In general, OPP staff stood back from these issues (once they had persuaded the first communities to begin). Once a lane had ensured that the finance was available, they would provide technical assistance only. The first challenge was one that the communities had to realize by themselves.

The scope of the sewer construction programme grew as more local groups approached OPP for technical assistance and the local authorities began to develop the mains into which the sewers could be integrated. The concept of component-sharing between people and government evolved. The inhabitants could finance, manage and maintain the construction of latrines, lane sewers and small secondary sewers (known as internal development), and the government could take responsibility for financing, managing and maintaining the large secondary sewers, trunk sewers and treatment plants (know as external development). To date, nearly 6000 lanes have developed their own sewer systems linked to sanitary pour-flush latrines serving over 90,000 housing units, using their own funds (the equivalent of around US$1.4 million) and under their own management. One indication of the appropriateness of the model developed by OPP is the fact that many lanes have organized and undertaken lane sewerage investments independently of OPP; another is the households' willingness to make the investments needed in maintenance. The main reason why low-income households could afford this is that the work cost one-sixth of what it would have cost if it had been undertaken by the state.

Women were very active in local groups; many were elected group leaders and it was often women who found the funds to pay for the sewers out of household budgets.

OPP understood the need to simultaneously improve technical, financial and organizational options. At the beginning, it was established to provide a pilot scheme for the government. Its experience taught it that the government generally had little interest in what it was trying to do. But as local residents became more interested and involved, so too did their elected representatives, who now found that they were dealing with people who had a good understanding of infrastructure investments. There are now many project-level agreements between OPP, local communities and state agencies. In all of these settlements, the state is doing much more than it was before, although it is working within a model of sanitation that has reduced its responsibilities.

The programme is now being replicated in eight cities in Pakistan by local NGOs, CBOs and local governments, and in 49 other settlements in Karachi by local governments and the government agency responsible for upgrading the informal settlements, the Sindh Katchi Abadi Authority.

Source: Hasan, Arif (1997), *Working with Government: The Story of OPP's Collaboration with State Agencies for Replicating its Low Cost Sanitation Programme*, City Press, Karachi, 269 pages; Orangi Pilot Project–Research and Training Institute (2002), *Katchi Abadis of Karachi: Documentation of Sewerage, Water Supply Lines, Clinics, Schools and Thallas, Volume One: The First Hundred Katchi Abadis Surveyed*, Orangi Pilot Project, Karachi, 507 pages.

like to be seen as the mechanisms for delivering better provision; many local politicians opposed the Orangi model and the community toilets in Mumbai because of this. Local bureaucracies may dislike it because it removes myriad possibilities of bribes (one reason why many local government officials disliked the community toilets described in Box 7.2 is that they removed the informal payments they received from private contractors who had previously built public toilets). Private sector companies and water kiosk operators or vendors will dislike the way it takes business from them. These are all factors that have to be overcome. OPP may now be regarded as a great success, but this was not always so. Early on, it was criticized by international experts for having the wrong approach, and it took many years for it to receive official recognition. Despite its name, OPP is not a 'pilot project' but a 20-year programme through which hundreds of thousands of people in low-income areas have obtained good quality sanitation in Karachi and in other cities in Pakistan.[13] For many years the municipal authorities did not recognize the validity of the approach, and local authorities did not consult OPP staff. But the growing influence of OPP can be seen not only in neighbourhood solutions but in developing city-wide policies and priorities. OPP helped to demonstrate to the provincial government that it did not need to take out a large external loan to improve the trunk sewers because there were much cheaper, more effective ways of doing so.[14] It has also produced the kinds of detailed neighbourhood plans which are needed for improving provision in low-income settlements – in effect, once again demonstrating the capacity of a local NGO to do a task that should ideally be done by local water and sanitation utilities.[15] It has helped to set up the Urban Resource Centre in Karachi to provide information to community groups and link them at city level to put more pressure on local government. In the process, a city-wide water and sanitation network of many city NGOs and CBOs has evolved.

Box 7.4 describes a programme in Luanda to improve water and sanitation provision. This can be considered as an approach rooted in model 2 above. Here, conventional water and sanitation systems serving each household are far too expensive for poor households, and are difficult for local government to organize and finance. A local NGO, Development Workshop–Angola – working with local government – has come up with a pragmatic response to the serious need for improved water and sanitation provision that fits local resource availabilities and institutional capacities. The hope is that, if peace is maintained in Angola and the economy picks up, the capacity to reach everyone in Luanda (and other places) with better water and sanitation provision, and to provide higher levels of provision to those who can afford it, will develop. The programme described in Box 7.4 is, in effect:

> *building local institutions from the bottom–up – and seeking to create trust and working partnerships between community organizations, local governments and the water company, in which each has defined roles and performance standards. But this kind of long-term support for institutional development is not one that most international funding agencies can support. Their support is more for capital investments in time-bound projects. Many external agencies also see privatization as the solution but this would be inappropriate for Luanda with its weak national private sector, public institutions too weak to manage privatization and a large part of the population with incomes too low to be attractive to private enterprises.[16]*

Here too, as in Karachi, the local authorities recognize the potential of a system where the official water companies concentrate on improving bulk water supply, while community organizations are responsible for the distribution and management of local systems.

This chapter has given two examples of the development of local solutions and local institutions that can improve water and sanitation provision in low-income neighbourhoods: the standpipes in Luanda and the lane sewers supported by OPP in different cities in Pakistan. There was also the example of the

Box 7.4 Building water and sanitation provision from the bottom–up in Luanda

Improving water and sanitation provision in Luanda is particularly problematic because:

- the population has grown rapidly, in part due to war which forced people to flee rural areas; Luanda's population has grown from 480,000 in 1970 to around 3.4 million today, in a country which has had more than 40 years of conflict and economic decline;
- for 20 years there has been almost no provision for extending water provision to the peri-urban areas where much of Luanda's population growth has taken place;
- conflict has damaged and inhibited the political and institutional foundations for ensuring basic service provision;
- local governments and the water company lacked the power and resources to address the deficiencies in water and sanitation (although recent reforms aim to make local governments more accountable and effective); and
- incomes among much of the population were too low to allow conventional solutions, yet there was no tradition of community provision (and government agencies were wary of working with community organizations).

Overall, 17 per cent of households report a water connection but only 10 per cent have an indoor water supply. Most of Luanda's population rely on water purchased from tankers, with prices varying from the equivalent of US$4 per cubic metre in an area close to a water company distribution tank to US$20 in an area far away from the river and from any water company connection. The proportion of families with provision for sanitation within their homes is low.

The NGO Development Workshop began work in Angola in 1981, at the invitation of the Angolan government, and initially its work concentrated on providing technical support to the government, working within the Ministry of Construction's Department of Urbanism. It set up a new bureau for the upgrading of *musseques* [peri-urban squatter areas]. In addition, a pilot project (Project Sambizanga) was initiated in one *musseque* which demonstrated two viable approaches to improving provision: community-managed public standpipes and family dry-pit latrines. It also demonstrated how an NGO could support residents' groups in developing and managing these models, and how to involve government organizations (even if they are weak and lacking in funding). It also made clear the need for water supply and sanitation models that could be managed and funded within the community.

From 1995 onwards a larger water programme developed, based on what had been learnt in Project Sambizanga. To date, this has built 200 public standposts in eight of the nine municipal areas of Luanda, each serving around 100 families. When the programme started, there were only ten working standpipes; many had been built at the end of the colonial period and in the early post-colonial period, but were no longer functioning because of the lack of management, protection and maintenance. For each standpipe, Development Workshop sought to develop a partnership between a local elected water committee that managed it, the water company and the local authority. Half the funds collected from users went to the water committee for management and maintenance (and to pay the wages of those who managed it), 30 per cent went to the water company and 20 per cent to the local authority. The community management worked well but it was often difficult to get the necessary support from the local government and the water company. For instance, it was difficult to make sure that the water company supplied water to the standpipe and, inevitably, community support for standpipes waned when there was no regular water supply; a programme is now underway to improve water mains provision. Local governments were often not supportive – for instance, in helping to deal with illegal connections – and, in some places, they took over the water management systems.

The latrine programme supported the construction of 5000 family latrines between 1995 and 2000 focusing on particular geographic areas, with the aim of getting 90 per cent or more of households in an area to invest in them. Mobilizers trained by Development Workshop encouraged and supported families in chosen areas to develop the latrines. The dry-pit latrine was found to be the most appropriate way to improve sanitation in the peri-urban areas – where water has to be carried to the home, so water-based latrines were not appropriate. In addition, dry-pit latrines are cheaper and need less maintenance than water-based toilets with septic tanks. Pour-flush toilets present a hazard, as their effluent generally goes into gullies or is dumped in rubbish lots. Much effort went into developing designs and squat plates that kept down costs and were appropriate to local soil conditions. Families were responsible for digging the pits, lining them (this was usually done by professional masons) and building the cabin. Development Workshop provided the only significant sanitation programme in Luanda during the 1990s for peri-urban areas.

Sustainable basic service provision

The intention of these programmes was to develop robust systems for water and sanitation (there was another programme for solid waste collection) that could work within a rapidly-growing city where much of the population live in self-constructed housing and have very low-incomes, and where local government is very weak. It was clear that low-income households were prepared to pay for water if they got a reliable service and the price was less than that charged by private water vendors. Thus, the challenge was to develop a model that provided such a service at a price people were prepared to pay, and which would cover the cost of the water and the standpost maintenance. There also had to be revenues for the water company, to encourage it to maintain the water supply to the standposts. Water committees were formed to operate the standposts, collect the revenue, ensure that the taps worked and were maintained, keep standposts clean, keep the drainage tube clear, register the number of days of water flow, and ensure that records of all payments and expenses were kept in a cash book. This meant developing community organizations that were accountable to residents, for which there was little precedent. It also meant developing community organizations that could manage finances and deal with conflict (including taking action against illegal connections). Following this, fora were developed through which the different community organizations involved in managing standposts could share their experiences and work together in seeking better services from the water company and from local authorities. The water company recognizes that it does not have the capacity to manage water supply at the community (*barrio*) level, and that it should concentrate on improving bulk water supply (ie, extraction from river, treatment and distribution through water mains).

Source: Cain, Allan, Mary Daly and Paul Robson (2002), *Basic Service Provision for the Urban Poor; The Experience of Development Workshop in Angola*, IIED Working Paper 8 on Poverty Reduction in Urban Areas, IIED, London, 40 pages.

toilets designed, constructed and managed by the communities in Pune and Mumbai, making better use of existing, locally available resources. Earlier chapters gave other examples: Chapter 3 included a description of a programme supported by WaterAid in low-income areas of Dhaka and Chittagong, which centred on providing public standpipes and shared, communal or public toilets. WaterAid-supported programmes in other nations have similar orientations in seeking to improve water and sanitation provision in ways that can be funded by local demand. All these programmes may be criticized for providing too little: why should low-income households not have the best provision supplied by external agencies? But if one provides high-quality systems for low-income households, necessitating large subsidies for each household reached, any available funding quickly gets used up and relatively few households benefit. If one develops a high-quality system in which the costs of provision and management are not covered, and the external subsidy then becomes unavailable, the system cannot work. The importance of these examples is in their potential for allowing much better quality provision to reach very large numbers of low-income urban households, even in cities where incomes are very low and local authorities weak. And no one can suggest that Mumbai, Dhaka, Chittagong, Luanda or Karachi are easy cities in which to develop self-financing, self-sustaining systems within low-income areas.

If model 2 outlined above is recognized as one that is valid for less prosperous urban centres and districts, then it will need different kinds of support. For instance, if it is appropriate to support in situ sanitation in each home (at least where plot size will allow it), support services will be required.[17] If pit latrines are common, they generally need efficient, affordable pit-emptying services; Box 7.5 gives an example of a technology to support this.

It is important to remember that the inhabitants of low-income areas will often want to install one of the lower-cost technologies initially, and then have the option of upgrading as the capacity to pay and the desire for more convenient systems increases.[18] In addition, external professionals must avoid making assumptions about what particular communities need. Community consultation is important for determining the most appropriate intervention in each neighbourhood, and external professionals often under-estimate the amount that low-income households are prepared to pay for good quality water and sanitation provision (for instance, for in-house connections rather than standpipes). In addition, in large and high-density residential areas, the cost of sewer systems per household may be comparable to on-site systems such as pit latrines, and the former will be much preferred by the inhabitants because they take up less space, remove wastewater and do not need emptying. But sewers can also be completely inappropri-

Box 7.5 Urban sanitation micro-enterprises: the UN-HABITAT Vacutug Development Project

In recent years, the problems associated with the disposal of human waste have escalated with the growth of unplanned settlements in urban areas in low- and middle-income countries. In these settlements, there are often more than 100 persons to each pit latrine. Although the latrines are now generally made of modern materials, the problem of renewing them when they become full has proved a difficult challenge. Often the settlements have no road access for disposal tankers, so a novel solution is needed. In association with a private sector engineering company and a Kenyan water NGO, UN-HABITAT has been developing a prototype technology called 'Vacutug'

that can empty latrines. The Vacutug is a 500-litre vacuum tank and pump driven by a small petrol engine mounted on a small cart. It can empty pit latrines or clean drains. The engine can also propel the cart on which it (and the tank) is mounted at speeds of up to 5 kilometres per hour, and the cart is small and manoeuvrable enough to go through the tight turns and narrow paths that characterize many informal settlements. The Vacutug can, on average, empty eight pits per day (the number depends on the distance between the pits and the disposal site). A micro-enterprise that used it earned over US$10,000 over a two-year period and employed four people.

UN-HABITAT have now launched the second phase of the project, expanding the operation and assessing the technology in a number of different conditions in different countries. The Vacutug is seen as a simple but very effective solution and is currently supported by the governments of UK, Ireland and Denmark. The programme is shortly to be expanded to many other cities on a partnership basis, and presents an ideal opportunity to greatly improve health aspects related to excreta disposal, while at the same time generating much-needed income for the urban poor.

Source: UN-HABITAT, *The Vacutug Development Project*, unpublished report, UN-HABITAT, Nairobi.

ate too – for instance, where water supplies are too irregular to allow toilets to be flushed, or in settlements where on-site sanitation is much cheaper and thus more affordable.

Governance for small urban centres

It is also important to evolve policies that support good quality water and sanitation in smaller urban centres – smaller in the sense of their actual size and population, or smaller in regard to their economic and political status within the nation's urban system (which often implies difficulties in getting sufficient resources).[19] Earlier chapters noted how most of the world's urban dwellers live in urban centres with under half a million inhabitants, and this includes a significant proportion in urban centres with fewer than 20,000 inhabitants. In most nations, this means that policies must be appropriate to hundreds (or, in some nations, thousands) of small urban centres, most of which have very weak local authorities and populations with very limited capacities to pay. The limited number of case studies of water and sanitation provision in smaller urban centres in Chapter 1 suggests that most people in such settlements do not

have access to piped supplies – and most of those who do have access to standpipes or water kiosks only. For most households in small urban centres in Africa, Asia and Latin America, provision for sanitation is totally dependent on what households install themselves, as there is no sewer system to which they can connect.[20]

Figure 7.3 is a schematic representation of how water and sanitation provision generally changes as urban centres get larger and wealthier. Of course, the extent to which provision conforms to this figure depends on many local factors, and there are likely to be many exceptions, including examples of good provision in relatively small and poor urban centres, and very inadequate provision in larger, relatively prosperous urban centres. In addition, there are many examples of large cities in low-income nations which are not wealthy and, of course, smaller cities that are.

A review of the issues regarding the sustainable management of water supply systems in small towns in Africa highlighted the great variation between different urban centres in the extent of provision for piped water, and the form that its management took (and could take). Table 7.2 summarizes the main characteristics and where they may

Figure 7.3 Schematic representation of how provision for water and sanitation often varies in smaller urban centres with increasing population and increasing wealth in low- and most middle-income nations

		Increasing number of people served with piped supplies, including growing number of households and businesses connected to piped supplies. Management capacity of water and sanitation agency developed with paid staff; more possibility of expansion based on locally generated revenues. Greater possibilities of sewers and drains construction and expansion of services to support on-site sanitation.
	Piped water supply developing, but most of those served by it reached only by standpipes. Limited capacity for organizations involved to cover costs; they are generally reliant on external funds for investments. No services for sanitation (quality of provision dependent on what households construct and maintain).	
No piped water supplies or, if there are, very small proportion of people have access to them. No services for sanitation (quality of provision dependent on what households construct and maintain for themselves).		

Size of urban centre →

Wealth of urban centre →

prove most appropriate. 'Delegated management' may include local governments delegating responsibility for provision to provincial or state agencies, which is common in smaller urban centres in many nations.

There is no clear distinction between 'villages' and 'small towns', especially since what is considered a small urban centre in one country would be considered a rural village in another. As noted in Chapter 3, a large proportion of the villages in India would be classified as small urban centres in other countries, as they fulfil their 'urban criteria'. Box 7.6 gives an example of a partnership between an NGO, a local government and a private company to improve provision for water in over 700 villages and various small urban centres in India.

Better governance and mechanisms for extending provision to unserved or inadequately served households

There are various mechanisms for improving or extending water and sanitation provision to unserved or inadequately served households. The two most important are slum and squatter upgrading programmes and programmes that support new homes with good water and sanitation provision that are affordable by those currently living in homes with inadequate provision. These are described in more detail below. Of course, there are other mechanisms, including: support for household investment in improved provision (as in the latrine construction programme in Luanda

Table 7.2 Main aspects of different management options for water supplies in small urban centres

	Community management	Municipal management	Delegated management
Ownership of the system	Can be owned by the community or by the (local) government. Ideally owned by the community	System owned by (local) government, normally a municipal water department	System owned by (local) government
Management of the system	By the community. For larger systems a community may employ professional management staff	Mainly by government (direct municipal management, independent public water body or mixed economy model with funds drawn from private sector), although sometimes by private sector or cooperative (eg, with CBO)	By private company or other operator on the basis of a contract
Monitoring	If done at all, normally by the community, but there may be some element of external monitoring (eg, of water quality)	Various branches of government. System monitored by local government or water department. If quality is monitored, then normally done by another branch of government	Remains with (local) government
Regulation	Normally de facto, left to the community. Ideally an independent regulator within the framework of a national strategy	By local government or an independent regulator within the framework of a national strategy	
Operation and maintenance	Either entirely by the community or with some external support (eg, pump mechanic)	By local government, except where under cooperative management. Sometimes with the external support of technical contractors	By the operator who holds the management contract. Operators may do it themselves or with sub-contractors, or with community bodies
Capital works and financing	Normally by an external agency – donor or government	Local government. Funded through either government budgets or through private sector under mixed economy model	Normally remains the responsibility of government
Cost-recovery	Frequently ad hoc. Can successfully cover small repairs but seldom larger repairs, and almost never capital works. Depends on system size and number of users	Through tariffs, water kiosk payments, etc. Under direct municipal management, no separation of water from other parts of the municipal budget; under autonomous municipal management, water run as an autonomous unit	Normally the responsibility of the operator, which is expected to maintain the system and sometimes take a profit from the revenues collected. However, often contains an element of government subsidy, and can remain wholly with government
Most suited to	Rural areas, simple systems, areas where government is weak	Larger towns with strong capacity, large and complex systems, 'wealthy' user base	A range of (urban) situations where operational capacity exists in the private sector and regulatory capacity exists in the public sector
Least suited to	Urban areas, complex systems, areas of resource constraint	Small towns, rural areas, ad hoc settlements where management capacity is weak or non-existent	Rural areas, areas where local government is weak and unable to enforce regulations/contracts

Source: Moriarty, P B, G Patricot, T Bastemeijer, J Smet and C Van der Voorden (2002), *Between Rural and Urban; Towards Sustainable Management of Water Supply Systems in Small Towns in Africa*, International Water and Sanitation Centre, Delft.

Box 7.6 Water supply in Ananthapur, India

Ananthapur, in the southern state of Andhra Pradesh, is one of India's most arid districts and has been continuously affected by drought for the last 15 years. Apart from the adverse impact of drought on the economy of the district, the inhabitants also suffer from many water-borne diseases, including fluorosis.

A project was developed and implemented over an 18-month period to provide over 700 villages and some small towns with better water supplies. This was undertaken as a partnership between Sri Sathya Sai Central Trust (an NGO), which mobilized the funding; the state government of Andhra Pradesh, which provided technical support; and Larsen and Toubro Ltd, a private sector company, which implemented the project. The initial project was designed for nearly 700 villages, but during the implementation phase the scope was enlarged to 731 villages and three towns, including the district headquarters. At present the project provides water to 0.9 million persons, although it was designed for 1.25 million persons.

The project has provided public standposts at suitable locations in the settlements. Close to half of all households in these settlements use the project water supply for drinking, cooking, bathing and washing. On average, nearly 300 litres of drinking water per family per day has become available. Water is also available throughout the year.

The quality of the water in the system is checked each day. Impurities, suspended particles, foul smells, fluorides and other harmful chemicals have been eliminated. Water-borne diseases due to excess fluoride, and its harmful effects on bones and teeth, have almost been eliminated. Field survey reports indicate that earnings and health have improved. Households have expressed a high level of satisfaction with the improved water supply system. Soft water has improved cooking practices, as boiling rice, pulses and vegetables does not take such a long time. The drudgery and time consuming nature of fetching water from long distances away has been cut.

The central and state governments' support was in the form of excise and sales tax concessions on the purchase of plant and machinery. Encouraged by the successful implementation of this project, excise and sales tax concessions have been granted universal application in India for all water supply projects initiated by the private sector. The state government also provided project-facilitating infrastructure, such as enhancing the road and electricity network, and coordinated different departments to ensure speedy approvals for the project works. The community voluntarily pooled its land for the project work, free of cost, and the project was implemented without any conflicts. The community did not ask for any compensation for crops damaged during the project work (which involved laying water pipes 1 metre below the ground level), and this helped to keep down project costs and avoid delays and obstruction.

The operation and maintenance of the water supply facilities have been entrusted to a newly constituted board under the chairmanship of the district collector. At present there are no tariffs. The operation and maintenance costs are meant to be covered by the government of Andhra Pradesh (through the board) and *gram panchayats* [rural local bodies] in the ratio of 70:30. *Gram panchayats* are expected to raise 30 per cent by collecting funds from the community, but this has proved difficult.

After completing the Ananthapur district water supply project, Sri Sathya Sai Central Trust has provided water to villages in other districts of Andhra Pradesh and is developing a project in the city of Chennai. The trust has also undertaken similar projects in other countries.

described above) or in connections to formal systems (including ways of making connection charges cheaper or more easily paid); support for communal provision (as in the community-managed public toilets in Pune and Mumbai described above); and support for private sector provision (small-scale or larger formal provision) to extend supplies.

Community upgrading

For most cities, slum and squatter upgrading programmes have particular importance for water and sanitation for two reasons. The first is that they have been the primary means by which governments and international agencies have improved provision for water, sanitation and drainage within low-income urban settlements over the last 30 years – even if most international agencies do not classify upgrading programmes as water and sanitation interventions. The second is that upgrading programmes recognize (whether formally or informally) the rights of the inhabitants of the area being upgraded to basic infrastructure and services, even though they may have occupied or developed the land illegally.

While many upgrading programmes have had serious limitations – for instance, in the inadequacies in the improvements to water and sanitation, and in the inattention to provision for maintenance – a new generation of upgrading programmes have sought to address these.[21] Perhaps more to the point, there is a recognition of the need to shift emphasis away from support for upgrading projects to developing the institutional capacity of city and municipal authorities to work continuously with the inhabitants of low-income settlements in upgrading the quality and extent of infrastructure and service provision.

Community-supported upgrading programmes provide perhaps the most important means of meeting the Millennium Development Goal of achieving, by 2020, a significant improvement in the lives of at least 100 million slum dwellers. They also provide an important means for achieving two other Millennium Development Goals: reducing the proportions of people without access to safe drinking water and sanitation (see the final section of this chapter for more discussion on this). This is largely because the unit cost of providing or improving provision to existing homes is generally much less than the cost of new homes with water and sanitation provision. In addition, upgrading is easier and quicker to implement on a very large scale because there is no need to acquire land and develop new sites. Box 7.7 gives an example of a programme in Nicaragua that provided support for municipal authorities' upgrading programmes, households' efforts to improve their homes and micro-enterprises. In effect, this was promoting improved water and sanitation provision by three routes:

1   support for neighbourhood upgrading schemes (which often included improved water and sanitation provision);
2   support for households' efforts to improve water and sanitation provision within the home (for instance, improved internal plumbing and better kitchens); and
3   support for micro-enterprises' efforts to increase household incomes, which in turn allowed more to be spent on water and sanitation services.

All three routes have importance if the Millennium Development Goal of ensuring significant improvements in the lives of 100 million slum dwellers is to be achieved.

Upgrading programmes are, in effect, a recognition of the current or potential role of low-income citizens and their organizations in building cities. They recognize that slums can be transformed from the bottom–up, through improvements in infrastructure and services (especially for water, sanitation and drainage) and support for the inhabitants' efforts to improve housing. They may also recognize the importance for the city economy of areas that might be officially designated as slums or illegal settlements.[22] As such, they are very different from policies supporting slum removals and the evictions that they entail. But support for upgrading generally developed for more pragmatic reasons. One was the widespread failure of public housing or low-cost housing programmes during the 1960s and 1970s to provide low-income groups with good quality housing in most nations.[23] Another reason, especially important in Latin America (although also evident in some other nations), was stronger local democracies; in many cities, a large part of the electorate lived in slums and squatter settlements, and many community organizations demonstrated their capacity to mobilize votes and negotiate with city authorities. However, it is still common for low-income people to be evicted from their homes with little or no compensation.[24] In most instances, each household evicted is another household without water and sanitation provision. If an eviction does not provide those evicted with adequate, acceptable alternative accommodation, in effect it does not remove slums but helps to create them elsewhere.

However, major new infrastructure works are needed in most cities – including efforts to provide water mains, trunk sewers and drains. While these can often be designed to produce little or no displacement of people, there are inevitably schemes that do require some resettlement. The critical local governance issue then is how these displacements are managed. Do they simply evict people from their homes and neighbourhoods, and so increase the number of people lacking water and sanitation provision (not to mention the

Box 7.7 The Experience of the Local Development Programme (PRODEL) in Nicaragua

The Local Development Programme (PRODEL) in Nicaragua provides small grants for infrastructure and community works projects, and loans and technical assistance for micro-enterprises and housing improvement. The programme also helps to develop the capacity of local institutions to implement these measures. Its immediate goal is to improve the physical and socio-economic conditions of families living in poor communities. Between 1994 and 1997, it was active in five municipalities and, from 1998, it became active in three more.

By the end of 1998, more than 38,000 families had benefited from the US$10.5 million programme – 48 per cent of the total population of the eight towns. Just over half of this funding was provided by the Swedish International Development Cooperation Agency (Sida) with the rest being mobilized locally, mostly from the households taking part and the municipal authorities. Between 1994 and 1998, the infrastructure and community works component supported 260 projects (up to US$50,000 per project) in 155 neighbourhoods with a total investment of US$4.4 million. Among the works funded were piped water supplies, sewers and drains, treatment plants, roads and footpaths, electrification and street lighting, health centres and day care centres, playgrounds, sporting facilities and sites for the collection, disposal and treatment of wastes. The communities contributed 132,000 days of work (volunteer and paid).

Housing improvement loans of US$200–1400 were provided to 4168 households to enable them to enlarge and improve their homes, including funding for indoor plumbing, the construction of additional rooms, the upgrading of kitchens and the repair or replacement of roofs. Loans of US$300–1500 supported 2400 small enterprises (most of which had more than one loan). Both loan programmes were serving low-income households – for instance, 70 per cent of the households that received housing improvement loans had monthly incomes of US$200 or less. Both achieved good levels of cost-recovery (and low default rates) despite the economic difficulties within Nicaragua. The funding recovered through loan repayments went to support new loans. More than 60 per cent of the housing improvement loans and 70 per cent of the micro-enterprise loans were taken out by women.

Source: Stein, Alfredo (2001), *Participation and Sustainability in Social Projects: The Experience of the Local Development Programme (PRODEL) in Nicaragua*, IIED Working Paper 3 on Poverty Reduction in Urban Areas, IIED, London.

other devastating impacts that evictions so often have on low-income households) – or do they use this opportunity to improve housing and basic service provision? Box 7.8 gives an example of a large-scale resettlement programme in Mumbai that worked with the people that were to be resettled and their organizations to minimize the disruption to their lives (and livelihoods), and provide alternative accommodation that was in a location and of a form that was acceptable to those who were resettled. They also got much better provision for water, sanitation and drainage in the places where they were resettled. In this instance, people were resettled not because of the need to build water mains and drains but because of the need to improve the railways, but the principles behind this project would hold for any resettlement programme.

Supporting new homes with provision

Extending water and sanitation provision in cities is achieved not only through extending provision to existing settlements but also through supporting provision in new settlements. Programmes that permit low-income households to acquire (or build) housing with good water and sanitation provision should be one of the principal means of expanding water and sanitation provision. There are many good examples of projects or programmes that have done so, and some are given below. They include serviced site schemes, where new house plots are laid out with provision for piped water to each plot (and sometimes provision for sanitation). The households who obtain the plots are then responsible for building their own homes (and financing the cost of doing so). Successful projects that help low-income groups to acquire land and develop their own homes that are well served with basic infrastructure (including water and sanitation provision) need to be developed into established city-wide programmes that provide constant support. One-off projects are rarely on a scale to provide for current and future needs. Ongoing programmes must also avoid the tendency evident in many official serviced

Box 7.8 People-managed resettlement programmes in Mumbai

Mumbai relies primarily on its extensive suburban railway system to get its workforce in and out of the central city; on average, over seven million passenger-trips are made each day on its five main railway corridors. But the capacity of the railway system is kept down by the illegal railway settlements that crowd each side of the tracks. By 1999, more than 20,000 households lived in shacks within 25 metres of the tracks, including many within less than a metre of passing trains. These households were located there because they had no other affordable option, as they needed the central location to enable them to get to and from work. Yet they had to face not only the constant risk of injury or death from the trains but also high noise levels, insecurity, over-crowding, poor quality shelters and no water and sanitation provision. Indian Railways, which owned the land, would not allow the municipal corporation to provide basic amenities for fear that this would legitimate the land occupation and encourage the inhabitants to consolidate their dwellings. So the inhabitants had to spend long hours fetching and carrying water, a task that generally fell to women. Most people had no toilet facility and had to defecate in the open. Discussions within the Railway Slum Dwellers' Federation (to which the majority of households belonged) made clear that most would be happy to move if they could get homes with secure tenure in an appropriate location.

A relocation programme was developed as part of a larger scheme to improve the quality, speed and frequency of the trains. This was unusual on three counts. First, it did not impoverish those who moved (as is

generally the case when poor groups are moved to make way for infrastructure development). Second, the actual move – involving some 60,000 people – was voluntary and needed neither police not municipal forces to enforce it. Third, the resettled people were involved in designing, planning and implementing the resettlement programme, and in managing the settlements to which they moved. The process was not entirely problem-free: for instance, Indian Railways started demolishing huts along one railway line and had cleared more than 2000 before the National Slum Dwellers' Federation and the NGO SPARC managed to get the state government to decree that the demolitions must stop. Land sites were identified to accommodate the evicted households and the federation was given the responsibility for managing the resettlement programme.

Perhaps the most important feature of this resettlement programme was the extent to which those who were to be resettled were organized and involved before the move. First, all huts along the railway tracks and their inhabitants were counted by teams of federation leaders, community residents and NGO staff. This was done in such a way that the inhabitants' questions about what was being done and how the move would be organized could be answered. Then maps were prepared with residents in which each hut was identified with a number. Draft registers of all inhabitants were prepared and the results were returned to communities for checking. Households were then grouped into units of 50 and these house groupings were used to recheck that all details were correct and to provide the basis for

allowing households to move to the new site together and live next to each other when they were resettled. Households could choose to move from one group to another. Identity cards were prepared for all those to be moved, and visits were made to the resettlement sites. Then the move took place: some households moved to apartments in completed units and others moved to transit camps as better quality accommodation was being prepared.

A series of interviews with the relocatees in January and February 2002 highlighted the support that the inhabitants gave to the resettlement and their pleasure in having secure, safe housing with basic amenities. No process involving so many people moving so quickly is problem-free: for instance, the schools in the area to which they moved (four railway stations from where they previously had lived) could not expand enough to cope with the number of children; many households had difficulties getting ration cards (which allowed them access to cheap food staples and kerosene); and the electricity company over-charged them because they were on communal meters. The resettlement would have been better if there had been more lead time, with sites identified by those to be relocated and prepared prior to the resettlement. But this programme worked much better than other large resettlement programmes, and has set precedents in regard to fully involving those to be relocated in the whole process. It is hoped that other public agencies in India will follow suit.

Source: Patel, Sheela, Celine d'Cruz and Sundar Burra (2002), 'Beyond evictions in a global city; people-managed resettlement in Mumbai', *Environment and Urbanization*, Vol 14, No 1, pages 159–172.

site programmes to lower unit costs by developing large concentrations of serviced sites in peripheral locations which are too far from income-earning opportunities. As with upgrading schemes, these need to be developed in

consultation with low-income groups.

Another approach is to provide financial support to low-income households to enable them to buy or build new homes which have better provision for water, sanitation and

Box 7.9 Community development in Namibia

The city of Windhoek allow groups of low-income residents to purchase land with communal water and sanitation provision services as communities. The city does not charge for the intrinsic value of the land but communities have to pay for the costs of extending bulk infrastructure and services to the plot of land that they are seeking to buy. They also have to make a contribution to the cost of the city road network.

Residents can repay the costs of this infrastructure over five years at an interest rate of 15 per cent a year. The cost of a plot of 180 square metres can be as low as 1500 Namibian dollars (Na$, US$120). Groups that are members of the Shack Dwellers' Federation of Namibia have established their own loan fund that they borrow from in order to upgrade communal services to individual plots. A further stage is to upgrade their shacks to concrete block houses. The

incremental development process ensures that development is affordable to many more households. It has been introduced because the municipality recognized that most urban residents cannot afford to pay for plots with individual infrastructure and services. The costs of plots and of upgrading from communal to individual services are also kept down by community organizations undertaking the individual water and sanitation connections and the construction of gravel roads.

Table 7.3 Comparison of the cost of land purchase, individual water and sanitation connections and gravel roads between municipal development and community development

	Municipal development	Community development
Windhoek	Na$10,000 for 300 square metres	Na$2100–3100 for 180 square meters (depending on area)
Walvis Bay	Na$12,000 for 300 square metres	Na$1500 for 300 square meters

Source: Namibia Housing Action Group (2000), 'Information collected in 15 urban areas in Namibia by the Shack Dwellers Federation of Namibia', Namibia Housing Action Group, Namibia.

drainage. Box 7.9 provides an example of how the city of Windhoek allows groups of low-income residents to purchase land with communal water and sanitation services, as communities, and then develop their own houses and improve water and sanitation provision. Note the dramatic differences in unit cost between conventional municipal provision and community development.

Support for low-income groups' savings schemes and for their acquisition of land with infrastructure on which they can organize the construction of their own homes is an important part of improving water and sanitation provision, as demonstrated by the large number of low-income households that have acquired better quality housing through community-managed schemes in India (within the National Slum Dwellers' Federation and Mahila Milan),[25] Thailand (with the support of the former Urban Community Development Office, now the Community Organizations Development Institute)[26] and South Africa (within the Homeless People's Federation).[27] This is an

approach that has to be demand-driven for low-income households; many government schemes to provide low-income households with sites and services on which they can build have been supply-driven, with the result that new sites were in the wrong location or were too expensive for low-income households. Box 7.10 gives an example of the community-managed housing developments undertaken by the South African Homeless People's Federation through which thousands of low-income households have acquired good quality homes with water and sanitation provision.

The costs of water and sanitation provision can also be brought down by community provision. People's Dialogue and the South African Homeless People's Federation have been seeking to reduce the cost of infrastructure through community management and community labour. In Joe Slovo Community (a self-help scheme near Port Elizabeth), residents have been working with a local engineer to reduce unit costs. It is anticipated that water, sanitation and gravel roads can be

Box 7.10 Community-managed housing development by the South African Homeless People's Federation

The South African Homeless People's Federation was established in 1994 to represent autonomous local organizations that had developed savings and credit schemes and were developing their own housing schemes. To date, more than 8000 households have obtained secure good quality housing with infrastructure and services through the schemes the federation has supported, and more than 10,000 have secure tenure.

Its national character, active membership, autonomy and high level of participation make it one of the most significant housing movements in Africa. With over 80,000 households within its member groups, power and decision-making are highly decentralized, with individual organizations responsible for their own development activity and direction. The local organizations are based around savings and credit schemes and all federation members are encouraged to save daily. By July 1999, there were 2000 savings schemes, 70,000 active savers and 3.5 million rand saved. The federation and the NGO that works with it – People's Dialogue for Land and Shelter – support member organi-

zations in the development of housing schemes and in obtaining official support for them. They also support the formation of new local organizations, largely through community-level exchanges.

One of the principal activities of the federation and of People's Dialogue on Land and Shelter has been to change the government's housing subsidy scheme. With the election of South Africa's first democratic (and non-apartheid) government in 1994, a new housing programme was set up with the aim of building 1 million houses within five years. A housing subsidy of up to 15,000 rand was available to low-income households. They did not receive the subsidy directly, but through a subsidized unit built by commercial developers. Most of the units built under this scheme were very small – usually a single core room and a latrine. Many were badly designed and constructed, and located on city peripheries far from available job opportunities. The federation lobbied for the subsidy to be available directly to low-income households who, through their savings schemes,

could organize the construction of their own homes and the development of their own neighbourhoods. Many member groups within the federation have shown how, with the support of this subsidy, they can build much larger, better quality housing than commercial developers.

Another problem with the housing subsidy is that it is only available to households that have legal tenure of a house plot. Thus, another major area of work for the federation and the People's Dialogue is to help member savings groups to negotiate with municipal authorities or other government agencies for land. Some housing savings groups have also resorted to land invasions when they have become frustrated by the delays or the broken promises of local authorities to provide them with land. Some savings schemes have purchased land on the market and the federation has a special fund (the uTshani Fund) that provides loans to help them do so.

Source: Baumann, Ted, Joel Bolnick and Diana Mitlin (2001), *The Age of Cities and Organizations of the Urban Poor: The Work of the South African Homeless People's Federation and the People's Dialogue on Land and Shelter*, IIED Working Paper 2 on Poverty Reduction in Urban Areas, IIED, London.

provided for between 3000 and 4000 rand per household (roughly US$300–400), half the cost of a contractor-provided system. But it has proved difficult to take the construction to a larger scale: local authorities put considerable pressure on residents to accept contractor-installed infrastructure and services, arguing that they cannot ensure the quality of community-installed systems, which they will have to maintain.

One reason why these examples from Thailand, South Africa, India and Namibia have importance is that they have a scale and a momentum that allows much larger-scale impacts, but were still based on local-demand-driven initiatives. The large scale is not achieved by replicating one model but is the sum of diverse local initiatives. One key reason for this is the constant interchange between

different projects to support collective learning. The model first developed in India by the alliance of SPARC, Mahila Milan and the National Slum Dwellers' Federation is now widely used by urban poor federations in many nations to learn how to develop and build their own homes and communities, and to negotiate appropriate support from local authorities, including adequate water and sanitation provision. Within this model:

- Communities identify needs and priorities and, through discussions within the federation and support NGOs, develop a strategy to address them. One or more communities agree to try out this strategy; some are successful, some fail.
- When a community-developed initiative works well, many other communities

visit it and discuss it with those who had been involved in it, and this stimulates a new generation of volunteers to try out the strategy and refine it to suit their local circumstances.

- The refined solution is then explored on a larger scale within the city and again is shared through exchanges. The federation builds a core team from those who implemented the solution, and this visits other cities to demonstrate how it worked and to expose more communities to innovation. It also puts pressure on local officials and politicians to support more community action.[28]

Better governance and the performance of water and sanitation utilities

As this chapter has stressed, conventional water and sanitation utilities do not provide the only model for improving urban water and sanitation provision. In some of the smaller or more deprived urban areas, they may not provide an appropriate model at all. But in most urban centres, they do have a critical role. Piped water networks are generally the least-cost means of distributing potable water to different parts of an urban area. Usually, pipes are also the least-cost means of getting water to individual urban residences. Networked sewerage systems are costly, and less expensive alternatives may be more appropriate. On the other hand, the disposal of human waste is a potentially hazardous activity, often best undertaken by a regulated utility, even when decentralized systems (such as septic tanks or pit latrines) are employed. Moreover, various environmental and health problems can arise if water is supplied without any system for the disposal of wastewater.

Many of the mechanisms described in the previous section rely on connections to piped water networks and sanitation systems that are run, for the most part, as integrated utilities. Conventional network expansion will also continue to be an important means of extending water and sanitation provision. Well run water and sanitation utilities are not only in a better position to engage with innovative

attempts to extend provision by civil society groups or private enterprises, but should be capable of initiating and implementing expansion plans.

Chapter 5 made clear how difficult it is to generalize about the appropriate organizational structure of a water and sanitation utility. It is possible for a utility to be operated by a public agency, a private enterprise, a public–private partnership or a cooperative. Regulatory frameworks can also vary. The regulatory framework can be designed to encourage a public utility to run on commercial principles (eg, by linking the utility's revenues to its sales) or to encourage a privately operated utility to serve the public interest (eg, by appropriate cross-subsidies). There are also important choices relating to the degree of centralization in the operation of both the utilities and the regulatory system.

Important as these organizational choices are, the quality of governance is usually more important. Not only does better governance increase the likelihood that the appropriate organizational choices will be made, but once those choices have been made it increases the likelihood that the chosen form will operate in the public interest. While weak or unrepresentative local governments are unlikely to be able to operate a public utility efficiently or equitably, they are also unlikely to be able to set up or supervise private sector participation efficiently and equitably. More generally, how the government relates to civil society, and how the utility is situated within this relationship, has a major influence on the functioning of water and sanitation utilities.

It is often claimed that when water and sanitation services are provided through a public utility, they become too politicized. A more accurate criticism is that they can become adversely politicized as the result of governance problems. When utilities become tools in the short-term pursuit of political gain, rather than in the long-term pursuit of the public interest, their maintenance is likely to suffer, investments are likely to be distorted, and even pricing policy is likely to be affected. In urban centres where a large share of the population lacks adequate water and sanitation, this can have serious repercussions for public health. Prices may be kept low at the expense of improving provision, because increasing water tariffs has immediate effects that cannot be hidden, while improving the quality of provision is a long-term process that is less likely to attract attention. Moreover, when residents do not trust the utility to use tariff increases to improve provision, they have good reason to resist higher tariffs, even if they would be willing to pay more to get better services.

If a public utility is operated with transparency, responsibility, accountability, participation and responsiveness to the needs of the people (all qualities of good governance, according to the Commission on Human Rights Resolution 2000/64), such problems are unlikely to arise. This ideal is unlikely to be achievable. However, improvements are often possible. Exactly what should be done depends on the local situation. In some situations it may be possible to set up a regulatory system that reduces the adverse political manipulation of water provision, while giving the public utility more of an incentive to serve the public interest. In other cases, it may be more important to address corruption problems, or simply to provide more finance. Private sector participation may be part of the solution in some situations, and contribute to the problem in others.

As indicated in Chapter 5, privately operated utilities can also suffer as the result of governance failures, and privatization can actually heighten the political conflicts surrounding water and sanitation provision – most notably when large contracts, international politics and foreign corporations are involved. Residents who do not trust their government to operate a utility in the public interest are unlikely to trust a private company brought in by that government (or forced upon the government by economic or political pressures). Where governance problems are severe, privatization may actually increase the opportunities for corruption, and involve public–private 'partnerships' of a pernicious variety. Under such circumstances, privatization can allow the government to abdicate its responsibilities towards its citizens, rather than providing the

means for meeting these obligations. As with public utilities, if the regulatory framework ensures transparency, responsibility, accountability, participation and responsiveness to the needs of the people, such problems are unlikely to arise. In practice, however, politics almost always do matter, regardless of the organizational structure of the utilities.

Governance is by no means the only obstacle to improving the operation of water and sanitation utilities. Utilities often have internal management problems, or lack the technical expertise and financial resources to provide services efficiently and undertake necessary investment programmes. Such problems were mentioned in earlier chapters, and are well documented in the policy literature on the water and sanitation sector. However, governance failures can also prevent technical and financial resources from being used effectively.

In short, better local governance, and the national legislation and administration to support this, should help address many of the problems that can prevent water and sanitation utilities from achieving their potential. An efficient and equitable regulatory system can help, whether the utility is public or privately operated. Privatization is not a solution to governance problems. When it is appropriate, privatization should emerge from good governance.

Better governance and integrated water resource management

As described in Chapter 6, integrated water resource management (IWRM) emphasizes the importance of water-relevant boundaries, including especially watershed boundaries. Some urban centres are heavily dependent on water resources that are being undermined by their own excessive withdrawals or by upstream activities in the same watershed. Not only can this make it more difficult to provide water to all residents, but the measures taken to address these water resource problems can be more or less supportive of their more vulnerable residents. Addressing these problems efficiently and equitably can be a serious challenge for local and national governments. The governance challenge is compounded by the need to coordinate across administrative areas (eg, a municipality and an upstream province), sectors (eg, water and agricultural sectors) and stakeholders (for some of whom basic human rights to adequate water and sanitation may be at risk).

IWRM has been driven more by concerns about aggregate water stress than by specific water scarcities in deprived areas. As discussed in Chapter 6, in urban centres where an appreciable share of the population lacks adequate water and sanitation provision, the demand-side aspects of IWRM need to be adjusted accordingly. Many of the mechanisms described in the previous sections of this chapter respond to these concerns. There are cities, however, where water resource problems are a major barrier to improving provision. Under such circumstances, whether and how these resource problems are addressed will make a major difference to all urban stakeholders, including those currently without adequate provision.

Even within the boundaries of an urban area, various water resource management issues can arise, preventing vulnerable households from accessing adequate water and sanitation. In a number of cities, groundwater aquifers are being depleted. The obvious response is for the government to regulate the use of groundwater to prevent excessive abstraction. In practice, however, there are often a wide range of competing interests and hydrological complexities that prevent this from being a simple solution.

In Jakarta, for example (as indicated in Chapter 4), the groundwater is saline in the northern parts of the city, but wells still provide an important source of water in many parts of the city, especially for low-income households. There have been discussions about charging a well tax. Moreover, the water concessions granted in the late 1990s can be read as giving the government the responsibility to ensure that residents switch to piped water when it is available. On the other hand, it is the use of deep wells that is depleting the deep water aquifer; the shallow aquifer used by most of the shallow household wells is more rapidly replenished, and the salination of the shallow aquifer is a long-standing phenomenon. Enforcing shallow well taxes or prohibitions would be difficult, and inflict considerable hardship. Moreover, the Indonesian constitution grants people the right to use water resources to meet basic needs. Thus, far from being a straightforward planning decision, regulating groundwater use raises a wide range of complex hydrological and political issues, involving the government's responsibilities and relations to both citizens and private enterprises.

When an urban centre's water resource problems stem from activities upstream, a conventional response has been to rely on the national government or some other extra-urban authority to address these problems. In a few cases, however, attempts have been made to develop explicit market or governance mechanisms that allow urban water needs to influence upstream activities. As indicated in Chapter 6, this has recently extended to attempts to create markets for environmental services. Box 7.11 summarizes an initiative in Ecuador, involving a water fund that is in part financed by the water utility of Quito. While such initiatives do little to ensure that the water and sanitation provision in currently deprived areas actually improves, they can at least help to prevent it from getting much worse.

Developing strong local information systems

It is obvious that cities seeking to improve water and sanitation provision need good information about the quality and extent of provision in each home, neighbourhood and city. The key need is detailed information on current levels of provision and current need, house by house, plot by plot, and neighbourhood by neighbourhood. Installing piped water supplies, sewers or drains requires detailed maps that include plot boundaries, roads and pathways. This most basic information base is lacking in most urban centres in Africa, Asia and Latin America, at least for large sections of the population. In most illegal and informal

---

Box 7.11 Quito's water conservation fund: pooling demand for watershed services through trust funds

Quito, the capital of Ecuador, is a city of over 1.5 million, located in an Andean valley at about 2800 metres above sea level. The city consumes roughly 7 cubic metres of water per second. Potable water is provided by a municipal public company. About 80 per cent of Quito's potable water comes from two protected areas. Water demands are growing, while financing for increasing supplies is tight. Moreover, even in the protected areas there are a number of activities threatening the city's water supplies. In 2000 the city established a water fund (Fondo del Agua) to finance the management and conservation of surrounding watersheds.

Finance is intended to come primarily from the fees levied on domestic, industrial and agricultural users, although some initial seed funds have been provided. Users may form associations to contribute to the fund. The main users include the Metropolitan Enterprise of Water and Sewer Systems in Quito, which uses 1.5 cubic metres per second for drink-

ing water and has already agreed to pay 1 per cent of sales, worth about $12,000 per month. In addition to direct payments by beneficiaries, it is possible that funds will continue to be supplemented from national and international sources.

On the supply side, the improved water supplies are to be achieved through investment in watershed protection, initially in the Cayambe-Coca (400,000 hectares) and Antisana Ecological Reserves (120,000 hectares) surrounding Quito. The area may be extended to incorporate the Condor Bioreserve. Glaciers in these areas store 1400 cubic metres of water. The area is inhabited by 27,000 people who use water for agriculture and extensive livestock grazing. Activities that could be financed through this scheme include: land acquisition in critical areas, the provision of alternative income for local residents, supervision, the implementation of agriculture best management practices, education and training.

The fund, which became operational in 2000, is managed by a private asset manager (Enlace Fondos) and has a board of directors with representatives from local communities, hydropower companies, the national protected area authority, local NGOs and government. The fund is independent from the government, but cooperates with the environmental authority to ensure complementarity with government programmes. The programme will be executed through specialized entities and will involve local participation. According to the fund's mandate, administration costs will be limited to 10–20 per cent of total expenditure.

Source: Echevarria, Marta (2002), 'Financing watershed conservation: The FONAG water fund in Quito, Ecuador', in Stefano Pagiola, Joshua Bishop and Natashia Landell-Mills, *Selling Forest Environmental Services*, London, Earthscan: and Landell-Mills, Natashia and Ina T Porras (2002), *Silver Bullet or Fools Gold? A Global Review of Markets For Environmental Services and their Impact on the Poor*, Instruments For Sustainable Private Sector Forestry Series, International Institute for Environment and Development, London.

---

settlements (where between a quarter and a half of the city population may live), there are not even maps of the settlement or records showing house and plot boundaries, let alone details of levels of provision for water, sanitation and drainage. This is why the information about the quality of provision for cities (and for urban populations in general) is so poor. It also means that there is more information on water and sanitation provision in the better served, better managed cities, which then biases discussions of issues towards them. For instance, some of the most detailed statistics about inequalities in water and sanitation provision within cities and between cities come from Brazil, so these statistics are widely used to give examples of inequities in provision.[29] Official statistics from Brazil also show differences in infant mortality rates between different districts in cities (and between different cities) and differences in life expectancy between cities. These reveal serious inequities.

But the inequities in water and sanitation provision (and in infant mortality rates and life expectancies) are likely to be far more dramatic in nations for which no such data are available – for instance, Haiti (within Latin America) or within most low-income nations in Africa and Asia.

Good information systems inevitably draw on many sources. Good censuses should have great importance because they are generally the only official data sources that collect information on conditions for each household (including water and sanitation provision). Thus, they can provide local authorities with information not only on conditions within the city but on conditions in each street and neighbourhood, so that investment and improvement programmes know which streets and neighbourhoods to prioritize. But it seems that few census bureaux or national statistical offices provide local governments with census data in a form that allows them to use it in small-area planning.[30] If they do, the data appear many years after the census was held. Ironically, the data from censuses – which should provide the information base for local decisions and actions – ends up being owned, controlled and used by national institutions. There is still an assumption among many government statistical offices that they are serving national government policy rather than the policies of local government. The recognition of the importance of local institutions and local action (or local governance) for good development and environmental management is well established.[31] But most nations have not changed their official information-gathering systems to serve this recognition.

In some of the poorest nations there has been no census for 10–20 years, so there is no information base at all on water and sanitation provision to each household. Governments and international agencies have placed increasing reliance on household surveys as an alternative to censuses. But the problem with these is that they are based on samples. They may be able to tell with great accuracy the percentage of households that are unserved by piped water supplies or rely on shared pit latrines (or how many are poor), but they cannot say where these households are. They are based on sample sizes that are representative nationally, not locally. The sample sizes may be large enough to allow a comparison of provision between rural and urban areas (and even to show levels of provision for the largest city), but they provide no information that is useful for local governments or local water and sanitation providers about where, within their jurisdictions, provision is inadequate. If it is accepted that national governments and international agencies should give more attention to improved local governance, then this also means designing data-gathering systems that serve local governance. At present, most official statistical services and donor-funded surveys do not do so.

Many city authorities who find themselves ill-served by the official national statistical services develop their own information bases. There is also a need for strong information systems from the bottom–up. Even where census data are available to local authorities in a form that provides the data for each street, they give few clues as to what underlies poor conditions. Census questions about water and sanitation can also be rather rudimentary. Fortunately, there are examples that show new ways to address this. One of the most remarkable examples is provided by the Pakistan NGO OPP, which has worked with low-income communities throughout Karachi to produce detailed maps showing each individual house plot and current forms of provision for water, sanitation and drainage in 100 low-income informal settlements, and is developing comparable plans in others.[32] Another example is provided by the Indian NGO SPARC working with the National Slum Dwellers' Federation and cooperatives of women pavement and slum dwellers (Mahila Milan) as they undertake slum censuses, primarily carried out by slum inhabitants working with community leaders and some external support. Many other organizations or federations formed by the urban poor have undertaken their own slum censuses or shack censuses, which give detailed information on each house, shack or plot in informal settlements into which official agencies rarely venture; the findings from one such shack census (from Huruma in Nairobi) were described in Chapter 1. Box 7.12 describes a community-based environmental management information system that allows the residents of a settlement to generate their own information system. Some city governments have recognized the potential of community-supported censuses or surveys to provide the information base for more effective policies.

Another source of bottom–up information of relevance to water and sanitation provision comes from community-based consultations. For instance, the community consultations that were central to the participatory budgeting process in Porto Alegre allowed those living in any neighbourhood to set priorities for government investment and action in their neighbourhood.[33] Much valuable information can also come from consultations with children and youth, as can be seen in the many cities that have developed permanent mechanisms for consulting children.[34] The Growing Up in Cities programme provides many examples of

Box 7.12 Empowering communities to generate their own information system: CEMIS

A community-based environmental management information system (CEMIS) has been developed by UN-HABITAT to promote effective management approaches that will help local authorities and communities to develop strong local information systems.

CEMIS, which has been applied in low-income communities in Accra (Ghana) and Jakarta (Indonesia) over a period of two years, has been developed as an open and flexible information and management system. Its main objective is to empower communities to monitor and assess their own living environments without external support and, based on the information gathered, to develop and manage the needed interventions. CEMIS has been developed to be as simple as possible; it makes use only of technologies that are appropriate for the host community.

The CEMIS process involves the following steps and modules:

1   Community preparation and mobilization in which community leaders are identified. The expected output is an increased community awareness of the inter-relationship between housing and environmental health.

2   Environmental risk assessment and monitoring. The communities, through self-assessment, are able to identify problems and priorities and monitor human settlement conditions and related environmental health risks.

3   Assessment of technological options, in which communities are enabled to select the most appropriate technologies. Besides technical information, communities also require information on installation, operation and maintenance costs, environmental and health impacts as well as options on how to manage the technology.

4   Assessment of effective demand, in which the resource base of the community is determined by the community itself. It assesses the community's willingness and commitment to contribute to specific inventions.

5   The fifth module is intended to enable communities to prioritize human settlement interventions based on the use of a criteria catalogue. The criteria catalogue includes information about the ranking of environmental problems and related strategic human settlement interventions. A further prioritization of human

settlement interventions is conducted, based on available technological information, options and available resources.

6   Community action planning and implementation, in which guidelines for planning, implementing and managing intervention are provided.

7   Monitoring and evaluation. This module provides tools for monitoring and evaluating human settlement intervention in communities.

The last module strives to strengthen the institutional framework developed by the project and the capacities developed to sustain CEMIS and improve living conditions.

In Module 2, a house card has been developed as a tool for community self-surveys and self-reporting.

Sources: For more details of the house card system, see Surjadi, C and A Dzikus (1998), 'CEMIS Indonesia: community-based assessment and monitoring of living conditions with the help of a house card' in J Breuste, H Feldmann and O Uhlmann (eds), *Urban Ecology*, Springer Verlag, Berlin/Heidelberg, New York. A detailed training manual on CEMIS is available from UN-HABITAT: Dzikus, A, B Jenssen, R Piesch and D Ridder (eds) (2000), *The Guide For Community Based Environmental Management Information Systems (CEMIS)*, Spring Centre, University of Dortmund, Germany and UN-HABITAT.

how to involve children in evaluating their communities, determining their priorities for change and helping to implement local improvements.[35] This involved local teams in a range of countries (including sites in the UK, Norway, the USA and Australia as well as in Argentina, South Africa, Poland and India).

International support for better local governance for water and sanitation

One reason why water and sanitation provision is so inadequate for much of the urban population of Africa, Asia and Latin America is that

national and international agencies saw this too much as a technical and financial problem. Their policies did not acknowledge the political aspects (or rather the fact that the problem could not be addressed without better governance). Slums and squatter settlements were seen as the problem, rather than the local government systems that did nothing to support low-income households in finding or building better quality homes. Large-scale investments in water and sanitation were made in cities with political systems that had no interest in improving conditions for low-income groups. Where they turned to privatization, it proved difficult to reconcile large private companies' interests and priorities with the slow, difficult and often expensive investments needed to ensure good provision for low-income groups.

If it is agreed that improving water and sanitation provision in urban areas depends on better local governance, one must ask how local governance can be improved. What role do international agencies have? It is very difficult for international agencies to know how to support good local governance; every city has a complex political economy of competing interests and changing circumstances that are difficult to understand, even for specialists who live and work in the city, let alone those who try to support city programmes from Washington, DC, Tokyo or London. National governments also do not want international agencies to support changes that reduce the resources they receive and can allocate, or to support their political rivals (in many instances, innovative city governments are from different political parties to those in power nationally).[36] There is little point in channelling funds to governments or NGOs to improve water and sanitation provision for low-income groups if there are no systems in place to ensure that they are spent in ways that are transparent and accountable to low-income groups. Box 7.13 gives an example of how UN-HABITAT is working with the international NGO ENDA-Tiers Monde and the government of Senegal in evaluating a successful community-based wastewater management system that ENDA-Tiers Monde developed, in order to gauge its suitability for application elsewhere.

One key task for international agencies is to support better national frameworks that in turn support better local governance. Figure 7.4 gives some examples of the kind of national support structures that can help better local governance, but these broad national changes need to be accompanied by support for local action that can deliver very specific changes that improve governance for water and sanitation on the ground.

There is also an obvious need for more funding, not only for water and sanitation but also for the means by which provision gets improved (which is not classified as water and sanitation). These include programmes supporting slum and squatter upgrading, serviced site schemes and credit schemes supporting low-income households' capacity to buy or build new homes. They also include programmes to strengthen good government and good governance at the municipal, city and national level, including addressing the issues highlighted in Figure 7.4. It is also obvious that significant improvements in provision will require more funding from all possible sources, including households, communities and local governments, as well as national governments and international agencies.

The current scale of external funding is not very large in relation to need. For instance, in Asia, as described in Chapter 3, external support provided around US$1 billion a year during the 1990s for urban water and $120 million a year for urban sanitation.[37] US$1 billion a year would cover the cost of providing 10 million people a year with a conventional house connection, but Asia's urban population was growing by around 35 million a year during the 1990s. Even if the money had been spent on standposts, it would not even have covered the increase in Asia's urban population, let alone dealt with the very large backlog. The investment of $120 million a year in urban sanitation would have reached less than 1 million people a year (or 10 million people over the decade) if spent on contractor-constructed sewer systems, and around 24 million over the decade if spent on pour-flush latrines or VIP latrines. This is very small in relation to need if it is accepted that around half of Asia's urban population (ie, some 700 million people) have inadequate provision.

The scale of the funding needed for urban water and sanitation may be considerably under-estimated for two reasons. First, estimates may be based on large under-estimations as to the number of people lacking adequate provision. This returns to the issue discussed in Chapter 1 regarding what is considered 'adequate' provision. If there were only 98 million urban dwellers in Asia in need of a better water supply (as all but these have 'improved' provision), the problem would be soluble financially. If there were 500 million urban dwellers in Asia in need of a better

---

Box 7.13 Replicating the Rufisque experience through the Water for African Cities Programme

As part of the Water for African Cities Programme, UN-HABITAT in association with the international NGOs ENDA-Tiers Monde and ONAS are providing assistance to the government of Senegal to evaluate a successful community-based waste-water collection, treatment and disposal system. The system, in an informal settlement called Rufisque, has been developed by ENDA and comprises a low-cost shallow sewerage system linked to a decentralized treatment plant, based on a lagoon system with floating macrophytes. The treated wastewater is used in a simple urban agriculture scheme and

also for aquifer recharge. The systems collect both grey and black water from over 500 households where water consumption is between 10–30 litres per person per day.

Although the demonstration project at Rufisque has been in operation for several years and has been acclaimed internationally, the national sanitation agency has been reluctant to advocate the technology nationally without a thorough evaluation. UN-HABITAT developed an evaluation approach and, together with the government of Senegal, identified appropriate experts to evaluate the project. All aspects of the initiative

are being evaluated, including socio-economic, technical and institutional aspects. The longer-term goal of the study is to ratify the method and produce national codes of practice and design manuals, so that the technology, together with recommended modifications, can be replicated nationally without compromising health and environment. In addition to providing an environmentally sound treatment and disposal method, the initiative will provide a source of income generation for some local residents through urban agriculture.

---

water supply, because the 402 million urban dwellers who have improved provision still have very inadequate provision, the picture changes rather dramatically. The second reason that the funding needs may be considerably under-estimated is the need for investment in infrastructure, facilities and institutions upstream of the pipes and downstream of the drains. But the scale of the necessary external funding may also be over-stated by under-estimating the extent to which local resources can and should be mobilized (for instance, the US$1.4 million spent by households in Orangi on developing their own sewer systems – see Box 7.3); or by under-estimating the extent to which unit costs can be reduced by community–NGO–local authority (and/or local utility) partnerships, which in turn reduces the gap between good quality provision and what low-income households can afford.

The many case studies on which Chapter 1 drew certainly suggest that the deficiencies are far larger and affect far more people than indicated by the official statistics about who has improved provision. For instance, if we took 'adequate' water to mean a regular piped supply available within the home or house yard, at least half of the urban population of sub-Saharan Africa and Southeast Asia have inadequate provision (and perhaps substantially more than this). In these

regions, it is not only most of the urban poor who lack provision but also large sections of the urban non-poor. The study by Hewett and Montgomery, whose findings were presented in Chapters 1 and 2, drew on demographic and health surveys from 43 low- and middle-income nations. It suggested that a large proportion of non-poor households in sub-Saharan Africa and Asia lack water on the premises (whether piped or from a well) – as well as most of the urban poor. If we take 'adequate' sanitation to mean an easily maintained toilet in each person's home, with provision for hand-washing and for the safe removal and disposal of toilet wastes, a very large proportion of the urban population of sub-Saharan Africa (50–60 per cent?) and more than half of the urban population in most low-income nations in Asia and Latin America are likely to have inadequate provision. Table 7.4 contrasts the different estimates as to the number of urban dwellers lacking water and sanitation provision – one based on 'improved provision' as defined by the 2000 WHO/UNICEF assessment, the other based on the interpretation of 'adequate provision' discussed in earlier chapters.

Estimates of the scale of funding needed could also change if consideration was given to the current or potential role of investments made by households, communities and local

Figure 7.4 The many factors that help support more effective action by local governments to improve provision for water and sanitation

National constitutions that support rights-based approaches and citizen organization and action to achieve it

Democratic pressures from the bottom–up; capacity of low-income groups to organize, make demands and negotiate with local governments

Democratic safeguards from the top–down; including effectiveness of guarantees on civil and political rights and support for local democracy (eg elected city councils and mayors) and procedures that strengthen it (eg, participatory budgeting)

Potential for urban governments to ensure good provision for water and sanitation

Decentralization; support from higher levels of government for urban governments with the power, capacity and revenue sources to meet their responsibilities

International conventions and action plans to which national governments have committed themselves (and which national judiciaries take note of)

National government commitment to implementing the Millennium Development Goals and supporting their implementation at local level

National legislation giving rights to those living in informal settlements and **independent judiciary**

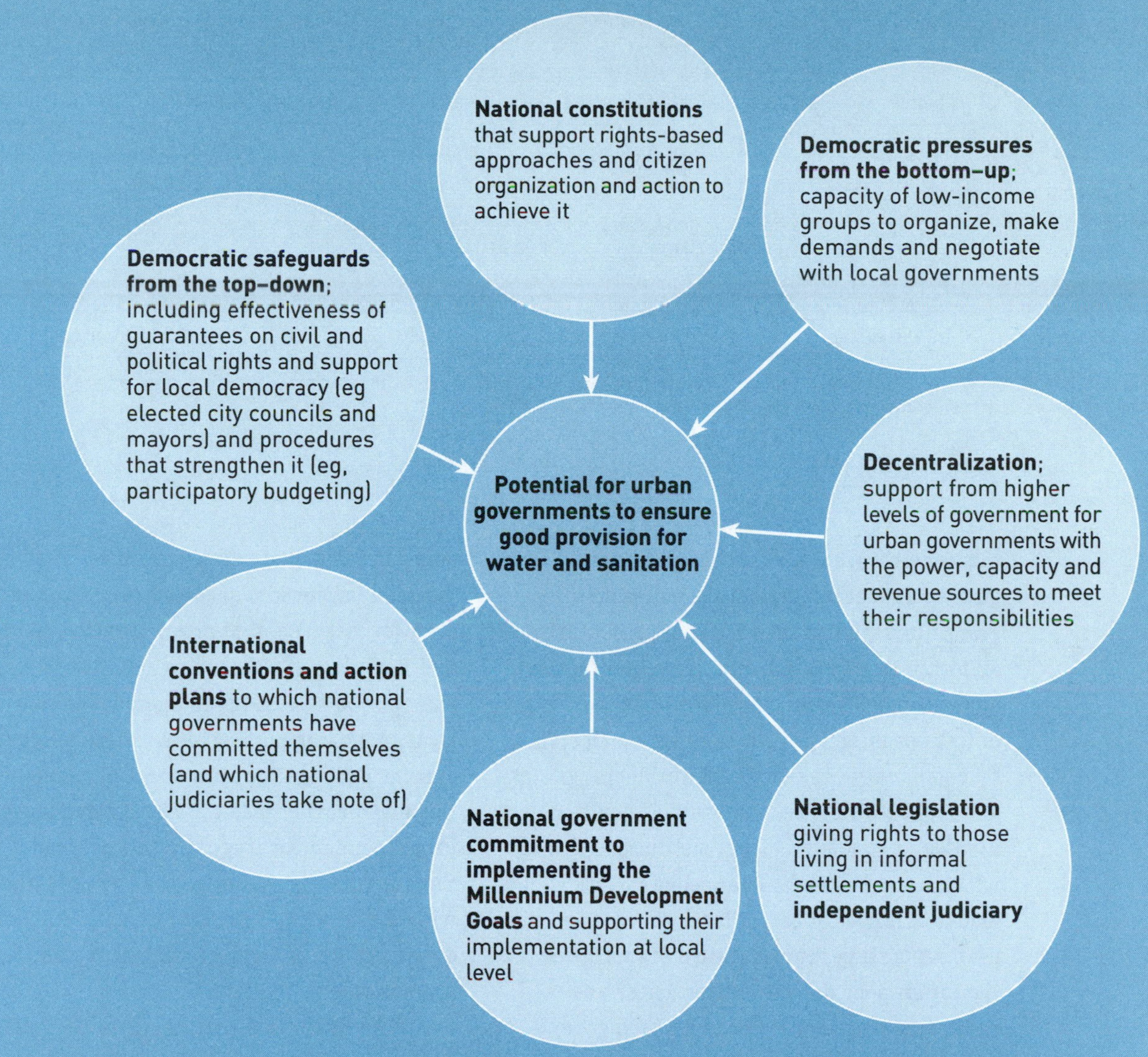

Source: Adapted from UNICEF – Innocenti Digest (2002), *Poverty and Exclusion among Urban Children*, Innocenti Research Centre, United Nations Children's Fund, Florence.

governments. But the official development assistance agencies were not set up to support households, communities and local governments; they work with and through national governments. Most seek to support local governments and some seek to support community initiatives (or steer their funding through other institutions that can), but this represents a small part of their funding for water and sanitation, except in nations where national governments have supported this. All official development assistance agencies have difficulties supporting a diverse range of 'cheap' initiatives because of the high administrative cost of doing so. However, if water and

sanitation provision is to be improved, international agencies will need to develop a greater capacity to support good local governance and support the investments and initiatives undertaken by households, communities and local governments. This inevitably means channelling more support to local governments that are committed to improving provision and less to local governments (or national governments) that are not. This can be awkward politically; it may mean some redirection of funds away from some of the poorest nations because of their government's lack of interest in improving water and sanitation provision and in the local governance structures that

Table 7.4 Different estimates as to the number of urban dwellers lacking provision for water and sanitation in 2000

Region	Number and proportion of urban dwellers without improved provision for:[a]		Indicative estimates for the number (and proportion) of urban dwellers without adequate provision for:[b]	
	Water	Sanitation	Water	Sanitation
Africa	44 million (15 per cent)	46 million (16 per cent)	100–150 million (circa 35–50 per cent)	150–180 million (circa 50–60 per cent)
Asia	98 million (7 per cent)	297 million (22 per cent)	500–700 million (circa 35–50 per cent)	600–800 million (circa 45–60 per cent)
Latin America and the Caribbean	29 million (7 per cent)	51 million (13 per cent)	80–120 million (circa 20–30 per cent)	100–150 million (circa 25–40 per cent)

Sources: a WHO and UNICEF (2000), *Global Water Supply and Sanitation Assessment 2000 Report*, World Health Organization, UNICEF and Water Supply and Sanitation Collaborative Council, Geneva, 80 pages; *b* based on the evidence presented in Chapter 1.

this requires. It is also inconsistent with poverty reduction goals, to penalize poor groups in nations that have unrepresentative and anti-poor governments. Here, international agencies need to consider how to support local initiatives directly, including those undertaken by community organizations, residents' groups and local NGOs. This will usually require new funding channels and local institutions through which such funding is channelled.[38] This is not incompatible with better local governance, in that supporting representative organizations of the urban poor develop better water and sanitation provision helps build such governance from the bottom–up.

There are many initiatives underway that respond to the recognition of the need for better local governance and that seek to help develop local governance capacities to improve water and sanitation provision. These include programmes specifically aimed at improving provision that have been mentioned in earlier chapters, such as the Water for African Cities and the Water for Asian Cities programmes and the World Bank's Water and Sanitation Program. Box 7.14 gives more details of the Water for African Cities programme. Many other international programmes can also help – including the Healthy Cities Programme, supported by the World Health Organization, the Child-friendly Cities Secretariat in UNICEF and the Sustainable Cities Programme supported by UN-HABITAT. There are also

many Local Agenda 21 programmes that have included improved water and sanitation provision, for instance in Manizales in Colombia[39] and Ilo in Peru.[40] There are also some examples of international agencies taking measures to support local institutional development and local governance. One example of this given earlier was the Local Development Programme in Nicaragua; although funded by Sida, it was a programme that worked directly with the municipal authorities and community organizations in eight urban centres and was accountable to them.[41]

The final issue that needs to be considered by international agencies is how to meet the Millennium Development Goals that relate to water and sanitation. This is the focus of the final section.

Water and sanitation and the Millennium Development Goals

There is now a formal commitment by most governments and international agencies to greatly improve water and sanitation provision, and specific targets have been set that have to be achieved by specific dates.[42] These arose from a special session of the United Nations General Assembly (the Millennium Assembly) in September 2000. The commitments made by this assembly were later re-organized into the Millennium Development

Box 7.14 The Managing Water for African Cities Programme

This is a collaborative initiative of UN-HABITAT and UNEP within the framework of the UN System-wide Special Initiative on Africa. The programme is collaborating with a variety of international agencies and donors, including the Water Supply and Sanitation Collaborative Council and the International Atomic Energy Authority. The programme is a direct follow-up to the Cape Town Declaration (1997), adopted by African ministers wishing to address the urgent need for managing water in African cities. The programme started in October 1999 and is the first regional initiative of its kind to support African cities to manage the growing water demand and protect their fresh water resources from the increasing pollution loads from cities. The programme's objectives are to:

• support African countries' efforts to address the growing urban water crisis and protect the continent's threatened water resources from urban pollution; and
• improve urban water resources management through awareness, the promotion of effective policies, programmes and investments, and building capacity at the city level in key national and regional institutions.

The programme addresses the following interlinked priorities:

• Operationalizing an effective water demand management strategy in demonstration cities to encourage efficient water use by domestic users, industry and public institutions. Work is underway in Abidjan (Côte d'Ivoire), Accra (Ghana), Addis Ababa (Ethiopia), Dakar (Senegal), Johannesburg (South Africa), Lusaka (Zambia) and Nairobi

(Kenya). Other cities have also applied to join the programme. In five cities, the programme has contributed to water sector reform; in three, environmental action plans have been utilized as a basis for the protection of water resources; and in six, awareness campaigns have been developed to engage high-level political support for water resources protection. Operational water demand management units have been established in six of the cities and have already demonstrated reduced water consumption by 35 per cent in pilot areas.
• Building capacity at city level to monitor and assess pollution loads entering fresh water bodies from different sources, and putting in place early warning mechanisms for the timely detection of emerging hot-spots of urban pollution.
• Enhancing regional capacity in the area of urban water resources management through information exchange, awareness raising, training and education. Over 10,000 copies of the newsletter are circulated in French and English.

The programme is implemented on two parallel tracks:

1   city demonstrations in the participating cities; and
2   region-wide activities focusing on information sharing and awareness raising on water conservation.

The focus of the city demonstrations is to support policy reforms, promote institutional changes, and build capacity at the city level to implement water demand management (addressing quantity) and pollution control

(addressing quality) programmes. The regional component includes the sharing of good practices and anchoring the capacity within selected regional resource centres. A high-level (ministerial) advisory group comprising responsible ministers from the seven participating countries provides oversight and guidance.

Development of the training and capacity-building component

The Netherlands' government is supporting a training and capacity-building component, and the programme is developing separate training programmes in terms of content, training methodology, duration and implementation for three target groups of professionals:

1   Policy- and decision-makers (managing directors and administrative/political heads) in utilities, ministries, regulatory bodies etc; training will be through seminars/exposures/ workshops, focusing on the sensitization of this target group, and will address policy, strategy and programme development issues.
2   Senior managers (heads of technical and financial departments); the training will address project planning, monitoring and coordination, evaluation and resource allocation issues.
3   Middle-level managers; workshops will address project preparation, implementation and management issues in the areas of water demand management and water quality management.

The government of Sweden is also supporting a schools water education programme.

Goals. The two most relevant goals for water
and sanitation are:

- Target 10: to halve, by 2015, the proportion of people without sustainable access
  to safe drinking water.
- Target 11: to achieve, by 2020, a significant improvement in the lives of at least
  100 million slum dwellers.

Task forces have been set up to advise the
United Nations on how these goals can be met,
and many international agencies are re-
orienting their goals and structures to respond
more effectively to these goals.

When the Millennium Development Goals
were drawn up, a goal for improvements in
sanitation was forgotten (or ignored).
However, the World Summit on Sustainable
Development in Johannesburg in 2002, when
endorsing the Millennium Development Goals,
added '...we agree to halve, by the year 2015,
the proportion of people who are unable to
reach or to afford safe drinking water (as
outlined in the Millennium Declaration) and
the proportion of people who do not have
access to basic sanitation...' The 2002 World
Summit also stressed the need for actions at
all levels to develop and implement efficient
household sanitation systems, improve sanitation in public institutions (especially in
schools), promote safe hygiene practices and
integrate sanitation into water resources
management strategies.[43]

What becomes clear from the discussions
in earlier sections of this chapter and in
Chapter 1 is that we do not know how many
urban dwellers have sustainable access to safe
drinking water in much of Africa, Asia and
Latin America, so there is no baseline from
which to assess what progress is being made.
The same is true for sanitation. It is possible
to monitor the proportion of urban populations
with access to improved sanitation (one of the
indicators suggested for monitoring), but not
to monitor the proportion with adequate or
good quality or safe sanitation in most of
Africa, Asia and Latin America and the
Caribbean. If we interpret the Millennium
Development Goals as requiring a halving by
2015 of the number of people without

adequate water and sanitation provision, at
least in urban areas, there is no basis for
assessing who has adequate provision now and
thus no basis for monitoring progress towards
these goals. It may be possible to reach agreement on what constitutes adequate provision
for water and sanitation and even to reach
agreement on the need for different criteria for
rural and urban areas. But this would imply
much more detailed assessments of water and
sanitation provision – for instance, including
data on quality, reliability, price and convenience (as outlined in Box 1.1).

There is an obvious need to broaden and
deepen the coverage of global and national
assessments of the quality of provision for
water, sanitation and hygiene in urban (and
rural) areas so that they show the proportion
of people with safe, regular, convenient and
affordable provision, as well as improved provision. This becomes all the more urgent as
development assistance agencies seek to meet
the explicit targets mentioned above.

Achieving more accurate and detailed
international statistics on people's access to
adequate provision for water and sanitation is
problematic. As the WHO and UNICEF *Global
Water Supply and Sanitation Assessment 2000
Report* explains, it is not possible to assess the
proportion of urban (and rural) populations
with safe drinking water in most nations (see
Chapter 1 for more details). Most censuses do
not have sufficient information on water and
sanitation provision to allow this. Nor do most
household surveys; as a review of the
demographic and health surveys noted, 'unfortunately, no data are collected in DHS surveys
on the money cost of water, the weekly or
daily variability of supply and perceived levels
of contamination, all of which would be important considerations in urban areas.'[44] This
review also pointed to the inadequacies of the
questions in these surveys regarding sanitation; few surveys sought to establish how
many households share each toilet, and no
information is gathered on the time costs of
access to shared facilities.[45] So at present,
there is no possibility of monitoring progress
towards the Millennium Development Goal
related to halving the number of people
lacking sustainable access to safe drinking

water. The only aspect that can be monitored is changes in the proportion of people with improved provision, but as Chapter 1 emphasized, this is not the same as safe provision or adequate provision.

To get more detailed data on water and sanitation provision for each city district and smaller urban centre (and rural area) would mean significant changes in the questions asked in censuses, which most national census bureaux would find problematic. Some low-income nations have had no census for many years. A more comprehensive set of questions on water, sanitation and hygiene can be introduced into household surveys, including demographic and health surveys or living standards measurement surveys. These can provide more accurate and detailed national statistics for urban and rural populations, but there is a reluctance among those who fund these surveys to increase the number of

questions. Moreover, if the goal is to improve water and sanitation provision, then what is needed is not surveys based on representative samples of rural and urban populations, but site-specific information for each city and smaller urban centre and each settlement within them. This information should document the deficiencies, and should be used by water and sanitation providers to plan improvements, or by local residents to articulate their demands (or even meet their own needs). If the Millennium Development Goals provide the impetus for better meeting local demands for better water and sanitation, at least some of the resulting improvements will be evident in the international statistics. It would be a great mistake to concentrate only on improving global statistics when what is needed is more accurate and detailed local statistics to support local actions.

 Notes and references

1. Although there are important economies of scale for many investments.

2. Mumford, Lewis (1991), *The City in History*, Penguin, London, 752 pages.

3. Recommendation C12 from the Recommendations for National Action endorsed at the UN Conference on Human Settlements (Habitat) in 1976.

4. See, for instance, the worries in recent years that New York's water supplies will become insufficient, which are in part explained by lower than average rainfall – see the report in the *New York Times*, 31 October 2002, B1–B2.

5. Hasan, Arif (1999), *Understanding Karachi: Planning and Reform for the Future*, City Press, Karachi, 171 pages.

6. UNCHS (HABITAT) (1996), *An Urbanizing World: Global Report on Human Settlements, 1996*, Oxford University Press, Oxford and New York; Hardoy, Jorge E, Diana Mitlin and David Satterthwaite (2001), *Environmental Problems in an Urbanizing World: Finding Solutions for Cities in Africa, Asia and Latin America*, Earthscan Publications, London, 470 pages.

7. Souza, Celina (2001), 'Participatory budgeting in Brazilian cities: limits and possibilities in building democratic institutions', *Environment and Urbanization*, Vol 13, No 1, pages 159–184; Melo, Marcus with Flávio

Rezende and Cátia Lubambo (2001), *Urban Governance, Accountability and Poverty: The Politics of Participatory Budgeting in Recife, Brazil*, Urban Governance, Partnerships and Poverty Research Working Papers 27, University of Birmingham, Birmingham, 201 pages. For a discussion of the negative influence of politicians on community-driven solutions, see also Asian Coalition for Housing Rights and Slum/Shack Dwellers International (2003), *Community-driven Water, Sanitation and Infrastructure*, ACHR, Bangkok.

8. Roberts, Ian (2000), 'Leicester environment city: learning how to make Local Agenda 21, partnerships and participation deliver', *Environment and Urbanization*, Vol 12, No 2, pages 9–26.

9. McCarney, Patricia L (1996), 'Considerations on the notion of "governance": new directions for cities in the developing world', in Patricia L McCarney (ed), *Cities and Governance: New Directions in Latin America, Asia and Africa*, Centre for Urban and Community Studies, University of Toronto, Toronto.

10. Democratic structures also provide no guarantee of the integration of ecological concerns, except in the extent to which they help prevent the passing on of ecological costs from one local government area to another.

11. See the case study of Seine Normandy within the forthcoming World Water Development Report, UNESCO, Paris.

12. Orangi Pilot Project developed into four autonomous institutions in 1988: OPP Research and Training Institute, Orangi Charitable Trust, Karachi Health and Social Development Association, and the OPP Society, which channels funds to these institutions – see Hasan, Arif (1997), *Working with Government: The Story of OPP's Collaboration with State Agencies for Replicating its Low Cost Sanitation Programme*, City Press, Karachi, 269 pages.

13. Hasan 1997, 1999, op cit.

14. Hasan 1999, op cit.

15. Orangi Pilot Project – Research and Training Institute (2002), *Katchi Abadis of Karachi: Documentation of Sewerage, Water Supply Lines, Clinics, Schools and Thallas, Volume One: The First Hundred Katchi Abadis Surveyed*, Orangi Pilot Project, Karachi, 507 pages.

16. Cain, Allan, Mary Daly and Paul Robson (2002), *Basic Service Provision for the Urban Poor; The Experience of Development Workshop in Angola*, IIED Working Paper 8 on Poverty Reduction in Urban Areas, IIED, London, 40 pages.

17. Good quality on-site sanitation can be developed in relatively small plots – see Cotton, Andrew and Darren Saywell (2001), *On-plot Sanitation in Low-income Urban Communities; Guidelines for Selection*, Water, Engineering and Development Centre (WEDC), Loughborough University, Loughborough.

18. Kalbermatten, J M, D S Julius and C G Gunnerson (1980), *Appropriate Technology for Water Supply and Sanitation: A Review of the Technical and Economic Options*, The World Bank, Washington, DC.

19. In research on smaller urban centres, 'small' urban centres are often taken to be settlements recognized by the government as 'urban' but with less than 20,000 inhabitants. 'Intermediate' urban centres have 20,000 to 100,000 inhabitants. See Chapter 9 of Hardoy, Jorge E and David Satterthwaite (1989), *Squatter Citizen: Life in the Urban Third World*, Earthscan Publications, London, 388 pages. But there is such variation between small urban centres of comparable sizes in (among other things) size, topography, settlement pattern, availability of fresh water, economic base and local government capacity that it is difficult to generalize about which forms of water and sanitation provision suit which size of urban centre. Clearly, there are important economies of scale, proximity and agglomeration for many aspects of piped water supplies, sewers and drains, although many operate at relatively low population sizes – see Linn, Johannes F (1982), 'The costs of urbanization in developing countries', *Economic Development and Cultural Change*, Vol 30, No 3, pages 625–648.

20. This is not always the case. For instance, Orangi Pilot Project-Research and Training Institute found that there were sewer systems into which household or community systems could connect in many urban centres in Pakistan.

21. See, for instance, Stein, Alfredo (2001), *Participation and Sustainability in Social Projects: The Experience of the Local Development Programme (PRODEL) in Nicaragua*, IIED Working Paper 3 on Poverty Reduction in Urban Areas, IIED, London; and Fiori, Jorge, Liz Riley and Ronaldo Ramirez (2000), *Urban Poverty Alleviation through Environmental Upgrading in Rio de Janeiro: Favela Bairro*, Development Planning Unit, University College London, London, 107 pages.

22. See for instance Benjamin, Solomon (2000), 'Governance, economic settings and poverty in Bangalore', *Environment and Urbanization*, Vol 12, No 1, pages 35–56, on the local economies of Bangalore.

23. Hardoy and Satterthwaite 1989, op cit.

24. COHRE and ACHR (2000), *Forced Evictions in Bangladesh: We Didn't Stand a Chance*, COHRE and ACHR Mission Report, Centre on Housing Rights and Evictions (COHRE) and Asian Coalition for Housing Rights (ACHR), Bangkok, 65 pages; COHRE (2002), *Forced Evictions: Violations Of Human Rights – Global Survey On Forced Evictions No 8*, Centre on Housing Rights and Evictions, Geneva, 133 pages.

25. Patel, Sheela and Diana Mitlin (2001), *The Work of SPARC and its Partners, Mahila Milan and the National Slum Dwellers' Federation in India*, IIED Working Paper 5 on Urban Poverty Reduction, IIED, London.

26. UCDO (2000), *UCDO (Urban Community Development Office) Update No 2*, Urban Community Development Office, Bangkok, 32 pages.

27. Baumann, Ted, Joel Bolnick and Diana Mitlin (2001), *The Age of Cities and Organizations of the Urban Poor: The Work of the South African Homeless People's Federation and the People's Dialogue on Land and Shelter*, IIED Working Paper 2 on Poverty Reduction in Urban Areas, IIED, London.

28. Patel and Mitlin 2001, op cit.

29. See Mueller, Charles C (1995), 'Environmental problems inherent to a development style: degradation and poverty in

Brazil', *Environment and Urbanization*, Vol 7, No 2, October, pages 67–84; also Stephens, Carolyn (1996), 'Healthy cities or unhealthy islands: the health and social implications of urban inequality', *Environment and Urbanization*, Vol 8, No 2, October, pages 9–30.

30. See Navarro, Lia (2001), 'Exploring the environmental and political dimensions of poverty: the cases of the cities of Mar del Plata and Necochea-Quequén', *Environment and Urbanization*, Vol 13, No 1, pages 185–199.

31. Hardoy, Mitlin and Satterthwaite 2001, op cit; UNCHS 1996, op cit.

32. OPP-RTI 2002, op cit.

33. Menegat, Rualdo (2002), 'Participatory democracy and sustainable development: integrated urban environmental management in Porto Alegre, Brazil', *Environment and Urbanization*, Vol 14, No 2, pages 181–206.

34. Riggio, Eliana (2002), 'Child friendly cities; good governance in the best interest of the child', *Environment and Urbanization*, Vol 14, No 2, pages 45–58; Guerra, Eliana (2002), 'Citizenship knows no age; children's participation in the governance and municipal budget of Barra Mansa, Brazil', *Environment and Urbanization*, Vol 14, No 2, pages 71–84; and Racelis, Mary and Angela Desiree M Aguirre (2002), 'Child rights for urban poor children in child friendly Philippine cities: views from the community ', *Environment and Urbanization*, Vol 14, No 2, pages 97–113.

35. Chawla, Louise (ed) (2002), *Growing Up in an Urbanising World*, Earthscan Publications and UNESCO Publishing, London and Sterling VA, 254 pages.

36. See, for instance, Montiel, René Pérez and Françoise Barten (1999), 'Urban governance and health development in León, Nicaragua', *Environment and Urbanization*, Vol 11, No 1, April, pages 11–26.

37. WHO and UNICEF (2000), *Global Water Supply and Sanitation Assessment 2000 Report*, World Health Organization, UNICEF and Water Supply and Sanitation Collaborative Council, Geneva, 80 pages.

38. Satterthwaite, David (2002), 'Local funds and their potential to allow donor agencies to support community development and poverty reduction', *Environment and Urbanization*, Vol 14, No 1, pages 179–188.

39. Velasquez, Luz Stella (1998), 'Agenda 21; a form of joint environmental management in Manizales, Colombia', *Environment and Urbanization*, Vol 10, No 2, pages 9–36.

40. López Follegatti, Jose Luis (1999), 'Ilo: a city in transformation', *Environment and Urbanization*, Vol 11, No 2, October, pages 181–202.

41. Stein 2001, op cit.

42. This section draws on a background paper prepared by Pietro Garau and Elliott Sclar, the co-chairs of the task force on meeting the Millennium Development Goal of achieving a significant improvement in the lives of at least 100 million slum dwellers.

43. Ibid.

44. Hewett, Paul C and Mark R Montgomery (2002), *Poverty and Public Services in Developing-country Cities*, Population Council, New York, 62 pages.

45. Ibid.

Index

Page references in *italics* refer to figures, tables and boxes